Teacher's Edition
From School to Work

J.J. Littrell, Ed. D.
Arizona State University
Tempe, Arizona

James H. Lorenz, Ed. D.
Middle Tennessee State University
Murfreesboro, Tennessee

Harry T. Smith, Ed. D.
Tennessee Technological University
Cookeville, Tennessee

Publisher
The Goodheart-Willcox Company, Inc.
Tinley Park, Illinois
www.g-w.com

ISBN: 978-1-59070-937-5
3 4 5 6 7 8 9 – 09 – 13 12 11 10

Contents

From School to Work

Prepare your students for the challenges of making the transition from school to work.

Topics include

- exploring the workplace
- exploring career options
- making plans for career success
- acquiring workplace skills
- developing personal skills for job success
- managing money
- growing toward independence

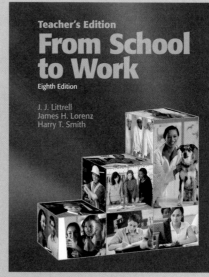

The Building Blocks of the Package

A complete package of materials is available to help your students learn and to help you teach effectively.

For Students

Student Text

Colorful headings, readable typeface, and logical organization facilitate reading comprehension and learning.

Interactive Student Text

This powerful CD contains the content of the printed text to allow easy viewing of pages. Also includes Web links and a search feature for checking individual chapters or the entire text.

Student Workbook

Includes various activities to help students review and apply chapter concepts.

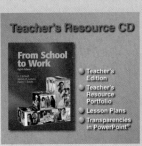

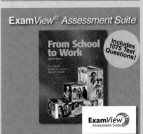

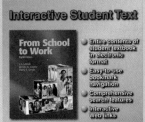

For Teachers

Teacher's Edition

The text provides a variety of teaching aids in the page margins to help you review and reinforce chapter content. Answer keys appear next to review questions.

Teacher's Annotated Workbook

Designed for presenting answers to workbook activities right where you need them.

Teacher's Resource Guide

Contains learning strategies, reproducible masters, blackline transparencies, and chapter tests.

Teacher's Resource Portfolio

Conveniently groups the content of the *Teacher's Resource Guide* into an easy-to-use binder! Includes color transparencies.

Teacher's Resource CD

Allows you to easily access the content of the portfolio and the *Teacher's Edition* of the text, plus show color transparencies in PowerPoint® and create daily lesson plans.

ExamView® Assessment Suite

This test generator CD lets you quickly and easily create and print tests from a test bank of hundreds of questions.

Teacher's PowerPoint® Presentations

Includes presentations for each chapter to reinforce key concepts and terms.

For Students and Teachers

A Companion Web Site

Motivates and engages students beyond the classroom with online flash cards, interactive quizzes, animated activities, and more. Provides answers in a secure site for teachers.

Introduction

From School to Work has been used primarily for classes that are involved in some form of career and technical education. It was originally designed for use in cooperative education programs that began appearing in 1968. In more recent years, new legislation expanded the scope of career and technical education to include a variety of approaches to work-based learning, the most significant of which are summarized below. Ongoing studies have made an effort to refine these approaches, broadening their impact and identifying a career-oriented focus that can be applied to *all* students. The culmination of these efforts is the career clusters.

Tech Prep

In 1985, Dale Parnell, a leading educator, proposed the *tech prep concept*—a blending of secondary and postsecondary programs leading to an associate's degree from a community, technical, or junior college. He stressed the need for more challenging math, science, communication, and technical courses that emphasized an applied approach to learning.

Tech prep programs combine at least two years of secondary and two or more years of postsecondary education in a sequential course of study without duplicated coursework, all leading to an associate degree, certification, or credential in a specific career field. These strategies must result in either jobs or further education.

The 1990 Carl D. Perkins Vocational and Applied Technology Education Act provided federal funds for the development of tech prep programs at the state and local levels. Tech prep became one of the most important efforts because of the soundness of its approach and the financial support of the Carl Perkins legislation. Continued funds for these programs were provided by The Carl D. Perkins Vocational and Technical Education Act of 2006 (also known as Perkins IV).

State Standards

To receive funding under Perkins IV, tech prep programs at the state and local levels must prove that they are providing students with the skills necessary for job success. If a program does not meet the Perkins criteria, an improvement program must be developed. If there is no improvement after three years, Perkins IV funding could be withheld from the program.

To verify the fulfillment of Perkins IV funding requirements, states developed standards on which to base their curricula. Teachers and instructors use these standards to make sure students learn the required skills and, therefore, achieve the requirements for continued funding under Perkins IV.

SCANS

In the past, states created many of their standards based on SCANS workplace competencies. In 1989, the U.S. Secretary of Labor convened a panel to identify the work-readiness competencies needed for success in the changing workplace. This panel was named the Secretary's Commission on Achieving Necessary Skills (SCANS). The Commission identified five workplace competencies and a three-part foundation of skills and personal qualities that workers need in order to perform effectively on the job.

The recommendations of the SCANS Commission had major implications for the high school curriculum. The workplace competencies and skills could not be learned apart from the real-world applications found in a systematic study of the workplace. States carefully reviewed course curricula to determine a natural fit between the existing course content and the workplace competencies and foundation skills.

Although the SCANS competencies set a precedent for emphasizing skills needed to succeed on the job, they did have some shortcomings. First, they did not require or show a progression of knowledge and skills in a career. In addition, over time the emphasis of career and technical education has evolved from just including a few jobs to addressing all careers. The importance of broad skills that apply to all areas as well as specific skills necessary for particular careers are now stressed. Finally, updates to The Carl D. Perkins Vocational and Technical Education Act between 1990 and 2006 changed the law's emphasis, due partially to legislation in the No Child Left Behind Act of 2001. Programs are now held accountable for the integration of academics, with the goal being to combine academic skills with employability skills.

The Career Clusters

In the mid 1990s, a project called Building Linkages began development, led by the Office of Vocational and Adult Education (OVAE). Building Linkages was funded in partnership by the U.S. Departments of Labor and Education. The goal of the project was to create a reliable set of standards for the integration of academics with workplace skills. Another goal was to show how higher levels of skills and knowledge lead to higher positions. Eventually the organization of the project emerged as career clusters, and The States' Career Clusters Initiative was launched in 2001.

The career clusters are introduced in Chapter 1 of *From School to Work* and are discussed in depth in Chapter 13. There are 16 career clusters, and among these are 81 different career pathways. Three levels of knowledge and skills exist in each cluster. The levels start with broad categories and move up to more specific categories. The *foundation* level applies to all levels of all careers. The *pathways* level lists the skills necessary for all careers in one cluster or employment area. The *specialty level* is the highest level of skill and knowledge within a given cluster.

Many of the knowledge and skills categories correspond to the SCANS competencies. All levels create employability, academic, and technical skills.

Integrating Academics

No matter what career path a student chooses, academic skills will be critical to his or her success. The No Child Left Behind Act of 2001 brought to national attention the importance of reading and mathematics to academic and personal success. The Act also instituted a program of accountability testing, placing high stakes on student achievement in key areas. The No Child Left Behind Act lists the following as core academic subjects in schools: English, reading, language arts, math, science, foreign languages, and civics and government, economics, arts, history, and geography.

Because achieving in these areas is so important, many career and technical education teachers are asked to incorporate academic standards into their curriculum. A career education course can support the core subjects by including subject matter from these areas as appropriate. Co-curricular projects with core subject teachers can also support students' growth and achievement in these areas.

The *From School to Work* program supports student growth and achievement in key academic areas in several ways. Some subjects (reading, language arts, math, science, social studies, and civics and government) are covered as background information to career education concepts. To promote connection to academic areas, at least two cross-curricular activities appear on the last page of each chapter within the section titled "Developing Your Academic Skills."

Reading, English, and Language Arts

The entire *From School to Work* student text is designed to encourage reading and understanding. Each chapter begins with a prereading question to engage student interest. The objectives, key terms, and key concepts are listed at the start of each chapter to focus on the information to come. Key terms are shown in bold to draw attention to the reader. The *Student Workbook* and the *Teacher's Resources* provide more activities designed to develop skills in English/Language Arts.

Math

Mathematics is a tool necessary for success in the workplace as well as in managing personal finances. Unfortunately, some students have not learned the basics of arithmetic and using numbers. To strengthen these skills, various math activities appear in the student text, the *Student Workbook,* and the *Teacher's Resources* as chapter content dictates.

Social Studies

Social Studies is an important part of explaining the full meaning of work and the reasons for the changing workplace. Psychology is especially helpful in understanding self and the importance of recognizing personal interests when deciding on and preparing for a satisfying career. Appropriate activities are found in the student text on the last page of each chapter under "Applying Your Knowledge and Skills" and "Developing Workplace Skills." Additional activities appear in the *Student Workbook* and *Teacher's Resources*.

Civics and Government

Any discussion of career education must include a discussion of how laws and other government influences affect work, workers, and the workplace. As students learn to prepare for a career, teaching them to become responsible citizens is also important. To strengthen student skills in these areas, appropriate activities appear on the last page of each chapter under "Developing Workplace Skills." Additional activities are in the *Student Workbook* and *Teacher's Resources* as chapter content dictates.

Meeting Academic Standards

In an effort to increase student proficiency with academic standards, all public schools are required to provide students with a high-quality education particularly in core academic subjects, such as mathematics and English and language arts. With an emphasis on developing a strong foundation for the workplace, each chapter-opening page of the *Teacher's Edition* of *From School to Work* lists the relevant standards supported by each chapter. You will find standards for the following academic areas:

- **Mathematics.** On applicable chapter opening pages, you will find the relevant national math standards. As you build your course curriculum, identify additional math standards that your students meet. These standards are reprinted with permission from *Principles and Standards for School Mathematics,* copyright 2000 by the National Council of Teachers of Mathematics. All rights reserved. The standards are listed with the permission of the National Council of Teachers of Mathematics (NCTM). NCTM does not endorse the content or validity of these alignments.

- **English Language Arts.** On the chapter-opening pages, you will also see a paraphrased version of one or more relevant English Language Arts standards. These standards represent the skills students will use and learn from reading the chapter. As you build your course curriculum, identify additional standards that your students meet from the *Standards for English Language Arts.* Please refer to the following chart for the complete wording of these standards from the *International Reading Association* and the *National Council of Teachers of English.*

Standards for English Language Arts

Standards for the English Language Arts, by the International Reading Association and the National Council of Teachers of English, Copyright 1996 by the International Reading Association and the National Council of Teachers of English. Reprinted by permission.

1. Students read a wide range of print and non-print texts to build an understanding of texts, of themselves, and of the cultures of the United States and the world; to acquire new information; to respond to the needs and demands of society and the workplace; and for personal fulfillment. Among these texts are fiction and nonfiction, classic and contemporary works.

2. Students read a wide range of literature from many periods in many genres to build an understanding of the many dimensions (e.g., philosophical, ethical, aesthetic) of human experience.

3. Students apply a wide range of strategies to comprehend, interpret, evaluate, and appreciate texts. They draw on their prior experience, their interactions with other readers and writers, their knowledge of word meaning and of other texts, their word identification strategies, and their understanding of textual features (e.g., sound-letter correspondence, sentence structure, context, graphics).

4. Students adjust their use of spoken, written, and visual language (e.g., conventions, style, vocabulary) to communicate effectively with a variety of audiences and for different purposes.

5. Students employ a wide range of strategies as they write and use different writing process elements appropriately to communicate with different audiences for a variety of purposes.

6. Students apply knowledge of language structure, language conventions (e.g., spelling and punctuation), media techniques, figurative language, and genre to create, critique, and discuss print and non-print texts.

7. Students conduct research on issues and interests by generating ideas and questions, and by posing problems. They gather, evaluate, and synthesize data from a variety of sources (e.g., print and non-print texts, artifacts, people) to communicate their discoveries in ways that suit their purpose and audience.

8. Students use a variety of technological and information resources (e.g., libraries, databases, computer networks, video) to gather and synthesize information and to create and communicate knowledge.

9. Students develop an understanding of and respect for diversity in language use, patterns, and dialects across cultures, ethnic groups, geographic regions, and social roles.

10. Students whose first language is not English make use of their first language to develop competency in the English language arts and to develop understanding of content across the curriculum.

11. Students participate as knowledgeable, reflective, creative, and critical members of a variety of literacy communities.

12. Students use spoken, written, and visual language to accomplish their own purposes (e.g., for learning, enjoyment, persuasion, and the exchange of information).

National Math Standards—Grades 9 Through 12

Number and Operations

- Understand numbers, ways of representing numbers, relationships among numbers, and number systems

- Understand meanings of operations and how they relate to one another

- Compute fluently and make reasonable estimates

Algebra

- Understand patterns, relations, and functions

- Represent and analyze mathematical situations and structures using algebraic symbols

- Use mathematical models to represent and understand quantitative relationships

- Analyze change in various contexts

Geometry

- Analyze characteristics and properties of two- and three-dimensional geometric shapes and develop mathematical arguments about geometric relationships

- Specify locations and describe spatial relationships using coordinate geometry and other representational systems

- Apply transformations and use symmetry to analyze mathematical situations

- Use visualization, spatial reasoning, and geometric modeling to solve problems

Measurement

- Understand measurable attributes of objects and the units, systems, and processes of measurement

- Apply appropriate techniques, tools, and formulas to determine measurements

Data Analysis and Probability

- Formulate questions that can be addressed with data and collect, organize, and display relevant data to answer them

- Select and use appropriate statistical methods to analyze data

- Develop and evaluate inferences and predictions that are based on data

- Understand and apply basic concepts of probability

Problem Solving

- Build new mathematical knowledge through problem solving

- Solve problems that arise in mathematics and in other contexts

- Apply and adapt a variety of appropriate strategies to solve problems

- Monitor and reflect on the process of mathematical problem solving

The School-to-Work Movement

In 1994, the School-to-Work Opportunities Act (STWOA) was passed. This federal legislation, jointly funded by the U.S. Departments of Labor and Education, provided venture capital to states and communities to implement programs connecting education with careers. Partnerships were created among business, labor, government, education, and community organizations. The goal was to combine learning in school with learning in the workplace so students see the relevance of their academic studies to their future life, explore career options, and learn basic occupational skills.

As of 2002, federal school-to-work funds were no longer available. At that time, states and local districts were expected to have school-to-work partnerships developed and be self-sufficient. Funds from The Carl D. Perkins Vocational and Technical Education Act of 2006 cannot be utilized for STWOA programs unless they also meet the criteria for Perkins IV. The future of school-to-work rests largely on support from state and local governments, the business community, and community-based organizations.

Strategies for Successful Teaching

You can make the *From School to Work* subject matter exciting and relevant for your students by using a variety of teaching strategies. Many suggestions for planning classroom activities are given in the various teaching supplements that accompany this text. As you plan your lessons, you might also want to keep the following points in mind.

Helping Your Students Develop Critical Thinking Skills

As today's students leave their classrooms behind, they will face a world of complexity and change. They are likely to work in several career areas and hold many different jobs. Young people must develop a base of knowledge and be prepared to solve complex problems, make difficult decisions, and assess ethical implications. In other words, students must be able to use critical thinking skills. These skills are often referred to as the higher-order thinking skills. Benjamin Bloom listed these as

- analysis—breaking down material into its component parts so its organizational structure may be understood

- synthesis—putting parts together to form a new whole

- evaluation—judging the value of material for a given purpose

In a broader perspective, students must be able to use reflective thinking in order to decide what to believe and do. According to Robert Ennis, students should be able to

- define and clarify problems, issues, conclusions, reasons, and assumptions

- judge the credibility, relevance, and consistency of information

- infer or solve problems and draw reasonable conclusions

Critical thinking goes beyond memorizing or recalling information. Critical thinking cannot occur in a vacuum; it requires individuals to apply what they know about the subject matter. It requires students to use their common sense and experience. It may involve controversy, too.

Critical thinking also requires *creative thinking* to construct all the reasonable alternatives, consequences, influencing factors, and supporting arguments. Unusual ideas are valued and perspectives outside the obvious are sought.

Finally, the teaching of critical thinking does not require exotic and highly unusual classroom approaches. Complex thought processes can be incorporated in ordinary, basic activities, such as reading, writing, and listening, if the activities are carefully planned and skillfully executed.

Help your students develop their analytical and judgment skills and to go beyond what they see on the surface. Rather than allowing students to blindly accept what they read or hear, encourage them to examine ideas in ways that show respect for others' opinions and different perspectives. Encourage students to think about points raised by others. Ask them to evaluate how new ideas relate to their attitudes about various subjects.

Debate is an excellent way to explore opposite sides of an issue. You may want to divide the class into two groups, each to take an opposing side of the issue. You can also ask students to work in smaller groups and explore opposing sides of different issues. Each group can select students from the group to present the points for their side.

Problem-Solving and Decision-Making Skills

An important aspect in the development of critical thinking skills is learning how to solve problems and make decisions. Some very important decisions lie ahead for your students, particularly those related to their future education and career choices.

Simulation games and role-plays allow students to practice solving problems and making decisions under nonthreatening circumstances. Role-playing allows students to examine others' feelings as well as their own. It can help them learn effective ways to react or cope when confronted with similar situations in real life.

Using Cooperative Learning

Because of the new emphasis on teamwork in the workplace, the use of cooperative learning groups in your classroom will give students an opportunity to practice teamwork skills. During cooperative learning, students learn interpersonal and small-group skills that will allow them to function as part of a team. These skills include leadership, decision making, trust building, communication, and conflict management.

When planning for cooperative learning, you will have a particular goal or task in mind. You will first specify the objectives for the lesson. Small groups of learners are matched for the purpose of completing the task or goal, and each person in the group is assigned a role. The success of the group is measured not only in terms of outcome, but also in terms of the successful performance of each member in his or her role.

In cooperative learning groups, students learn to work together toward a group goal. Each member is dependent on others for the outcome. This interdependence is a basic component of any cooperative learning group. Students understand that one person cannot succeed unless everyone succeeds. The value of each group member is affirmed as learners work toward their goal.

The success of the group depends on individual performance. Groups should be mixed in terms of abilities and talents so there are opportunities for the students to learn from one another. Also, as groups work together over time, the roles should be rotated so everyone has an opportunity to practice and develop different skills.

You will also need to monitor the effectiveness of the groups, intervening as necessary to provide task assistance or help with interpersonal and group skills. Finally, evaluate students' achievements and help them discuss how well they collaborated with each other.

Helping Students Recognize and Value Diversity

Your students will be entering a rapidly changing workplace—not only in matters pertaining to technology, but also in the diverse nature of its workforce. The majority of the new entrants to the workforce are women, minorities, and immigrants, all representing many different views and experiences. The workforce is aging, too, as the ranks of mature workers swell. Because of these trends, young workers must learn how to interact effectively with a variety of people who are considerably unlike them.

The appreciation and understanding of diversity is an ongoing process. The earlier and more frequently young people are exposed to diversity, the more quickly they can develop skills to bridge cultural differences. If your students are exposed to various cultures within your classroom, the process of understanding cultural differences can begin. This is the best preparation for success in a diverse society. In addition, teachers find the following strategies for teaching diversity helpful:

- Actively promote a spirit of openness, consideration, respect, and tolerance in the classroom.

- Use a variety of teaching styles and assessment strategies.

- Use cooperative learning activities whenever possible and make sure group roles are rotated so everyone has leadership opportunities.

- When grouping students, have each group's composition as diverse as possible with regard to gender, race, and nationality. If groups present information to the class, make sure all members have a speaking part.

- Make sure one group's opinions do not dominate class discussions. Seek out the unexpressed opinions of others, if necessary.

- If a student makes a sexist, racist, or similarly offensive comment, ask the student to rephrase the comment in a manner that it will not offend other class members. Remind students that offensive statements and behavior are inappropriate in the classroom.

- If a difficult classroom situation arises involving a diversity issue, ask for a time-out and have everyone write down his or her thoughts and opinions about the incident. This helps to calm the situation and allows you time to plan a response.

- Arrange for guest speakers who represent diversity in gender, race, and ethnicity, even though the topic does not relate to diversity.

- Have students change seats occasionally throughout the course and introduce themselves to their new "neighbors" so they become acquainted with all their classmates.

- Several times during the course, ask students to make anonymous, written evaluations of the class. Have them report any problems that may not be obvious.

Assessment Techniques

Various forms of assessment need to be used with students to evaluate their achievement. Written tests have traditionally been used to evaluate performance. This method of evaluation is good to use when assessing knowledge and comprehension. Other methods of assessment are preferable for measuring the achievement of the higher-level skills of application, analysis, synthesis, and evaluation.

Included in the *From School to Work* teacher supplements are two means of assessing learning. For each chapter in the text there is a reproducible *Review and Study Guide.* These are especially helpful for students who have difficulty drawing important information from their reading. Also included for each chapter is an objective test.

The *Facts in Review* sections in the text can be used to evaluate students' recall of important chapter concepts. The activities suggested in each chapter's last page provide more opportunities for you to assess your students' abilities to use critical thinking, problem solving, and application.

Performance Assessment

When you assign students some of the projects described in the text, a different form of assessing mastery or achievement is required. One method that teachers have successfully used is a rubric. A *rubric* consists of a set of criteria that includes specific descriptors or standards that can be used to arrive at performance scores for students. A point value is given for each set of descriptors, leading to a range of possible points to be assigned, usually from 1 to 5. The criteria can also be weighted. This method of assessment reduces the guesswork involved in grading, leading to fair and consistent scoring. The standards clearly indicate to students the various levels of mastery of a task. Students are even able to assess their own achievement based on the criteria.

When using rubrics, students should see the criteria at the beginning of the assignment. Then they can focus their effort on what needs to be done to reach a certain level of performance or quality of project. They have a clear understanding of your expectations of achievement.

Though you will want to design many of your own rubrics, several generic ones are included in the front section of three *From School to Work* supplements: *Teacher's Resource Guide, Teacher's Resource Portfolio,* and *Teacher's Resource CD.* These are designed to assess the following:

- *Individual Participation*
- *Individual Reports*
- *Group Participation*

These rubrics allow you to assess a student's performance and arrive at a performance score. Students can see what levels they have surpassed and what levels they can still strive to reach.

If your students are involved in work-based learning, you will probably have their supervisors use a form of rubric to evaluate their trainees' performance on the job. A sample of such an evaluation form is show in *From School to Work* on pages 64–65 of the student text. Some of the criteria for evaluation included on this form are cooperation, initiative, courtesy, job knowledge, and punctuality. The performance standards are described in detail so students know exactly what they need to do to improve their work performance.

Portfolios

Another type of performance assessment that is frequently used by teachers today is the portfolio. A *portfolio* consists of a selection of materials that students choose to document their performance over a period of time. Students select their best work samples to showcase their achievement. These items might provide evidence of employability skills as well as academic skills. The items appropriate for students to include in the portfolios they prepare for a job search are listed on page 338.

The portfolio is assembled at the culmination of a course to provide evidence of learning. A self-assessment summary report should be included that explains what has been accomplished, what has been learned, what strengths the student has gained, and what areas need improvement, if any. The students may present portfolios to the class. The items in the portfolio can also be discussed with the teacher in light of educational goals and outcomes. Portfolios should remain the property of students when they leave the course.

Portfolio assessment is a powerful evaluation tool for both students and teachers. It encourages self-reflection and self-assessment of a broader nature. Traditional evaluation methods of tests, quizzes, and papers have their place in measuring the achievement of some course objectives, but other assessment tools should also be used to fairly assess the achievement of all desired outcomes.

Teaching the Learner with Special Needs

The students in your classroom will represent a wide range of ability levels and needs. Special needs students in your classes will require unique teaching strategies. The chart on the next page provides descriptions of several of the types of special needs students you may find in your classes, followed by some strategies and techniques to keep in mind as you work with these students. You will be asked to meet the needs of all your students in the same classroom setting. It is a challenge to adapt daily lessons to meet the demands of all your students.

Learning Disabled*
Description

Students with learning disabilities (LD) have neurological disorders that interfere with their ability to store, process, or produce information, creating a "gap" between ability and performance. These students are generally of average or above-average intelligence. Examples of learning disabilities are distractibility, spatial problems, and reading comprehension problems.

Teaching Strategies

- Assist students in getting organized.
- Give short oral directions.
- Use drill exercises.
- Give prompt cues during student performance.
- Let students with poor writing skills use a computer.
- Break assignments into small segments and assign only one segment at a time.
- Demonstrate skills and have students model them.
- Give prompt feedback.
- Use continuous assessment to mark students' daily progress.
- Prepare materials at varying levels of ability.
- Shorten the number of items on exercises, tests, and quizzes.
- Provide more hands-on activities.

Mentally Disabled*

The mentally disabled student has subaverage general intellectual functioning that exists with deficits in adaptive behavior. These students are slower than others their age in using memory effectively, associating and classifying information, reasoning, and making judgments.

- Use concrete examples to introduce concepts.
- Make learning activities consistent.
- Use repetition and drills spread over time.
- Provide work folders for daily assignments.
- Use behavior management techniques, such as behavior modification, in the area of adaptive behavior.
- Encourage students to function independently.
- Give students extra time to both ask and answer questions while giving hints to answers.
- Avoid doing much walking around while talking to MD students as this is distracting for them.
- Give simple directions and read them over with students.
- Use objective test items and hands-on activities because students generally have poor writing skills and difficulty with sentence structure and spelling.

Behaviorally Emotionally Disabled*

These students exhibit undesirable behaviors or emotions that may, over time, adversely affect educational performance. Their inability to learn cannot be explained by intellectual, social, or health factors. They may be inattentive, withdrawn, timid, restless, defiant, impatient, unhappy, fearful, and unreflective; lack initiative; have negative feelings and actions; and blame others.

- Call students' names or ask them questions when you see their attention wandering.
- Call on students randomly rather than in a predictable sequence.
- Move around the room frequently.
- Improve students' self-esteem by giving them tasks they can perform well, increasing the number of successful achievement experiences.
- Decrease the length of time for each activity.
- Use hands-on activities instead of using words and abstract symbols.
- Decrease the size of the group so each student can actively participate.
- Make verbal instructions clear, short, and to the point.

*We appreciate the assistance of Dr. Debra O. Parker, North Carolina Central University, with this section.

Academically Gifted	Limited English Proficiency	Physical Disabilities
Academically gifted students are capable of high performance as a result of general intellectual ability, specific academic aptitude, and/or creative or productive thinking. Such students have a vast fund of general knowledge and high levels of vocabulary, memory, abstract word knowledge, and abstract reasoning.	These students have a limited proficiency in the English language. English is generally their second language. Such students may be academically quite capable, but they lack the language skills needed to reason and comprehend abstract concepts.	Includes individuals who are orthopedically impaired, visually impaired, speech impaired, deaf, hard-of-hearing, hearing impaired, and health impaired (cystic fibrosis, epilepsy). Strategies will depend on the specific disability.

Academically Gifted	Limited English Proficiency	Physical Disabilities
<ul><li>Provide ample opportunities for creative behavior.</li><li>Make assignments that call for original work, independent learning, critical thinking, problem solving, and experimentation.</li><li>Show appreciation for creative efforts.</li><li>Respect unusual questions, ideas, and solutions these students provide.</li><li>Encourage students to test their ideas.</li><li>Provide opportunities and give credit for self-initiated learning.</li><li>Avoid overly detailed supervision and too much reliance on prescribed curricula.</li><li>Allow time for reflection.</li><li>Resist immediate and constant evaluation. This causes students to be afraid to use their creativity.</li><li>Avoid comparisons with other students, which applies subtle pressure to conform.</li></ul>	<ul><li>Use a slow but natural rate of speech; speak clearly; use shorter sentences; repeat concepts in several ways.</li><li>Act out questions using gestures with hands, arms, and the whole body. Use demonstrations and pantomime. Ask questions that can be answered by a physical movement such as pointing, nodding, or manipulation of materials.</li><li>When possible, use pictures, photos, and charts.</li><li>Write key terms on the board. As they are used, point to them.</li><li>Corrections should be limited and appropriate. Do not correct grammar or usage errors in front of the class, causing embarrassment.</li><li>Give honest praise and positive feedback through your voice tones and visual articulation whenever possible.</li><li>Encourage students to use language to communicate, allowing them to use their native language to ask/answer questions when they are unable to do so in English.</li><li>Integrate students' cultural background into class discussions.</li><li>Use cooperative learning where students have opportunities to practice expressing ideas without risking language errors in front of the entire class.</li></ul>	<ul><li>For visually and hearing-impaired students, seat them near the front of the classroom. Speak clearly and say out loud what you are writing on the board.</li><li>In lab settings, in order to reduce the risk of injury, ask students about any conditions that could affect their ability to learn or perform.</li><li>Rearrange lab equipment or the classroom and make modifications as needed to accommodate any special need.</li><li>Investigate assistive technology devices that can improve students' functional capabilities.</li><li>Discuss solutions or modifications with the student who has experience with overcoming his or her disability and may have suggestions you may not have considered.</li><li>Let the student know when classroom modifications are being made and allow him or her to test them out before class.</li><li>Ask advice from special education teachers, the school nurse, or physical therapist.</li><li>Plan field trips that can include all students.</li></ul>

Using Other Resources

The following list includes sources of information and materials that may be useful to you and your students. Please note that information provided here may have changed since publication.

Career-Related Sites

The following sites provide career exploration and planning tools, résumé-writing tips, job listings, workplace statistics, and career education information.

The Armed Services Vocational Aptitude Battery (ASVAB)
www.military.com/ASVAB

Career Builder
(866) 438-1485
careerbuilder.com

Career Magazine
(610) 878-2800
careermag.com

Career Resource Center
careers.org

CareerOneStop
(877) 348-0502
careeronestop.org

Career Voyages
careervoyages.gov

Mapping Your Future
mapping-your-future.org

Monster
(800) MONSTER
monster.com

My Future
myfuture.com

O*NET Online
online.onetcenter.org

Occupational Outlook Handbook
stats.bls.gov/oco

States' Career Clusters Initiative
careerclusters.org

U.S. Army: Partnership for Youth Success
goarmy.com

U.S. Bureau of Apprenticeship and Training
doleta.gov/OA/bat.cfm

U.S. Bureau of Labor Statistics
(202) 691-5200
stats.bls.gov

U.S. Department of Labor Employment and Training Administration
(800) US-2JOBS
doleta.gov

Trade and Professional Groups

These and other trade and professional organizations provide career information. Usually it is industry specific.

Air-Conditioning and Refrigeration Institute
(703) 524-8800
ari.org

American Association of Family and Consumer Sciences
(800) 424-8080
aafcs.org

American Bankers Association
(800) BANKERS
aba.com

American Bar Association
(800) 285-2221
abanet.org

American Chemistry Council
(703) 741-5000
plasticsinfo.org

American Culinary Federation
(800) 624-9458
acfchefs.org

American Design Drafting Association
(731) 627-0802
adda.org

American Dietetic Association
(800) 877-1600
eatright.org

American Medical Association
(800) 621-8335
ama-assn.org

American Society of Furniture Designers
(336) 617-3209
asfd.com

American Society of Interior Designers
(202) 546-3480
asid.org

Association for Career and Technical Education
(800) 826-9972
acteonline.org

Institute of Food Technologists
(800) IFT-FOOD
ift.org

International Association of Culinary Professionals
(800) 928-4227
iacp.com

International Association of Lighting Designers
iald.org

National Association for the Education of Young Children
(800) 424-2460
naeyc.org

National Association of Home Builders
(800) 368-5242
nahb.com

National Council of Better Business Bureaus
bbb.org

National Institute for Automotive Service Excellence
(888) ASE-TEST
asecert.org

National Research Center for Career and Technical Education
(800) 678-6011
nccte.org

National Restaurant Association
(800) 424-5156
restaurant.org

Small Business Administration
(800) 827-5722
sba.gov

General Information

These sites provide information that prepares students for gaining independence as they transition to their future roles in the workplace.

American Financial Services Association
(202) 296-5544
afsaonline.org

American Savings Education Council
(202) 659-0670
choosetosave.org

Credit Union National Association, Inc.
(800) 356-9655
cuna.org

Federal Communications Commission
(888) CALL-FCC
www.fcc.gov

Federal Deposit Insurance Corporation (FDIC)
(877) 275-3342
fdic.gov

Federal Trade Commission Bureau of Consumer Protection
(877) FTC-HELP
ftc.gov/bcp

Food and Drug Administration (FDA)
(888) INFO-FDA
www.fda.gov

Insurance Information Institute
(800) 331-9146
iii.org

Internal Revenue Service
(800) 829-1040
www.irs.gov

Internet Fraud Watch
fraud.org

Jump$tart Coalition for Personal Financial Literacy
(888) 45-EDUCATE
jumpstart.org

National Council on Economic Education
(800) 338-1192
ncee.net

National Fraud Information Center
(800) 876-7060
fraud.org

Occupational Safety and Health Administration (OSHA)
(800) 321-OSHA
osha.gov

Securities and Exchange Commission (SEC)
(202) 942-8088
sec.gov

Social Security Administration
www.ssa.gov

Students Against Destructive Decisions (SADD)
(877) SADD-INC
saddonline.com

Teen Consumer Scrapbook
atg.wa.gov/teenconsumer

Teenager's Guide to the Real World: Money Really Matters
(888) 294-7820
bygpub.com

U.S. Consumer Product Safety Commission
(800) 638-2772
www.cpsc.gov

U.S. Equal Employment Opportunity Commission
(800) 669-4000
eeoc.gov

Note: Phone numbers and Web addresses may have changed since publication. For some entries, reaching the correct Web site may require keying *www.* into the address.

Incorporating Career and Technical Student Organizations

Career and Technical Student Organizations (CTSOs) have been a vital part of career and technical education since 1918. Currently, the U.S. Department of Education recognizes eight organizations.

CTSOs Officially Recognized by the U.S. Department of Education		
Short Name	**Full Name**	**Web Site**
BPA	Business Professionals of America	www.bpa.org
DECA	DECA—An Association of Marketing Students	www.deca.org
FBLA/PBL	Future Business Leaders of America/Phi Beta Lambda	www.fbla-pbl.org
FCCLA	Family, Career and Community Leaders of America	www.fcclainc.org
FFA	National FFA Organization	www.ffa.org
HOSA	Health Occupations Students of America	www.hosa.org
SkillsUSA	Formerly VICA–Vocational Industrial Clubs of America	www.skillsusa.org
TSA	Technology Student Association	www.tsaweb.org

Federal career and technical education funds can be used to support activities of these CTSOs. Many states require that CTSOs be incorporated as a co-curricular activity in career and technical subjects. The CTSOs offer a wide variety of activities that can be adapted to almost any school and classroom situation. A brief introduction to CTSOs follows. If you would like more details, visit their Web sites.

Purpose

The purpose of CTSOs is to assist students in acquiring knowledge and skills in career and technical areas as well as leadership skills and experience. These organizations achieve these goals by enlisting teacher-advisors to organize and lead local chapters in their schools. Support for teacher-advisors and their chapters is often coordinated through each state's education department. The chapters elect officers and establish a program of work. This program of work can include a variety of activities, including community service, co-curricular projects, and competition preparation. Student achievement in specified areas is recognized with certificates and/or public acknowledgement through awards ceremonies. Competition is the most visible activity of CTSOs, but not the only one.

Competitive Events

Competitive events are a main feature of most CTSOs. The CTSO develops events that enable students to showcase how well they have mastered the learning of specific content and the use of decision-making, problem-solving, and leadership skills. The competitive events also give the winners the opportunity for public recognition of their achievements. Each CTSO has its own list of competitive events and activities. Members develop career and leadership skills even though they may not participate in or win competitions.

Scope and Sequence

A *Scope and Sequence Chart* is located at the end of the introduction. Since *From School to Work* focuses on career preparation, the organizing concepts are the 10 categories of knowledge and skills that are linked to the career clusters:

- academic foundations
- communications
- problem solving and critical thinking
- information technology applications
- systems
- safety, health, and environment

- leadership and teamwork

- ethics and legal responsibilities

- employability and career development

- technical skills

This special resource is provided to help you select for study those topics that meet your curriculum needs. Bold numbers indicate chapters in which concepts are found.

Marketing Your Program

Many students and their parents may have preconceived ideas about what the career education curriculum includes. You need to identify these preconceptions and, if necessary, gently alter them to give students and their parents a more accurate idea of what your class entails.

To get your public relations campaign started, create a newsletter to inform parents about what their children will be studying in your class. You can also use copies of these promotionally to encourage students to enroll in your class. Post copies of flyers around your school or pass them out to students. You might ask some of your former students what they feel they have gained from taking your class and add some of their ideas to the flyer. (If you decide to use direct quotations, be sure to get permission from your students.)

Students and their parents are not likely to be the only ones who are not totally aware of the importance of career education classes. You can make people more aware through good public relations. It pays to make the student body, faculty, and community aware of your program. With good public relations, you can increase your enrollment, gain support from administrators and other teachers, and achieve recognition in the community. Following are some ways to market your program:

- Create visibility. It is important to let people know what is going on in your program. Ways to do this include announcements of projects and activities at faculty meetings and in school bulletins or newspapers, displays in school showcases or on bulletin boards, and articles and press releases in school and community newspapers. Talk up your program with administrators, other teachers, and students. Invite them to visit your classes.

- Interact with educators in other subject matter areas. Career education is related to many fields of learning. You can strengthen your program and contribute to other disciplines by cooperating with other teachers. You can coordinate the teaching of chapter material with other departments in your school that might be covering related information. The more interaction you can generate, the more you promote your class.

- Contribute to the education objectives of the school. If your school follows stated educational objectives and strives to strengthen specific skills, include these overall goals in your teaching. For example, if students need special help in developing verbal or writing skills, select projects and assignments that will help them in these areas. Show administrators examples of work that indicate student improvement in needed skills.

- Serve as a resource center. Career education is of practical use and interest to almost everyone. You can sell your program by making your department a resources center of materials related to career exploration and job hunting. Invite faculty members, students, and parents to tap into the wealth of information available in your classroom.

- Generate involvement and activity in the community. You are teaching concepts that students can apply in their everyday life. You can involve students in community life and bring the community into your classroom through field trips, surveys, presentations from guest speakers, and interviews with businesspeople and community leaders. You may be able to set up cooperative projects between the school and community organizations around a variety of topics.

- Connect with parents. If you can get them involved, parents may be your best allies in teaching career education classes. Let parents know when their children have done good work. Moms and dads have had experiences related to many of the issues you discuss in class. Call on them to share individually or as part of a panel addressing a specific topic. Parents can be a rich source of real-life experience. Keep them informed about classroom activities and invite them to participate as they are able.

- Establish a student sales staff. Enthusiastic students will be your best salespeople. Encourage them to tell their parents and friends what they are learning. You might create bulletin boards or write letters to parents that focus on what students are studying in your classes. Ask students to put together a newsletter highlighting their experiences in your career education class. Students could write a column from your department for the school paper.

Goodheart-Willcox Welcomes Your Comments

We welcome your comments and suggestions regarding *From School to Work* and its supplements. Please send any comments you may have to the editor by visiting our Web site at www.g-w.com or writing to

Editorial Department
Goodheart-Willcox Publisher
18604 West Creek Drive
Tinley Park, IL 60477-6243
www.g-w.com

Scope and Sequence Chart

In planning your program, you may want to use this scope and sequence chart to identify the major concepts presented in each chapter of *From School to Work*. Concepts relate to the career cluster knowledge and skills. Refer to the chart to select topics that meet your curriculum needs. Bold numbers indicate chapters in which concepts are found.

Part 1: Work-Based Learning

Academic Foundations

1: Career knowledge and skills

2: Study and learn; Improve your reading skills; Take notes

Communications

1: Career knowledge and skills; Transferable skills

2: Follow the training plan; Practice good study habits; Improve your reading skills; Participate in class

3: Cooperation; Courtesy; Accepting criticism

Information Technology Applications

2: Practice good study habits; Organize your schedule; Take notes

Systems

1: Opportunities to learn on the job

2: Practice good study habits; Organize your schedule

Safety, Health, and Environment

2: Know the law; Fair labor practices; Safe labor practices

3: Personal appearance; Good health and fitness

Leadership and Teamwork

1: Benefits of learning on the job; Cooperative education

2: Participate in class

3: Performance; Initiative; Cooperation; Courtesy

Ethics and Legal Responsibilities

2: Get a social security number and a work permit; Abide by the training agreement; Follow the training plan; Know the law; Fair labor practices; Safe labor practices

3: Ethics in the workplace

Employability and Career Development

1: Exploring the world of work; Career clusters; Workplace exploration; Opportunities to learn on the job; Cooperative education; Internship; Benefits of learning on the job; Preparing for career success; Career knowledge and skills; Transferable skills

2: Your training station; Abide by the training agreement; Follow the training plan; Know the law; Fair labor practices; Safe labor practices

3: Personal qualities needed on the job; Positive attitude; Good attendance; Punctuality; Performance; Initiative; Cooperation; Courtesy; Personal appearance; Good health and fitness; Accepting criticism

Technical Skills

1: Career knowledge and skills; Transferable skills

2: Practice good study habits; Take notes

Part 2: Skills for Success

Academic Foundations

6: Using a calculator; Addition, Subtraction, Multiplication, Division; Using fractions; Decimals, and percentages; Fractions, Decimals; Percentages; Taking measurements; Linear measuring; Area measuring; Digital measuring; Using the metric system; How the system works; Making conversions

11: Reading and approving minutes

Communications

4: Characteristics of an effective team; Stays focused; Works for the common good; Managing conflict; Address the conflict; Develop an acceptable solution; Implement and evaluate

5: Effective communication; Listening skills; Reading and comprehension skills; Writing and keyboarding skills; Business letters; Parts of a business letter; Types of business letters; Appearance of a business letter; Appearance of a business envelope; Memos; Parts of a memo; Appearance of a memo; Business reports; Nonverbal communication; Speaking skills; Talking on the phone; Speaking to a group; Shift changes

9: Call for help

10: Leadership and group dynamics in the workplace

11: Order of business; Call to order; Reports of officers; Standing committee reports; Special committee reports; Unfinished business; New business; Program; Announcements; Adjournment; Making a motion; Amending a motion; Tabling a motion

Problem Solving and Critical Thinking

4: Problem solving; Steps in problem solving; Aids in problem solving; Managing conflict; Know when to intervene; Address the conflict; Identify the source and importance of the conflict; Identify possible solutions; Develop an acceptable solution; Implement and evaluate

6: Analyzing data; Understanding mean, median, and mode; Using charts and graphs

Information Technology Applications

5: Talking on the phone; Communication technology; Voice mail; Cellular phones; Walkie-talkies; Headsets; Teleconferencing and videoconferencing

6: Using a calculator

7: Technology today; Computer hardware; Peripherals; Software tools; Internet;

E-mail; Wireless technology; Troubleshooting; Impact of technology; Technology on the job; Technology at school; Technology in the home; Computers in the future

Systems

4: Teams in the workplace; Role of team in the workplace; Characteristics of an effective team; Shares leadership; Rotates team roles; Stays focused; Works for the common good

6: Using the metric system; How the system works; Making conversions

7: Technology today; Troubleshooting

9: Follow safety precautions; Follow universal precautions; Follow emergency evacuation procedures

10: Dynamics and groups

11: Order of business

Safety, Health, and Environment

8: Good health; Eat well-balanced meals; Get enough sleep; Stay active; Good grooming; Clean body; Smooth shave; Healthy complexion; Clean hair; Attractive hands; Fresh breath

9: What causes accidents? Lack of knowledge and skills; Environmental hazards; Poor safety attitudes; Unsafe behavior; Costs of accidents; Costs to you; Costs to the employer; Costs to the economy; Preventing accidents; Stay healthy; Use machines and tools properly; Wear protective clothing and use protective equipment; Follow safety precautions; What to do when an accident occurs; Call for help; Provide first aid; Follow universal precautions; Follow emergency evacuation procedures; Workplace violence; Role of government in protecting your health; OSHA; EPA; CDC

Leadership and Teamwork

4: Teams in the workplace; Pros and cons of the team approach; Role of the team in the workplace; Stages of team development; Characteristics of an effective team; Shares leadership; Works for the common good

5: Informal communication channels; Shift changes

10: Leaders and authority; Skills and qualities

technology, and communications; Business, management, and administration; Education and training; Finance; Government and public administration; Health science; Hospitality and tourism; Human services; Information technology; Law, public safety, corrections, and security; Manufacturing; Marketing, sales, and service; Science, technology, engineering, and mathematics; Transportation, distribution, and logistics; Education and training requirements; Future occupational trends

14: Career research resources; Evaluating careers; Educational requirements; Work hours; Work conditions; Pay: starting and potential; Personal lifestyle and goals

15: Career decisions; Making a career plan; Making work decisions

Technical Skills

14: Career information guides; Internet; One-stop career centers

---

Part 4: The Job Hunt

Academic Foundations

16: Finding job openings; Want ads; Trade and professional journals

17: Skill tests; Written honesty tests; How to take preemployment tests

18: Learn about the employer and the job

Communications

16: Searching the Internet; Before you apply; Preparing a personal fact sheet; Developing a home page; Contacting an employer by telephone; Letter of application

17: Skill tests; Situational tests; Polygraph tests; Written honesty tests

18: Preparing for an interview; Make a list of questions to ask; List the materials to take with you; Be prepared for questions; Practice for the interview; Interview; Dinner interview; After the interview; Accepting a job offer; Rejecting a job offer

Problem Solving and Critical Thinking

16: Finding job openings

17: Situational tests; Armed services vocational aptitude battery; How to take preemployment tests

18: Make a list of questions to ask; Be prepared for questions

Information Technology Applications

16: Searching the Internet; Developing a home page

Leadership and Teamwork

16: Finding job openings; Networking; Direct employer contact; Preparing a personal fact sheet; Preparing a résumé

17: Skill tests; Psychological tests; Situation tests; Written honesty tests

18: Preparing for the interview

Ethics and Legal Responsibilities

16: Job application forms; Illegal questions on job applications

17: Written honesty tests; Medical examinations; Drug testing

18: Be prepared for questions

Employability and Career Development

16: Finding job openings; Before you apply; Preparing a personal fact sheet; Job résumés; Job résumé information; Preparing a résumé; Job portfolio; Developing a home page; Contacting an employer by telephone; Letter of application; Job application forms

17: Skill tests; Psychological tests; Situational tests; Polygraph tests; Written honesty tests; Medical examinations; How to take pre-employment tests

18: Preparing for an interview; Interview; Dinner interview; After the interview; Accepting a job offer; Rejecting a job offer

Technical Skills

16: Searching the Internet; Preparing a personal fact sheet; Preparing a résumé; Contacting an employer by telephone; Letter of application; Job application forms

17: Skills tests

Part 5: Job Satisfaction

Academic Foundations

20: Language

22: Pricing your product or service; Obtaining licensing; Financial record keeping

Communications

19: Relating to others at work; Working with your supervisor; Working with coworkers; Your conduct and job success

20: Language; Facing sexual harassment or discrimination; Discouraging the behavior; Taking action

22: Importance of small business; Choosing a location

Problem Solving and Critical Thinking

19: Handling job stress; Evaluating job performance

20: Promoting diversity in the workplace; What employees can do

21: Business management

22: Opportunities for entrepreneurs; Planning your own business; What does it take to succeed? Choosing a business; Choosing a location

Information Technology Applications

19: Training opportunities

22: Choosing a location

Systems

19: Relating to others at work; Performance rating; Unions; Must you join a union? Organization of unions; Collective bargaining

21: How businesses are organized; Proprietorship; Partnership; Corporation; How businesses are structured

22: Financial record keeping

Safety, Health, and Environment

19: Handling job stress

20: Diversity, rights, and discrimination

22: Zoning, licensing, and permits

Leadership and Teamwork

19: Relating to others at work; Working with your supervisor; Working with coworkers; Making a job change

20: Benefits of diversity in the workplace; Promoting diversity in the workplace; What employers are doing; What employees are doing

21: Business management

22: Planning your own business; What does it take to succeed? Choosing a business; Choosing a location; Pricing your product or service

Ethics and Legal Responsibilities

19: Your conduct and job success; Being fired

20: Diversity, rights, and discrimination; Law and discrimination; Types of discrimination in the workplace; Sexual harassment in the workplace

21: Limited government involvement

22: Legal and financial issues; Choosing your business structure; Zoning, licensing, and permits; Obtaining financing; Financial record keeping; Professional assistance

Employability and Career Development

19: Your first day on the job; Relating to others at work; Your conduct and job success; Handling job stress; Evaluating job performance; Job probation; Performance rating; Training opportunities; Changes in job status; Promotion; Lateral move; Demotion; Making a job change

20: Diversity trends in the United States; Cultural heritage; Language; Religion; Gender; Age; Disability; Benefits of diversity in the workplace; Promoting diversity in the workplace; What employers are doing; What employees can do; Facing sexual harassment or discrimination; Discouraging the behavior; Taking action

21: Business management

22: Importance of small business; Opportunities for entrepreneurs; Advantages of entrepreneurship; Disadvantages of entrepreneurship; Types of business ventures

Technical Skills

19: Evaluating job performance; Training opportunities

22: Pricing your product; Financial record keeping

Part 6: Managing Your Income

Academic Foundations

23: Forms of income; Wages; Salary; Commission; Piecework; Tips; Bonus; Profit sharing; Fringe benefits; Understanding your paycheck; Taxes; Types of taxes; Preparing tax returns; Filing your first tax return

24: Budgeting your money; Establish financial goals; Estimate your monthly income and expenses; Balance your budget; Keep track of income and expenses; Evaluate your budget

25: Understanding credit; The cost of credit; Using credit wisely

26: Writing checks; Balancing a checkbook; Computerized personal financial management; Understanding interest; Investing your money

27: Financial responsibility laws

Communications

23: Filing your first tax return

24: Be an informed consumer; Understanding advertising and other promotional methods; Exercising your consumer rights; Know the right way to complain

25: Establishing credit; Credit agreements

26: Banking by phone; Making deposits; Writing checks

27: Choosing an insurance company, agent, and policy; Filing an insurance claim

28: Family roles; Building relationships; Balancing family and work roles; Community involvement; Consulting a lawyer

Problem Solving and Critical Thinking

24: Establish financial goals; Evaluate your budget; Understand advertising and other promotional methods; Decide where to shop; Develop shopping skills; Consumer fraud; Avoiding consumer fraud

25: Credit agreements; Shopping for credit; Should you use credit? Dealing with credit problems

26: Choosing a financial institution; Investing your money; Making investments

27: Buying auto insurance; Choosing an insurance company, agent, and policy

28: Using leisure time effectively; Managing your time; Voting

Information Technology Applications

23: Filing your first tax return

24: Establish financial goals; Balance your budget; Keep track of income and expenses; Consumer fraud; Identity theft

26: Electronic banking; Online banking; Electronic funds transfer; Automated teller machines; Debit cards; Computerized personal financial management

Systems

23: Taxes; Types of taxes

24: Budgeting your money; Establish financial goals; Estimate your monthly income; Balance your budget; Keep track of income and expenses; Managing your consumer spending; Develop shopping skills

26: Recording changes to your account; Balancing a checkbook; Understanding interest; Retirement accounts

27: Health insurance; Life insurance

28: Balancing family and work roles; Managing your time; Court system; Small claims court

Safety, Health, and Environment

23: Worker's compensation; Medical care benefits; Disability income; Rehabilitation benefits; Death benefits; Unemployment insurance

25: Federal credit laws

26: Choosing a financial institution; Automated teller machines; Debit cards; Safe-deposit boxes

27: Automobile insurance; Health insurance; Group health insurance; Home insurance; Life insurance; Whole life insurance; Term life insurance; Universal life insurance

28: Maintaining the home; Family and Medical Leave Act; Family-friendly benefits and policies; Obeying the law

Leadership and Teamwork

28: Working from home; Citizenship responsibilities; Community involvement; Criminal law; Civil law

Ethics and Legal Responsibilities

23: Taxes; Types of taxes; Preparing tax returns; Filing your first tax return

24: Exercising your consumer rights and responsibilities; Use consumer protection services; Use government protection agencies; Avoiding consumer fraud

25: Federal credit laws; Using credit wisely; Should you use credit? Dealing with credit problems

26: Recording changes to your account

27: Financial responsibility laws; Filing an insurance claim

28: Citizenship responsibilities; Community involvement; Voting; Obeying the law; Criminal law; Civil law; Consulting a lawyer; Small claims court

Employability and Career Development

23: Understanding your paycheck; Taxes; Types of taxes; Social security; Social security benefits; Medicare benefits; Medicaid benefits; Worker's compensation; Medical care benefits; Disability income; Rehabilitation benefits; Death benefits; Unemployment insurance

24: Use consumer protection services; Establishing financial goals

26: Retirement accounts

27: Employer-sponsored insurance programs

28: Balancing family and work roles; Managing your time; Using community resources; Family-friendly workplace; Family and Medical Leave Act; Family-friendly benefits and polices

Technical Skills

24: Budgeting your money

26: Electronic banking; Online banking; Electronic funds transfer; Automated teller machines; Debit cards; Computerized personal financial management

28: Managing your time; Using community resources

From School to Work

J.J. Littrell, Ed. D.
Arizona State University
Tempe, Arizona

James H. Lorenz, Ed. D.
Middle Tennessee State University
Murfreesboro, Tennessee

Harry T. Smith, Ed. D.
Tennessee Technological University
Cookeville, Tennessee

Publisher
The Goodheart-Willcox Company, Inc.
Tinley Park, Illinois
www.g-w.com

Copyright © 2009

by

The Goodheart-Willcox Company, Inc.

Previous editions copyright 2006, 2004, 2000, 1996, 1991, 1987, 1984
All rights reserved. No part of this work may be reproduced, stored,
or transmitted in any form or by any electronic or mechanical means
including information storage and retrieval systems without the prior
written permission of The Goodheart-Willcox Company, Inc.
Manufactured in the United States of America.

Library of Congress Catalog Card Number 2008017454

ISBN 978-1-59070-936-8
3 4 5 6 7 8 9 – 09 – 13 12 11 10

Library of Congress Cataloging-in-Publication Data

Littrell, Joseph J. (Joseph Junior), 1920-
  From school to work / J.J. Littrell, James H. Lorenz, Harry T. Smith.
    p. cm.
  Includes index.
  ISBN 978-1-59070-936-8
  1. Education, Cooperative--United States. 2. Students--Employment-
-United States. 3. Career education--United States. 4. School-to-work
transition--United States. I. Lorenz, James H. II. Smith, Harry T. III.
Title.
  LC1049.5.L58 2009
  370.113--dc22
                                     2008017454

Introduction

From School to Work will help you—a student preparing for the workplace—make a smooth transition from the classroom to a satisfying job. This book discusses the world of work, your place in it, and what it takes to succeed. You will learn about your responsibilities to your school and your employer while participating in a work-based learning program.

Future success in the workplace requires important skills and qualities. With this book, you will develop valuable thinking skills and personal qualities that make you a more capable person and valuable worker. You will improve your ability to read, write, speak, listen, and solve math problems. The book will also help you develop the workplace know-how needed to perform well on a job.

While participating in a work experience, you will start preparing for a full-time career. *From School to Work* guides you through career planning and job hunting. It prepares you for the challenges you will face when you live on your own. You will also learn how to manage your income wisely so you can build a secure and satisfying life.

Welcome to From School to Work

As you prepare for the workplace, *From School to Work* will help you learn to succeed in school and in your future career. The student edition includes these features:

A Colorful, Easy-to-Read Design

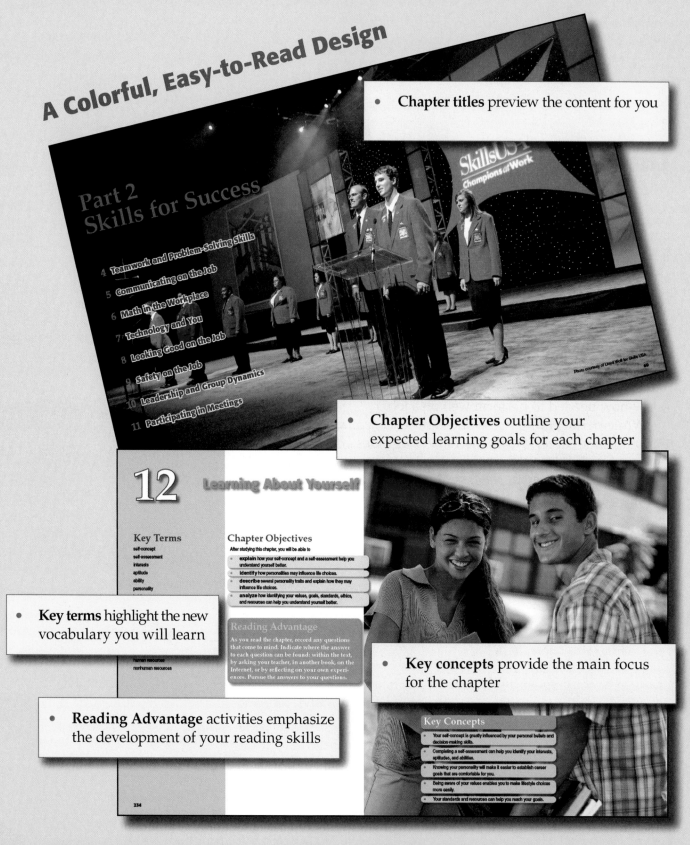

- **Chapter titles** preview the content for you

- **Chapter Objectives** outline your expected learning goals for each chapter

- **Key terms** highlight the new vocabulary you will learn

- **Key concepts** provide the main focus for the chapter

- **Reading Advantage** activities emphasize the development of your reading skills

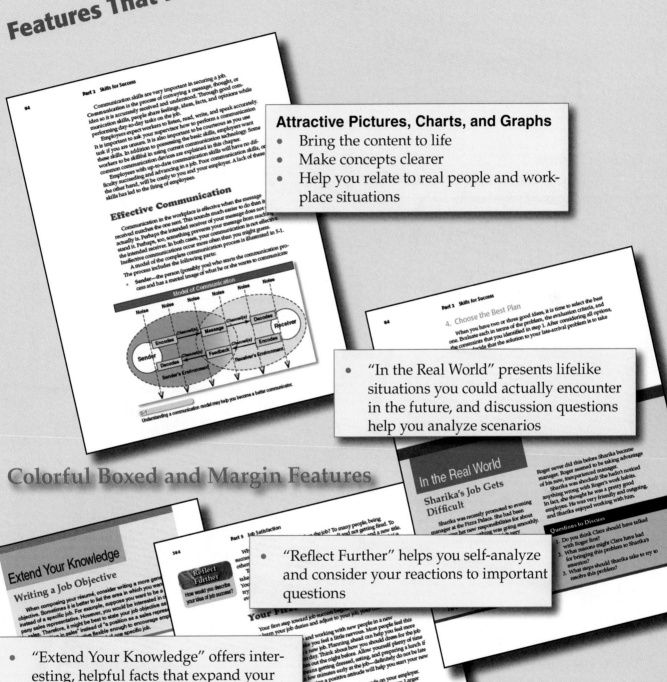

Features That Help You Relate to Content

5

Attractive Pictures, Charts, and Graphs
- Bring the content to life
- Make concepts clearer
- Help you relate to real people and work-place situations

- "In the Real World" presents lifelike situations you could actually encounter in the future, and discussion questions help you analyze scenarios

Colorful Boxed and Margin Features

- "Reflect Further" helps you self-analyze and consider your reactions to important questions

- "Extend Your Knowledge" offers interesting, helpful facts that expand your understanding of important topics

New Terms appear in bold type where they are defined

- "Thinking It Through" promotes your higher-level thinking skills and aids class discussion

Reviews to Reinforce Your Learning and Challenge Your Thinking Skills

Facts in Review
- Reinforces your recall of chapter content

Developing Your Academic Skills
- Relates the Career Education content to academic curriculum areas such as math, English, science, and social studies

Applying Your Knowledge and Skills
- Allows you to practice and develop skills needed for various occupations

Summary
- Provides a review of major chapter concepts

Information Technology Applications
- Focuses on the use of technology, such as the Internet and software programs

Developing Workplace Skills
- Helps you build the skills employees need to succeed on the job

Career Clusters to help you plan for your future

Extend Your Knowledge

Using the Career Clusters

Ask your teacher or guidance counselor for advice on investigating the career clusters at www.careerclusters.org. Examine two clusters that the career clusters you may decide to pursue. What new facts did you learn

The Sixteen Career Clusters

The Career Clusters icons are being used with permission of the States' Career Clusters Initiative, 2008.
www.careerclusters.org

All occupations in the U.S. workforce are addressed within these 16 career clusters.

Chapter 1
- Provides an introduction and overview to the 16 clusters

Chapter 13
Brief Summaries
- Explain the types of occupations covered and the qualifications needed for career entry
- Bring the career clusters to life with photos of workplace settings

Health Science

Health care is the fastest-growing industry in the United States, so careers in this cluster are in high demand. The career pathways include therapeutic and diagnostic services, health information, support services, and biotechnology research and development.

Pathways and Career Options
- Show examples of the many career choices available

About the Authors

Joseph J. Littrell, the original author of this text, taught industrial and vocational education to teachers in training at Arizona State University. Littrell began his career teaching industrial education in Nebraska and Oregon public schools. Later he taught engineering at the University of Missouri. He earned degrees from Peru State College in Nebraska, the University of Minnesota, and the University of Missouri.

James H. Lorenz is professor emeritus and chair of the department of engineering technology and industrial studies at Middle Tennessee State University. He has taught graduate and undergraduate teacher certification courses and undergraduate drafting courses for over 25 years. Lorenz conducts numerous in-service training programs for teachers and has directed SkillsUSA activities at district and state levels. He began his career teaching drafting and graphic arts at the secondary level. Lorenz holds degrees from the University of Wisconsin-Stout, the University of Minnesota, and the University of Georgia.

Harry T. Smith is professor of curriculum and instruction at Tennessee Technological University where he has served as program supervisor of industrial education since 1986. Smith's primary responsibility is teaching instructional media technology and occupational education licensure courses to undergraduate and graduate students in the college of education. Earlier, Smith taught industrial education at the secondary level in Missouri and the postsecondary level in Missouri and Michigan. Smith holds degrees from Northeast Missouri State, Central Missouri State, and Michigan State Universities.

Reviewers

The authors and publisher are grateful to the following reviewers who provided valuable input to this edition.

Lynne Bryla
Applied Arts Coordinator
Lake Park High School
Roselle, Illinois

Dr. Diane Ross Gary
Education Consultant
Connecticut State Department of Education
Hartford, Connecticut

John Hernandez
Diversified Career Preparation Instructor
East Central High School
San Antonio, Texas

Rheta Hughey
Family and Consumer Sciences Teacher Coordinator
West End High School
Birmingham, Alabama

Annie Hunter Clasen
Instructor
Aparicio-Levy Technical Center
Tampa, Florida

Peggy Pearson
Diversified Career Technology Coordinator
Simmons Career Center
Plant City, Florida.

Contents in Brief

Contents

Part 2
Skills for Success

**Part 3
Career Planning**

Part 4
The Job Hunt

17

18

Part 5
Job Satisfaction

19

Part 6
Managing Your Income

Part 1
Work-Based Learning

1

Making the Transition from School to Work

Key Terms

job

occupation

career

career clusters

job shadowing

work-based learning programs

school-to-work programs

school-to-work coordinator

program coordinator

training station

supervisor

work-based mentor

training sponsor

cooperative education

internship

transferable skills

Chapter Objectives

After studying this chapter, you will be able to

- **identify** what students should consider when trying to make a career decision.

- **explain** how a work-based learning program is organized.

- **list** the purpose and types of work-based learning programs available.

- **describe** the benefits of the work-based learning programs for students and employers.

- **identify** the career knowledge and skills that all students should develop.

Reading Advantage

Read the review questions at the end of the chapter *before* you read the chapter. Keep the questions in mind as you read to help you determine which information is most important.

Achieving Academic Standards

English Language Arts

- Read print and non-print texts to acquire new information and to respond to the needs and demands of society and the workplace. (IRA/NCTE, 1)
- Apply strategies to comprehend, interpret, evaluate, and appreciate texts. (IRA/NCTE, 3)
- Use different writing process elements appropriately to communicate. (IRA/NCTE, 5)

Key Concepts

- To find the job that is right for you, you will need to explore the options available.

- Work-based learning programs can help you prepare for the world of work.

- Participating in a work-based learning experience has many benefits.

- Career clusters knowledge and skills and transferable skills can help you succeed on the job.

Resource

Getting to Know Your Classmates, Activity A, WB

Reflect

Identify two personal interests and match them to two occupational areas. What types of work experiences have you had that match your areas of interest?

Chances are you will spend more time working than doing any other activity in your lifetime. Deciding what to do to earn a living is one of the most important decisions you will ever make. Like any important decision, having all the information you need improves your chance of making a good one.

Before making a career decision, you will need to become familiar with the workplace and the requirements of different occupations. Basic information about the world of work can be obtained in many ways— through school counselors, the Internet, and library resources. It is very important, however, to confirm what you learn about the work world through actual exposure to the workplace.

Exploring the World of Work

Reflect Further

What work-related skills have you learned through school courses and extracurricular activities? What jobs use these skills?

A key concern of people entering the workplace is finding a job they enjoy. A **job** is a task performed by a worker, usually to earn money. It is rare for a person to stay at the same job for a lifetime and not want increased variety, responsibility, and pay. These are provided by a series of more challenging jobs. When work requires the use of related skills and experience, that work is called an **occupation**. However, an occupation is not a career. A **career** is a progression of related occupations that results in employment and personal growth.

Each person is unique, so your idea of the ideal career will not match someone else's. Making a good career decision requires knowing yourself, your strengths, and your interests. It also involves knowing about the different types of jobs that make up the workplace.

The Career Clusters

One of the best ways to learn about careers is by studying the **career clusters**, the 16 groups of occupational and career specialties. Reading the titles of the career clusters is the simplest way to begin thinking about the 16 basic career areas, 1-1.

Students usually begin thinking about their future in the workplace by trying to imagine themselves in different work settings. They consider how well different occupations match their talents, abilities, and interests. Eventually, they narrow down the many choices to two or three careers that seem most interesting. For an overview of the career clusters and the interests and abilities important to each, see Chapter 13, "Learning About Careers."

Each cluster includes several career directions, called *career pathways*. Within each pathway are various occupations ranging from entry-level to very challenging. All the career choices within a given pathway require a set of common knowledge and skills. This means the related careers require very similar programs of study. Being prepared for more than one career in a related field allows more flexibility when you are ready to look for a job.

Extend Your Knowledge

Using the Career Clusters

Ask your teacher or guidance counselor for advice on investigating the career clusters at www.careerclusters.org. Examine two clusters that include careers you may decide to pursue. What new facts did you learn during the search? Did your research help you move closer to making a career decision?

The career clusters are important because they are part of a broad plan that links school preparation to career success. The plan was developed by educators, employers, and professional groups. These experts carefully examined what students must know and be able to do in order to be prepared to handle any given job. With the help of teachers and counselors, you will develop a study plan matched to your career goals. Compatible activities and learning experiences will be added as you refine your career choice.

Discuss

Are you familiar with these career clusters?

Reflect

Which cluster listed in Chart 1-1 seems most interesting to you?

The Sixteen Career Clusters

The Career Clusters icons are being used with permission of the States' Career Clusters Initiative, 2008, www.careerclusters.org

1-1

All occupations in the U.S. workforce are addressed within these 16 career clusters.

Workplace Exploration

Making a career decision is not always easy because there are hundreds of choices to consider. Attending career events at school and listening to guest speakers are activities that can help you decide. These speakers can provide practical information on what it takes to get into their fields.

Another way to explore the workplace is by participating in field trips to different employers in your community. You can help arrange field trips as part of a class project. Most employers are happy to conduct group tours during slow business periods. You can also try contacting a company that interests you and visit on your own.

Another way to learn more about the world of work is through job shadowing. **Job shadowing** is following a worker on the job and observing what that job involves. If you know someone who has a job that sounds interesting, ask if it is possible to spend some time with him or her at work. The experience may last a few hours or a couple days, but it always requires the permission of the employer.

Volunteering is another way to learn about work. Animal shelters, recycling centers, and many other nonprofit operations rely on volunteer help. By volunteering, you can observe different types of work while contributing to activities that benefit your community.

Thinking It Through

Who would you like to observe on the job? Where can you volunteer and observe a work setting unfamiliar to you?

Opportunities to Learn on the Job

Several types of school programs are designed to prepare students for work. They are called **work-based learning programs** because they provide students with job training. They are also called **school-to-work programs**.

Work-based learning programs bridge the gap between school and work. They help students make the adjustment from full-time students to full-time employees, 1-2. Students attend classes and work part-time alongside full-time employees in business and industry. These programs give students an opportunity to learn in two places—school and work. The programs are especially valuable to students who want to succeed in a full-time occupation right after high school. For students planning to attend a technical school or college, these programs can help them decide which study plan to pursue

Work-based learning opportunities do not just happen. They are developed by contacting businesses and convincing them to work as partners with high schools for the benefit of students. Finding business partners and handling the details of creating and operating a school-to-work program can be a full-time job.

Students in work-based learning programs have a special teacher or counselor at the school assigned to them called a **school-to-work coordinator**. Another common term for this important person is **program coordinator**. The program coordinator works on the student's behalf to help make the work-based learning experience successful. He or she

Resource

Work-Based Learning: How It Works, color transparency CT-1, TR

Discuss

What tours or field trips have students taken that broadened their knowledge of the world of work?

Vocabulary

Discuss the definition of the term *work-based learning*. List five ways you expect to benefit from this program.

Discuss

What are the implications of the term *school-to-work*?

consults with everyone who must be informed about your progress. This person also provides the information, support, and help you will need to solve problems and make decisions.

Your contact with your future employer is through the program coordinator. He or she is responsible for reviewing your application for work experience. An effort is then made to match your occupational goals with an available work experience.

The coordinator carefully discusses your qualifications for a work experience with one or more potential employers before you are assigned to a training station. A **training station** is a job site where a student works to learn job skills. A training station may be a manufacturing company, hospital, hair salon, bank, construction site, auto service center, or some other workplace. The training stations available to you depend on the type of work-based learning program you follow and the cooperating employers in your area. Usually you are responsible for providing your own transportation from school to work.

Thornridge High School

1-2
Work-based learning is designed to help students make smooth transitions from their classrooms to meaningful jobs.

When you report to the job on your first day of work, you will be introduced to your supervisor. The **supervisor** is your boss in the workplace. He or she explains what is expected of you on the job and evaluates how well you do your work. The supervisor is responsible for the training station and your job training.

The supervisor explains the job and the company as much as possible, but often assigns an assistant to help you with day-to-day questions. This helper is called a **work-based mentor**. Another common term for this worker is **training sponsor**. He or she is an employee who knows how to do the job and teach you to do it well. Students tend to form friendships with their mentors and feel more relaxed when they are around.

Remember, the work-based learning experience is a three-way relationship involving you, your program coordinator, and the employer, 1-3. You have the most to gain from this relationship—professionalism, skills, knowledge, and work experience. Two common types of work-based learning programs available to you are cooperative education programs and internships.

Reflect Further

What might be discussed with a school-to-work coordinator that wouldn't be discussed with another teacher? Why is a student's relationship with his or her mentor different from that with teachers?

Cooperative Education

Cooperative education is a school program that prepares students for an occupation through a paid job experience. Cooperative education programs are also called *co-op programs*. They team a school with a local employer who agrees to hire a student part-time and pay an hourly wage. The employer provides job training to help a student prepare for a career goal.

Resource

Candidates for Work-Based Education, Activity B, WB

Discuss

What are the differences between a supervisor and a mentor?

For a work experience to be successful, the program coordinator and the workplace mentor must work together cooperatively with the student.

Reflect Further

How might a work-based learning experience affect your career plans?

Note

Remind students that in addition to providing experience, an unpaid internship can be listed under "Work Experience" on a résumé. This can be very important to people trying to find their first job.

Discuss

What are some benefits of working as an intern?

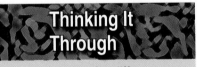

How are the different work-based learning programs similar? How are they different? Which type of program is best for you?

At school the student takes classes for approximately a half-day to meet requirements for graduation. The student also takes a cooperative education class taught by the coordinator to learn how to set career goals, apply for jobs, and manage finances. The student earns credit toward graduation for both the cooperative education class and the work experience.

Internship

An **internship** is a school program providing paid or unpaid work experience for a specified period to learn about a job or an industry. Students participate in this supervised work experience by enrolling as they would for a class. Instead of attending a formal class, however, the student works or volunteers at a temporary position during or after school hours and earns credit toward graduation.

A variety of internships are available to provide many different learning opportunities. An internship may involve routine duties as well as specially designed projects. Students must usually work for a specific number of hours and prepare a formal report that records their experiences. The school offering the internship establishes specific requirements.

In the Real World

A New Outlook for Tony

At 7:30 on a February morning in northern Texas, it's very cold! It seemed even colder to Tony when his car didn't start. The engine coughed once, then twice, and finally started. Tony muttered to himself, "Eleven more car payments to make, and it needs a new battery."

As Tony drove to school, he thought about quitting and looking for a job. During his three years in high school, he experienced nothing but discouragement. Freshman year was okay, but school had become a drag since then.

Tony didn't fail any of his classes, but he didn't study much either. Three reasons accounted for Tony's lack of enthusiasm. First, he had no goals for his future. His study habits were very poor. Finally, he had recently burdened himself with monthly car payments.

Tony was considering dropping out of high school when a friend suggested applying for the cooperative education program. The friend said, "You go to school for half the day and work part-time. You get paid for your work and school credit for the job."

"Oh, I've heard about that," Tony said, "but how do I get into the program?"

"See Mr. Lamas, the program coordinator. You had two courses in auto mechanics and enjoy working on cars. Maybe you can get a job at an auto repair shop. Then you won't need to quit school."

Tony met with Mr. Lamas and applied for the cooperative education program. The day Tony was accepted, his outlook on life seemed to change. All summer Tony looked forward to his senior year and his cooperative work experience.

During his senior year Tony worked for an auto service center. He learned how to tune car engines and repair brakes, transmissions, and other car parts. He also learned something about running a business. It was hard work, but Tony enjoyed it. Not only did Tony pay for his car and learn new skills, but he also made the B honor roll in his last semester.

Questions to Discuss

1. Why do you think Tony's outlook on life changed when he was accepted into the cooperative education program?
2. Why do you suppose Tony's grades improved in his senior year?
3. How did the cooperative education experience benefit Tony?
4. What do you think would have happened to Tony if he had quit high school?

Benefits of Learning on the Job

Participating in a work-based learning experience has many benefits. School-to-work programs can help students in the following ways:

- *Gaining on-the-job experience.* Every occupation requires certain skills and knowledge as basic job requirements. The work-based experience helps you develop these needed requirements. It also helps students make the personal transition from school to work.

- *Acquiring marketable skills.* By working in a real job under real working conditions, you develop skills that are useful in your job now. These skills will also help you get other jobs in the future.

Discuss

Do you know someone who has dropped out of school who might have benefited from a work-based learning program?

Resource

The Benefits of a Work-Based Learning Experience, transparency master 1-1, TR

- *Recognizing career goals.* Work-based learning gives you a chance to test some of your career interests. You can discover what you like to do and are able to do. In addition, you can discuss your career goals with others at work as well as in school.

- *Learning to work with others.* You will learn to communicate with a variety of people, including supervisors, coworkers, and customers. As a new employee, you learn how to conduct yourself in a work situation.

- *Earning money.* Many school-to-work programs provide opportunities to earn an income. The expression "earn while you learn" applies to work-based learning.

Employers benefit from work-based learning programs, too. They earn recognition in the community for their willingness to help young people. They receive interested part-time workers who are eager to learn and do a good job. Also, employers get the opportunity of a short-term labor supply they can pair with short-term projects. However, employers often are so pleased with the job performance of students that they offer them full-time employment after they graduate.

Preparing for Career Success

It is true that different jobs require different skills and knowledge. However, different jobs also require certain similar abilities in all workers, no matter what jobs they hold. Companies try to hire workers who possess the knowledge and skills needed for workplace success.

Career Knowledge and Skills

Preparation for the world of work begins long before you actually have a job. Workplace readiness involves the knowledge and skills you are learning now.

Employers have identified what learners and employees should know and be able to do to be successful in their work. Their recommendations were condensed to a top-10 list of essential knowledge and skills. This brief list is used to identify the specific requirements of a given career, 1-4.

For example, thinking logically, reading, and writing are skills you strengthen through class participation and homework. They are the same skills used by a worker when communicating with coworkers. In the workplace, being able to write instructions for coworkers can mean the difference between getting the job done well or having it totally confused.

Possessing the required knowledge and skills makes employees more valuable to their employers. When you focus on a career goal, you will recognize the link between the 10 brief terms and specific career requirements. You will have many opportunities to develop the necessary knowledge and skills long before you join the workforce. Taking advantage of these opportunities will help you develop to your full potential.

Career Knowledge and Skills	
Basic Knowledge or Skill	**Expression of a Career Requirement**
Academic foundations	Knowing how to read, write, make presentations, and listen well, and use math and science principles
Communications	Using illustrations to convey complex concepts
Problem solving and critical thinking	Analyzing, synthesizing, and evaluating data
Information technology applications	Using Internet searches, presentation software, and writing/publishing applications
Systems	Understanding the roles within the team, work unit, department, and organization
Safety, health, and environment	Knowing and following the procedures required by health and safety codes
Leadership and teamwork	Demonstrating integrity, perseverance, self-discipline, and responsibility
Ethics and legal responsibilities	Behaving in ways that are appropriate for the workplace
Employability and career development	Recognizing what needs to be learned or accomplished to gain a promotion
Technical skills	Correctly using the technological systems and equipment common to a chosen career

1-4
The 10 knowledge and skills required in all careers appear in the left column. The right column shows examples of how they are used to identify the requirements of specific careers.

Reflect Further

What skills or qualities are evident in the workers you most admire?

Resource

The Benefits of School-to-Work Programs, Activity D, WB

Discuss

Discuss the term *work smarter*. Ask students to identify ways in which they could improve their grades and overall school performance by working smarter.

Resource

What Are Your Workplace Skills? Activity E, WB

Thinking It Through

How can you use classroom and school activities to develop transferable skills? How can you use activities outside school to achieve the same goal?

Transferable Skills

Often the skills used in one job are also used in another. These are called **transferable skills**. A specialized skill such as speaking a second language is an example. People who possess transferable skills can easily use them in other jobs that require them.

Specialized skills are not the only skills that qualify as transferable skills. Broader skills such as good writing, problem-solving, and leadership skills are transferable skills, too. Your future success will depend on developing skills that can be used now and applied to future work opportunities. This means using the skills you develop as a student and transferring them to a work-based learning program. There you will polish your skills and learn other skills, all of which can be transferred later to a full-time job.

Continue developing transferable skills. They make you a more capable person and help expand the knowledge and skills you will need in the workplace.

Summary

Making a good career decision involves studying the career clusters and knowing about the many career choices available. It also requires knowing one's abilities and interests. Participating in career events, taking field trips, job shadowing, and volunteering are some ways to obtain first-hand advice on careers.

Work-based programs give students the opportunity to gain work experience while still in school. Of the various work-based learning experiences available, most are paid. Participating in these programs helps students prepare for a career goal. In a work-based learning experience, the student gains work experience through a part-time job with a local employer. The employer helps the student develop skills under actual work conditions. The program coordinator guides the student through a successful work experience.

While on the job, students gain marketable skills as they get experience in an occupation. They learn how to conduct themselves in work situations and gain job skills. Employers benefit by helping young people in the community and by gaining a valuable employee at the same time. They give interested students training that can lead to full-time employment after graduation.

It is important for students and workers to know certain knowledge and skills to achieve success in the workplace. Many of the skills are transferable from school to work and from job to job.

Facts in Review

1. True or false. Jobs, occupations, and careers always involve work that is done for pay.
2. The different career choices existing within each career cluster are called career _____.
3. List two ways for students to gain actual exposure to the workplace besides holding a job or participating in a work-based learning program.
4. Briefly explain how a work-based learning program is organized.
5. Who is usually responsible for providing transportation for the student from school to work?
6. Who is in charge of a training station?
7. Which work-based learning program(s) may consist of an unpaid work experience?
8. Name four benefits of a work-based learning program.
9. When should students develop the knowledge and skills they will need in their future careers?
10. Identify five transferable skills.

Resource

Review and Study Guide for Chapter 1, reproducible master 1-3, TR

Answers to *Facts In Review*

1. false
2. pathways
3. (List two:) field trips, job shadowing, volunteering
4. A school-to-work coordinator matches the student's occupational goals to available work-based learning experiences. An employer hires the student part-time for on-the-job training. The student goes to school part-time to meet graduation requirements.
5. the student
6. the job supervisor
7. internship
8. (List four:) gaining on-the-job experience, acquiring marketable skills, recognizing career goals, learning to work with others, earning money
9. while in school
10. (List three:) speaking a second language, writing skills, problem solving, leadership

Developing Your Academic Skills

1. **English.** Select a topic related to your current job, research information on it, and write a paper. Make sure all the information is communicated clearly. Use proper grammar and research-paper formatting.

2. **Social Studies.** Research the history of the U.S. Department of Labor at www.dol.gov. Write a report on the reasons for creating the department, as stated in its founding legislation in 1913.

Information Technology Applications

1. Use a drawing program to diagram a comparison of the two types of work-based learning programs described in this chapter: cooperative education versus an internship. Use the diagram to show commonalities shared by both programs as well as characteristics unique to each.

2. Do an Internet search to identify different types of work-based learning programs offered to high school students throughout the United States. Write a brief description of each program and prepare a spreadsheet or chart to summarize your findings.

Applying Your Knowledge and Skills

1. **Leadership and Teamwork.** Work with a small group of classmates to list the adjustments students may encounter as they make the transition from full-time students to full-time employees. Share your findings with the class.

2. **Communications.** Write a half-page summary explaining why you enrolled in a work-based learning program and what you expect to gain from your experience.

3. **Employability and Career Development.** Investigate volunteer opportunities in your community. Report on one that appeals to you. Identify how the volunteer activity contributes to preparing individuals for a future job.

4. **Problem Solving and Critical Thinking.** Work with a small group of classmates to develop a plan for exploring the world of work. The plan should include a variety of possible experiences including Internet and library searches, guest speakers, field trips, job shadowing, and volunteering. Include the names and telephone numbers of speakers and companies to visit.

5. **Communications.** Form a discussion group with a small group of classmates to discuss what work means to each individual. Which do you see more often—people treating work as a problem or as an opportunity? Discuss what may inspire workers to view work as fun and exciting.

Developing Workplace Skills

Working with a small group of classmates, interview a former student of the school who participated in a work-based learning program. (The person you interview can be someone you know or a person whose name is provided to you by the school-to-work coordinator.) Determine how the former student's work experience helped him or her develop the knowledge and skills needed in the workplace. Show your findings in a concise chart and briefly report them to the class.

2

Understanding Work-Based Learning

Key Terms

interview

social security

work permit

training agreement

training plan

training station report

Fair Labor Standards Act (FLSA)

minimum wage

Equal Pay Act

Equal Employment Opportunity
  Commission (EEOC)

priority

summarizing

Chapter Objectives

After studying this chapter, you will be able to

- **explain** what your school expects of you as a student in a work-based learning program.

- **summarize** the effects of the Fair Labor Standards Act on workers.

- **identify** ways you can improve your learning skills.

Reading Advantage

Arrange a study session to read the chapter with a classmate. After you read each section independently, stop and tell each other what you think the main points are in the section. Continue with each section until you finish the chapter.

Achieving Academic Standards

English Language Arts

- Read print and non-print texts to acquire new information and to respond to the needs and demands of society and the workplace. (IRA/NCTE, 1)
- Use different writing process elements appropriately to communicate. (IRA/NCTE, 5)

Math

- Compute fluently and make reasonable estimates. (NCTM)

Key Concepts

- Your training station is the location of your work-based learning.

- A social security card is required for work. Depending on your age, you may also need a work permit.

- A training agreement outlines the purposes of the work-based program and defines the responsibilities of everyone involved.

- The training plan lists attitudes, skills, and knowledge that you plan to learn during the work experience.

- Several laws cover fair labor practices and safe labor practices.

- The study skills you use in the classroom are just as important as the job skills you will learn.

Reflect Further

As a school-to-work student, what behaviors will your school's leaders expect of you? How might their expectations for you differ from those for students not in school-to-work programs?

Note

The school-to-work program will be a critical test of your ability to manage time effectively.

Resource

Getting a Social Security Card, Activity B, WB

Activity

Devise a way to memorize your social security number.

Thinking It Through

When is a social security number needed? How might your social security number be used illegally?

As a student in a work-based program, your daily schedule may be different from those of other students. Your behavior will be governed by certain state and federal laws that did not affect you before. You may need to adjust to new school and work hours. You will meet new people and accept new responsibilities. You will spend more time on your own, which means you will have more freedom. Your success in a work-based learning program depends a great deal on how well you handle your freedom and responsibilities.

Your Training Station

You will receive on-the-job training at a school-approved training station. This is the location of your work-based learning. Your program coordinator will help you find a suitable training station and send you for an interview. An **interview** is a planned meeting between a job applicant and an employer. During or after your interview, the employer will show you where the person selected for the job will work.

The employer may interview several other students for the same job. After the interviews, the employer will decide whether to hire you or another student. Once an employer has agreed to hire you, you are ready to prepare for your work experience.

Get a Social Security Number and a Work Permit

A social security card is a requirement for work. **Social security** is the federal government's program for providing income when earnings are reduced or stopped by retirement, disability, or death. Employers use social security numbers for reporting earnings to the federal government for income tax purposes. Social security numbers are also used for enrollment in health insurance or retirement programs offered by the employer, among other reasons.

Most people in today's society are required to have a social security number to perform everyday activities. For example, you need a social security card to open a savings account. You may even need one to enroll in school or get a driver's license. Your social security number should be kept private and given only to people who need to know it. The Social Security Administration suggests you ask the following questions before giving out your social security number: Why is my number needed? How will my number be used? What happens if I refuse? What law requires me to give my number? You can learn more about the proper use of social security numbers at www.ssa.gov.

If you have lost your social security card, you must apply for a replacement card at a social security office, 2-1. You should also apply for a replacement card if you change your name. Generally, apply for a social security number at least two weeks before you will need it. You must show evidence of your age, identity, and U.S. citizenship or immigrant status when you apply.

If you are under age 16 (under age 18 in some states), you will also need a work permit. A **work permit** makes it legal for a student underage to work for an employer. A work permit limits the number of hours a student can work each school day and the types of jobs a student can do. Work permits may be issued by schools. Check with your school to see if you will need a permit before you begin work.

2-1

After your social security application is processed, you will receive a social security card with your name and number on it.

Abide by the Training Agreement

During your work experience, you will be expected to assume the responsibilities outlined in an agreement between you, your school, and your employer. This is called a **training agreement**, 2-2. It may have different names or formats depending on your specific school-to-work program.

A training agreement is similar to a contract. It outlines the purposes of the work-based program and defines the responsibilities of everyone involved. The agreement requires signatures from you (the student), your parent(s) or guardian, the school coordinator, and the employer and sometimes the school administrator. Although the wording varies from school to school, all training agreements serve the same general purposes:

- To assure the employer that the student is committed to the work experience.

- To assure the student that the employer is committed to training him or her to do the job.

- To assure the parent(s) or guardian that the student is involved in a well-planned educational experience.

- To assure the school-to-work coordinator that all parties understand their responsibilities and are committed to the student having a successful work experience.

Resource

The Training Agreement Benefits All, color transparency CT-2A, TR

Resource

Training Agreement Responsibilities, Activity A, WB

Thinking It Through

Why is it important for students, employers, parents or guardians, and teachers to sign a training agreement?

Work-Based Learning Program Training Agreement

Program _____ Coordinator _____

Student _____ Birth Date _____ Social Sec. No. _____

Training Station _____ Supervisor's Name _____

Training Station Address _____ Student's Job Title _____ Program Code ____

Training Station Phone _____ Student's Hourly Wage _____

Teacher _____ through _____
                                              (Date)

Duration of Training Period: _____
                              (Date)

(Employment will terminate at the end of the training period for purposes of this agreement.
Employment beyond the ending date of the agreement will be at the option of the employer
and the employee and will not be governed by the terms of this agreement.)
===

The items below identify the obligations of all parties to this agreement. If additional
information is required by any party, it should be added at the time the agreement is signed.

The Cooperating Training Station Employer/Mentor

1. Will provide an average minimum of fifteen hours of work/training per week.
2. Will provide the student with supervision by a qualified and experienced work-based mentor.
3. Will provide the student with the same consideration given other employees in regard to safety, health, social security, and other general employment conditions.
4. Will not use the student to replace any regular employee.
5. Will direct the participation of the student in the occupational experience as detailed in the training plan with the objective of assisting the student in understanding the nature of the occupation and the responsibilities and opportunities it involves.
6. Will keep a daily record of the student's attendance and will report attendance and progress to the program coordinator as requested.
7. Will not assign the student to hazardous tasks. (OSHA, Fair Labor Standards Act)
8. Will not assign the student to drive.
9. Will immediately notify the program coordinator of any unsatisfactory development.
10. Will provide insurance against accidents on the premises when the student is on the job.
11. Will develop a training plan for the student with the aid of the program coordinator.
12. Will pay the student a wage or salary comparable to other trainees.
13. Will be responsible for compliance with all state and federal laws governing employment of student learners.
14. Will provide time for the training station supervisor to confer with the program coordinator to discuss progress of the student and to assist in determining grades.

The Student

1. Will report promptly to the training station on the days and hours mutually arranged with the employer/mentor.
2. Will notify the employer/mentor and the program coordinator well in advance when absence is unavoidable.

(continued on next page)

2-2

A training agreement outlines the purposes of the work-based learning program and defines the responsibilities of everyone involved.

3. Will cooperate with the employing supervisor, engage in the assignment as a learning experience, observe all rules of the company, and observe safety rules.
4. Will make a weekly written report to the program coordinator.
5. Will remain in the program for the entire school year.
6. Will take an active part in the selection of a workstation and all that is involved in maintaining a good relationship with the employer/mentor.
7. Will participate in the related student organization activities.
8. Will not be permitted (without approval from the program coordinator) to work on days when he/she is absent from school.

The Program Coordinator

1. Will, with the assistance of the employer/mentor or training supervisor, prepare a training plan of tasks to be learned on the job and related topics to be taught in school. A copy of this training plan will be kept on file with the employer/mentor, the program coordinator, and the student.
2. Will make provision for all school-to-work students to receive the regularly scheduled instruction.
3. Will visit each student a minimum of once per quarter at the training station and meet with the person to whom the student is responsible while employed.
4. Will endeavor to adjust all complaints with the cooperation of all parties concerned and will have the authority to transfer or withdraw a student.

The Parent or Guardian

1. Will agree to the conditions of the student's participation in the work-based learning program.
2. Will be responsible for the student's conduct both in school and on the job.

Special Considerations

_____

_____

_____

I fully understand the above conditions and I agree to cooperate in their implementation:

_____   _____
Student's Signature   Parent's (or Guardian's) Signature

_____   _____
Employer's/Mentor's Signature   Program Coordinator's Signature

The parties to this agreement do not discriminate on the basis of race, color, national origin, sex, handicapping condition, religion, creed, or limited English proficiency.

The employers in this agreement are affirmative action/equal opportunity employers. They comply with Title IX of the Educational Amendments of 1972, the Rehabilitation Act of 1973, the Vietnam Era Veterans' Readjustment Assistance Act of 1974, and the Americans with Disabilities Act of 1990.

2-2

Continued.

Reflect Further

Why are training plans an important part of the school-to-work program? What might be some consequences of falsifying a progress report?

Follow the Training Plan

In addition to the training agreement, there is the **training plan**. It consists of a list of attitudes, skills, and knowledge that you plan to learn during the work experience. The plan is usually developed by you, your program coordinator, and the employer. The purpose of the plan is to help you progress on the job toward your career goals. Like training agreements, training plans vary in form. Some are detailed plans, while others consist of a few general statements describing what you will learn.

Another purpose of the training plan is to formally identify your training supervisor on the job. The supervisor is responsible for the training station and your on-the-job training. This is the person your program coordinator contacts about your progress.

To help everyone evaluate your progress, most schools require students to keep a weekly or monthly job record. This is a progress report known as a **training station report**. Each week or month you write down the duties you performed and the attitudes, skills, and knowledge you learned at work. Periodically you and your program coordinator check your accomplishments to see if you are progressing toward the goals listed in your training plan. During these evaluation checks, you learn how much you have accomplished and what you still want to achieve, 2-3. Your supervisor will also do a formal evaluation of the tasks on the training plan each grading period.

2-3

Periodically you and your program coordinator will meet to evaluate the progress you are making in your work experience.

Know the Law

There always are school rules and regulations to follow. Now that you will be working away from school as part of your school assignment, there will be new rules governing your actions. Some of these are covered in your training plan and agreement. Others may involve state or federal laws.

Fair Labor Practices

The **Fair Labor Standards Act (FLSA)** protects workers from unfair treatment by their employers. Passed in 1938, the law deals with relationships between employees and employers.

Resource

Your Training Plan—An Important Component, color transparency CT-2B, TR

Resource

Step-by-Step Training Plan, reproducible master 2-1, TR

Resource

The Training Plan, Activity C, WB

All employees who work for employers involved in interstate or international commerce are covered by this act. Therefore, any business producing, handling, or selling a product or service outside the state must comply with this law. Employees who work in education and health care are also covered. In fact, there are few workers who are not covered by the Fair Labor Standards Act.

If an employee feels that rights protected by fair labor laws have been violated, he or she may complain. Complaints should be directed to the Employment Standards Administration or the Wage and Hour Division of the U.S. Department of Labor. Complaints are investigated by government officers. If an employer is found in violation of the law, the business may be prosecuted in court and fined. You can learn more about the FLSA from the Fair Labor Standards Act Advisor at www.dol.gov/elaws/flsa.htm and Youth Rules at www.youthrules.dol.gov.

Minimum Wage

An FLSA amendment established the creation of a minimum wage. **Minimum wage** is the lowest hourly rate of pay that most employees must receive. Employers, of course, may pay more than minimum wage, but they cannot pay employees less. The minimum hourly rate is set by the federal government. It is changed periodically to meet the needs of inflation and recession.

Some employees are excluded from the minimum wage law by specific employer exemptions. For instance, food service workers who earn tips can lawfully be paid less than minimum wage. It is also lawful to pay employees less during a training period when they first start a new job. Trainees, too, may be paid less than minimum wage.

Overtime Pay

Another FLSA amendment sets guidelines for overtime pay to employees. Overtime must be paid at a rate of at least 1½ times the employee's regular pay rate. Overtime is paid for each hour worked in excess of the maximum hours allowed. For example, suppose an employee who earns $8.00 an hour works 44 hours in a workweek. The employee is entitled to at least 1½ times $8.00, or $12.00, for each hour over 40. That person's pay for the week is $320.00 for the first 40 hours plus $48.00 for four hours of overtime—a total of $368.00.

Saturdays, Sundays, and holidays are treated like any other day of the week. Employers are not required to pay overtime on weekends and holidays unless the hours worked exceed the maximum allowable. Like minimum wage, some employees are exempt from receiving overtime pay.

Thinking It Through

Do you know what the current minimum wage is? Do you think requiring a minimum wage is important? Why?

Discuss

Why is attitude an important part of obtaining and maintaining employment?

Enrich

Contact a legislator or search the Internet and obtain a copy of the FLSA. Review the provisions of the law.

Enrich

Debate the pros and cons of minimum wage.

Activity

How much would an employee make who works 50 hours a week at $4.80 per hour?

Students working in school-based learning programs are considered trainees, not employees. Consequently, this law will not apply to you during your work-based learning experience. However, some employers may pay overtime voluntarily.

Equal Pay

An amendment to the Fair Labor Standards Act resulted in the **Equal Pay Act** of 1963. This law requires equal pay to employees of both sexes for doing equal jobs. Jobs performed under similar working conditions that require the same level of skill, effort, and responsibility are considered equal, 2-4.

Pay exceptions may occur for differences in seniority, skill, productivity, services performed, or shift work. Any violation of equal pay requirements encountered by employees should be reported to the **Equal Employment Opportunity Commission (EEOC)**. This U.S. agency oversees equal employment opportunities for all Americans. You can get more information from any of its offices, which are listed in most phone books under *U.S. Government*, or at www.eeoc.gov. (Also refer to Chapter 20, "Diversity and Rights in the Workplace.")

2-4
The Equal Pay Act guarantees this woman the same wage as that paid to a man for performing this job.

As a trainee, you will not be entitled to the same pay level as an employee. However, your pay as a trainee should match the pay that other trainees receive for doing the same work.

Child Labor Standards

The FLSA child labor provision is designed to serve two functions. It protects the educational opportunities of children. It also prohibits the employment of children in jobs that may be hazardous to their health or well-being. Your state may have laws that are stricter than these provisions particularly as they apply to full-time students:

- 18-year-olds are no longer subject to federal child labor laws. They can work at any job for any number of hours.

- 16- and 17-year-olds can work at any nonhazardous job for any number of hours. (Hazardous jobs include operating motor vehicles or power-driven machinery, working with explosives, and jobs in construction, demolition, and other fields.)

- 14- and 15-year-olds may work outside school hours in various nonmanufacturing, nonmining, and nonhazardous jobs, but for no longer than three hours per school day or 18 hours per school week. During nonschool periods, they may work no longer than eight hours per day or 40 hours per week. Also, their work may not begin before 7 a.m. or extend past 7 p.m. (9 p.m. in the summer).

A special provision applies to 14- and 15-year-olds enrolled in an approved work experience through school. They may be employed for up to 23 hours per school week and three hours per school day even during school hours.

The minimum age for most nonfarm work is 14. However, young people of any age may deliver newspapers or work for parents in a nonfarm business. They may also perform in radio, television, movie, or theatrical productions.

Thinking It Through

What is the purpose of child labor laws? Do you think child labor laws help or hurt your chances to get ahead?

Safe Labor Practices

Safety in the workplace is so important that it is the sole focus of one government agency. The *Occupational Safety and Health Administration (OSHA)* sets and enforces safety and health standards for workers. The agency's goal is to prevent accidents and injuries in the workplace. Their Web site can be found at www.osha.gov.

Employers must provide a safe workplace, but workers are required to follow all safety rules. Before you begin working, your supervisor will review the specific safety rules that apply to your training station. (For more information about OSHA and workplace safety, see Chapter 9, "Safety on the Job.")

Study and Learn

School-to-work students sometimes say "I want to work, not study." You will need to do both to be successful in your work-based learning experience and your future career. Part of your success in the program may depend on your desire to study and learn. The study skills you use in the classroom are just as important as the job skills you will learn. That is why it is important to complete all class assignments.

To complete your assignments, you need to study to the best of your ability. Sometimes this means making an extra effort to improve your study skills. However, your efforts will reap benefits now and in the future. You can use your attitudes, skills, and knowledge to complete your education and finish school. As you move into your future career, you will be able to use many of the same skills.

Discuss

What are some possible results of not following workplace safety rules?

Activity

Read a copy of an instruction bulletin related to a certain job task. Discuss why it is important to study.

In the Real World

What Will School Ever Do for Me?

Susan loved her job at the automotive parts store, and she did it well. She knew where to find any item a customer needed and sometimes helped customers install parts in their cars. She often came to work early and stayed late. Her boss was very impressed with her work and her attitude and gave her very high marks on her monthly performance reviews.

Susan loved her job, but hated school. She couldn't wait to graduate. With her poor grades getting worse, however, she wasn't sure she *would* graduate. Quitting school was an idea she seriously considered. She just couldn't see any value in her classes. After all, she was doing great on her job and that was all that mattered, or so she thought.

One day her program coordinator took her aside and told her she could no longer stay in the work-based learning program due to failing grades in English and American History. Susan was angry. "That's not fair!" she said. "I'm doing good at my job, and English and history ain't got nothing to do with it."

Questions to Discuss

1. Did Susan have a right to be angry?
2. Was the program coordinator right in removing Susan from the program?
3. What is the relationship between English and history classes and succeeding in the world of work?

Reflect Further

When and where do you study best? Do you prefer silence or some background sounds? How can you avoid distractions that interfere with your studying?

Enrich

Demonstrate with another student how you should respond during an evaluation at a work site. Demonstrate both positive and negative (but constructive) comments.

Note

Emphasize that many employers observe attitude first, then knowledge and skills second.

Practice Good Study Habits

Learning to study is not difficult. The key to success starts with improving your study habits. To develop good study habits, practice the following study points:

- *Keep a separate notebook for each class.* A spiral notebook can help you organize your notes and assignments.

- *Make sure you clearly understand the assignment.* When you do not understand what to do, ask the teacher.

- *Complete your class assignments every day.* This is especially important during the classroom portion of your experience. Your teacher will give you assignments related to your job experiences and personal life. The knowledge and skills you will gain by completing these assignments will help you succeed in both school and work.

- *Set aside a time and place to study.* If possible, study at the same time every day. Make sure the atmosphere is appropriate for the way you learn best, 2-5.

- *When it is time to study, begin immediately.* Go to your study place with an attitude that studying is the only thing you want to accomplish. Do not waste time daydreaming or thinking of other things to do.

- *Study in small segments of time.* Two separate 30-minute study periods may be better for you than a one-hour study period.

- *Do the more difficult assignments first.* Studying only the easy subjects may leave little time for harder assignments.

- *Use your computer.* The Internet can help you research topics quickly. However, be careful. Not all information posted on the Internet is accurate. Internet addresses that end in *.gov* (government agencies) and *.org* (official organizations) are usually the most reliable. Word processing software is a great way to take notes as well as improve your writing skills. Spreadsheets can help organize and prioritize your assignments.

2-5
The school library is an ideal place to study if you prefer quiet surroundings.

Organize Your Schedule

As a student working part-time, learning to organize your schedule is an important skill. You may want to develop a daily schedule to help balance your time for work, study, and recreation. You can do this by making a list of all the important tasks you must do each day. Then you can arrange your list in order of priority. **Priority** means ranking first in a "to do" list. When items are ranked by priority they are listed from first to last.

A list of things to do helps you decide which tasks are most important and which must be done ahead of others. Because both school and work are important to you in this program, tasks for both should be done well and on time. Getting organized helps you use time wisely each day.

Thinking It Through

What important tasks must be done tomorrow? Which should be done first, next, and so forth? By listing tasks ahead of time, are you more likely to do them well and on time?

Resource

Your Study Habits, Activity E, WB

Resource

Organizing Your Schedule, Activity F, WB

Resource

Reorganizing Your Weekday Schedule, reproducible master 2-2, TR

Reflect Further

How can you improve your reading skills? Who can you see for help?

Improve Your Reading Skills

The skill that is basic to all studying and schoolwork is reading. The better you read, the more effective studying will be and the more you will learn. Some readers may take more time to read and complete their assignments. However, a person's reading skills can be improved. The more a person reads, the easier and faster reading becomes. Some readers improve their reading skills by setting aside more time for studying and reading. They also get special help by joining a reading improvement program at school.

To understand the written material better, think about what you are reading before you begin. Observe the chapter title, the subheads, the photos, and the charts. What are the main ideas the writer is trying to express? When you know the main ideas, reading becomes easier.

Do not just focus on single words. Read sentences and paragraphs to understand the details of an idea. It takes many words together to express a thought, idea, or fact. Read the assignment more than once and reread sections you do not understand. The first reading will help you understand the main idea. Additional readings will help you understand details.

Participate in Class

Pay close attention to the teachers in all your classes, even in the classes you dislike. Be a good listener. Focus on the teacher or speaker and think about what is being said. Also, be sure to sit where you can see and hear well.

If you do your assignments regularly, it is easier to make contributions during class. State facts as you know them. Ask questions about ideas or facts that you do not completely understand. Even lessons that seem uninteresting take on new meaning when you get involved in the discussion and participate in class, 2-6.

2-6

Participating in class can help you learn more and enjoy the time you spend at school.

Activity

In your work experience notebook, list your daily tasks in order of most important to least important.

Activity

Prioritize six tasks in three situations and justify the reasons for your prioritization.

Extend Your Knowledge

More Notes on Notes

Taking notes in class helps reinforce learning and identifies the most important points in the material you are studying. The more organized your notes are, the more helpful they will be when you study. Start by writing the lesson title or topic and the date at the top of the page. During class, record the main headings and leave space for adding comments. Do not try to write entire sentences, just a few words or phrases to help you remember the main ideas. After class or during study time, review your notes and complete the ideas and facts you want to remember.

Take Notes

Many students improve their learning skills by taking notes while or after they read an assignment. They go back to each page, section, or paragraph, and write down the main ideas in a study notebook. This is called **summarizing**. Summarizing helps you remember what you have read. It also helps you review the information for a test.

When taking notes, organize them by chapter or date, whichever is best for you. Write the notes in your own words and be brief. Just summarize the main idea and write it in your notebook. Do not try to copy the idea word for word from the book.

You may want to consider using a computer to take notes. Computer notes are more legible and easier to edit. You will find it easy to search for specific terms or assignments. A laptop computer will enable you to take notes in class. However, it is important to resist the temptation to play games or search the Internet.

Reflect Further

What can you do to be a better class participant?

Discuss

In class, do you take better notes if you are prepared? Is there a disadvantage to making too many notes?

Summary

Students in work-based learning programs work with their program coordinators to find a suitable training station. To apply for a job, a social security card is needed, and so is a work permit in some cases. Students also need to complete a training agreement. This agreement outlines the purposes of the work-based learning program. It also defines the responsibilities of the parent or guardian, employer, school, and student. A training plan is developed to show the attitudes, skills, and knowledge students are expected to learn on the job. Most labor laws only govern employees, but some apply as well to school-to-work students in the workplace.

Students in work-based learning are expected to do their jobs well and keep pace with their school studies. Practicing good study habits and keeping schedules organized are important skills for success in the program. Students can improve their reading skills by trying to read more often. Participating in class, taking good notes, and summarizing key points are also helpful ways to improve learning skills.

Facts in Review

1. Before beginning a school-to-work program, how can a student know his or her training station?
2. True or false. A person can wait to get a social security card after starting work.
3. What questions should you ask before giving out your social security number?
4. What are the purposes of a training agreement?
5. What are the purposes of a training plan?
6. How do the school-to-work student and the program coordinator determine if the goals of the training plan are being met?
7. What is the overtime pay rate?
8. What jobs are considered equal?
9. At what age can a person work at any job for an unlimited number of hours?
10. List five ways a student can develop good study habits.
11. Define *summarizing*.

Resource

Review and Study Guide for Chapter 2, reproducible master 2-3, TR

Answers to *Facts In Review*

1. by visiting it at the job interview
2. false
3. Why is my number needed? How will my number be used? What happens if I refuse? What law requires me to give my number?
4. to assure the employer that the student is committed to the work experience, to assure the student that the employer is committed to training the student to do the job, to assure the parents/guardian that the student is involved in a well-planned educational experience, to assure the program coordinator that all parties understand their responsibilities and are committed to the student having a successful work experience
5. to help the student progress toward his or her career goals through the work-based experience
6. by reviewing the training station report and evaluation checks
7. 1½ times the person's regular pay rate
8. jobs performed under similar working conditions that require the same level of skill, effort, and responsibility
9. 18 years
10. (List five:) keeping a separate notebook for each class, making sure he or she clearly understands the assignments, completing assignments daily, setting aside a time and place to study, beginning to study immediately when time to, studying in small segments, doing the difficult work first, using the computer
11. briefly restating the main idea of each page, section, or paragraph

Developing Your Academic Skills

1. **Math.** Determine how much a person would earn annually working 20 hours a week at minimum wage. Is this an adequate salary for a high school student? Determine the yearly salary of a person working full-time for minimum wage. Is this amount adequate to support one person? Compare this amount with a yearly salary based on the minimum wage ten years ago.

2. **English.** Read selections from *The Grapes of Wrath* by John Steinbeck, *The Jungle* by Upton Sinclair, or other literature related to labor conditions. Report on how conditions described in these books have led to and been changed by labor reform.

Information Technology Applications

1. Research and review software designed to improve reading skills. Give reports on the effectiveness of the programs.

2. Gather information on the history of OSHA from their Web site, www.osha.gov. Give an oral report on your findings to the class.

Applying Your Knowledge and Skills

1. **Problem Solving and Critical Thinking.** Identify at least six instances where you may be required to provide your social security number. Use the Internet and personal interviews to answer the following questions for each instance. Why is my number needed? How will my number be used? What happens if I refuse? What law requires me to give my number?

2. **Employability and Career Development.** Take a close look at the training agreement related to a work-based learning experience at your school. Make a list of the responsibilities of the school-to-work student as outlined in the agreement. Rank the responsibilities in their order of importance. Which responsibility do you consider most important? Why?

3. **Communications.** Research the work conditions and labor practices that were common before the Fair Labor Standards Act was passed. Write a paper, with sources documented, to report your findings.

4. **Employability and Career Development.** Determine what the minimum wage currently is and when the rate was last changed. Based on a 40-hour workweek, what would be the annual salary before taxes for a person making the minimum wage?

Developing Workplace Skills

New job responsibilities added to your school and leisure activities will place new demands on your time. Develop a two-column spreadsheet for each day of the week to help you allocate your time wisely. Record the times of day in one column and the scheduled activities in the other. Keep a detailed daily journal for your first week of work. Afterward, consider if changes are needed. In a brief report to the class, explain what you learned through this exercise.

3

What Your Employer Expects

Key Terms

attitude

self-esteem

individual responsibility

initiative

self-management

sociability

ethics

integrity

confidential

work ethic

constructive criticism

job evaluation

Chapter Objectives

After studying this chapter, you will be able to

- **explain** what your employer expects of you as a worker.
- **identify** things you can do to promote good working relationships with your supervisor and coworkers.

Reading Advantage

Think of a movie you have seen that relates to this chapter. Sketch a scene from the movie or write a brief description. As you read the chapter, visualize the characters in the movie. How would the scene be different if the characters had read this chapter?

Achieving Academic Standards

English Language Arts

- Read print and non-print texts to acquire new information and to respond to the needs and demands of society and the workplace. (IRA/NCTE, 1)
- Use a variety of technological and information processes to gather and synthesize information and to create and communicate knowledge. (IRA/NCTE, 8)
- Use spoken, written, and visual language to accomplish their purposes. (IRA/NCTE, 12)

Key Concepts

- Personal qualities are important to your job success.

- Your personal qualities will affect how you relate to your supervisor and coworkers.

- Accepting constructive criticism will help you improve your job performance.

Resource

An Employer's View, Activity A, WB

Resource

Personal Qualities on the Job,
Activity B, WB

Your employer will make a major investment in time and money to help you become an effective employee. He or she will have certain expectations of you as a result. Chances are many of these expectations will not be unique to your employer. All employers appreciate good work habits, honesty, willingness to learn new skills, and the ability to get along well with others.

Personal Qualities Needed on the Job

Reflect Further

Give an example of an attitude you have observed at your place of work. Was it positive or negative? Do you enjoy working with someone with a bad attitude? Why or why not?

As an employee, there are certain guidelines your employer will expect you to follow. Your employer will expect you to have a positive attitude, attend work regularly, be on time for work, and perform well on the job. Your company or business will also expect you to be honest, show initiative, be loyal, and be cooperative. You are expected to be courteous and well groomed as well. Your ability to meet these expectations will depend partly on your health and fitness.

You may be thinking you have many responsibilities to meet as an employee. You are right! When you work for someone else, you will need to follow his or her rules. Employers expect the people they hire to use their attitudes, skills, and knowledge to help the business operate and make a profit. Your employer will expect you to do the same and to work to the best of your ability.

Positive Attitude

Your attitude will play a big part in your success on the job. An **attitude** is an outlook on life. It reflects how you feel and think about other people and situations.

What types of employee and employer attitudes have you observed on the job? If people have positive attitudes, they usually get along well with other people and enjoy sharing ideas. They tend to be friendly, cheerful, and treat others with respect. People with negative attitudes do not get along well with other people. They may complain, argue, or get angry easily. Some are unhappy and withdraw from others.

A positive attitude is beneficial to your employer and to you. Your employer expects you to have a good attitude while you are working, 3-1. When you take a positive approach to your work, you tend to be more productive. Your work performance improves. This makes you a more valuable employee and helps you get along well with other people.

To a great extent, your self-esteem determines your attitudes. **Self-esteem** is having confidence and satisfaction in yourself. It is a measure of how you see yourself. People who think they will fail have low self-esteem. People who think they will succeed have a positive outlook on life and high self-esteem.

In the Real World

What Bad Attitude?

Carlos started his morning discussing a recent order with a customer on the telephone. The customer ordered additional memory for her computer over a week ago and still had not received it. Carlos explained that he took the order correctly and sent it immediately to the shipping department. He told the customer it was not his fault she had not received her order.

The customer said she did not care whose fault it was. She had already paid for the memory and expected prompt delivery as promised. Carlos insisted it was not his problem and that the customer needed to call the receptionist and ask to talk with someone in the shipping department. The customer became so angry she told Carlos to cancel her order and slammed down the receiver.

Carlos lost his temper. He called the customer back and said, "You had no right to hang up on me. I deserve to be treated with respect!" The customer hung up again without saying a word. Still angry, Carlos called the customer back, but she refused to answer.

Questions to Discuss

1. Who is responsible for the confrontation?
2. How could Carlos have handled the situation differently?
3. Is there ever a good reason for showing disrespect to a customer?

3-1
By having a positive attitude, this employee conveys that she enjoys her job.

Discuss

List the many ways an employee's attitude can affect a company.

Enrich

Select an adult role model and research how attitude helped him or her to achieve goals.

Good Attendance

Both the employer and the school will expect you to be at work every working day. When a person is absent, it causes extra work for others. Poor attendance also reduces the effectiveness of the work experience.

Because absenteeism is a major concern of employers and teachers, many schools require students and parents to read and sign an absenteeism policy. This type of policy stresses the importance of regular attendance at school and at work. By signing the policy, students are saying they will attend school, work regularly, and notify their employer and coordinator if they must be absent. Violating this policy may cause the student to be dismissed from work and the school-to-work program.

Students with good attendance records avoid asking for time off from work to do personal errands. Scheduling doctor appointments, car repairs, and other personal needs outside work hours is best. In case of illness, death in the family, or an emergency, you should contact your employer and your coordinator to explain your absence from work.

Being dependable also means being reliable. A reliable person does not need to be watched because he or she always does what is expected. The important jobs in a company go to reliable workers.

Punctuality

Constantly arriving late to work is one employee practice that irritates employers. Being late may make your employer think you are not interested in your job. Frequent lateness indicates an "I don't care" attitude. Being late is inconsiderate and is not tolerated in the working world. You cannot make up being late one day by going in early the next day. You must be on time every day, 3-2.

Do not make the mistake of thinking that occasionally being a few minutes late will make little difference. It makes a big difference and you will be noticed. It is your responsibility to be at your job at starting time or earlier, never later. Plan your schedule so you will always be on time. If you take a bus to work and arrive late, you will need to catch an earlier one. If you drive, bicycle, or walk, allow plenty of time for delays caused by bad weather or heavy traffic. In other words, you should make it a policy to be five minutes early, not one minute late. Being late is a bad habit that can be costly to you and the company. Develop the good habit of being prompt.

Some companies require workers to check in and out by punching a time clock or starting a computer. These methods clearly show when employees arrive late or leave early. If you do not follow your work schedule, the company may subtract a percentage of your pay.

Performance

Although you will be learning new skills on the job, your employer will expect you to have some basic attitudes, knowledge, and skills in your area of employment. If you will be employed as an office assistant, you will need to have keyboarding skills. You cannot expect your employer to teach you the basics of a skill you should already possess.

You will be expected to possess **individual responsibility**, or a willingness to answer for your conduct and decisions. People without individual responsibility try to "pass the buck" rather than answer for their own failures. Even competent workers make mistakes, but they admit them and work to correct them.

3-2

Being on time shows that you care about your job and are considerate of your coworkers.

Your employer will also expect you to put forth your best effort while on the job. As a beginner, you probably will not be expected to do as much as an experienced worker. However, you will be expected to have the same work standards. If you are a secretary, you will not be expected to create a business letter as fast as an employee with five years of experience. You will, however, be expected to complete a letter correctly and accurately. As you gain more experience, you will be expected to increase your speed. Working quickly and efficiently should be one of your goals at work.

Discuss

Can an immature person possess individual responsibility?

Organizational Ability

The ability to organize your time and work assignments is another important skill. The difference between average and excellent workers is often not how hard they work, but how well they prioritize assignments. "Work smarter, not harder" is a phrase frequently quoted in business and industry.

Your work assignment may include a variety of tasks. In many cases you will need to work on several tasks at the same time. You will be expected to learn to determine the order in which the tasks need to be completed. For example, while you are sorting the mail, your supervisor may ask you to run some copies she needs for an important meeting. Then, before you get to the copier, the telephone rings with an urgent request to deliver an important message. How do you decide what needs to be done first?

Many factors can affect your decision. These may include important deadlines, your supervisor's priorities, the importance of the assignments, and the time you have available. It is also important to develop time management skills such as those discussed in Chapter 28, "Managing Family, Work, and Citizenship Roles." However, if you are uncertain as to what is most important, it is always best to consult your supervisors or mentor.

Reflect Further

What affect will your ability to organize and prioritize assignments have on your overall job performance? How will it affect your supervisor's performance?

Initiative

When at work, your supervisor and work-based mentor will tell you what your job is. When one project is done, you are expected to immediately start working on the next without someone reminding you. This quality is called **initiative**. It means making oneself do what is necessary.

Another term for initiative is **self-management**. Employers want employees with self-management for the obvious reason: they cannot afford employees who work only when reminded. They need independent thinkers who can recognize what needs to be done next.

Looking for new skills to learn on the job is another way to show initiative. Once you have gained some job experience, your employer will expect you to find tasks to do without being told. Use common sense, however, and do not try to do work that you are not qualified to do.

Cooperation

To be effective at your job, it is important for you to get along with your supervisor and coworkers. This is a sign of sociability. **Sociability** is interacting easily with people. On the job, you will need to be sociable with employees, customers, and everyone else you meet. Being sociable will make it easier for you to do your job well and get ahead.

To be cooperative, accept your share of the work and perform your job to the best of your ability. Make sure you follow directions carefully. Always ask questions when you do not understand how to do a certain task.

Be friendly, respectful, and considerate of other workers' feelings. A smile and a few minutes of friendly conversation are good ways to promote good working relationships. Also be enthusiastic about your job. Expressing enthusiasm will help you become a part of the working team, 3-3.

Thinking It Through

If a student intern leaves her boring job to help a coworker with a more interesting project, is this a sign of initiative?

Discuss

Have students share examples of tasks they performed on their jobs that were not requested or expected. What was the supervisor's reaction? Did this type of initiative ever get them in trouble?

Vocabulary

Define the term *cooperation* and give one negative and one positive example.

Discuss

Is it possible to become too sociable on the job? What are some signs?

3-3

Being cooperative and enthusiastic will help you get along well with your coworkers.

Being Part of a Team

Many employers now consider teamwork to be the key to competing successfully in the workplace. You may be asked to work as a member of a team to meet the demands of your employer. Being a team member of a company work group is similar to playing on a basketball or soccer team. Success is measured in terms of the team's success, not the individual's.

A company will ask you to join its team based on what you can contribute to its success. This chapter discusses some important characteristics of a good employee, such as a proper attitude, good attendance, punctuality, and cooperation. These characteristics become even more important as you work closely with coworkers. Failure to come to work, for example, not only affects your performance but also the team's. If you are absent, your coworkers must do their jobs plus yours to keep the team on target.

Every individual has certain strengths and weaknesses. Often the difference between a good team and a championship team is finding the right people to play the right positions. In the workplace you need to be honest about your strengths and weaknesses. You must be willing to play the position that helps the team most. As a beginning worker, your role may often be one of a support or bench player. Play the role effectively and be a member your team can rely on.

A key to working successfully on a team is getting to know and trust your fellow team members. You must be willing to admit when you have problems or make a mistake. You also must be able to share your feelings and ideas with others.

Finally, you must be willing to put the team's goals ahead of your personal goals. Ask questions concerning the purpose of the group. Be sure you can state the team's long-term and short-term goals. Understand why the team's goals are important and how they fit in the company's overall plan.

Working with Your Supervisor

Your supervisor has the role of seeing that work gets completed. The supervisor is also responsible for the quantity and quality of the product or service your department produces. When one or both is lacking, the supervisor must take the necessary steps to correct the problem. The supervisor may suggest a new way of getting the job done. The supervisor may also ask employees to work faster or change roles within the team.

You need to realize that your supervisor probably has a supervisor to whom he or she must report. Therefore, your performance on the job directly influences your supervisor's job performance. This, in turn, affects the progress of your employer.

Reflect

What personal characteristics does teamwork require? Do you possess these characteristics? Are you willing to develop them?

Resource

Case Study: A Worker's Attitude on the Job, reproducible master 3-1, TR

Discuss

Does a supervisor's tone of voice always reflect his or her attitude?

Reflect Further

Do you feel that members of a work team should vote on important matters? If so, do you believe that each member's vote should have equal weight?

Reflect Further

What should you say to your supervisor if you are assigned a task you do not want?

Reflect Further

Describe your idea of the perfect supervisor. Could your idea of the perfect supervisor differ from your coworkers'?

3-4

Make a special effort to work with your supervisor and to respect his or her decisions.

At times you may be assigned tasks that you would rather not do. Very few workers enjoy sweeping the floor or washing windows, but these are jobs that must be done. You must remember that you are a beginner. Beginners start with basic tasks and work their way up. Accept the tasks you are given with a pleasant attitude and perform them as well as you would any others.

Sometimes you may not mind the tasks you are assigned but dislike the way you are told to do them. Different supervisors have different ways of supervising. You may have the type of supervisor that shouts orders and gives no explanation. These people tend to be impersonal and strictly business-focused. This type of boss is likely to say, "Bob, clean up the storeroom before you leave work today and make sure you do a good job."

Other types of bosses make requests rather than give orders. They usually explain *what* they want done and *why*. This type of boss might say, "Bob, there will be an inspection at the plant tomorrow, and everything needs to look as nice and clean as possible. I would like you to be in charge of cleaning the storeroom today. I am sure you will do a good job."

Most of us prefer the second type of boss, but sometimes we get the type that shouts orders. No matter what type of boss you have, work *with* your supervisor, not *against* him or her, 3-4. Try to adapt to his or her style of management. You will find all types of people in the work world. Prepare yourself to get along with them all.

Discuss

What attitudes should be maintained to keep a positive outlook as you begin your career working in lower-level jobs?

Extend Your Knowledge

Customers and Courtesy

If you deal with customers on the job, being courteous to them is important. While on the job, you are the employer's representative. Consequently, you should treat customers with the courtesy your employer desires. "The customer is always right" is a motto many employers follow. Learning to be patient and considering others' rights and feelings will help you become a successful employee.

Courtesy

Being courteous means showing concern for other people and being mannerly with them. Courtesy can help you get along with your supervisor, coworkers, and customers. Showing respect for your employer is a form of courtesy. Being polite and considerate to your coworkers is another form of courtesy. Being polite instead of rude will also make your job more pleasant.

Personal Appearance

In many jobs, a worker's personal appearance has a great deal to do with his or her success. Your appearance is a reflection of you. While on the job, you should try to look your best. A neat, clean appearance starts with good grooming. Clean, neatly combed hair; clean hands; and trimmed nails show cleanliness.

Your clothes are also important to your personal appearance. Wearing clean, neat clothes that are appropriate for your job shows that you take pride in yourself. Before you go to work, think about your appearance. How do you look to your employer, coworkers, or customers?

Thinking It Through

What types of hairdo, jewelry, and clothing are very popular now, but are not appropriate for the workplace?

Good Health and Fitness

Your employer expects you to be alert when you arrive on the job and remain so for the entire workday, no matter how long or short it is. Your alertness and job performance will depend on your health and fitness. To stay healthy and physically fit, you need to follow three basic guidelines:

- Eat well-balanced, nutritious meals.

- Get adequate sleep and rest.

- Stay physically active and exercise regularly. See 3-5.

Discuss

Does an employer have a right to set standards of appearance regarding hair length, style of dress, and personal hygiene?

Note

Many companies have fitness centers for employees to use during breaks and before or after hours. How does a company benefit from this arrangement?

3-5
Regular exercise will help you
stay healthy and physically fit.

Reflect Further

As an employer, would
you keep an employee
found loafing on the
job, taking company
supplies home, or
stealing money from
coworkers?

Discuss

Have students discuss examples
of questionable, and possibly
unethical, behaviors observed in
the workplace.

Looking and feeling your best is nearly
impossible if you get five hours of sleep nightly,
never exercise, skip breakfasts, and have soda
and potato chips for lunch.

In addition to good physical health, you
need to stay healthy and fit mentally. You may
be in perfect physical health but appear pale
and ill if you are unhappy. To keep mentally
fit, remember to make time for play as well as
work. Set aside time to spend with friends and
to participate in new activities. Exercising your
brain is just as important as exercising your
body.

Ethics in the Workplace

A very important personal quality in the
workplace involves ethics. **Ethics** is a guiding
set of moral values. Long-term success for a
business is due in a large part to the ethics
practiced by its employees. People with ethical behavior use moral values
to guide their actions. They do what society considers right and fair.

Outright lying, cheating, and stealing are clear examples of unethical
behavior in the workplace, but some examples are not so obvious.
Consider the employee who uses the company phone to make personal
phone calls. This is unethical in two ways. The employee is wasting
the company's money on a nonbusiness call and using work time for
personal matters instead of doing the job.

Employers know that workers who disregard moral values will
disregard company values, too. Consequently, they look for workers
whose behavior reflects moral values. People who firmly follow moral
values have **integrity**. The fact that employers consider this quality
necessary for effective workers indicates how highly they value integrity
in the workplace.

Behaving ethically is often a step above behaving legally. For
example, it may not be against the law for you to speak badly about
your boss behind her back, but it is unethical to do so. Ethical behavior
involves such qualities as honesty, confidentiality, and loyalty. These
personal qualities play a part in shaping a person's work ethic.

Honesty

Your employer expects you to do an honest day's work for an honest
day's pay. That means doing the job you are assigned and not wasting
time. An employee who loafs on the job is actually stealing time away
from his or her employer. Employers cannot afford to pay employees for
services not performed.

Being honest on the job also includes not taking your employer's supplies for personal use. If you work in a grocery store, this does not mean you can take groceries without paying for them. If you work in an office, this does not mean you are entitled to take home paper, pens, tape, and other supplies. Businesses have been known to go out of business due to the dishonesty of their employees.

Anyone caught stealing company supplies or property from coworkers can expect to be fired. Once a person has a reputation for being dishonest, it is difficult for that person to get hired anywhere else.

Honesty not only involves what you do; it may also involve what you *do not* do, but should. Knowing that someone is stealing from the company and failing to report it is another form of dishonesty. When you learn that a coworker is doing something illegal or against company policy, you have an obligation to report it to your supervisor. If the activity involves your supervisor, then report the matter to your program coordinator who will help decide what steps to take. Always keep your school-to-work coordinator informed of any unethical behavior you report or observe at work.

Confidentiality

There are many times on the job when employees have the opportunity to hear or see something that should be kept private, 3-6. Perhaps you will learn of new products the company will make, new employees it will hire, or old plants it will close. Such company matters

Reflect Further

Should you report unethical behavior you observe in the workplace?

3-6
In the workplace, treat the work done by others as confidential.

Discuss

Have students give examples of the type of honesty that involves not doing something that should be done.

Resource

Personal Traits, Activity C, WB

Discuss

What are some reasons employees share confidential information with others when they know they shouldn't? What are some strategies to help avoid the temptation to share confidential information?

In the Real World

Michael Shares a Secret

Michael arrived at work early one morning for his job at a furniture distribution warehouse. When he entered the building, he saw his supervisor, Doug, in his office. The office door was open, so Michael stepped inside to say good morning. It was then that he noticed that Doug was checking out a dating Web site.

Doug looked startled when Michael entered and quickly shut down the computer. He laughed nervously and said that he had reached the site in error as he searched for the Web site of Love's Furniture Company. Michael said he could see how that could happen and left the office. He felt a little embarrassed since he knew Doug was married.

However, later that morning Michael decided to share what he had seen with a group of coworkers during their morning break. He embellished the story and made it seem like his supervisor was actively searching for a date. He conveniently left out how Doug said he had reached the site in error. All his coworkers had a good laugh. As Michael walked away, he saw Doug standing within earshot.

Questions to Discuss

1. How do you think Michael's supervisor felt?
2. How do you think Michael felt when he knew his supervisor had overheard his conversation?
3. What should Michael do next?
4. What should Doug do next?
5. How could Michael have avoided the situation?

are **confidential**, or private, and should not be shared with those who do not need to know. Discussing these matters with outsiders could harm the company's future and give its competition an unfair advantage.

Just as you keep company matters private, you should also keep personal matters about coworkers private. You would not want someone to reveal private facts about you, and you should never do this to others. Discussing the private matters of others may make you popular with those who spread office gossip, but your reputation with your supervisor will suffer. You will not be viewed as a person who can be trusted for important jobs.

Loyalty

Loyalty means being faithful to your coworkers and to your employer. Workers who are loyal to their employers are proud of their company and the products or services it provides. These workers speak well of their companies inside and outside the workplace. Therefore, you need to always display a positive attitude about your work and your employer.

Resource

Follow These Signs to On-the-Job Success, color transparency CT-3, TR

Reflect

Is there ever a conflict between honesty and loyalty? What is an example?

If you disagree with policies or decisions your employer or supervisor makes, talk with your program coordinator about them. Do not criticize the decision of your supervisor, and never gossip with coworkers at your workstation. Most likely your coordinator will be able to help you understand why such policies and decisions were made. He or she can also help you decide how to deal with problem situations.

The Work Ethic

Closely related to ethical behavior is a person's work ethic. **Work ethic** is how you feel about your job and how much effort you put into it. People with a strong work ethic view their work as a vital part of their lives. They arrive at work early, take pride in their work, and always do their very best. How dedicated a person is to a job reflects the strength of his or her work ethic.

Accepting Criticism

One more responsibility your supervisor has is giving constructive criticism. **Constructive criticism** is pointing out a weakness to analyze it and cause improvement. The goal of constructive criticism is not to embarrass an employee, but to help that person do a better job. The term *constructive* indicates that a positive motive prompts this type of criticism. Graciously accepting constructive criticism is a mark of a person who wants to improve.

The only way you will know how to work better is by being told how or shown a better way. For example, being ordered to work faster is not very helpful, but hearing tips on how to gain speed is. Another way your supervisor may use constructive criticism is by asking you why you are not working as fast as your coworkers. This remark will inspire you to analyze the situation and find one or more answers.

Constructive criticism helps workers improve their skills so they can work more efficiently. This, too, is the purpose of a **job evaluation**, which is a written review of your work performance by your supervisor. During your work-based learning experience, your supervisor will be asked to evaluate your job performance and provide constructive criticism. A sample job evaluation form is shown in 3-7. Your supervisor's evaluation should help you and your program coordinator identify your strengths and weaknesses at work.

As an employee, it is your responsibility to accept criticism and improve your performance. Listen to what your supervisor says and follow his or her suggestions. Be thankful your supervisor takes an interest in your work and wants to help you do your best on the job.

Reflect Further

How do you think employers feel about employees with a weak work ethic? Does the average American have a strong work ethic? Would you prefer to work with someone having a weak or a strong work ethic?

Resource

Dependability and Work Ethic, Activity D, WB

Activity

Role-play giving and receiving constructive criticism in work situations.

Resource

Employer Job Evaluation, Activity E, WB

Thinking It Through

What is the purpose of a job evaluation? When your supervisor discusses something you did wrong on the job and shows you the correct way to do it, how should you react?

Student Evaluation

Student: _____ Training Station: _____

Evaluation Period: _____ Evaluator: _____

Instructions: Please place a check mark on the line preceding the statement that most accurately describes your student-learner's attitude or performance. Evaluate each category without regard to the student's rating in any other category.

1. Cooperation _____ **Comments** ___

_____ A Gets along well with others; is friendly with others.
_____ B Cooperates willingly; gets along with others.
_____ C Usually gets along with others.
_____ D Does not work well with others.
_____ E Is antagonistic; pulls against rather than works with others.

2. Initiative _____

_____ A Is resourceful; looks for tasks to learn and do.
_____ B Is fairly resourceful; does well by himself/herself.
_____ C Does routine work acceptably.
_____ D Takes very little initiative; requires urging.
_____ E Takes no initiative; has to be instructed repeatedly.

3. Courtesy _____

_____ A Is very courteous and very considerate of others.
_____ B Is considerate and courteous.
_____ C Usually is polite and considerate of others.
_____ D Is not particularly courteous in action or speech.
_____ E Has been discourteous to the public and staff.

4. Attitude Toward Constructive Criticism _____

_____ A Accepts criticism and improves greatly.
_____ B Accepts criticism and improvement noted.
_____ C Accepts criticism and tries to do better.
_____ D Doesn't pay much attention to criticism.
_____ E Doesn't profit by criticism; resents it.

5. Knowledge of Job _____

_____ A Knows job well and shows desire to learn more.
_____ B Understands work; needs little supervision.
_____ C Has learned necessary routine but needs supervision.
_____ D Pays little attention to learning job.
_____ E Has not tried to learn.

6. Accuracy of Work _____

_____ A Very seldom makes errors; does work of very good quality.
_____ B Makes few errors; is careful, thorough, and neat.
_____ C Makes errors; shows average care, thoroughness, and neatness.
_____ D Is frequently inaccurate and careless.
_____ E Is extremely careless.

7. Work Accomplished _____

_____ A Is fast and efficient; production is well above average.
_____ B Works rapidly; output is above average.
_____ C Works with ordinary speed; work is generally satisfactory.
_____ D Is slower than average.
_____ E Is very slow; output is unsatisfactory.

(continued on next page)

3-7

Many factors are considered when you are evaluated on the job.

8. Work Habits ———————————————— **Comments** ——
_____ A Is industrious; concentrates very well.
_____ B Seldom wastes time; is reliable.
_____ C Wastes time occasionally; is usually reliable.
_____ D Frequently wastes time; needs close supervision.
_____ E Habitually wastes time; has to be watched and reminded of work.

9. Adaptability ————————————————
_____ A Learns quickly; is adept at meeting changing conditions.
_____ B Adjusts readily.
_____ C Makes necessary adjustments after considerable instruction.
_____ D Is slow in grasping ideas; has difficulty adapting to new situations.
_____ E Can't adjust to changing situations.

10. Personal Appearance ————————————
_____ A Is excellent in appearance; always looks neat.
_____ B Is very good in appearance; looks neat most of the time.
_____ C Is passable in appearance; but should make effort to improve.
_____ D Often neglects appearance.
_____ E Is extremely careless in appearance.

11. Punctuality ————————————————
_____ A Never tardy except for unavoidable emergencies.
_____ B Seldom tardy.
_____ C Punctuality could be improved.
_____ D Very often tardy.
_____ E Too frequently tardy.

12. Dependability ———————————————
_____ A Never absent except for an unavoidable emergency.
_____ B Dependable.
_____ C Usually dependable.
_____ D Not regular enough in attendance.
_____ E Too frequently absent.

13. Identify major strengths of this student-learner.
14. Identify any major weakness in the attitude or performance of this student-learner.
15. Is improvement needed in any particular skills related to the student's job?
16. List the dates the student-learner was absent from work during this grading period.
   Did the student-learner call in to report his or her absence?
   _____ Yes   _____ No
   Were the reasons for absence justifiable?
   _____ Yes   _____ No

Student Comments _____

_____

Student Signature _____ Date _____
Evaluator's Signature_____ Date _____

Summary

Meeting your employer's expectations will help you be successful on the job. Your employer expects you to keep a good attitude, attend work regularly, be on time, perform well on the job, and show initiative.

As an employee, you are expected to use your skills and training to the best of your ability. Learning to cooperate and show courtesy is important. A neat, clean personal appearance shows that you take pride in yourself. Keeping yourself healthy and physically fit will help you meet your employer's expectations. Displaying high ethical standards such as honesty, confidentiality, loyalty, and a strong work ethic is essential. Learning to accept criticism will help you continue to improve your job performance.

Resource

Review and Study Guide for Chapter 3, reproducible master 3-2, TR

Answers to *Facts In Review*

1. self-esteem
2. A worker's absence causes extra work for others and reduces the effectiveness of the work experience.
3. Contact the employer and the school coordinator to explain the absence.
4. standards
5. by looking for work and doing it without being told, by looking for new skills to learn on the job
6. accept his or her share of the job and do the best work possible
7. It helps a worker get along with coworkers, supervisors, customers, and others.
8. by having clean, combed hair; clean hands; trimmed nails; and clean, neat, appropriate work clothes
9. Eat well-balanced, nutritious meals. Get adequate sleep and rest. Stay physically active and exercise regularly.
10. because the employee is stealing time from the employer
11. confidentiality
12. Talk to the program coordinator about it.
13. The person likes his or her job and puts great effort into it.

Facts in Review

1. What personal quality is linked to a person's attitudes on the job?
2. Why is it important to be at work every working day?
3. What should a student do if unable to attend school and work?
4. Although a beginning worker probably will not be expected to do as much as an experienced worker, the new worker will be expected to have the same work _____.
5. Describe how to show initiative to an employer.
6. What can a student worker do to show a desire to cooperate with his or her supervisor and coworkers?
7. Why is courtesy to others important to success on the job?
8. How can an employee look his or her best at work?
9. What three basic guidelines should be followed to stay healthy and physically fit?
10. Why is loafing on the job a form of dishonesty?
11. When workers keep private matters private, they are exercising _____.
12. When student workers find it difficult to be loyal to their employer because of a disagreement with policies and decisions, what should be done?
13. What does it mean when someone has a strong work ethic?

Developing Your Academic Skills

1. **Social Studies.** Research changes in acceptable attire in the last century. Write a report answering the following questions: How has the dress code for the workplace changed? Why are these differences apparent? What is considered proper attire for the workplace today? Why are certain types of clothing unacceptable in the workplace?

2. **English.** Write a paper on a subject being studied in the English class. Trade papers with another student and critique each other's work. Make sure to use only constructive criticism. Return the paper and look over the critiques you received. Discuss how the corrections make you feel. Also evaluate whether making the recommended changes would improve your paper.

Information Technology Applications

1. Evaluate yourself using the criteria in Figure 3-7. Use graphing software to make a graph showing areas in which your work is satisfactory and areas in which you could improve.

2. Using presentation software, prepare a report on the personal qualities needed for success on the job. Discuss why each is important. Also address how developing skills and good habits now will affect your career later in life. Present your report to the class.

Applying Your Knowledge and Skills

1. **Problem Solving and Critical Thinking.** Write a brief description of a positive example of how an employee handled a sensitive situation with a customer. Analyze what factors contributed to the outcome. Repeat the activity for a negative example.

2. **Ethics and Legal Responsibilities.** A student intern decided to leave his workstation early one Friday although the supervisor had not given the student permission to do so. Discuss in class what, if anything, the supervisor and the program coordinator should do about this student's behavior.

3. **Employability and Career Development.** List the actions that might cause a student to be fired from his or her work experience. Discuss in class why each behavior might deserve this action.

4. **Communications.** Conduct interviews with at least two employers to determine the importance of dependability, promptness, honesty, and getting along with others. Report your findings to the class.

Developing Workplace Skills

Divide into groups to research workplace ethics and make a group report to the class. Use a variety of sources including the library, Internet, and personal interviews. Explain the importance of having high ethical standards in the workplace. Find some case studies to provide examples of negative effects caused by the unethical behavior of some companies and/or employees. What were the results of this unethical behavior for the company and/or the employee? What, if anything, did the company do to counteract the negative image created by the unethical behavior?

Part 2
Skills for Success

Photo courtesy of Lloyd Wolf for Skills USA

4

Teamwork and Problem-Solving Skills

Key Terms

interpersonal skills
team
quality
quality assurance
quality control
functional team
cross-functional team
multifunctional team
self-directed team
norm
goal
Gantt chart
problem
problem solving
criteria
constraint
Pareto Principle
brainstorming
compromise
consensus
conflict

Chapter Objectives

After studying this chapter, you will be able to

- **describe** the importance of teamwork in the workplace.
- **recognize** how teams develop and work effectively.
- **explain** the problem-solving process.
- **demonstrate** how to manage conflict.

Reading Advantage

Draw a comic strip that shows two employees having a conversation about what you think will be covered in this chapter. After reading the chapter, draw another comic strip that incorporates what you learned.

Achieving Academic Standards

English Language Arts

- Read print and non-print texts to acquire new information and to respond to the needs and demands of society and the workplace. (IRA/NCTE, 1)
- Apply strategies to comprehend, interpret, evaluate, and appreciate texts. (IRA/NCTE, 3)

Math

- Select and use appropriate statistical methods to analyze data. (NCTM)
- Apply and adapt a variety of appropriate strategies to solve problems. (NCTM)

Key Concepts

- The American workplace has changed over time.

- Teams are often used in the workplace.

- Effective teams share leadership, rotate team roles, stay focused, and work for the common good.

- Knowing how to manage conflict is important in the workplace.

Working well with others is an important skill for future success at work. First and foremost, it requires good **interpersonal skills**. People with good interpersonal skills are friendly and sensitive to the needs of others. They communicate well and know how to listen. These skills are important in solving problems, working on teams, and dealing with customers. Using interpersonal skills well is an expectation in today's workplace.

Working with others can be fun and rewarding. It can also be frustrating and irritating. This chapter explains the importance of working as a team member in the workplace and ways to promote team harmony. A **team** is a small group of people working together for a common purpose.

Changing Nature of the Workplace

4-1

Today, even repetitive jobs often require special skills, reasoning ability, or creativity.

Not too long ago, many American workers were expected to leave their ability to think at the door when they entered the workplace. Managers made the decisions, and workers followed their orders. Workers spent long hours doing repetitive tasks that often required little or no formal training or creative thinking, 4-1. These jobs paid a good wage and provided good benefits. Workers could count on holding a lifelong job with one company that provided their families with a high standard of living.

This style of management worked well for decades. It helped make the United States the top manufacturing country in the world. After World War II, however, the business world began to change. The U.S. economy boomed, and new products were in such great demand that production hardly kept pace. Competition as we know it today did not exist because products sold out easily. There was a willing buyer for everything made. Since products sold out quickly in the United States, product quality was not a major concern.

No single definition of **quality** exists in the workplace, but it generally means a commitment by everyone in an organization to exceed customer expectations. The terms **quality assurance** and **quality control** have the same meanings. These terms refer to a variety of strategies used by a company to ensure that its products and services are of the highest quality. Several of these strategies, such as the team approach, the Gantt chart, problem solving, consensus building, and Pareto analysis, are discussed later in this chapter. They are all part of a "Total Quality" strategy involving meeting customer needs, employee involvement, and continuous improvement.

American industry failed to embrace many of these concepts and, as a result, the quality of many products built in the United States declined during the 1950s, 1960s, and 1970s. This lack of attention to quality began to hurt American industry. More information on quality can be found at the Web site of the American Society for Quality (www.asq.org).

The first major challenge to U.S. industry was led by Japan. The quality of Japan's products at the end of World War II was so low that most were considered unreliable. The entire Japanese economy suffered when sales slowed. As a result, the companies in Japan redesigned their workforce around a way of managing that focused on quality. This plan began in the United States but was abandoned when quantity, not quality, became the main goal.

Japan's companies, however, decided to put quality first. They learned to compete with companies throughout the world. The automotive and electronics industries were prime examples. Cars, cameras, and television sets from Japan set the worldwide standards for quality for these products. They were rated higher than American products. The rebirth of industries in Japan and other countries led to worldwide competition. Communications and transportation improved.

The failure to compete on the world market negatively affected the morale of American workers. Many felt defeated and depressed when faced with the better quality and lower prices of overseas products. Many, too, lost their jobs when U.S. companies could not find buyers for their more expensive, lower quality products. As a result, a surplus of U.S. workers with outdated skills could not find work.

This lesson resulted in a number of changes in the workplace. The U.S. industry refocused on quality, making it the number one goal. See 4-2. This shift in focus increased the role of typical workers. They were no longer expected to leave their ability to think at the door. Workers were expected to help solve problems and make decisions on work methods, quality, and finances. Successful companies began using teams of workers to solve problems once handled by top managers. Most importantly, these changes created a need for a more highly educated American workforce.

This major adjustment in how work is performed continues to affect the workplace today. Employers want workers who are comfortable working with others and sharing ideas. They expect workers to stay knowledgeable about their work and continually make improvements. Employers want workers who can work with others, solve problems, and manage conflict. As a result, the quality of American products has been on the rise.

Discuss

Why is competition on a world-wide scale so important today? Is this condition here to stay?

Reflect

Does your employer give you or your coworkers the responsibility to make some decisions without asking the supervisor? Does this make the job easier?

Thinking It Through

How does competition affect quality? Give examples from athletics or other areas that indicate how competition affects quality.

4-2

Companies have quality control departments to constantly check the quality of products coming off production lines.

Resource

Handling Problems in Teams,
Activity A, WB

Activity

Have the class develop a list
of the pros and cons of team
membership based on their real-
life experiences.

Teams in the Workplace

More and more companies are now using teams to help solve problems and increase productivity in the workplace. Depending on its purpose, the typical number of members on a team ranges from 5 to 15 people.

Pros and Cons of the Team Approach

The team approach has a number of advantages for both the employer and the employee. As a rule, teams reach better and more creative decisions than individuals. One reason for this is the greater amount of information obtained by a group compared to the efforts of an individual. The saying "two heads are better than one" certainly applies to teams. One team member's comments will often inspire ideas from others. This can lead to creative new ideas that would have never surfaced if several individuals had worked alone. See 4-3.

When research needs to be done, several people can gather information more quickly than one person can. Team members are more likely to make plans work when they are involved in the decision-making process. They can even make a poor plan work well if they agree with the idea. Effective teams make individuals feel better about themselves and the quality of their work. Members may feel they are accomplishing more than they could as individuals.

There are disadvantages to the team approach, too. Teams usually take more time to reach a decision than individuals do. Working with a group can be very frustrating, especially if the team is not effective. Personality clashes can develop which create an unpleasant working environment. Some people just are not good team members and make life difficult for others. It may take weeks or even years to develop an effective team. Some teams never fully develop, and production may suffer during this period.

4-3

Successful teamwork produces results that exceed what any single individual could do in the same amount of time.

DECA

As you can see, a team approach is not always best. It depends on the situation and individuals involved. In fact, some individuals can be more productive and creative than teams in a lot less time. Therefore, important considerations for employers are *when* and *how* to involve teams in the workplace.

Role of the Team in the Workplace

Teams in the workplace are formed for different purposes. Generally, three common types of teams exist: functional, cross-functional, and multifunctional.

Functional Teams

All members of a **functional team** have similar skills and expertise although they would not be able to perform one another's jobs. They usually work in the same department. Functional teams solve problems based on their understanding of the work to be done and each team member's unique contribution. For example, a functional team for plant maintenance might be composed of a variety of workers such as electricians, plumbers, and air-conditioning specialists. They would have a common knowledge of the department's role in keeping a plant running and could help solve maintenance related problems.

Cross-Functional Teams

A **cross-functional team** consists of workers from different areas within a company who are assigned to work on a specific project. See 4-4. Members are selected based on their expertise and ability to make a unique and meaningful contribution. For example, a team whose purpose is to create a new car design might consist of representatives of the company's design, manufacturing, marketing, and financial departments. The marketing representative could share information on special features that help the car sell better. The manufacturing representative would comment on the company's ability to build the new design. Working together, their goal would be to produce a well-designed car that is relatively easy to build and can be profitably sold at a reasonable price.

Multifunctional Team

Members of a **multifunctional team** have been cross-trained so each person is able to perform the duties of all the other team members.

Reflect Further

What teams have you joined? Did you always enjoy working on the team? Were there times when you disliked being a member of the team?

Reflect

Do you work better alone or with others? To what degree does the type of task affect the way you work?

Discuss

With which type of team have you had the most experience: a team composed of members with similar skills or members with different skills?

4-4

Cross-functional teams consist of people from different parts of the organization who can contribute different types of expertise.

Thinking It Through

When teams are productive in the workplace, do you think more or fewer top managers are needed?

Enrich

Take a field trip to a local company that uses various team approaches to observe teams in action. Have the students interview team members regarding the responsibilities each team has.

Example

Compare the behavior of class members on the first day of class to one month later. Point out the behavior similarities to the forming stage of team development.

Reflect Further

In your experience, what can help new members feel comfortable on a team? What can make them feel uncomfortable?

An example might be a team of workers who assemble automobile air conditioners. Each member of the team would be able to perform all the jobs on the assembly line. When a worker is ill or takes a rest break, another team member can step in and do the job without further instruction.

Each of the previous teams could perform as a self-directed team. A **self-directed team** has been given full responsibility for carrying out its assignment. The members of the team must set work-related goals and objectives. They identify priorities, set budgets, develop work plans, and solve problems. Self-directed teams evaluate their own progress and often hire, train, and evaluate their team members. For example, if a worker becomes seriously ill, the team decides whether to hire a temporary replacement or to have the team members work overtime.

Stages of Team Development

You cannot group strangers together and expect them to perform well right away. Because teams are composed of people, they go through stages of development just as people do. It takes time for team members to learn to work together.

Team development evolves in stages. One way to identify these stages is the following set of terms: *forming*, *storming*, *norming*, and *performing*. These stages were developed by group dynamics expert Dr. Bruce Tuckman. Generally team members do not begin to work well together until the last two stages. However, not all teams make it to stage four. Some teams may not make it past stages one or two.

Stage 1. Forming

Teams go through the forming stage when they first come together. At this stage the team members may feel good about what the team can do. Individuals may be excited about being chosen for the team.

In many cases, members of the team do not know each other very well. They may feel uncomfortable, afraid to speak, and full of doubts. They may not understand why the team was formed or what is expected of them. During this stage, team members become acquainted. They also discuss the purpose of the team. There may be no leadership, or someone may step up and take charge.

Stage 2. Storming

Disagreements are likely to occur when team members get to know each other better. Team members may distrust or not understand one another. They may even question why the team was formed. See 4-5.

There may be disagreements over how the team operates, who is in charge, or when and where the team meets. Sometimes these conflicts are discussed openly during meetings. In other cases team members

4-5
Members of new teams may have disagreements while they get to know and trust one another.

may talk behind others' backs. There may be personality clashes and arguments. As a result, team members may find it hard to work together and make decisions. However, this is also the stage when members begin to trust each other and share their feelings more openly.

Stage 3. Norming

At this stage, team members begin to work together and leaders emerge. Teams resolve the disagreements that began during stage 2. The members openly discuss issues, listen to one another, and become more involved. They feel good about themselves and the team. They accept the team's decisions and are willing to work hard to carry them out.

The title of this stage comes from the scientific term *norm*. A **norm** is a pattern that is typical in the development of a social group.

Stage 4. Performing

This is the highest level of team performance. The positive feelings that developed during stage 3 continue to grow. Members are committed to the team and the organization. They take responsibility for making improvements and examine the best way for the team to function. Different team members may take charge depending on the task at hand. The team works at maximum efficiency in this stage.

Characteristics of an Effective Team

A good, effective team is no accident. It is a sign of a team that has reached the highest level of development, the *performing* stage. The members of a team in the performing stage assume leadership and other team roles as needed. They stay focused and work for the common good.

Reflect Further

If you were the leader of a team whose members were split on which direction to follow, what would you do?

Discuss

Why does conflict tend to arise as people become better acquainted?

4-6

An effective team is led by the member most expert in the subject. When the mission is accomplished and a new goal is identified, the most qualified team member then leads the group.

Reflect Further

Do you prefer to follow your plans or those of others? Why?

Shares Leadership

Leadership on effective teams is shared among the members. Often the person who knows the most about a given problem serves as team leader until the problem is resolved. When a new problem is faced, the most expert person on that issue becomes the next team leader, 4-6.

When leadership is shared, everyone feels responsible for the success or failure of the team. All members of the group are more willing to make decisions and take responsibility for them. Leadership does not mean telling others what to do. Instead, it involves helping the team move forward. A leader listens and encourages the team members. People who like to control others are not very effective team leaders.

Rotates Team Roles

A good team keeps everyone involved. One way to accomplish this is to assign roles to members. Besides rotating the role of leader, other roles are assigned to different members, too. This is particularly true in team meetings. The roles that rotate among members are shown in 4-7.

These roles may vary depending on the needs of the team. Taking turns performing the roles increases interest in the team's activities. The team leader one week may be the recorder next week.

Stays Focused

An effective team consists of members always aware of their mission. There are several ways to keep the team's focus on its mission.

4-7

For a team to work effectively, all these roles must be filled.

Team Roles
• **Leader**—sets the team's agenda and helps the group make progress
• **Encourager**—inspires everyone to participate and makes certain that everyone's opinions are heard
• **Taskmaster**—keeps the group focused on achieving its goal(s)
• **Critic**—questions the assumptions expressed and decisions made
• **Recorder**—keeps detailed notes

Discuss

What are some problems that may arise from shared leadership? What if two individuals feel qualified to become the leader and try to assume control?

Discuss

What other roles might team members play?

Resource

Examining Team Roles, reproducible master 4-1, TR

- *Using humor effectively*—relaxes team members and helps them focus on the issues. There are times when groups become too frustrated or tense. A humorous comment helps to release the tension. However, make sure humor is never used to "put down" or embarrass another team member.

- *Taking a break*—can also relieve pressure, reduce tension, and get a team back on track. It can be a few minutes or a few days long, depending on the situation. Team members often return with fresh ideas and more positive attitudes even after a ten-minute break.

- *Listing goals*—helps team members continually move forward. A **goal** is what you want to attain. For example, a work team may work toward the goal of reducing department injuries in June by 50 percent. Concentrating on the steps everyone must take to achieve that goal keeps the team focused.

One tool for staying focused is a **Gantt chart**. This is a graph that shows the steps of a task divided across a timetable. See 4-8. Team members can tell at a glance what phase of the goal should be in progress.

Reflect

Think of examples in which humor was used effectively and ineffectively in a group setting.

Example

Share one or two goals you have for this class. Explain how having these goals helps improve your teaching.

Resource

Using a Chart as a Scheduling Tool, Activity B, WB

Works for the Common Good

Members of effective teams agree on what they are trying to do. The team members are able to set and meet deadlines. They encourage each other and celebrate both team and individual accomplishments. Effective teams make sure everyone understands the plan and helps carry it out. The team checks on the way it operates to see if it can work better.

Advertising Plan									
	Week 1	Week 2	Week 3	Week 4	Week 5	Week 6	Week 7	Week 8	Week 9
Buy advertising space.	▓	▓							
Run magazine ads.			▓	▓					
Run newspaper ads.				▓	▓	▓	▓		
Run TV commercials.						▓	▓	▓	
Run in-store promotions.							▓	▓	▓
Measure sales; evaluate plan.									▓

4-8

A Gantt chart provides an easy way to see if team activities are proceeding as planned.

In the Real World

Pit Crews Are Team Players

Pit crews are critical to the success of professional racecar drivers. The crew may include a chief mechanic, general manager, driver assistant, "fuel" person, "tire" person, transportation personnel, and others. Pit crews must set up the pit hours before a race. They make sure gasoline, tires, and anything else they may possibly need is available in the pit.

Before the race, the pit crews wheel pit buggies and huge toolboxes into the pit area. The equipment and supplies include jacks, spare chassis, drink holder with extended handle for the driver, brush with extended handle to clean the car's grill, and spare shocks. Three gas cans, each containing 11 gallons of fuel, are placed in the pit. There is also a broom in the pit for cleanup, and a gas catch-can to catch excess fuel during a fill-up. There are various lubricants, mufflers, lug nuts, sets of spare tires, and sometimes even a spare steering wheel. The list of items needed during a race is quite lengthy. If something is needed in a race and is not in the pit, a crew member must run to the garage to get it. That takes valuable racing time.

Around the pit buggy, five air wrenches are carefully placed. Hoses connecting them with nitrogen tanks are coiled and secured so nobody trips over them. The nitrogen tanks provide the pressure needed to operate the wrenches.

Probably one of the most important tools used during pit stops is a two-way radio. Before the driver comes down pit road, he can tell his crew about any problems the car has. He can talk with his crew for instructions, such as when to pit and how many tires will be changed.

Only seven crew members are allowed over the pit wall at any time to work on the car, so special tricks are used to perform the work at lightning speed. Pit crews can change four tires and add 22 gallons of fuel to the car in less than 28 seconds. The actual fueling process on a stock car only takes ten or eleven seconds.

For the driver to win the race, the team has to function like clockwork. Each member has to know his or her job well and be highly skilled. The successful team not only helps the driver win a race but also assures a safe race without injuries.

Questions to Discuss

1. What characteristics of an effective team are evident in a pit crew at a professional car race?
2. To what stage of team development has a racecar pit crew evolved?
3. How does teamwork solve the problems associated with driving racecars in competition?

Problem Solving

Reflect

What are some problems you have faced in your life? Do they fall within this definition of *problem*?

A **problem** exists when there is a difference between reality (what you have) and expectation (what you want). **Problem solving** is the process of making an expectation a reality. The methods used to solve problems are the same for individuals and teams.

Employers are finding that many benefits occur when workers are given more responsibility for solving work problems. Workers take greater pride in their work and employee morale increases, 4-9.

4-9
Large construction projects present many problem-solving challenges. After solving them, workers often feel strongly attached to the finished projects.

Employees also tend to support an action plan they helped develop and complete successfully. Employers expect their workers to be able to solve problems.

Solving problems as a team will involve the same basic steps as solving them as an individual. The important difference is that everyone should be involved as much as possible to keep the team functioning effectively. Problem solving skills can be developed if you learn and follow several basic steps.

Discuss

What are some reasons people don't take time to really analyze a problem?

Steps in Problem Solving

Knowing the steps involved in solving problems will increase your success rate. See 4-10. Although the following steps are listed in a recommended order, it is not simply a matter of doing one step at a time. Very often information you obtain at one step may send you back to a previous step. As you gather data in step 2, for example, you may find that you did not fully do step 1. When this occurs, simply go back to the beginning and proceed once again though the steps.

Problem-Solving Steps
1.   Identify and analyze the problem.
2.   Collect and analyze data.
3.   Consider possible solutions.
4.   Choose the best plan.
5.   Implement the plan.
6.   Observe, evaluate, and adjust.

4-10
Learning the problem-solving process will increase your confidence in your ability to solve problems.

1. Identify and Analyze the Problem

Unsuccessful problem-solvers tend to jump right in and start trying to find solutions. Successful problem-solvers take time to identify and analyze the problem. It is very important to learn as much as you can about the problem before taking any action.

Do you understand what the problem is? Can you state it accurately? For example, you may not be getting along well with your employer. A major cause for this friction is your frequent tardiness to work. Usually your friends give you a ride to work and pick you up late. Simply stated, however, the problem is your late arrival to work caused by riding with your late friends. The friction with your boss is only a result of the problem.

The first step in solving a problem is to state it accurately. As you try to determine the basic problem, you will identify factors related to the problem. These factors will be useful when you consider possible solutions in step 3. The factors to consider are criteria and constraints.

- **Criteria** are standards you use to find the best solution. Without the criteria to help make an evaluation, it is difficult to know if the problem is really solved. For this example, you may need a solution that incorporates the following criteria: *arriving five minutes early to work* and *arriving dressed in your work uniform*. Evaluation criteria will have an important influence on which solution you choose.

- **Constraints** are factors that may restrict or hinder your ability to solve the problem. One hindrance to arriving on time at work may be *not having your own car*. Another constraint may be *having just 50 minutes between your last class and the time work starts*. At this point your identification and analysis of the problem would resemble the chart in 4-11.

2. Collect and Analyze Data

In this step, you collect and analyze data related to the problem and ask yourself certain questions. What do you need to know about the problem that you do not already know? What information is available to help you solve the problem? Do you have everything you will need? If not, can you obtain what you need or must you make adjustments?

4-11

A careful examination of a problem pinpoints all the important factors.

Identifying the "Late Arrival" Problem

Problem
- Late arrival at work caused by riding with friends who are usually late

Criteria
- Arriving five minutes early to work
- Arriving dressed in uniform

Constraints
- No car
- Just 50 minutes between the last class and the time work starts

As you go through this process, other questions may arise. These questions will vary depending on the type of problem being solved. For example, what type of public transportation is available? Can you get a ride to work from more reliable friends, relatives, or coworkers?

You can gather data at the same time you develop your questions. This information should help you better understand the problem and provide ideas for possible solutions to it. If it does not, you may need to go back and reconsider how you identified and analyzed the problem.

One of the problems in collecting data is organizing it in a form that team members can easily understand and apply. Pareto analysis is one strategy for accomplishing this. The **Pareto Principle** states that as a general rule, 20% of causes produce 80% of the effects, or 20% of the effort produces 80% of the results. If you can discover which areas to concentrate on, you will be much more productive in solving problems and accomplishing goals. For example, imagine that 100 students were surveyed to determine the type of fund-raiser in which they would be willing to participate. Forty-four percent would prefer a car wash, while 30 percent prefer a candy sale. The remaining 26 percent of responses are divided among four other activities. The students conclude that if they concentrate on just the car wash and candy sale, they will have the largest percent of student participation.

Once you are satisfied that you have accurately defined the problem and collected all important data, you can focus on possible solutions.

Resource

The Pareto Principal, transparency master 4-2, TR

Discuss

Why is quantity more important than quality when first trying to identify possible solutions to a problem?

3. Consider Possible Solutions

This is the first step in actually solving the problem. Your first concern is the quantity of ideas you develop, not their quality. Try to think creatively. Even wild ideas may have some later value. Keep your ideas simple and brief at first. Do not worry about details. See 4-12.

Some possible solutions to the problem of tardiness may be to take a cab, ride the bus, or buy a car. Once you list various ideas, you can begin to narrow the list. Now is the time to think about the quality of your ideas. If you do not have enough money to buy a car or take a taxi, these are not practical solutions to your problem. Keep your evaluation criteria in mind, but do not be overly concerned about that at this point. Add more detail to the ideas that seem workable. You may even consider combining several ideas. This process should result in a few workable solutions.

4-12

Brainstorming can help groups generate many ideas in a short period of time.

4. Choose the Best Plan

When you have two or three good ideas, it is time to select the best one. Evaluate each in terms of the problem, the evaluation criteria, and the constraints that you identified in step 1. After considering all options, you may decide that the solution to your late-arrival problem is to take the city bus.

5. Implement the Plan

You should now be confident that you have a good workable answer to your problem. You know what bus to catch and where to catch it. It is time to carry out your plan.

In the Real World

Sharika's Job Gets Difficult

Sharika was recently promoted to evening manager at the Pizza Palace. She had been performing her new responsibilities for about two weeks and everything was going smoothly. She was really enjoying it and felt very competent as a manager.

Then one night, Clare, her top server, came to her with a problem. Clare was very upset. She explained that she was doing all the work while Roger, the other night server, did very little. He left tables for her to clean. He often pretended to be too busy to handle some of his assigned tables and left them for her to handle. He even took tips belonging to her. Clare said

Roger never did this before Sharika became manager. Roger seemed to be taking advantage of his new, inexperienced manager.

Sharika was shocked! She hadn't noticed anything wrong with Roger's work habits. In fact, she thought he was a pretty good employee. He was very friendly and outgoing, and Sharika enjoyed working with him.

Questions to Discuss

1. Do you think Clare should have talked with Roger first?
2. What reasons might Clare have had for bringing this problem to Sharika's attention?
3. What steps should Sharika take to try to resolve this problem?

Extend Your Knowledge

Success Brings Confidence

Do you feel apprehensive about problem solving in the workplace? As you become more successful at solving problems, your confidence will grow. The combination of knowing how to solve problems and having the confidence to try is very important. New problems will seem less intimidating when you are more confident of your abilities. You will soon find yourself looking forward to the challenges of problem solving.

6. Observe, Evaluate, and Adjust

This is one of the most important steps in the problem-solving process. Even the best plans may not go smoothly at first. Therefore, the plan must be carefully watched and evaluated. Perhaps adjustments are needed. It is also important to allow flexibility in your plan.

Again consider the evaluation criteria you developed when you identified the problem. The success or failure of your plan will depend to a great extent on how well your plan meets the evaluation criteria. If the plan fails this test, it may need to be abandoned. When that happens, return to step one to reexamine the problem.

To continue with our example, it is now time to check how well taking the bus solves the problem. Is it a dependable solution? Do you arrive at work five minutes early each day? Do you have enough time to dress into your work uniform before catching the bus? If this solution does not meet your evaluation criteria, discover why. Perhaps there is a better way to solve your problem.

Aids to Problem Solving

For a team to solve problems well, all members should be involved in each step of the process. Brainstorming, compromise, and consensus are tools that help teams through the problem-solving process.

Brainstorming

Brainstorming is a group technique used to develop many ideas in a relatively short time. It can be used during a number of different steps in the problem-solving process. However, it is a very good way to identify answers to a problem. The quality of the ideas is not a major

Thinking It Through

Is it easier to solve a big problem alone or with help? Which is faster?

Discuss

Why is self-confidence such an important factor in the ability to solve problems?

Enrich

Research and write a report on the problem-solving strategies of one or two great inventors, such as Benjamin Franklin or Thomas Edison.

Brainstorming Strategy

- Have the team sit in a semicircle to encourage discussion.

- Present the topic to the group.

- Have one member of the group offer his or her idea.

- Have someone record the ideas on a board or flip chart located so all can see. Do not criticize or discuss the merits of the ideas.

- Continue around the circle as each person states one idea. (It is permissible to build on someone else's ideas.) A person with nothing to contribute may pass.

- Continue around the circle as many times as necessary to identify all ideas.

- Discuss and evaluate the ideas.

concern during brainstorming. The purpose is to identify as many ideas as possible. No idea is considered too ridiculous. See the chart in 4-13 for a common way to hold a brainstorming session.

Compromise

One way to solve a problem is through compromise. **Compromise** is when each side gives up something of value to help solve a problem. All sides accept the idea, but no one may feel it is the best one. This is because they gave up something that was important to them to reach the compromise.

Voting is often used to reach a compromise. However, the people who vote for an issue may feel more positive about carrying it out than those who vote against it.

Consensus

Another way to solve a problem is through consensus. A **consensus** is when all members of a group fully accept and support the decision. It is much more difficult to reach than a compromise. When all members agree with a decision, they are more likely to be excited about carrying it out. Ideas must be thoroughly discussed and understood by all team members before a consensus can be reached. As a result, the process often leads to new and more creative ideas that neither side considered in the beginning. There is no need to vote since everyone fully supports a decision reached by consensus.

A major problem with achieving consensus is that it is very time consuming. Therefore, you may not want to try to reach a consensus for all decisions.

Managing Conflict

As you work with others, whether as individuals or in teams, disagreements are bound to occur. More serious disagreements are called conflict. **Conflict** is a hostile situation resulting from opposing views. It is important that you know how to handle conflict so it does not become a destructive force in the workplace. See 4-14.

In a traditional work setting, a permanent manager supervises a group of employees. That manager is responsible for managing conflict. In teamwork arrangements, however, the individuals have a responsibility to prevent destructive conflict among team members. The person temporarily assigned to lead the team has a special responsibility. The steps to managing conflict are shown in 4-15.

4-14
Stress, frustration, anger, and even illness can result from conflict in the workplace.

Know When to Intervene

Disagreements are not always bad. Constructive disagreements often lead to improvements in the workplace. One of the first decisions you must make when they arise is whether to become involved. It is sometimes best not to act. What seems terribly important at the moment may later seem unimportant or even trivial. Sometimes your action may even make a difficult situation worse.

Steps in Managing Conflict
• Know when to intervene.
• Address the conflict.
• Identify the source and the importance of the conflict.
• Identify possible solutions.
• Develop an acceptable solution.
• Implement and evaluate.

4-15
Knowing how to manage conflicts when they occur is part of being an effective team player.

Reflect

Have you ever intervened in a situation and later realized it was a mistake? Have you ever stayed uninvolved when you should have become involved? What lessons did you learn from both?

Thinking It Through

Which of the problem-solving aids do representatives in Congress use?

Often avoiding or ignoring a serious disagreement only postpones the time when conflict will result and action will be required. As a rule, it is time to consider action when the team or individual's happiness and/or productivity are affected.

Address the Conflict

When you have decided to take action, there are some rules you should follow. The first consideration, and perhaps most important, is to take a positive approach. Accept disagreement as a natural part of the group process. Then try to follow the golden rule as you address the situation. Treat others as you would want to be treated. Try to understand the issue from the other person's point of view. Try to protect the person's self-esteem. Do not ever try to embarrass someone.

Whenever possible, try to avoid addressing the problem in front of others. Find a quiet place to resolve the conflict so you will not be distracted. Talk directly to the person or persons involved, 4-16. Demonstrate control by speaking in a calm, firm, constructive way. Use "I" messages as you discuss the problem. For example, you might say: "I really felt embarrassed when you shouted at me" rather than "You should know better than to shout at other people." "You" messages tend to put people on the defensive.

4-16

When you find two or more people causing conflict at work, it is best to discuss the problem openly with them at the same time.

Identify the Source and Importance of the Conflict

The next step in resolving conflict is to state the problem openly. Encourage each person to describe the problem as he or she sees it. Be sure there is a real problem, not simply a misunderstanding. Be specific in the discussion rather than general. Try to get people to focus directly

Reflect

Did the last person who disciplined you use I or you messages? Did the person's approach make a difference regarding how you felt?

Discuss

What are some ways to encourage each person involved in a conflict to express the problem from his or her own viewpoint?

on the problem. Imagine someone is continually late for team meetings. Is that the problem, or is tardiness a sign of a larger problem? What is the real problem?

Keep an open mind as the problem is discussed. Focus on getting all the facts expressed. Avoid making snap judgments and jumping to conclusions.

Identify Possible Solutions

Be sure everyone involved understands that each individual is responsible for both the problem and the solution. Anyone who is not involved in the matter should not be included in the discussion. Ask for comments and possible solutions from all sides and discuss the pros and cons.

Develop an Acceptable Solution

Focus on behavior that can be changed, not something a person cannot control. At the end of the discussion, summarize what has been decided and what action will be taken. Make sure everyone understands his or her role in solving the problem.

Implement and Evaluate

Once an agreeable solution has been reached, it is time to try it. Be willing to become involved in carrying out the plan. Avoid thinking it is not your problem. Be sure to check periodically to make sure teamwork has improved to a satisfactory extent. If not, it may be time to bring the concerned parties back together and try again to resolve the conflict. You could address the conflict from the beginning or return to the point where the breakdown occurred.

Reflect Further

When was the last time you were involved in a conflict with another person? How was it resolved? How did you feel afterward? Could it have been handled differently? If so, how?

Resource

Team Problem-Solving Case Study, Activity D, WB

Resource

Teamwork and Problem-Solving Terms, Activity E, WB

Summary

At the end of World War II, American products were so much in demand that quality was sacrificed for the sake of increasing production. Then the Japanese adopted some strategies that focused on quality and helped them make products preferred around the world. The success of the Japanese caused American companies to refocus on quality. These and other changes required workers who could solve problems and work in teams.

The team approach offers advantages to both the employer and the employee. Different teams are used for different purposes, but all teams that work effectively share common qualities. It takes considerable time to develop into an effective and smooth running team.

Knowing the basic steps in problem solving will increase your confidence in your ability to solve problems. Being able to accurately identify and analyze problems is the first and most important step in the problem-solving process.

When a team solves a problem, there is the added challenge of keeping the members involved in the process. A good team leader knows when to try to reach consensus and when to be satisfied with compromise. As you work with others on a team, it is important that you are able to understand and manage conflict effectively.

Resource

Review and Study Guide for Chapter 4, reproducible master 4-4, TR

Facts in Review

1. When did American companies begin relying on teamwork?
2. What are three possible advantages of teamwork?
3. What are three possible disadvantages of teamwork?
4. What three common types of teams are used in the workplace?
5. Briefly describe the four stages of team development.
6. What are the four characteristics of an effective team?
7. Name three ways to keep the team focused.
8. Briefly list the problem-solving steps.
9. List and describe the three considerations important in identifying and analyzing a problem.
10. What is the Pareto Principle?
11. Why is it important to check how well a specific plan solves a specific problem?
12. True or false. When brainstorming, the most important consideration is the quality of the ideas generated.
13. True or false. In a decision involving compromise, everyone involved feels that the decision is the best one.
14. List the steps in managing conflict.
15. Why should "I" messages be used when attempting to resolve conflicts?

Answers to *Facts In Review*

1. when quality became the number one goal and workers were expected to solve problems and make decisions
2. (List three:) better decisions, more creative decisions, faster gathering of information, good quantity and quality of work, enhanced feelings about self and work
3. (List three:) longer delays, greater frustrations, personality clashes, an unpleasant working environment, poor production
4. functional team, cross-functional team, multifunctional team
5. Members come together in the forming stage. Members clash and disagree in the storming stage. Members work cooperatively and leaders emerge in the norming stage. The team works as a unit at maximum efficiency in the performing stage.

6. shares leadership, rotates team roles, stays focused, works for the common good
7. by using humor, taking a break, and listing goals
8. Identify and analyze the problem; collect and analyze data; consider possible solutions; choose the best plan; implement the plan; observe; evaluate, and adjust the plan.
9. a problem, which is stated accurately; the criteria, or standards used to find the best solution; the constraints, or factors that hinder finding a solution
10. a general rule that 20% of the causes produce 80% of problems and 20% of effort produces 80% of the results
11. If the plan does not solve the problem, it may mean the problem was defined incorrectly.

(continued)

Developing Your Academic Skills

1. **Science.** To stress teamwork in the workplace, work in teams on an experiment. Divide tasks equally among team members. Write reports on how each member's contribution was instrumental in making the experiment a success, and relate this to the necessity of teamwork in the workplace.
2. **Science.** Discuss the steps in the scientific method. Compare and contrast the scientific method with the steps in problem solving.
3. **Social studies.** Research the labor movement following World War II and its long-term effects on the American workplace. Also study the growth of business in Japan after the war.

Information Technology Applications

1. Use the Internet to research a current topic involving conflict resolution, such as a strike or political situation. Use the information to debate the topic in class.
2. Use the Internet to research aspects of the changing workplace. The Web site for the Department of Labor, www.dol.gov, contains information about working in the 21st century.
3. Conduct an Internet search on one of the following problem-solving tools, which were not covered in this chapter: benchmarking, cause-effect diagram, control chart, force-field analysis, nominal group technique, or histogram. Write a brief paper describing the technique and how it is used.

12. false
13. false
14. Know when to intervene; address the conflict; identify the source and importance of the conflict; identify possible solutions; develop an acceptable solution; implement and evaluate.
15. "You" messages tend to put people on the defensive.

Applying Your Knowledge and Skills

1. **Communications.** Invite someone who has been employed for 40 or more years to speak to your class on how the workplace has changed over that period.
2. **Leadership and Teamwork.** Ask someone to speak to your class who works in a team setting. Ask him or her to share experiences related to each of the four stages of team development.
3. **Problem Solving and Critical Thinking.** Set up a situation where two of your classmates are having a disagreement. Select another classmate to act as moderator and demonstrate the steps in resolving a conflict as discussed in the text. Conclude the activity by having your class discuss the pros and cons of the techniques used in the role-play.
4. **Employability and Career Development.** Organize and conduct a brainstorming session on a work-related problem. Try to involve people outside the school in your group.
5. **Leadership and Teamwork.** Form a team of four to six members. Identify a problem for the team to solve and role-play the four stages of team development: forming, storming, norming, and performing. End the role-play with a discussion of how members felt during each of the stages.

Developing Workplace Skills

Work with three or four classmates to examine the personal traits needed to contribute to effective teamwork. Begin by developing a checklist of traits needed in effective team members. Then, brainstorm ways for promoting the development of each trait. From your brainstorming ideas, create a student handout listing helpful tips for developing traits that contribute to good teamwork. Title it "Tips for Acquiring Teamwork Traits" and use a computer software program to enhance its appearance.

5

Communicating on the Job

Key Terms

communication
sender
encoder
message
channel(s)
receiver
decoder
feedback
noise
hearing
listening
comprehension
margin
block-form
modified block-form
memo
nonverbal communication
voice mail
cellular phone
walkie-talkie
multitasking
teleconferencing
videoconferencing
informal communications
commuting

Chapter Objectives

After studying this chapter, you will be able to

- **determine** how well you listen and how you can perfect this skill.
- **identify** ways you can improve your reading and comprehension skills.
- **write** business letters, memorandums, and reports.
- **identify** ways you can improve your speaking skills when interacting with others.
- **describe** technological tools in the workplace that aid communications with others.

Reading Advantage

Write the main headings in the chapter, leaving space under each heading. As you read the chapter, write three main points that you learned from reading each section.

Achieving Academic Standards

English Language Arts

- Read print and non-print texts to acquire new information and to respond to the needs and demands of society and the workplace. (IRA/NCTE, 1)
- Use spoken and written language to communicate effectively. (IRA/NCTE, 4)
- Use a variety of technological and information processes to gather and synthesize information and to create and communicate knowledge. (IRA/NCTE, 8)

Key Concepts

- Good communication skills are necessary for performing most jobs.

- Written communication in the workplace includes business letters, memos, and business reports.

- Nonverbal messages use expressions and body language to communicate instead of written or spoken words.

- Practicing can help you improve your speaking skills.

Reflect

How does ineffective communication work to your disadvantage in school and on the job?

Discuss

Identify the possible effects of poor basic skills on your job and your personal life.

Resource

Effective Communication, Activity A, WB

Communication skills are very important in securing a job. **Communication** is the process of conveying a message, thought, or idea so it is accurately received and understood. Through good communication skills, people share feelings, ideas, facts, and opinions while performing day-to-day tasks on the job.

Employers expect workers to listen, read, write, and speak accurately. It is important to ask your supervisor how to perform a communication task if you are unsure. It is also important to be courteous as you use these skills. In addition to possessing the basic skills, employers want workers to be skillful in using current communication technology. Some common communication devices are explained in this chapter.

Employees with up-to-date communication skills will have no difficulty succeeding and advancing in a job. Poor communication skills, on the other hand, will be costly to you and your employer. A lack of these skills has led to the firing of employees.

Effective Communication

Communication in the workplace is effective when the message received matches the one sent. This sounds much easier to do than it actually is. Perhaps the intended receiver of your message does not understand it. Perhaps, too, something prevents your message from reaching the intended receiver. In both cases, your communication is not effective. Ineffective communications occur more often than you might guess.

A model of the complete communication process is illustrated in 5-1. The process includes the following parts:

- **Sender**—the person (possibly you) who starts the communication process and has a mental image of what he or she wants to communicate

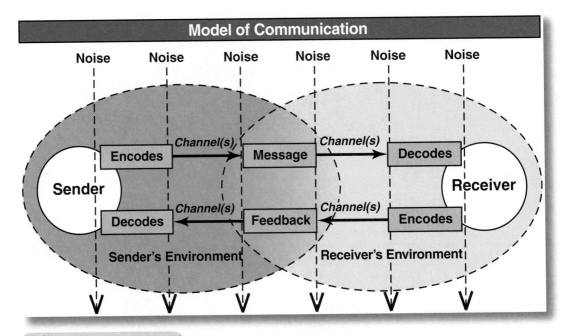

5-1

Understanding a communication model may help you become a better communicator.

- **Encoder**—the sender's mind, which forms a mental image of the message being sent
- **Message**—something that is understood by the senses (usually something spoken, written, or printed)
- **Channel(s)**—how the message is delivered (by voice, a printed document, an image, or another means)
- **Receiver**—the person who gets the message
- **Decoder**—the receiver's mind, which forms a mental image of the message received
- **Feedback**—a clue that reveals what message was received
- **Noise**—anything that interrupts the message

As you can see, the communication process is more complex than just speaking or writing to another person. The minds of both the sender and the receiver of the message are actively involved. The reaction of the message receiver signals what he or she understood. If the reaction is unusual or unexpected, it can mean that the receiver got the wrong message.

If you ask a coworker, for example, where office supplies are located, you expect an answer. If he continues staring at the computer screen, the feedback may indicate that he did not hear you. When the coworker answers with directions to the office supplies, you know your message is understood. In some cases, feedback is not necessary because you know the message was correctly communicated. However, the only way to be certain a message is understood is by providing feedback to the sender.

Noise is any interference that distorts the meaning of the message. Noise can be a mechanical sound, such as a ringing phone, loud conversation, or squeaky machines. Noise can also be a psychological factor that takes many forms. An example of psychological noise is when a customer does not hear you because of anger over a failed product. Psychological noise can also result from personality conflict between the sender and receiver. Psychological noise is very common and affects most conversations.

Practically every communication in the workplace is an opportunity for a breakdown to occur. By recognizing this possibility, you are more likely to make a greater effort to communicate accurately.

Listening Skills

Some people never seem to listen. They become so involved in what they will say that they do not bother to listen to others. Have you ever encountered people who seem to be thinking about something else when you are talking to them? Do you ever do the same to others?

Sometimes listening is considered the same as hearing, but it is not. **Hearing** is recognizing sound. **Listening** involves understanding what you hear. For communication to occur, a message must be sent, received, and understood. Therefore, if a person is not listening when a message is sent, communication does not take place.

Reflect

Recall a recent conversation you had. Identify and explain each part of your communication as it relates to the communication model.

Resource

How Well Do You Listen?
Activity B, WB

Resource

Using Good Listening Skills,
reproducible master 5-1, TR

Reflect Further

Have you ever expressed a message that wasn't understood? If so, why did the communication break down? What part(s) of the communication model failed?

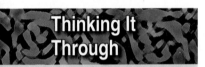

Thinking It Through

Is it possible to talk to someone but not communicate?

People often fail to listen when they are in the following situations:

- *They are interrupted.* A person's ability to listen is affected when someone walks into the room, a telephone rings, or other people are talking nearby.

- *They think they know what will be said.* Sometimes people only listen to part of a conversation because they think "I've heard this before."

- *They do not agree with what is said.* When people do not agree with what is said, they often block the information from entering their minds. They refuse to listen to the speaker.

- *They are having difficulty hearing.* People do not listen when they cannot hear well. For example, you may stop listening when someone is speaking so softly you cannot understand what is said.

- *They are distracted by the speaker.* Sometimes the speaker has distracting mannerisms, speaks in a monotone, or does not make eye contact with the audience. This discourages listening.

- *They do not understand the words.* Not knowing the meanings of words used by the speaker handicaps the listener.

- *They start thinking about something else.* When people allow their minds to wander, they fail to concentrate on what is being said.

To be a good listener, you concentrate on what is said, 5-2. You do not let yourself become distracted. You block out everything except the voice of the speaker. Do not interrupt the speaker unless you do not understand what is being said. Then ask the speaker to explain in more detail what he or she is saying. Being a good listener will help you be a better worker. Listening is a skill you can improve with practice.

5-2

A good listener pays attention to what is being said and shows a sincere interest in what the speaker is saying.

Reading and Comprehension Skills

Reading and comprehension skills are important in the workplace. In almost every work situation, you will be expected to read many types of printed materials that involve your job. Reading skill involves more than just being able to sound the words aloud. It involves **comprehension**, or the ability to understand the material. To be an effective employee, you will need to understand the memos, reports, books, directions, and other documents associated with your job.

In the Real World

Are You Listening, Quentin?

At a department meeting, Quentin's supervisor introduced a new process that the company will begin using in the manufacture of their products. He explained that the new process would require a large new machine. In order to make room for the new machine, all the other machines in the department would need to be relocated. He said, "This new semiautomatic machine will be placed along the east wall. All other machines will be placed along the north and west walls."

The supervisor began to explain how the heavy equipment should be moved. Suddenly Quentin said, "Why don't we put the new machine along the east wall?"

The room became silent. The supervisor replied that the idea was a good one, but had already been discussed.

Embarrassed, Quentin said, "I'm sorry. I didn't hear you."

The supervisor had spoken loud enough for everyone to hear him easily. Quentin had perfect hearing, but he wasn't paying attention. Most of his coworkers laughed at him, shaking their heads.

Questions to Discuss

1. On a scale of 1 (poor) to 10 (excellent), what rating do Quentin's listening skills deserve?
2. Do you think Quentin's coworkers were rude to him? What might this incident do to Quentin's reputation?
3. What can you learn from Quentin that would make you a better listener?

In Quentin's case, for example, comprehension is important. He will be operating new technical equipment. He knows he must read the instruction manuals and carefully follow directions to operate the machines safely. As a result, he will avoid an accident and prevent damage to the machines. His skill in reading and understanding what he reads will benefit him and his employer. He will gain some new skills. This could help him advance on the job. His skills will save his employer time and money.

Being able to read the printed materials at your training station will help you do the job well. Good reading and comprehension skills can help you find information quickly and save time. You can also gain new knowledge and skills through reading that can help you advance to a better job.

Discuss

When you see an unfamiliar word, do you look it up or try to understand its general meaning without checking the definition?

Activity

List the documents you and your coworkers are required to read on the job.

Even good readers can improve their reading skills. Sharpening these skills will help you read faster and remember more of what you read. The following guidelines may help you become a better reader:

- *Read with a purpose.* Before you start to read, you should know why you are reading something. Then you can focus on reading the information you really need. For example, Quentin will read the instruction manuals so he can operate the machines safely. Your purpose might be to learn something new or to find answers.

- *Look over the material you are reading first.* Once you have a purpose for reading, you can decide how fast you want to read. Read quickly if you want just the main ideas. Do this by reading the first paragraph, main headings, and last paragraph. This tells you what information is covered. If you have to remember detailed information, read more slowly. Look over the material first, and then go back and read it carefully. Quentin will follow these guidelines as he reads through the manuals.

- *Try to read for meaning.* The best way to remember what you read is to concentrate. Do not let your mind wander. After you finish reading a section of material, think about the main ideas. Picture these ideas in your mind. This will help you understand what you read. Another way to understand the meaning of what you read is to organize and outline the main ideas in your mind or on paper. This can help you understand the writer's message.

- *Try to improve your vocabulary.* Improving your vocabulary is very important to improving comprehension. As you read, you will find one or more words you do not know. Sometimes you can determine the meaning by the way the word is used in the sentence or paragraph. If the meaning still is not clear, use a dictionary to check the word's meaning. You may even come across certain words or terms that relate to the type of work you do. Many businesses have their own special vocabulary. These special words are used to describe products or operations for that specific business. They also make communication among employees more efficient. Learning these words or terms can help you read and understand job-related materials.

As Quentin reads his manual, he will find several new technical terms. He can ask his coworkers what the terms mean or check a dictionary; or they can use the grammar check on the computer. Either method will help him do his job well.

Writing and Keyboarding Skills

Many employers consider written communication skills one of the most important job skills an employee can have. Why? The main reason is few people possess this skill. Poor communication causes employers to lose business and money. Therefore, the ability to write a message clearly and accurately is an important skill to have in the working world.

Extend Your Knowledge

Accurate Keyboarding Is a Job Skill

Keyboarding skill is not the same as writing skill. In fact, some of the fastest and most accurate keyboarders do not compose messages. They simply key-in existing data and become skilled by doing it often. Keyboarding is a tool often associated with office work. However, this skill is needed even in manufacturing plants where machines are controlled with computers and keyboards.

Good writing skills involve composing written or printed communications. It requires the presentation of clear, logical thoughts. Writing skills become especially important as you advance on the job.

Today, few written communications in the workplace are handwritten except quick notes. The vast majority of written and printed communications in the workplace are prepared with a computer keyboard. When people key-in data well, they are applying their typing skills to a computer keyboard, 5-3. You may wish to take a keyboarding course to learn the correct procedures.

Basic keyboarding skill is a tool to help you compose workplace communications. The basic types of written communications in the workplace include business letters, memorandums, and reports.

Thinking It Through

How can poor writing skills prevent a person from getting ahead on the job?

Business Letters

Writing a business letter is different from a personal letter to a friend or relative. When writing a personal letter, you can use your own style of writing. You can write just as you would talk to the person face to face. You can write on bright red stationery or yellow paper with polka dots. Also, you do not ordinarily keep a copy of every personal letter you write.

Letters written in the workplace, however, are more formal. There are certain parts that should be included in every business letter. There are certain styles that are considered acceptable. There are certain ways business letters should appear. Word processing programs often have a variety of templates for writing business letters. Keeping a copy of every business letter you write is also important.

5-3

Keyboard skills are essential in today's workplace.

Parts of a Business Letter

Most business letters have eight standard parts—the return address, date, inside address, salutation, body, complimentary close, signature and name, and reference initials. Each part is described here and identified in 5-4.

- *Return address*—tells the reader from where the letter came. Most companies have their return addresses printed on their stationery, which is called *letterhead*. (If you are using blank paper for a business letter, you will need to add the return address. See 5-5.)

- *Date*—tells the reader when the letter was written. (If you are using blank paper, the date appears with the return address as shown in 5-5.)

- *Inside address*—includes the name, business title, and address of the person to whom the letter is written. It is the same address as that on the envelope.

- *Salutation*—is the greeting that precedes the body of the letter. The most widely used salutation is *Dear Mr.* (*Mrs., Ms.,* or *Miss*) *Jones.* If you are writing to a group of men and women, you can use *Gentlemen* or *Ladies.* If you know the person on a first-name basis, you can write *Dear Terry.* A colon (:) always follows the salutation.

- *Body*—contains the message.

- *Complimentary close*—formally ends the message. Most business letters have one of the following closings: *Sincerely, Yours truly,* or *Cordially.* A comma follows the closing.

- *Signature, printed name, and business title*—follow the complimentary close. You should sign your name in ink above your printed name. Usually you sign both your first and last name. If you are on a first name basis with the person to whom you are writing, simply sign your first name. Your business title appears directly below your name.

- *Reference initials*—identify the writer of the letter and the typist. Below your business title, your initials as the writer of the letter usually appear in capital letters. These are followed by a colon or slash and the typist's initials in lowercase letters. The common forms used are *MLD/ch* and *MLD:ch.* If the writer of the letter is also the typist, then only one set appears or no initials at all.

Thinking It Through

If a business letter is missing one or more of the standard parts, does this reflect badly on the company, the person who wrote it, or the one who keyed-in the letter?

H.B. Jones Welding

812 N. 7th Avenue

Kansas City, Missouri 65100

Return address

November 15, 20xx

Date

Acme Welding Supply
999 Camden St.
St. Louis, MO 63000

Inside address

Dear Sir or Madam:

Salutation

Please send me information about the new Acme welding machines you advertised in the Welding Journal last month. My company rebuilds heavy road construction equipment, and we need to replace five of our welding machines.

Body

If you have a salesperson in the Kansas City area, we would appreciate having him or her call us at 876-555-4567 or e-mail us at acme@acme.com.

Sincerely,

Jackie Jones

Complimentary close

Jackie Jones
Purchaser

Signature and typed name

JRJ/ra

Reference initials

5-4
Most business letters have eight standard parts.

687 Sunnybrook Lane
Clinton, IL 60466
November 20, 20xx

Acme Welding Supply
999 Camden Street
St. Louis, Missouri 63000

To Whom It May Concern:

I understand your company rebuilds and repairs road construction equipment. I am an owner of a small road-repair business who works primarily on local country roads. I need to have an asphalt paving machine repaired as soon as possible.

Please contact me so I know what to do to get this machine repaired. Can one of your representatives identify its problem and fix it on site? I would appreciate a phone call at your earliest convenience. My 24-hour number is 815-555-3231.

Sincerely,

William Brown
President

5-5

The main purpose of a request letter is to get the reader to do something for you.

Types of Business Letters

A business letter is usually written for one of three reasons:

- to request information, merchandise, or service
- to send good news or a neutral message
- to deliver bad news

To address these different reasons, there are three main types of business letters: request letters, good news and neutral-message letters, and bad-news letters. The type of message you communicate will determine which type of letter to write and what information to include. The following are guidelines for writing each type of letter.

Request Letters

When the main purpose of your message is to ask the reader to do something, you are writing a request letter. In this case, it is important to cover three points.

- Introduce your request and state why you are making it.
- Include any details necessary for the reader to respond to your request correctly.
- State clearly what action you want the reader to take and when.

For example, if you are ordering merchandise, it is important that you include the name of the merchandise, quantity wanted, order or catalog number, size, color, and any other important information. Also, give the reader the name and address to which the merchandise should be sent. Tell the reader when the order is needed and how it will be paid.

In the closing paragraph, you should also include a statement of appreciation. You might write this: "I would appreciate a phone call at your earliest convenience," as shown in 5-5.

Good-News and Neutral-Message Letters

Letters that answer requests; grant favors; express appreciation; or make announcements about events, policies, and procedures can be written by the good-news/neutral-message letter plan. These types of letters are usually easy to write because you tell the reader something pleasant or not controversial.

In a good-news/neutral-message letter, there are three important points to tell the reader.

- State the news or the main idea.
- Explain any details, facts, or reasons that relate to it.
- End the letter on a positive and friendly note.

For example, suppose your job is to fill a mail order for a customer. If the customer ordered four items and you only have three items in stock, explain when the other item will be sent. Thank the customer for doing business with your company. Let the person know you will be glad to fill future orders. If your company is also sending information about a new product or service, provide complete information about it and how to obtain it. See 5-6.

Activity

Write a letter requesting information.

Activity

Write a good-news letter to an imaginary individual who has just won a million dollars.

Acme Welding Supply
999 Camden Street
St. Louis, Missouri 63000

November 20, 20xx

Ms. Jackie Jones, Purchaser
H.B. Jones Welding
812 N. 7th Avenue
Kansas City, MO 65100

Dear Ms. Jones:

Thank you for your letter requesting information about our new Acme welding machine. Enclosed is a booklet describing the machine to familiarize you with its exceptional features.

Ken Adams is our Acme welding machine representative in the Kansas City area. He would be happy to demonstrate the welding machine to you and answer any questions you may have about its use for your company. Ken will be calling you this week to arrange a visit.

Again, thank you for your interest. Ken will be happy to fill an order for you if you decide the Acme welding machine or any of our other products will meet your needs.

Sincerely,

Larry Smith

Larry Smith
Sales Manager

LS/rb

5-6

Good-news or a neutral-message letter is written when answering requests, granting favors, expressing appreciation, or making announcements about events, policies, and procedures.

Bad-News Letters

Acknowledging orders you cannot fill, turning down requests, and announcing news about price increases or discontinued services are examples of bad-news messages. The wording of bad-news letters is very important. You want to tell the reader the bad news without the reader forming a bad impression of your company.

Usually there are four important points to tell the reader:

- Say something positive that interests the reader, yet relates to the bad news.

- Explain why the request cannot be granted or why the situation must be different from the way the reader wants it.

- Offer a constructive suggestion or an alternative.

- End the letter on a friendly, positive note.

Thank the reader sincerely for making the request, but indicate that it cannot be filled and explain why. For example, maybe your company does not carry the exact item requested but a very similar product that may interest the reader. Perhaps you can direct the reader to a company that does carry the item. Finally, express continued interest in the reader, and invite him or her to contact you in the future. See 5-7.

Thinking It Through

Before you begin writing any type of business letter, why should you first decide what type of letter is needed?

Appearance of a Business Letter

A key factor that influences the appearance of a letter is the space devoted to margins. A **margin** is the blank space around the printed or written material. A letter needs top, side, and bottom margins. The top margin is usually formed by the space around the company's letterhead. Ideally, margins should be the same size all around the letter so they frame the message like a picture. To do this, companies usually stock two sizes of stationery: the normal 8½ × 11-inch and a smaller size.

Although the office assistant is usually responsible for the appearance of a letter, the writer also needs to know how a business letter should look. Most business letters are arranged in one of two ways: block form and modified-block form.

With the **block-form** letter, all parts begin at the left margin and paragraphs are not indented. The good-news letter in 5-6 is in block form on stationery with a letterhead. If you type a letter on blank paper, the return address should also begin at the left margin. Since all parts of the letter begin at the left margin, this is the faster style to key-in.

With the **modified block-form** letter, all parts begin at the left margin except the return address (if keyed-in), date, complimentary close, name, and signature. Also, the paragraphs of the body may be indented. The bad-news letter in 5-7 is a modified block-form.

The placement of the parts of a letter is also important. If the return address is keyed-in, it is usually placed on line 12 with the date keyed-in directly below it. On letterhead stationery, the date should appear about two lines below the last line of the company letterhead, which is usually line 14.

Activity

Write a bad-news letter informing a customer that the price of the item ordered has increased 20 percent. Your letter will return the customer's check, written for the former price.

Resource

Combining Good and Bad News, Activity E, WB

Activity

Obtain a copy of an actual business letter. Write a critique of the style and content.

Activity

Do you see more business letters in block or modified-block form?

Acme Welding Supply
999 Camden Street
St. Louis, Missouri 63000

December 2, 20xx

Mr. J. T. McRae
McRae & Sons Construction
110 East Rd.
Independence, MO 65923

Dear Mr. McRae:

Thank you for your order for three Acme welding machines.

Since the demand for this newest welding device has far exceeded our sales expectations at this time of year, we are temporarily out of stock. However, our production manager has assured me that a new supply of welding machines will be available within ten days.

You can plan on receiving a rush shipment of your welding machines by December 15. We are confident you and your employees will agree that the performance of these lightweight welding machines far surpasses every-thing you have used to date.

Sincerely,

Larry Smith

Larry Smith
Sales Manager

LS/rb

5-7

The main purpose of a bad-news letter is to tell the reader unfavorable news without the reader forming a bad impression of your company.

The inside address is placed two to eight lines below the date, depending on the length of the letter. The shorter the letter, the more lines you should leave between the date and the inside address. The salutation appears two lines below the inside address. The body of the letter begins two lines below the salutation. It is single-spaced with double spacing between paragraphs. The complimentary close is two lines below the last line of the body. About four lines below the complimentary close, the name and business title should appear. This allows room for the person's signature. Two lines below the business title is the location of the reference initials.

Most business letters are printed on white or off-white paper. They should appear neat and clean with no smudges, fingerprints, or creases.

Appearance of a Business Envelope

Business envelopes should repeat the inside address of the business letter slightly below the center point of the envelope. The return address should appear in the upper-left corner. This address includes the full name and address of the person sending the communication. The return address is especially important if, for any reason, the letter cannot be delivered.

The U.S. Postal Service appreciates the use of uppercase letters on envelopes because these work best with their scanning equipment. Many businesses, however, continue to use upper- and lowercase letters. Always include the two-letter state abbreviation developed by the Postal Service and the zip code.

Memos

When you want to send a written message to someone at work, you do not send a business letter—you send a memorandum. A memorandum, or **memo**, is an informal written message from one person or department to another person, persons, or department(s) in the same company. It may be a short note to remind others of a coming event or to explain a new company rule. Memos are short because they usually deal with only one subject. Therefore, they tend to be fast and easy to write. Memos may be sent as hard copy or as e-mail.

Parts of a Memo

The standard parts of a memo are described here and shown in 5-8.

- *Date*—This indicates when the memo was written. The date can be expressed completely as November 10, 20xx, or abbreviated as 11/10/xx. The abbreviated date is more informal. Which choice is a better choice depends on the situation and your company's style.

Thinking It Through

When might it be better to communicate with a business letter instead of a phone call?

Activity

Explain to another student how to fold an 8½×11-inch business letter to fit a 4¼×9½-inch envelope.

Reflect

What are some topics in your work setting that would be appropriately covered in a memo?

Resource

Writing Memos, Activity F, WB

Department of Industrial Technology

Memo

Date:	October 22, 20xx
To:	Jim Jenkins, Director Warehouse Chemical Stores
From:	Joe Larks, Foreman Production Lab – Room 30
Subject:	RUSH – Sulfuric Acid

We are using our last bottle of sulfuric acid. Please send 20 gallons of concentrated sulfuric acid to our department by 10:00 a.m. tomorrow. Thanks.

5-8

Memos are usually short, informal messages that deal with one subject.

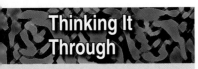

Thinking It Through

What kind of a message is ideal in memo form where you, a parent, or a friend works? What topics do you think are too lengthy for a memo?

- *To*—The names of the person(s) or department(s) receiving the memo appear here. If the memo is going to just one person with whom you work closely, you may use a first name or nickname, such as *Kesha*. However, you should refer to your reader by title and position if the person is a superior or someone unfamiliar to you, or if the memo will be filed as a record. In these situations, you would use *Kesha Jones, Personnel Manager*.

- *From*—The name of the person or department sending the memo appears here. Whether you include the first name only, the full name, or full name and business title depends on the situation. More formal situations require a full name and business title.

- *Subject*—After this heading, briefly state the purpose of the memo. For example, if you are requesting office supplies, the subject line of your memo might be *Office Supplies Needed*. Sometimes *RE*, a shortened expression for *regarding*, is used instead of *SUBJECT*.

- *Body*—This contains the message. The same general guidelines that apply to writing business letters also apply to memos. The big difference is length since a memo can be as short as one sentence.

Appearance of a Memo

Some businesses may have a special type of stationery to use for memos. It may have *Memorandum* and the company's name at the top of the page. If your company does not have memo stationery, regular typing paper can be used.

In most cases, a memo format is available on your computer at work. You simply key-in the information after each heading. Although there are no set guidelines for typing memos, here are some tips for memo placement. The words *Date*, *To*, *From*, and *Subject* should be followed by colons at the left margin. There should be one line of white space between each heading. The body of the memo should begin under the subject line after one or two lines of white space, regardless of the length of the message. The message is usually single-spaced.

Thinking It Through

How does the appearance of a memo differ from that of a business letter?

Activity

Write a memo on a topic directly related to your work setting.

Activity

Ask your employer for two or three non-confidential memos. Critique the memos in class.

Enrich

Write a formal report to your school's alumni on how well your athletic and academic teams did last season.

Business Reports

Business reports are written to present a new idea, explain a problem that needs action, or summarize work done to date. They are usually written to help the receiver(s) understand a significant business situation, solve a business problem, or make a decision. Business reports are either formal or informal.

Formal reports are usually long and about complex problems. They usually include a cover, title page, table of contents, introduction, body, summary, and bibliography. They often include graphs, tables, and illustrations to explain specific points.

Informal reports are generally short and usually include just the body of the message, like the body of a letter or memo. Weekly reports on sales, number of phone calls received, and department accomplishments are examples of informal reports. Often the information appears on company reporting forms.

As with letters and memos, you will need to plan what you want to include in a report before you begin writing:

- *Define the purpose.* Why are you writing the report? What do you need to tell the receiver?

- *Consider who will receive the report.* Who wants or needs the report? How much detail do they need or prefer?

- *Determine what ideas to include.* What points will you need to cover to accomplish the report's purpose?

When preparing any report, write clearly, concisely, and accurately. Present the facts objectively. This means you should make sure you do not let your personal feelings about the subject influence what you report.

Nonverbal Communication

Nonverbal communication can affect the content of what people try to communicate more than what is said or heard. **Nonverbal communication** is any message that does not use written or spoken words. People alter the meaning of what they say with facial expressions, gestures, and the way in which they sit and stand.

It is important to be aware of what messages your actions as well as your words convey. Make an effort to match your nonverbal communications with your feelings and the messages you are trying to send. For example, when you sit tall in a chair and make direct eye contact you appear interested. When you lean back, slouch, or look away from a speaker, you appear disinterested, 5-9.

Greeting someone with a smile and firm handshake makes you appear happy to meet them. Using a limp handshake and staring at the floor may make you appear unconfident or disinterested. Sitting beside an individual may indicate a willingness to discuss differences and reach a solution. Standing directly in front of someone's face, practically nose to nose, may show a readiness to fight.

5-9

What message does this nonverbal communication send?

Reflect Further

Have you ever misunderstood a nonverbal message from someone? What happened? How can communicators make sure their messages are clear?

Speaking Skills

When you began talking as a young child, you probably learned one or more new words every day. Now that you are older, you routinely use thousands of words. However, good speaking skill requires more than knowledge of words. You must also be able to use words effectively.

Resource

Speaking Skills, reproducible
master 5-4, TR

Activity

Record an informal conversation
with someone to evaluate your
speaking skills. Suggest ways to
improve your skills.

Employers consider speaking skills so important that they cite them as one of the basic skills needed by effective workers. How good are your speaking skills? If they need improvement, you can accomplish that with practice. Follow these guidelines when you speak to others.

- *Speak clearly and distinctly.* Avoid running words together such as *whydoncha* for *why don't you*. If necessary, talk more slowly. If you have a tendency to mumble, try opening your mouth a little wider when talking. Always be sure not to talk with food or anything else in your mouth.

- *Speak to the listener.* Whether you speak to one person or more, establish eye contact. This will help hold each listener's attention and show that you are interested in the conversation, 5-10. When you speak, use words the listener will understand.

- *Speak with a friendly and courteous tone.* Try to phrase what you want to say in a positive way. When you find it necessary to use criticism, be ready to offer a constructive idea. Avoid arguing and complaining.

- *Use Standard English.* This means you should use standard grammar and pronunciation when speaking. *Bob came here yesterday* is Standard English. *Came Bob yesterday here* is not. The person who uses Standard English on the job appears more competent and better educated.

- *Talk "with" the listener, not "to" the listener.* Keep messages short and understandable. Make sure your messages are received correctly. You may want to ask questions such as "What do you think?" or "What are your feelings about this?" This gives the listener a chance to provide feedback. From the listener's comments, you will know if your messages have been understood.

Reflect Further

Which of the guidelines
for improving speaking
skills do you need to
practice most?

5-10

Speaking directly to a person
and making eye contact
will help hold the listener's
attention.

In the Real World

The Telephone Puzzle

Kesha dialed a business telephone number. After the telephone rang six times, she heard someone pick up the receiver. Then she heard voices in the background, but nobody spoke. Eventually, a voice said, "Hulooo."

"Is this the Acme Company?" Kesha asked.

"Yeah," was the loud reply.

"This is Kesha Jones. I would like to speak to Gordon Brown, please."

"Watcha wan hem fir?"

"I'm calling to cancel a luncheon meeting for tomorrow that Mr. Brown is scheduled to attend at the Hilton Hotel."

"I don't know nothin' about that," came the reply.

"Would you please connect me with Mr. Brown or his assistant," Kesha said before hearing a dial tone.

The dial tone meant that her call had been disconnected. As Kesha considered how to get the urgent message to Mr. Brown, she tried to review in her mind what she might have said to trigger so much confusion during the call.

Questions to Discuss

1. If you were Kesha, what mental picture would you have of the person who answered the phone? Would this person's behavior influence your opinion of the Acme Company?
2. What do you think the person who answered the telephone at Acme Company should have said to Kesha? What should the person have done?
3. What confusion, if any, did Kesha cause?

Talking on the Phone

Using the telephone in the workplace is one of the quickest ways to communicate. A one-minute telephone call, if handled properly, can save hours or even days in communication time. If you have a job that involves a telephone, it is important to use good telephone manners. The way you communicate over the telephone can help or hurt your employer.

Here are some pointers to improve your telephone skills at work. When the telephone rings, answer it immediately. Greet the caller pleasantly and give the name of your company, your department, or your own name. Your supervisor will probably tell you what greeting to use. You may say something like "Good morning, the Acme Company, may I help you?"

When talking, hold the phone about one inch from your lips and speak directly into the transmitter. Speak clearly and say each word distinctly. Do not eat, drink, or chew gum while speaking on the phone. Always be courteous to the caller even if it is a wrong number.

Be sure to keep a message pad or paper and pen close to the telephone so you can write down messages. When taking a message, record the following:

- date
- time of the call
- name of the caller
- name of the person who should receive the message
- message

Thinking It Through

How should you end a business call? Why?

Reflect Further

How do you feel about speaking in front of others? Do you feel calmer when you're well prepared?

Thinking It Through

Do you know anyone who doesn't get nervous before speaking? What is their secret?

Activity

Have a classmate quietly create a telephone message, then say it aloud as you write down all the important information.

Resource

Your Speaking Skills, Activity H, WB

Discuss

Why is it best to outline your speech rather than write every detail?

After writing down the message, read it back to the caller to make sure you recorded the information correctly. If you are not sure how to spell a person's name or a company's name, ask the caller to spell it for you. It is important for you to copy down the message exactly.

When calling a person, plan your call in advance. For example, if you are placing an order for company supplies, be sure you have all the facts you need in front of you. Know what you want to say and how you want to say it.

When any business call comes to a close, end the conversation pleasantly. If you made the call, thank the person for his or her assistance or cooperation. If you received the call, you may want to thank the person for calling. Remember, the impressions you make on others will influence the impressions they will have of you and your company.

Speaking to a Group

At school you have probably spoken in front of a group. You have probably given oral reports in some of your classes. Perhaps you have spoken in front of a club or participated in a public speaking contest.

Practically all occupations require some form of public speaking. As an employee, you may be asked to guide a tour group through your department. You may be asked to make a sales pitch to a group of buyers or speak at a meeting. You will probably be asked on many occasions to explain your ideas to a group of coworkers. Regardless of the type of work you do, having the ability to speak in front of a group will help you be a better communicator on and off the job.

Most people are afraid to speak in front of a group because they are afraid they might say or do something foolish. That becomes less of a problem when you speak on a familiar topic. You may be thinking you do not know much about anything, but you do. You are an expert on yourself. You could talk confidently about where you live, where you go to school, where you work, and what your interests and hobbies are. You are the expert on what you do at your training station—the tasks you perform and the skills you learn. Knowing your subject is half the work in public speaking. The other half is preparing your presentation.

When preparing your speech, outline the main thoughts you want to convey to your audience. Try to limit yourself to five main points or less. Then organize your points in a logical order. For example, suppose you will speak about refinishing furniture, a hobby of yours. You decide there are three main points to include:

- different types of finishes to use

- a step-by-step explanation of how to refinish furniture

- materials and equipment needed for refinishing

After reviewing these, you decide the most logical point to mention first is a step-by-step explanation. Next, you decide you want to describe the material and equipment needed. This leaves the discussion of finishes last. Therefore, you decide to organize the points as follows:

1. a step-by-step explanation of how to refinish furniture

2. materials and equipment needed for refinishing

3. different types of finishes to use

Now you have a speech, but how do you deliver it? Here is one easy rule to follow—tell them what you plan to tell them; tell them; then tell them what you told them. This simply means identify your main points, discuss them, then summarize them.

When you begin with an overview of your plans, catching the audience's attention is important. You may want to tell a funny story related to your subject or one that will lead into your subject. You may also want to tell a personal experience related to the subject. Then go through your points one by one. Finally, summarize the points.

Before giving your speech, practice! Practicing will help you know what you want to say and when. See 5-11. You will also want to practice timing to make sure your speech is not too long or short. If you are not given a time limit, then limit yourself. It is best not to speak longer than twenty minutes. This will allow some time for answering questions from the audience.

When delivering your speech, avoid reading from your notes. Use note cards instead. You should speak to your audience, not read to them. As you speak, project your voice so everyone can hear you clearly. It is also important to look at the people to whom you are talking. Making eye contact will help you hold your audience's attention.

Your appearance when making a presentation is also important. Dress appropriately for the occasion and the audience. If speaking to classmates in your English class at school, dress as you would for school. If speaking to a group of employers about your cooperative work experience, dress more formally. Always make sure you look clean and neat.

Remember, when you give a speech, you are simply sharing a message with others. Give it with confidence and enthusiasm. Also, before giving your speech, look back at the communication model and be sure you are sending and encoding exactly what you want the audience to receive.

Communication Technology

The way people communicate in the workplace has changed due to technology. Few employers can afford to let their employees take extra

Discuss

Fear of public speaking is the general public's number one fear. Why do you think that fear ranks so high?

Reflect

How did you feel before and after you last spoke in front of a group? Were any of your fears realized?

Activity

List what you fear most about speaking in front of a group. Devise a plan to help you deliver your speech with confidence.

5-11
Practicing your speech is especially important when visual aids are part of the presentation.

Reflect Further

What do you need to do to deliver better speeches in the future?

Discuss

What impresses you most, both positively and negatively, about the latest communication technology?

time to prepare handwritten letters, memos, directions, and instructions. All forms of communication have become electronic in nature because of the speed provided and time saved.

Manufacturing, construction, service, entertainment, and all other types of businesses are dependent on a variety of communication tools. Employees are using electronic communications on a daily and hourly basis. The communication equipment in use includes, telephones, headsets, and many other tools. (You will learn about *e-mail*, or electronic mail, in Chapter 7, "Technology and You")

Using Voice Mail

When you leave messages, be sure to

- speak clearly and say each word carefully.

- give your name and telephone number twice, at the beginning and the end.

- keep your message brief, but explain the reason for your call.

- give the date and time of your message (even though many voice-mail systems do that automatically).

- let the person know the best time to reach you.

5-12

These tips will help you use voice mail effectively.

Voice Mail

One common phone feature that you will be expected to handle is voice mail. **Voice mail** allows callers to leave recorded messages. Some of your work may involve directions left for you in your voice mail. Keeping messages short and to the point is important when using a voice mail system. Sometimes you are not warned that your call will be disconnected after a certain number of seconds. The best advice is to be ready to quickly cover the key facts before leaving a voice mail message. Follow the guidelines in 5-12.

Cellular Phones

The etiquette used when recording voice mail messages also applies to using a cellular phone. A **cellular phone** is a type of wireless phone. In most cases involving a cellular call, both parties are charged for the call. Consequently, the person receiving your call will want you to deliver it as quickly as possible. Before making a cellular call, take a few moments to gather your thoughts so you can deliver your message fast and courteously.

Cellular phones are a common communication tool and are used more often than traditional phones by many people. Cellular phones have the advantages of being easy to carry and the convenience of providing an instant communication link wherever you are, 5-13. Within a few seconds after a communication is sent, it is received.

You may be issued a cellular phone in your job. Make sure your recorded greeting is professional. Your employer may provide you with a specific format for your greeting. It is very important you understand exactly how your employer expects you to use this phone. Some employers will allow personal calls on a company cellular phone, but others will not. Some employers will allow personal calls only if you pay for those calls. It is also important to discuss with your

5-13

Telephone access anytime anywhere is the reason for increasing dependence on cellular phones in the workplace.

employer the types of calls that may be made with these phones because cellular calls are not always private. In many instances, your calls may be overheard and recorded by others.

Walkie-Talkies

Similar to a cellular phone but limited to short-distance calling, a **walkie-talkie** is also a very common communication tool on a job. Walkie-talkies aid communications between workers separated by a distance of a couple miles or less.

Walkie-talkies can be used to help a crane operator position a load accurately and safely with directions from an assistant standing beyond hearing range. They may also be used by surveyors in the field, construction workers on a skyscraper, and factory workers in different departments. These short-range communication devices are very important in search-and-rescue missions as well as in military applications.

Headsets

Many employees use headsets as part of their job. One example is the headset worn by employees in fast-food establishments. One employee on a headset may be listening to the orders being taken at the drive-in window by a coworker speaking into a headset. (Doing more than one job at a time is called **multitasking**.) Headsets allow employees to hear related tasks being done by others.

Many employees working at computer terminals are also required to wear headsets. See 5-14. Some firemen driving a fire truck wear a headset that allows them to keep in contact with the fire station while in route to an emergency. Using a headset should not be a concern since your employer will provide the necessary training.

Teleconferencing and Videoconferencing

Flying people to meetings in other cities can be very costly for an employer. However, technology can link people together in various locations to hold a productive meeting. Participants can be as near as the next office or as far as another country. There are two ways that employees separated by distances can meet: through teleconferencing and videoconferencing.

Using a phone to conduct a meeting with participants in different locations is **teleconferencing**. Through the use of speakerphones in each location, everyone can contribute comments while hearing what the others are saying. During a teleconference, it is important to speak loudly and clearly. Also, it is helpful when people identify themselves each time they speak so everyone knows *who* is saying *what*. Teleconferencing is a widely used business tool.

5-14

Workers quickly adjust to wearing headsets while working at a terminal.

Videoconferencing involves two or more people communicating through a video and voice linkup, 5-15. Some basic videoconferencing guidelines are important for a high-quality conference. How will you feel if your caller refuses to turn on the camera? How alert will you appear on screen if your caller is boring you with a long and aimless conversation? How do you think the dress and other physical features seen on the video screen will affect the conversation? There are many professional and social questions associated with use of this technology.

Informal Communication Channels

Informal communications are sometimes more informative than formal communications in the workplace. On the other hand, sometimes these communications are merely gossip. It will be up to you to distinguish the useful from the useless information.

Informal communications may be defined as unscheduled communication with coworkers that occur by chance inside and outside the workplace. Informal communications may relate to your job, coworkers, or employer. Sometimes it may relate to your employer's reputation in the industry or the local community. Informal communications are common during travel between home and work, shift changes, or breaks.

5-15

Videoconferencing is becoming more widely used for a large variety of purposes.

METNET, Helena College of Technology

Commuting

Regularly traveling back and forth to work is called **commuting**. When you make that trip with coworkers, it is an opportunity to share information about work. The trip can be very frustrating in some places due to heavy traffic and crowds. For many other people, however, the trip to work is a pleasant time when friendships are made. Very open conversation may take place related to both work and family.

Shift Changes

When you are on a job where informal communications take place during shift changes, it is important to listen carefully. The person working at the job before your shift begins may have information about events on the previous shift that may affect you. While these communications may take place during an informal discussion, the details may be critical for you to know. Listen carefully, ask key questions, and think about how the information told to you may affect your job performance.

Work Breaks

Work breaks may involve informal conversations at a water cooler, in a break room, or while in route to or from breaks. Depending on the size of the business, you may take breaks with many people or just one or two, 5-16. Informal communications at work are necessary and should be enjoyable.

During informal communications, it is important to keep in mind you are still "on the clock" and responsible to your employer. At times it is tempting to discuss other employees, your superiors, and topics related to both work and social situations. Remember, some people do not keep confidences, and anything you say may be passed on to anyone else. It is best to confine your discussions to subjects that relate to your employment and are harmless social conversations.

5-16

Work breaks are opportunities to relax and become better acquainted with your coworkers.

Summary

Communication is important to success on the job. The four basic communication skills include listening, reading, writing, and speaking. Developing nonverbal skills can also improve success on the job.

Listening skills involve understanding what you hear. When speaking to others, talk clearly and distinctly. Always use Standard English. Keep messages short and talk "with" the listener.

Reading skills are improved by learning to read with a purpose. Look over the material first, then read carefully to understand the meaning.

Written business communications include letters, memos, and reports. Reports may be written for use inside or outside the company. Sometimes a specific format is used.

When speaking to a group, select a topic you know. Limit your speech to five or fewer main points and practice before giving it.

Many new tools are being used to speed and improve communications in the workplace. Employees must learn to use them efficiently and ethically. It is important to use informal channels carefully and only for reasons that are positive.

Resource

Review and Study Guide for Chapter 5, reproducible master 5-5, TR

Answers to *Facts In Review*

1. to know how to communicate well and where communication breakdowns may occur
2. (List four:) when interrupted, when they think they know what will be said, when they do not agree with what they hear, when they cannot hear well, when distracted by the speaker, when they don't understand the words, when their thoughts wander
3. Reading is sounding out the words, while comprehension is understanding them.
4. because they are used to operate computers, which are used in practically all types of jobs
5. return address; date; inside address; salutation; body; complimentary close; signature, printed name, and business title; reference initials
6. request information, merchandise, or service; send good news or a neutral message; deliver bad news
7. letters that answer requests, grant favors, express appreciation, or make announcements
8. There is an additional step in writing a bad-news letter—to offer a constructive suggestion or alternative.

Facts in Review

1. Why is it important to understand the model of the complete communication process?
2. What are four reasons why people fail to listen?
3. What is the difference between reading and comprehension?
4. Why are computer application skills so important?
5. What are the eight standard parts of a business letter?
6. What are the three main reasons for writing business letters?
7. Name four examples of letters expressing good-news or neutral messages.
8. What steps in writing a good-news letter differ from writing a bad-news letter?
9. Why is it important to word bad-news letters carefully?
10. What are the ways people communicate nonverbally?
11. Name five guidelines that are important to follow when speaking to others.
12. What is the proper way to handle a business call?
13. What information should you write down when taking a telephone message?
14. What is an easy rule to follow to help you deliver a good speech?
15. Why should you practice before giving a speech?
16. List four important communication tools in the workplace and the main reason for each one's use.
17. Give three examples of occasions for informal work-related communications to occur between workers.
18. What are some hazards of informal communications?

9. to prevent the reader from forming a bad impression of your company
10. by facial expressions and body movement
11. Speak clearly and distinctly; speak to the listener; use a friendly and courteous tone; use standard English; talk "with" the listener, not "to" the listener.

(continued)

Developing Your Academic Skills

1. **Speech.** Prepare a speech and deliver it during class. Critique classmates' speeches for grammar and pronunciation. Give specific examples when incorrect grammar or pronunciation made a message unclear. What might be the reactions to these mistakes in the business world?

2. **English.** Practice writing different types of business letters. Exchange your letters with a partner and check for proper format, spelling errors, and content.

Information Technology Applications

1. Have you ever used technology to communicate and received a message that was vague or misleading? Why was the message unclear? Why is it important to speak clearly and use proper grammar when using technology to communicate?

2. As a class, debate the usefulness of videoconferencing as a business tool. Research videoconferencing to prepare for the debate. If possible, visit a business with videoconferencing technology to see how it works before the debate.

Applying Your Knowledge and Skills

1. **Leadership and Teamwork.** Practice your listening and speaking skills by having a conversation with another classmate about any topic. When one person is speaking, the other listens. Neither person may respond to any statement without first summarizing what the other person has said. Incorrect summaries must be clarified before the conversation continues.

2. **Employability and Career Development.** Demonstrate the correct way to do the following:
   A. answer the telephone at work
   B. take a telephone message
   C. place a telephone order

3. **Communications.** Prepare a three- to five-minute speech on how to give a speech. Present it to the class.

4. **Academic Foundations.** Interview two coworkers. Ask for specific examples of how they use reading skills on the job. Make a list of the types of materials they must read. Give a brief report to the class.

Developing Workplace Skills

Work with two classmates to practice the speaking and listening skills needed for good telephone communications. One person will create a detailed business message, tape it on a recorder, and play it back for the others to silently write a telephone message. Then the written messages should be read and compared to the taped message. Determine what important details, if any, were left out. Analyze why these errors may have occurred.

12. Answer the phone immediately; be pleasant; use the appropriate greeting; speak clearly; do not speak with anything in your mouth; always be courteous.

13. the date, time of call, name of the caller, name of the person who should get the message, the message itself

14. Tell them what you plan to tell them; tell them; then tell them what you told them.

15. to help you know what to say when and how

16. (List four:) voice mail—to leave messages; cellular phone—to let you call anywhere and anytime; walkie-talkie—to communicate across short distances; headset—to hear related tasks being done by coworkers; teleconferencing—to allow the voice linkup of people in different locations; video conferencing—to allow the voice and video linkup of people in different locations

17. commuting, shift changes, work breaks

18. gossiping, not keeping confidential the comments expressed, misunderstandings with coworkers

6

Math in the Workplace

Key Terms

common fraction

decimal fraction

percent

area measurement

metric system

meter

gram

liter

degree Celsius

mean

median

mode

table

line graph

bar graph

circle graph

pictograph

Chapter Objectives

After studying this chapter, you will be able to

- **explain** how to count change correctly.
- **use** a calculator properly.
- **perform** basic mathematical computations.
- **read** linear measurements and determine area measurements.
- **demonstrate** how to measure in metrics and make conversions to and from metric measurements.
- **explain** the value of mean, median, and mode.
- **communicate** math data accurately in charts and graphs.

Reading Advantage

Describe how this chapter relates to another class. Make a list of the similarities and differences.

Achieving Academic Standards

English Language Arts

- Read print and non-print texts to acquire new information and to respond to the needs and demands of society and the workplace. (IRA/NCTE, 1)
- Apply strategies to comprehend, interpret, evaluate, and appreciate texts. (IRA/NCTE, 3)
- Conduct research on issues and interests by gathering, evaluating, and synthesizing data from a variety of sources to communicate discoveries. (IRA/NCTE, 7)

Math

- Understand numbers, ways of representing numbers, relationships among numbers, and number systems. (NCTM)
- Understand meanings of operations and how they relate to one another. (NCTM)
- Compute fluently and make reasonable estimates. (NCTM)
- Apply appropriate techniques, tools, and formulas to determine measurements. (NCTM)
- Understand patterns, relations, and functions. (NCTM)
- Understand and apply basic concepts of probability. (NCTM)

Key Concepts

- Knowledge of fractions, decimals, and percentages are necessary on the job and can help you figure credit card charges, payroll deductions, taxes, and sales markdowns.

- Linear and area measurement are the two basic measurement skills you may be expected to use in the workplace.

- Understanding and using the metric system is necessary for manufacturers to compete worldwide.

- Understanding mean, median, and mode and using charts or graphs are effective ways in which you can analyze data.

Reflect Further

What math skills do you possess that are important in your career choice? What math skills must you acquire?

Arithmetic and math skills are considered basic to workplace effectiveness. Companies expect their employees to have the minimal math skills required for whatever position they are seeking. It is assumed that the basic math skills of addition, subtraction, multiplication, and division are acquired before entering high school. If job applicants lack required math skills, it will be their responsibility in most cases to acquire them. While some companies offer programs to teach these skills, they do not feel they must do so.

The type of math skills required of you at work will be determined by the job you hold. Your job may require you to operate a cash register and make change for customers or use a calculator. You may be required to perform relatively simple calculations with fractions, decimals, and percentages. You may be expected to take exact measurements and figure areas. You may even need to develop charts and graphs to show data from your work.

Whether your job is working as a department manager in a clothing store, a restaurant chef, a nurse's aide, or a bank teller, some math will be essential. As you decide your career choice, you should also acquire the math skills associated with that job. Often a higher level of math skills will result in better job opportunities and a higher salary for you.

Making Change

6-1

Few transactions with customers are as important as giving them correct change.

Making change for customers is a necessary skill for success in many places of employment. The skill of making change is required of salespeople in fast-food establishments, retail stores, entertainment businesses, and taxi companies. Knowing how to make change correctly is important for providing customer satisfaction and avoiding embarrassment to you, 6-1.

When a customer makes a purchase, the change you return is determined by the amount of money the customer has given you. Suppose the customer buys a music CD that costs a total of $17.31 including tax. The customer gives you a $20 bill. You will probably have a cash register that figures the change for you—in this case, $2.69. You would then give the customer the following change:

- 4 pennies (4¢)
- 1 nickel (5¢ + 4¢ = 9¢)
- 1 dime (10¢ + 9¢ = 19¢)
- 2 quarters (50¢ + 19¢ = 69¢)
- 2 one-dollar bills ($2 + 69¢ = $2.69 total)

You would count the change while you hand it to your customer. For example, you would say, "$17.31 and '4' (*the pennies*) equals $17.35… and '5' (*the nickel*) equals $17.40… and '10' (*the dime*) equals $17.50… and '50' (*the quarters*) equals $18… and two dollars (*the bills*) equals $20." By counting the change in this manner you are helping make sure the customer receives the correct change. You are also making sure your cash register will balance at the end of your shift.

Using a Calculator

The calculator is an instrument that can help you solve math problems more quickly. It can add, subtract, multiply, and divide as well as perform other math operations. A pocket calculator is inexpensive and easy to use, 6-2. Some cell phones also have a calculator feature that can be used.

To operate a calculator properly, you need to enter information and instructions correctly. Entries are made by pressing certain numbers and symbols on the keyboard. The information you enter appears above the keyboard in the display area. Check the display area after you have entered a number to be sure the number is correct.

The most common symbols you will find on a calculator and the function each performs are shown in 6-3. Operate a calculator to make sure you understand each function. Press the *on* key, and follow these steps to add, subtract, multiply, and divide 63 and 21.

6-2

Learning to use a calculator can make math homework easier.

Using a Calculator	
Key	**Function**
C	Clears all entries.
CE	Clears last entry.
.	Enters the decimal point.
+	Adds.
−	Subtracts.
×	Multiplies.
÷	Divides.
%	Figures the percentage.
=	Figures the answer.

6-3

The location of the keys on a calculator may vary from model to model, but they perform the same functions.

Resource

Counting Change, reproducible master 6-1, TR

Discuss

Why is it important to have basic math skills as well as know how to use a calculator?

Resource

Using a Calculator,
Activity B, WB

Addition

To add 63 and 21:

1. Enter 63 by pressing 6 and then 3. (63 should then appear on the display.)

2. Press the + key.

3. Enter 21 by pressing 2 and 1. (21 should appear on the display.)

4. Press the = key. (Look for the sum, 84, on the display.)

Subtraction

To subtract 21 from 63:

1. Enter 63.

2. Press the – key.

3. Enter 21.

4. Press the = key. (The answer is 42.)

Multiplication

To multiply 63 by 21:

1. Enter 63.

2. Press the × key.

3. Enter 21.

4. Press the = key. (The answer is 1,323.)

Division

To divide 63 by 21:

1. Enter 63.

2. Press the ÷ key.

3. Enter 21.

4. Press the = key. (The answer is 3.)

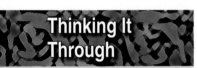

Thinking It Through

Name some of the tasks at home and at work for which people use calculators.

Using Fractions, Decimals, and Percentages

Many people have difficulty understanding fractions, decimals, and percentages. These concepts are necessary for many everyday uses, such as figuring credit card charges, payroll deductions, taxes, and sales markdowns. Knowledge of these concepts is basic to any specialized math skills your future job may require.

Fractions

A **common fraction** is one or more parts of a whole number, 6-4. Common fractions are written with one number over or beside the other as follows:

$$\frac{1}{3} \text{ or } 1/3 \qquad \frac{13}{15} \text{ or } 13/15 \qquad \frac{5}{9} \text{ or } 5/9$$

The number written above or before the line in a fraction is the numerator. The *numerator* is the number of parts present in the fraction. The number below or after the line in a fraction is called the denominator. The *denominator* is the number of parts into which the fraction is divided.

$$\frac{3}{5} \quad \begin{array}{l} \text{numerator} \\ \text{denominator} \end{array}$$

When reading a common fraction, you always read the numerator first, then the denominator. The fraction *3/5* is read three-fifths.

6-4

One of the windowpanes from this quartered window represents 1/4 of the window. One wedge of a pie cut into six equal parts is 1/6 of the pie.

Decimals

You will frequently work with decimals, which are a special type of fraction. A **decimal fraction** is a fraction with a denominator (or multiple) of 10, such as 100, 1000, and 10,000. When writing a decimal fraction, you omit the denominator and place a dot, called a *decimal point*, in front of the numerator. Therefore, the fraction 1/10 becomes .1 as a decimal fraction. Both are read the same: one-tenth.

The quantity of numbers to the right of the decimal point lets you know what multiple of 10 the denominator is. When there is one number to the right of the decimal point, the decimal is read as tenths. Two numbers to the right of the decimal point are read as hundredths. Three numbers to the right of the decimal point are thousandths; four numbers are ten-thousandths.

.1 =	1/10 =	one-tenth
.01 =	1/100 =	one-hundredth
.001 =	1/1000 =	one-thousandth
.0001 =	1/10,000 =	one ten-thousandths

Decimal fractions are usually easier to work with than common fractions, and they are used in many ways. For example, decimal fractions are used to figure sales tax and calculate the number of miles you travel. Decimals are also used in our money system to separate dollars from cents.

Discuss

Explain how fractions are used in everyday life.

Activity

State the ratio of the number of boys to the total number of students in class as a fraction. What is the ratio of girls?

Enrich

Develop a pie chart showing the fraction of time you spend each day eating, sleeping, working, studying, and attending school.

Extend Your Knowledge

Decimals

Another good example of decimals is their daily use at service stations. Decimals are used with most gasoline pumps in the United States to indicate gallons of gas pumped, such as 14.34 gallons. Also, some tire manuals may state the minimum thickness of a tire in decimals. If you are working in a tire center, this use of decimals is very important. Can you think of other ways decimals are used?

Because decimals are easier to write and compute than fractions, fractions are often changed into decimals to figure math problems. To change a fraction into a decimal, you divide the denominator into the numerator. For example, to change 5/8 into a decimal, you divide 5 by 8 as follows:

$$
\begin{array}{r}
.625 \\
8\overline{\smash{)}5.000} \\
\underline{48} \\
20 \\
\underline{16} \\
40 \\
\underline{40}
\end{array}
$$

Activity

Provide problems in which students must convert fractions to decimals.

Activity

What is the sale price for a $29.95 item at 10%, 15%, and 20% off?

The answer in a division problem is the *quotient*. When changing a fraction to a decimal, the number of decimal places in the quotient must be the same as the number of zeros you add to the numerator. If the division does not come out evenly, you carry it out as many decimal places as needed for the answer. Carrying the division to four or five decimal places is usually the most you would ever need.

Percentages

A very common mathematical term is **percent**, which means *per hundred*. By using percentages, you examine a number by dividing it into one hundred parts. The simplest example is a dollar, which divided into 100 parts, equals 100 pennies. One penny—just one of the dollar's 100 parts—is 1/100th of the whole. The use of a percentage sign (%) is an easier way to show this relationship. One penny is 1% of the dollar, 10 pennies is 10%, and 100 pennies is 100%, or one whole dollar. A percent can easily be converted back to decimal form with the use of a decimal point in the right place, as follows:

Thinking It Through

Does your state charge a sales tax on goods and services purchased?

If yes, what percentage rate is charged?

100%	=	1
10%	=	.1
1%	=	.01
.1%	=	.001
.01%	=	.0001

Whole numbers need no decimal point since a fraction is not present. Consequently, 100% is expressed simply as 1. However, 150% converted to decimal form is the fraction 1.5 because there is a whole number with a fraction.

The following examples show several uses of percentages in the workplace:

- If the unemployment rate in your state is 7%, it means 7 of every hundred employable people are not employed, or 7 per 100 people.

- If the profit on a pair of water skis priced at $259.00 is 30%, the seller will make $78.00.

- The new company opening in your hometown will hire 51% of its employees locally. The business estimates it will need 780 employees. Consequently, at least 398 local residents will have jobs with the new company.

Check each of these examples to be sure you understand how percentages were used. See 6-5.

Taking Measurements

Being able to measure accurately is one of the basic skills employers expect of their employees. Regardless of your career, basic measurement skills are essential. Do not be like the person who answered, "Gosh, maybe 25," to the question: "How many quarters are in an inch?"

Linear Measuring

Linear measurement is measuring straight or curved lines with a ruler, yardstick, or tape measure. Some examples include measuring the length of a proposed sidewalk, the distance around a pool, the height of a doorway, or the depth of a computer desk.

Linear measuring tools are commonly divided into equal parts called inches. Each inch is divided into equal fractional units consisting of halves (1/2), quarters (1/4), eighths (1/8), and sixteenths (1/16). Linear measuring skills require accurate measuring to at least 1/16 of an inch. More precise rulers also have the smaller divisions of thirty-seconds (1/32) and sixty-fourths (1/64).

The drawing in 6-6 shows an inch divided into sixteenths. Note that the one-inch line is the longest. The 1/2-inch line is next in length, followed by the 1/4-inch line and the 1/8-inch line. The 1/16-inch line is the shortest.

When measuring, it is usually best to measure to the smallest fraction marked on your ruler. Most rulers are divided into sixteenths. Unless you need greater precision, measuring to within 1/16 inch is acceptable.

Remember, too, fractional measurements are always reduced to their lowest terms. For example, a measurement of 12/16 is expressed as 3/4; 4/16, as 1/4; and 2/4, as 1/2.

6-5
Practically every sales event uses percentages to determine the lowered prices.

Resource

Fractions, Decimals, and Percentages, Activity C, WB

Activity

Measure the width of different doorways in your school.

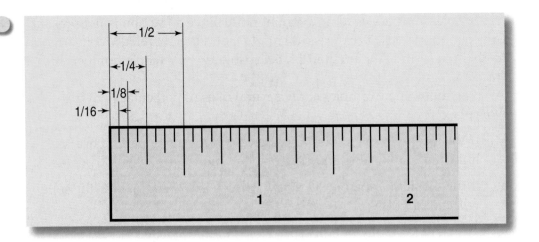

Area Measurement

Area measurement is simply finding how much space is within the border of a geometric shape. The area may be a simple shape, such as square, rectangle, parallelogram, triangle, or circle. See 6-7. You need to take linear measurements well to figure area measurements accurately.

Four-Sided Shapes

A square has four sides, all the same length. A rectangle and a parallelogram have two pairs of sides of different lengths. All three of these shapes use the same formula for measuring area:

$$Area = base \times height$$

If your employer wants you to measure a wall for new wallpaper, you will need to know the total wall area. If the windowless wall is 18-feet wide and 7-feet 6-inches high, the equation is written as follows:

$$Area = 18 \text{ ft.} \times 7.5 \text{ ft.} = 135 \text{ sq. ft.}$$

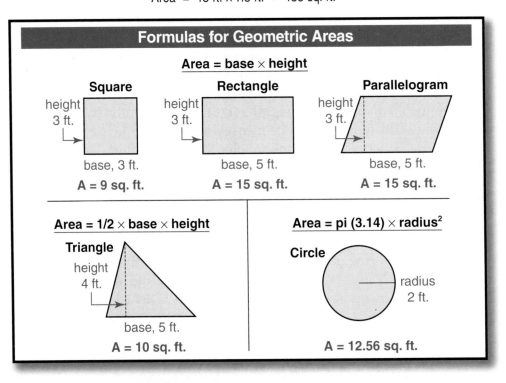

Formulas for Geometric Areas

Area = base × height

Square — height 3 ft., base, 3 ft. — **A = 9 sq. ft.**

Rectangle — height 3 ft., base, 5 ft. — **A = 15 sq. ft.**

Parallelogram — height 3 ft., base, 5 ft. — **A = 15 sq. ft.**

Area = 1/2 × base × height

Triangle — height 4 ft., base, 5 ft. — **A = 10 sq. ft.**

Area = pi (3.14) × radius²

Circle — radius 2 ft. — **A = 12.56 sq. ft.**

Note the linear measurement *7-feet 6-inches* was converted to the decimal *7.5* to make multiplication easier. Area is always expressed in squared units. This is true no matter what measuring unit is used—feet, inches, meters, yards, miles, or some other linear measure.

Triangles

For figuring the area of a triangle, the formula is:

Area = 1/2 × base × height

If you are asked to make a triangular sail for a customer's boat, you must first calculate the area of the sail. If the height of the sail measures 24 ft. and the base measures 20 ft., you have the basic facts needed to figure the answer:

Area = 1/2 × 20 ft. × 24 ft. = 240 sq. ft.

The total area of the finished sail is 240 square feet, but extra fabric will probably be needed for sewing seams.

Circles

The formula for calculating the area of a circle is:

Area = pi × radius^2

Suppose you work for a landscaping company that is installing a circular fishpond. You must calculate the area of the pond to determine how much waterproof fabric will be needed to line the surface. The pond has a 3-ft. radius and sides 2 ft. high. Therefore, the waterproofing fabric must have a radius of 5 ft. to cover the bottom and sides of the pond. You would multiply pi (3.14) times the radius squared (5^2). Pi is often written with the Greek symbol π. The formula will then appear as:

Area = 3.14 × 25 sq. ft. = 78.5 sq. ft.

Again, as in the example of the boat sail, extra fabric may be needed for sewing seams.

Digital Instruments

It is important for employees to be receptive to new technologies. One type of newer technology being applied in the workplace is digital measuring. Digital measuring is the process of using instruments to directly read distance, size, temperature, and other measurements.

Digital tools are becoming more common in the workplace and at home. One of the latest tools in basic measuring technology is the digital tape measure, 6-8. A memory chip holds the measurement seen in the display. The measurement can be displayed in regular or metric measures. Measuring can even be accomplished in very dark areas by pushing a button to store the measurement in memory until the user has enough light to see the display.

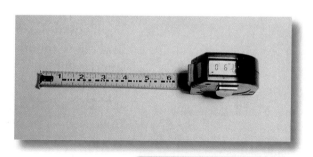

6-8

Digital measuring instruments, like this tape measure, are becoming very common.

Activity

Calculate the area of a triangle formed by drawing a line diagonally from corner to corner across a standard sheet of paper.

Activity

Calculate how many feet of waterproofing fabric are needed if the sides of a pool are 3 feet high.

Reflect

With the use of digital measuring instruments, is it important to measure accurately with conventional measuring tools?

In the Real World

Markie's Secret

Markie was very excited about his new job working on a housing construction crew. He enjoyed working outdoors. The variety of jobs gave him a chance to learn many skills. He learned to frame a complete house as well as install a roof and attach siding. Markie learned almost every job associated with carpentry and building a house. His skills with tools did not go unnoticed among his fellow crew members and his superintendent.

As time passed, Markie became the lead member on the crew. He began to fill in for crew members that were absent. His superintendent began depending on him to take full responsibility for the work done by his crew. Markie was well-liked by his crew members. He never suspected what would happen in the next few weeks.

Markie's superintendent pulled him aside late one afternoon and explained that he would take another position in the company next month. "Would you like to follow me around for a few weeks to learn the ropes and become the next superintendent of the residential work crews?" the superintendent asked.

Markie pretended to be thrilled, but deep inside he knew he could never be superintendent. He knew his secret would become apparent within the first few days he took on that responsibility. Although the position would give him a better salary, more status within the company, and more job security, he could not accept it.

"I am happy with my present job," Markie said to his superintendent. "I want to keep this job and stay where I am." Markie then walked away with his secret.

What was Markie's secret? As superintendent he would be responsible for all aspects of the construction. This included reading blueprints and checking the accuracy of the construction. To do that, Markie would have to read measurements, use fractions and decimals, and know simple geometry.

Markie had no math skills. In fact, he always asked his crew members to do the necessary math anytime it was needed. He even hid his lack of math skills from them!

Questions to Discuss

1. Do you know anyone who hides his or her lack of math knowledge?
2. Do you know anyone that thinks math is too difficult to learn?
3. What could Markie have done to enable himself to take advantage of this opportunity for promotion?

Reflect Further

What occupations can you list that use various measuring skills? Give specific examples.

Digital thermometers are already in daily use. They are very accurate and allow the user to directly read the actual temperature rather than interpret it from the numbers and lines drawn on a traditional thermometer scale.

The use of digital instruments usually leads to more accurate readings. Keep a positive attitude toward new technologies when you are interviewing for a job.

Using the Metric System

To measure distance, weight, volume, and temperature, most countries use the International System of measurement, or the metric system.

The **metric system** is a decimal system of weights and measures, like our money system. The metric system uses the **meter** to measure distance, the **gram** to figure weight, the **liter** to measure volume, and the **degree Celsius** to determine temperature.

Although the United States may eventually convert to the metric system, it still uses the U.S. system of measurement. Inches, feet, yards, and miles are used to measure distance. Ounces and pounds are used to figure weights. Pints, quarts, and gallons are used to measure volume, and Fahrenheit degrees are used to determine temperature.

Many U.S. manufacturers use the metric system to compete in the world market. Speedometers on U.S. cars show kilometers-per-hour as well as miles-per-hour. The U.S. manufactures 35-millimeter film for 35-millimeter cameras, not 1.365-inch film for 1.365-inch cameras. Soda is bottled in liter bottles, not gallon bottles. Many businesses also use the metric system to repair and service foreign products.

Since metrics is a widely used system of measurement, you may work with it on the job. Therefore, you need to learn how to measure in metrics and make metric conversions.

How the System Works

Metric units increase and decrease in size by 10s. To increase the amount, you move the decimal point one place to the right or multiply by 10. To decrease the amount, you move the decimal point one place to the left or divide by 10.

Think about how you write one dollar ($1.00). If you move the decimal point one place to the right, you increase the amount 10 times and make it ten dollars ($10.00). Move the decimal point one more place to the right, and you have one hundred dollars ($100.00). This is ten times more than $10.00. Any metric unit works the same way. In 6-9 you can see how dollars and meters are similar because they are both based on a decimal system.

The metric system has seven basic units, four of which are commonly used and will be discussed in this textbook: meter, gram, liter, and degree Celsius. Scientists, mathematicians, and engineers mainly use the other three units. In the metric system, one of six prefixes can be added

Thinking It Through

Why do many U.S. manufacturers and businesses use both the U.S. system and metric system of measurements?

Discuss

What are the pros and cons of the United States using the metric system?

Resource

How Do You Measure? color transparency CT-6, TR

Discuss

What products do you use that are measured in metric?

Our Money System Compared to the Metric System			
Dollars		**Meters**	
$1,000.00	1,000	1,000 m	1 kilometer—km
100.00	100	100.0 m	1 hectometer—hm
10.00	10	10.00 m	1 dekameter—dam
1.00	1	1.000 m	1 meter—m
.10	1/10	.1000 m	1 decimeter—dm
.01	1/100	.0100 m	1 centimeter—cm
.001	1/1,000	.0010 m	1 millimeter—mm

6-9

The metric system is similar to our money system because they are both based on a decimal system. Here, dollars are compared to meters.

6-10

The six prefixes indicate different levels of value.

Units of Measure in the Metric System				
Prefix	**Number**	**Distance**	**Weight**	**Volume**
kilo	1,000	kilometer (km)	kilogram (kg)	kiloliter (kl)
hecto	100	hectometer (hm)	hectogram (hg)	hectoliter (hl)
deka	10 1	dekameter (dam) meter	dekagram (dag) gram	dekaliter (dal) liter
deci	.1	decimeter (dm)	decigram (dg)	deciliter (dl)
centi	.01	centimeter (cm)	centigram (cg)	centiliter (cl)
milli	.001	millimeter (mm)	milligram (mg)	milliliter (ml)

to a meter, gram, or liter to show its level of value, 6-10. *Deci, centi,* and *milli* can be added to identify smaller measurements. *Deka, hecto,* and *kilo* can be added to identify larger measurements. The most commonly used prefixes are *centi, milli,* and *kilo.*

Meter

A meter (m) is a little longer than one yard. It is used to measure the dimensions of a room, the length of a racetrack, and fabric lengths. A kilometer (km) is just over a half mile, or 5/8 of a mile. It is used to measure the distance between cities and the altitude of a plane in flight. A centimeter (cm) is about the length of one-half inch. Body measurements such as chest, waist, and hip measurements are given in centimeters. One millimeter (mm) is about the thickness of a dime. It is used to measure short lengths such as camera film and small hardware.

Gram

One gram (g) is a very small weight, much less than one ounce. A United States dollar bill weighs about one gram. The gram is used to measure other lightweight items such as spices. A kilogram (kg) is about 2.2 pounds, or 35 ounces. Body weights and freight weights are figured in kilograms. A grain of sand and items too small to see without a microscope are measured in centigrams (cm) or milligrams (mg).

Liter

A liter (l) is a little more than a quart. Gasoline and motor oil are sold by the liter and so are bottles of soft drinks and cartons of milk. Large tanks of liquids are measured in kiloliters (kl). Volumes less than a liter such as paint, cooking oil, and recipe ingredients are usually measured in milliliters (ml).

Activity

Sketch a football field, basketball court, or major league baseball park. State the dimensions in meters and calculate the playing area.

Reflect

Think of one item you use that provides information in each of the following metric measures: gram, liter, and degree Celsius.

Resource

Math Skills Refresher, reproducible master 6-2, TR

Activity

Practice converting U.S. measurements to metric measurements, then convert metric to U.S. measurements.

Degree Celsius

One degree Celsius (°C) is a little more than two degrees Fahrenheit. Water freezes at 0°C, or 32°F, and water boils at 100°C, or 212°F. A comfortable room temperature is 20°C, and a warm sunny day is about 25°C. Normal body temperature is 37°C, or 98.6°F.

Making Conversions

The best way to learn the metric system is to "think metric." This means measuring in metric instead of measuring with the U.S. system and changing the number to metric. However, there may be times when you need to change a U.S. system measurement to a metric measurement or vice versa. This is called making conversions. Chart 6-11 shows how to

Thinking It Through

Discuss the advantages and disadvantages of using the metric system of measurement.

Resource

Working with Metrics, Activity E, WB

Making Conversions (approximate)					
Converting to Metric			**Converting from Metric**		
When You Know	Multiply By	To Find	When You Know	Multiply By	To Find
Distance			**Distance**		
inches	25.4	millimeters	millimeters	0.04	inches
inches	2.54	centimeters	centimeters	0.39	inches
feet	0.3	meters	meters	3.28	feet
yards	0.91	meters	meters	1.09	yards
miles	1.61	kilometers	kilometers	0.62	miles
Weight			**Weight**		
ounces	28.35	grams	grams	0.04	ounces
pounds	454	grams	grams	0.002	pounds
pounds	0.45	kilograms	kilograms	2.2	pounds
Volume			**Volume**		
fluid ounces	29.57	milliliters	milliliters	0.03	fluid ounces
pints	0.47	liters	liters	2.11	pints
quarts	0.95	liters	liters	1.06	quarts
gallons	3.79	liters	liters	0.26	gallons
Temperature			**Temperature**		
Fahrenheit	0.56 (after subtracting 32)	Celsius	Celsius	1.80 (then add 32)	Fahrenheit

6-11

This chart can help you convert measurements to and from the metric system.

make conversions to and from the metric system. To use the chart, look up the unit you know in the left column and multiply it by the known quantity in the middle column to find your conversion.

Suppose you need to learn how many meters are in a strip of 15 yards of fabric. According to the chart, you multiply 15 by 0.91 to find the length of a 15-yard piece of fabric in meters. The answer is 13.65 meters.

Analyzing Data

In the workplace, it is a very common practice to analyze data in a variety of ways to fully understand the subject. Two ways are discussed here: understanding mean, median, and mode; and using charts or graphs.

Understanding Mean, Median, and Mode

Mean, median, and mode are three ways to analyze data. The **mean** is the mathematical average of the data. You find it by totaling all your numbers and dividing by the quantity of numbers you have. The **median** is the number exactly in the middle when the data is listed in ascending or descending order. The **mode** is the number(s) that occurs most frequently. There may be none, one, or more.

Each method of examining data has its own advantages and disadvantages. When most people use the word *average*, they generally refer to the mean. However, some may refer to the median or the mode. It is possible for all three to be identical, but this rarely occurs.

When interviewing for a job, for example, suppose you want to know if a salary offer from a certain company is good or should be better. You need to know how the offer compares to the salaries of others with that job. Suppose you ask about the average salary received by company employees with that position title. Using the salaries in 6-12, do you think the mean, median, or mode would be quoted to you as the average salary of similar employees? Suppose the employer says, "The average salary of people who work in that job is $32,000, but we will offer you $28,000." Listening to that sentence alone, the offer sounds quite fair.

Analyzing Data			
Eleven employees with various levels of experience and years of service hold the same job title within a company at the following salary levels. Examine the mean, median, and mode for this data.			
Employee Salaries			
$28,500	$31,000	$32,000	$32,000
$32,000	$36,000	$37,500	$37,500
$62,500	$91,500	$124,000	

Mean   = $49,500
Median = $36,000
Mode   = $32,000 (occurs three times) and
　　　　　　 $37,500 (occurs twice)

6-12

The mean, median, and mode help with the analysis of statistics.

However, your salary offer is $4,000 below the lowest mode, $8,500 below the median, and $20,500 below the mean.

What the figures in 6-12 do not show are the factors that explain the salary differences. These may include years of experience, educational levels, special abilities, and other factors important to the employer. It would be far more helpful to know how your salary offer compares to that recently offered to employees of similar ability and experience. Knowing the mean, median, and mode of that data would be far more helpful in considering yours.

Again referring to 6-12, suppose the employee earning $28,500, the lowest salary for that job, wants a pay raise. To justify a raise in pay, what figure should she or he quote as the "average" company salary—the median, mean, or mode? Why?

Using Charts and Graphs

Charts and graphs are used to display information quickly and clearly. They are commonly used in books, magazines, newspapers, and on TV. When done well, charts and graphs make data easier to comprehend, compare, and use.

Often the terms *chart* and *graph* are used interchangeably. Charts may take many forms. The five basic types of charts are described as follows:

- Simple **table**—arranges data in rows and columns.

- **Line graph**—shows the relationship of two or more variables. It can also show trends across periods of time.

- **Bar graph**—shows comparisons between categories. Sometimes multiple lines or bars are used.

- **Circle graph**—shows the relationship of parts to the whole.

- **Pictograph**—presents information with the use of eye-catching images.

When a graph presents mathematical data, special care must be taken to make sure the data is presented accurately. The elements of the visual must be drawn to correct mathematical scale. A computer with the appropriate software can do the job easily. Using the computer to create graphics will be discussed in more detail in Chapter 7, "Technology and You."

Graphs should be planned carefully in advance so wrong proportions do not confuse the facts. It is important to know exactly what information you want to deliver. That is the first step to determining the best way to convey data visually.

Reflect Further

Do you believe some people will use the mean, median, or mode in ways to prevent you from knowing the complete picture? How can you prevent this?

Reflect Further

On what specific TV programs or newspaper sections have you seen charts and graphs?

Resource

Common Types of Charts and Graphs, reproducible master 6-3, TR

Enrich

Survey the birthdays of all students in your class. Prepare three different types of charts or graphs to present the information.

Summary

Learning and using basic math to solve problems are important skills for all students to have. The basic math operations of addition, subtraction, multiplication, and division should be learned prior to entering high school. Knowing how to use fractions, decimals, and percentages are also necessary math skills used often at work, school, and home.

When handling money on the job, workers have a special responsibility to count change accurately for customers. To solve math problems quickly and easily, a calculator is often used. To operate a calculator properly, information and instructions must be entered correctly.

Measuring distances on the job also requires math skills. A basic measuring tool is the ruler, which determines linear measurements. Knowing linear measurements is the first step to figuring area measurements. Linear and area measurements can be determined by using U.S. or metric measures. Converting to and from metric measures is simplified by using conversion charts.

Employers use many ways to analyze data. One common way is to compare the mean average, median, and mode. Another way is to plot data on charts and graphs. When displaying figures and other mathematical data in graphics, it is important to make sure the parts of the graph are proportionate to the data.

Resource

Review and Study Guide for Chapter 6, reproducible master 6-3, TR

Answers to *Facts In Review*

1. addition, subtraction, multiplication, division
2. It is important for providing customer satisfaction and avoiding embarrassment.
3. by reading the numerator first then the denominator
4. Both are nine-sixteenths.
5. by dividing the denominator into the numerator
6. .08
7. a part of a whole expressed in hundredths; by multiplying 40 by .06
8. square, rectangle, parallelogram

Facts in Review

1. What four basic math skills should students have before entering high school?
2. How does your ability to correctly count change affect the impression the customer has of you?
3. How do you read a fraction?
4. How would you read the fraction 9/16 and the decimal fraction .9?
5. How do you change a fraction into a decimal?
6. How do you write 8/100 as a decimal fraction?
7. What is a percentage? How do you find 6% of 40?
8. *Area = base × height* is the formula for finding the area of what shape(s)?
9. What is the formula for finding the area of a circle?
10. The metric system is a decimal system, which means it is based on units of _____.
11. What are the basic units of measure for distance, weight, volume, and temperature in the U.S. system of measure?
12. What are the basic units of measure for distance, weight, volume, and temperature in the metric system of measure?
13. What is another term for mathematical average?
14. True or false. The number of modes a group of numbers may have is none, one, or more.
15. What are the five basic types of charts?

9. Area = pi (3.14) × radius²
11. distance = inch, feet, yard, miles; weight = ounce, pound; volume = pint, quart, gallon; temperature = Fahrenheit degrees
12. distance = meter; weight = gram; volume = liter; temperature = Celsius degrees
10. weights and measures
13. mean
14. true
15. table, bar graph, line graph, circle graph, pictograph

Developing Your Academic Skills

1. **Math.** Working with a partner, use fake money to practice counting back change to each other.

2. **Science.** Take the temperatures of three different liquids in degrees Celsius. Then convert the temperatures to degrees Fahrenheit. Record your findings.

3. **Language Arts.** Using Internet or print sources, research the origins of the prefixes *kilo*, *hecto*, *centi*, and *milli*. Give examples of other words that begin with these prefixes. Explain how knowledge of these prefixes can make using the metric system easier. Write a brief essay of your findings.

Information Technology Applications

1. Take measurements of five different items in the classroom using digital and standard tape measures. Record your findings. Also take your temperature using a digital and standard thermometer. Which type of measuring tool did you find easier to use? Explain why.

2. Using the Internet, research workplace accident statistics. Using the computer, prepare several types of graphs for these statistics. Present your completed graphs in class.

Applying Your Knowledge and Skills

1. **Academic Foundations.** If you are given a $50 bill for a $21.15 purchase, how much change would you hand back to the customer? How would you count the change to the customer?

2. **Problem Solving and Critical Thinking.** At the beginning of next month, Bob will receive a 10% raise. If his hourly wage is now $8.00, how much will his new hourly wage be? How much more money will he earn per eight-hour day? How much more money will he earn per 40-hour week?

3. **Technical Skills.** Estimate the length and width of your classroom in feet/inches and in meters. Then measure the two distances with a yardstick and meter stick. What were your estimated U.S. and metric measurements? What were the actual U.S. and metric measurements? Did you do better at estimating U.S. measurements or metric measurements? Explain.

4. **Leadership and Teamwork.** With the help of a classmate, measure your height in centimeters.

Developing Workplace Skills

Find the high and low temperatures for each day last week in your county or city. Use a calculator or a computer to determine the mean, median, and mode for the daily high temperatures. Do the same for the daily lows. To present your information, use the computer to create a line or bar graph.

Working with a small group of four or five classmates, present your graph. Give a two-minute summary of what you learned through this exercise and what difficulties you had creating the graph.

As each graph is presented, the group should analyze it for accuracy and clarity of the data communicated. Ways to improve the graph should be discussed after each presenter's summary.

7

Technology and You

Key Terms

hardware

central processing unit (CPU)

USB flash drive

peripherals

software

World Wide Web

copyright

e-mail

troubleshooting

globalization

lifelong learning

computer literate

E-learning

multimedia

Chapter Objectives

After studying this chapter, you will be able to

- **identify** aspects of computer technology that are most frequently used on the job.
- **explain** various computer applications being used today.
- **analyze** the advantages and disadvantages of using the Internet and e-mail at work.
- **describe** the role of technology in the workplace, school, and home.

Reading Advantage

As you read the chapter, take notes in a presentation software program. Make one slide for each of the main headings. List three to four main points on each slide. Use the finished presentation to study for tests.

Achieving Academic Standards

English Language Arts

- Read print and non-print texts to acquire new information and to respond to the needs and demands of society and the workplace. (IRA/NCTE, 1)
- Apply strategies to comprehend, interpret, evaluate, and appreciate texts. (IRA/NCTE, 3)

Key Concepts

- Being familiar with computer technology is crucial for job success.

- Follow your employer's guidelines when using technology on the job.

- Technology has influenced the way tasks are accomplished on the job, at school, and in the home.

Thinking It Through

What types of computers are sold at the stores in which you shop?

Technology Today

Rapid advances in technology are continually causing your home, school, and work environments to change. Computers are commonly used in many ways to transmit information and make tasks easier. Workers are expected to have basic computer skills. However, they must also be able to adjust quickly to new roles and responsibilities as technology continues to change. Your ability and willingness to learn new technology will help you succeed in the workplace.

The computer and the Internet increasingly impact today's lifestyles. It is assumed that most teens have a working knowledge of computers and basic operations, 7-1. Understanding how to use computers and the Internet is a necessity. Students preparing for the workplace must also learn how to use the tools and technology common to their chosen profession.

Computer Hardware

Small desk-size computers are called *personal computers* (PCs). One popular type of personal computer is the *laptop*. This is a lightweight, portable computer about the size of a notebook. It is especially useful for college students, traveling salespeople, and other professionals who spend much of the workday away from an office, 7-2. The physical equipment in computer systems is the **hardware**. The hardware includes the computer itself and all the items needed to use it except software.

A computer's power depends on the speed of its processor and the amount of memory it has. The **central processing unit (CPU)**, also called the *processor*, controls what is done with the data received.

7-1

Most children today begin using computers at an early age.

This is the component that performs the computer's functions. Processor speeds are measured in frequencies of megahertz (Mhz) and gigahertz (Ghz).

Random Access Memory (RAM) allows data to process quickly. Computers vary in the amount of RAM they have. The amount of memory is measured in *megabytes (MB)* and *gigabytes (GB)*. The more RAM a computer has, the more programs it can run, and the faster the programs can run. The total RAM capacity of personal computers on the market will continue to increase as buyers demand computers with more memory and speed. Generally, it is a good idea to buy a computer with as much memory and as fast a processor as you can afford. Even if you do not require much power when you purchase the computer, you may need it later for software upgrades.

Video cards can also help a computer run faster. A video card helps the computer process complex graphics, such as those found on the Internet or in games.

Methods of Storing Data

Data is either stored in the computer's memory or sent to a secondary storage device. The internal hard disk drive, or *hard drive*, stores the data to operate the computer as well as all information entered by the user. Secondary storage devices are also used to store information. These storage devices include writable CDs, DVDs, and USB flash drives.

Writable CDs (originally called *CD-Recordable*) are referred to as CD-Rs. They hold large amounts of data, but once data is saved to a CD-R, it cannot be erased. On the other hand, CD-Re-Writable discs (CD-RWs) can be erased and used to record repeatedly. As technology improves, the amount of data that may be stored on a CD will probably increase. See 7-3.

DVD-Recordable discs (DVD-Rs) are primarily used to record videos, although they can also be used to store data. DVD-Rs hold much more data than CD-Rs. Data can only be written to (or "burned to") a DVD-R once.

A **USB flash drive** can also be used to store data for extended periods of time. A USB flash drive is also known as a *thumb drive, keychain drive*, or *jump drive*. This tiny unit can be plugged into a computer's USB port and recognized as a storage device. Once data has been saved to the device, it can be plugged into another computer to transfer the data. For this reason, it is a convenient method of backing up data.

Your workplace may connect its computers through a closed *network*. This means that multiple terminals can share information with one another. A *local area network (LAN)* is a network that covers a small area,

7-2

A laptop is portable and takes up little space.

Discuss

The speed of a computer's processor may limit the software a computer can use. What factors might indicate you need a processor upgrade?

Discuss

Why might a USB flash drive be more convenient than a CD-RW or DVD-R for people who must regularly transfer data from one computer to another?

such as an office building. Through your network, you may be able to save information to a server. A *server* is a computer with extensive memory that is connected to other computers. The workers at individual workstations can save information to folders on the server, retrieve information from the server, and share files with coworkers. Most businesses regularly back up information saved to the server as a precaution.

No matter what method you use to save files, *file management* is necessary. This means keeping your files organized and easily retrievable in an appropriate structure. Your company may dictate how files should be managed. Perhaps each employee must maintain files for each project. Keeping files in the appropriate folders will help prevent the server from becoming cluttered with unidentified files and unneeded information.

Peripherals

Peripherals include output and input devices—anything that can be plugged into your CPU. Output devices include monitors and printers. Input devices include keyboards, mice, scanners, digital cameras, and webcams.

A *scanner* is a device that passes an electron beam over an image, allowing the image to be stored in the computer's memory. The stored data can then be retrieved as an image that may be viewed on the computer monitor and modified electronically. Scanners can also be used to input large amounts of text and thereby save hours of keyboarding. To save space, you can buy a printer that includes a scanner.

Digital cameras have almost entirely replaced traditional film cameras. With these cameras, photos are captured to memory cards (or *compact flash cards*) instead of film. The cameras can be plugged into a computer's USB port, and transferring photos to the computer's hard drive. There the images can be modified, stored, or sent to others. Most digital cameras feature a viewing screen on which the user can see the image as soon as the picture is taken. See 7-4.

Webcams are used to transmit videos to the Internet. They are usually plugged into computers and can provide a continuous feed. They are often used for videoconferences or video chatting. These cameras generally provide lower-quality pictures than those of a camcorder.

Software Tools

Computers cannot operate without being told what to do. Hardware is the equipment; **software** provides the instructions. A computer can be instructed to do a variety of tasks depending on the software used.

There are two types of computer software: operating system software and application program software. *Operating system software* directs the use of the computer's hardware. In the case of PCs, either the

7-4
Digital cameras are easy to use and allow you to immediately see the photo you have taken.

Activity

Investigate information on popular word-processing software brands and their capabilities.

Windows® operating system or the Mac OS® operating system is used. Operating system software makes it possible for the computer to use compatible application programs.

Application program software gives the computer directions to do specific tasks, 7-5. Some tasks include word processing, data formatting, or Internet browsing. Many of these programs are already installed on new computers. These programs may be purchased at computer stores or purchased online for download.

Word Processing

The ability to quickly enter, edit, store, and print words with a computer is *word processing*. The computer also makes it easy to add charts, pictures, and other graphics to documents. Adding formatting, such as margins and line spacing, is as simple as clicking your mouse. Most word processing programs have features for checking spelling and grammar. Files can be saved to the hard drive or other storage using the *Save as* option.

Spreadsheets

Spreadsheets are documents that organize text and/or numbers in rows and columns, 7-6. The software is used to organize data into specific formats and perform mathematical computations. Formulas are applied to rows or columns so figures adjust automatically when new data is entered according to the user's needs.

7-5
This program helps the user make precise graphs based on the data that has been entered.

Reflect Further

Have word processing programs entirely replaced typewriters? For what tasks might typewriters still be used?

Spreadsheets are used extensively in all areas of financial accounting. They also provide an organized way to view numerous figures about business performance. For example, store managers may use spreadsheets to track the effect of various weekly promotions and marketing strategies on sales.

7-6

Spreadsheets are used whenever a large quantity of numbers are analyzed.

Reflect Further

Do you agree with the following statement? "Computers are smart."

Discuss

What are the differences among such software tools as word processing, spreadsheets, and databases? How might each be used at home and in the workplace?

Activity

Use desktop publishing or presentation software to inform others about the key topics described in this chapter.

Enrich

Use desktop publishing software to publish a monthly school-to-work newsletter.

Thinking It Through

Where can you learn how to operate computer software programs for word processing, spreadsheets, databases, presentation software, and desktop publishing?

Databases

Databases are computer files that organize a large collection of related information. A database is like a file folder in which groups of related records are stored and cross-referenced. Depending on the chosen reference category, or *field*, one or more parts of the file can be retrieved. Information can be entered or sorted by field. The information in a database can also be merged into documents in other programs, such as a word processing document.

Sometimes databases are used to track customer purchasing habits or the costs of materials from different suppliers. For example, suppose your sales force wants to keep track of the action to take with each customer after a sales call. By inputting data about the visits to a database, four separate lists can be printed to help the sales department know whom to visit again, phone, send more information, or simply leave alone.

Desktop Publishing

PCs can be used to create, edit, and produce newsletters, reports, and other documents. This ability is called *desktop publishing*. It requires the use of software that formats the copy, offers various type styles and sizes, and creates page layouts. The software allows the user to create graphics and add photos and other visuals.

Documents made with desktop publishing have the same high-quality look as those prepared professionally. One system is used for the entire publishing process from creation to printing.

Businesses, schools, organizations, and government offices use desktop publishing. Newsletters, business reports, sales materials, and even books are prepared using this method. Rapid improvements in technology coupled with more affordable equipment has caused a revamping of the printing industry. The result is a dramatic rise in desktop publishing.

Presentations

Presentation software is a program that allows the user to create electronic presentations similar to slide shows. Text and images can be inserted on each slide, as well as notes for the speaker. Then, as the speaker gives the presentation, he or she moves the slide show forward by clicking the mouse or a remote.

The presentation can incorporate video and sounds if desired. The speaker can also prepare informative handouts for the audience by printing the presentation in different formats.

The Internet

The *Internet* consists of thousands of computer networks around the world joined together. It is the largest computer system in existence. This network allows connected computers to exchange information and access resources at speeds and volumes once considered impossible. See 7-7.

When you access the Internet, you are *online*. To get online, you first need a computer with the appropriate software, a modem, and a connection. That connection is usually provided by a phone line, cable line, or digital subscriber line (DSL). Wireless connections are also very popular.

In addition, you need an Internet service provider. This may be your local phone company, cable company, or a commercial service provider. Usually for a monthly fee, you receive the software and the ability to go online 24 hours a day. Various other fees may also apply.

The **World Wide Web** is the part of the Internet that carries messages having pictures, color, and/or sound. It contains huge collections of documents on sites called *Web sites.* These sites are maintained by various educational institutions, companies, organizations, government agencies, and individuals. Because Web sites contain colorful formats, many are entertaining as well as informative. To view material on the World Wide Web, you will need a *browser.* This is a type of program that allows you to access and view Web sites.

The program that searches for Internet information is called a *search engine.* You can find information faster and more accurately by searching for significant key words or an exact phrase. This will help limit the search results to most relevant Web site links.

Activity

Go online and research the variety of browsers available to users of the World Wide Web. What are the key features of each? Which browser best suits your needs?

Enrich

How has society changed as a result of 24-hour-a-day access to the Internet? What are the positive and negative effects?

Note

Remind students not to give out personal contact information when using various Internet sites. Predators can easily take advantage of such information and cause students harm.

Resource

Investigating Web Sites, Activity B, WB

7-7
The Internet allows a person who works at home to instantly share information with those working in the office.

Thinking It Through

To check the reliability of information obtained from an unfamiliar Internet source, what would you do?

Note

Some Internet works fall in the realm of *public domain* and are unprotected by copyright, such as those found on government Web sites or items that precede copyright law.

Reflect Further

Why do people post music, images, and writings on the Internet if they don't want them to be accessible to others?

Information Ownership

The Internet itself is not owned or controlled by any single person, organization, or country. Anyone can place any type of information on the Internet, whether accurate or not. Consequently, when using online references, you should focus on using reliable sources and check the accuracy of information provided by unfamiliar sources. Currently, there are no government regulations, and little information on the Internet is censored. This may change, however, in the future.

Who owns the information available on the Internet? Any individual who creates an original item and posts it on the Internet owns its **copyright**, or legal right. This is true whether the item has a copyright notice or not. Writings, art, and music are all protected under copyright law. Therefore, if you write a story and post it on the Internet, someone else cannot make copies of it and sell it. Doing so is considered *plagiarism* and is against the law. If you post a photo, it is illegal for someone to use it without your permission.

In a like manner, you cannot copy information, art, or music posted on the Internet for personal use or claim it as your own. You cannot copy material and pass it along to others without permission. Most text, music, and movie files must be purchased before they are downloaded. It is illegal to copy and distribute most music, software, photographs, and literature. If you want to use any of these items as a reference, you will first need the owner's permission. The owner will probably insist that you place a credit line next to the material to identify ownership.

Note that the law protects *original* works. Works based on characters or situations copyrighted first by other parties are not protected and, technically, cannot be published without permission. An exception to this law is parody, which is considered "fair use" under United States law.

Responsible Use of the Internet

If you use the Internet at home, you are largely responsible for self-censorship. When you go online at work and school, your employer and your school administration have the right and responsibility to limit the time you can spend and the sites you can search. It is important to follow the Internet usage guidelines at both work and school. See 7-8.

If your employer gives you access to the Internet, there are responsibilities that go with that privilege. Company executives responsible for Internet policies may monitor the following:

- Internet sites visited
- type and quantity of data downloaded
- amount of time spent on the Internet

7-8

If you have Internet access at work, remember that your employer may monitor your use.

In the Real World

Bocheta's Blunder

Bocheta was employed the summer before her senior year in high school at a store that ships packages worldwide. Her job was to greet customers and assist them with packaging and shipping their items. She had been working there for four weeks and was making a very good impression with her work habits.

Once in a while, Bocheta would have downtime between customers. There was a computer with Internet access that the employees used for a variety of job-related chores. The employees were occasionally allowed to use the computer for surfing and e-mailing friends.

One morning, after taking care of a dozen customers, Bocheta had some free time. She decided to e-mail her boyfriend and discuss the good times they'd had over the weekend. She had written several paragraphs when a customer came in the door. She stopped to take care of the customer and quickly returned to the e-mail. As she was writing, another customer came in and looked at the various sizes of shipping boxes hanging on the wall.

Bocheta knew she had to quickly close her e-mail and send it so she could assist the customer. In her haste, Bocheta accidentally addressed the e-mail to a group mailing, which was a list of store managers as well as regional managers. They all received the e-mail she intended to send to her boyfriend.

Questions to Discuss

1. How will this mistake affect Bocheta's work reputation?
2. Was Bocheta wrong in sending such an e-mail?
3. What would you do if you were Bocheta's boss? (Consider that the e-mail was also sent to the regional managers.)

Many employers will state in their employee handbook that "all communications are the property of the employer." Employees should not expect personal privacy while working for that company. In the overwhelming majority of court cases in which employees claimed an invasion of privacy, the courts have sided with employers.

Internet Threats

When you are online at work, it is important to be aware of issues that can cause problems to your computer. Viruses are one type of computer threat. *Viruses* are programs created with the intent to harm others' computers. Viruses can corrupt programs, take up memory, or delete files. They can be transmitted from an infected computer to others. This usually happens when files are shared through a network, transmitted via a storage device, or opened from an e-mail attachment.

Most businesses will protect their technology with anti-virus software. However, you must be careful about opening unknown files or clicking on suspicious Internet links. Remember that your computer and coworkers' computers are the property of your employer. Accidentally installing a virus could damage your computer and others.

Activity

Read several recent articles about people who have plagiarized copyrighted materials. What penalties did they face for their actions? Write a summary of your findings to share with the class.

Discuss

What types of Internet activities might employers monitor? Why is personal privacy an unrealistic expectation for employees who use company computers at work?

Reflect Further

Have you ever accidentally introduced a virus to a computer? What did you learn from this experience?

Discuss

Why is it important for employees to keep their passwords and other confidential technology information private?

Discuss

For what other purposes is e-mail sometimes used instead of the telephone?

Activity

In your own words, write 12 sentences or less summarizing basic e-mail etiquette.

Activity

Compose an e-mail message to an employer or a school requesting information about a specific product or study program. Print the message for your teacher's review prior to sending it.

Hacking is accessing a computer or network system without being authorized to do so. A hacker breaks through the security on a computer or network to gain access to the data it contains. The purpose may be a prank, such as vandalizing a company's Web site. It may be something more sinister, such as gaining electronic access to a company's or individual's financial information. Usually, a company will have protection to help prevent hacking. This may include a *firewall,* or encryption on their security system. It is also important for employees to keep their passwords or other confidential technology information private.

Hacking and creating or purposely sending viruses are unethical practices. Participating in either of these Internet threats on the job would most likely result in your dismissal. These acts are also considered crimes that can have legal consequences.

E-Mail

E-mail is the shortened term for *electronic mail,* which is a message delivered to your computer from another. E-mail is now a standard communications tool in business, government, and education. Much faster than old-fashioned mail, it can travel to people around the world in seconds.

Etiquette

E-mail is a less formal type of communication. E-mail messages tend to resemble memos and are usually very brief. Like all other forms of business communication, however, e-mail has a set of basic guidelines for proper and accepted use. Any e-mail you send from work should follow correct grammar, spelling, and punctuation rules. Using e-mail effectively and professionally may be essential to your employment success. See 7-9.

7-9

E-mail sent from work should be composed with the same thought and care as the letters and memos you write.

Using E-Mail at Work

- **Check grammar, spelling, and punctuation.** Your e-mail may be viewed as regular business correspondence, so appearance counts.

- **Be positive.** A positive tone to your messages will make them more understandable and will also get better responses from the receivers.

- **Do not yell.** Using all upper-case letters is considered YELLING. Use upper- and lowercase letters, just as you would in business reports or letters.

- **Fill the e-mail window accurately.** Be sure to completely and accurately fill in the information for *To, From*, and *Subject*.

- **Make the subject line informative.** A few carefully chosen words tell receivers what they need to know. Otherwise too much time may be wasted trying to understand the nature and importance of your message.

- **Remember that e-mail is not private.** Write messages that are appropriate for others in the company to read. Also remember that your e-mail may be considered a legal document.

In the Real World

E-Mail in the Workplace

Jodie was thrilled to have an internship with a large bank as an office assistant. The job required excellent computer skills, and she took great pride in meeting the bank's high standards. She was especially happy to be working with a family friend, Mrs. Collins, who managed the bank's office.

Several times this week, she overhead Mrs. Collins say, "It's such a pleasure to work with someone who is so capable." Jodie wanted Mrs. Collins to think she could handle any assignment.

"Please e-mail Mr. Raja in the loans department and tell him his monthly report is ready," Mrs. Collins told Jodie. Jodie often sent e-mail from home to friends, so she followed that pattern and sent this message:

Your monthly report is ready :-). Please pick it up. *S*

Jodie realized after sending the message that Mr. Raja had no way of knowing who she was or what report she meant, so she quickly sent another message.

BTW your monthly report from Mrs. Collins' office is ready to pick up :-D.

Jodie expected to see Mr. Raja step off the elevator within minutes. After several hours passed, she began to question if she sent the message to the correct e-mail address. She decided to send a message that would definitely get his attention:

FYI YOUR MONTHLY REPORT FROM MRS. COLLINS' OFFICE HAS BEEN WAITING FOR YOU SINCE NOON :-(.

A few days later, Mrs. Collins asked Jodie to explain what she e-mailed to Mr. Raja. He had called to complain about "the confusing messages and rude behavior of someone named Jodie."

Questions to Discuss

1. Do you think Jodie sent confusing messages?
2. Was Jodie's behavior to Mr. Raja rude?
3. How should business e-mail look compared to e-mail sent to friends from home?
4. In business e-mail, do you recommend using shorthand and emoticons, such as *S*, :-), BTW, :-D, FYI, :-(, and others? Do you know what they mean?

It is likely that your company will have an e-mail policy that restricts content and defines how it should be used in the workplace. E-mail can be an efficient tool if it is used properly, but avoid substituting e-mails for personal conversations. Composing e-mails takes up more time than talking.

Do not use e-mail to spread gossip or rumors. Avoid opening chain mail or spam. (*Spam* is unsolicited e-mail that may contain viruses or unsafe links.) Never forward chain mail or spam to others. Never use work e-mail to forward jokes or any other inappropriate messages.

Wireless Technology

Wireless technology is becoming increasingly popular in the workplace. Wireless technology uses radio waves to transmit over small areas. Tools such as a wireless mouse and keyboard can give workers more flexibility on the job. Other tools allow for easier communication between coworkers or employees and customers.

Thinking It Through

What are the differences and similarities between writing a business letter that will be sent via regular mail and an e-mail letter?

Activity

Rewrite Jodie's e-mail message in an appropriate business format. Be sure that Mr. Raja would clearly understand the content of the message.

Using a PDA helps busy people keep track of important details.

Reflect Further

How would your life be different if wireless technology didn't exist?

Information can be exchanged among a variety of wireless devices. This technology can allow team members to stay in contact with one another within or outside a work environment. It can also allow workers to monitor other electronic devices. Wireless technology includes mobile phones, headsets, and personal digital assistants.

Personal digital assistants (PDAs) are handheld computers. PDAs have a touch screen and can be used as a calendar, address book, calculator, and clock. PDAs that use wireless technology can be used as mobile phones, for browsing the Internet, or to send and receive text messages. PDAs are available under a variety of brand names. See 7-10.

Laptop computers can also make use of wireless technology to connect to the Internet and access e-mail. Many public places, such as stores and restaurants, are now *hotspots*. This means they provide wireless Internet access to people with compatible devices. Many people find this access convenient, 7-11. However, this service is not necessarily free, so check before using it to see if there is a charge. In addition, this access may not be secure from hackers or viruses. If you use a hotspot, make sure you have up-to-date anti-virus protection on your laptop.

Troubleshooting

When you work with technology on a daily basis, you are bound to run into glitches. Sometimes a problem may occur with your computer hardware. At other times, the problem may be with a specific software

7-11

This man uses a hotspot at a café to access the Internet while stopping for a quick cup of coffee.

Discuss

What are the similarities and differences between laptop computers and PDAs? When might you use each?

Discuss

Why is up-to-date virus protection important when using hotspots?

program. **Troubleshooting** includes the basic steps you can take to solve a computer problem.

Before asking for technical support, take a few moments to see if you can solve the problem yourself. If the problem seems to be with hardware, check power and connection cables. Also try *rebooting*, or turning your computer off and on. This may help clear up some software problems as well. For individual software questions, try searching the help files for answers before consulting a supervisor or coworker.

If the problem appears to be more complicated, such as a lack of sufficient memory to run a program, contact your employer's technical support. Do not attempt to fix problems by yourself. Your employer will probably have guidelines about issues such as downloading software upgrades. You will not want to do anything without permission that could result in harming your computer. Remember, the equipment you use on the job is your employer's property.

The Impact of Technology

We have become a *technological society*. This means most information is spread through the use of technology. Technology is

Extend Your Knowledge

Learn the Lingo

You may use the following terms all the time, but do you really know what they mean?

cookies—data sent to your computer from Web sites that track and record your activity on the site

hypertext—text that links to other information within a document or on another Web page

IP address—four sets of numbers separated by dots; used to identify every computer connected to the Internet

LISTSERV®—a type of management program that sends messages to many e-mail addresses on a mailing list; should not be used to describe generic lists

protocol—rules for the ways computers communicate with one another

URL—uniform resource locator; the specific address for a Web page or document

---

Thinking It Through

Why should you refrain from trying to fix complicated computer problems at work even if you think you know what to do?

Activity

Develop a personal troubleshooting checklist to use when a problem occurs with your computer hardware at home or at work. Once you run through all the items on your list, then seek technical support help.

Activity

Brainstorm a list of ways that technology and the Internet impact your life at school and work. Compare your list with those of your classmates. What are the similarities and differences?

Note

Computer and software capabilities change daily. Be sure to supplement this chapter with the latest information.

Resource

Essential Technology Skills Self-Check, Activity C, WB

Reflect Further

How do you think computer technology will affect your employment?

everywhere. It plays a part in most of our actions and activities. The emergence of technology has had a huge impact on businesses and the economy.

Most people in the United States have access to computers. Those who cannot afford a home computer may use computers at school. Most libraries have computers available for limited use. Any student who does not have at least basic computer experience will be at a major disadvantage in the job market.

Technology on the Job

Within the past few decades, business and industry have become entirely dependent on computers and computer software. Without computer capability, companies could not survive in today's marketplace. Whether an organization produces goods or provides a service, computers are used extensively in successful organizations. See 7-12. Many of the computer applications used in the workplace are also used in schools and homes.

7-12

Keeping track of ticket payments and passenger seating assignments are common computerized operations at a busy airline.

Internet Uses

Practically every business now maintains a Web site to promote itself in the same way it uses TV and magazine advertising. The Web site may advertise and sell company products and/or services. Customers are usually able to place orders directly by accessing the site, thus making the site a sales tool.

Employees also use computers and the Internet in the workplace to conduct online research and gather information they need for their work. The Internet allows employees in many locations to view real-time events. *Real-time* refers to something that is occurring now.

Many people are able to use the Internet to work out of the office. This is convenient for salespeople or other employees who must spend significant time at other locations. The Internet also allows people to work from their homes, yet stay connected to the office.

Discuss

What concerns you about using computers on the job?

Enrich

Take a field trip to a local advertising or printing company to observe how employees use desktop publishing and other computer software.

Resource

The Impact of Technology, Activity D, WB

Globalization

One of the effects of technology in the workplace is globalization. **Globalization** means that interrelations among nations of the world are strengthening, with particular effects on the global economy. This is partially due to increased communication in the business world. Information can travel from one side of the globe to the other in the blink of an eye.

The result is that nations are more likely to engage in trade, as well as share resources. These resources include labor, goods, and services.

Global Positioning

The *global positioning system (GPS)* is a highly accurate satellite-based navigation system. It operates in all types of weather, providing continuous worldwide coverage. Signals from four or more satellites are used to display the user's position anywhere in the world. This highly accurate data is collected and saved on memory cards.

GPS is a relatively new communication system that can be applied to many businesses. It is used for surveying, tracking people and objects, operating vehicles and robots, the precision approach and landing of aircraft, and many emergency services.

In the field of agriculture, GPS has numerous applications. It is helpful in controlling the application of agricultural chemicals and locating insect or weed problems. GPS is also used for field preparation, controlling planters, watershed mapping, controlling pesticide runoff, and mapping the proximity of agriculture to endangered species. GPS may now be used to direct vehicle drivers and fishermen to their destinations.

Lifelong Learning

Computers in the workplace are here to stay. They greatly increase productivity and reduce labor costs. When employers add or upgrade technology systems, employees will need to adjust to the new systems and new procedures. See 7-13.

Reflect Further

In what ways can computer technology reduce the price of consumer products?

Enrich

What are some ways that globalization impacts commerce in the local community?

Resource

GPS Basics, color transparency CT-7, TR

Enrich

Interview several workers and list the specific ways they use computers at work.

Resource

Using Computers in the World of Work, reproducible master 7-2, TR

Discuss

What are some ways that lifelong learning will impact all workers?

7-13

These firefighters use laptop computers to see maps showing the fastest routes to an address and the location of nearby hydrants.

Photo courtesy of Herald-Citizen, Dayna Bagby

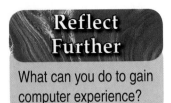

Reflect Further

What can you do to gain computer experience?

The adjustments may be difficult and may require new ways of working. More than ever, employers will expect workers to be flexible and adjust to changes in the workplace. This process, called **lifelong learning**, will be ongoing over a worker's entire career.

Employees may need to take classes to become acquainted with, and proficient at, using new technologies. Workers may also consider joining groups that would help them learn new skills. A worker who is open to keeping up with developing technologies will be highly valued in the workplace. On the other hand, workers who cannot adjust may find themselves left behind to handle the jobs requiring fewer skills.

7-14

Taking advantage of all the computer experiences offered in school will help you develop your computer skills.

Reflect

Think about how adaptable and flexible you are in all situations. How might your adaptability and flexibility impact your career throughout life?

Technology at School

The vast majority of jobs involve a computer, but are not focused on them. Most jobs, however, will require you to use a computer in some manner. School systems across the nation are responding to employer demands to teach students to become **computer literate**. This means knowing how to operate a computer and the basic software programs. Many states teach computer skills as a prerequisite for graduation. Students who gain these important skills will have a definite advantage when interviewing for most jobs.

Try to take advantage of every opportunity you have to gain experience in using computers while you are still in school, 7-14. Take a keyboarding class. Become familiar with word processing and other software programs by taking classes in these subjects.

Expect to get advanced computer instruction at the postsecondary level. Technical schools, community colleges, and universities offer many courses in computer technology. Most schools offer evening classes so you can work full time and still continue your education. If your place of employment uses computers, volunteer to learn how to operate them. School and workplace computers are sometimes different, so take advantage of any learning opportunities where you work.

E-Learning and Distance Learning

E-learning, or electronic learning, is teaching through the use of computers or related technology. E-learning can take the form of virtual classrooms, online testing, and Web-based training. *Blended learning* occurs when these methods are used to supplement traditional classroom teaching methods.

E-learning can also be used as distance learning. *Distance learning* is used to teach students who are not physically present in the same building as the teacher. In the past, distance learning was accomplished through correspondence courses. Now, students can take advantage of class Web sites, e-mail, and instant messaging to complete online courses. It is even possible to earn degrees through E-learning.

Specialized Education

The type of technology you use on the job will depend on where you work and what you do. Based on your career objective, you may take specialized courses that acquaint you with specific types of technology and applications. Computer technology has created many new career opportunities. If you enjoy working frequently with computers, you might consider a career described in 7-15.

Computer Careers

- **Computer operators**—set the computer's controls, load the software, and monitor operations and/or output devices

- **Computer programmers or software developers**—write the instructions for computer applications software

- **Data entry keyers**—use keyboards to enter data into computer systems

- **Service technicians**—repair computers, printers, and related hardware when they break down

- **Support specialists**—train users of new computer programs and networks; provide technical assistance to users

- **Systems analysts**—resolve computer user and computer program problems; analyze existing systems to make improvements

- **Systems engineers**—manage mainframes; develop and manage computer networks; plan ways to computerize business tasks

- **Tool programmers**—write coded instructions that operate machine tools (such as drill presses, lathes, and milling machines) used in manufacturing precision-machined metal parts

- **Web programmers, Web managers, or Webmasters**—create, maintain, and update organizations' Web sites

---

Thinking It Through

What role will computer technology have in your continuing education?

7-15

Careers in the computer field offer an ever-growing list of opportunities.

Discuss

What are some additional ways that computers can be used at school?

Enrich

What computer-literacy skills might you need to participate in E-learning opportunities?

Activity

Take on the "each one, teach one" philosophy and tutor a fellow student in learning how to operate a computer and basic software programs.

Resource

Computer-Related Careers, Activity E, WB

A *programmer* is a person who writes computer programs. Sometimes no application program software is available to perform a specific task that needs to be done. In such a case, a new program needs to be written. Programmers usually know several different computer languages that are used to write the new programs.

Demand is high for talented people who can design multimedia. **Multimedia** is the use of two or more communication methods, such as audio, video, images, and text. Web pages and instructive CDs are considered multimedia. As the shift toward greater use of technology continues, more multimedia designers will be needed.

Computer-aided drafting and *computer-aided design (CAD)* are two tasks that use computer graphics. CAD is the use of computers and graphics software to assist a drafter or designer in preparing a drawing. These tools increase productivity and accuracy. CAD is also used in architectural drawings of buildings, including floor plans, electrical plans, elevations, and sectional views, 7-16.

Thinking It Through

Are there certain skilled occupations where a computer is unlikely to be used?

7-16

This screen of a CADD system shows how an architect might use the program to create housing designs.

Discuss

What are the job-requirement differences between computer programmers and multimedia designers?

Enrich

Research the specific job and skills requirements for multimedia designers. Write a short report to share with the class.

Discuss

How do drafters and designers use CAD software?

Enrich

Have a student with CAD experience demonstrate CAD software to the class.

Technology in the Home

In the home, almost every room has some type of appliances. Computers are used in audio systems, entertainment systems, major and portable appliances, heating and cooling equipment, and automobiles. While an in-depth understanding of how these computers operate is not essential, it is important to understand their significance to daily life.

Using computers to communicate can help family members stay connected. Through e-mail, family members may stay in touch with others in distant locations. With some Internet providers, chat services are free and, therefore, a considerable savings compared to phone calls.

Entertainment is another product of the computer age. Software manufacturers provide a wide variety of entertainment options. You can find computer programs that simulate real-life experiences. You can play thousands of different games. Movies can be viewed on computers equipped with the appropriate software.

Many people use software and the Internet to balance checkbooks and make banking transactions such as paying bills and transferring funds. Common software programs also help families maintain household inventories, write wills, and keep records of monthly expenses. See 7-17.

7-17
Money management programs simplify the task of household budgeting.

Computers in the Future

From one year to the next, advances in computer technology are impossible to predict. Computers become more powerful, and at the same time, more affordable. They play a major role in entertainment, information, communication, and research functions.

It is very important to accept the changes and the challenges they present. It is equally important to continue learning about computers after high school so your skills meet the computer literacy level expected by employers. It does not matter what career area you choose. Knowing how to use a computer will certainly improve your chances of finding a good job.

Activity

Write a summary about the different types of tasks people can handle at home on a computer.

Enrich

Use database software to develop a list of the names, addresses, telephone numbers, and e-mail addresses of your family members and friends.

Reflect Further

Consider this statement: Computers are taking jobs away from people.

Enrich

Investigate the use of "smart" technology to operate all systems in a home. Use presentation software to present your findings. Predict when such technology might be commonplace in most homes.

Summary

Workers today are expected to be able to use personal computers. A computer's power depends on the speed of its processor and the amount of memory it has. Secondary storage devices are necessary to back up and transfer data. Many different kinds of peripherals are available to enter and receive data. Software programs give computers directions for specific tasks. Uses of the computer in the workplace include word processing, spreadsheet creation, and desktop publishing.

When using the Internet and e-mail in the workplace, be sure to follow your employer's guidelines. These tools can be effective if used properly. However, be aware of threats to your employer's property due to misuse.

Computers are commonly used in schools and homes. They have brought about numerous changes in the workplace. Many new jobs have been created that involve the use of computers. Some require specialized training in a specific computer application, but most will need workers who are computer literate and willing to adapt to changes. It will be to your advantage to learn all you can about using computers in order to compete for the best jobs.

Facts in Review

1. How are processor speeds measured?
2. List three secondary storage devices.
3. List four examples of peripherals.
4. Which device is used to automatically input images and text into the computer?
5. To write a term paper free of spelling and punctuation errors on a computer, what type of software is needed?
6. Explain the value of spreadsheets.
7. Who owns the copyright of an image posted on the Internet?
8. What aspects of an employee's use of the Internet may be monitored in the workplace?
9. How are computer viruses spread?
10. List five guidelines for using e-mail in the workplace.
11. Explain the concept of lifelong learning.
12. What is the difference between blended learning and distance learning?
13. What is multimedia?
14. Give two examples of how computer technology is used in the home.

Resource

Review and Study Guide for Chapter 7, reproducible master 7-3, TR

Answers to *Facts In Review*

1. frequencies of megahertz (Mhz) and gigahertz (Ghz)
2. (List three:) CD-Rs, CD-RWs, DVD-Rs, USB flash drive, network
3. (List four:) monitors, printers, keyboards, mice, scanners, digital cameras, webcams
4. scanner
5. word-processing software
6. They organize large amounts of numbers and data into specific formats and perform mathematical computations.
7. the creator of the image
8. the Internet sites visited, type and quantity of data downloaded, amount of time spent on the Internet
9. Files from an infected computer are shared through a network, transmitted via a storage device, or opened from an e-mail attachment.
10. (List five:) Check grammar, spelling, and punctuation. Be positive. Don't "yell." Fill the e-mail window accurately. Make the subject line informative. Remember that e-mail is not private. Follow your employer guidelines for e-mail use. Avoid substituting e-mails for personal conversations. Do not use e-mail to spread gossip or rumors. Avoid opening chain mail or spam. Never forward chain mail or spam to others. Never use work e-mail to forward jokes or any other inappropriate messages.
11. Lifelong learning is the ongoing process of being flexible and adjusting to technology changes in the workplace.
12. Blended learning is the use of E-learning to supplement traditional classroom teaching methods. *Distance learning* is used to teach students who are not physically present in the same building as the teacher.
13. the use of two or more communication methods, such as audio, video, images, and text
14. (List two:) record keeping, communications, educational uses, entertainment

Developing Your Academic Skills

1. **Social Studies.** Research privacy laws. Then break into groups and debate if computer communications should be included in these laws.
2. **Science.** Research the technology that makes computer processors work. How has this technology changed over time? How have these changes affected the size, cost, and availability of computers?

Information Technology Applications

1. Research a job of your choice to discover what computer skills you would need for that job. List the necessary skills in a report. Indicate which skills you already possess. Describe where and how you might acquire skills they do not possess.
2. Using the Internet, research E-learning courses available. What schools offer them? What is the cost? What technology is used to conduct them? What credit does the student receive for taking the course? Summarize your findings in a written report.

Applying Your Knowledge and Skills

1. **Communications.** Research and write a report on one of the newest computer applications used in the workplace. What makes this technology cutting edge? How does it differ from earlier technology? What function will this technology fulfill in the work world? Present your findings to the class.
2. **Employability and Career Development.** Ask the employed members of your family how computers are used where they work. Ask if they had to learn how to use different devices and programs, and how they accomplished this. How long did it take? Make a list of the responses and report them to your class.
3. **Ethics and Legal Responsibilities.** Research cases where individuals or companies took legal action against people writing "fanfiction." What laws govern this popular area of writing? How are these cases usually settled?

Developing Workplace Skills

Working with two classmates, determine all the ways you can access the Internet and the costs associated with each. Then determine which plan your group prefers, and present your choice to the class. Determine among yourselves how to divide the tasks.

8

Looking Good on the Job

Key Terms

nutrients

Dietary Reference Intakes (DRIs)

MyPyramid

Dietary Guidelines for Americans

grooming

hygiene

dermatologist

Chapter Objectives

After studying this chapter, you will be able to

- **explain** how your health habits, grooming habits, and clothes influence your appearance and the way other people see you.

- **explain** the guidelines you need to follow to develop and maintain a healthful lifestyle.

- **describe** the grooming habits you need to practice to stay neat and clean.

- **evaluate** your wardrobe and make wise clothing selections for school, work, and other occasions.

- **demonstrate** how to care for clothes properly and follow the clothing care labels.

Reading Advantage

As you read the chapter, write a "top ten" list of important concepts.

Achieving Academic Standards

English Language Arts

- Read print and non-print texts to acquire new information and to respond to the needs and demands of society and the workplace. (IRA/NCTE, 1)
- Apply strategies to comprehend, interpret, evaluate, and appreciate texts. (IRA/NCTE, 3)

Math

- Compute fluently and make reasonable estimates. (NCTM)

Key Concepts

- To maintain a healthful lifestyle you need to eat well-balanced meals, get enough sleep, and stay physically active.

- Planning a well-balanced diet is easier when you follow the guidelines established in MyPyramid and the Dietary Guidelines for Americans.

- Good grooming skills are essential to getting and keeping a job.

- Dressing right for a job includes wearing clothes that are appropriate for the work you will be performing.

- Taking proper care of your clothes will help them look better and last longer.

Thinking It Through

How can your appearance influence a person's first impression of you?

When you meet someone for the first time, what do you notice right away? Most people notice a person's appearance. In fact, people tend to form first impressions about others based on their appearance. That includes employers. Many employers assume that people who take pride in their appearance are likely to take pride in their work as well.

Looking good on the job involves more than wearing the "right clothes." Your health and grooming habits as well as your clothes influence your appearance. What impressions do you think others form of your appearance? "I want to succeed at this job" is the impression you should want to make at work. You can do this by keeping yourself in good physical condition, keeping neat and clean, and dressing appropriately.

Good Health

Reflect Further

What do you do to help stay in good physical health?

Looking good on the job begins with a healthy you. Good grooming and nice clothes will make very little difference if you are in poor physical health. That is because your health affects everything about you. It affects the way you look and feel.

To develop a healthful lifestyle, there are three basic steps to follow. You need to eat well-balanced meals, get adequate sleep, and stay active. Following these steps will not only make you look more attractive, it will help you be more alert and productive on the job.

Eat Well-Balanced Meals

What you eat does affect your appearance, so a good diet is important for good health. What are the benefits to you? Eating the right foods and regular balanced meals will help you look good and feel good.

Choose Healthful Foods

Reflect

What kind of first impression do you make?

Resource

MyPyramid, color transparency CT-8, TR

Activity

Examine the label from a snack you eat regularly. Determine the percentage of nutrients it contains. Compare it to the guidelines for a healthful diet.

The foods you eat play an important role in keeping you alive and healthy. Eating the right foods supplies your body with the nutrients it needs to develop and grow. **Nutrients** are the chemical substances in foods that nourish your body. These substances build and repair your body cells as well as help your body function properly.

There are six groups of nutrients that are essential to the body: carbohydrates, fats, proteins, vitamins, minerals, and water. Most foods contain more than one of these essential nutrients. However, no one food contains all the nutrients you need to stay healthy. That is why eating a variety of foods each day that supply the essential nutrients is so important.

The **Dietary Reference Intakes (DRIs)** are guidelines established by the U.S. government to help you know how much of each nutrient you need every day. You can learn more about DRIs by visiting the U.S. Department of Agriculture Food and Nutrition Information Center Web site at www.fnic.nal.usda.gov.

Planning a balanced diet is easier when you follow certain guidelines. **MyPyramid** is a personalized eating plan that gives amounts of food to consume in five basic food groups. See 8-1. Each of the food

Resource

MyPyramid Plan, Activity A, WB

MyPyramid
STEPS TO A HEALTHIER YOU
MyPyramid.gov

GRAINS	VEGETABLES	FRUITS	MILK	MEAT & BEANS
Make half your grains whole	Vary your veggies	Focus on fruits	Get your calcium-rich foods	Go lean with protein
Eat at least 3 oz. of whole-grain cereals, breads, crackers, rice, or pasta every day	Eat more dark-green veggies like broccoli, spinach, and other dark leafy greens	Eat a variety of fruit	Go low-fat or fat-free when you choose milk, yogurt, and other milk products	Choose low-fat or lean meats and poultry
1 oz. is about 1 slice of bread, about 1 cup of breakfast cereal, or ½ cup of cooked rice, cereal, or pasta	Eat more orange vegetables like carrots and sweetpotatoes	Choose fresh, frozen, canned, or dried fruit		Bake it, broil it, or grill it
		Go easy on fruit juices	If you don't or can't consume milk, choose lactose-free products or other calcium sources such as fortified foods and beverages	Vary your protein routine — choose more fish, beans, peas, nuts, and seeds
	Eat more dry beans and peas like pinto beans, kidney beans, and lentils			

For a 2,000-calorie diet, you need the amounts below from each food group. To find the amounts that are right for you, go to MyPyramid.gov.

| Eat 6 oz. every day | Eat 2½ cups every day | Eat 2 cups every day | Get 3 cups every day; for kids aged 2 to 8, it's 2 | Eat 5½ oz. every day |

8-1

Eating the recommended amounts from each of the food groups daily provides a well-balanced diet. Your age, sex, and activity level determine the amounts you should eat for the calorie level you need.

groups provides a set of important nutrients. The plan includes foods from the following groups:

- grains
- vegetables
- fruits
- milk
- meat and beans

Selecting foods from each of these groups at each meal will help supply your daily nutrient needs. MyPyramid advises you to eat oils sparingly. You can use the MyPyramid food guidance system by accessing the www.MyPyramid.gov Web site.

Another way to help you choose healthful foods is to follow the **Dietary Guidelines for Americans**. Developed by the United States Department of Agriculture, these guidelines work together to promote good health. Use these guidelines along with the MyPyramid system when you choose or prepare foods. The Dietary Guidelines provide this advice:

- Make smart choices from every food group. Focus on fruits, eat a variety of vegetables, get calcium-rich foods, make half your grains whole, and keep your protein lean.

- Find your balance between food and physical activity. Being physically active will help you burn the calories you consume from foods.

- Get the most nutrition out of your calories. Eat nutrient-dense foods that provide large amounts of vitamins and minerals compared to the number of calories they supply. The most nutrient dense forms of foods are those that are lowest in fat and free of added sugars.

Eat Regularly

When you eat can be just as important as what you eat. Think about your daily meal schedule. Do you eat breakfast in the morning before school, or do you skip it because you want to sleep late? Do you grab a high-sugar snack for lunch on your way to work, or do you pack a nutritious lunch?

The number and types of meals you eat every day can be affected by your schedule. If you have an active schedule, you may have less time for regular meals. However, skipping meals or eating only one big meal a day does not promote good health. Snacks are also a part of your daily meal plan, so try to select nutritious snacks such as fresh fruits or vegetables. Eating regular meals, starting with breakfast, is the best way to maintain your energy throughout the day and stay healthy.

Get Enough Sleep

Getting enough sleep is an important health habit with plenty of benefits for you. You will be at your best at school and at work if you get plenty of sleep every night.

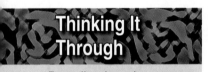

Thinking It Through

Describe the advantages of following the MyPyramid guidelines.

Activity

Track the amount of fat you consume in a day by checking the labels of the foods you eat. Compare your consumption of fat to the guidelines for a healthful diet.

Enrich

Invite a dietitian to speak about healthful eating habits.

When you have an active schedule, finding time to get enough sleep can be difficult. Not getting enough sleep can affect you in different ways. You may tire easily and become short tempered. A drop in muscle coordination may result. The quality of your work may suffer, too. Your ability to concentrate and learn may become more difficult. That can lead to mistakes or cause accidents on the job.

Getting the right amount of sleep will help you develop a more healthful lifestyle. As you sleep, your body builds and repairs itself. You feel more energetic during the day and are in a better mood. As a result, you feel more alert and are more productive.

How do you know if you are getting enough sleep? Because you are active and still growing, your sleep needs may differ from others' needs. Most people need eight to ten hours of sleep; some need more and some need less. By using your own judgment, you can best determine your sleep needs. Cutting down your activities is one way to allow more time for sleep, if you need it. When you awake feeling refreshed and alert, you will know you had enough sleep.

Stay Active

The *Dietary Guidelines for Americans* also provide fitness advice:

- Be physically active each day.

- Include conditioning and resistance exercises.

Your good health is not complete without regular physical activity. When good nutrition and physical activity work together, health and well-being improves. Also, body weight stays in a healthy range.

Your body benefits from physical activity in many ways. You can improve your heart and blood circulation, increase your lung capacity, and improve your digestion. As you exercise, you strengthen your muscles and make them more flexible. Your coordination and your posture improve as a result. Activity can help you control your weight and resist infectious diseases. In addition to helping you relax, it can help relieve anger, stress, and depression.

Exercise of any type can be helpful. Walking, jogging, team sports, or household chores are examples of good physical activities. If you spend most of your time going to school or work, watching TV, or using the computer, you need to get started on your fitness plan! Inactivity offers no benefits to you and may even lead to health problems later in life.

The following guidelines will help you get started:

- Aim for a healthful weight and work to maintain it. Find ways to increase activity as a part of your daily routine. Take stairs instead of elevators. Walk or bike instead of riding.

- Add an exercise plan if you need more activity in your day. If you are happy with your plan, you will probably stick to it. Try joining a group program or exercising with a friend if you do not think you can exercise on your own, 8-2.

Thinking It Through

How can your sleep schedule affect your performance at school and at work?

Reflect

Are you getting enough rest? If not, how can you change your schedule to incorporate more rest?

Resource

Exercise Regularly, Activity B, WB

Enrich

Use the exercise guidelines to develop a weekly exercise plan for yourself.

- Increase activity gradually. This gives your body time to adjust to more physical demands.

- Include activities that improve your respiration and circulation, such as jogging or aerobic dancing. Exercises that develop your muscle strength, coordination, and flexibility, such as gymnastics, are also important for fitness.

- Accumulate at least 60 minutes of moderate physical activity most days of the week, preferably daily. Moderate activity is walking two miles in 30 minutes.

Good Grooming

Good **grooming** means taking care of yourself and looking your best. It is essential to getting and keeping a job. When it comes to good grooming, there are two words you need to remember—cleanliness and neatness. You need to be clean and neat from your head to toe every day on the job.

A Clean Body

Keeping your body clean is called good **hygiene**. To help you stay clean, you need to bathe or shower and use a deodorant or antiperspirant every day. Everyone perspires, even in winter. When you perspire, bacteria grow and cause body odor. Frequent bathing with soap and water removes the bacteria and body odor. However, you usually do not have time to bathe several times a day. That is why it is important for you to use a deodorant or antiperspirant.

Both deodorants and antiperspirants help control body odor by interfering with the growth of bacteria. Antiperspirants also help reduce the flow of perspiration. A deodorant or antiperspirant should be applied daily after you bathe. There are many different varieties to choose from. You may want to use a roll-on, solid, gel, or aerosol form, either scented or unscented. Experiment to find out which brand will work best for you.

In the Real World

The Case of the Disappearing Coworkers

Brent works for Industrial Design Graphics as a graphic illustrator. His department always takes a midmorning break. He and his coworkers enjoy going to the lunchroom, relaxing, and chatting about a variety of topics.

Over the past few weeks, however, Brent has noticed people moving further away from him at the break table. In fact some people have been going elsewhere during the break. Brent wondered why people were not meeting as a group in the break room anymore.

Brent asks, "Where is everyone? Why aren't we all meeting for breaks like we did before?"

You know the answer because it has been a topic of discussion behind Brent's back. Brent has an offensive body odor. You are the only other person in the room when he asks these questions.

Questions to Discuss

1. How would you answer Brent's questions?
2. Do you feel a friend should have advised Brent about his need for good grooming before it became a public issue?

A Smooth Shave

To shave or not to shave is a decision both men and women have to make. Men need to decide if they want to shave their facial hair or grow a mustache, beard, or both. Women need to decide if they want to shave their legs and underarms.

Some men want to have a mustache or beard. However, there are some employers who object to facial hair, especially beards. They prefer the clean-shaven look. These employers often think a clean-shaven man gives a better impression of their company.

Whatever decision you make, the general rule is to be neat and clean. If you want your face neatly shaved, do not go to work with stubble on it. For most men, this means they must shave every day. See 8-3. If you choose to have a beard or mustache, wash it regularly with a mild soap and keep it neatly combed and shaped. An unkempt beard or mustache will certainly give a sloppy appearance. Also be sure the style of beard or mustache you choose is suitable to your hairstyle and face shape.

8-3

For the clean-shaven look, most men shave every day.

Enrich

Invite a dermatologist to speak to the class on proper skin care.

Discuss

How does a person's age relate to possible skin problems?

Enrich

Invite a hairstylist to speak to the class about hair care and styles.

Most young women in the United States choose to shave their legs and underarms because they think it gives a neater appearance. Women who do not shave may be considered less concerned about their appearance. Shaving under the arms can also help reduce perspiration odor.

The decision to shave or not to shave is yours. Remember, however, that many employers have preferences regarding how their employees appear to others.

Healthy Complexion

Sometimes your complexion can be the most difficult part of your body to keep looking good. Many young people often have problems with oily skin. This may contribute to skin problems such as pimples and acne. Regardless of the type of skin you have you can keep it looking clean by caring for it properly.

All skin types should be cleansed regularly with warm soapy water or a cleanser to keep the skin free of bacteria, dirt, and oils. You should see a dermatologist if your skin is extremely oily and acne becomes a problem. A **dermatologist** is a doctor who specializes in treating skin. This type of specialist will be able to recommend the best cleansers and cosmetics for your skin.

Clean Hair

The hair has often been called a person's "crowning glory" because it can greatly enhance personal appearance. That is why it is so important to keep your hair clean and neatly styled. Hair care involves three major steps: shampooing, conditioning, and styling.

Once hair is cleaned and conditioned, it needs to be styled. You should choose a style that will suit the texture of your hair, the shape and size of your face, and your lifestyle, 8-4. You may want to consult a hairstylist to help you choose the best style for you. Hairstylists are trained to analyze hair and facial features and to cut and style hair accordingly.

8-4

Choosing a hairstyle that is right for you can help you look your best.

Attractive Hands

Because your hands are in sight most of the time, they are an important part of your appearance. You need to keep your hands and fingernails clean and manicured.

If your hands and nails get heavily soiled on the job, like an auto technician's do, you may need to use a special soap to get them clean. A nailbrush can also help you wash away dirt and oil from under and around the nails.

Extend Your Knowledge

Hairstyle Computer Programs

Hairstyle computer programs are now available over the Internet and are being used at certain salons. These programs can help you see what you will look like with a hairstyle before you even change your hair. Whatever style you choose, be sure it is one you can care for easily.

Fresh Breath

Your mouth plays an important role in your appearance. Because the mouth draws so much attention, you need to have clean teeth and fresh breath.

Teeth are an important part of your mouth, your breath, and your smile. To help keep your teeth clean and healthy, your breath fresh, and your smile bright, you need to brush your teeth regularly. You also need to floss your teeth often and schedule regular checkups with your dentist, 8-5. Caring properly for your teeth can also help you avoid cavities and gum disease.

In addition to brushing, some people find it helpful to gargle with a mouthwash to avoid bad breath. You may want to try a mouthwash as well. Whatever ensures good breath for you, do it daily! You do not want to be caught with bad breath on the job, especially if you work closely with others.

8-5

For healthy teeth and gums, schedule regular dental visits.

Discuss

What are some possible causes of bad breath? What are some remedies?

Discuss

Is there a link between nutrition, healthy hair, and good breath? If so, what?

Dressing for the Job

Many people feel they have a right to wear whatever they want to work. However, employers also have the right to expect employees to dress appropriately for work. For example, some employers may view shorts or jeans as inappropriate dress. Therefore, most companies have established a dress code that their employees are expected to follow. If you choose not to dress appropriately for the job, your employer can always hire another worker who will.

The first step to dressing right for the job is to wear clean clothes. You also need to make sure your clothes fit properly and are appropriate for the work you will be doing. To help you decide what is appropriate to wear to work, think about the responsibilities you will have on the job. Will you be lifting and bending? Will you be handling food? Will you be working at a desk in an office?

If you are likely to get dirty and greasy, you will need clothes that are appropriate for those conditions. For example, an auto mechanic needs durable clothes to withstand wear, tear, grease, and oil. Similar clothing is needed for service station workers, carpenters, plumbers, factory workers, farmers, and construction workers. Many of these workers may even wear coveralls to protect their clothes.

Outside workers need clothes that will protect them from rain, snow, cold, and the sun. Other workers may need to wear safety clothing like a hard hat, safety shoes, safety glasses, or earplugs. Outdoor and safety clothing are usually needed for miners, welders, chemists, brick masons, and some construction and factory workers.

For health reasons, hospital workers, food handlers, and dental assistants must take extra care to stay clean and wear clean clothes. Many of these workers wear uniforms or lab coats that can be cleaned easily. See 8-6. Employees who work in laboratories or in food service may also be required to wear hairnets. These prevent their hair from falling into their work.

Clothing choices are important for office and business workers like salespeople, receptionists, office clerks, and cashiers because these workers come in contact with the public. A company wants workers who will make a good impression on customers and the general public so they will form a good impression of the company.

In general, female office workers should wear nice slacks with a blouse or sweater, or a skirt or dress with hose. Male office workers should wear nice slacks; a shirt and tie, shirt and sweater, or a dressy, open-collar shirt; and possibly a sports jacket. Workers should avoid inappropriate clothes such as tight pants, unbuttoned shirts, and miniskirts. Tight, skimpy, or revealing dress can send the wrong message to coworkers and customers.

Another good way to help you decide what is best to wear is to make sure you are aware of your company's dress code. You can also observe what others wear to work. If most of the workers tend to dress conservatively, you may want to dress this way also. If many of the employees wear nice jeans to work, you may feel comfortable wearing jeans as well. Some companies do not want their employees to have excessive tattoos or body piercings. If you are still in doubt about what is appropriate, ask your work supervisor or school-to-work coordinator. He or she will be able to give you some good suggestions.

8-6

In the health professions, wearing clean uniforms or lab coats is a job requirement.

Caring for Clothes

Even the best quality clothes will not look good if you do not care for them properly. Taking proper care of your clothes will help them look better and last longer. Clothes that are clean, neatly pressed, and mended will also help you have an attractive appearance.

Caring for clothes on a routine basis will keep clothes in good condition and ready to wear. For example, do not just pull off your clothes, wad them up, and throw them on the floor. Take an extra minute to remove your clothes carefully and put them away properly. Be sure to undo buttons, snaps, and zippers before removing a garment. This will help you avoid tearing or stretching the garment out of shape.

After each wearing, check clothes for stains, tears, and missing buttons, 8-7. Be sure to remove stains right away. The longer a stain stays in a fabric, the harder it will be to remove. Small repairs, such as sewing on a button or mending a split seam, do not take long. Everyone can learn how to do these simple mending jobs.

If clothes do not need cleaning or mending, you may want to air them in an open room before storing. Then fold knits and sweaters neatly and store them in drawers or on shelves. Hang blouses, dresses, shirts, skirts, trousers, and jackets.

When clothes and accessories need cleaning, be sure to follow the directions on clothing care labels, laundry products, washers, and dryers. Washing clothes the correct way will keep them from fading, shrinking, and wrinkling unnecessarily.

Care Labels

Before buying clothing, you should always check the care label to learn how the garment should be cleaned. Should it be machine-washed in warm water, hand-washed in cold water, or dry-cleaned? Can it be dried in a dryer, or should it drip-dry on a hanger? Should it be ironed with a cool iron or not ironed at all? Ask a salesperson to explain a garment's care label if the information is not clear.

It would be impractical for a child care worker or telephone repair person to buy work clothes that must be dry-cleaned. Unless you are in a job where you must wear suits, buy work clothes that can be machine washed and dried. Wash-and-wear and permanent press clothes are great for work because they are easy and inexpensive to keep clean.

Reflect Further

How much money each month is spent on the care of your clothing?

8-7

It is better to take care of stains, rips, and other clothing problems right away so items will be ready to wear after they are cleaned.

Enrich

List the types of stains commonly found on your clothing. Use Internet or print sources to research the appropriate treatment for each.

Summary

Your health is reflected in the way you look. A healthful lifestyle is achieved through proper eating, sleeping, and exercise habits. By following the guidelines set up in MyPyramid, you can learn to develop good eating habits. You can also make sure you are getting the nutrients your body needs to keep you healthy. You need to get enough sleep every night to be alert and function your best at school or at work. The Dietary Guidelines for Americans provide helpful advice for adding physical activity into your daily routine.

Looking good on the job also involves a neat, clean appearance. This depends on many factors, such as a clean body, proper skin care, neatly groomed hair, and clean hands. It also depends on wearing clothes appropriate for the job you perform. Caring for your clothes properly will help them look better and last longer.

Facts in Review

1. What three factors influence your appearance?
2. What is the impression you should want to make at work?
3. Name the three steps to follow to stay in good physical health.
4. What information can you learn from the Dietary Reference Intakes?
5. Name the five basic food groups in the MyPyramid food guidance system.
6. What are three key recommendations given in the Dietary Guidelines for Americans?
7. List three benefits of getting the right amount of sleep.
8. List five physical benefits of physical activity.
9. In addition to the physical benefits, what other benefits does physical activity provide?
10. List six good grooming practices you can follow for a neat, clean appearance.
11. Why is it important to read clothing care labels before buying a garment?

Resource

Review and Study Guide for Chapter 8, Reproducible Master 8-2, TR

Answers to *Facts In Review*

1. your health, grooming habits, and clothes
2. a desire to succeed at the job
3. Eat well-balanced meals; get adequate sleep; stay active.
4. how much of each nutrient you need every day
5. grains, vegetables, fruits, milk, and meat and beans
6. Make smart choices from every food group; find your balance between food and physical activity; get the most nutrition out of your calories.

7. (List three:) to look rested and alert, to feel refreshed, to stay healthier, to be more productive, to give the body time to heal and repair itself
8. (List five:) better heart and blood circulation, greater lung capacity, improved digestion, stronger muscles, increased muscle flexibility, better coordination, improved posture, weight control, resistance to infectious diseases
9. relieve anger, stress, and depression
10. (List six:) Bathe or shower; use deodorant or antiperspirant; shave cleanly; use proper skin care for your complexion type; shampoo and condition hair; style hair; keep hands and fingernails clean; brush teeth; freshen breath; dress in clean, neat clothes.
11. to learn how to properly clean the garment

Developing Your Academic Skills

1. **Science.** Choose one nutrient and write a report on its function in the body. Include health problems that can develop if the body gets too little of the nutrient. Share your finished report in an oral presentation to the class.
2. **Language Arts.** Prepare a presentation on grooming. Be sure to explain why grooming is important to health as well as appearance. Share your presentation with the class.
3. **Math.** Determine what clothes you would need for work. Develop a spending plan that will help you get the most clothing items for your money.

Applying Your Knowledge and Skills

1. **Safety, Health, and Environment.** Find out what fitness programs are available to you in your community. Develop your own fitness program and keep a record of your activity and progress for one month.
2. **Communications.** Interview a human resources manager from a company about the importance of good grooming in getting and keeping a job. Write a brief report and present it to the class.
3. **Academic Foundations.** Make a daily and weekly schedule of good grooming habits.
4. **Communications.** Interview a hairstylist on choosing a hairstyle and proper hair care. Write a report of your findings.

Information Technology Applications

1. Using the Internet, research different types of popular high-tech exercise equipment. Could people still use these exercise techniques if the technology was not available? Using the computer, prepare a report of your findings.
2. Use the MyPyramid Tracker program at www.mypyramid.gov to keep a food diary of your meals for one week. At the end of the week, study your results to see if you are following the recommendations in MyPyramid and the Dietary Guidelines for Americans. Write a brief summary of what you have learned about your eating habits.

Developing Workplace Skills

Working with a classmate, list three different types of dress or items of clothing you have seen worn by people from different cultures. Use the Internet to research the history of these and learn their special use or significance to their cultures. Decide in which careers those forms of dress or clothing items would be appropriate and in which they would not. Make a brief oral presentation to the class summarizing what you learned and the decisions you made. Use pictures or drawings to show classmates the items you researched.

9

Safety on the Job

Key Terms

environmental hazards

safety-conscious

ergonomics

disability

workers' compensation

flammable

National Safety Council

first aid

tourniquet

universal precautions

workplace violence

Occupational Safety and Health Administration (OSHA)

citation

material safety data sheet (MSDS)

Environmental Protection Agency (EPA)

Centers for Disease Control and Prevention (CDC)

National Institute for Occupational Safety and Health (NIOSH)

Chapter Objectives

After studying this chapter, you will be able to

- **describe** the causes of accidents on the job.

- **describe** how the costs of accidents can affect you, the employer, and the economy.

- **identify** safety procedures workers can follow to avoid and prevent accidents.

- **define** workplace violence and describe possible steps for prevention.

- **explain** what the Occupational Safety and Health Administration, Environmental Protection Agency, and Centers for Disease Control and Prevention do to protect people's health and safety.

Reading Advantage

Imagine you are a business owner and have several employees working for you. As you read the chapter, think about what you would like your employees to know. When you finish reading, write a memo to your employees and include key information from the chapter.

Achieving Academic Standards

English Language Arts

- Read print and non-print texts to acquire new information and to respond to the needs and demands of society and the workplace. (IRA/NCTE, 1)

- Apply strategies to comprehend, interpret, evaluate, and appreciate texts. (IRA/NCTE, 3)

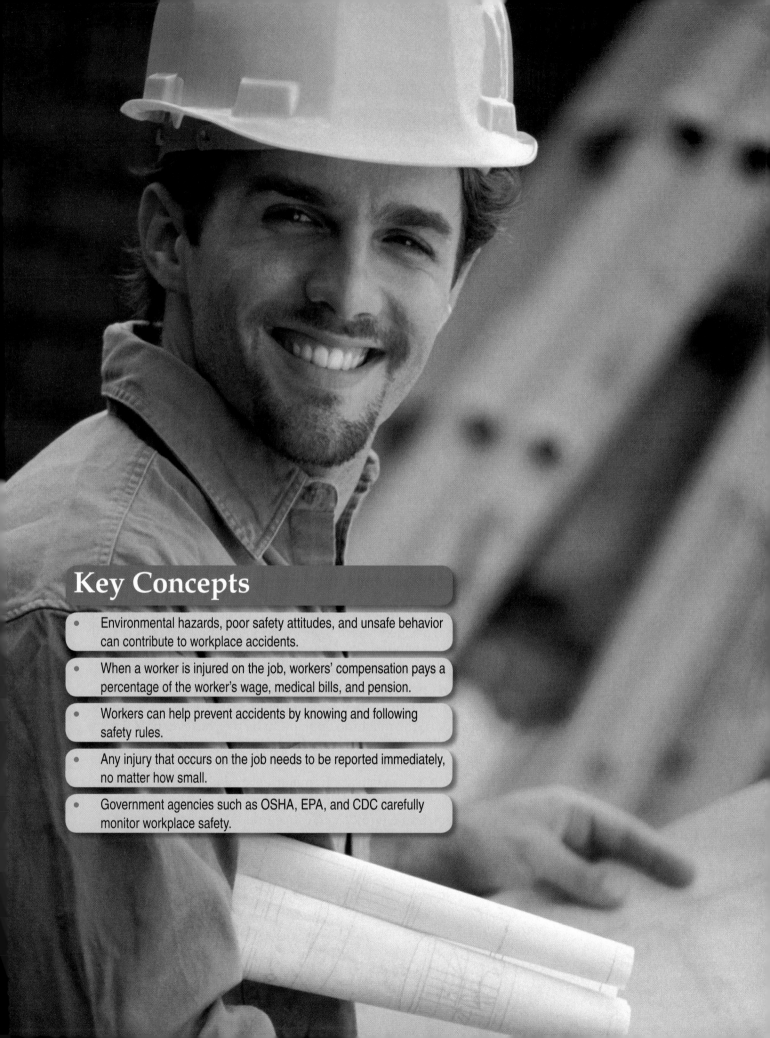

Key Concepts

- Environmental hazards, poor safety attitudes, and unsafe behavior can contribute to workplace accidents.

- When a worker is injured on the job, workers' compensation pays a percentage of the worker's wage, medical bills, and pension.

- Workers can help prevent accidents by knowing and following safety rules.

- Any injury that occurs on the job needs to be reported immediately, no matter how small.

- Government agencies such as OSHA, EPA, and CDC carefully monitor workplace safety.

Accidents and injuries are not pleasant. No one wants to get hurt on the job or see anyone else get hurt. Workplace accidents can also cause damage to equipment. Injured workers and damaged equipment cost an employer time and money. Workers that are new to a job are more likely to have accidents than experienced workers.

Working safely is the responsibility of every worker and employer. Preventing an accident is much better than living with the results of a serious one. Although jobs in some occupations have high accident rates, accidents can occur anywhere. People are not perfect. However, many accidents can be prevented when people are alert, careful, and aware of the potential dangers around them.

What Causes Accidents?

Directly or indirectly, people cause accidents. According to researchers, accidents are most often caused by

- lack of knowledge or skills

- environmental hazards

- poor safety attitudes

- unsafe behavior

Lack of Knowledge and Skills

Workers need training to do their jobs accurately and safely. Otherwise, mistakes and accidents are more likely to occur. Workers with less than one year of work experience account for a large percentage of all occupational accidents each year. A worker's knowledge and skill are especially important when working with machinery, equipment, chemicals, or hazardous materials.

Workers who operate machinery should learn as much as possible about the equipment before they begin operating it. They should know exactly what to do if the machine appears to be overheating or if something gets caught in it. Workers should never attempt to operate a piece of machinery they are not trained to use.

Learn as much as you can about materials and chemicals before you use them on the job. What you do not know can be dangerous to you and other workers. Some liquids can cause fires or explosions when used improperly. Some materials that were once thought to be safe are now known to be harmful to your health and may cause cancer or even death. Common examples are asbestos, lead, and mercury. Protect yourself when handling any materials or chemicals by using caution and following label directions.

Lack of knowledge and skill can cause accidents in any job—not just jobs involving machines. For example, consider what happened to Bob on his first day as a waiter at a nice restaurant. All the waiters carry their trays of orders high on their shoulders and gracefully place them on

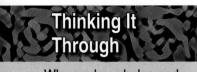

stands for serving. When Bob picked up his first order, he attempted to do the same. However, half his tray of food scattered across the floor and the other half fell on his customers. Bob tried to perform a task before he developed the skill to do it.

You need to be aware of the things you can and cannot do. Do not pretend to know how to do something you are unfamiliar with. Seek out information about a job you do not know how to do. Make sure you have the knowledge and the skills to perform the task correctly and safely before you begin. See 9-1. Some companies provide employees with on-the-job training before they are expected to perform tasks on their own. Be sure you are familiar with your companies training policies so you know what is expected of you.

To learn a new skill, watch a skilled worker perform the task. Then ask the worker to show you step-by-step how to do the task. Next, perform the task slowly yourself. Have the skilled worker watch you to make sure you do each step correctly. Afterward, practice doing the task until you can do it safely and accurately.

Enrich

Prepare a skit demonstrating common road hazards. Record the skit for future classes.

9-1

Workers can avoid many accidents if they learn how to operate machines properly.

Hazards on the Road

Traffic accidents are a leading cause of accidents and deaths among teens. Although many drive safely and responsibly, a good number do not. As a result, state and federal authorities are cracking down on teen driving in general. Lack of driving experience is the primary reason for teen traffic accidents. Another leading cause is a greater tendency to take risks.

As a school-to-work program participant, your employer will take a special interest in your driving record. In many cases, employers do not permit students who lose their drivers license to keep their jobs. If using a car to get to work is a must, a valid drivers license and a record free of moving violations is usually a requirement for employment. See 9-2.

9-2

If you are not careful and do not have a good driving record, you will probably not qualify for a work-based learning experience that requires a car to get to work.

Environmental Hazards

The very nature of the work environment can influence the number of accidents that are likely to occur on the job. Possible dangers or unsafe conditions in the workplace are known as **environmental hazards**. These hazards exist in every type of working environment—from jobs involving mechanical equipment to automated offices. However, accidents occur more often in dangerous jobs because more environmental hazards exist.

Extend Your Knowledge

Teen Driving Laws

Federal and state laws limit how much driving teens can do as part of their jobs. No employee under 17 may drive on public roads as part of the job. For 17-year-olds, "only occasional and incidental" driving on the job is permitted. Some examples are running errands or making deliveries. However, there are specific limits on what is allowed regarding the following: distance traveled, number of passengers, type of material transported, number of trips made, and hours spent driving per day and per week. In areas where a state law is stricter than the federal law, the state law must be followed. Federal and state laws are subject to change. Be sure to keep up-to-date on changes in the laws.

It is not surprising, for example, that more accidents happen in construction jobs than in office jobs. Construction workers come in contact with a greater number of hazards more often. These hazards include heavy equipment, ladders, hand and power tools, electricity, heights, and many other potential dangers.

Hazards in Dangerous Work

Environmental hazards exist in many industries besides construction, 9-3. For instance, workers in logging, mining, agriculture, and meat

9-3

Can you identify the environmental hazards in these working conditions?

Discuss

Is a driver's license a right or a privilege?

Resource

Protection from Environmental Hazards, Activity B, WB

Enrich

Use Internet or library resources to determine the 10 most hazardous occupations.

processing are also involved in dangerous work. People involved in dangerous work must be safety-conscious. Being **safety-conscious** involves knowing the job hazards and taking appropriate steps to avoid accidents.

The first step in protecting yourself against job hazards is to know how dangerous your job is. Many employers spend considerable time and money in trying to reduce the number of on-the-job accidents. They offer safety programs, use safer equipment, and train workers in an effort to provide a safe work environment.

The government keeps statistics on workplace injuries and detects trends as new job dangers surface. One problem affecting many workers is repetitive-motion injuries. These injuries result from making the same motion over and over again. Repetitive-motion injuries result in tingling sensations and sharp shooting pains. Destruction of nerve endings and loss of mobility in the limb can result. The science of examining motions and how to perform them properly is referred to as **ergonomics**.

Hazards in the Office

Office workers can also come in contact with unsafe conditions in their workplace. Safe design of office equipment and improved air quality are some of the safety concerns being studied by companies. In modern offices, safely automating the office while respecting workers' health and safety needs are growing issues. Repetitive-motion injuries are a common problem. See 9-4. Companies realize that identifying and correcting unsafe conditions will permit workers to perform their duties safely and productively.

Sometimes office workers forget to follow simple safety procedures at work because they feel safe in an office. Most accidents that do occur are caused by a combination of careless people and unsafe conditions. Leaving boxes in walkways or leaving file drawers open are examples of workers creating safety hazards. Recognizing safety hazards and then correcting them are important safety practices for all office workers to follow.

Poor Safety Attitudes

Not taking the right attitude toward safety can put you and others in danger. A poor safety attitude can lead to accidents. Read what happened to the following workers.

- Joan decides to stop wearing her safety glasses when drilling metal at work. She said they were too hot and uncomfortable to wear. The next week a metal chip flew into her eye, causing her to have surgery.

- One of David's jobs at the warehouse is to stack boxes of merchandise. When the stack of boxes reaches a certain height, David is supposed to start another stack. One day David did not bother to start a new stack. Later that day the stack of boxes fell on another worker and caused him a minor head injury.

Reflect Further

What are some other environmental hazards faced by workers?

What hazards do you face on your job?

Discuss

Describe the safety training you received at your workstation.

Vocabulary

Write a one-page report describing how the term *ergonomics* relates to your workstation.

Activity

Research your state's current eye safety legislation and share it in class.

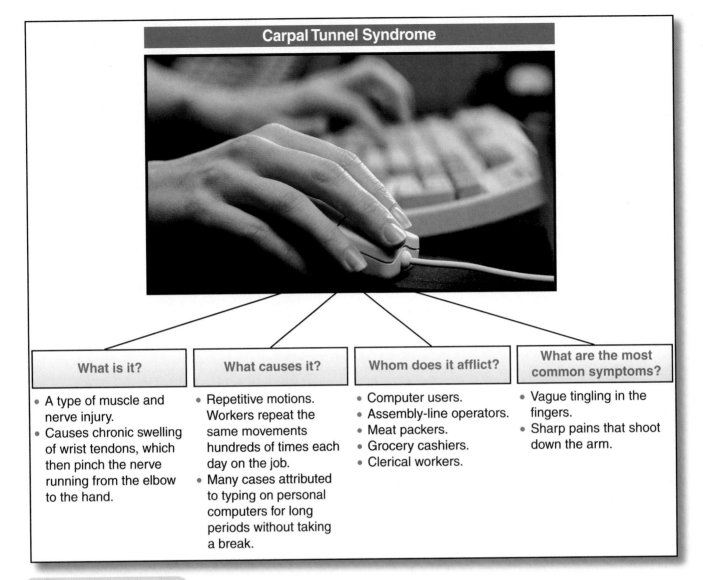

Carpal Tunnel Syndrome

What is it?	What causes it?	Whom does it afflict?	What are the most common symptoms?
• A type of muscle and nerve injury. • Causes chronic swelling of wrist tendons, which then pinch the nerve running from the elbow to the hand.	• Repetitive motions. Workers repeat the same movements hundreds of times each day on the job. • Many cases attributed to typing on personal computers for long periods without taking a break.	• Computer users. • Assembly-line operators. • Meat packers. • Grocery cashiers. • Clerical workers.	• Vague tingling in the fingers. • Sharp pains that shoot down the arm.

9-4

The most familiar repetitive-motion injury is known as carpal tunnel syndrome.

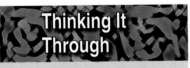

Thinking It Through

How does a person's attitude affect job safety?

Juan works in an office as a word processor. One afternoon while he was on break, he carried a cup of water back to his desk. He did not realize he spilled some water in the hallway at the top of the stairs. The water could not be seen on the tile floor until it was too late. Two coworkers came around the corner, slipped, and fell—one hurting his back after falling down several stairs.

You and every worker need to "think safety." Safety rules are developed to protect you and others. Get into the habit of doing tasks the safe way. Wear the proper clothes and use the proper equipment, 9-5. Follow all safety procedures exactly. Do not assume that a safe environment happens automatically.

Enrich

Interview someone who has a repetitive-motion injury. How can workers prevent such injuries?

Unsafe Behavior

People who do not consider or practice safety on the job have poor safety attitudes. People with these attitudes cause many accidents. The

9-5

For the safety of others, food service workers need to follow certain safety rules such as wearing chef's hats and washing their hands before handling food.

following stories are all examples of unsafe behavior that should be avoided:

- *Recklessness.* Near the end of a workday, two woodworkers start telling jokes. No one bothers to turn off the circular saw. Jokingly, one worker pushes the other, who loses her balance, falls against the circular saw, and cuts her arm.

- *Bad temper.* Mike works as a chef's helper in a restaurant. During the lunch rush, another worker yells at him to hurry up. While he is chopping lettuce, Mike angrily yells back. As he does, his knife slips and cuts his finger so deeply that the bleeding would not stop without stitches. Mike reacted without thinking. By losing control of his temper, he was the prime target for an accident.

- *Lack of consideration.* An office worker takes a file from the bottom drawer of the file cabinet and does not bother to close the drawer. Another worker walks around the corner and trips over the open drawer, 9-6.

- *Disobedience.* Latrice works at a local machine shop. Because she operates machinery, she is told not to wear jewelry on the job. She refuses to take her ring off for fear of losing it. As a result, her ring caught on a revolving tool and she loses her finger. Following instructions and obeying company safety rules would have saved Latrice from serious injury.

Enrich

Develop a bulletin board display that promotes safety on the job.

Reflect

Do any of your coworkers have attitudes that promote unsafe conditions? What can you do to improve such situations?

9-6

Keeping aisles in the workplace clear helps prevent accidents.

- *Carelessness.* After mopping the hallway, Pete forgets to put up signs that say "Caution Wet Floor." A customer walks in, slips on the wet floor, and injures his hip. Pete's carelessness created an unsafe condition that caused pain and injury to someone else.

- *Laziness.* Tyrone is an example of an accident waiting to happen. He will soon start working on an electric circuit located across the room from the master lockout switch. He thinks the circuit has been properly shut off and locked out, but he is not sure. Anyway, he decides it is too far to walk to check. Tyrone receives an electrical shock and burn.

- *Fatigue.* Marie works two jobs to make extra income. Sometimes she does not even have time to eat after her first job before starting the evening job. In spite of the long hours, Marie feels she can keep up the pace. One night several weeks later, she fell asleep while operating her machine. The machine jams and Marie seriously injures her arm. She is unable to continue working. If Marie had been alert, she might have avoided her accident. A lack of rest and poor diet caused her fatigue. Getting plenty of rest and eating properly would have helped her operate at her best. See 9-7.

- *Impatience.* A file clerk decides to climb the shelves in the storage room to get a box of file folders instead of using a stepladder. The clerk loses her footing, falls backward, and fractures her elbow.

Besides the unsafe behaviors described here, other factors can cause unsafe behavior that may lead to accidents. On-the-job safety can also be influenced by a person's emotional state or the use of drugs or alcohol.

Reflect Further

What are some other examples of unsafe work behavior you have seen or heard? How can these behaviors be changed to prevent accidents?

9-7

Workers on dangerous sites must stay alert and cautious.

Discuss

Give examples of occasions when someone's carelessness or forgetfulness led to an accident.

Resource

Job Safety Checklist, reproducible master 9-1, TR

- *Emotional state.* The way people feel on the job can influence their attitudes about safety. Extreme emotions can make them less concerned about their personal safety. That means when they are very happy, angry, tired, or depressed, they are more likely to have an accident. Thinking about their personal problems or not paying attention to their work can affect their job performance. To play it safe, they need to stay in full control of their emotions. Keeping focused on their work is a good way to practice safety and avoid injury.

- *Use of drugs or alcohol.* These substances can lead to accidents on the job. They can slow down a user's responses and reflexes. This makes it difficult for a worker to react quickly or accurately to a dangerous situation. Even a routine job can become hazardous when a worker cannot concentrate or coordinate movements well. The use of these substances does not have to take place on the job to affect job performance. Many substances stay in the body hours or even days after their use. The abuse of drugs and alcohol has become such a problem that many companies now conduct preemployment and random drug tests.

Unsafe behavior is a threat to everyone's safety. Try to avoid these behaviors while you are on the job. Thinking about and practicing safety is the best way to develop a good safety attitude.

Costs of Accidents

The costs of work-related accidents are high. Billions of dollars are spent each year to cover the medical costs and wage losses of people who become victims of accidents. Everyone—you, your employer, and the economy—feels the effects in some way.

The Costs to You

You may not realize the importance of your health and safety until you have an accident. What is the cost to you? An accident can cost you financially and personally. It could lead to lost time on the job, possible wage loss, and even a job loss. A serious injury could cost you your career. If you cannot perform your job, you may be forced to make a career change or train for another type of work.

A serious disability could forever prevent you from working. A **disability** is a permanent job-related injury. Dealing with an injury can be difficult. Often there is no amount of money that could ease the suffering or personal loss that results from an accident.

The Costs to the Employer

Work injuries from accidents cost employers time and money. As the result of an accident, production slows down when a worker cannot perform his or her duties. Finding another experienced worker to replace

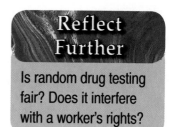

Reflect Further

Is random drug testing fair? Does it interfere with a worker's rights?

Discuss

Everyone experiences emotional extremes. What can you do when your emotional state may negatively affect your job performance and safety?

Discuss

What should be done if you know or suspect a coworker is under the influence of drugs or alcohol on the job?

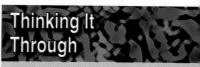

Thinking It Through

What are the costs to you if you are injured or equipment is damaged due to an accident on the job?

In the Real World

Is Safety Everyone's Business?

Cleon had been on his job as a forklift operator for just a few weeks when he noticed two press operators not following company safety rules. They wore their safety glasses and shields only when the supervisor was in the area. In addition, one of the operators frequently disabled a safety switch so he could produce work faster and, thus, create more "down" time to relax. They always quickly put on their glasses and reactivated the safety switch whenever the supervisor appeared.

Cleon was very concerned for the safety of his fellow workers. Both his school-to-work coordinator and his workplace mentor constantly stressed the importance of safety and of reporting unsafe conditions. Cleon approached the worker who was not wearing his safety glasses and said, "Felix, I know wearing glasses is uncomfortable, but you really should wear them. You could be hit by a piece of molten metal off your press and be blinded for life!"

Felix gave Cleon a blank stare, smiled slightly, and returned to his work.

Cleon persisted, "Why won't you wear them? Don't you care about your eyesight?"

At that, Felix spun around and said angrily, "Why don't you mind your own business! You've been here a few weeks and you think you know everything. I have been operating this press for six years and have never been injured. The safety glasses and shields make it more difficult for me to see the work. I can't get any work done with them on."

Cleon became a little nervous at Felix's sudden outburst and turned to walk back to his forklift. However, he couldn't resist a last comment and said, almost under his breath, "I'll bet your supervisor wouldn't appreciate your speed if he knew you were violating safety rules."

Felix heard the comment, grabbed Cleon by the shoulder, and spun him around. Felix then grabbed Cleon by the front of his shirt and started to throw a punch. He said, "If you ever say anything to the supervisor about me or Roy, I'll catch you outside the plant and you'll be sorry you were ever born!"

Cleon backed down quickly. He said, "I'm sorry, I was only kidding. I'll never say anything to the supervisor. What business is it of mine anyway?"

From that day on, Cleon vowed to concentrate only on his job. He ignored every unsafe condition he saw while operating the forklift except those that involved his own safety.

Questions to Discuss

1. Do you think Cleon was right in confronting Felix about his unsafe behavior? Should he have talked to his school coordinator or workplace mentor first?
2. Was Cleon legally bound to report safety violations? Was he morally bound to do so?
3. Did Cleon make the right choice in deciding to mind his own business? How would you have handled the situation?

the injured worker is sometimes difficult. Other workers must also produce more goods and services to make up the cost of work injuries. The time required to give first aid, investigate the accident, and write up the accident report is also part of the cost. In addition to production loss, the employer may have to deal with possible lawsuits or fines.

Most workers are covered by **workers' compensation** if they are injured on the job. This is insurance against loss of income from work-related accidents. The employer rather than the employee pays the premiums for this type of insurance.

When workers are injured, they are entitled to certain benefits. Workers' compensation pays a percentage of the worker's regular wage, medical bills, and pension. The program covers other benefits, too. These benefits include income for disability or death and insurance against diseases caused by working conditions.

All states in this country have workers' compensation laws, although they may differ slightly from state to state. Each state's Department of Labor administers this program. They can provide more information about workers' compensation laws in your state.

The Costs to the Economy

How do work-related accidents affect the nation's economy? Accidental deaths or disabling injuries affect many workers in the workforce. Billions of dollars are paid nationwide each year to injured workers covered under workers' compensation. This money covers wage losses, medical costs, and insurance administration costs. Employers may be affected by factors such as lower production and higher insurance premiums. This means higher prices for goods and services that are passed on to the consumer. Eventually, everyone pays for the high cost of accidents and injuries.

Preventing Accidents

Preventing accidents is everyone's responsibility. On the job, you share that responsibility with your employer. Doing what you can to prevent accidents will help make your workplace safer.

What can you do to prevent accidents? Learning to do your job correctly is a good way to start. Think and act safely while you are on the job. Avoid unsafe acts and correct any unsafe working conditions. Know and follow safety rules to help prevent accidents. Following these other safety procedures will also help you prevent accidents:

- Stay healthy.
- Use machines and tools properly.
- Wear protective clothing and use protective safety equipment.
- Follow safety precautions.

Stay Healthy

Being alert and healthy is the best way to do your job well and safely. You can stay healthy by eating properly and getting adequate sleep. This practice cuts down fatigue. Fatigue on the job can lead to unsafe behavior that causes an accident. If you become ill while on the job, stop working. Your illness affects your performance and may cause you to injure yourself or someone else. Report your illness to your supervisor.

Reflect Further

Why is workers' compensation important to you if you are injured?

Enrich

Invite someone who has suffered a job-related injury to speak to the class.

Resource

Accident Prevention, Activity C, WB

Activity

Write a safety pledge stating what you will do to ensure your safety on the job.

Regular exercise will help you stay alert and physically fit. This is especially important for jobs requiring physical activity. However, it will also improve the performance of workers in jobs that are demanding mentally instead of physically.

Use Machines and Tools Properly

Many machines and tools can be dangerous if not handled properly. Never operate any type of machinery without receiving proper operating instructions and supervision. See 9-8. If you do not know, ask! When you use any machines or tools, work at a safe speed. Taking shortcuts, rushing, or taking chances could lead to a costly accident. Keep all work areas around machinery clean. Scraps of material or oil can cause a worker to slip or fall.

Hand tools should be used and maintained properly. Choose the right tool for the job to get it done safely. Tools should be kept clean and in working condition. Sharpen dull tools and replace broken handles. All tools should be properly stored when not in use.

9-8

Workers learn how to use the specialized tools of their trade by working with experienced employees.

Use the Computer Properly

Today many jobs involve using a computer in one form or another. Eyestrain and repetitive-motion injuries are two problems commonly associated with extended computer use. The following tips can help you avoid many health problems.

- Use a large monitor, if possible, and place it slightly below eye level and 18 to 28 inches from your eyes.

- Place your computer in a position that avoids glare from other light sources.

- Place reference material close to you on an appropriate holder to avoid unnecessary head movements.

- Use dark lettering on a light background on your monitor display. Be sure to keep it sharply focused.

- Clean your screen regularly.

- Blink your eyes frequently to help them stay moist.

- Adjust your chair to a proper height for you.

- Maintain good posture and keep your muscles relaxed.

- Take frequent short breaks to stand up, stretch, and rest your eyes. Exercise your wrists and fingers frequently.

Discuss

Under what circumstances should you skip work because of illness? Whom should you notify and when?

Enrich

Demonstrate exercises and proper stretching techniques to prevent repetitive-motion injuries from using the computer for long periods of time.

Wear Protective Clothing and Use Protective Equipment

Certain jobs require special protective clothing and equipment to prevent injury to the worker. Wear properly fitted clothes, especially if you work with moving machinery. Protect your feet by wearing hard-toed safety shoes on construction and industrial sites. Hard hats are required safety equipment in the construction industry. Dust masks or protective breathing devices are necessary around dust, chemical sprays, and biological agents. See 9-9. Protective gloves and clothing are needed when handling chemicals. Wear protective eye equipment and hearing protection when needed. Always be sure to follow company policies and procedures.

Follow Safety Precautions

Closely following basic safety precautions is another way for you to help prevent accidents. Practicing safety on the job includes using ladders safely, washing hands frequently, lifting properly, preventing fires, and keeping work areas neat.

Use Ladders Safely

Many jobs require the use of ladders. Ladders should be handled with care. Choose the right ladder for the job. Check the ladder to be sure it is in good condition. Avoid using metal ladders near electrical equipment or high-voltage wires because metal conducts electricity. Someone

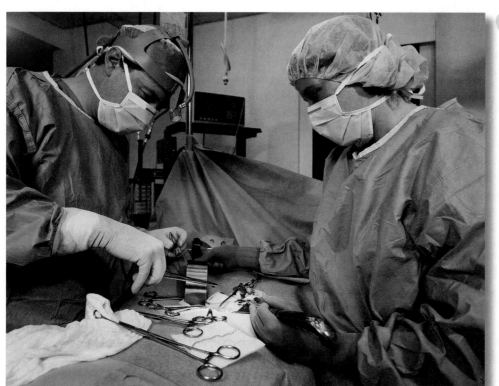

9-9
Some employees are required to wear special clothing and protective devices to keep them safe from environmental hazards.

standing on or touching the ladder could be seriously injured or killed if electricity comes in contact with the ladder.

Ladders should be placed firmly on level ground to prevent tipping. The base of extension ladders should be placed the proper distance from the wall or building they are leaning against. Make sure the ladder is strong enough to support you and the tools and materials you use. To avoid a fall, place the ladder within an arm's length of your work. Face the ladder when you climb up or down.

Wash Hands Frequently

Proper and frequent hand washing has proven to be a major factor in preventing the transmission of communicable diseases. Be sure to wash your hands after using the restroom and before eating or handling food. The following general procedure is recommended. Of course, if you work in a clinical setting or know you have been exposed to an infectious agent, stricter guidelines may apply.

1. Wet your hands with warm running water.

2. Apply soap to all surfaces of your hands and fingers.

3. Vigorously rub your hands together for 10 to 15 seconds. Be sure to generate friction on all surfaces of your hands and fingers. Take extra care to remove dirt from under your fingernails.

4. Remove all soap by thoroughly rinsing your hands.

5. Dry your hands using a paper towel or electric hand dryer if available.

Lift Properly

Using proper lifting procedures can help prevent injury. Lifting heavy objects incorrectly or lifting too much at one time can cause strains or back injuries. To lift properly, use your leg muscles because they are stronger than your back. Keep your back straight and your knees bent when you lift a heavy object from the floor. Do not try to lift more than you can handle. Instead, ask for assistance or learn to use a mechanical aid, such as a crane or hoist, to assist you.

Prevent Fires

The best way to avoid a fire is to prevent it from starting. Faulty electrical wiring and careless smoking are the main causes of many fires. However, some workplaces now prohibit smoking in the building or limit smoking to designated areas only. This decreases the risk of fire. Other causes of fire may include: faulty heating equipment, unattended open flames in labs or kitchens, and grease buildup in kitchen hoods. Another cause of fire is the careless use of **flammable** liquids. These are liquids that ignite easily and burn rapidly, such as gasoline.

A fire needs oxygen, fuel, and heat to start. You can extinguish a fire by removing any one of those elements. Fire extinguishers are designed to help put out fires. There are four different types of fire extinguishers, each one designed to fight a specific type or class of fire. Using the wrong type of extinguisher could actually make the fire worse or injure the person operating it. Be sure you know if the extinguisher is designed for the type of fire you are fighting before using it, 9-10.

You can help prevent a fire on the job by following these other safety tips:

- Keep your work area clean.

- Do not store oily rags and paper in open containers. They could eventually ignite.

- Keep containers of flammable liquids tightly closed. Store in a cool area.

- Do not overload electrical wires. They could short-circuit and cause a fire.

- Use matches and lighters only in designated areas.

If a fire should occur in your work area, follow your company's fire plan. Review the plan periodically so you will know what to do before the need arises. Above all, stay calm.

If you are selected to assist during a fire emergency, you will receive extra training in the use of fire extinguishers. If no specific fire plan exists, there are some general guidelines to follow. See 9-11.

Activity

Identify your employer's emergency procedures for fire, tornado, earthquake, and emergency notification of relatives.

Enrich

Demonstrate how to use a fire extinguisher.

Classes of Fires	
Ordinary **A** **Combustibles**	Class A fires involve wood, paper, cloth, rubber, many plastics, and other ordinary combustible materials. Water or solutions containing a large percentage of water stops these fires.
Flammable **B** **Liquids**	Class B fires involve flammable liquids, gases and similar materials such as greases, oils, tars, and oil-base paints. Stopping these fires requires smothering (or exclusion of air) and the interruption of the chemical chain reaction.
Electrical **C** **Equipment**	Class C fires involve Class A or B fires in or near live electrical equipment. A nonconductive agent must be used in the fire extinguisher to prevent injury to its operator.
Combustible **D** **Metals**	Class D fires involve combustible metals such as magnesium, titanium or sodium. Special extinguishing agents and techniques are needed for fires of this type.

9-10

There are four classifications of fires, and each needs a specific type of fire extinguisher.

Being Prepared for a Fire

- Know what action you will take before the need arises.

- Know where the fire exits, alarms, and extinguishers are located.

- Find out how to use the fire alarm.

- Confine the fire by closing all windows and doors.

- Rescue persons in immediate danger if possible.

- Use the telephone to report a fire to the fire station or operator.

- Give the correct company name, address, and location of the fire.

- Participate in practice fire drills so you know how to leave the building safely.

9-11

Review fire safety guidelines often to avoid panic in case of a fire.

Reflect Further

What can you and other workers do to prevent many common accidents on the job?

Activity

Develop a daily strategy for students to keep the work-based learning classroom orderly and safe.

Keep Work Areas Neat

Good housekeeping helps reduce hazards in the work area. Keeping your work area neat and clean will prevent accidental tripping, slipping, or being struck by falling objects. Pick up any scraps and wipe up spills immediately. Place safety cones or caution signs on freshly mopped floors so they can be seen from all directions. Store tools in a safe area after use. Do not leave any items on stairs or in walkways where someone might trip or fall.

You can find more information related to accident prevention through the **National Safety Council** at www.nsc.org. It is the nation's leading advocate for safety and health. The National Safety Council's mission is "to educate and influence people to prevent accidental injury and death."

What to Do When an Accident Occurs

No matter how careful people are, accidents do happen. When an accident occurs, it is very important to stay calm. Very often, the difference between staying calm and panicking is preparation. Prior training will teach you what to do in an emergency, and it could help save an injured person's life.

Be sure to report any injury that occurs on the job, no matter how small. Even a small scratch could lead to blood poisoning.

Call for Help

Call for help as soon as it is safe to do so. Who you call will depend on the extent of the accident or sudden illness. In cases of serious injury or illness you will want to telephone for professional help. Often phoning 9-1-1 or your local emergency number accomplishes this. The Poison Control Center should be contacted immediately for accidents involving any type of poison. Review your company's emergency policy so you know what to do if an accident occurs. You may also need the help of bystanders in making the phone call, assisting the injured, or controlling traffic.

When making the telephone call, be sure to explain the nature of the accident and what type of aid has been provided. Identify the location of the accident and the telephone number of the phone you are using. Then stay on the line until the emergency provider gets all the information needed and hangs up.

In the Real World

It Is Just a Scratch

The cleanup bell had already rung in cabinet-making class and Clarisa was running late. Her tools had not been put away and her workbench was covered with shavings. Her boyfriend was waiting at the door, and the floor sweeper was on her to hurry as she was holding up dismissal of the entire class. So rather than take time to pick up the brush hanging on the side of the cabinet, she just used her arm to sweep the shavings to the floor. As she did so she felt a sting on the palm of her hand and noticed a light scratch near her right thumb. She knew her teacher, Mr. Gonzales, required her to report all accidents immediately but she just could not take the time now.

The next morning Clarisa noticed a slight redness around the scratch. However, it was so small she had to think twice to remember how she had received it. When she entered her cabinet making class she decided not to report her accident. She did not want to hear another one of Mr. Gonzales' lectures on the importance of safety and how critical it was to follow all class rules.

A few days later red streaks appeared on her hand and arm. She developed a fever and began to feel very ill. It was only then that Clarisa decided to report her illness to the school nurse. After two weeks in the hospital she was on her way to recovery from a near fatal case of blood poisoning.

Questions to Discuss

1. Would you have reported the accident when it first occurred? Why or why not?
2. What should Clarisa have done when she first noticed the scratch?
3. Do you think Mr. Gonzales's stern approach to safety contributed to Clarisa not reporting the accident?
4. Is there a way Mr. Gonzales could stress the importance of safety and not discourage students like Clarisa from reporting accidents?
5. Do you think Clarisa will think differently about Mr. Gonzales's approach to following safety rules?

Provide First Aid

First aid means giving an ill or injured person immediate, temporary treatment before proper medical help arrives. Try to receive formal first aid training before or while you are on the job. The Red Cross is one organization that provides training classes in first aid and CPR. Online first aid training is available as well. You should have a reason for everything you do. These basic lifesaving steps are shown in 9-12.

To stop the bleeding, use a tourniquet as a last resort. A **tourniquet** is a long, thin strip of cloth or other material twisted tightly around the body to restrict blood flow.

Follow Universal Precautions

Whenever an accident occurs that involves loss of blood or vomiting, there is a danger of spreading serious viral infections like AIDS

Activity

Research and report on the American Red Cross procedures for basic first aid.

9-12

Follow these basic life-saving steps before medical help arrives.

Activity

Interview the person at your workstation who is trained in universal precautions. Summarize the interview in a one-page paper.

Giving First Aid

1. Remain calm.

2. Rescue the person from the hazardous situation if it is possible to do so alone.

3. Do not move the person unless there is an immediate threat of further injury.

4. Check to make sure nothing is in the injured person's mouth or throat that could interfere with breathing.

5. Stop any bleeding by applying pressure to the wound.

6. Help to prevent shock by keeping the person warm and flat on his or her back with the head low.

7. Call for medical help.

8. Stay with the injured person until medical help arrives.

or hepatitis B. **Universal precautions** are the following steps designed to help prevent the spread of infection.

1. Use protective barriers such as appropriately designed masks, gowns, gloves, and eye protection.

2. Always wear latex gloves when handling blood.

3. Remove the first glove by touching the outside of that glove with your other gloved hand. Remove the second glove with your bare hand by touching only the inside of the second glove. To remember this procedure, think of the phrase *glove to glove-side, skin to skin-side*.

4. Dispose of gloves in a plastic bag labeled *contaminated*.

5. Wash your hands after handling blood even if gloves were worn. See 9-13.

6. If blood has made contact with any part of your body, wash or rinse (if eyes) thoroughly and see a doctor immediately.

9-13

Wash your hands thoroughly after coming in contact with blood.

One or more persons at your workplace should be trained in universal precautions. Whenever possible, rely on that person to handle accidents where a loss of blood occurs. Call him or her first!

Follow Emergency Evacuation Procedures

As in the case of some fires, there may be a time when a situation becomes so severe that it will require an evacuation of a portion or all of a facility. In other situations, such as a tornado warning, it may be more important to go to a safe place in the building rather than leave. Your employer should have specific guidelines for these situations.

It is very important that you know and understand what you are expected to do. Look for posted copies of floor plans that show emergency exits and evacuation routes. Determine their location in advance so you will be able to find them in an emergency. Many companies conduct emergency drills. Take these drills very seriously. How you behave in an actual emergency could end up saving your life and the lives of others.

Workplace Violence

Workplace violence is a very serious problem for the American worker. **Workplace violence** involves violent acts or threatening behavior that occur in the workplace or at a company function. Each week thousands of individuals are victims of workplace violence. Actual numbers are hard to determine as many of these instances go unreported.

Attacks of violence in the workplace may be physical or psychological. For example, physical attacks may include shooting, hitting, pushing, or kicking. Psychological attacks may involve harassment, swearing, or verbal or written threats. The individuals involved in workplace violence may not be current or former employees. They could be customers or someone associated with an employee such as a spouse or even a friend.

There are many possible motives for workplace violence. Some may include robbery, domestic problems, or personality conflicts. It could be an employee who feels he or she has been fired or disciplined unfairly. Another cause for workplace violence could even be imagined problems by someone who is mentally unstable. Many people see workplace violence simply as an extension of the violent society in which we live.

As you can see, workplace violence is a very complex issue. There are no easy solutions for prevention. However, there are some things you should keep in mind. For example, where you work is an important factor. Retail and fast food businesses tend to be more prone to violence. While murder is one of the leading causes of death on the job, the vast majority of workplace murders are robbery-related. Many businesses

Thinking It Through

Why is it important to be extra careful when assisting a person who is bleeding or vomiting?

Reflect

Have you received a copy of your employer's emergency-action plan? What does it direct you to do?

Activity

Use the Internet to research articles about workplace violence. Write a brief report of your findings to share with the class.

Discuss

What factors might contribute to violence in the workplace?

In the Real World

Not in Nathan's Job Description

Nathan was proud of his promotion to assistant stockroom attendant. The factory, which manufactured lighting fixtures, was one of the city's largest employers. He felt confident that he was well prepared to handle all the duties of his new job. Then one day something unexpected happened to Nathan that made him unsure of his capabilities.

One of his new responsibilities was to deliver lamp parts to workers in the plant. They would then take the parts and perform grinding and polishing operations prior to final painting and assembly.

One morning he delivered a box of parts to Hunter for final grinding. He was expecting the friendly greeting he usually got from workers on his morning rounds. However, Hunter looked rather upset. He did not smile but scowled and said: "Take them back. I have too much to do already." Nathan replied that he was just doing what he had been told to do by his boss, Mr. Mathews, and he would not take them back. At that point Hunter jumped up and stood face to face within a few inches of Nathan. His fists were clenched and his face was red. He screamed, "OK leave them! But I am going to find you at lunch and knock your teeth out!"

Nathan was shocked and scared. He was not sure what to say or do. He just turned and walked away acting as brave as possible.

Questions to Discuss

1. Could something besides the workload be bothering Hunter?
2. Should Nathan have taken the parts back to the stockroom? Why or why not?
3. Do you think Nathan should have said something in response to Hunter's outburst? If so, what?
4. What should Nathan do next?

have now installed bulletproof glass, video surveillance, and alarm systems. Some businesses have even changed the way cash is handled in response to this problem. You need to be aware of the potential dangers whenever you are handling cash and follow established guidelines.

The **Occupational Safety and Health Administration (OSHA)** is a government agency that sets and enforces job safety and health standards for workers. OSHA recommends that employees take the following steps to help prevent workplace violence. However, following them will not guarantee you will not become a victim. You can learn more about causes and prevention of workplace violence by visiting the OSHA Web site at www.osha.gov/.

- Learn how to recognize, avoid, or diffuse potentially violent situations by attending personal safety training programs.

- Alert supervisors to any concerns about safety or security and report all incidences immediately in writing.

Resource

Workplace Violence Awareness, Activity D, WB

Resource

Safety Committee Presentation, Activity E, WB

- Avoid traveling alone or in unfamiliar locations or situations whenever possible.

- Carry only minimal money and required identification into community settings.

The Role of Government in Protecting Your Health

The government plays an important role in promoting safe working environments. It makes and enforces laws that promote health and safety on the job. These laws led to the creation of three government agencies that carefully monitor workplace safety: The Occupational Safety and Health Administration (OSHA), the Environmental Protection Agency (EPA), and the Centers for Disease Control (CDC).

OSHA

The Occupational Safety and Health Act is a national act passed by Congress in 1970. The act calls for safe and healthful working conditions. Under this act, the Occupational Safety and Health Administration (OSHA) was formed. Most employees are covered under the act. Some who may not be covered are: self-employed persons, independent farmers, and workers covered under other legislation. Also, OSHA does not cover employees of state and local governments unless they are in one of the states with OSHA-approved safety programs.

OSHA provides workplace inspection, training, and education programs. It also enforces the law, making sure that required health and safety standards exist in the workplace. To an employer who does not comply, OSHA gives a **citation**, which is a summons to appear in court, and may charge one or more fines.

Employers and employees both have certain responsibilities under the law. OSHA makes it mandatory for each employer to provide all its employees a safe place to work—free from safety and health hazards. The employer is also responsible for following the standards set forth by OSHA and making sure employees follow safety procedures. Employees, on the other hand, are expected to adhere to OSHA health and safety standards and follow these rules:

- Read the OSHA poster at your job site so that you know your rights and responsibilities.

- Follow OSHA safety standards and your employer's standards.

Resource

Protective Devices and Procedures, Activity F, WB

Reflect

Where is the OSHA safety standards poster located at your place of employment?

Enrich

Review your employer's safety standards. How do they compare with those established by OSHA?

Note

Determine if you have received the required information under OSHA's *Hazardous Chemical Right to Know* provisions.

Reflect

What is the procedure you need to follow for reporting injuries on the job?

Enrich

Review copies of the material safety data sheets (MSDS) at your workstation. Are there any hazardous materials that do not have an MSDS?

- Report any injury that occurs on the job.
- Wear personal protective equipment when required. A list of some of the most common protective devices and the protection each provides is shown in 9-14.
- Use safety devices properly.
- Participate in fire drills and other safety practices.
- Report unsafe working conditions and practices. If your employer does not correct the situation, request OSHA to make an inspection. A state or federal OSHA office is located in each state.

An important provision of OSHA is the *Hazardous Chemical Right to Know*. As an employee, you have the right to know about any hazardous chemicals in your workplace and be trained to handle and use them. This includes container labeling and other forms of warning. Your employer is also required to have a **material safety data sheet (MSDS)** for each hazardous material. These sheets provide information on the specific hazards involved and procedures for their safe use. Your employer must train you to recognize and avoid the hazards present in these materials. See the OSHA Web site at www.osha.gov/ for more information about OSHA programs.

9-14

Some of the protective devices OSHA requires workers to wear are listed here.

Examples of Personal Protective Equipment	
Equipment	**Protects Against**
Leather gloves and apron shields	Welding burns
Gloves	Cuts and abrasions
Safety goggles and face shields	Eye injuries
Hard hats and safety shoes	Injuries from falling objects
Rubber gloves, aprons, and face shields	Burns from acids, caustics, and alkalies
Asbestos gloves and leggings	Burns from flames and hot metal
Ear plugs and earmuffs	High frequency sounds
Masks and respirators	Harmful gases

EPA

Keeping the environment safe and clean is a major concern for everyone. Pollution not only damages the environment, it can cause serious health hazards and diseases. The **Environmental Protection Agency (EPA)** is another government agency that works to make this country a safer place to live. The agency was formed for the purpose of protecting the environment. The EPA works to eliminate environmental hazards such as air and water pollution. Other environmental concerns regulated by the EPA include: toxic waste disposal, pesticide standards, and radiation monitoring.

To help reduce pollution, the EPA has attacked industrial smokestack pollution, auto exhaust emissions, and contaminated rivers and lakes. As a result of the agency's work, many cities now have cleaner air. Some rivers and lakes have been reopened for fishing and swimming. Many toxic waste sites have been improved.

The EPA also conducts research on the effects of pollution and provides assistance to states and cities working to prevent pollution. You can learn more about the EPA regulations and programs by visiting their Web site at www.epa.gov/.

Reflect Further

Do you feel safer knowing federal agencies are dedicated to helping maintain your health and safety?

CDC

The **Centers for Disease Control and Prevention (CDC)** is part of the United States Department of Health and Human Services. CDC works with worldwide, state, and local health agencies to protect the public from health threats. CDC's activities include conducting research, promoting public health policies, and providing leadership and training. Mysterious deaths or illnesses are often sent to CDC for investigation. You can find a variety of health-related information at the CDC Web site, www.cdc.gov/.

The **National Institute for Occupational Safety and Health (NIOSH)** is an arm of the Centers for Disease Control and Prevention. It is specifically responsible for conducting research and making recommendations for the prevention of work-related injury and illness. NIOSH information related to young worker safety and health may be found on their Web site at www.cdc.gov/niosh/topics/youth.

Discuss

The EPA is frequently in the news. What current issue(s) do you associate with this agency?

Activity

Use the Internet to search for information about OSHA, EPA, CDC, and NIOSH. Choose one of the organizations and prepare a presentation based on your findings.

Summary

Safety is everyone's responsibility—especially on the job. Many accidents are caused by a lack of knowledge and skills.

The costs of accidents affect everyone. An injured worker must personally deal with the injury. The employer's costs include lower production, training or hiring another worker, and dealing with possible lawsuits or fines. The economy is affected by losses in the workforce, billions of dollars paid for accidents, and higher costs of goods and services as a result.

Practicing safety can prevent many accidents. Wearing protective clothing and using safety equipment will help protect the worker from environmental hazards. Workers can reduce job hazards by using ladders and lifting properly, preventing fires, keeping work areas neat, and washing hands frequently. Workers should also know what to do when an accident does occur. This involves properly reporting the accident, knowing first aid steps, and following universal precautions and proper evacuation procedures.

Workplace violence continues to be a major problem for American workers. It is important that workers are alert to possible dangers and know how to respond.

Resource

Review and Study Guide for Chapter 9, reproducible master 9-3, TR

Answers to *Facts In Review*

1. lack of knowledge and skills, environmental hazards, poor safety attitudes, unsafe behavior
2. none
3. Seek information on how to perform the job; make sure you have the knowledge and skills to perform the task correctly and safely before you begin.
4. Watch a skilled worker perform the task; have the worker give you a step-by-step lesson; perform the task slowly yourself while the skilled worker watches; practice the task until you do it safely and accurately.
5. (List three. Student response.)
6. (List five:) recklessness, bad temper, lack of consideration, disobedience, carelessness, laziness, fatigue, impatience, emotional state, use of drugs or alcohol
7. time, money
8. Stay healthy; use machines and tools properly; wear protective clothing and use safety equipment; follow safety precautions.

Facts in Review

1. What are the four main causes of accidents?
2. What workplace is free of accidents?
3. If you do not know how to operate a machine or perform a task, what should you do before trying to do it on your own?
4. Describe a good way to learn a new skill.
5. Give three examples of workers not taking the right attitude toward safety.
6. List five reasons for unsafe behavior on the job that could lead to an accident.
7. What are the costs to an employer if a worker is injured on the job?
8. Identify four basic ways to prevent accidents in the workplace.
9. When is it particularly important to wash your hands?
10. Describe the steps to follow when washing your hands.
11. What three requirements are needed to start a fire?
12. What are the important procedures to remember when following universal precautions?
13. Define *workplace violence*.
14. What does *OSHA* do?
15. According to OSHA, what are employees required to do?
16. How does the EPA help keep the environment safe and clean?

9. after using the restroom, before eating or handling food
10. Wet hands with warm water; apply soap to all areas of hands; rub hands together for 10 to 15 seconds; remove dirt from under fingernails; rinse hands removing all soap; dry hands with a paper towel or electric hand dryer.
11. oxygen, fuel, heat
12. Use protective barriers. Always wear latex gloves when handling blood. When removing gloves, never touch the outside of the glove with your bare hand. Dispose of gloves in a plastic bag labeled contaminated. Wash hands after handling blood, even if gloves were worn. If blood has made contact with any part of your body, wash thoroughly and see a doctor immediately.

(continued)

Developing Your Academic Skills

1. **Science.** Using Internet or print sources, research materials or chemicals that can be harmful, such as asbestos, lead, and mercury. Write a brief report of your findings.
2. **Health.** Using Internet or print sources, research the hazards of drug and alcohol abuse in the workplace. Prepare a presentation based on your findings.
3. **Social Studies.** Prepare a report on the role of government agencies such as OSHA, EPA, and CDC in monitoring workplace safety.

Information Technology Applications

1. Using the Internet, research workers' compensation laws in your state. These might be found on the Web site of your state's Department of Labor. Write a report of your findings.
2. Explore the OSHA Web site at www.osha.gov/. What procedure should a worker follow if unsafe working conditions or practices exist and have not been corrected at the worker's company? Write a brief essay of your findings.
3. Visit the EPA Web site at www.epa.gov/. Search for information about how the agency works to protect the environment and your health. Write a one-page report to present to the class.
4. Investigate the CDC Web site at www.cdc.gov/. Create a paper describing a major news event in which CDC has played an important role.

13. *Workplace violence* involves violent acts or threatening behavior that occur in the workplace or at a company function.
14. OSHA is a government agency that sets and enforces job safety and health standards for workers.
15. Read the OSHA poster; follow employer and OSHA safety standards; report any workplace injury; wear the required protective equipment; use safety devices properly; participate in fire drills and other safety practices; report unsafe working conditions and practices.

Applying Your Knowledge and Skills

1. **Employability and Career Development.** List two examples of accidents that have occurred in your type of work. Write a paragraph about each one, describing what happened. Then write another paragraph about each, explaining how the accident might have been prevented.
2. **Communications.** Collect information about job safety, including safety tips and procedures, that relate to your job. Use this information to write a brief report about safety on your job site.
3. **Systems.** Contact two local employers. Ask them to discuss safety training or any programs they use for their employees' safety.
4. **Safety, Health, and Environment.** Locate at least three fire extinguishers in your school or place of employment. Determine the type of extinguisher and the last date of inspection. Then write a paper summarizing your findings. State why you feel the specific type of extinguisher was used in the location you found it.
5. **Problem Solving and Critical Thinking.** Using Internet or print sources, identify at least 3 examples of workplace violence that have occurred in the last six months. Briefly describe the events and recommend changes in company policy that could help to prevent future occurrences of each event.

Developing Workplace Skills

Identify a hazardous occupation that requires the wearing of personal protective equipment. Determine what the equipment is by conducting research at the library, on the Internet, and/or by visiting a worker in that occupation. Make a list and describe the purpose of each piece of equipment. Indicate the source(s) of your information.

16. by punishing polluters, researching the effects of pollution, and providing pollution-prevention assistance to states and cities

10

Leadership and Group Dynamics

Key Terms

leadership

position authority

earned authority

vision

delegate

dynamics

group dynamics

career and technical student organizations
(CTSOs)

Chapter Objectives

After studying this chapter, you will be able to

- **explain** the different types of authority leaders possess.
- **identify** the skills and qualities of a good leader.
- **explain** group dynamics and the effect of good leadership.
- **describe** the school groups and career and technical student organizations in which you can participate and develop good leadership skills.
- **explain** the value of good leadership and group dynamics in the workplace.

Reading Advantage

As you read the chapter, write a letter to yourself. Imagine you will receive this letter in a few years when you are working at your future job. What would you like to remember from this chapter? In the letter, list key points from the chapter that will be useful in your future career.

Achieving Academic Standards

English Language Arts

- Read print and non-print texts to acquire new information and to respond to the needs and demands of society and the workplace. (IRA/NCTE, 1)
- Apply strategies to comprehend, interpret, evaluate, and appreciate texts. (IRA/NCTE, 3)
- Use spoken and written language to communicate effectively. (IRA/NCTE, 4)
- Use a variety of technological and information processes to gather and synthesize information and to create and communicate knowledge. (IRA/NCTE, 8)

Key Concepts

- Good leaders can learn and develop qualities such as honesty, dependability, and loyalty.

- Environmental factors such as room temperature and lighting can have an effect on group dynamics.

- Leadership skills can be developed in school through participation in activities such as band, sports, or career and technical student organizations.

- Leadership experiences are very valuable when applying for a job.

Photo courtesy of DECA

Reflect Further

Describe two people you know—one who uses position authority in a positive way and one in a negative way. Identify a person who has made the shift from position to earned authority.

Companies realize production quantity and quality increase when employees work together effectively. As teams are emphasized more in the workplace, leadership and team skills are becoming essential for success.

Think of groups with which you are involved. Consider the individuals who lead these groups. What traits do they possess? What do you think causes others to follow them? **Leadership** is the capacity to direct a group. The person who uses this ability is the *leader*. Usually this is a person who can influence others and demonstrate authority.

Leaders and Authority

A leader may be officially appointed by his or her organization. On the other hand, the person may simply be viewed as the leader by his or her teammates or coworkers. These two cases represent the two types of authority that exist.

Once a person is named team leader, manager, president, or a similar title, he or she has position authority. **Position authority** gives a person certain powers as defined by the source of the title, which usually is the company management. It is an authority that automatically goes with the title and is not to be questioned. Team members usually have no option but to follow the directions of the person with position authority. As shown in 10-1, position authority tends to be short-lived and may not be deserved.

Position authority is much less effective than the other type of authority, which is earned authority. **Earned authority** is power granted by the other members of the group. The leader is viewed by team members as the most knowledgeable, experienced, or capable member of the group. Even when a leader with earned authority has difficulties, the team rallies behind its leader. Members feel comfortable in questioning the leader if disagreements arise. Earned authority is usually the most effective type of authority and tends to be lasting.

Position authority and earned authority are the two general types of leadership that exist in the workplace. They determine the effectiveness of groups and teams. It is important for a person with position authority to gain earned authority as early in the leadership term as possible. The type of leadership a person uses affects the team or work group's interactions.

Types of Authority

Position Authority

- Is granted by a higher authority
- May or may not be deserved
- Is not to be questioned by those with less authority
- Tends to be short-lived
- Is usually less effective than earned authority

Earned Authority

- Is granted by those with less authority (subordinates)
- Is deserved (earned)
- May be questioned at any time by those with less authority
- Tends to be lasting, even in difficult times
- Is usually more effective than position authority

10-1

It is important to understand how position authority and earned authority affect teamwork.

Resource

What Makes a Leader?
Activity A, WB

Skills and Qualities of a Good Leader

Different types of leadership are needed for different roles. The governor of a state may need different leadership qualities than a military leader or a business leader. There are some common qualities all leaders need. As you become involved with school clubs and work groups, think about the leadership qualities good leaders possess. A good friend or a nice person may not make a good leader.

What qualities do good leaders possess? First of all, good leaders must have **vision**. This means knowing what is most important to the group and how to achieve it. Followers tend to support the leader whose vision most closely resembles their own thoughts on the group's future direction. See 10-2.

To carry out their vision, leaders need special skills. Many of the skills that make a good leader are shown in 10-3. One of the skills is the ability to **delegate**. That means assigning responsibility or authority to another person. The only way for most work to get done is to assign some of it to others. Letting group members be responsible for certain projects makes them feel involved and more committed.

In addition to leadership skills, good leaders usually have certain personal qualities that help them lead others. These qualities include

Photo courtesy of FCCLA

10-2

A common way leaders convey their vision is by speaking to the membership about proposed changes and ideas.

Extend Your Knowledge

Leadership Skills

Leaders are needed in every occupation at all job levels. Business and industry look for and reward workers with leadership skills. Developing your leadership skills can help you be a better worker. School groups and career and technical organizations can provide that opportunity for you.

Reflect

Who would you be willing to follow anywhere with no questions asked?

Activity

List local community and business leaders. What positive leadership qualities does each person possess?

10-3

The skills expected of a good leader can be developed.

Resource

What Does It Take to Lead? color transparency CT-10A, TR

Activity

Recall a recent positive event that occurred in school and identify the group dynamics that affected it. Repeat the activity for a work-based event.

Reflect

Review the leadership skills in 10-3. How many of these skills do you possess?

Leadership Skills

Good leaders have the ability to

- motivate group members to support a vision and achieve goals.
- assume responsibility for the duties of the office or position.
- show confidence and keep a group focused.
- analyze situations clearly and take decisive action when needed.
- take risks and explore new ways of achieving goals.
- maintain enthusiasm and a positive attitude.
- encourage team spirit and cooperation among members.
- listen to others and respond to their views.
- delegate assignments and recognize the accomplishments of others.
- welcome new ideas.
- set a good example.
- work for group success, not personal success.
- do a fair share of the work.
- stay up-to-date on important issues.

Thinking It Through

What are some qualities of bad leadership?

Is it true that leaders have all the power? Is it important for leaders to know all the answers?

Thinking It Through

What are some reasons teams lack or lose motivation? Is the leader responsible for this?

Is it more important to be a good leader or a good follower?

---

honesty, imagination, the desire to work hard, and good communication skills. Not everyone has these qualities or the ability to lead others. However, many of the qualities needed to become a good leader can be learned and developed with practice.

Dynamics and Groups

Dynamics may be defined as underlying causes of change or growth. The fact that you attend high school causes change or growth within you, so the *dynamics* of high school impact your life. Dynamics may be one or many forces. Your personality is one such dynamic force. Whether consciously or unconsciously, your dynamic personality impacts group activity.

Group dynamics are the interacting forces within a human group. These forces include your own personality and the personalities of all other members of the group. See 10-4. A spirit of cooperation fosters positive dynamics, while anger and jealousy foster the opposite. The dynamics may also include environmental factors such as seating arrangement, room temperature, lighting, and size and location of a meeting room.

Whether you work with few or many people, group dynamics are present. The dynamics of groups in the workplace affect the work environment, quality of the product, and reputation of the company in the eyes of the customers and the competition. Your understanding of basic dynamics and their effect in the workplace is important.

You have an impact on group dynamics at work, in school, and at home. When you function within a group that has positive dynamics, you benefit personally. Some of the benefits you receive are the following:

- greater self-esteem

- greater understanding of others and respect for their differences

- improved communication and relationship skills

- improved ability to work with people from diverse backgrounds

- greater job satisfaction

- better understanding of how to work with others smoothly and productively

- pride in a job well done

Besides the personal benefits individuals achieve, a team also benefits from positive group dynamics. See 10-5. Your teams will be more able to accomplish the following:

- Understand how individuals contribute to the group's progress.

- Learn how to utilize the talents of each person on the team.

- See a task to its completion.

- Accomplish objectives and, perhaps, exceed goals.

Photo courtesy of FBLA

10-4

Working with the different talents and ideas of team members is part of group dynamics.

Resource

Evaluating Leaders, Activity B, WB

Discuss

What are some examples of positive dynamics you have observed within a group?

Tech Prep
Showcase
Gold

Photo courtesy of Lloyd Wolf for SkillsUSA

10-5

Working efficiently as a team member leads to great rewards.

In the Real World

Follow the Leader

Dara could not be happier. The company just announced her appointment to technical department director. She recently graduated from one of the toughest universities in her engineering field with high honors. Now she held a top job at an excellent company. It seemed everything was perfect until her first day on the job.

There she soon learned that the employees of her department did not welcome her with open arms. In fact, many treated her with suspicion.

As the weeks went by, Dara realized things were not getting done in the way she wanted. She also learned that department members were secretly discussing their assignments with Michael, the person with the most experience and longest service in the department.

Although the assignments were getting done well and on time, Dara resented Michael's interference. She especially disliked the fact employees were not doing things in the way she directed. However, she could not argue with the fact that their methods seemed to produce better results than hers would have. Still, she disliked the way Michael was intruding on her authority.

"I'm really not happy with your inability to be a cooperative team member," Dara yelled at the first opportunity she saw Michael at his desk alone.

"What are you talking about?" Michael asked.

"Do you think I don't see through your plan to take my job?" Dara replied.

"I'm only trying to help," Michael explained. "Besides, there are certain ways we do things here, and your methods are different."

"If the company wanted things done according to your methods, you would be the director, but you're not. Now, start following directions and quit telling others how to do their jobs," Dara warned.

Michael never said anything to his coworkers about the incident, but that did not matter. Several department employees were working around the corner and heard every word. They immediately told the others and soon the entire company was gossiping about it. Ever since that day, department employees did their work precisely as Dara dictated, but silently they hoped she would transfer to another department.

Questions to Discuss

1. Who has position authority? Who has earned authority?
2. Does this department have good leadership? Explain.
3. Who is responsible for the poor group dynamics of this department?
4. What should Dara do to improve group dynamics?
5. How should she work with Michael?

Leadership and Group Dynamics in School

You have many opportunities in school to develop leadership qualities. As you work on developing these qualities, you also contribute in a positive way to group dynamics. Participation in various school teams, groups, or clubs can help you develop leadership and teamwork skills you can use on the job. Under the direction of a good leader, groups are motivated to make many worthwhile accomplishments.

There are many activities and contests designed to help you develop leadership skills to your maximum. If you are not already a member of a school group, consider joining the debate team, newspaper staff, or drama club. Band, chorus, sports, and other activity groups that interest you are also good choices. Student group activities and projects tend to center around five areas:

- professional activities
- civic activities
- service activities
- social activities
- fund-raising activities

Professional activities enhance the professional improvement of students. They include such activities as club meeting programs related to an occupational field, field trips, and an employer-employee banquet. Skill contests are also considered professional development activities, 10-6. They help students improve and expand their career-related attitudes, knowledge, and skills.

Civic activities are student group projects that serve the school and community. Projects range from helping improve the school or community to participating in fairs, trade shows, and other community events.

Service activities involve projects that emphasize the need for sharing. Making a contribution to a charity, visiting a nursing home, and making and delivering fruit baskets to shut-ins are examples of service activities.

Social activities are also an important part of student groups. Social activities include parties, picnics, and socializing after meetings. The employer-employee banquet is also considered a social activity as well as a professional one.

Resource

Leadership and Group Dynamics, Activity C, WB

Enrich

List 10 civic activities appropriate for a class project and vote for one to do this year.

Reflect

What groups are you involved in? What groups would you like to learn more about?

10-6
Skill contests are held periodically by the career and technical student organizations. This was at a national SkillsUSA contest.

Photo courtesy of SkillsUSA

Fund-raising activities are necessary to finance all the other activities of the group. Service projects and social functions are types of activities that may require fund raising. See 10-7.

Of course, there is no limit to the types of activities an organization may sponsor. The limit is set only by the creativity of its members and officers. For a club to be successful, its members need to work willingly and enthusiastically on club activities. An active member of an organization participates in two or more of the following ways:

- attends meetings
- learns parliamentary procedure
- serves on a committee
- supports and/or participates in organization activities
- holds an office, if elected or appointed

If you want to be part of an active organization, you and all its members must work for the good of the group. Everyone cannot be the president, but every member can do his or her part. Members can assume leadership roles by freely volunteering to handle their fair share of the work. Assess your own abilities and decide what you can do best for your organization. Taking an active role in an organization can help you develop as a person, a leader, and a team member.

Reflect Further

What leadership experiences can you gain from membership in your favorite organization? How can those experiences make you more employable?

Activity

Identify two ways you can become active (or more active) in a school or community organization and report your progress to the class.

Resource

Career and Technical Student Organizations, color transparency CT-10B, TR

Career and Technical Student Organizations

Some of the best opportunities for developing interpersonal skills are through **career and technical student organizations (CTSOs)**. These organizations have leadership and teamwork skills as major objectives.

Your school most likely has a student organization that is related to your vocational interests. If there are no available career and technical organizations in your career interests, one can be started with your school's approval. Career and technical student organizations help reinforce and expand what students learn in the classroom and on the job. Students can participate in CTSOs on the local, state, and national levels. The CTSOs commonly found in schools are described on the following pages.

10-7

Some student groups raise money for service projects, such as this walkathon for the March of Dimes.

Photo courtesy of National Foundation-March of Dimes

Business Professionals of America

Business Professionals of America (BPA) is one of the main national Career and Technical Service Organizations. Middle school, high school, and college students may join BPA. Students focus on getting ready for careers in business, management, administration, and information technology. BPA continues to grow and now has over 51,000 members in over 2,300 chapters. BPA's Workplace Skills Assessment Program (WSAP) offers students a chance to demonstrate knowledge in problem solving and workplace skills. Students may also learn leadership skills by joining in annual competitions. Students may choose to compete in events offered in any of the following categories:

- Financial Services
- Administrative Support
- Information Technology
- Management/Marketing/Human Resources

In addition to helping students, BPA also assists educators. BPA provides resources to supplement classroom curriculums that are based on national standards. You can learn more about Business Professionals of America by visiting their Web site at www.bpanet.org.

DECA—An Association of Marketing Students

DECA is the association for marketing students. See 10-8. It has chapters in all 50 states, Guam, Puerto Rico, Canada, Germany, and Mexico. DECA currently has over 180,000 members. It offers programs for both high school and college students. DECA helps students develop team and leadership-building skills. Members have a chance to join in leadership programs as well as a co-curricular competitive events program. Any students interested in membership in DECA may have a career interest in one of the following areas:

- Marketing, Sales, and Service
- Management and Entrepreneurship
- Business Administration
- Hospitality
- Finance

Photo courtesy of DECA

10-8

By participating in DECA, you can develop your skills while pursuing a career in marketing or business.

Discuss

Where do leaders acquire their qualities? Where do they earn the experience to lead?

Activity

List two ways in which team members can work together. Then list two team benefits and two personal benefits.

DECA also assists educators. They provide programs and materials to supplement classroom curricula that are based on the national standards. These programs focus on leadership development, community service, skill assessment, and academic skill development. You can learn more about DECA by visiting their Web site at www.deca.org.

Future Business Leaders of America

Future Business Leaders of America (FBLA) is a student business organization. It is dedicated to preparing students for careers in business and business-related fields. FBLA has divisions for middle school, high school, and postsecondary students. FBLA also has a professional division for business people. See 10-9. The high school division is currently the largest. It has approximately 215,000 members nationwide. FBLA offers career recognition programs that are specifically created for each of their divisions.

FBLA also offers annual competitive events at state leadership conferences. Top state winners of these events may then participate in the annual competitive events at the national leadership conference. To assist students in the transition from school to work is the mission of FBLA. You can learn more about Future Business Leaders of America by visiting their Web site at www.fbla-pbl.org.

10-9

FBLA members provide a valuable resource for networking.

Photo courtesy of FBLA

National FFA Organization

National FFA Organization prepares members for leadership and careers in agricultural science education, 10-10. This includes the food, fiber, and natural resources industry. National FFA Organization was founded in 1928. It now has over 500,000 members. There are currently 7,358 chapters throughout the United States, Puerto Rico, Guam, and the Virgin Islands. The National FFA Organization does

10-10

You can pursue a career in agricultural science education and develop your leadership skills by joining the National FFA Organization.

Photo courtesy of the National FFA Organization

not consider itself a "club." It does consider itself a part of the following
three core areas in the agricultural science education program:

- Classroom/laboratory instruction
- Supervised agricultural experience programs
- FFA student organization activities

The combining of these three components helps students within the
National FFA Organization. Students can develop their potential for leadership, personal growth, and career success. The organization also offers
members a chance to participate in annual agricultural science education
competitive events. It is called their Career Development Events (CDEs.)
program. To become a member of the National FFA Organization, students must have an existing FFA chapter at their school. Students must
also be between the ages of 12 and 21. You can learn more about the
National FFA Organization by visiting their Web site at www.ffa.org.

Family, Career and Community Leaders of America

Family, Career and
Community Leaders of America
(FCCLA) is a dynamic and effective nonprofit national student
organization that helps young
men and women become leaders, 10-11. It
addresses important personal, family, work,
and societal issues through Family and
Consumer Sciences Education. FCCLA has
more than 220,000 members and nearly 7,000
chapters from 50 state associations and the
District of Columbia, Puerto Rico, and the
Virgin Islands. FCCLA offers many programs
and competitions students can participate in.
These help students develop leadership and
daily life skills. Some of the programs FCCLA
offers include the following:

- Career Connection is a program that works
  with students through individual, team,
  and competitive events. It helps students
  discover their career interests and develop
  a career plan.

Photo courtesy of FCCLA

10-11

FCCLA provides you with
many opportunities to
develop your leadership and
teamwork skills.

- Dynamic Leadership is a program that offers project ideas, activities, and information about leadership. It helps members expand their skills.

- Leaders at Work is a national program. It provides projects that encourage students to build leadership skills. It also helps students get ready for career success.

- STAR (Students Taking Action with Recognition) Events are competitive events. Members can enter to demonstrate their leadership ability and skills.

You can learn more about the programs FCCLA has to offer by visiting the FCCLA Web site at www.fcclainc.org.

Activity

If your school does not have a chapter of the organization in which you are interested, contact the appropriate state or national office.

Enrich

With a classmate, identify all the student organizations included in the latest yearbook. List them and describe their activities.

Health Occupations Students of America

Health Occupations Students of America (HOSA) is a career and technical student organization. The U.S. Department of Education and the Health Occupations Education Division of the American Vocational Association endorse it. HOSA was formed in 1976. It now has about 90,000 members with 44 charters in the United States. HOSA helps support career opportunities in the health care industry. They also try to improve the quality of health care people receive. HOSA is part of a student's health and health science-related course work.

HOSA offers members a chance to join in annual competitive events. These events give students opportunities for knowledge, skill, and leadership development. Students can compete in events for health science professions, emergency preparedness, leadership, and recognition events. You can learn more about HOSA by visiting their Web site at www.hosa.org.

Technology Student Association

The Technology Student Association (TSA) provides competitions and programs for middle and high school students with a strong interest in technology, innovation, design, and engineering. These activities prepare TSA members for the challenges of a dynamic world by promoting personal growth, leadership, and problem solving skills in students. TSA reaches 150,000 members in over 1,500 chapters nationwide.

TSA hosts an annual conference that features middle school and high school level competitions. See 10-12. Members can compete in a broad range of areas such as robotics, CAD, engineering, film, manufacturing, and leadership. TSA's competitive events, as well as its other programs and activities are intended to extend student understanding of science, technology, engineering, and mathematics (STEM). The overall focus of TSA is to promote the development, impact, and potential of technology and careers in technology. You can learn more about the Technology Student Association by visiting the Web site at www.tsaweb.org.

Reflect Further

Which career and technical student organizations may have the most to offer you? Which interest you most?

10-12

Team competitions in various technology-related events are a feature of TSA.

Photo courtesy of TSA

Discuss

Where would leaders be without followers? What skills are required of followers?

SkillsUSA

SkillsUSA is a national non-profit organization. It is for high school and college students as well as teachers. SkillsUSA joins students, teachers, and industry together. It creates a strong,

skilled workforce for America. SkillsUSA helps students get ready for careers in technical, skilled and service occupations, and health occupations, 10-13. SkillsUSA offers members programs that will provide education experiences. They focus on leadership, teamwork, character development, and citizenship.

- The Professional Development Program (PDP) teaches students 84 workplace skill competencies. This is done through a series of lessons.

- The Work Force Ready System provides assessments for career and technical education that are supported by industry, education, and policy leaders.

- Student2Student Mentoring allows older high school students to mentor younger students.

- The Career Skills Education Program teaches employability and life skills. This program is strictly for college students.

- CareerSafe is a 10-hour online training program. It gives students basic knowledge of safety. It also provides a credential for the job market.

Developing the student's technical, academic, and employability skills is the goal of SkillsUSA. You can learn more about the programs SkillsUSA has to offer by visiting their Web site at www.skillsusa.org.

Photo courtesy of Lloyd Wolf for SkillsUSA

10-13

SkillsUSA offers many competitive events you can participate in to help prepare you for joining the workforce.

Leadership and Group Dynamics in the Workplace

Working well with coworkers, serving customers, and taking a leadership role are skills employers expect workers to possess. All of these interpersonal skills are considered necessary for working effectively in today's workplace. When employees do not have these skills, they may fall short of customer expectations and lose business.

The driving force behind company decisions is profit. Regardless of their social or professional contributions to communities, if companies do not make a profit, they do not survive. Survival is dependent on a quality workforce that possesses strong leadership and teamwork skills.

Think of a health services organization with thousands of employees, two hospitals, and several clinics. The group dynamics on both a large and small scale greatly influence the success or failure of this company. Customer satisfaction and service depend on the ability of groups to function smoothly. Good leaders can make this happen. Dissatisfied customers mean the organization is not doing its job well and may be sacrificing its future.

Leadership experiences are very valuable when you apply for a job, 10-14. Employers look for experiences that indicate you can take responsibility and perform well in a group. Be sure to add your membership in school groups and career and technical student organizations to your résumé. Students who do not participate in groups or organizations are at a disadvantage when interviewing for a job. Employers know students with a record of group interaction usually make better employees.

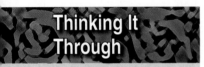

Thinking It Through

Do you think a company can be successful with bad leadership?

Photo courtesy of DECA

10-14

Becoming actively involved in an organization moves you one step ahead of others when seeking employment.

Summary

Leadership is a very important employability skill. Understanding the necessity of both position and earned authority is key to your success in the workplace. Good leaders have certain qualities and abilities to help them carry out their leadership roles. As people work on teams, group dynamics affect the group's work and decision-making processes.

Participating in school teams, clubs, and groups can help students develop their leadership skills. Career and technical student organizations are especially useful for learning how to work with and lead a group. Through group activities, you will expand your attitudes, knowledge, and skills to contribute to the goals and objectives of the organization. Leadership experience while in school prepares students to demonstrate leadership skills in the workplace.

Facts in Review

1. Define *leadership* and give three examples.
2. List five qualities of position authority.
3. List five qualities of earned authority
4. List five skills that are important for a good leader to have.
5. Name two environmental forces that may contribute to group dynamics.
6. List four ways you may personally benefit from being a member of a group.
7. Name three ways a person can actively participate in a group's activities.
8. What is the purpose of career and technical student organizations?
9. Name five examples of CTSOs.
10. How can participating in a CTSO help you get a job?

Resource

Review and Study Guide for Chapter 10, reproducible master 10-2, TR

Answers to Facts In Review

1. Leadership is the capacity to direct a group. (Examples are student response.)

2. granted by higher authority, may not be deserved, is never questioned by those with less authority, is generally short-lived, is usually less effective than earned authority

3. granted by subordinates, is deserved, may be questioned by subordinates, tends to be long-lasting, is usually more effective than position authority

4. (List five. See Chart 10-3 on page 204.)

5. (List two:) seating arrangement, room temperature, lighting, room size, room location (Students may justify other answers.)

6. (List four:) more self-esteem, better understanding of others and respect for their differences, improved communication and relationship skills, more able to work easily with people of diverse backgrounds, greater job satisfaction, pride in a job well done

7. (List three:) attends meetings, learns parliamentary procedure, serves on a committee, supports/participates in organization activities, holds an office

8. to reinforce and expand what is learned in the classroom and on the job

9. (List five:) Business Professionals of America; DECA-An Association of Marketing Students; Future Business Leaders of America; National FFA Organization; Family, Career and Community Leaders of America; Health Occupations Students of America; Technology Student Association; SkillsUSA

10. Employers seek employees with the strong leadership and teamwork skills that career and technical student organizations help develop.

Developing Your Academic Skills

1. **Language Arts.** Using Internet or print sources, research how communication skills improve group dynamics. Write a report of your findings. Give an oral presentation of your report in class.

2. **Science.** Working in a group, prepare a research project involving future trends in Science-related careers. Elect a team leader for your group. After the project is finished, hold a group discussion about leadership in relation to the success of your project.

3. **Social Studies.** List at least three examples of recent civic activities conducted by student groups. Write a brief essay on how these activities benefit the community.

Information Technology Applications

1. Using the Internet, explore the Web sites of the career and technical student organizations listed in this chapter. Choose the organization you are most interested in and write a one-page report based on your findings.

2. Using the Internet, research famous leaders and qualities that made them great leaders. Prepare a presentation of your findings.

Applying Your Knowledge and Skills

1. **Academic Foundations.** Find a story in the local newspaper that involves a team and discusses the roles of each team member.

2. **Problem Solving and Critical Thinking.** Contact a member of a team or organization in your school of which you are not a member. Discuss the group dynamics of that organization.

3. **Leadership and Teamwork.** Working with two classmates, develop a list of ways a person with position authority can make the transition to earned authority.

4. **Systems.** Become an active member in an organization and take a leadership role, either as an officer or as a contributing member of a committee.

5. **Employability and Career Development.** Join an organization and compete in a leadership or skills competition.

6. **Communications.** Write a short story on being a contributing member or leader of a nonschool organization.

Developing Workplace Skills

List the traits you already possess as a productive member of a team, then list the traits you want to develop or improve. Explain how you lead (or would lead) a team effectively by listing the leadership traits you already possess. Also list the leadership traits you want to develop or improve. Prepare a one-page chart with four columns to list the traits in each category.

Identify one or more groups that can help you develop the traits you lack or need to improve. Explain how these groups can help in a brief written report. Give both pages to a trusted teacher or counselor and ask for a confidential review. Can the reviewer recommend any other traits to list or groups to explore? Record the reviewer's recommendations and refer to your lists as needed.

11

Participating in Meetings

Key Terms

parliamentary procedure

bylaws

quorum

standing committees

special committees

main motion

secondary motion

Chapter Objectives

After studying this chapter, you will be able to

- **identify** reasons for meetings.
- **explain** the order of business most organizations follow.
- **describe** the difference between a main motion and a secondary motion.
- **demonstrate** how to make, amend, and table a motion.
- **analyze** the two methods most groups use to nominate and elect officers.

Reading Advantage

Take time to reread sentences or paragraphs that cause confusion or raise questions. Rereading will clarify content and strengthen your understanding of key concepts.

Achieving Academic Standards

English Language Arts

- Read print and non-print texts to acquire new information and to respond to the needs and demands of society and the workplace. (IRA/NCTE, 1)
- Apply strategies to comprehend, interpret, evaluate, and appreciate texts. (IRA/NCTE, 3)
- Develop an understanding of and respect for diversity in language use across cultures. (IRA/NCTE, 9)
- Use spoken, written, and visual language to accomplish their purposes. (IRA/NCTE, 12)

Key Concepts

- Meetings are held to conduct the business of an organization or company. Parliamentary procedure is used to conduct the most important meetings.

- Meetings can be more efficient and productive when group members are aware of the procedures for conducting meetings.

- Standing committees are permanent committees within an organization, while special committees are created for a specific purpose.

- Organizations usually nominate and elect new officers once a year.

- When attending work meetings, be prepared and have any questions well thought-out.

Thinking It Through

Why is it important for the leader of an organization to know how to conduct meetings?

If you have ever been a member of an organization, committee, or group, you may have noticed that many group meetings are conducted in similar ways. Most organizations base their meetings on what is known as **parliamentary procedure**. This refers to an orderly way of conducting a meeting and discussing group business. The purpose of parliamentary procedure is to help groups conduct meetings in an efficient and fair manner.

Why Have Meetings?

Meetings of school organizations have two important purposes. Developing socialization skills is one purpose. The other purpose is to conduct the business of the organization.

In the workplace, meetings are held only for business reasons. Some of the reasons may include deciding how to divide the department workload, brainstorming new ideas, and updating staff on important events. This type of meeting is commonly referred to as a *casual meeting*, where strict guidelines are not followed. However, it costs the company money every time a meeting is held. Workers are pulled away from their jobs and not accomplishing work. As a result, everyone at a work-related meeting is expected to stay alert, make appropriate contributions, and not waste time. Knowing how to conduct meetings efficiently helps to achieve these goals.

Parliamentary procedure is used to conduct the organization's most important meetings. These include meetings with stockholders or the board of directors and other meetings in which the group's decisions must be recorded.

Parts of a Formal Meeting

1. Call to order
2. Reading and approving of minutes
3. Reports of officers
4. Standing committee reports
5. Special committee reports
6. Unfinished business
7. New business
8. The program
9. Announcements
10. Adjournment

11-1

Learning parliamentary procedure can help you become a more active group member.

Order of Business

Many organizations follow a similar procedure for conducting meetings. This procedure or order of business is based on *Robert's Rules of Order*, the famous book on parliamentary procedure. The order of business usually follows the pattern shown in 11-1, unless otherwise specified in the organization's bylaws. The **bylaws** are rules and regulations that govern the organization.

All members of the organization have a right to participate in each meeting. In order to understand parliamentary procedure and participate in this type of meeting, you need to be familiar with the terms in 11-2. When group members understand the meanings of these words, meetings can proceed much more smoothly and productively.

Terms Used in Parliamentary Procedure

Adjourn—To end a meeting

Agenda—A list of things to be done and discussed at a meeting

Amend the motion—To change the wording of a motion that has been made

Aye—The formal term for yes (pronounced eye)

Bylaws—The rules and regulations that govern the organization

Chair—The presiding officer at a meeting, such as the president or chairperson

Debate—To speak for or against a motion. Every member has a right to debate an issue

Majority—At least one more than half of the members present at the meeting

Minutes—A written record of the business covered at a meeting

Motion—A recommendation by a member that certain action be taken by the group

Nay—The formal term for no

Quorum—The number of members who must be present to legally conduct business at a meeting

Second the motion—The approval of a motion by another member

Table the motion—To delay making a decision on a motion

The floor—The right to speak in a meeting without interruption from others

11-2

The terms used in parliamentary procedure date back to medieval England.

Resource

Understanding Parliamentary Procedure, reproducible master 11-1, TR

Resource

Terms Used at Meetings, Activity A, WB

Call to Order

The president or presiding officer of the group calls the meeting to order. He or she does this by rapping a gavel on a wooden block and saying, "The meeting will now come to order."

To proceed with the business part of the meeting, there must be a quorum present. A **quorum** is a majority of members or the number of members stated in the rules of the group.

Reading and Approving Minutes

After calling the meeting to order, the president asks the secretary to read the minutes of the previous meeting. The secretary stands and reads the minutes, 11-3. The president sits during the reading of the minutes.

After the reading, the president stands and says, "You have heard the minutes of the previous meeting. Are there any corrections or additions?" At this point, any member may stand and explain corrections or additions that need to be made to the

11-3

In a formal meeting, the person who has the floor usually stands.

minutes. If there are no corrections, the president will say, "The minutes stand approved as read." If there are corrections and they are made, the president will then say, "The minutes stand approved as corrected."

Reports of Officers

At this time, the president calls on the vice-president, secretary, and treasurer to give any reports they may have. Often, the only officer who reports at every meeting is the treasurer. The purpose of the treasurer's report is to inform the officers and members of the group's financial status. The report should include any expenses paid since the last meeting, any income taken in, and the balance in the treasury. The balance is the amount of money that exists in the group's account.

Standing Committee Reports

After the reports of officers, the president calls on each chairperson of the standing committees for a progress report. **Standing committees** are the permanent committees of the group such as the membership committee and the program committee. These committees are identified in the organization's bylaws.

Special Committee Reports

Reflect Further

Why do you think it is important for a committee to report to the group at every meeting?

While standing committees are permanent, **special committees** are established for a specific purpose or a short period. Examples of special committees are a homecoming parade float committee and a spring picnic committee.

A special committee has a certain job to do. After the committee completes its job and properly reports it to the group, the committee disbands. During the life of the committee, however, the chairperson is asked to report on their progress at every group meeting.

Unfinished Business

The president starts this part of the meeting by asking, "Are there any items of unfinished business that need to be discussed today?" Unfinished business might include motions that have been tabled.

Suppose at the last meeting there was a motion to sell candy as a fund-raising project. However, there was not enough time to discuss the motion and vote on it, so the motion was tabled. Discussing and voting on the motion to sell candy as a fund-raising project, therefore, is unfinished business.

New Business

At this point in the meeting, the president says, "The next order of business is new business. Is there any new business?" New business includes such things as discussing future group activities, setting dates for activities, and presenting bills for payment. From this discussion, special committees may be formed to plan special activities. If decisions are not made on items of new business, they are usually discussed at the next meeting as unfinished business.

The Program

At this time, the president says, "The program committee will now present the program." The president calls on the program committee chairperson who introduces the speaker or the program presentation. At the end of the program, the program committee chairperson thanks the speaker or participants. Then he or she returns the meeting to the president.

To prevent wasting the time of program speakers and presenters, some groups have their programs right after the call to order. Then their business meetings follow. This, too, is an acceptable order of business, 11-4.

Photo courtesy of Lloyd Wolf for SkillsUSA

11-4

The program speaker or presentation may follow the call to order or new business.

Announcements

Following the program, the president should ask, "Are there any announcements?" This is the time to announce the scheduled date and time of the next meeting and to remind members of any special activities occurring before the next meeting. Any type of announcement can be made, such as a thank-you to a committee for doing a good job. Sometimes refreshments are served after the meeting. They, too, should be announced.

Adjournment

In order for the president to end the meeting, there must be a motion from one of the members to adjourn. The president can also ask for a motion to adjourn. After a motion and a second to the motion, the president declares the meeting adjourned.

Motions

Members of a group are responsible for making motions and discussing them. There are two types of motions—a main motion and a secondary motion.

A **main motion** is a suggestion for the group members to consider. It includes one item of business. The requirements for a main motion are as follows:

- It must be made at a time when no other business is before the meeting and in proper order of business. It must also be made by a member who has the floor.

- It must be seconded by another member.

- It must be stated by the chair.
- It may always be discussed.
- It must be handled in a manner acceptable to the group.

A **secondary motion** is one that can be made while a main motion is being considered. The purpose of a secondary motion is to amend the main motion or postpone action on the motion. Secondary motions made while discussing the main motion must be voted on before voting on the main motion.

Making a Motion

Here is an example of the proper way to make a motion. Amy thinks it would be a good idea for her group to have a fund-raising project to increase the amount of money available to spend on group activities. At the next meeting when the president asks if there is any new business, Amy stands up and says, "Madame President."

The president recognizes Amy by calling her name, "Amy."

Amy says, "I move that we have a fund-raising project to make more money available for group activities."

Kevin, another group member, agrees and says, "I second the motion."

Then the president says, "It has been moved by Amy and seconded that we have a fund-raising project to make more money available for group activities. Is there any discussion?"

As the presenter of the motion, Amy explains why she thinks the group needs more money in its budget. Then other members comment about the motion. Individually, they stand, address the president, are recognized, and voice their opinions.

11-5

To vote in favor of a motion, members raise their hands or say "aye."

When the comments end, the president asks, "Is there any further discussion?" If no more speakers rise, the president calls for a vote by saying, "We will now vote on the motion to have a fund-raising project. All in favor of the motion say 'aye' (or raise your hand)." See 11-5. The president counts the *yes* votes. "Those opposed say 'no' (or raise your hand)." The president counts again. "The ayes have it. The motion to have a fund-raising project passes."

Amending a Motion

Suppose Randy, a member of Amy's group, is not exactly satisfied with Amy's motion. He is in favor of having a fund-raising project, but he feels all the money earned should be used toward the group's end-of-the-year banquet. During the discussion of the main motion, Randy decides to amend the motion. He stands and says, "Madame President." After being recognized by the president, Randy continues, "I move to amend the motion by changing the words *group activities* to *the end-of-the-year banquet*." Barbara, the secretary, seconds the motion.

Extend Your Knowledge

Committee Meetings

Before each committee meeting is over, there should be a review or summary of the items discussed. After the meeting is adjourned, the chairperson prepares a written committee report and presents the report at the next chapter meeting.

The president handles this secondary motion just as she did the main motion. She says, "It has been moved by Randy and seconded that the pending motion be amended by changing the words *group activities* to *the end-of-the year banquet*. Is there any discussion?" The group can then discuss their views on this motion. After the discussion, the president calls for a vote on the amendment.

The amendment is always dealt with prior to taking action on the main motion. If the amendment passes, the issue before the group is the motion as amended. If the amendment does not pass, the issue is the original motion.

Tabling a Motion

Tabling a motion is another secondary motion that can be made. The purpose of this motion is to postpone the group from making a decision on the main motion. A member might make this motion because he or she feels the motion would have a better chance of passing at a later date. A member might also table a motion if the business meeting is running long.

The motion to table a motion is not debatable. Consequently, the president states the motion and goes straight to a vote. Again, the majority vote rules.

Committees

The work done by committees is a very important part of an organization, 11-6. In fact, most groups depend on their committees to plan and initiate all the activities.

Committee chairpersons are either elected by the group or appointed by the president. In certain cases, some are elected while others are appointed. The method for determining chairpersons is described in a group's bylaws.

Once elected or appointed, each chairperson asks two or more people to serve on the committee. When a committee is formed, the chairperson arranges a place and time for a meeting. At the first meeting

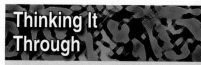

Thinking It Through

Explain how a group member makes a motion.

Note

Share the three ways to properly amend a motion: inserting or adding, striking out, and striking out and inserting.

Activity

Have students review the constitution and bylaws of one of their student organizations to determine how committee chairpersons are selected.

11-6

Committees may need to meet regularly after school to plan and discuss upcoming events.

In the Real World

A Speech or a Tour?

Your group has decided to organize a professional development activity for its members. Professional development activities will help members enhance their employability skills. Some possible professional development activities include listening to invited speakers, attending state and national conferences, participating in leadership and skill development activities, and visiting workplace sites.

Gustavo Cavallaro, the president of your organization, has called for a meeting of the membership today after school. It is rumored some members of your organization want to invite the president of Jogalong, Inc., a manufacturer of popular sports apparel, to speak at the next scheduled meeting. You and some other members would prefer to tour the Jogalong factory where the apparel is made. You see this as a better learning opportunity. Therefore, you and your friends decide to be ready with a well-thought recommendation to have a fund-raiser to cover the expenses of transportation to tour Jogalong's factory.

After discussing what needs to be done, your group realizes at least two transactions must take place at the meeting this afternoon. First of all, you or a fellow member must make a motion that a tour of Jogalong, Inc. be planned rather than a speech from the company president. Secondly, you need to be prepared to propose an activity to raise the funds for transportation to Jogalong's factory.

Between classes, you check with Gustavo and find out the rumor is true. You quickly let the other members who prefer the tour know that you want to meet during lunch hour. During that time you will plan how to bring your tour idea to the floor for discussion.

Questions to Discuss

1. How could you persuade a majority of members to vote favorably for the tour?
2. Should you be prepared to list the necessary steps to secure transportation?
3. What would you recommend to raise the money needed for transportation to the Jogalong factory?

Resource

Case Study: The Drama Club Meeting, reproducible master 11-2, TR

the chairperson explains what the committee is expected to do and asks for suggestions from the members. Every member should feel free to participate and discuss options for the committee. However, committee members should talk about the tasks of the committee and not stray from the subject. Part of the job of the chairperson is to guide the discussion and keep the committee focused on the business at hand.

Reflect Further

Why do you think active committees are important to the success of an organization?

Electing Officers

Most groups nominate and elect new officers once a year. The method of nominating officers is outlined in a group's bylaws. Organizations usually nominate officers by one of two methods: accepting nominations from the floor or appointing a committee to nominate a list of candidates.

Nominations from the floor are made by a member simply saying, "I nominate Li Wen for president." (Nominations do not need to be seconded.) The chairperson waits for further nominations. After waiting a reasonable length of time, the chair asks if there are any further nominations. If there are none, he or she declares the nominations closed for the office of president and proceeds to the next office. When there is a large group participating, it is customary to have a motion to close the nominations. The motion requires a two-thirds vote.

Other groups have a nominating committee prepare a list of candidates to present to the group. Some groups have the committee select only one person for each office, while others have at least two people nominated. On the day of the election, the committee presents the candidates to the group. After the nominations have been presented, the president will usually ask, "Are there any further nominations from the floor?" Therefore, it is still possible for members to make nominations from the floor even if a committee prepares a list of candidates. Usually, however, no further nominations are made because the committee was assigned to do the job.

Following nominations, the president will then take a vote to determine the new slate of officers. A vote will be held for each office if there is more than one candidate. If there is only one nomination for each office, the president can take a vote for the entire slate of officers. A majority vote will make the candidates official officers.

> **Reflect Further**
>
> How does a group you have participated in accept nominations for officers from the floor?

Participating in Meetings at Work

There will be times meetings will be called by one of your superiors. You may feel the meeting is a waste of time, or you may be looking forward to it. Use the following guidelines when you participate in meetings.

1. Be on time. Being late is a sign of disrespect.

2. Be prepared. Do any necessary homework prior to the meeting. Have any questions well thought-out.

3. Do not monopolize the conversation. There are times to speak and times to listen.

4. Contribute by making statements rather than always asking questions.

5. Do not allow others to intimidate you. Give yourself 'think time' before responding to any personal attacks.

6. Do not chew gum or engage in other similar inappropriate habits.

7. Try to read 'nonverbal' signals accurately. This may require your taking time to get to know the other members in the room fairly well.

8. Turn your cell phone off. You can pick up your messages after the meeting.

9. Never skip a meeting. If you have to be absent, be sure to let the presiding person know in advance.

10. Stick to the topic. You make notes to yourself regarding unrelated topics to be brought up at another time.

Resource

Organization Constitutions and Bylaws, Activity C, WB

Enrich

In groups of four or five students, role-play a typical committee meeting. Assign each committee a purpose and topic. Have students take turns serving as chair.

Resource

Conducting a Meeting, Activity D, WB

Summary

Meetings are held for several reasons. In the workplace, meetings are always held for business reasons. It is important for all members of the group or organization to have an opportunity to participate.

Parliamentary procedure is a ten-step method used by most organizations in conducting meetings. The presiding officer makes sure the meeting is conducted properly by following this procedure. As group members learn about parliamentary procedure and participate in meetings, they can become more active in their organization.

During a meeting, members make motions to help plan group activities and discuss business. After a member makes a motion, another member can discuss a change to the motion by amending it. Tabling a motion postpones a group decision on the main motion.

Committees play an important part in every organization. Committee members are responsible for planning, discussing, and initiating most of the group's activities.

Most groups nominate and elect officers once a year. Officers are nominated by a nomination from the floor or by a committee appointed to nominate a list of officers. The candidates who receive the majority of votes are then elected to office.

Facts in Review

1. List two reasons for student organization meetings.
2. What is the purpose of parliamentary procedure?
3. What does it mean to have a quorum?
4. Give one example of each: a standing committee and a special committee.
5. How does unfinished business differ from new business?
6. What are the requirements for a main motion?
7. Explain the difference between a main motion and a secondary motion.
8. Which is voted on first—a main motion or a secondary motion?
9. Why might a member move to table a motion?
10. Name the two ways most organizations nominate new officers.

Resource

Review and Study Guide for Chapter 11, reproducible master 11-3, TR

Answers to *Facts In Review*

1. to develop socialization skills, to conduct the business of the organization
2. to conduct meetings and discuss group business in an orderly way
3. to have the number of members necessary to legally conduct group business
4. (List one of each:) standing committee—membership or program committee; special committee—parade float or spring picnic committee (Students may justify other answers.)
5. Unfinished business includes motions that have been tabled, but new business is an issue discussed for the first time.
6. must be made when no other business is under discussion; must be made in the proper order of business; must be made by the member who has the floor; must be seconded by another member; must be stated by the chair; may be discussed; must be handled in a manner acceptable to the group
7. A main motion is an item of business for the group to consider. A secondary motion is made while considering a main motion for the purpose of changing the main motion.
8. secondary motion
9. to postpone a vote until a time when the motion has a better chance of passing; to postpone discussion due to lack of time
10. by accepting nominations from the floor or appointing a committee to nominate a slate of officers

Developing Your Academic Skills

1. **Social Studies.** Working in a group, practice parliamentary procedure. Take turns role-playing the roles of officers giving reports and making and seconding motions. How does parliamentary procedure make speaking out in a group easier? Write a brief essay of your experience.

2. **Language Arts.** Watch the movie *1776*. How did Congress use parliamentary procedure in the film? Write a one-page report comparing and contrasting your understanding of parliamentary procedure to that used in the film. Read your report aloud in class.

Information Technology Applications

1. Design a Web page for a career and technical student organization to promote the group's bylaws as well as a schedule of meetings and events.

2. Use a word processing program to create a template for keeping an organization's meeting minutes organized. Organize a file system for storing the minutes.

Applying Your Knowledge and Skills

1. **Communications.** Obtain and read a copy of the constitution and bylaws of a school organization to which you belong or might like to join. Then answer the following questions:
   A. What is the order of business the organization should follow?
   B. What is a quorum?
   C. What are the organization's standing committees?
   D. How should officers be nominated and elected?
   E. How should committee chairpersons be selected?

2. **Leadership and Teamwork.** Role-play in class the proper way to make a motion and amend a motion. Take turns role-playing the group leader, a member making a motion, and a member amending the motion.

Developing Workplace Skills

Imagine you are presiding over a formal meeting. (If you have already done so, refer to that experience for this exercise.) Explain how you will use (or have used) the resources of time, money, materials, and people efficiently. Summarize your comments on one page and be prepared to report the main points to the class.

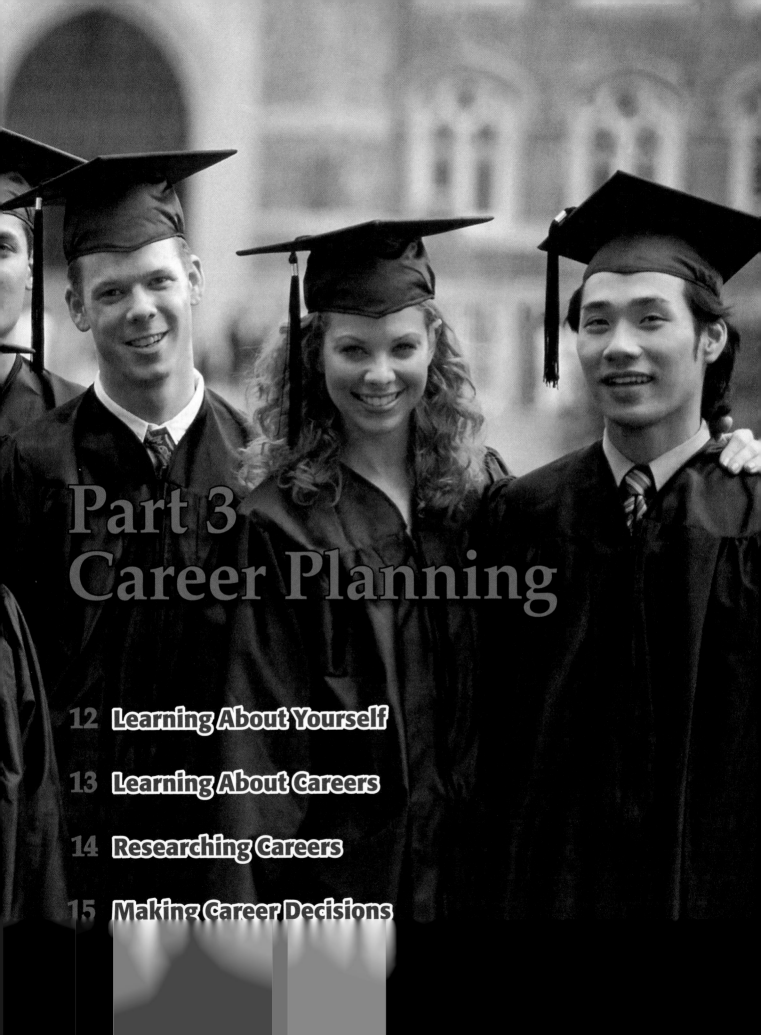

Part 3
Career Planning

12

Learning About Yourself

Key Terms

self-concept

self-assessment

interests

aptitude

ability

personality

habit

values

lifestyle goals

short-term goal

long-term goal

standards

standard of living

resources

human resources

nonhuman resources

Chapter Objectives

After studying this chapter, you will be able to

- **explain** how your self-concept and a self-assessment help you understand yourself better.
- **identify** how personalities may influence life choices.
- **describe** several personality traits and explain how they may influence life choices.
- **analyze** how identifying your values, goals, standards, ethics, and resources can help you understand yourself better.

Reading Advantage

As you read the chapter, record any questions that come to mind. Indicate where the answer to each question can be found: within the text, by asking your teacher, in another book, on the Internet, or by reflecting on your own experiences. Pursue the answers to your questions.

Achieving Academic Standards

English Language Arts

- Read print and non-print texts to acquire new information and to respond to the needs and demands of society and the workplace. (IRA/NCTE, 1)
- Apply strategies to comprehend, interpret, evaluate, and appreciate texts. (IRA/NCTE, 3)
- Develop an understanding of and respect for diversity in language use across cultures. (IRA/NCTE, 9)
- Use spoken, written, and visual language to accomplish their purposes. (IRA/NCTE, 12)

Key Concepts

- Your self-concept is greatly influenced by your personal beliefs and decision-making skills.

- Completing a self-assessment can help you identify your interests, aptitudes, and abilities.

- Knowing your personality will make it easier to establish career goals that are comfortable for you.

- Being aware of your values enables you to make lifestyle choices more easily.

- Your standards and resources can help you reach your goals.

Activity

Make a list of the positive characteristics that make you unique. Identify the characteristics you do not possess now but hope to add to the list someday.

Resource

Choosing a Career? These Pieces Need to Fit, color transparency CT-12, TR

Discuss

Identify a recent positive event at work or school. How did it affect your self-concept?

Resource

How I See Myself, Activity A, WB

Have you taken time to sit quietly by yourself and think about your strengths and weaknesses? Do you know what you want to do in life? How do you define *success* and *happiness*? What are the characteristics and qualities that make you the person you are?

Success and happiness in life involve more than just letting things happen. Success and happiness involve learning about yourself and making the best use of your skills. To be successful you need to know as much as possible about yourself. What skills do you have? What do you do well? What type of work appeals to you? Would you be more successful in a business or an educational setting? Is your personality more suited to becoming a teacher or an engineer?

What are the principles and beliefs that you consider important? Is earning a lot of money important to you? Is having a challenging and responsible job important? Do you want to have a family? In other words, what do you want to achieve and how will you achieve it?

Your answers to these questions are the foundations from which you will make all your decisions. The more you know about yourself, the better prepared you will be to make decisions about your education, career, and lifestyle.

Your Self-Concept

Part of learning about yourself is thinking about your self-concept. **Self-concept** is the mental image you have of yourself, 12-1. As you go through adolescence, you may feel two interacting forces pulling you. One force is the need to become increasingly independent. The other force is a need to feel good about who you are and what you do. Development and constant changing of your self-concept is a lifelong process.

As you attempt to become more independent, your self-concept is very important. As you develop your self-concept, you may be directed in many ways. Your close friends may help you believe in your own ability to cope with pressure. On the other hand, some peer groups can have a negative influence. Classmates who believe it is okay to lie or cheat are examples of negative influences. Your personal beliefs and decision-making skills will greatly influence your self-concept.

For you to develop a strong, positive self-concept, it is important to

- believe in your capabilities
- believe you can control your life
- exercise self-discipline and self-control
- use effective communication skills
- demonstrate flexibility and integrity

You will find that these skills do not develop in isolation. They are dependent on one another. For example, deciding not to experiment with drugs will require you to use your decision-making skills and communication skills. Self-discipline and self-control must be used also.

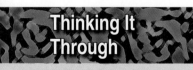
Thinking It Through

When people have a negative self-concept, what might they do to feel better about themselves?

It is important to have a person in your life who exerts a strong positive influence and steers you clear of risky behavior and its pitfalls. This person may be a mentor, coach, big brother or sister, or just a special friend. It is helpful to have basic positive values to rely on and a special person to talk with when you are facing negative temptations. Adolescence is a time when you develop the attitudes, knowledge, and skills that will directly impact your self-concept for the rest of your life.

Self-Esteem

When you have a positive self-concept, you also have confidence and satisfaction in yourself. This is self-esteem. It is a feeling of self-worth. Positive self-esteem means you recognize and value your uniqueness. You are proud of who you are and what you do, 12-2.

Self-esteem is a type of self-respect. People with high self-esteem believe they can handle life's challenges. People with low self-esteem often tend to see themselves as failures and, consequently, avoid everyday challenges.

Photo courtesy of SkillsUSA

12-1

Positive accomplishments lead to positive self-concepts about yourself.

Making a Self-Assessment

Self-assessment is the process of taking stock of your interests, aptitudes, and abilities. Through self-assessment you are better able to plan your future. You will find it easier to select hobbies and elective courses in school. You will also find it easier to make plans for your life. Sometimes self-assessment techniques may involve thinking exercises or written or electronic testing. Whatever method is used, take the process of self-assessment seriously.

What Are Your Interests?

To know and understand yourself, you need to analyze your interests. Your **interests** are the activities, events, and ideas you like. What do you enjoy doing the most? How do you like to spend your time? What are your hobbies? What do you like most in school? What would you do if you had spare time? Make lists for each answer. Your lists of answers should help you identify careers that will be interesting to you.

Sometimes people have a hard time determining their interests. One day a person may have a strong interest in becoming a teacher but later have little interest in teaching. It is important for you to get involved in a variety of positive activities. Interests are learned, so unless you

Resource

Identifying Personal Interests, Activity B, WB

Discuss

Do interests always match a person's talents?

12-2
Pride in your accomplishments is a sign of high self-esteem.

have tried something, you do not know for sure if you have an interest in it. You are more likely to meet people and develop different interests as you experience new activities.

In your work-based learning experience, you may discover new career interests. You may also realize that an earlier career interest now seems uninteresting. Learning about different careers and occupations helps you determine what careers interest you. Job shadowing experiences can also be a good way to help you understand what duties are involved with a job.

If you find it hard to identify your interests, talk to others. Listen to those who know you well. Your friends and family members may be able to help you recall the activities you have enjoyed the most or the projects you have done well. Also ask others about their careers and what they like most and least about them.

Another way to become more aware of your interests is to take an activities preference inventory. Most high school guidance departments are prepared to give preference tests to students. The inventory is designed to help you determine if you prefer working with people, objects, or ideas. You are usually given several activities and asked to select the one activity that appeals to you most. After completing the inventory, you are given a key to interpret the results.

If the inventory indicates you would primarily enjoy working with people, you may want to consider a career in social work, teaching, sales, or health care services. If the inventory points to objects, you might want a job as a fashion illustrator, auto technician, baker, or machine operator. An interest in ideas would suggest careers in publishing, advertising, or marketing. These are only a few examples of the types of careers related to people, objects, and ideas.

Keep in mind that one person or test cannot tell you what to do with your life. They can only provide direction and help you consider possibilities of which you may not have been aware. It is up to you to make the final decisions about your career goals. The information in 12-3 may help you become more aware of your interests and understand how interests relate to choosing a career.

What Are Your Aptitudes?

To be successful in a career, you need to have more than just an interest in it. You also need to have an aptitude for it. An **aptitude** is a person's natural physical and mental talents for learning. If you have an aptitude for a certain skill, you will be able to learn the skill easily and perform the skill well.

Career Interest Concepts	
Concepts	**Examples**
There are many interest areas in a career.	A grain farmer may have an interest in growing vegetables, working for himself, and operating machinery. The farmer might also have an interest in athletics or upholstering, but these interests are not needed in farming.
People have interest areas they do not want to pursue as a career.	An auto technician may have gardening as a hobby but may not want an occupation as a farmer or horticulturist.
Genuine interest is important for success in any career.	Working at something you like is more pleasant.
Everyone has many interests.	A person may have interests in music, athletics, mechanical things, and people.
Different careers may involve similar or the same interests.	A salesperson, politician, teacher, and lawyer are interested in working with people and, in some way, influencing them.

12-3

As you think about your career interests, consider these basic concepts.

Enrich

Invite a guidance counselor to speak about career inventory instruments.

Activity

As a class project, have students select one occupational theme and develop a bulletin board showing all the interrelated careers.

Resource

Case Study: A Writer's Career Choice, reproducible master 12-1, TR

If you have an aptitude for writing, for example, perhaps you could become a successful newspaper writer or Web site contributor. On the other hand, if you do not have this aptitude and still try to become a writer, doing well in that career may forever be a struggle for you. Be realistic about your aptitudes. Become aware of your mental and physical limitations as well as your strengths.

What Are Your Abilities?

You are born with certain aptitudes, but you must develop your abilities. Everyone has an ability of some kind. An **ability** is a task or skill you have already developed. Abilities are learned through training and practice.

Abilities are developed more easily if you have related aptitudes. For example, if you have physical aptitudes for rhythm and coordination, you will probably excel quickly in a ballroom dancing class. If you have very little aptitude for dancing, hard work and genuine interest can help you overcome low aptitudes and develop abilities. By taking dancing lessons on a regular basis and practicing dancing, you can develop the ability to dance.

Your interests, aptitudes, and abilities all need to be considered in career planning. Most people are usually interested in the activities they do best, but sometimes that may not be the case. A person may want to become a professional basketball player but not have the physical aptitude for the sport. Sometimes a person may have the ability to play a musical instrument but not have the interest to do so. The ideal situation is to have the mental and physical aptitudes and abilities that relate to a career that interests you, 12-4.

Thinking It Through

Why do you need to consider your interests, aptitudes, and abilities when career planning?

Extend Your Knowledge

Aptitude Tests

To learn more about your aptitudes, ask your guidance teacher if your school gives any aptitude tests such as the General Aptitude Test Battery (GATB). By taking these tests, you will get a better idea of the kinds of careers in which you have the best chances for success.

12-4

This worker combined his interest in helping people with his therapy skills and became a physical therapist.

Resource

Your Personality and Career Choices, reproducible master 12-2, TR

Activity

Schedule yourself to take an aptitude test if you have not done so recently.

Resource

Identifying Your Personality Traits, Activity C, WB

Your Personal Characteristics

Your personal characteristics make you distinct and separate from everyone else. These characteristics are a combination of your personality traits and your behavioral habits.

Personality Traits

Reflect Further

How do you think others would describe your personality? Is it possible for a person to completely change his or her personality?

Everyone has a personality. **Personality** influences how a person thinks and feels. It influences how you interact with different people in different situations. Your personality even influences the way other people feel about you.

Different careers require different personality traits. That is why it is important to consider your personality when establishing your career goals. Suppose a person has a quiet, reserved personality and likes to spend a lot of time alone reading. This person probably would not enjoy a career in sales. Being successful in sales requires an outgoing personality and spending much time talking with others. Knowing your personality will make it easier to establish career goals that are comfortable to you. See 12-5 for a list of personality traits and some career areas that complement each.

Habits

When you do something the same way every time it is called a **habit**. Your daily life includes many habits, such as the way you stand, sit, talk, walk, and gesture when speaking. The habits you form are a part of your personality, and they influence the way others see you.

Habits can be good or bad. For example, arriving to work and school on time every day is a good habit. Being late frequently is a bad habit. It is wise to examine your habits periodically. Do you have good grooming habits? Do you have annoying mannerisms? What new habits would you like to establish? What old habits would you like to change? See 12-6.

Personality and Careers	
Personality Trait	**Ideal Career Area**
Helpful	Food, hotel, and passenger services
Artistic	Decorating, creative writing, performing
Detail-oriented	Reporting, bookkeeping, engineering
Enterprising	Sales, promotions, demonstrations
Questioning	Inspections, research, repair services
Protective	Child care, law enforcement, emergency services
Social	Teaching, interviewing, coaching

12-5
You will be happier if you select a career that suits your personality traits.

Your Values

Values are the principles and beliefs that you consider important. The values you have influence your decisions and actions. That is why it is important for you to become aware of them. To most people, friendship, honesty, good health, and compassion are important. Education,

12-6
Food habits are some of the hardest habits to change.

Activity

Identify five career areas you believe fit well with your personality.

Resource

Matching Traits and Abilities to Jobs, Activity D, WB

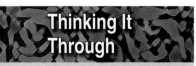

Thinking It Through

How can your habits have a negative or positive influence on the way others see you?

Enrich

Develop a list of eight values you believe everyone should possess. Discuss in class.

Discuss

Would you feel comfortable working with employees whose values and ethics were completely different from yours?

Reflect

Your values are subject to change over time. How have yours changed?

popularity, new cars, a happy family life, and money are also important to many people. Examine *what* is important to you and *why*. Identifying the ideals and objects that are important to you will help you develop your career goals, 12-7.

For instance, being able to wear blue jeans and casual clothes to work may be important to you. Then you probably would not be happy in a situation where suits or dress clothes are required. If you prefer a quiet, comfortable environment, you would probably dislike a noisy, bustling factory.

Identify your values. Then rank them in order of importance. Your values guide your behavior and help you develop a sense of direction in your life. Being aware of them will also enable you to make lifestyle choices more easily. For example, suppose you list a challenging job and a well-paying job as two of your values. However, you rank a challenging job near the top of your list and a well-paying job lower down. Therefore, you could probably conclude that a challenging job would be more important to you than a boring job with higher pay.

Ethics

Have you ever heard people say, "She is not ethical" or "He lacks basic ethics"? They are referring to the set of moral values that guide the person's conduct. It is important to remember that the ethics of individuals determines the ethics of a group.

When a person calls in sick to school on a sunny spring day, takes credit for another student's work, or lies to a friend, the ethics of that person are not positive. It may be said the person's behavior is unethical.

Several things influence the ethics of people. School pressures, family demands, work conditions, finances, peer pressure, and even goals may influence ethics. The way people handle these influences determines their ethics.

12-7

If you value spending time with young children, you would probably enjoy a career working with or teaching children.

In the Real World

Reporting Travel Expenses

Juliet is going on a business trip. It is a good opportunity for her to find new clients for her company and enjoy herself at the same time. She realizes the importance of doing a good job, but if she spends too much, she may upset her boss and get stuck with the bill. It is very important for Juliet to abide by the company's policy on travel expenses.

Juliet also has to take a mental inventory of her own values and ethics. She knows these will affect how she reports her travel expenses.

While most companies do not object to employees rounding up expenses to the nearest dollar, they consider it dishonest to turn in a receipt for an expense an employee did not have. For example, Juliet's employer says she is allowed to spend $32 on dinner. She knows it is dishonest to turn in a receipt for the entire $32 if she just grabs a hamburger and cola. In some restaurants, Juliet will be offered the temptation to cheat. Some eating establishments present the customer with the actual bill, along with a blank bill on which the customer may write any amount.

On her trip, Juliet meets an old friend from another company and they decide to go out together to eat. After the meal when the checks are presented, Juliet learns that her friend Cara is not required to turn in receipts for meals. Cara is simply reimbursed a certain fixed amount per day.

Cara pays for her meal, knowing that her reimbursement is automatic. Juliet considers taking Cara's receipt and turning it in with her expense account. The boss will probably think that Juliet was being a good salesperson by taking a potential client to lunch. In this way, Juliet will make some extra money.

Juliet does not tell Cara her plan, but Cara knows and simply hands her receipt to Juliet. Before heading back to their hotels, the friends promise to meet again tomorrow.

"Let's go to a real expensive place tomorrow," Juliet said. "We deserve it."

"Can you afford it?" Cara asked.

"I'll find a way," replied Juliet.

Questions to Discuss

1. Is Juliet, Cara, or both guilty of unethical behavior?
2. If ethical behavior had been used, how would this story change?
3. What should Juliet do when she makes out her expense account after the trip?

When conflicts of ethics arise, it is helpful to carefully study all the pros and cons of different possible reactions to a situation. Take a long-term view and decide what decisions or behaviors are best for you. What actions will you take to resolve the conflict? Will your actions conflict with your conscience? Are these actions acceptable by society's standards?

Your Goals

Goals are what you want to attain. A person's goals are usually based on his or her values. For example, John likes listening to music on a good stereo system. However, John's system does not work very well anymore. John has set a goal to buy a new stereo system in a year by saving a portion of each paycheck. As this example shows, goals and values are related. Values express thoughts and feelings and goals put them into action. Like values, goals influence and shape the decisions you make.

Activity

Discuss the actions that demonstrate a willingness to learn. Identify one benefit for taking such actions.

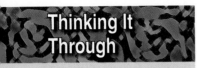

Thinking It Through

Why do values and goals differ for different people? Why do values and goals usually change as people grow older?

Have you thought about your goals? What do you want to do with your life? What do you want to accomplish?

The first step in setting and achieving goals is to make a list of what you really want from life. These are your **lifestyle goals**. Deciding where you want to live, if you want a family, and how much money you need to make to be comfortable are all examples of lifestyle goals. Also be sure to include both short-term goals and long-term goals. A **short-term goal** is a goal you want to reach tomorrow, next week, or within a few months. Getting an *A* on your next English assignment, becoming an officer in a school organization, and improving your tennis game are examples of short-term goals. A **long-term goal** is a goal that may take several months or years to achieve. Completing school, starting a career, and buying a car are examples of long-term goals. See 12-8.

One important factor to remember when setting goals is to be realistic. Do you really want to reach that goal? Is it possible for you to reach? What will it cost in terms of time, energy, and money? Is the goal in keeping with your values? Setting well-defined, realistic goals can help you develop a sense of direction and purpose in life.

Standards

Standards are accepted levels of achievement. There are standards for dress, cleanliness, food and drug safety, and school grades, to name a few examples. Electrical products must meet certain safety standards before they are given a seal of approval. People in professions such as law and medicine must meet certain standards before they can practice their professions, 12-9.

Individuals also have their own personal standards, called standards of living. A person's **standard of living** refers to the goods and services considered essential for living. For some, an elegant residence, gourmet food, and frequent world travel are essential. For many people, their standard of living consists of a comfortable home, occasional restaurant meals, and weekend trips close to home.

Standards are closely related to values and goals. You will have high standards for whatever you consider important and set goals to achieve. For example, if you place importance on making the school honor roll and set aside time to study regularly, your standards for grades would be high. On the other hand, if you do not care much about clothes and pay little attention to the quality and style of clothing you wear, your standards for clothes would not be high.

What are your standards regarding work? Do you strive to do your very best on the job or do you just put in your hours? Do you have high standards for the way you look and dress? What are your standards for education? Knowing your own standards and what you expect from life can help you understand yourself better. This can help you establish satisfying lifestyle goals.

12-8

Getting married after you complete your education and begin your career is an example of a long-term goal.

Enrich

Read the biography of a prominent person and determine how that person set goals.

Activity

Write down two long-term goals. Then list short-term goals that will help you reach them.

Resources

Resources are all the things you have or can use to help you reach your goals. To know yourself well, you need to recognize your resources. What resources do you have? What are your human resources? What are your nonhuman resources? **Human resources** are the resources you have within yourself such as skills, knowledge, and experience. See 12-10. Determination, motivation, and imagination are also valuable human resources. **Nonhuman resources** generally are the material things you have or can use to achieve goals such as money, tools, clothes, and community resources. Time is also a nonhuman resource.

Identifying your resources helps you identify your strengths and weaknesses. For example, if you know you have artistic talents (a human resource), you will probably be successful pursuing a career in art. If you want to go to college or postsecondary training but do not have enough money (a nonhuman resource), you may apply for a scholarship, get a loan, or work part-time. Knowing your strengths and limitations can help you set realistic goals for your life and career.

12-9
Paramedics must pass certification tests to assure they are skilled in giving aid to people in life-threatening situations.

12-10
Your skills, knowledge, and experiences are valuable human resources.

Reflect Further

What do you consider your most valuable human and nonhuman resources?

Photo courtesy of the National FFA Organization

Resource

Values, Goals, Standards, and Resources, Activity E, WB

Resource

A Learning Review, Activity F, WB

Summary

Learning all about yourself can help you make decisions about the career that is right for you. As you learn about yourself, your interests, aptitudes, abilities, personality, habits, and values, you will be able to make decisions about your life, education, and career.

Before you choose a career, you need to know and understand yourself. You can start by looking at your interests. What do you enjoy doing the most? To be successful in a career, you need to have more than an interest in it. You need to consider your aptitude or ability to perform the duties required for that career as well.

You also need to consider your personality when choosing a career. Matching your personality with a suitable career will increase your chances for success and happiness on the job.

Knowing your values can help you make choices in your career and set your lifestyle goals. You can use your values to help guide your behavior and give some direction in your career choice. Once you know your values, you can also use them to help you set goals. The way you achieve your goals will depend on your own personal standards and the resources available to you.

Facts in Review

1. Name four perceptions or skills important for a positive self-concept.
2. Why is it important for you to learn as much about yourself as possible at this point in your life?
3. What is *self-assessment*?
4. What two things can you do to help you identify your interests?
5. What is an activities preference inventory?
6. Explain the difference between an aptitude and ability. Give an example of each.
7. How is it possible to overcome low aptitudes?
8. Why is it important to consider your personality when choosing a career?
9. How do values influence personal behavior?
10. What determines the ethics of a group?
11. How are standards closely related to values and goals?
12. What nonhuman resource does everyone have in common?

Resource

Review and Study Guide for Chapter 12, reproducible master 12-3, TR

Answers to *Facts In Review*

1. (List four:) Believe in your capabilities; believe you can control your life; exercise self-discipline and self-control; use effective communication skills; demonstrate flexibility and integrity.
2. The more a person understands himself or herself, the better prepared he or she is to make decisions about a career and the future.
3. The process of taking stock of your interests, aptitudes, and abilities.
4. Talk to others; take an activities preference inventory.
5. a test designed to help a person determine a preference for working with people, objects, or ideas
6. Aptitudes are natural talents, while abilities are performance skills that may have been learned. (Student response for example.)
7. through hard work and genuine interest
8. because different careers require different personalities
9. Values determine what a person considers important, which guides one's actions.
10. the ethics of the individuals in the group
11. The things you consider important and set goals to achieve are the things for which you will have high standards.
12. time

Developing Your Academic Skills

1. **Language Arts.** Choose a character from a story or novel you are currently reading. Write a report on how the character's self-concept influences his or her successes or failures.
2. **Social Studies.** With a partner, debate how ethical and unethical behavior played a part in American politics in the last 10 years. Should ethics be an issue to consider when electing leaders? Why or why not?

Information Technology Applications

1. Using a software program of your choice, create a chart of your interests, aptitudes, and abilities. Do your interests complement your aptitudes and abilities? What might the chart indicate about your future careers? Write a brief summary of your findings.
2. Using word-processing software, create an ethics survey. Write a list of questions to ask other students. For example, ask students how they feel about cheating on homework or tests in school. Also question whether students feel stealing products or coming in late to work is cheating on the job. (Make sure the survey forms do not include blanks for names.) Tally the survey results and write a report for the school paper.

Applying Your Knowledge and Skills

1. **Problem Solving and Critical Thinking.** List twelve things you like to do. Beside each activity on your list, note whether it involves mainly people, objects, or ideas. Evaluate your responses to see if you can form any conclusions about your interests and how they might influence your job choices.
2. **Employability and Career Development.** Ask your guidance counselor about taking an aptitude test. If available, take an aptitude test and discuss the results with your counselor.
3. **Ethics and Legal Responsibilities.** Describe how people could show that they place importance on the following: honesty, friendship, education, good health, and compassion.
4. **Systems.** Make a list of your lifestyle goals. Be sure to include several short-term and long-term goals you might want to achieve.
5. **Employability and Career Development.** Make a list of possible careers that would match your interests and aptitudes. Then write down any transferable skills that would correspond to these careers.

Developing Workplace Skills

Write several paragraphs describing yourself by using the following terms: abilities, aptitudes, values, ethics, habits, interests, personality, resources, self-concept, self-esteem, and standards. (You may use singular or plural forms of the terms.) Underline or circle the first use of each term. Share your paper with a trusted teacher, counselor, or friend, and ask for his or her comments.

13

Learning About Careers

Key Terms

myth
logistics
e-marketing
associate degree
bachelor's degree
occupational trends

Chapter Objectives

After studying this chapter, you will be able to

- **identify** myths regarding employment in nontraditional jobs.
- **explain** the differences among the career clusters.
- **describe** the wide range of jobs within career clusters.
- **select** careers and occupations that interest you.
- **list** occupations with the greatest number of job openings and their educational requirements.

Reading Advantage

Describe how this chapter relates to a chapter you read earlier in the semester.

Achieving Academic Standards

English Language Arts

- Read print and non-print texts to acquire new information and to respond to the needs and demands of society and the workplace. (IRA/NCTE, 1)
- Conduct research on issues and interests by gathering, evaluating, and synthesizing data from a variety of sources to communicate discoveries. (IRA/NCTE, 7)
- Use a variety of technological and information processes to gather and synthesize information and to create and communicate knowledge. (IRA/NCTE, 8)

Key Concepts

- Your interests, aptitudes, abilities, values, and goals influence your career choices.

- Myths about employment can put artificial limits on your career choices.

- The career clusters and pathways can help you learn about careers that fit all aspects of who you are and want to become.

- Occupations require different levels of education and training, but those requiring more often pay better.

- You will have an easier time of finding a job if the occupation you want is in demand.

As you learned in Chapter 12, there are many aspects about yourself that can impact your entire life—especially when selecting a career. You might ask yourself "How will my interests, aptitudes, and abilities influence my career choices? What career options fit my abilities, values, and goals for the future?"

When seeking the answers to these questions, it is helpful to reflect on past, current, and future factors that influence career options, 13-1. As you read the following paragraphs, think about your interests, aptitudes, and abilities. How might your values and goals, as well as beliefs and traditions, influence your career choices? How can the career clusters help you find a career that fits?

Traditional and Nontraditional Careers

Reflect Further

What traditions or beliefs do you hold that may influence your career options?

The beliefs and traditions of a society often dictate which groups should hold which jobs. For example, careers involving children and the family were once traditionally reserved for women. Careers that were typical for one gender but not the other are called *nontraditional*. A man working as a nurse and a woman working as a bricklayer are examples of nontraditional careers. In a society that respects equal rights for all workers, job skills are more important than tradition.

There are many myths regarding people employed in nontraditional careers. A **myth** is an unfounded belief or notion. Figure 13-2 examines some of these myths. As you look for a suitable career, it is important to remember that myths place artificial limits on your options. If you can do a job well, employers who focus on job skills, not myths, will welcome you.

Using the Career Clusters

Some of the most important and up-to-date resources to help you make career decisions are the career clusters. As you recall, the career clusters group occupations by common knowledge and skills. While reading about the career clusters and the occupations they include, think about your interests, aptitudes, and abilities. What careers spark your interest? Do they link to interests that ignite your passion? Do these careers fit your aptitudes and abilities? How might certain careers link to your values and goals?

13-1

Reflecting on all aspects of who you are can help you make wise career decisions.

Myths Regarding Employment in Nontraditional Jobs

Myth	Fact
Myth #1: Women in clerical jobs dress so well that surely they make more money than trade workers.	**Fact:** This is not true. Consider the difference in the following entry-level weekly salaries: • Office clerk: $456 • Food service cook: $392 • Receptionist: $440 • Secretary: $528 • Chemical technician: $1,173 • Drafter: $840 • Electrician: $839 • Welder: $604 *Note: While current salaries may differ, pay gaps between positions remain.*
Myth #2: Men aren't nurturing or sensitive enough to work with small children, the elderly, or the sick as caregivers.	**Fact:** Besides the many caring fathers, grandfathers, and brothers who often care for family members, many men are successful elementary school teachers, nurses, paramedics, nursing assistants, and other professional caregivers. (Male caregivers provide excellent role models for young children and help erase many of the negative stereotypes about men.)
Myth #3: Women are not strong enough to work as skilled laborers.	**Fact:** The average woman is strong enough to work as a skilled laborer because modern machinery and tools have made many jobs easier. Also, women can build strength while on these jobs.
Myth #4: Men who work in nontraditional careers aren't very masculine.	**Fact:** Men in nontraditional careers come in all sizes, shapes, and types. They are as manly as men in other career fields.
Myth #5: Work in the trades can be dirty and women don't like to get messy.	**Fact:** Women traditionally do "dirty" jobs such as changing diapers, gardening, and housecleaning.
Myth #6: Men who choose nontraditional careers aren't skilled or strong enough to be employed in traditionally male careers.	**Fact:** Men choose nontraditional careers because of their interests, skills, and abilities. They have the capacity to perform skilled tasks, such as dispensing medicine to the sick, and they work in conditions that require strength, such as lifting nursing home residents.
Myth #7: Women who work in the trades are too rough and tough to be feminine.	**Fact:** Just because a female wears rugged work clothes and gets dirty doesn't mean she is any less feminine.
Myth #8: Men in nontraditional careers earn less money than men employed in traditional careers.	**Fact:** Men in nontraditional careers, especially those who own their own business or work as a supervisor, can earn more than men employed in traditional careers.
Myth #9: Females don't have the math ability for work in the trades.	**Fact:** Using math is not a gender-related activity. Practice and a desire to learn determine how well a person performs math.

13-2

Men and women are pursuing nontraditional careers in great numbers.

Discuss

What aspects about yourself impact your life—especially the career choices you might make?

Discuss

What are some other employment myths you have heard regarding the inability of some people to perform certain jobs?

Resource

The Sixteen Career Clusters, color transparency CT-13, TR

Agriculture, Food & Natural Resources

People who have jobs in this cluster work with food products and processing, power, and structural systems and plants and animals. Careers in natural resources, environmental services, and agribusiness are also included in this cluster.

Fewer jobs involve traditional farming and ranching. Many careers involve working with food science and technology to discover new food sources, analyze food structure and content, and develop new ways to process, preserve, package, and store food. Workers in natural resources focus on improving the present and future quality of life, conserving natural resources, and preserving wildlife. Conservation scientists help solve problems affecting the use of land, water, and air. Foresters plan and supervise the growing, protection, and use of trees. Environmentalists work to resolve

problems related to pollution and hazardous waste disposal. Animal scientists study genetics, nutrition, and reproduction.

Entry-level jobs are available. Although some knowledge and skills are learned on-the-job, many technical jobs require two or more years of advanced training. Professionals, such as engineers and scientists, must have a four-year college degree or beyond.

The demands of an expanding population, globalization, and increasing public awareness on nutrition and diet will result in strong job opportunities in the future. Many of these specialists work for government agencies, such as the U.S. Department of Agriculture, the Environmental Protection Agency, or the National Park Service. Private employers include mining and logging operations, landscapers, and oil companies.

Pathways and Career Options

The Career Clusters icons are being used with permission of the: States' Career Clusters Initiative, 2008, www.careerclusters.org

Food Products and Processing Systems

Agricultural Salesperson ▪ Agricultural Communications Specialist ▪ Business-Educator ▪ Food Scientist ▪ Meat Processor ▪ Toxicologist ▪ Biochemist ▪ Nutritionist ▪ Dietician ▪ Food Broker ▪ Food Inspector ▪ Meat Cutter-Grader ▪ Meat Science Researcher ▪ Food Meal Supervisor ▪ Cheese Maker ▪ Microbiologist ▪ Produce Buyer ▪ Bacteriologist ▪ Food & Drug Inspector ▪ Bioengineer ▪ Biochemist ▪ Food & Fiber Engineer ▪ Food Processor ▪ Storage Supervisor ▪ Fieldhand ▪ Quality Control Specialist

Plant Systems

Bioinformatics Specialist ▪ Plant Breeder & Geneticist ▪ Biotechnology Lab Technician ▪ Soil & Water Specialist ▪ Crop Farm Manager ▪ Agricultural Educator ▪ Plant Pathologist ▪ Aquaculturalist ▪ Botanist ▪ Tree Surgeon ▪ Education & Extension Specialist ▪ Commodity Marketing Specialist ▪ Grain Operations Superintendent ▪ Forest Geneticist ▪ Golf Course Superintendent ▪ Greenhouse Manager ▪ Grower ▪ Farmer ▪ Rancher ▪ Custom Hay & Silage Operator ▪ Agricultural Journalist

Animal Systems

Agricultural Educator ▪ Livestock Producer ▪ Poultry Manager ▪ Equine Manager ▪ Veterinarian ▪ Veterinary Assistant ▪ Feedlot Specialist ▪ Animal Scientist ▪ Embryo Technologist ▪ Livestock Buyer ▪ Wildlife Biologist ▪ Livestock Geneticist ▪ Animal Nutritionist ▪ Dairy Producer ▪ Livestock Inspector ▪ Pet Shop Operator ▪ Feed Sales Specialist ▪ Animal Health Salesperson ▪ Meat Science Researcher ▪ Reproductive Physiologist ▪ Embryo Transfer Technician ▪ USDA Inspector

Power, Structural and Technical Systems

Machine Operator ■ Electronics Systems Technician ■ Agricultural Engineer ■ Agricultural Extension Engineering Specialist ■ Heavy Equipment Maintenance Technician ■ Recycling Technician ■ Waste Water Treatment Plant Operator ■ Parts Manager ■ Welder ■ Machinist ■ Communication Technician ■ GPS Technician ■ Agricultural Applications Software Developer ■ Programmer ■ Computer Service & Technical Support Technician ■ Information Lab Specialist ■ Remote Sensing Specialist

Natural Resource Systems

Cartographer ■ Wildlife Manager ■ Range Technician ■ Ecologist ■ Park Manager ■ Environmental Interpreter ■ Fish & Game Officer ■ Logger ■ Forest Technician ■ Log Grader ■ Pulp & Paper Manager ■ Commercial Fishermen ■ Fishing Vessel Operator ■ Soil Geology Technician ■ Geologist ■ Mining Engineer ■ Fisheries Technician ■ Water Monitoring Technician ■ Hydrologist ■ Fish Hatchery Manager

Environmental Service Systems

Pollution Prevention & Control Manager ■ Pollution Prevention & Control Technician ■ Environmental Sampling & Analysis Scientist ■ Health & Safety Sanitarian ■ Environmental Compliance Assurance Manager ■ Hazardous Materials Handler ■ Hazardous Materials Technician ■ Manager ■ Water Environment Manager ■ Water Quality Manager ■ Waste Water Manager ■ Toxicologist ■ Recycler ■ Solid Waste Technician, Manager, Specialist, or Disposer

Agribusiness Systems

Bank, Insurance Company, or Government Program Field Representative ■ Farm Investment Manager ■ Agricultural Commodity Broker ■ Agricultural Economist ■ Farmer ■ Rancher ■ Feedlot Operator ■ Farm Manager ■ Breeder ■ Dairy Herd Supervisor ■ Agricultural Products Buyer ■ Animal Health Products Distributor ■ Livestock Seller ■ Feed or Farm Supply Store Manager ■ Produce Commission Agent ■ Agricultural Chemical Dealer ■ Chemical Sales Representative

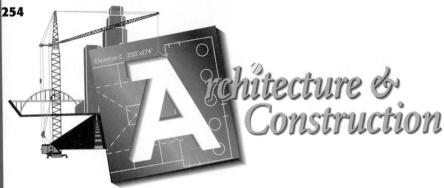

Architecture & Construction

People with careers in architecture and construction are involved in design and pre-construction planning, construction, and maintenance of structures. They may design, build, restore, or maintain homes, bridges, industrial plants, dams, hospitals, highways, and shopping malls. Some careers may involve landscape architecture, urban planning, and interior design.

Architects design the structures to be built. Engineers supervise the building of structures and make sure construction plans are structurally sound. Skilled craft-workers, such as carpenters, bricklayers, roofers, plumbers, and electricians actually build the structures.

You must be licensed before practicing as an architect. After earning a four-year college degree and working as an intern-architect for about three years, you must pass all parts of the Architect Registration Examination (ARE) in order to become licensed.

Community colleges, technical institutes, and career-technical schools offer certificate and degree programs, ranging from one to three years, for many architecture and construction jobs. Architects, engineers, and construction managers require at least a four-year college degree. Specific job requirements may range from on-the-job training to advanced degrees for other occupations in this cluster.

The employment outlook for careers in this cluster remains steady, especially for workers in design and construction. Those who have broad skills in the area of maintenance operations will have favorable job options in a slower-than-average growth area.

Pathways and Career Options

Design and Preconstruction

Architect ▪ Drafter ▪ Regional & Urban Planner ▪ Designer ▪ Industrial Engineer ▪ Materials Engineer ▪ Environmental Designer ▪ Civil Engineer ▪ Programmer▪ Mechanical Engineer ▪ Electrical Engineer ▪ Preservationist ▪ Environmental Engineer ▪ Surveyor ▪ Fire Prevention & Protection Engineer ▪ Cost Estimator ▪ Electrical & Electronic Engineering Technician ▪ Civil Engineering Technician ▪ Environmental Engineering Technician ▪ Surveying & Mapping Technician ▪ Interior Designer ▪ Landscape Designer ▪ Specifications Writer ▪ Building Code Official ▪ Computer Aided Drafter ▪ Renderer ▪ Modeler

Construction

General Contractor & Builder▪ Construction Foreman ▪ Estimator ▪ Project Inspector ▪ Sales & Marketing Manager ▪ Education & Training Director ▪ Safety Director ▪ Construction Inspector ▪ Subcontractor ▪ Field Supervisor ▪ Mason ▪ Iron & Metalworker ▪ Carpenter ▪ Electrician ▪ Boilermaker ▪ Electronic Systems Technician ▪ Carpet Installer ▪ Sheet-Metal Worker▪ Security & Fire Alarm Systems Installer ▪ Concrete Finisher ▪ Tile & Marble Setter ▪ Landscaper ▪ Elevator Installer ▪ Roofer ▪ Painter ▪ Plasterer ▪ Paperhanger ▪ Drywall Installer▪ Plumber ▪ Pipe Fitter ▪ Heating, Ventilation, Air Conditioning, & Refrigeration Mechanic ▪ Electrician

Maintenance and Operations

General Maintenance Contractor ▪ Construction Engineer ▪ Construction Manager ▪ Estimator ▪ Facilities Engineer ▪ Environmental Engineer ▪ Demolition Engineer ▪ Project Inspector ▪ Manufacturer's Representative ▪ Highway Maintenance Worker ▪ Equipment & Material Manager ▪ Maintenance Estimator ▪ Security Controls Manager ▪ Preservationist ▪ Remodeler ▪ Safety Director ▪ Construction Inspector ▪ Service Contractor ▪ System Installer ▪ Electrician ▪ Boilermaker ▪ Cost Estimator ▪ Sheet-Metal Worker ▪ Hazardous Materials Remover ▪ Steamfitter

Arts, A/V Technology & Communications

If you have creative talents along with strong communication, math, and science skills, this may be the career area for you. These diverse career pathways include visual and performing arts, audio and video (A/V) technology, and film. Journalism and broadcasting, telecommunications, and printing technology are other career directions. The job outlook remains steady for the foreseeable future.

People who work with A/V technology may design, install, or operate audio and video equipment. Those who work in journalism and broadcasting prepare and present information about local, state, national, and international events. Jobs in the performing arts range from actors, dancers, and musicians to instructors, playwrights, and scriptwriters. Costume designers plus lighting and stage crews complete the behind-the-scenes work in performing arts.

Those who work with print technology complete many printing-process tasks to transform text and photos into magazines and books. Working with computers and communications equipment is key to telecommunications. Through a variety of art media, visual artists bring concepts, thoughts, and feelings to life.

Preparation for these careers begins early in life and continues through high school and into adult life. It requires self-discipline and hard work. Although most jobs require some training beyond high school, employment requires talent, not just training and years of experience.

Some entry-level jobs require on-the-job training or an apprenticeship. Most technical jobs require one, two, or three years of training at a technical or community college. Careers in management, education, and journalism may require four-year degrees and beyond.

Pathways and Career Options

Audio and Video Technology and Film

Video Systems Technician ■ Video Graphics, Special Effects, & Animation Designer ■ Audio-Video Designer & Engineer ■ Technical Computer Support Technician ■ Audio-Video System Service Technician ■ Audio Systems Technician

Printing Technology

Graphics & Printing Equipment Operator ■ Lithographer & Platemaker ■ Computer Typography & Composition Equipment Operator ■ Desktop Publishing Specialist ■ Web Page Designer

Visual Arts

Commercial Photographer ■ Commercial Interior Designer ■ Residential & Home Furnishings Coordinator ■ Graphic Designer ■ Computer Aided Design Technician ■ Fashion Illustrator ■ Textile Designer ■ Commercial Artist ■ Illustrator ■ Artist ■ Gallery Manager ■ Fashion Designer ■ Curator

Performing Arts

Production Manager (Digital, Video, or Stage) ■ Cinematographer ■ Video Editor ■ Dancer ■ Playwright ■ Screen Writer ■ Screen Editor ■ Script Writer ■ Director & Coach ■ Set Designer & Painter ■ Performer ■ Actors ■ Musician ■ Costume Designer ■ Make-Up Artist ■ Stagecraft Designer & Lighter ■ Stagecraft Sound Effects & Acoustics Coordinator ■ Composer ■ Conductor ■ Music Instructor

Journalism and Broadcasting

Audio & Video Operations ■ Station Manager ■ Radio & TV Announcer ■ Editor ■ Journalist ■ Reporter ■ Broadcast Technician ■ Control Room Technician

Telecommunications

Telecommunication Technician ■ Installer ■ Telecommunication Computer Programmer & Systems Analyst ■ Telecommunication Equipment, Cable, or Line Repairer

Business, Management & Administration

Careers in this cluster involve skills that businesses need to keep productive and running smoothly. Management, business financial management and accounting, and human resources are some career options. Business analysis, marketing, and administration and information support are also included in this cluster. Broad skills in planning, organizing, and evaluating business operations are essential. Businesspeople also need good computer skills, common sense, decision-making skills, and problem-solving abilities.

Business managers form policies and direct the operations of corporations, nonprofit groups, and government agencies. Financial managers and accountants create and use accounting systems to analyze and prepare financial reports. People who work in business analysis find cost-effective ways to do business. They also uphold business values and strategies. Marketing workers may do market research and promote, sell, and maintain products and services. Workers in administration and information support use technology to gather and deliver information and perform other office duties.

Some entry-level jobs may require certification and a two-year or four-year degree. Most jobs in this career cluster require a four-year degree from a college or university. Top managers, financial analysts, and human resources specialists often need advanced degrees beyond their four-year degrees. Work experience is often a requirement in addition to a degree. Business expansion and complexity will result in faster-than-average growth for the careers in this cluster.

Pathways and Career Options

Management

Entrepreneur ■ Chief Executive ■ General Manager ■ Accounting Manager ■ Accounts Payable Manager ■ Assistant Credit Manager ■ Billing Manager ■ Business & Development Manager ■ Compensation & Benefits Manager ■ Credit & Collections Manager ■ Payroll Manager ■ Risk Manager ■ Operations Manager ■ Public Relations Manager ■ Human Resources Manager ■ Management Analyst ■ Facilities Manager ■ Association Manager ■ Meeting & Convention Planner ■ Administrative Services Manager ■ Sports & Entertainment Manager ■ First Line Supervisor ■ Public Relations Specialist ■ Senior Manager ■ Management Trainee

Business Financial Management and Accounting

Accountant ■ Accounting Clerk ■ Accounting Supervisor ■ Adjuster ■ Adjustment Clerk ■ Assistant Treasurer ■ Auditor ■ Bookkeeper ■ Budget Analyst ■ Budget Manager ■ Billing Supervisor ■ Cash Manager ■ Controller ■ Chief Financial Officer ■ Finance Director ■ Certified Public Accountant ■ Accounts Receivable Clerk ■ Cost Accountant ■ Financial Accountant ■ Billing Clerk ■ Payroll Accounting Clerk ■ Merger & Acquisitions Manager ■ Price Analyst ■ Top Collections Executive ■ Top Investment Executive ■ Treasurer

Human Resources

Human Resources Manager ■ Human Resources Coordinator ■ Industrial Relations Director ■ Compensation & Benefits Manager ■ Employee Assistance Plan Manager ■ Training & Development Manager ■ Corporate Trainer ■ Arbitrator ■ Employer Relations Representative ■ Affirmative Action Coordinator ■ Equal Employment Opportunity Specialist ■ Pay Equity Officer ■ Interpreter & Translator ■ Organizational Behaviorist ■ Occupational Analyst ■ Compensation, Benefits, & Job Analyst ■ Human Resources Information Systems Specialist ■ Meeting & Convention Planner ■ Employment Interviewer ■ Personnel Recruiter

Business Analysis

Systems Analyst ■ E-commerce Analyst ■ Requirements Specialist ■ Marketing Analyst ■ Operations Research Analyst ■ Business Consultant ■ Business Analyst ■ Budget Analyst ■ Product Manager ■ Price Analyst

Marketing

Marketing Manager ■ Sales Manager ■ Assistant Store Manager ■ Department Manager ■ Salesperson ■ Customer Service Supervisor ■ Customer Service Clerk ■ Research & Development Manager ■ Small Business Owner & Entrepreneur ■ E-commerce Manager & Entrepreneur ■ Demonstrator & Product Promoter ■ Telemarketer ■ Wholesale & Retail Buyer ■ International Distribution Manager ■ Warehouse Manager ■ Logistics Manager ■ Market Researcher ■ Public Relations Specialist ■ Media Coordinator ■ Graphic Designer ■ Event Manager ■ Distribution Worker ■ Traffic, Shipping, & Receiving Clerk ■ Copywriter

Administration and Information Support

Administrative Assistant ■ Executive Assistant ■ Office Manager ■ Medical Front Office Assistant ■ Information Assistant ■ Desktop Publisher ■ Customer Service Assistant ■ Data Entry Specialist ■ Receptionist ■ Communications Equipment Operator ■ Computer Operator ■ Court Reporter ■ Stenographer ■ Dispatcher ■ Shipping & Receiving Worker ■ Records Processor ■ Medical Transcriptionist ■ Library Assistant ■ Order Processor ■ Word Processor ■ Typist ■ Legal Secretary ■ Paralegal

Education & Training

Do you have the ability to inspire and motivate others? Are you sensitive to their varying needs? If you do, a career in education and training may be an option for you. This career area includes teaching and training, professional support services, administration, and administrative support.

Teaching gives you a chance to influence the lives of many students. Highly skilled educators use a variety of teaching methods to help students achieve. Those who work in professional support services—such as psychology, counseling, or social work—help students meet personal, family, and career needs. Strong leadership and management of day-to-day school activities are important skills for school administrators.

Highly skilled teachers spend many of their nonteaching hours upgrading their teaching skills in order to enhance student performance. When compared to many other professional jobs, such as doctors or lawyers, wages for careers in this cluster are often lower. However, benefits and job security are very good in comparison to many other careers. Professionals in this career cluster work in either public or private schools.

Although some entry-level jobs exist, most jobs in this cluster require a four-year-college degree and licensing or certification. Some jobs in professional support services and administration require advanced college degrees. The high demand for highly skilled education and training professionals leads to an excellent job outlook.

Pathways and Career Options

Administration and Administrative Support

Superintendent ■ Principal ■ Administrator ■ Supervisor & Instructional Coordinator ■ Education Researcher ■ Test Measurement Specialist ■ College President ■ Dean ■ Curriculum Developer ■ Instructional Media Designer

Professional Support Services

Psychologist (Clinical, Developmental, or Social) ■ Social Worker ■ Parent Educator ■ Counselor ■ Speech & Language Pathologist ■ Audiologist

Teaching and Training

Preschool Teacher ■ Kindergarten Teacher ■ Elementary Teacher ■ Secondary Teacher ■ Special Education Teacher ■ Teacher Aid ■ College & University Lecturer ■ Professor ■ Physical Trainer ■ Coach ■ Child Care Director ■ Child Care Worker ■ Child Life Specialist ■ Nanny ■ Early Childhood Teacher & Assistant ■ Group Worker & Assistant ■ Human Resource Trainer

Finance

Finance careers involve the management and use of money. The career pathways in this cluster include financial and investment planning, business financial management, banking, and insurance. Strong interpersonal and communication skills are key qualities for these workers.

Financial and investment planners help individuals and businesses make wise investment decisions. Business financial managers analyze and prepare financial reports. Jobs in banking and related services range from bank tellers to loan officers to credit analysts. People who work with insurance services help individuals and businesses protect themselves from financial losses.

Careers in finance exist in all parts of the economy. Some of the most desirable finance jobs are in sales and stock trading. Trading can be very stressful and requires a thorough knowledge of markets and financial instruments. Although it can be difficult to get started in this business, the rewards are high to a person with great sales skills.

Employment opportunities in finance will likely be steady in the foreseeable future. Some entry-level finance positions are available to those with a high school diploma and strong math and communication skills. A four-year college degree or advanced training is required for most of the careers in this cluster. Many require special certifications beyond a college degree. Earnings in this cluster vary significantly depending on the occupation.

Pathways and Career Options

Financial and Investment Planning

Personal Financial Advisor ▪ Tax Preparation Professional ▪ Securities & Commodities Sales Agent ▪ Investment Advisor ▪ Brokerage Clerk ▪ Brokerage Assistant ▪ Development Officer

Business Financial Management

Accountant ▪ Financial Analyst ▪ Treasurers, Controllers & Chief Revenue Agent ▪ Auditor ▪ Economist ▪ Tax Examiner ▪ Collector ▪ Revenue Agent

Banking and Related Services

Credit Analyst ▪ Loan Officer ▪ Bill & Account Collector ▪ Teller ▪ Loan Processor ▪ Customer Service Representative ▪ Data Processor ▪ Accountant ▪ Internal Auditor ▪ Compliance Officer ▪ Debt Counselor ▪ Title Researcher & Examiner ▪ Abstractor ▪ Credit Report Provider ▪ Repossession Agent ▪ Network Service & Operations Manager

Insurance Services

Claims Agent, Examiner, & Investigator ▪ Claims Clerk ▪ Insurance Appraiser ▪ Underwriter ▪ Actuary ▪ Sales Agent ▪ Customer Service Agent ▪ Processing Clerk ▪ Direct Marketing

Government & Public Administration

This career area involves working in a government position or on issues related to government matters. Seven pathways make up this cluster. They include governance, national security, foreign service, planning, revenue and taxation, regulation, and public management and administration. Places of work range from nonprofit organizations to overseas locations to local, state, or federal governments.

People enter government and public service for a variety of reasons. Some want to help shape environmental regulations or public or foreign policy. Others desire to serve the president or protect national security for the Department of Defense. Yet others make social, economic, and environmental decisions as they help plan communities, highways, airports, and other public spaces. Those who work with revenue and taxes make sure that citizens and businesses pay their taxes. They also review tax returns and collect overdue taxes. People who work in the regulatory industry help protect peoples' health and safety by making sure that industries and businesses follow the law. Managers and administrators who handle public resources must have strong technical skills in budgeting and managing personnel.

The training and education needed to enter a career in this cluster range from on-the-job training to advanced college degrees. Government job opportunities exist in every career area, and employment opportunities in state and local governments are increasing. This is due to population changes and a growing demand for public services.

Pathways and Career Options

Governance

President ■ Vice President ■ Governor ■ Lieutenant Governor ■ Mayor ■ Cabinet Level Secretary (Federal or State) ■ Representative (Federal or State) ■ Senator (Federal or State) ■ Assistant, Deputy, & Chief of Staff ■ Commissioner (County, Parish, or City) ■ Commissioner (State Agency) ■ Congressional Aide ■ Legislative Aide ■ Legislative Assistant ■ Specialist ■ Lobbyist ■ Policy Advisor

National Security

National Security Advisor ■ Staff or Field Officer ■ Electronic Warfare Specialist ■ Combat Operations Officer ■ Infantry Field Officer ■ Artillery Officer ■ Air Defense Artillery Officer ■ Special Forces Officer ■ Nuclear Weapons Officer & Specialist ■ Missile & Space Systems Officer ■ Military Intelligence Specialist ■ Signals Intelligence Officer ■ Surface Ship Warfare Officer ■ Submarine Officer ■ Combat Control Officer ■ Combat Engineer ■ Combat Aircraft Pilot & Crew ■ Airborne Warning Control Specialist ■ Intelligence & Counterintelligence Agent or Specialist ■ Intelligence Analyst ■ Cryptographer

Foreign Service

Ambassador Foreign Service Officer ■ Consular Officer ■ Administrative Officer ■ Political Officer ■ Economic Officer ■ Diplomatic Courier

Planning

Business Enterprise Official ■ Chief of Vital Statistics ■ Commissioner ■ Director (Various Agencies) ■ Economic Development Coordinator ■ Federal Aid Coordinator ■ Census Clerk ■ County Director ■ Census Enumerator ■ Census Planner ■ Program Associate ■ Global Imaging Systems Specialist

Revenue and Taxation

Assessor ■ Tax Auditor ■ Internal Revenue Investigator ■ Revenue Agent & Officer ■ Tax Examiner Assistant or Clerk ■ Inspector General ■ Tax Attorney ■ Tax Policy Analyst

Regulation

Business Regulation Investigator ■ Chief of Field Operations ■ Code Inspector or Officer ■ Equal Opportunity Officer, Inspector, Investigator, or Examiner ■ Chief Bank Examiner ■ Bank Examiner ■ Aviation Safety Officer ■ Border Inspector ■ Cargo Inspector ■ Election Supervisor ■ Enforcement Specialist ■ Immigration Officer

Public Management and Administration

City Manager ■ City Council Member ■ City or County Clerk ■ Court Administrator or Clerk ■ Executive or Associate Director ■ Officer ■ General Service Officer ■ Management Analysis Officer ■ Program Administration Officer

Health Science

Health care is the fastest-growing industry in the United States, so careers in this cluster are in high demand. The career pathways include therapeutic and diagnostic services, health information, support services, and biotechnology research and development.

People who work in health sciences have a variety of responsibilities. Those in therapeutic services—physical therapists, doctors, nurses, and others—provide care and treatment through direct patient contact. People who work in diagnostic services help detect, diagnose, and treat diseases or injuries. Those who manage medical data and patient information need strong computer-science skills. Workers in support services, such as dietary technicians or hospital maintenance engineers, create a healthful environment for health services. Scientists in biotechnology study ways to diagnose and treat human diseases.

The rapid growth of health-science technology and a quickly aging population are leading to a high demand for health-science workers. Entry-level jobs in health information require on-the-job training or certification. Most other careers in this cluster require a four-year-college degree or advanced college degree. Some also require a license or certification.

About half of all health-science workers find employment at hospitals. Many others find work at clinics, pharmacies, nursing homes, public health agencies, and private offices. Researchers in biotechnology find work at universities, government agencies, or major health organizations.

Pathways and Career Options

Therapeutic Services

Acupuncturist ■ Anesthesiologist Assistant ■ Art, Music, or Dance Therapist ■ Athletic Trainer ■ Audiologist ■ Certified Nursing Assistant ■ Chiropractor ■ Dentist ■ Hygienist ■ Dietician ■ Emergency Medical Technician ■ Home Health Aide ■ Licensed Practical Nurse ■ Massage Therapist ■ Medical Assistant ■ Mortician ■ Occupational Therapist or Assistant ■ Optometrist ■ Paramedic ■ Pharmacist ■ Pharmacy Technician ■ Physical Therapist or Assistant ■ Physician ■ Physician's Assistant ■ Psychologist ■ Registered Nurse ■ Respiratory Therapist ■ Social Worker ■ Speech & Language Pathologist ■ Veterinarian

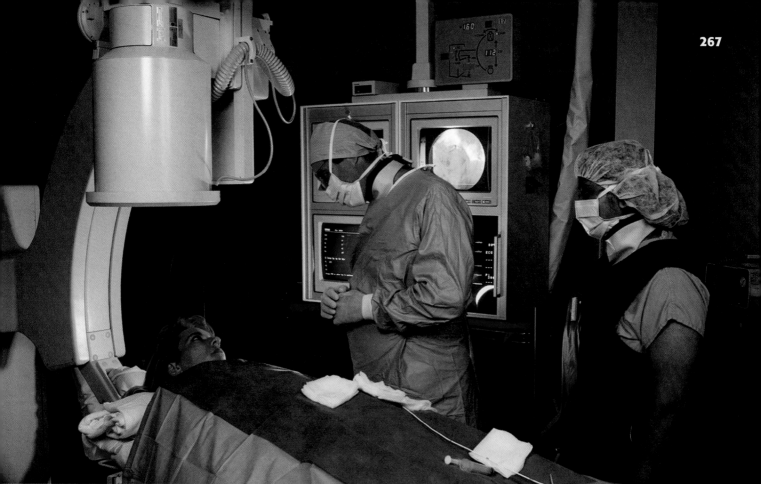

Diagnostics Services

Cardiovascular Technologist ■ Clinical Lab Technician ■ Computer Tomography (CT) Technologist ■ Cytotechnologist ■ Diagnostic Medical Sonographer ■ Electrocardiographic (ECG) Technician ■ Electronic Diagnostic (EEG) Technologist ■ Exercise Physiologist ■ Geneticist ■ Histotechnician ■ Histotechnologist ■ Magnetic Resonance (MR) Technologist ■ Mammographer ■ Pathologist ■ Pathology Assistant ■ Phlebotomist ■ Medical Technologist ■ Clinical Laboratory Scientist ■ Nuclear Medicine Technologist ■ Positron Emission Tomography (PET) Technologist ■ Radiologic Technologist ■ Radiographer ■ Radiologist

Health Informatics

Admitting Clerk ■ Applied Researcher ■ Community Services Specialist ■ Data Analyst ■ Epidemiologist ■ Ethicist ■ Health Educator ■ Health Information Coder ■ Health Information Services ■ Healthcare Administrator ■ Medical Assistant ■ Medical Biller ■ Patient Financial Services Coordinator ■ Medical Information Technologist ■ Medical Librarian & Cybrarian ■ Patient Advocate ■ Public Health Educator ■ Reimbursement Specialist ■ Social Worker ■ Transcriptionist ■ Unit Coordinator ■ Utilization Manager

Support Services

Biomedical Engineer ■ Clinical Engineer ■ Biomedical Technician ■ Clinical Technician ■ Environmental Services Worker ■ Facilities Manager ■ Food Service Worker ■ Hospital Maintenance Engineer ■ Industrial Hygienist ■ Materials Manager ■ Transport Technician

Biotechnology Research and Development

Biochemist ■ Bioinformatics Associate ■ Bioinformatics Scientist ■ Bioinformatics Specialist ■ Biomedical Chemist ■ Biostatistician ■ Cell Biologist ■ Clinical Trials Research Associate ■ Clinical Trials Research Coordinator ■ Geneticist ■ Genetics Lab Assistant ■ Lab Technician ■ Microbiologist ■ Molecular Biologist ■ Pharmaceutical Scientist ■ Quality Assurance Technician ■ Quality Control Technician ■ Regulatory Affairs Specialist ■ Research Assistant ■ Research Associate ■ Research Scientist ■ Toxicologist

Hospitality & Tourism

With increasing leisure time and personal income, many people have more resources for eating out, travel, and recreation. Career options in the area of hospitality and tourism focus on food and beverage services, lodging services, travel, and all types of recreation. Those who work in this industry must have exceptional customer-service skills. They like demanding and diverse work. These workers must also have a solid foundation in math, science, and technical skills.

Chefs prepare and serve food with the help of cooks, servers, and hosts. Lodging managers—with the help of reservationists, bellhops, housekeepers, and front-desk clerks— check guests in and out, meet all their needs, and keep the hotel clean. Travel agents need strong organizational skills and sales abilities to help people plan trips and make lodging and travel reservations. Recreation workers help guests enjoy amusement parks, museums, zoos, unfamiliar cities, and other recreation services.

Many jobs in hospitality and tourism require no specific education. Workers—such as front-desk clerks, housekeepers, and cooks—often receive on-the-job training. However, managers of large resorts, hotels, restaurants, and amusement parks usually complete a four-year college degree. Managers may also have advanced training and certifications. People can acquire education and training at high schools, technical institutes, and two-year or four-year colleges and universities.

The job outlook for hospitality and tourism careers remains steady. Wages may vary greatly depending on the area of the country and type of facility.

Pathways and Career Options

Restaurants and Food and Beverage Services

General Manager ■ Food & Beverage Manager ■ Kitchen Manager ■ Catering & Banquets Manager ■ Service Manager ■ Maitre'd ■ Restaurant Owner ■ Baker ■ Brewer ■ Caterer ■ Executive Chef ■ Cook ■ Pastry & Specialty Chef ■ Bartender ■ Restaurant Server ■ Host ■ Banquet Server ■ Cocktail Server ■ Banquet Set-Up Employee ■ Bus Person ■ Room Service Attendant ■ Kitchen Steward ■ Counter Server ■ Wine Steward

Lodging

Front Office Manager ■ Executive Housekeeper ■ Director of Sales & Marketing ■ Director of Human Resources ■ Director of Security ■ Controller ■ Food & Beverage Director ■ General Manager ■ Quality Assurance Manager ■ Owner & Franchisee ■ Communications Supervisor ■ Front Desk Supervisor ■ Reservations Supervisor ■ Valet Attendant ■ Door Attendant ■ Laundry Supervisor ■ Room Supervisor ■ Laundry Attendant ■ Maintenance Worker ■ Bell Captain ■ Shift Supervisor ■ Sales Professional ■ Night Auditor ■ Front Desk Employee ■ Concierge ■ Guestroom Attendant ■ Van Driver

Travel and Tourism

Executive Director ■ Assistant Director ■ Director of Tourism Development ■ Director of Communications ■ Director of Visitor Services ■ Director of Sales ■ Director of Marketing & Advertising ■ Director of Volunteer Services ■ Events Manager ■ Sales Manager ■ Destination Manager ■ Convention Services Manager ■ Travel Agent ■ Event Planner ■ Meeting Planner ■ Special Events Producer ■ Tour & Travel Coordinator ■ Tourism Assistant ■ Tour Guide ■ Tourism Marketing Specialist ■ Transportation Specialist ■ Welcome Center Supervisor ■ Motor Coach Operator ■ Interpreter

Recreation, Amusements, and Attractions

Club Manager & Assistant Manager ■ Club Membership Developer ■ Parks & Gardens Safety & Security ■ Parks & Garden Ranger ■ Resort Trainer & Instructor ■ Gaming & Casino Manager ■ Gaming & Casino Dealer ■ Gaming & Casino Security & Safety ■ Fairs & Festival Facility Manager ■ Fairs & Festival Promotional Developer ■ Theme Parks & Amusement Parks Area Ride Operations Manager ■ Theme Parks & Amusement Parks Group Events Manager ■ Historical, Cultural, Architectural, or Ecological Site Guide or Exhibit Developer ■ Museum, Zoo, or Aquarium Animal Trainer & Handler

Human Services

Careers in human services relate to family and human needs. If you like to help others, one of these careers may be for you. People who enter these careers often desire to protect, nurture, or provide a service for others in need. Career pathways include services in early childhood development, counseling and mental health, family and community, personal care, and consumer services.

In early childhood development, workers nurture, teach, and care for children. Counselors and other mental-health workers help people with family and personal problems, mental-health issues, and career-related decisions. Family and community services workers—such as social workers, grief counselors, and geriatric workers—help people with crises or other needs that impact daily living. Personal care workers may help people enhance their appearances or develop fitness. Helping people make financial decisions, buy or sell real estate, or purchase quality insurance or consumer products are just a few contributions of those focused on consumer services.

Most positions in this cluster are growing faster than average. Some entry-level jobs may require a high school diploma and a few community college courses. Other careers may require two-year, four-year, or advanced college degrees. Many careers may require state licenses or certification. Strong communication skills combined with solid science and technology skills will benefit anyone seeking a career in human services.

Pathways and Career Options

Early Childhood Development and Services

Childcare Facility Director ■ Childcare Facility Assistant Director ■ Elementary School Counselor ■ Preschool Teacher ■ Educator for Parents ■ Nanny ■ Teachers' Assistant ■ Childcare Assistant or Worker

Counseling and Mental Health Services

Clinical & Counseling Psychologist ■ Industrial-Organizational Psychologist ■ Sociologist ■ School Counselor ■ School Psychologist ■ Substance Abuse & Behavioral Disorder Counselor ■ Mental Health Counselor ■ Vocational Rehabilitation Counselor ■ Career Counselor ■ Employment Counselor ■ Residential Advisor ■ Marriage, Child, & Family Counselor

Family and Community Services

Community Service Director ■ Adult Day Care Coordinator ■ Volunteer Coordinator ■ Licensed Professional Counselor ■ Religious Leader ■ Religious Activities & Education Program Director ■ Human Services Worker ■ Social Services Worker ■ Vocational Rehabilitation Counselor ■ Employment Counselor ■ Career Counselor ■ Vocational Rehabilitation Service Worker ■ Leisure Activities Coordinator ■ Dietician ■ Geriatric Service Worker ■ Adult Day Care Worker ■ Residential Advisor ■ Emergency & Relief Worker ■ Community Food Service Worker ■ Community Housing Service Worker ■ Social & Human Services Assistant

Personal Care Services

Barber ■ Cosmetologist, Hairdresser, & Hairstylist ■ Shampooer ■ Nail Technician, Manicurist, & Pedicurist ■ Skin Care Specialist & Esthetician ■ Electrolysis Technician ■ Electrologist ■ Funeral Director ■ Mortician ■ Embalmer ■ Funeral Attendant ■ Personal & Home Care Aide ■ Companion ■ Spa Attendant ■ Personal Trainer ■ Massage Therapist

Consumer Services

Consumer Credit Counselor ■ Consumer Affairs Officer ■ Consumer Advocate ■ Certified Financial Planner ■ Insurance Representative ■ Small Business Owner ■ Banker ■ Real Estate Services Representative ■ Financial Advisor ■ Investment Broker ■ Employee Benefits Representative ■ Hospital Patient Accounts Representative ■ Customer Service Representative ■ Consumer Research Department Representative ■ Consumer Goods or Services Retailing Representative ■ Market Researcher ■ Account Executive ■ Sales Consultant ■ Event Specialist ■ Inside Sales Representative ■ Field Merchandising Representative ■ Buyer

Information Technology

Do you find the ever-changing world of computer technology fascinating? With work available in every segment of society, information technology (IT) careers are among those most in demand. The IT career pathways include network systems, information and support services, programming and software development, and interactive media.

Network specialists analyze, implement, and maintain computer systems critical to corporate business. They may devise systems by which employees in a worldwide company can view information at the same time. Information support workers implement computer systems and provide technical support to all users.

Programming and software developers must comprehend computer operating systems and programming languages. They often work with cutting-edge technologies to meet the future IT needs of businesses and individuals. Web designers, animators, and graphic artists have one thing in common—they all work with interactive media. People in these careers design and produce interactive multimedia that meet a variety of needs from sales and marketing to entertainment.

Depending on the occupation, training and education can be obtained at some high schools, technical colleges, two-year colleges, and four-year colleges or universities. Because IT specialists must be well versed in all factors affecting their industry, continuing education is often a requirement beyond a college degree. In addition to computer skills, people in these careers need strong science, math, and communication skills.

Pathways and Career Options

Network Systems

Data Communications Analyst ▪ Information Systems Administrator ▪ Information Systems Operator ▪ Information Technology Engineer ▪Technical Support Specialist ▪ User Support Specialist ▪ Telecommunications Network Technician ▪ Network Administrator ▪ Network Analyst ▪ Network Engineer ▪ Network Operations Analyst ▪ Network Security Analyst ▪ Network Transport Administrator ▪ Systems Administrator ▪ Systems Engineer ▪ Lead PC Support Specialist ▪ Systems Support Lead

Information Support and Services

Data Administrator ▪ Data Analyst ▪ Data Modeler ▪ Database Administration Associate ▪ Database Developer ▪ Knowledge Architect ▪ Systems Administrator ▪ Technical Writer ▪ Desktop Publisher ▪ Instructional Designer ▪ Online Publisher ▪ Technical Support Analyst ▪ Call Center Support Representative ▪ Customer Service Representative ▪ Product Support Engineer ▪ Sales Support Technician ▪ Systems Analyst ▪ Technical Support Engineer ▪ Testing Engineer ▪ Application Integrator ▪ Business Continuity Analyst ▪ Cross-Enterprise Integrator ▪ Data Systems Designer ▪ E-Business Specialist ▪ Electronic Transactions Implementer ▪ Information Systems Architect

Interactive Media

2D & 3D Artist ▪ Animator ▪ Audio & Video Engineer ▪ Media Specialist ▪ Media Designer ▪ Instructional Designer ▪ Multimedia Author ▪ Multimedia Developer ▪ Multimedia Specialist ▪ Producer ▪ Production Assistant ▪ Programmer ▪ Streaming Media Specialist ▪ Virtual Reality Specialist ▪ Web Designer ▪ Web Administrator ▪ Web Page Developer ▪ Web Site Developer ▪ Webmaster

Programming and Software Development

Applications Analyst ▪ Applications Engineer ▪ Business Analyst ▪ Computer Engineer ▪ Data Modeler ▪ Operating Systems Designer & Engineer ▪ Operating Systems Programmer ▪ Operating Systems Analyst ▪ Program Manager ▪ Programmer ▪ Analyst ▪ Software Applications Specialist ▪ Software Applications Architect ▪ Software Applications Design Engineer ▪ Software Applications Development Engineer ▪ Quality Assurance (QA) Specialist ▪ Software Applications Tester ▪ Systems Analyst ▪ Systems Administrator ▪ Test Engineer

Law, Public Safety, Corrections & Security

911

With strong interest in public safety and national security, careers in law, public safety, and corrections, are increasingly in demand. Keeping citizens and the country safe is the core mission of this career area. Career pathways include working in corrections, emergency and fire management, security and protection, law enforcement, and legal services.

Careers range from probation officers to firefighters to criminal investigators and lawyers. Corrections workers have the responsibility to watch over those under arrest, awaiting trial, and serving time for crimes committed. Firefighters, emergency medical technicians, and other emergency workers keep citizens safe during all types of disasters. Often they are first on the scene to give help and treatment.

Security and protective services workers may check credentials and inspect packages of people entering or leaving businesses. Police officers and other workers protect citizens and their property by enforcing laws, investigating crimes and accidents, and arresting criminals. While adhering to a strict code of ethics, legal services personnel—such as judges, lawyers, and paralegals—uphold the legal system, which impacts all aspects of American life.

U.S. citizenship and no felony convictions are the basic requirements of most jobs in this career area. Some jobs require a high school diploma and work experience. Others require formal training, such as at fire-fighting or police academies, plus two-year or four-year college degrees or law degrees. Some careers require passing written exams or tests of physical strength and endurance.

Pathways and Career Options

Correction Services

Warden ■ Jail Administrator ■ Mid-level Manager ■ Program Coordinator & Counselor ■ Public Information Officer ■ Correctional Trainer ■ Case Manager ■ Community Corrections Practitioner ■ Probation & Parole Officer ■ Corrections Educator ■ Corrections Officer ■ Detention Deputy ■ Support Staff ■ Youth Services Worker ■ Facility Maintenance Worker ■ Transport Officer ■ Food Service Staff ■ Medical Staff ■ Dietitian

Emergency and Fire Management Services

Emergency Management & Response Coordinator ■ Emergency Planning Manager ■ Emergency Medical Technician ■ Firefighter ■ Manager & Supervisor ■ Rescue Worker ■ Manager & Supervisor ■ Forest Fire Inspector & Investigator ■ Hazardous Materials Responder ■ Dispatcher ■ Training Officer ■ Grant Writer & Coordinator

Security and Protective Services

Security Director ■ Security Systems Designer & Consultant ■ Information Systems Security Specialist ■ Computer Forensics Specialist ■ Private & Corporate Investigator ■ Loss Prevention & Security Manager ■ Security Trainer & Educator ■ Security Sales Representative ■ Loss Prevention Specialist ■ Life Guard ■ Ski Patrol Officer ■ Security Systems Technician ■ Private Investigative Assistant ■ Security Sales Assistant ■ Transportation Security Supervisor ■ Executive Protection Officer ■ Certified Security Officer ■ Armored Car Guard ■ Control Center Operator ■ Uniformed Security Officer ■ Security Clerk ■ Transportation Security Technician

Law Enforcement Services

Animal Control Officer ■ Bailiff ■ Child Support Investigator ■ Missing Persons Investigator ■ Unemployment Fraud Investigator ■ Criminal Investigator & Special Agent ■ Gaming Investigator ■ Bomb Technician ■ Highway Patrol ■ Immigration & Customs Inspector ■ Police & Detective Manager & Supervisor ■ Police Detective & Criminal Investigator ■ Police, Fire, & Ambulance Dispatcher ■ Police & Patrol Officers ■ Private Detectives & Investigator ■ Sheriff ■ Deputy Sheriff ■ Training Officer ■ Transit & Railroad Police ■ Park Ranger ■ Evidence Technician ■ Federal Marshall

Legal Services

Attorney ■ Case Management Specialist ■ Court Reporter ■ File & Document Manager ■ Information Officer ■ Investigator Judge ■ Law Clerk ■ Legal Assistant ■ Legal Secretary ■ Magistrate Mediator & Arbitrator ■ Negotiator ■ Paralegal

Manufacturing

Careers in the manufacturing cluster involve skills in planning, managing, and making raw materials into quality products. The cluster pathways involve production, process development, and equipment maintenance and installation, inventory control. They also include quality, health, safety, and environmental assurance.

Production workers use machinery and tools to assemble everything from electronics to modular homes. Design engineers and production managers work with product design and the overall manufacturing process to make quality products. Equipment technicians perform emergency repairs and also do routine maintenance on equipment, machines, and tools. Quality assurance workers make sure products and services meet customer standards.

People who work with **logistics**—the handling of operational details—and inventory control oversee all aspects of production from delivering raw materials to shipping products. Environmental and safety engineers focus on the safe use of equipment and a safe and healthy work environment.

The job outlook in manufacturing will grow faster than average especially for people with broad skills. Some careers, such as those in quality control, may see a decline as automation increases. Skilled jobs, such as machinists and welders, are usually learned through apprenticeships or at technical schools or two-year community colleges. Engineers, scientists, and production managers need at least a four-year degree. Some careers require special licenses or certification in addition to education and training.

Pathways and Career Options

Production

Assembler ■ Automated Manufacturing Technician ■ Bookbinder ■ Calibration Technician ■ Electrical Installer & Repairer ■ Extruding & Drawing Machine Setter ■ Extrusion Machine Operator ■ Foundry Worker ■ Grinding, Lapping, & Buffing Machine Operator ■ Hoist & Winch Operator ■ Instrument Maker ■ Large Printing Press Machine Setter ■ Milling Machine Set-Up Operator ■ Millwright ■ Tool & Die Maker ■ Welder ■ Tender & Cutter ■ Painter ■ Pattern & Model Maker ■ Precision Layout Worker ■ Production Associate ■ Sheet Metal Worker ■ Solderer & Brazier

Manufacturing Production Process Development

Design Engineer ■ Electrical & Electronic Technician & Technologist ■ Electronics Engineer ■ Engineering Technician & Technologist ■ Engineering Technician ■ Industrial Engineer ■ Labor Relations Manager ■ Manufacturing Engineer ■ Manufacturing Technician ■ Power Generating & Reactor Plant Operator ■ Precision Inspector, Tester, & Grader ■ Process Improvement Technician ■ Production Manager ■ Purchasing Agent ■ Supervisor

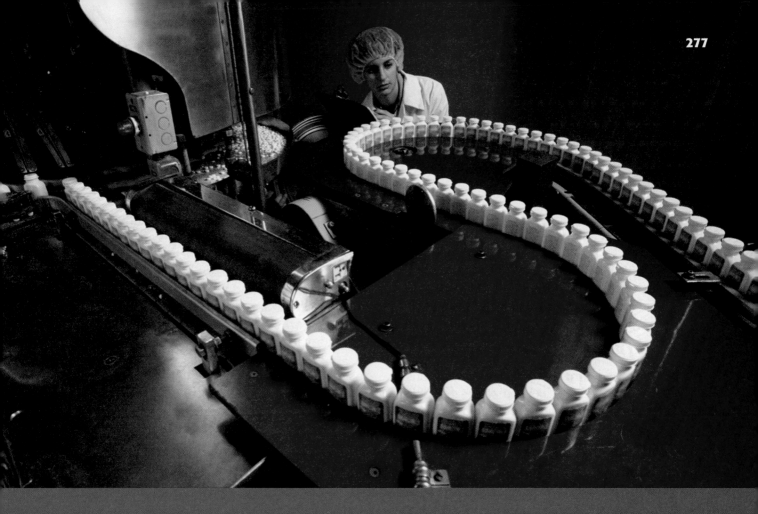

Maintenance, Installation, and Repair

Biomedical Equipment Technician ■ Boilermaker ■ Communication System Installer & Repairer ■ Computer Installer & Repairer ■ Computer Maintenance Technician ■ Electrical Equipment Installer & Repairer ■ Facility Electrician ■ Industrial Facilities Manager ■ Industrial Machinery Mechanic ■ Industrial Maintenance Electrician ■ Industrial Maintenance Technician ■ Instrument Calibrator & Repairer ■ Instrument Control Technician ■ Fixture Designer ■ Laser Systems Technician ■ Major Appliance Repairer ■ Meter Installer & Repairer ■ Millwright ■ Plumber, Pipe Fitter & Steam Fitter ■ Security System Installer & Repairer

Quality Assurance

Calibration Technician ■ Inspector ■ Lab Technician ■ Process Control Technician ■ Quality Control Technician ■ Quality Engineer ■ Statistical Process Control (SPC) Coordinator

Logistics and Inventory Control

Communications, Transportation, & Utilities Manager ■ Dispatcher ■ Freight, Stock, & Material Mover ■ Industrial Truck & Tractor Operator ■ Logistical Engineer ■ Logistician ■ Material Associate ■ Material Handler ■ Traffic, Shipping, & Receiving Clerk ■ Material Mover ■ Process Improvement Technician ■ Quality Control Technician ■ Traffic Manager

Health, Safety, and Environmental Assurance

Environmental Engineer ■ Environmental Specialist ■ Health & Safety Representative ■ Safety Coordinator ■ Safety Engineer ■ Safety Team Leader ■ Safety Technician

Marketing, Sales & Service

If you crave variety and enjoy a fast-paced environment, a career in marketing, sales, and service may be perfect for you! Careers in this cluster include all the jobs involved in buying, distributing, marketing, and selling products, and providing follow-up service to customers. Related jobs include finding new customers and tracking marketing data.

Managers and entrepreneurs direct the advertising, marketing, sales, and public relations for small businesses or major companies. Specialists in sales and marketing move goods and services to businesses and individuals. Merchandise managers and buyers predict trends and buy merchandise accordingly. Sales associates and store managers focus on selling and providing customer service.

Developing strategies to promote goods and services are key to those who work in marketing and promotions. Market researchers gather information about consumer needs and use it to predict and plan new products. A logistics engineer often works closely with a warehouse manager to control the movement and storage of raw materials and finished goods. Specialists handle **e-marketing**, which is the use of computer technology to market goods and services.

The overall demand for employees in this cluster remains high. Those with computer skills and college degrees will have more opportunities in management. Many entry-level jobs exist in sales. However, employment opportunities are greater for those who attend community colleges or technical schools that offer one-, two-, or three-year programs, or colleges and universities that offer four-year degrees. Wages vary by occupation, level of responsibility, and work experience.

Pathways and Career Options

Management and Entrepreneurship

Entrepreneur ■ Owner ■ Small Business Owner ■ President ■ Chief Executive Officer ■ Principal ■ Partner ■ Proprietor ■ Franchisee ■ Administrative Support Representative ■ Independent Distributor

Professional Sales and Marketing

Inbound Call Manager ■ Channel Sales Manager ■ Regional Sales Manager ■ Client Relationship Manager ■ Business Development Manager ■ Territory Representative ■ Key Account Manager ■ National Account Manager ■ Account Executive ■ Sales Engineer ■ Sales Executive ■ Technical Sales Specialist ■ Retail Sales Specialist ■ Outside Sales Representative ■ Industrial Sales Representative ■ Manufacturer's Representative ■ Telemarketer ■ Customer Service Representative ■ Field Representative ■ Broker ■ Agent ■ Solutions Advisor ■ Sales & Marketing Associate

Buying and Merchandising

Store Manager ■ Retail Marketing Coordinator ■ Merchandising Manager ■ Merchandise Buyer ■ Operations Manager ■ Visual Merchandise Manager ■ Sales Associate ■ Stock Clerk ■ Receiving Clerk ■ Sales Manager ■ Department Manager

Marketing Communications and Promotion

Advertising Manager ■ Public Relations Manager ■ Public Information Director ■ Sales Promotion Manager ■ Co-op Manager ■ Trade Show Manager ■ Circulation Manager ■ Promotions Manager ■ Art & Graphics Director ■ Creative Director ■ Account Executive ■ Account Supervisor ■ Sales Representative ■ Marketing Associate ■ Media Buyer & Planner ■ Interactive Media Specialist ■ Contract Administrator ■ Copywriter ■ Research Specialist ■ Research Assistant

Marketing Information Management and Research

Database Manager ■ Research Specialist & Manager ■ Brand Manager ■ Marketing Services Manager ■ Customer Satisfaction Manager ■ Research Project Manager ■ Constituent Relationship Management (CRM) Manager ■ Forecasting Manager ■ Strategic Planner ■ Product Planner ■ Planning Analyst ■ Director of Market Development ■ Database Analyst ■ Research Associate ■ Frequency Marketing Specialist ■ Knowledge Management Specialist ■ Interviewer

Distribution and Logistics

Warehouse Manager ■ Materials Manager ■ Traffic Manager ■ Logistics Manager ■ Transportation Manager ■ Inventory Manager ■ Shipping & Receiving Clerk ■ Logistics Analyst & Engineer ■ Distribution Coordinator ■ Shipping & Receiving Administrator

E-Marketing

Fulfillment Manager ■ E-Merchandising Manager ■ E-Commerce Director ■ Web Site Project Manager ■ Internet Project Director ■ Brand Manager ■ Forum Manager ■ Web Master ■ Web Designer ■ Interactive Media Specialist ■ Internet Sales Engineer ■ Site Architect ■ User Interface Designer ■ On-line Market Researcher ■ Copywriters ■ Designer ■ Account Supervisor ■ Customer Support Specialist

Science, Technology, Engineering & Mathematics

Workers in this cluster use math and the scientific process in laboratory and testing services, and also conduct research. Often their work leads to discoveries that have the potential to improve life. Careers in this cluster are available in two areas: science and mathematics or engineering and technology.

Careers in science and mathematics range from teacher to physicist to statistician to lab technician. Workers use science and math to deal with real-world issues, such as solving environmental problems or preventing certain health conditions.

Engineers and technologists often specialize in biotechnology or distinct areas of engineering—civil, electrical, mechanical, aerospace, or chemical engineering. They use scientific principles to design new machinery, build new roads and bridges, or develop systems to prevent pollution or reduce energy usage.

Some entry-level jobs require a two-year degree from a community college or technical institute. Most careers in this cluster, including entry-level lab technicians, require a four-year degree from a college or university. Advanced degrees are common among engineers, scientists, technologists, and mathematicians. Some careers require certification, too.

Because of the critical nature of work in this cluster, the employment outlook remains very strong. Scientists and mathematicians who learn to use equipment in industrial and government settings may have a competitive edge over other job seekers. The need for technologists and engineers will increase as technology advances and employers need to improve and update product designs and manufacturing processes.

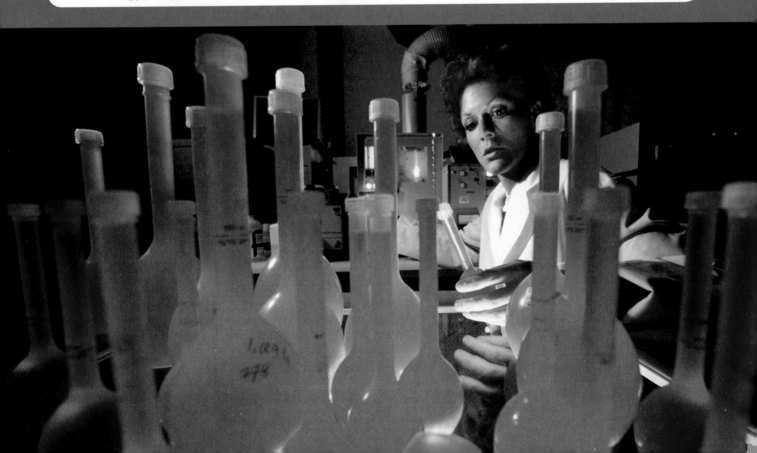

Pathways and Career Options

Engineering and Technology

Aerospace Engineer ■ Application Engineer ■ Automotive Engineer ■ Biotechnology Engineer ■ Chemical Engineer ■ Civil Engineer ■ Energy Transmission Engineer ■ Environmental Engineer ■ Facilities Technician ■ Geothermal Engineer ■ Hazardous Waste Technician ■ Human Factors Engineer ■ Industrial Engineering Technician ■ Licensing Engineer ■ Marine Engineer ■ Materials Engineer ■ Materials Lab & Supply Technician ■ Mechanical Engineer ■ Metallurgic Engineer ■ Mining Engineer ■ Nuclear Engineer ■ Operations Research Engineer ■ Packaging Engineer or Technician ■ Petroleum Engineer ■ Plastics Engineer

Science and Math

Research Chemist or Technician ■ Science Teacher ■ Lab Technician ■ Scientific Visualization & Graphics Expert ■ Statistician ■ Analytical Chemist ■ Anthropologist ■ Applied Mathematician ■ Archeologist ■ Astronomer ■ Astrophysicist ■ Atmospheric Scientist ■ Biologist ■ Botanist ■ Computer Aided Design (CAD) Operator ■ Cartographer ■ Chemist ■ Cosmologist ■ Demographer ■ Dye Chemist ■ Ecologist ■ Economist ■ Environmental Scientist ■ Geneticist ■ Geologist ■ Geophysicist ■ Geoscientist ■ Hydrologist ■ Inorganic Chemist ■ Mammalogist ■ Marine Scientist ■ Materials Analyst or Scientist ■ Mathematician ■ Metallurgist ■ Meteorologist

Transportation, Distribution & Logistics

Transportation by road, rail, water, and air offers many employment options. These careers focus on effective planning, efficient management, and safe movement of products and people. Related careers focus on planning, managing, and maintaining the equipment, facilities, and systems used.

Transportation workers, such as pilots and bus drivers, operate vehicles that transport freight and people. Others ensure safety, security, and timely delivery. Logistics and distribution employees plan and schedule transportation, shipment periods, and delivery dates. Workers in warehousing and distribution use cutting-edge tracking software to sort, label, and schedule customer deliveries. They also ensure accurately loaded shipments.

Some workers maintain, repair, and service transportation vehicles and the facilities that house them. Traffic engineers may plan, manage, and regulate the basic framework of public transportation systems. Employees in health, safety, and environmental management conduct research and find ways to keep the environment safe and clean. Workers in sales and service sell transportation services to new customers and manage transportation needs of existing customers.

As one of the fastest growing segments of the economy, this career cluster offers many high-demand, high-wage work options. Many entry-level positions require on-the-job training or a special certificate (such as a Commercial Driver's License–CDL for truck drivers). Others require two-year or four-year degrees from a college or university. Entry-level positions for urban and regional planners often require an advanced degree.

Pathways and Career Options

Transportation Operations

Air & Space Transportation Manager ■ Airplane Pilot & Copilot ■ Flight Attendant ■ Air Traffic Controller ■ Aircraft Cargo Handling Supervisor ■ Rail Dispatcher ■ Locomotive Engineer ■ Railroad Brake, Signal, & Switch Operator ■ Train Crew Member ■ Yard Worker ■ Water Transportation Manager ■ Captain ■ Sailor & Marine ■ Ship & Boat Captain ■ Ship Engineer ■ Motorboat Operator ■ Bridge & Lock Tender ■ Truck, Bus, & Taxi Dispatcher ■ Truck Driver ■ Bus Driver ■ Taxi Driver ■ Bus Dispatcher ■ Subway & Streetcar Operator

Logistics Planning and Management Services

Logistician ■ Logistics Manager ■ Logistics Engineer ■ Logistics Analyst ■ Logistics Consultant ■ International Logistics Manager

Warehousing and Distribution Center Operations

Warehouse Manager ■ Storage & Distribution Manager ■ Industrial & Packaging Engineer ■ Traffic, Shipping, & Receiving Clerk ■ Production, Planning, & Expediting Clerk ■ First-Line Supervisor & Manager ■ Laborer & Material Mover ■ Machine & Vehicle Operator ■ Laborer & Freight Stock Material Mover ■ Car, Truck, & Ship Loader ■ Packer & Packager

Facility and Mobile Equipment Maintenance

Facility Maintenance Manager & Engineer ■ Industrial Equipment Mechanic ■ Industrial Electrician or Electronic Technician ■ Aerospace Engineering & Operations Technician ■ Aircraft Mechanic, Service Technician, or Engine Specialist ■ Power Plant Mechanic ■ Aircraft Body & Bonded Structure Repairer ■ Motorboat Mechanic ■ Ship Mechanic & Repairer ■ Rail Car Repairer & Mechanic ■ Signal & Track Switch Repairer ■ Motorcycle Mechanic ■ Automotive Body Repairer or Service Technician ■ Diesel Engine Specialist

Transportation System Infrastructure

Urban & Regional Planner ■ Civil Engineer ■ Engineering Technician ■ Surveying & Mapping Technician ■ Government Service Executive ■ Environmental Compliance Inspector ■ Air Traffic Controller ■ Aviation Inspector ■ Traffic Engineer ■ Traffic Technician ■ Motor Vehicle Inspector ■ Freight Inspector ■ Railroad Inspector ■ Marine Cargo Inspector ■ Vessel Traffic Control Specialists ■ Public Transportation Inspector ■ Government Agency Manager, Regulator, or Inspector

Health, Safety, and Environmental Management

Health & Safety Manager ■ Industrial Health & Safety Engineer ■ Environmental Scientist & Specialist ■ Environmental Science & Protection Technician ■ Environmental Manager & Engineer ■ Environmental Compliance Inspector ■ Safety Analyst

Sales and Service

Marketing Manager ■ Sales Manager ■ Sales Representative (Transportation & Logistics Services) ■ Reservation, Travel & Transportation Agent or Clerk ■ Customer Order & Billing Clerk ■ Cashier, Counter, or Rental Clerk ■ Cargo & Freight Agent ■ Customer Service Manager ■ Customer Service Representative

Education and Training Requirements

Often people are not aware of the educational requirements for various occupations. Having the education necessary to enter a profession of choice is highly important.

Jobs that do not require a degree or technical training after high school usually provide on-the-job training. Often, these are lower-paying positions that people use as stepping-stones to better jobs. See 13-3 for a list of the 10 most available jobs through 2016 for workers without a degree or technical training.

Many jobs require at least an **associate degree**. This is a two-year college degree. Sometimes students take a two-year program to jumpstart a career. Once working, they seek additional education and training. See 13-4 for a list of the 10 most available jobs through 2016 for those with an associate degree.

About 20 percent of jobs may require at least a four-year degree, or a **bachelor's degree**. The belief that everyone needs a bachelor's degree is simply not true. These jobs are usually higher paying than those requiring less education. See 13-5 for a list of the 10 most available jobs through 2016 for individuals with a bachelor's degree.

By examining the career clusters and the information that accompanies them, you can learn to identify occupations that offer good job prospects. Look for occupations that are in high demand or are growing. Also, notice which occupations show declining numbers. If you choose a career in such a field, recognize that finding work may be more challenging.

Future Occupational Trends

What are the jobs of the future? No one knows for sure, but researchers continue to study **occupational trends**. These are research predictions regarding the jobs that will most likely be needed in the future.

Top 10 Jobs Through 2016 That Do Not Require a Degree	
Occupations	**Total Job Openings**
Retail salespersons	5,034,000
Office clerks, general	3,604,000
Cashiers (except gaming)	3,382,000
Combined food preparation and serving workers (including fast-food)	2,955,000
Customer service representatives	2,747,000
Janitors and cleaners (except maids and housekeeping cleaners)	2,732,000
Waiters and waitresses	2,615,000
Truck drivers—heavy and tractor-trailer	2,053,000
Nursing aides, orderlies, and attendants	1,711,000
Maids and housekeeping cleaners	1,656,000

U.S. Bureau of Labor Statistics

Top 10 Jobs Through 2016 Requiring an Associate Degree	
Occupation	**Total Job Openings**
Registered nurses	3,092,000
Computer support specialists	624,000
Legal secretaries	308,000
Paralegals and legal assistants	291,000
Radiologic technologists and technicians	226,000
Dental hygienists	217,000
Medical records and health information technicians	200,000
Engineering and mapping technicians	192,000
Respiratory therapists	126,000
Veterinary technologists and technicians	100,000

U.S. Bureau of Labor Statistics

13-4

These jobs require a two-year college degree.

Resource

Retail Salespersons, reproducible master 13-2, TR

Resource

Occupation Interview, Activity B, WB

Resource

Occupational Interests, Activity C, WB

Top 10 Jobs Through 2016 Requiring a Bachelor's Degree	
Occupation	**Total Job Openings**
Elementary school teachers (except special education)	1,749,000
Accountants and auditors	1,500,000
All other business operations specialists	1,261,000
Secondary school teachers (except special and career/technical education)	1,096,000
All other teachers (primary, secondary, and adult)	805,000
Computer software engineers, applications	733,000
Computer systems analysts	650,000
Construction managers	564,000
Computer software engineers, systems software	449,000
Network systems and data communications analysts	402,000

U.S. Bureau of Labor Statistics

13-5

These higher-paying jobs require at least a bachelor's degree

Reflect Further

What additional technological and societal trends will likely impact careers of the future?

One such trend is the ever-growing number of service-related jobs. These jobs are expected to account for most of the new jobs generated by 2016. The majority of new service positions will be in business, health, and social services.

Advances in technology and changes in society shape occupational trends. Some important societal changes that are shaping U.S. occupations include an aging population, increased concern over health and fitness, high interest in recreation and entertainment, and new ways of communicating based on new technologies.

All 16 career clusters are important sources of future jobs. You and your peers will likely work in 10 or more jobs for five or more employers before retirement. Some of the occupations you will hold may not exist today. This means it is your responsibility to manage your own career and watch for new opportunities.

Keep career flexibility in mind as you explore various occupations. Success in tomorrow's workplace will require self-reliant individuals who can easily adapt to change, transfer skills to new situations, and learn new skills.

Summary

A good way to begin exploring careers is to think about factors that influence your options. These factors may include your interests, aptitudes, and abilities. Your values and goals are influences, too. When exploring careers, avoid placing limits on the types of occupations to consider. You are likely to work in several different occupations during your career.

Then explore the 16 career clusters and their pathways to learn about the wide range of jobs within each cluster pathway. You can identify specific jobs that interest you and examine them in more detail.

It is important to understand the trends that show growth or change in occupational areas. Areas of growth usually provide the most high-demand job opportunities. Occupations are available for people who have different levels of education and training, but the jobs that require more knowledge and skills usually pay better. Ultimately, each individual is responsible for choosing a suitable occupation and taking advantage of career-enhancing opportunities.

Resource

Review and Study Guide for Chapter 13, reproducible master 13-3, TR

Answers to *Facts In Review*

1. interests, aptitudes, abilities, values, and goals
2. List two. Student response.
3. Name six. Student response.
4. (List three:) planning, organizing, evaluating, computer skills, common sense, decision-making skills, and problem-solving skills
5. upgrading teaching skills to enhance student performance
6. interpersonal, communications, and math skills
7. Job increases are due to population changes and a growing demand for public services.
8. Workers in therapeutic services provide direct patient care and treatment, while those in health information manage medical data and patient information.
9. Name six. Student response.

Facts in Review

1. What factors influence careers you choose from the career clusters?
2. List two myths related to nontraditional jobs—one for each gender.
3. Name at least six examples of careers in the arts, audio/video technology, and communications cluster.
4. List at least three skills all businesspeople need.
5. How do highly skilled educators use many of their nonteaching hours?
6. What skills do people need to build a foundation for a finance career?
7. Why are government career opportunities increasing?
8. Contrast the job responsibilities for health-science workers in therapeutic versus health information services.
9. Name six careers in the human services cluster.
10. In addition to computer skills, what key skills do workers in information technology careers need?
11. What are the basic requirements for most jobs in the law, public safety, corrections, and security career cluster?
12. Why will demand for scientists, technologists, and engineers increase?
13. What is the difference between an *associate* degree and a *bachelor's* degree?
14. What occupation in 2016 will offer the greatest number of jobs to people with no degree?

10. science, math, and communication skills
11. U.S. citizenship, no felony convictions
12. Technological advances will cause employers to improve and update product designs and manufacturing processes.
13. two years of college (associate) versus four years of college (bachelor's)
14. retail salesperson

Developing Your Academic Skills

1. **English.** Use Internet and print resources to research the origins of traditional jobs. Identify which periods in history prompted a break from traditional roles in the workplace. Write a brief report summarizing your findings.

2. **Science.** Interview a science teacher about the importance of understanding science principles as they relate to various occupations. What skills are most important? Share your findings with the class in an oral report.

Information Technology Applications

1. Use presentation software to give a talk on a career of your choice. Incorporate photos into the presentation by scanning images or downloading them from the Internet. Clearly identify the source of each image by keying this line under each: *Photo courtesy of (name of group or organization).*

2. Search the Internet for the term *emerging occupations* and the occupations associated with this term. Write a brief summary indicating which emerging occupations were listed as most *in demand*.

Applying Your Knowledge and Skills

1. **Problem Solving and Critical Thinking.** Select a career that interests you and research the past employment opportunities that it presented. Cite examples of societal changes that have affected career opportunities in the last 10 years and plot these changes on a timeline.

2. **Employability and Career Development.** List at least five occupations from any of the career clusters that interest you. Then identify the school subjects and the knowledge and skills that relate to each job. Have you taken any of these subjects or do you plan to take them in the future? In what other ways could you prepare yourself for these jobs?

3. **Communications.** Choose one example of societal change discussed in this or a previous chapter. Write a report explaining the positive and negative aspects of that change on career opportunities.

Developing Workplace Skills

Conduct an in-depth study of the varied aspects of occupations related to your interest area. Select a preferred career and forecast a job profile 10 years from now by using information from the U.S. Bureau of Labor Statistics and the *Occupational Outlook Handbook*. (Both are accessed through www.bls.gov.) In your job profile, include information about how economic, technological, and societal trends may impact your career. Keep the profile in your personal career file for future reference.

14

Researching Careers

Key Terms

The Occupational Information Network (O*Net™)

Career Voyages

CareerOneStop

One-Stop Career Centers

occupational training

transfer

registered apprenticeship

fringe benefits

dual-career family

Chapter Objectives

After studying this chapter, you will be able to

- **Identify** different types of career research sources.
- **demonstrate** how to research careers and occupations.
- **evaluate** careers based on educational requirements, work hours, work conditions, pay, and personal lifestyles and goals.

Reading Advantage

Before reading, skim the chapter and examine how it is organized. Look at the bold or italic words, headings of different colors and sizes, bulleted lists or numbered lists, tables, charts, captions, and boxed features.

Achieving Academic Standards

English Language Arts

- Read print and non-print texts to acquire new information and to respond to the needs and demands of society and the workplace. (IRA/NCTE, 1)
- Apply strategies to comprehend, interpret, evaluate, and appreciate texts. (IRA/NCTE, 3)
- Conduct research on issues and interests by gathering, evaluating, and synthesizing data from a variety of sources to communicate discoveries. (IRA/NCTE, 7)
- Use a variety of technological and information processes to gather and synthesize information and to create and communicate knowledge. (IRA/NCTE, 8)

Key Concepts

- By using the Internet, you can access a wealth of career information such as One-Stop Career Centers. These centers provide you with a wide range of employment, education, and training services.

- Occupational training, apprenticeships, and education through the Armed Forces are several ways of furthering your education besides attending college.

- In order to evaluate careers thoroughly, you must examine work hours, work conditions, and starting and potential pay. You also need to consider how the career would fit with your lifestyle choices and goals.

Perhaps you have wondered, "How do I find the best career for me?" The answer is research. You need to research the careers that match your job interests and skills as well as offer the job opportunities you want.

Career Research Sources

Many sources are available to help you research careers. These include local and school libraries, career information guides, the Internet, guidance counselors, career conferences, and your own observations and conversations. However, it is up to you to do the research. You must take the initiative to find information about the careers that interest you. The more information you learn about careers, the more likely you will be to select a satisfying one.

Libraries

Your local and school libraries are important sources of career information. Many books, brochures, magazines, Web sites, DVDs, CDs, and other sources are available on careers, occupations, job searching, and training. Once you begin your career information search, you will probably be amazed at the number of sources available.

As you begin researching careers, be sure to check your libraries periodical section. Magazine articles are one of your best sources for current career information. The *Occupational Outlook Quarterly*, which is published by the U.S. Department of Labor, is a good source for providing up-to-date career information. It can also be accessed online at www.bls.gov/opub/ooq/ooqhome.htm.

Additional magazine articles can be found by checking *The Readers' Guide to Periodical Literature*. This guide indexes articles that appear in major magazines. It lists articles alphabetically by subject, such as *careers*. The guide also lists the title of the article, name and date of the magazine, and page number(s).

Some libraries have pamphlet files for specific occupations. These files often contain career booklets published by large companies or professional associations. They may also contain current newspaper articles related to careers. See 14-1.

Other sources of career information include nonprint materials such as DVDs, CDs, and videotapes. Most libraries also have computers available for you to use so you can access career sites on the Internet.

If you have any trouble locating information, do not hesitate to ask a librarian for help. If you know what careers you want to research, a librarian can help locate the materials related to your interests.

Thinking It Through

Why is it important to research careers before choosing one?

Discuss

What are some ways to learn about careers beyond those listed on this page?

Resource

Library Research, Activity A, WB

Reflect Further

What types of career planning information are available in your school's guidance office?

Career Information Guides

The U.S. Department of Labor provides the following valuable career information guides. These guides help you learn about occupations and career options. They can usually be found in your local or school library or school guidance office. These guides are also available online.

- The *Occupational Outlook Handbook* (www.bls.gov/oco) describes the training and education needed for various occupations. It lists expected earnings, working conditions, and future job prospects. The *Occupational Outlook Handbook* also lists related occupations and sources of more in-depth information for specific careers. This guide is updated every two years.

- The *Career Guide to Industries* (www.bls.gov/oco/cg/cgjobout.htm) describes the training and education needed for various occupations. It shows expected earnings, working conditions, and future job prospects, and provides links to information about each state's job market. This guide can be used as a companion with the *Occupational Outlook Handbook*.

14-1

You can learn more about careers and what interests you by using the resources at your local library.

The Internet

If you have access to the Internet, a wealth of career information is at your fingertips. For example, the U.S. Department of Labor guides described in the previous section are also online. In addition, the following government Web sites are good sources to explore as you conduct your career research:

- *The U.S. Department of Labor Employment and Training Administration* (www.doleta.gov) is a resource for students, parents, guidance counselors, and others. It offers information and related Web sites for career exploration and planning. It also offers tools for examining your interests and personality to help identify suitable careers. Information on training and apprenticeships, applying to college, and pursuing a career in the Armed Forces is also provided. Selecting career-related topics from this large Web site's index is one of the best ways to see all the information it offers.

Activity

Select a career cluster that sparks your interest. Research a minimum of five jobs within that cluster using one of the career information guides listed on this page.

- **The Occupational Information Network (O*NET™)** system is gradually replacing the former resource, the *Dictionary of Occupational Titles.* The O*Net™ system provides the latest information needed for effective training, education, counseling, and employment of workers. The O*Net system offers three valuable features. The *O*Net Database* (www.onetcenter.org) identifies and describes the key components of over 900 modern occupations. *O*Net Online* (www.online.onetcenter.org), a Web-based viewer, lets students, professionals, and job seekers explore a variety of occupations, prerequisite skills, and earning potential. The *O*Net Career Exploration Tools* (www.onetcenter.org) are a set of assessments that help students and job seekers identify their interests and abilities so they can search for careers that match their preferences.

- **Career Voyages** (www.careervoyages.gov/) is sponsored by the U.S. Departments of Labor and Education. *Career Voyages* contains valuable information for students, parents, job seekers, and career advisors. It has information on career clusters, emerging industries, and education and training needed for in-demand occupations. The site also provides videos and links to other career information for each industry.

- **CareerOneStop** (www.careeronestop.org) is sponsored by the U.S. Department of Labor. It helps students, job seekers, and career professionals explore the outlook and trends for all types of careers. It provides information about the training required for jobs and the earnings potential for specific occupations by state. You can use the library at this site to explore your career interests, assess your skills, and link to other career exploration sites.

  America's Career InfoNet (www.careerinfonet.org) is part of *CareerOneStop.* This Web site provides education and training information and earnings potential. It also provides assessment tools so job seekers can determine their interests and abilities.

  America's Service Locator (www.servicelocator.org) is a part of *CareerOneStop.* This Web site connects job seekers to employment opportunities available at One-Stop Career Centers. **One-Stop Career Centers** coordinate government employment offices at local, state, and national levels to provide a wide range of employment, education, and training services. *America's Service Locator* provides the job seeker access to any state's job bank to find current employment opportunities.

Beyond these government-sponsored sources, you can locate other Internet sites for career research by using the search term *careers.* Some of these sites are listed in 14-2. As a general rule, you will find that many of the Web sites for researching careers are sponsored by government agencies or universities. If you are searching for a specific job online, make sure you use more specific search terms. Many companies also have their own Web sites with career information and job postings. (Using the Internet to search for jobs is discussed further in Chapter 16, "Applying for Jobs.")

More Web Sites for Researching Careers		
Source	**Internet Address**	**Description**
Mapping Your Future	www.mapping-your-future.org	Career planning and financial aid information for students and families from agencies linked to the Federal Family Education Loan Program
My Future	www.myfuture.com	Career assistance for teens
Career Resource Center	www.careers.org	Online job research center
Career Magazine	www.careermag.com	Career research site for job seekers from *Career* magazine
Career Path	www.careerpath.com	Career exploration and planning site for job seekers
Note: Internet addresses and content are subject to change without notice.		

14-2

Dozens of nongovernment Web sites, generally from educational institutions, are available for researching careers. These are some examples.

One-Stop Career Centers

Many cities have federally mandated career centers as part of America's One-Stop Career Center System. By coordinating local, state, and national resources, One-Stop Career Centers can provide employment counseling and assessment, information on job trends, and assistance in filing unemployment insurance. The centers also help individuals find job training and government funds to help pay training costs.

Different names are used for the centers in different states. You can find the center nearest you by contacting your state employment office and asking for the location of the closest One-Stop Career Center. You can also locate the center nearest you by visiting Web sites such as *America's Service Locator* (www.servicelocator.org). An online search using the search term *One-Stop Career Centers* can also guide you to additional resources.

Guidance Counselors

Guidance counselors also play an important role in providing career information. When you want to know more about a specific occupation, a guidance counselor can direct you to the information you need. Many guidance counselors keep career files in their offices that contain up-to-date information about different occupations and their educational requirements.

If you are in the process of trying to determine a career interest, a guidance counselor can help you explore your options. A guidance counselor will help you consider career options in relation to your abilities and personal goals. He or she can also answer questions about entry requirements and costs of schools, colleges, and training programs that offer the education you need to prepare for a specific career.

Discuss

How can job listings provide helpful information to a person seeking general information about careers?

Resource

Your Guidance Counselor, Activity C, WB

Career Conferences

Schools often have career days when representatives from various occupations, professions, and schools are available to speak to interested students. Sometimes a local community college or chamber of commerce sponsors these events. Be sure to participate in these programs and talk with representatives to learn more about your career options.

Informal Interviews and Personal Observations

If possible, have informal interviews with workers who are in jobs that interest you. See 14-3. An informal interview is a discussion for seeking advice. Having a chance to actually talk with workers will give you insight into their occupations. Your guidance counselor can help you identify key people who can tell you more about a given career area. Most will be glad to talk with you if you keep the interview brief and talk at a time that is convenient for them.

By asking key questions, you can find out what kind of training is important and how workers got their first jobs. You can also ask workers what they like most and least about their jobs. Informal interviews with people will help you learn more about a specific occupation and the business world in general. Discussions with workers will also help you make future job contacts and practice interviewing.

You can also learn more about a career by staying alert to happenings around you. While at school and at work, you observe people working every day. Do any of their jobs interest you? Sometimes a newspaper story or a TV program will reveal facts about a certain career that catches your attention. Perhaps your friends tell you about people they know who love their jobs.

When you learn of a career that seems promising, become your own career investigator. Gather facts and talk with people who can provide more information as you search for the right career.

14-3

Interviewing a worker in a career that interests you can help you find out what qualifications and training you may need.

Evaluating Careers

As you research career options, be sure to evaluate them carefully. For each career you explore, you should be able to answer the following questions:

- What educational requirements are needed?

- What are the general work hours?

- Under what conditions would you be working?

- How much pay could you expect to earn?

- How would this career fit into your lifestyle and goals?

Finding the answers to these questions will help you choose a more satisfying and rewarding occupation.

Educational Requirements

Education is often the most important consideration when evaluating careers. The career you choose will determine the training and education you need. You may already be in the process of learning skills for an occupation in your high school classes. Most occupations, however, require further training after high school.

Do the occupations that interest you require further education? How much time, effort, and money are you willing to spend on your education? Can you receive the education you need through training? Could you learn the skills you need through an apprenticeship? Will you need a college degree? Should you consider career training through the Armed Forces? The amount of training and education you obtain will influence your earnings and your opportunities for job advancement, 14-4.

Occupational Training

Occupational training prepares a person for a job in a specific field. Training can be received through occupational schools, skill centers, community colleges, company training programs, and correspondence or online programs. Since the quality of training can vary from one source to another, it is important to investigate a training program before you enroll.

If you choose to attend an occupational school, skill center, or a community college, be selective. Make sure the school has up-to-date equipment and facilities to provide you with up-to-date training. There are many fine occupational schools with excellent instructors. There are also schools that will be willing to take your money, but fail to provide you with the training you need. Your guidance counselor or school-to-work coordinator can help you evaluate occupational schools so you choose an appropriate one.

Resource

Sources for Career Research, Activity E, WB

Enrich

Develop an annual budget that honestly reflects your desired lifestyle. Will your job preferences support that lifestyle?

Resource

Job Education Benefits, reproducible master 14-1, TR

Activity

Interview people who have entered the job market through occupational training.

Reflect Further

What are the educational requirements for the careers that interest you?

14-4

How much you invest in your education and training will influence your future earning potential.

Reflect Further

What factors should you consider when choosing a provider of occupational training?

Activity

Select an industry and identify one technological change, either current or past, that is linked to the industry. Describe one positive and one negative outcome of the change.

Some companies will train employees for specific skills needed within their companies. Company trainers, through regular class instruction, may offer employees training. In some cases, trainers from outside the company may be brought in to provide instruction. Company training offers employees the chance to develop and improve their job skills on site.

If you live in an isolated area, you may find correspondence or online courses are a good way to further your education. See 14-5. These courses are often offered through community colleges and universities as well as private correspondence schools. Students complete the course requirements at home and mail their work to the school for evaluation and course credit. Many schools are now offering these courses online. Students are able to submit assignments and communicate directly with teachers through e-mail. Educating yourself by this method usually requires a great deal of self-discipline since the motivation to do the work must come from you.

Be sure to check the quality of any correspondence or online course carefully before enrolling. Check the school's reputation with prospective employers. If you plan to attend a school later but take a few correspondence courses now, make sure your course work will **transfer**. Courses transfer when one school accepts the credit given by another. Be especially suspicious of courses that eliminate the lab work or hands-on experience that is required of courses taught in traditional settings.

Apprenticeships

If you enjoy technical skills and want to learn a specific trade, an apprenticeship may be right for you. Employment opportunities and earnings are good for those who complete apprenticeships. An *apprenticeship* is a combination of on-the-job training and related classroom instruction in which workers learn the practical and theoretical aspects of a highly skilled occupation. Skills are actually learned under the supervision of a skilled tradesperson.

In Chapter 1, "Making the Transition from School to Work," you learned about the programs offered in some high schools called *youth apprenticeships*. Graduation from these programs may lead to immediate employment, but several more years of training are usually required. The training is gained through a **registered apprenticeship**. This is an advanced training program that operates under standards approved by the Office of Apprenticeship. The Office of Apprenticeship is a division of the U.S. Department of Labor.

There are approximately 28,000 apprenticeship programs registered with the Office of Apprenticeship. New programs are continually being added. See 14-6 for a sample listing of several job categories for which an apprenticeship program exists. Complete details on registered apprenticeships can be obtained by directly contacting the U.S. Department of Labor Office of Apprenticeship (www.doleta.gov/OA/eta_default.cfm). You can also view information on apprenticeship programs at the *Career Voyages* Web site (www.careervoyages.gov/). For additional information, you can conduct your own Internet search using the search term *apprenticeship programs*.

A high school diploma or equivalent certificate is the general requirement for entering an apprenticeship. However, application requirements may differ in various states and from one trade to another. An applicant must be at least 16 years of age and meet the program qualifications. Generally, applicants prove they have the ability, aptitude, and education to master the basics of the occupation and complete the related instruction required in the program. See 14-7. Many apprentice programs are difficult to enter. In some training programs, it is not unusual to have several hundred applicants for 25 new apprentice positions.

Apprentice programs require that the apprentice learn the entire trade, not just parts of it. This is accomplished by breaking down each trade into basic skill blocks. As apprentices complete each block, their skill and

14-5

Online courses offer you the convenience of furthering your education through the use of your computer.

Examples of Apprenticeship Programs	
• Air Transport Pilot	• Graphic Designer
• Automotive Technician Specialist	• Hotel/Restaurant Management
• Boiler Operator	• Machinist
• Catering	• Medical Transcriptionist
• Certified Nursing Assistant	• Mechanic
• Computer Operator	• Paramedic
• Computer Programmer	• Pharmacy Technician
• Construction Worker	• Pipelayer
• Dental Assistant	• Press Operator
• Dispatchers	• Tool and Die Maker
• Electricians	• Truck Driver
• Estimators and Drafters	• Welder

14-6

There are many apprenticeship programs for you to consider besides these.

Activity

Gather information on apprenticeships related to a career cluster that interests you. Write a report of your findings.

Activity

Carefully study the actual costs of a college degree for a program that interests you. Brainstorm ways you may cut those costs.

Discuss

Identify the two- and four-year colleges in your area and the programs they offer.

Extend Your Knowledge

Apprenticeship Programs

Joint employer and labor groups, employer associations, and individual employers sponsor apprenticeship programs. Apprenticeship training offers individuals a chance to earn while they learn. In addition to a paid 40-hour work week that includes on-the-job training, apprentices are required to attend related training on selected evenings and/or weekends. Wage increases are granted as apprentices gain experience through increased time in training.

understanding of the trade grows and their pay increases. A basic math skills test is usually required for admission to a large number of apprentice programs. Most apprenticeships take about four years to complete.

A College Education

14-7

Most unions with apprenticeships have people anxious to help you process your application.

A high school education or occupational training is adequate for many occupations. Professional occupations in certain fields, however, often require a one- or two-year technical program or a four-year college education.

Consider the examples of an architectural drafter and an architect. An architectural drafter is someone who makes drawings of buildings to be built, while the architect is the person who designs the buildings. Two years of training at an occupational school or a two-year college prepares an architectural drafter. However, it takes five or six years of college with two to three years of work experience to become a registered architect. Although the two occupations are in the same field, the job of an architect requires advanced training. Since an architect has more training and education than an architectural drafter, the architect has more skills to use on the job. Therefore, the architect is able to earn a higher salary.

If a four-year college is part of your career plans, be sure to choose a college or university that can help you achieve your career goals. For example, if you want to become a mechanical engineer, choose a school that has a reputable engineering department. To find out which colleges offer the programs that interest you, begin by talking with your guidance counselor. A guidance counselor can help you review college catalogs and evaluate the programs they offer.

Compare different colleges and universities on the basis of reputation, entry requirements, cost, and convenience. Then apply to the school or schools you would like to attend. Sometimes it is best to apply to more than one school. Because of certain entry requirements, some schools may not accept you. Also, applying to more than one school gives you time to reconsider your alternatives. A college education is an investment in your future, so you will want to make your choice carefully.

Armed Forces

Each year the Armed Forces provide thousands of men and women educational training that can be used in both military and civilian careers. Training is available for clerical and administrative jobs, skilled construction work, electrical and electronic occupations, auto repair, and hundreds of other specialties. See 14-8.

Receiving educational training through a branch of the Armed Forces has a number of advantages. There is little or no cost to the student for training. The student gets paid while being trained. In addition, the student receives many benefits, such as paid vacations, paid health care programs, free housing, and opportunities for travel and advancement.

Military life does have its disadvantages, however. It is more disciplined than civilian life. People in the military must follow orders regarding what they wear, where they go, and what they do. When a person joins a branch of the Armed Forces, that person must stay for three, four, or six years, or until the end of his or her contract. People in the military cannot leave or resign before the end of their terms if they decide they do not like military life.

Joining the military may be right for you if you want education and training beyond high school. You must be willing to conform to the military way of life and work well with others.

Work Hours

In the workplace, different jobs involve different work hours. A baker may start work at 4 a.m., while a night security guard may start at 7 p.m. When some people are beginning their workdays, others are ending their jobs to go home. What work hours would you prefer? Would you mind working long workdays or irregular hours? Would you prefer a seasonal occupation?

Thinking It Through

Why is it important to be selective when choosing a college?

Activity

Invite a recruitment officer of a branch of the Armed Forces to speak about military-related career opportunities.

Discuss

Do you know someone with current or recent military experience? How has it helped his or her career search?

14-8

The Armed Forces offer a variety of educational opportunities and training programs.

In the Real World

What Career for Alicia?

Alicia, a senior in high school, is a very talented person, especially in art. She sketches, uses watercolors, and paints with oils. Many of her illustrations have been printed in the school newspaper. Alicia designs and makes her own clothes. She also designed the costumes for all the school plays held during the past two years.

Alicia has done well in all her subjects and every activity she has pursued. That is part of her problem. She has so many interests and skills that she does not know which career to choose. Her current problem is trying to decide what type of training or educational program to take.

At the suggestion of her guidance counselor, Alicia wrote down what she hoped to accomplish over the next five to ten years. She wrote down these goals:

- to work in the interior design or graphic arts industry
- to work in a career that offers possibilities for travel

Alicia began thinking about the career areas that interested her. She realized that talking to people in similar careers might help her make a career decision. Her guidance counselor recommended several professionals who were willing to talk to Alicia about their careers. When it came time to actually phone them for appointments, however, Alicia always found other things to do.

After much soul-searching, Alicia believed that an interior design career suited her best. She learned that a four-year degree was required. Fortunately, a university that taught the program at a campus relatively close accepted her. She spent one year there before realizing that interior design was not for her.

She missed painting, sketching, and seeing her work used in publications. When a local advertising agency heard of her interest in a graphic arts career, they offered her a good-paying job on the spot. She was told about a visual arts program at the local community college that offered courses to broaden her skills. She also learned that the Armed Forces needed graphic artists and would pay the education expenses of a person who showed promise in that area. Now faced with so many options, Alicia does not know what to do.

Questions to Discuss

1. Did Alicia research her career interests well?
2. How could Alicia have improved her career research?
3. What would you advise Alicia to do?
4. What have you learned from Alicia's experience that may help you make a career decision more wisely?

It is important to consider working hours in your career planning. For example, if you know you want to work daytime hours during weekdays only, you may not want to consider a career in nursing. As a nurse, you may be required to work afternoon and night shifts as well as weekends and holidays. If you do not enjoy working in an office building all day, five days a week, then a less-confining occupation may be better. A career in sales, construction, or police work would enable you to move around from place to place.

Most employees work forty hours a week. Office workers usually work from 9 a.m. to 5 p.m. on weekdays. Factory and service employees

Discuss

After studying careers more, have your career interests changed? How?

work in eight-hour shifts for any five days of the week. They may work the morning shift, 7 a.m. to 3 p.m.; the afternoon shift, 3 p.m. to 11 p.m.; or the night shift, 11 p.m. to 7 a.m. Some employees work 10 hours a day, four days a week. Other workers are allowed to set their own work schedules so long as they include a core period when all department employees must be present, such as 10 a.m. to 2 p.m.

Many occupations require people to work irregular hours as needed, 14-9. People in real estate and insurance sales often work evening hours and weekends in order to schedule appointments with their clients. Some doctors also work irregular hours on occasion. An obstetrician may be called to deliver a baby any time of the day or night.

Some occupations are seasonal, such as farming field crops, playing professional sports, and operating a ski resort. Farmers usually work their longest hours when the crops must be planted, fertilized, and harvested. Athletes work many hours just before and during their playing seasons, but are off the rest of the year. Winter ski resort owners only operate during cold, snowy months.

Work Conditions

When evaluating occupations, you should also consider the conditions in which you will be working. Are there certain environmental, physical, or mental conditions that you find uncomfortable? Would you be opposed to working in dusty, dirty, noisy, steamy, or freezing conditions? Would you dislike lifting boxes, climbing ladders, or sitting at a desk all day?

Do you prefer following a set routine over and over like an assembly line or factory worker? Would you prefer a job with constant variety so no two days are alike? Do you want to work alone or in a team with others?

Every job has desirable and undesirable working conditions. See 14-10. You will want to choose the job that will most satisfy you.

Reflect

Do your career interests match the working conditions you would prefer? Are you willing to tolerate lesser conditions until you move up the career ladder?

Reflect Further

What work conditions would you avoid? Describe the ideal work conditions.

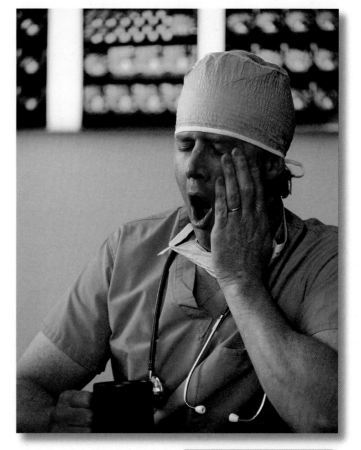

14-9

Doctors often have to work long and irregular hours and may be called to work anytime.

14-10

Traveling a lot and not working in an office appeals to some people and may be an undesirable work condition for others.

The Pay: Starting and Potential

Although an occupation should not be selected just on the basis of earnings, pay is an important aspect to consider. How much money do you expect to earn during the first year? How much do you want to earn after two years or five years?

Learn what wages or salaries you can expect to earn in the occupations that interest you. What is the starting pay? How much do experienced workers earn? Can you support yourself on that amount of income? Could you support a family? Will additional education be necessary for significant pay increases in the future?

The amount of the paycheck is not the only financial consideration. Does the company provide any fringe benefits? **Fringe benefits** are financial extras in addition to the regular paycheck. Medical and life insurance coverage, paid vacation and sick time, bonuses, and retirement plans are examples of fringe benefits. You may be further ahead financially with a lower paying job that includes excellent benefits than with a higher paying job having few or no benefits.

Personal Lifestyle and Goals

When you evaluate your career interests, you may also want to consider how your career will fit your life. In matching yourself to the right career, think about your personal lifestyle and goals, 14-11. How would certain careers affect your lifestyle choices? Your career can affect many important aspects of your future—where you live, your income, your friends, and your family. What are your future goals? Do you want to complete school and start a career? Do you plan on marriage and a family? Knowing your personal goals can help you make a wiser decision about your future career.

If your goals include marriage, how will you manage a marriage and a career? Discussing both marriage and career goals before planning to marry and have a family is important. If you and your spouse plan to have careers outside the home and raise a family, you will be part of a **dual-career family**. This means managing the demands of a career as well as family responsibilities.

A dual-career family can be a beneficial arrangement for both spouses. They can experience personal growth in their careers and contribute to the family's income. Opportunities for sharing home and family tasks can help strengthen a marriage. For couples with children, relationships may improve within the family if both spouses work. Children may become more independent. When the mother works outside the home, this may give the father more time with the children. He may also share in the household tasks.

Managing a dual-career family can also lead to problems. Caring for a home and children can be difficult when a couple works. Spouses may have different working hours. For example, one spouse may work during the day while the other spouse works at night. This may create problems in managing personal schedules, child care, and household tasks. One spouse may be transferred to another city, interfering with the other spouse's career plans. Home and family responsibilities may not be equally shared.

Career-oriented parents often have difficulties fitting child care into their work schedules. Child care within the home may be more convenient, but most parents take their children to a child care center or home. Some employers recognize this concern by providing on-site child care facilities for their employees. Other employers may help pay part of the cost of child care at child care facilities close to the work site.

The demands of a dual-career family can cause physical and emotional strains. To manage these, family members need to work together as a team. See 14-12. When family members accept and share household responsibilities, they learn cooperation, self-worth, and appreciation of each other.

Making a career decision can be complex. It should be taken very seriously since it will greatly impact your future. Gain a deep understanding of yourself and gather all the facts you can about your career interests before making a decision. Then consider your personal lifestyle and goals. Careful thought and planning should help guide you toward your career decision.

14-11

Listing your personal goals can help you evaluate how well a career choice is likely to fit your lifestyle.

14-12

When spouses have the same working hours, they are more able to smoothly coordinate family responsibilities.

Summary

By using the many sources available to help you research careers, you can find information about those that interest you. The Internet is a very valuable research tool. Schools and local libraries are also important sources of all types of career information. Using career information guides can help you learn more about different career options. Guidance counselors can provide up-to-date career information or help you explore your career interests. Attending career conferences or talking with workers employed in jobs that interest you is another way to research career choices.

Evaluating careers of interest is the best way to choose the best option for you. You will need to consider the educational requirements, work hours, work conditions, and pay levels for each career. Most importantly, you should consider how well a given career would fit your personal lifestyle and goals. Managing a career and family can be an important consideration when evaluating your career choices.

Resource

Review and Study Guide for Chapter 14, reproducible master 14-2, TR

Answers to *Facts In Review*

1. (List five:) libraries, career information guides, the Internet, guidance counselors, career conferences, informal interviews, personal observations

2. periodical section

3. *Occupational Outlook Handbook, Career Guide to Industries*

4. (Student response.)

5. provides career information, compares job requirements to personal interests and abilities, answers questions about educational requirements and suitable educational institutions

6. (List two:) to gain insight into their careers, to practice interviewing skills, to develop future job contacts

7. (List four:) What educational requirements are needed? What are the work hours? What are the work conditions? What pay level can be expected? How will the career fit the person's lifestyle and goals?

8. (List four:) occupational schools, skill centers, community colleges, company training programs, correspondence or online courses

9. (List five. See Chart 14-6 on page 297.)

Facts in Review

1. Name five sources available to help research careers.

2. Where is a good place to begin your library research?

3. Name two career information guides published by the U.S. Department of Labor that can help you identify occupations and career options.

4. What information can you obtain from the Internet that will help a career search?

5. How can a guidance counselor help a student learn more about careers?

6. Name two reasons for talking to people who work in jobs that interest you.

7. List four questions that can help determine how well a person is suited to a specific career.

8. Where can you receive occupational training?

9. Name five examples of a registered apprenticeship.

10. What are the advantages and disadvantages of receiving educational training through a branch of the Armed Forces?

11. Why is it important to consider a job's work hours when planning a career?

12. Why should fringe benefits be considered when selecting a career?

13. Why is it important to consider personal lifestyle and goals in evaluating a career?

14. Describe the benefits and problems that a dual-career family may experience.

10. advantages—pay little or nothing for training, receive pay and benefits, have opportunities for travel and advancement; disadvantages—must adhere to strict discipline, must follow orders regarding what to do and wear, cannot leave or resign before one's term expires

11. because a job's work hours will greatly determine a person's lifestyle

12. because their dollar value can exceed that of a higher paying job with few or no benefits

13. because a career can affect where one lives as well as one's friends, income, and family

14. (Student response. See pages 302-303.)

Developing Your Academic Skills

1. **Language Arts.** Take a tour of your school or local library. Experiment with using resources such as the *Reader's Guide to Periodical Literature*.

2. **Math.** Using Internet or print sources, search for a basic math skills test as admission to an apprenticeship program. Practice your math skills by completing the test.

3. **Social Studies.** Using Internet or print sources, research the history of one branch of the Armed Forces of the United States. Prepare a one-page report of your findings and include examples of current programs offered.

4. **Speech.** With a group of classmates, debate the effect of dual careers on today's family.

Information Technology Applications

1. Practice using your school or local library's technology systems, such as online card catalogs or CD indexes. Write a brief report of your experiences.

2. Using some of the Web sites listed in this chapter, research five careers that interest you. Print out the information found on these careers. Prepare a presentation of the information to share with the class.

Applying Your Knowledge and Skills

1. **Academic Foundations.** Choose three careers that interest you. Then go to your school or local library, search the Internet, and read two articles that directly relate to each career. Reread one of the six articles and write a one-page report about it.

2. **Employability and Career Development.** Using one of the U.S. Department of Labor's career information guides, look up three careers that interest you. For each career determine the following: training and education needed, expected earnings, working conditions, and job prospects for the future. Record your findings and share them with the class.

3. **Communications.** For each one of three careers that interest you, locate a successful person in each career and interview him or her to learn the following about each job: general job duties, working conditions and hours, necessary skills, recommended education and training, and future career outlook. Summarize your findings in a written report for your personal resource file.

Developing Workplace Skills

Select one career, acquire all the information you can, and become a class expert on it. Research the career area to find information on the following seven categories: basic job responsibilities, potential employers, general work conditions, educational/training requirements, other job qualifications, salary (starting and average), and sources of additional information.

Using a word processing program, create a one-page fact sheet with the seven headings and the main facts for each. Put the occupation's title on the top of the page and your name on the bottom.

Exchange fact sheets with a classmate and review each other's sheets for completeness and clarity. Discuss the improvements that each recommends for the other's sheet. Prepare a final copy of your fact sheet and turn it in. Copies of the fact sheet will be distributed to interested students who may come to you with additional questions to answer about the career.

15

Making Career Decisions

Key Terms

decision-making process

routine decisions

major decisions

career plan

entry-level job

advanced-level job

career ladder

Chapter Objectives

After studying this chapter, you will be able to

- **explain** the decision-making process.
- **apply** the decision-making process to developing a career plan.
- **identify** other applications for the decision-making process.

Reading Advantage

On separate sticky notes, write five reasons why the information in this chapter is important to you. Think about how this information could help you at school, work, or home. As you read the chapter, place the sticky notes on the pages that relate to each reason.

Achieving Academic Standards

English Language Arts

- Read print and non-print texts to acquire new information and to respond to the needs and demands of society and the workplace. (IRA/NCTE, 1)
- Apply strategies to comprehend, interpret, evaluate, and appreciate texts. (IRA/NCTE, 3)
- Use a variety of technological and information processes to gather and synthesize information and to create and communicate knowledge. (IRA/NCTE, 8)
- Use spoken, written, and visual language to accomplish their purposes. (IRA/NCTE, 12)

Math

- Compute fluently and make reasonable estimates. (NCTM)

Key Concepts

- Using the seven steps of the decision-making process helps you make major decisions carefully and logically.

- Developing a career plan will help you succeed in achieving your career goals.

- A career ladder shows a sequence of related jobs that are available at different educational levels.

- Using decision-making skills can positively affect your personal life, the decisions you make at work, and your purchasing decisions.

Resource

The Steps in Making a Career Decision, color transparency CT-15, TR

Discuss

Share a humorous example of a wrong decision you made.

Resource

Examining Decisions, Activity A, WB

Reflect

How many wrong decisions have you avoided?

Reflect Further

What are some routine decisions you make every day? What major decisions have you made?

Thinking It Through

What are the advantages of using the decision-making process to address a complex problem or decision?

As Enrico sat at the kitchen table, he shook his head and stared at the blank paper before him. Enrico had an assignment for English class: to write a two-page paper about his career plans.

Seventeen-year-old Enrico never seriously thought about a career for himself. This assignment forced him to sit down and think about his future. Enrico has no idea about what he wants to do after graduation. He wondered if there is some logical way to make such an important decision.

Enrico was right. There is a proven way to make important decisions. It is called the **decision-making process**. It is a seven-step process for making important decisions carefully and logically.

The Decision-Making Process

Making decisions is something you do every day. From the minute you get up in the morning, you begin making decisions. You decide what to wear, what to eat, and what time to leave for school. These **routine decisions** are made often. They are so minor you probably do not even know you are making them.

There are other decisions that take a little more thought, such as deciding which movie to see or what music to buy. These decisions usually require some thought but are generally very easy to make.

Then there are the major decisions. **Major decisions** are the toughest because they guide your career and personal life. Deciding whether to go to college, get married, or buy a car are major decisions. These decisions are significant because they take considerable resources and tend to have long-lasting effects, 15-1.

If you become a manager or supervisor on the job, you will also have major decisions to make. You may need to decide whether to hire or fire an employee. You may need to decide how to sell and market a new product. These are decisions that not only affect you, but also affect the company and the people with whom you work.

If you make a wrong decision about something that is not very important, the decision normally does not affect your life to any great extent. For example, Bill decided to buy his father a blue shirt for his birthday, but he bought the wrong size. Although Bill made an error, he was able to take the shirt back and exchange it for the right size. A wrong decision was made, but it was corrected with little effort and time.

On the other hand, if you make a wrong decision about something important, the decision may greatly influence your life. For example, Diane decided to be a dentist just because her father was one. She went through college and dental school and then realized she had made a big mistake. Being a dentist the rest of her life was the last thing she wanted to do. In fact, she only chose dentistry because she did not take the time to investigate other careers.

Now Diane realizes that teaching art is the career for her, and she wants to return to college for the required degree. Diane spent most of her college years unhappy about her career decision. She wasted thousands of dollars on an education she does not want to use. Now she must work a couple of years as a dentist to pay for her college expenses and a new loan for more education. Diane's quick career decision influenced her a great deal. It caused her much unhappiness as well as future financial problems.

Decision-Making Steps

When you have major decisions to make, you need to approach them carefully and logically. The decision-making process helps you do this. There are seven steps to follow when facing big decisions. They are summarized in 15-2 and explained here.

1. *Define the problem.* The first step is determining what the question or concern is and its importance to your life.

2. *Establish goals.* Set specific goals for yourself. Then identify what you want to accomplish from the decision you will make.

3. *Identify resources.* Make a list of the resources available to help you reach your goals. Include your human resources (such as aptitudes and abilities) as well as nonhuman resources (such as a car and savings account).

15-1

Deciding to get a college degree is a major decision because it usually involves considerable time, effort, and money.

4. *Consider the alternatives.* Explore all the options open to you, and weigh the advantages and disadvantages of each. A good way to test alternatives is to ask yourself the following questions: Will this decision have a bad effect on me or anyone else? Will it help me reach my goals? Is it illegal? Will I be happy with it?

5. *Make a decision.* Choose an alternative that will help you reach your goals. If you have carefully thought through these steps, you will probably be happy with the decision you make.

6. *Implement the decision.* Put the plan into action.

7. *Evaluate the results.* Judge how successful your plan was. Did your decision solve the problem or address the question completely? Are your goals being met? Are you satisfied with the results of the decision? Evaluating the results of a decision will help improve your future decision-making skills.

Resource

The Decision-Making Process,
Activity B, WB

Discuss

Is tardiness to class a problem or the symptom of a problem?

Career Decisions

Some of the hardest decisions to make are career decisions. Many people have no idea what they want to do for a living. They go from job to job and never really think about their future.

Your own career is too important for that. Career decisions are major decisions that influence your entire future. They need to be made with careful thought and planning. The work you choose will largely determine the way you live, people you meet, money you earn, and satisfaction you get from life. See 15-3.

You probably know some people who never really made a career decision; they just stayed in the first job they held. Some took any available job and hoped that it would lead to a fulfilling career. Some let their parents pick a career for them. Others chose the same career their best friends selected. Do you really think you would be satisfied letting someone else make decisions for you and not take the time to make them yourself? With the decision-making process, choosing a career can be easy and a great deal of fun.

Making a Career Plan

Once you know how to make important decisions by using the decision-making steps, it is time to apply that skill to developing a career plan. What career will be best for you? Before that all-important question can be answered, you must first take a careful self-assessment. This means you need to know the following about yourself:

*   interests, aptitudes, and abilities
*   strengths and weaknesses
*   significant personality traits

- values

- short- and long-term goals

- resources

Earlier chapters of the text covered all these areas to prepare you for the important exercise of making a career decision. The career you choose should use your special strengths and abilities, yet challenge you to develop others. See 15-4.

Especially compare your interests and skills. It is important that they match if you want to be successful in your career plans. It is not critical that they match exactly right now because you have not had enough time to develop all your skills. This is very common for high school students and recent graduates.

You may also have skills that you do not want to build a career around. For example, you may be an excellent fry cook or food server as a result of working in a fast-food restaurant. If you do not want to hold these or similar jobs for the long term, disregard the skills that relate exclusively to them. Concentrate instead on the skills necessary to pursue your desired career.

Once you decide what type of career interests you most, it is important to identify what it will take to fulfill that dream. This is called a career plan. A **career plan** is a list of steps to take to reach a career goal. While a career plan does not assure success, it greatly improves your chances of finding jobs that provide happiness and personal fulfillment. For example, Chris is a junior high school student who wants to become a conservation scientist. Her career plan is shown in 15-5. A career plan analyzes the steps a person will take to achieve the desired career goal. In Chris's case, for example, she must graduate from college first to be eligible for a job in her chosen career area.

A career plan is sometimes called a *career path* because it shows the steps that lead to a career goal. A career plan examines the following within each step:

- extracurricular and volunteer activities

- work or job experience

- education and training requirements

Notice how Chris's career plan states what she will do at each step to help obtain her career goal. Notice, too, that each level of the career plan builds upon the previous one. As each step is completed, Chris gains increased knowledge and experience. Focusing on your goal will help you determine the best steps for achieving it.

15-4

If you have a strong interest in computers, you may be suited to a career in computer engineering or computer software development.

Activity

Brainstorm other skills of an excellent food server that may relate to a completely different career. (Some possible answers are: exceptional neatness, courtesy with customers, good powers of persuasion, and fast and accurate execution of orders.)

Discuss

If an excellent opportunity becomes available, should you pass it up because it is not part of your career plan?

Extend Your Knowledge

Career Planning

It is important to determine if the career you are considering is really what you expect. Examine whether it offers the satisfaction, salary, and benefits you want. Many people find that high-salaried jobs do not always provide the total satisfaction they expected. Jobs that pay a bit less often provide more enjoyment and happiness in the long run. As you plan your career, keep in mind what will be most satisfying to you.

Career Plan for a Conservation Scientist			
	Extracurricular and Volunteer Activities	**Work Experience**	**Education and Training**
During Junior High School	• Help nonprofit groups and senior citizens with yard upkeep. • Select life science or environmental themes for fairs and competitive events.	Mow lawns and raise nursery plants for sale during summers.	For optional or extra-credit work, select topics and do projects pertaining to environmental or life sciences.
During High School	• Help waste recycling and land management efforts in the area. • Assist county conservation programs. • Attend public meetings on environmental matters.	Work part-time at a tree or plant nursery or in the gardening department of a local store.	Take a college preparatory program emphasizing biology and chemistry.
During College	• Help local groups identify and correct environmental problems.	Work part-time at a local conservation reserve, zoo, or botanical garden.	Take a B.S. degree program in the physical or environmental sciences in the preferred field.
After College	• Stay involved in local environmental matters and volunteer expertise as needed.	Work full-time as a conservation scientist for the state's conservation department.	Consider obtaining an advanced degree.

15-5

A career plan helps you map a path to the achievement of a career goal.

Creating a Career Ladder

There is no single route to achieving a career goal. Your resources, abilities, and values will direct a course that is best for you. When you first begin working full time or join a new employer, you will most likely be assigned to an entry-level job. An **entry-level job** is work for beginners who lack experience or specialized training. By acquiring special skills, knowledge, and experience, you prepared yourself for an **advanced-level job**.

Each career is composed of a sequence of related jobs—from entry-level to advanced—that are available at different educational levels. This is known as a **career ladder**. The example in 15-6 shows a series of job options at different levels for a person preparing to become a conservation scientist. Chris selected some of these jobs for her career plan. Each rung of the ladder presents some job possibilities for that level of education and training. The most complex jobs at the top of the ladder require the most education and training.

Remember, a career plan can be developed for any career goal, and any number of different routes can be used to reach the goal. A career plan is simply a road map to help you get to your destination, but as the driver, you are in charge. Your career plan should be updated every time there is a change in your goals or resources.

Using the Decision-Making Process

The decision-making process is a skill you can use throughout your life for making major decisions. Besides helping you achieve the career of your dreams, it can help with other important considerations in life. Learning decision-making skills can positively affect your personal life, the decisions you make at work, and your purchasing decisions.

Resource

Creating a Career Ladder, reproducible master 15-1, TR

Reflect

Do you want to work at the same job for your lifetime or at various jobs offering different challenges?

Resource

Preparing a Career Ladder, Activity D, WB

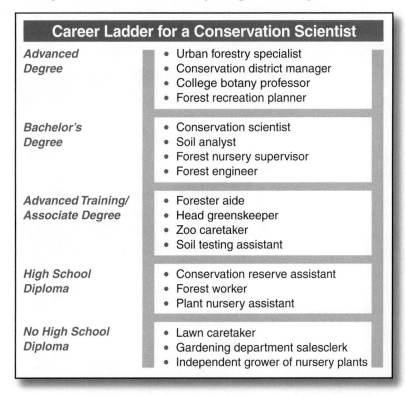

Career Ladder for a Conservation Scientist

Advanced Degree	• Urban forestry specialist • Conservation district manager • College botany professor • Forest recreation planner
Bachelor's Degree	• Conservation scientist • Soil analyst • Forest nursery supervisor • Forest engineer
Advanced Training/ Associate Degree	• Forester aide • Head greenskeeper • Zoo caretaker • Soil testing assistant
High School Diploma	• Conservation reserve assistant • Forest worker • Plant nursery assistant
No High School Diploma	• Lawn caretaker • Gardening department salesclerk • Independent grower of nursery plants

15-6

A career ladder shows job options for a career goal at different educational levels.

In the Real World

To School or Work?

Jerry will graduate from high school at the end of the year and wants a career in food service. He became interested in food service when he began his work-based learning experience as a cook's helper in a local restaurant. After four months of work, he now helps the chef develop new recipes.

1. Problem—Jerry must decide what type of career he wants in food service. He thinks he wants to be a chef, but that requires further training and Jerry wants a break from school. He does not want to spend the rest of his life as a cook's helper. Jerry wishes he could start being a chef right away.

2. Goals—He made the following list:
   - to become a successful chef in a large city restaurant
   - to work with friendly, creative coworkers and supervisors
   - to earn a good salary and have job security
   - to eventually own and manage a fine restaurant

3. Resources—Jerry has these resources:
   - knowledge of food service (from classroom work)
   - experience as a cook's helper at a local restaurant
   - strong desire to succeed in the food service industry and willingness to work hard
   - high school degree with good grades (nearly completed)

4. Alternatives—Jerry researched information on food service careers. He talked with a manager of a fast-food restaurant, two restaurant owners, and a noted chef in a large restaurant. From these conversations, he realized he had three options for pursuing a career as a chef:
   - Option 1—to earn a two-year culinary arts degree at a college or culinary institute
   - Option 2—to continue working as a cook's helper while taking food service courses at a community college
   - Option 3—to enter a three-year chef apprenticeship program

5. Decision—Jerry chose Option 3 because it would provide chef's training and on-the-job pay. Most of his training would take place in the commercial kitchen with highly qualified food service professionals. Only a few hours each week would involve classroom instruction.

6. Implementation—Jerry immediately sent for an application and applied for an apprenticeship. He knew it was important to apply early since entry into the program is very competitive.

7. Evaluation—Due to Jerry's good grades, food service experience, and enthusiasm, he was accepted into an apprenticeship program. From day one of the apprenticeship, he knew it was the right decision. Now Jerry looks forward to completing the apprenticeship and working as a professional chef.

Questions to Discuss

1. How did Jerry's list of career goals help him make a decision?
2. How did Jerry's list of resources help him move closer to his career goals?
3. How did research play an important role in Jerry's decision making?
4. If Jerry had not taken the time to plan his career carefully, what might have been the consequence?

Making Personal Decisions

Along with career decisions, you often need to make major decisions relating to your personal life. For example, major decisions may involve dating, getting engaged, choosing a marriage partner, or choosing a college. Should you have a family before you establish a career? Should you continue your education after you choose a career? Is marriage part of your future? These decisions have the potential for affecting your entire life. See 15-7.

Some decisions involve your lifestyle and health. These decisions might involve how to fit exercise into your daily routine or follow a nutritious diet. Relationships with your family, friends, or coworkers often involve decision making. You may want to decide whether or not to confront a friend who shoplifts. Should you buy a house or live in an apartment? There are many important decisions to make in life.

Making Work Decisions

You make decisions every day at work that can affect you and others. Sometimes they are simple; at other times they involve gathering facts and making a choice. For example, you may want to strengthen your relationships with your coworkers and improve your job performance. The decision might involve accepting a job promotion or transferring to another department. Asking for a raise, changing your work schedule, or finding a new job are other decisions you may need to make.

Activity

A student volunteer may present the "In the Real World" feature to the class and lead the discussion.

Resource

Decisions, Decisions, reproducible master 15-2, TR

Enrich

Select a short-term problem and solve it using the decision-making process.

Resource

Decision-Making Case Studies, reproducible master 15-3, TR

15-7
Many people with happy family lives credit successful careers as a key reason.

In the Real World

What Next for Vic?

Vic worked as a welder's helper since high school for a small family-owned company whose business was rebuilding heavy vehicle equipment. After Vic graduated, his boss offered him a full-time job with the company and Vic accepted. Within five years, Vic became shop supervisor and was practically running the place.

Then the boss retired, his son became company president, and everything changed. Vic was discouraged because his dream to move up and become part owner of the business seemed gone. With the new boss in charge, a lot of changes occurred. Many employees were fired and new work policies were posted. Then the boss hired a good friend who had as much experience as Vic. Now Vic was concerned about his future with the company. He no longer felt secure about his job and wondered if he, too, would be replaced.

1. Problem—Vic needs to decide what to do about his career, particularly his long-term goal of owning and operating his own business.
2. Goals—To help solve his problem, Vic wrote down a list of the things he wants to achieve:
   - to learn as much as possible about rebuilding and operating heavy vehicle equipment
   - to feel secure about a job
   - to make enough money to support a family comfortably
   - to own a rebuilding business
3. Resources—Vic also wrote down the resources he has to help him:
   - eagerness to learn everything about the heavy equipment rebuilding business
   - willingness to work hard to succeed
   - considerable experience in welding (seven years), heavy equipment work (six years), and supervision (three years)
4. Alternatives—After outlining his goals and resources, Vic outlined his options:

   - to continue working for the company and hope the new boss will eventually sell it
   - to talk with the new boss about his future with the company and interest in becoming part owner
   - to go to college part-time to get a business degree and continue saving money to start a rebuilding business
   - to borrow money to begin or buy a rebuilding business
   - to look for a job with another company
5. Decision—After careful thought, Vic chose two alternatives. He decided to talk with his new boss about his future with the company and his interest in becoming a part owner. By doing this, he would learn what the boss's plans are for him and if there is any possibility of buying a part of the company. Vic also decided to pursue a business degree part-time and put more money into savings for a future business.
6. Implementation—The following week Vic talked to his boss, enrolled in a business course at the community college, and began a monthly savings plan.
7. Evaluation—Talking to his boss was one of the best decisions Vic ever made. He learned that his boss was very pleased with his work and was planning to give him more responsibility for running the business. His boss even said he might sell the entire company in four or five years, but would definitely pay half of Vic's school expenses for courses that would help him do a better job for the company.

Questions to Discuss

1. How do you think the decision-making process helped Vic make his decisions?
2. How did Vic's goals help him make his decisions?
3. Do you think Vic made the right decisions at this point in his career? Why?
4. What can you learn from Vic's experience?

Making Consumer Decisions

Because so many goods and services are available to you as a consumer, making choices can be difficult. Making major purchases, such as a new car or computer, require careful thinking and planning before you buy. You can use the decision-making process to help you make more satisfying choices. See 15-8.

Throughout your life you will make consumer choices about food, clothing, transportation, energy, and housing. You must also make financial decisions about budgeting, saving, or investing. Buying a car is one example of a decision that may affect your life for several years. Should you buy a new car or a used one? For how many years should you make monthly payments? Can you afford the insurance and maintenance costs? The decision-making process is especially helpful when you face important decisions.

15-8

The decision-making process is especially helpful when making an expensive purchase because it forces you to investigate all your alternatives.

Summary

You make many types of decisions every day. Some are routine, while others require more thought and time. Major decisions are the hardest to make since they affect your life in many ways. Career decisions are major decisions that require careful thought and planning. They influence your entire future.

When making any major decision, you can use the decision-making process to help you sort your thoughts. By following each step of the process, you can determine the best choice and work toward the results you want.

Decision-making skills can be used to develop a career plan. First, you must recognize what you know about yourself. Then you can determine the type of career goal that will satisfy you. A career plan will help you decide how to achieve a chosen career.

The decision-making process is a skill you can use in other areas. When making important decisions, you can use this skill to help manage your life and make better choices.

Facts in Review

1. Why should a person be extra careful when making major career and personal decisions?
2. List and explain the seven steps to logical decision making.
3. What is the purpose of step three in the decision-making process?
4. What questions can be asked to test the alternatives for solving a problem or making a decision?
5. What is the purpose of the last step in the decision-making process?
6. The career a person chooses can largely determine what four factors?
7. Name two ways some people make career decisions other than using the decision-making process.
8. Name at least four factors that should be considered when taking a self-assessment before making a career decision.
9. True or false. A student's career plan should never change.
10. Besides career decisions, for what other matters can the decision-making process be used?

Resource

Review and Study Guide for Chapter 15, reproducible master 15-4, TR

Answers to *Facts In Review*

1. because the decisions tend to have long-lasting effects
2. Define the problem; establish goals; identify resources; consider alternatives; make a decision; implement it; evaluate results. (Explanation is student response.)
3. to identify resources so a person knows what is available to help reach a goal
4. Will the decision have a bad effect on me or anyone else? Will it help me reach my goals? Is it illegal? Will I be happy with it?
5. to evaluate results so decision-making skills are improved in the future
6. how you live, who you meet, what you earn, what satisfaction you get from life
7. (List two:) take any job and hope for the best, let parents decide, let friends decide
8. (List four:) interests, aptitudes, abilities, strengths, weaknesses, significant personality traits, values, short- and long-term goals, resources
9. false
10. personal decisions, work decisions, consumer decisions

Developing Your Academic Skills

1. **Math.** Pretend you are making a major purchase, such as a car, and apply the decision-making process to this purchase. Research any information you will need to consider, such as cost, insurance, and reliability. Be sure to consider long-term repercussions of your decisions. Record your plan.

2. **Language Arts.** Use the decision-making process to help narrow your career choices or choose a specific career. Describe each factor considered in the decision-making process, including your goals, resources, and alternatives to consider. Prepare an oral or written plan.

Information Technology Applications

1. Using the computer, make a flowchart applying the seven steps in the decision-making process to a real-life decision.

2. Using tables in a word processing program, prepare a personal career plan.

Applying Your Knowledge and Skills

1. **Problem Solving and Critical Thinking.** Apply the decision-making process to a major decision (other than a career decision) you might face within a year or two. Write down the problem, your goals, resources, alternatives, and the decision you would make. What are the pros and cons of using the decision-making process to solve problems and make decisions? Discuss your opinions with the class.

2. **Employability and Career Development.** Using Internet or print sources, determine today's average salaries within three career areas that interest you. For each career area, research the different salary levels for four jobs with different educational requirements—no high school diploma, high school diploma, postsecondary training, associate degree, bachelor's degree, or advanced degree.

Developing Workplace Skills

Using Internet or print sources, complete an educational and training plan for a career preference. Refer to the *Occupational Outlook Handbook* as one of your references. Using a word processing program, create two career plans that begin with entry into high school. Chart one career plan through postsecondary education and the other, through a training program. (The plans should resemble 15-5.) Keep these in your personal career file as references.

Part 4
The Job Hunt

16

Applying for Jobs

Key Terms

networking

résumé

personnel/human resource department

blind ads

personal fact sheet

reference

portfolio

letter of application

Chapter Objectives

After studying this chapter, you will be able to

- **explain** how to find job openings.
- **create** job résumés, letters of application, and portfolios.
- **prepare** job application forms correctly.

Reading Advantage

After reading each section (separated by main headings) stop and write a three- to four-sentence summary of what you just read. Be sure to paraphrase and use your own words.

Achieving Academic Standards

English Language Arts

- Read print and non-print texts to acquire new information and to respond to the needs and demands of society and the workplace. (IRA/NCTE, 1)
- Use spoken and written language to communicate effectively. (IRA/NCTE, 4)
- Use a variety of technological and information processes to gather and synthesize information and to create and communicate knowledge. (IRA/NCTE, 8)
- Use spoken, written, and visual language to accomplish their purposes. (IRA/NCTE, 12)

Key Concepts

- Job hunting requires using all resources available to find job openings.

- A personal fact sheet will help you write letters of application, prepare job résumés, and fill out application forms.

- A well-written résumé can help you stand out to an employer.

- A short, carefully worded letter of application should accompany each résumé you submit.

- An application form must be filled out completely and neatly.

HELP WANTED

Once you know what kind of job you want, you are ready for the job hunt. Half the battle of job hunting is finding job openings. The other half is getting interviews with employers.

To be successful on the job hunt, you need to have a plan. First, list all the companies where you would like to work. Second, prepare a résumé summarizing your education, work experience, and other qualifications for the job you want. Finally, contact the person in each company who has the responsibility to hire you.

Finding Job Openings

Job hunting takes work. Job openings will not wait for you; you must find them. To find available jobs, locate employers who are looking for a worker with your qualifications.

How do you find these employers? You can find them through a variety of sources. Some excellent sources of job leads include friends, relatives, and networking. **Networking** is talking with people and establishing relationships that can lead to more information or business. Other sources of job leads include school placement services, direct employer contact, want ads, trade and professional journals, state and private employment services, and the Internet.

Try using most or all these sources in your job hunt. The more sources you use, the more job openings you will likely find. Then, you will have a better chance of finding a job you really like instead of taking the first job that becomes available.

Friends and Relatives

Friends and relatives can be excellent sources of job leads. They may know employers who need a person with your skills. They may also know people who do the kind of work that interests you and places where these job openings exist.

When you mention your job search to friends and relatives, be sure to explain the type of job you want. Also, give them copies of your résumé. A **résumé** is a brief history of a person's education, work experience, and other qualifications for employment. (Résumés are discussed later in this chapter.) The more your friends and relatives know about you, the more able they are to talk about your skills and abilities to potential employers.

You should not be bashful about asking friends and relatives for job leads, but do not expect them to find a job for you. It is your responsibility to check job leads, arrange interviews, and "sell" yourself to a future employer.

Networking

Networking can begin long before you look for that first job. Networking involves developing contacts with people who are interested in you and are willing to help your search. It is a group of individuals

Thinking It Through

Why use several sources of job leads instead of just one or two to hunt for a job?

Thinking It Through

When you ask friends and family members for help with your job search, what do they need to know about you? Why should they have a copy of your résumé?

who know you, your interests, and your abilities. As you develop your network of contacts, you may eventually be in a position to help others. A good network of contacts should benefit all who are involved.

Both social and professional networks can help you find a job. A strong professional network, however, may be more important. This type of network includes people who are in a position to help you make job contacts. You can develop strong networks by taking part in a variety of activities. For example, you will meet local employers serving as guest speakers and judges when you participate in career and technical student organization activities. (These student organizations are described in Chapter 10, "Leadership and Group Dynamics.") If you impress these employers, they may offer you a job months or even years after the competition. The more contacts you make and the more you demonstrate your ability to work hard and effectively, the stronger your network will become.

School Placement Services

Many schools have a placement office or a school or vocational counselor to help students find jobs in the community. Students are usually asked to register with the placement office. When a job becomes available, the placement office then contacts qualified students for job interviews.

Your school placement office can be a good source for job leads, but you may be one of many selected to interview for available jobs. Competition is often stiff, so do not depend on your school as the only source of job leads. Investigate and use the many other sources available to you.

Direct Employer Contact

One of the best ways to find job openings is to contact employers directly. Many of the people who use this method of job hunting are successful in finding a job. To help you make a list of possible employers, look through the Yellow Pages in your phone book. Visit your chamber of commerce and public library. Ask your friends and relatives for contacts. Be sure to record the names, addresses, and phone numbers of all employers that may have the job you want. Also, do not overlook the job possibilities where you work now or have worked in the past.

Once you have a list of employers, begin contacting the person in each company who is responsible for hiring. A good place to find this person is the company's personnel or human resource department. The **personnel/human resource department** handles various responsibilities related to employment. These include screening potential job candidates, interviewing applicants, filing the necessary employee paperwork, and overseeing company benefits such as health insurance and vacation time. The person responsible for hiring is often the department director or manager. He or she will know the available jobs and the procedure to follow when applying for them.

Activity

Begin developing your network by listing individuals who may be helpful in your job search. Explain what help each can provide.

Enrich

Invite a school counselor to speak about placement services.

Note

Your state's *Directory of Manufacturers* would be an excellent source. It is available in most public libraries.

Enrich

Invite the personnel director from a local business to speak about proper procedures to follow when applying for a job.

Reflect Further

How many people in your network of contacts are willing to help you find a satisfying job? How can you enlarge your network?

In companies without a personnel department, the person to contact may be the manager of the specific department or even the president. If you know someone working for the company, ask him or her who to contact. You may also request permission to mention this person's name when inquiring about an opening. It is always helpful to know an employee of the company who can speak positively about you.

When you know who to contact at the organization, write a letter or make a phone call to express interest in working there. The interview process may be very formal or informal, depending on the employer. Companies that employ only a few people may invite job seekers to visit and fill out an application form. After a short interview, the job seeker may be hired within an hour. Larger companies and government agencies often require a screening process that usually takes much longer, sometimes weeks or even months.

Want Ads

Newspaper advertisements are another source of job leads, 16-1. They are listed in newspapers under a section called *classified ads* or *want ads*. These ads provide much information about the job market while furnishing job leads. You can learn which types of jobs are most available, what skills are needed for certain jobs, and what salaries are common. This basic information about the job market is helpful to all job seekers.

The best day to find want ads is Sunday. The Sunday edition of newspapers tends to have more ads than papers published any other day. When reading ads, look through all the jobs listed. Sometimes an interesting job appears under the most unlikely heading. As you read, you will see unfamiliar word abbreviations. Chart 16-2 lists the most commonly used abbreviations in want ads and the words they represent.

As you job hunt, you may find blind ads. A **blind ad** does not include the name of a company or contact person. Instead, you may be asked to respond to a post office box or fax number. Blind ads are used by employers for many reasons. They may want to avoid the time and expense of responding to a large number of applicants. A company with a poor public image may use blind ads to attract people who would not otherwise apply. In some cases, a company may want to keep the job opening a secret from their current employees. In any case, your chance of receiving a response to a blind ad is very slim. Blind ads are difficult to respond to since you know little about the position or the company. If you do decide to respond, address your cover letter to a specific position title, such as *Human Resources Manager*, and include a copy of your résumé.

Administrative Assistant
Architecture firm seeks an exp'd, organized detail oriented admin asst. Must have extensive knowledge of Microsoft Word & Excel. Please fax resume to UDG, Inc. 466-4851 e-mail: udgc@designgroup.com

AUTO MECHANIC
Wanted, exp'd w/own tools. Great pay/benefits pkg. Apply M-F, 9-5pm. Dempster & Waukegan Amoco, 8801 Waukegan Rd., Morton Grove, IL 966-4448

BOOKKEEPER-FULL TIME
Lincoln Pk. property mgmt co needs exp'd person to handle computerized rents, receivables, billing and ledgers! Fax resume & sal history: 281-1246
DIMENSIONS MANAGEMENT

CUSTOMER SERVICE
Professional association needs Customer Service Representatives. Good verbal skills and proficiency with computers needed. Good benefits. Down-town location. Fax resume to: Customer Service Department
795-0747

DRIVERS WANTED!
For upscale food delivery service
EARN UP TO $500 + /WEEK
• Flexible hrs to fit your sched
• Part & full time positions avail
• Cash paid out every night
• Must have dependable car with valid drivers lic & proof of insurance
NOW HIRING 50 DRIVERS
Call Camille at 664-1600 x635

Factory
Machine Operator, entry level. Operate metal machining equipment. Good mechanical & math skills req'd. Salary dependent on training/exp. Resume to:
P.O. Box 803883, M4341 Chicago, IL 60680

Food Service
RELIEF COOK
With sanitation cert. Exp needed. Call Norma Smith 8am-1pm, M-F, 847-8061. California Gardens Nursing

X-RAY TECH
City & Suburban openings for exp'd Tech. Hosp & office settings full/part time. All shifts. $16 to $18 hrly. w/bnfts. Spectrum Health Services 630-4400

HUMAN RESOURCES-ASST
Prestigious Loop investment banking firm needs degreed HR asst w/several years exp. Handle pre-employment processing, set-up interviews, other HR duties. Word/Excel skills.
FAX 372-3182.

RECEPTIONIST & MORE
■ **ADVERTISING** ■
Get your foot in door to our nat'l. assn. You will learn promotions, sales/mrktg., adv., etc. Help organize & attend annual convention. Promotable.
368-1383

■   RETAIL SALES   ■
Exp'd Furniture Sales people are needed for either Full or Part-Time positions. Interior design background is a plus. Fax resume to: 267-1182.
■   Or call: 267-1825   ■

TEACHER
Daycare center needs Teacher for infant/toddler room. Expe-rience preferred. Degree in early childhood or related field, or an equivalent combination of training and experience. Send resume to: Haymarket Center, Attn: Pat Allen, Director of Human Resources, 108 N. Sangamon, Chicago, IL 60607 or fax 226-8048. No Phone Calls. equal opportunity employer m/f

16-1
Reading the classified ads in the local newspaper can help you find job openings.

Circle the ads that match your job interests and abilities. Then answer them as soon as possible. The longer you wait to apply, the more likely the jobs will become filled by other applicants.

Unfortunately, most job openings are not advertised. The want ads represent only a fraction of the total number of jobs available. Consequently, you should not rely solely on want ads to find a job.

Trade and Professional Journals

Most trades and professions publish their own magazines and journals, sometimes with job ads. Most of the ads seek experienced workers. In national publications, the jobs may be located anywhere in the United States or abroad. Journals published by state and local chapters are usually more helpful in providing local job leads.

Trade and professional journals contain up-to-date information about the latest developments and trends in a given field. Reading them will help you know your occupational area better and become more informed for job interviews.

Government Employment Services

State employment offices are located in most large cities and towns. These offices are available to help job seekers find job openings within and outside government. The offices may have different names in different states. To locate your nearest state employment office, look in your local telephone directory under the name of your state. For example, in Chicago the state employment office is listed under *Illinois (State of), Employment Service.*

To use this free job service, you must fill out an application at a state employment office. An employment counselor will interview you to determine your skills and interests. If a job becomes available for which you qualify, the office will arrange an interview for you. Keep in mind, however, that only a small percentage of job seekers find a job through state employment services. Therefore, register for work at a state office, but use other job sources to find job leads.

As you read in Chapter 14, the U.S. Department of Labor Employment and Training Administration (www.doleta.gov/jobseekers) sponsors a variety of Web sites. These are designed to assist workers in career development. These sites include information about specific jobs, such as education

Abbreviations in Want Ads	
Abbreviations	**Words**
appt	appointment
ass't	assistant
avail	available
ben or bene	benefits
co	company
EOE	Equal Opportunity Employer
exc	excellent
exp	experience
hrs	hours
hs grad	high school graduate
med	medical
mfg	manufacturing
morn/aft/eve	morning/afternoon/evening
nego	negotiable
ofc	office
p/t or PT	part-time
pos	position
pref	preferred
ref	references
req	required
sal	salary
temp	temporary
w/	with
wpm	words per minute

16-2

To understand the information in want ads, become familiar with common abbreviations.

Resource

Checking Want Ads, Activity A, WB

Enrich

Read the newspaper want ads and list the openings for which you are presently qualified. Next, list openings for which you wish you were qualified. What training would you need to qualify for the jobs you desire?

Enrich

Visit your school and public libraries and review trade journals related to the occupations that interest you.

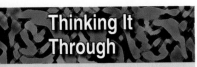

Thinking It Through

Does your school have a placement office or a school or vocational counselor to help students find jobs in the community? What must you do to use these services?

requirements, predicted job market growth, and salary ranges. Some sites also include tools to help the user assess personal skills and abilities.

Many of the Web sites may be accessed through CareerOneStop (www.careeronestop.org). These include

- O*NET Online (www.online.onetcenter.org)
- Career Voyages (www.careervoyages.gov)
- America's Career InfoNet (www.acinet.org)
- America's Service Locator (www.servicelocator.org)

Private Employment Agencies

Private employment agencies are in the business of helping employers locate workers and job seekers locate jobs. To stay in business, agencies must charge fees for their services. They either charge the job seeker or the employer. For most entry-level jobs, the job seeker can expect to pay the fee. For most high-paying professional jobs, the fee is usually paid by the employer. When employment agencies advertise job openings in the want ads, they usually state "fee paid" if the employer is paying the fee.

If you apply to a private agency, you may be asked to sign a contract concerning the payment of fees. Be sure to read and understand all conditions of any contract before signing it. Make sure you know exactly what you are agreeing to pay if you take a job the agency locates for you.

Before registering with a private agency, ask your school coordinator or counselor if any particular agency is recommended. Some agencies specialize in placing people in certain jobs, such as office, technical, or sales jobs.

Only a small percentage of job hunters find jobs through private agencies so you should not spend a great deal of time with them. Concentrate your efforts on other job-finding methods.

Reflect Further

What are some disadvantages of using a private employment agency to search for a job? Under what conditions might you use one?

Activity

Find the address of the One-Stop Career Center nearest you.

Enrich

Have students visit one of the Web sites listed and write a short paper describing how the resource is helpful in finding a job.

Activity

Locate a private employment agency in your area and learn about its services and fee requirements.

Searching the Internet

Imagine finding a job in your town, state, another state, or even another country without leaving the comfort of your home. Searching for jobs has become that easy. Many people have great success locating jobs using the Internet.

If you have access to the Internet in your home, it is possible to search Internet sites providing employment information and job listings for thousands of employment options. See 16-3. If you do not have a computer at home, most public libraries provide Internet access. Also, most local high schools have Internet access.

The government Web sites discussed earlier are good places to start your search since they provide a wealth of information about the job market. Job-search sites often list jobs by type, title, and location. For example, you could search for jobs in automotive sales in the Los Angeles area. These sites may also list educational requirements for various careers, allow you to post your résumé, and provide direct links to companies with openings.

In the Real World

Jan's Job Search

Jan was a recent graduate of a Wyoming business college. She decided to try to find a job by using the Internet. After picking a recommended Web site, Jan selected her key search words: *business*, *Cheyenne*, and *marketing*. Immediately she found 34 jobs meeting her criteria.

She selected one: an assistant to a business administrator at a university close to home. Four weeks later, Jan was hired at a good starting salary.

Although she did not use it while exploring the job options, Jan could have used the Web site's online calculator. This feature allowed her to key in her salary expectations and examine how her salary might adjust to the cost of living in various cities. In this way, she could learn where her starting salary would stretch farthest and allow her a good standard of living.

Questions to Discuss

1. Do you feel Jan's method of searching for a job was appropriate?
2. Why did Jan choose *business*, *Cheyenne*, and *marketing* as search words?
3. What other search words might Jan have used?
4. When should a job seeker use the online calculator?

16-3

Job search Web sites list job openings and may also provide some information about companies placing the ads.

Enrich

Share statistics on the cost-of-living averages for various cities.

You can also learn about job openings with many of the larger employers. By accessing a company's home page, you will find information about the company itself, its business, and its products or services. In addition, it may announce job openings or give directions for applying for a position. In many cases you can correspond directly with the company through the posted e-mail address.

By checking the Coca Cola Company's Web site (www.cocacola.com), for example, you can learn new details about this worldwide company, based in Atlanta, Georgia. The information will help you determine if a job with some branch of the company seems right for you. With the new information, you can develop a better letter of application and become better prepared for an interview. Interviewers are impressed with people who take the time to become familiar with their company and ask intelligent questions about it. (The interview process is discussed in detail in Chapter 18, "Interviewing for Jobs.")

These job-search services are usually free, but you should check possible costs before using the service. Also, you should research the credibility of the company before providing personal information. Remember, whatever information you provide is potentially available to everyone on the Internet. Items such as your name, address, and telephone and social security numbers become public information.

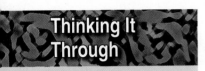

Thinking It Through

Why should you use caution when posting private information on the Internet? How might your information be used dishonestly?

Before You Apply

You may want to contact a long list of employers. However, before you begin applying for jobs, it is important to record all key facts about yourself in one place. This is your **personal fact sheet**. A personal fact sheet helps you write letters of application, prepare job résumés, and fill out application forms, 16-4.

Preparing a Personal Fact Sheet

Begin your personal fact sheet by identifying yourself. Write your name, address, and phone number. Do not include your social security number. If you should lose or misplace your fact sheet, someone else could use this number to access important personal financial information. However, you will need to memorize your number so you have it available when needed. If you have an e-mail address to use, include it here. Also, list your date of birth. (Some jobs may require certain heights and weights, so it is wise to keep track of these facts, too.)

Next, summarize your education. Include the names of your junior high, high school, and any other school such as college or trade school. List enrollment and graduation dates by month and year. Also record your grade average: with a letter such as "A average" or "B average," or with a grade point such as "3.0 on a 4.0 scale." All job application forms do not request all this information, but you will be prepared for those that do.

Activity

Locate three companies on the Internet and describe the types of job information available from each.

Activity

Develop a list of 12 possible employers to contact using six employment resources. Compile a list for two occupations.

Resource

Preparing a Personal Fact Sheet, reproducible master 16-2, TR

Personal Fact Sheet

Name _____

Address _____

Telephone _____

E-mail _____ Date of birth _____

Education	Name	Location	Date Attended	Date Graduated	Grade Average
Junior high school	_____	_____	_____	_____	_____
High school	_____	_____	_____	_____	_____
College	_____	_____	_____	_____	_____
Training school	_____	_____	_____	_____	_____
Other	_____	_____	_____	_____	_____

Work Experience

Name of employer _____

Address _____
        (street address)   (city)   (state)   (zip)

Telephone _____ Employed from _____ to _____
                                              (mo./yr.)   (mo./yr.)

Job title _____ Supervisor _____

Starting salary _____ Final salary _____

Job duties _____
_____

Name of employer _____

Address _____
        (street address)   (city)   (state)   (zip)

Telephone _____ Employed from _____ to _____
                                              (mo./yr.)   (mo./yr.)

Job title _____ Supervisor _____

Starting salary _____ Final salary _____

Job duties _____
_____

Skills _____

Honors and Activities _____
_____

Hobbies and Interests _____
_____

References

Name/Title _____

Address _____

Telephone (daytime) _____ E-mail _____

Name/Title _____

Address _____

Telephone (daytime) _____ E-mail _____

Name/Title _____

Address _____

Telephone (daytime) _____ E-mail _____

16-4

Having a personal fact sheet can help you fill out job application forms thoroughly and accurately.

Who would you ask to be your references? Why choose these particular people?

Then list all your work experiences. For each employer, write the name, address, telephone number, and employment dates. Also record your job title, duties, supervisor's name, and beginning and ending salary. Be sure to list part-time jobs and volunteer work such as babysitting, delivering papers, mowing lawns, or helping at a hospital.

Other types of information to record are your skills, honors, activities, hobbies, and interests. Under *Skills*, list what you do well that relates to the jobs you seek. For example, if you apply for secretarial jobs and you are a fast, accurate word processor, list *keyboarding* as a skill. Under *Honors and Activities*, list the school and community organizations in which you have participated. Also list awards received, club offices held, and other important accomplishments. Under *Hobbies and Interests*, list the activities you enjoy, especially those that relate to your job interests.

You will also need a list of three or four references. A **reference** is a person who knows you well and is willing to discuss your personal and job qualifications with employers. Former teachers, employers, and club advisers make good references. Be sure to ask permission before listing someone as a reference. You will also want to accurately record each person's name, title, address, and daytime telephone number. Most application forms require this information. If the reference uses an e-mail address, also record it. Both personal and professional references may be listed, but do use relatives.

Job Résumés

A résumé summarizes a person's educational background, work experiences, and other qualifications for employment. A résumé is usually sent to an employer with a letter of application or given to an employer with a completed application form. Reading a résumé is a quick and easy way for an employer to learn about an applicant.

A well-prepared résumé can help draw an employer's attention to your qualifications. It can help you get a job interview. It can also help give the employer a starting point for conducting the job interview.

Job Résumé Information

An example of a well-written résumé is shown in 16-5. It includes all the information that is important for an employer to know about the applicant. Your résumé should be concise. One page is best, especially early in your career. Avoid using words such as *I* or *me*. Résumé writing follows trends; use the Internet and other resources to determine what is current.

At the top of the résumé is the information an employer needs to know first: your name, address, telephone number, and e-mail address. Be sure to include your zip code and telephone area code. You want to make sure the employer can quickly contact you if he or she wants to hire you. However, avoid listing your cell phone number. Employers may contact you in situations where it is hard for you to try to make a good first impression. Do not use an e-mail address that sounds unprofessional. For example, GoofySam@server.net may turn off prospective employers.

Reflect

Have you conducted yourself in a manner that would make individuals want to serve as a reference for you?

Activity

List the names, addresses, and telephone numbers of individuals who would make good references. Contact each and obtain permission.

Note

Discuss the format and content of the résumé example on page 333.

MARY R. POSTON
1036 Spring Street
Milwaukee, Wisconsin 53172
(414) 555-3214
mposton@provider.com

Job Objective   Entry-level job as a receptionist or office assistant leading to a position as an office manager.

Education   Washington High School, Milwaukee, WI
20xx-20xx   Majored in business training, graduating June 20xx. Skilled in keyboarding, accounting, Excel, and Microsoft Word. Can operate dictaphone and copy machine.

Work Experience   Office Assistant, Watkins Insurance Agency, Milwaukee, WI
20xx-20xx   As a cooperative education student employee, typed, filed, and operated the
telephone and office machines. Handled some correspondence for the office manager.

Summer 20xx   Grill Crewperson, McDonald's Restaurant, Milwaukee, WI
Responsible for cooking and preparing the food and keeping the work area clean.

Honors and Activities   Member of the Office Educational Association for two years. Secretary during senior year.
Member of the Student Council during junior year.
Member of the high school marching band for four years.
Member of 4-H for eight years.

Hobbies   Coached youth soccer team (3 years).
Maintains personal Web site.

References   References available on request.

16-5
A well-written résumé impresses potential employers and encourages them to learn more about you.

Extend Your Knowledge

Writing a Job Objective

When composing your résumé, consider writing a more general job objective. Sometimes it is better to list the area in which you want to work instead of a specific job. For example, suppose you want to be a company sales representative. However, you would be interested in other jobs in sales. Therefore, it might be best to state your job objective as "a challenging position in sales" instead of "a position as a sales representative." This makes your job objective flexible enough to encourage employers to consider you for related jobs instead of one specific job.

Beneath this block of information, the résumé is organized into headings. This makes it easy to read. You may want to have the same headings used in 16-5 or something similar when preparing your own résumé. The order in which you list the headings may also vary. If you think your work experience will be more important to your employer than your education, list work experiences before education. Experiment first to develop a résumé that will work best for you. Use key words such as *high school diploma*, *Excel*, and *office assistant*. These represent skills and experiences employers feel are important. Key words are particularly important in electronic résumés, because employers may perform a computer search for these terms. Want ads are an excellent source for key words.

You may want to use résumé writing computer software. Several excellent programs will help you organize and format your information into a professional appearance. The headings most often used in résumés are shown here.

Job Objective

The first heading in a résumé is usually *Job Objective*. Sometimes this heading is called *Job Wanted*, *Position Wanted*, or *Career Objective*. The purpose of stating a job objective is to give the employer some idea of the type of job you seek. This is the most important part of your résumé. It is the first thing the employer reads. He or she may not read any further if the job objective is poorly written or does not match the job opening.

If you are interested in more than one type of job, you may need to write different job objectives. For example, consider the person who would be happy working either as an office assistant or airline reservations assistant. That person would most likely need to write different job objectives for these two jobs and, therefore, separate résumés. Preparing a résumé with word processing software allows the quick and easy creation of different résumé versions.

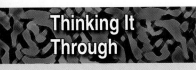

Thinking It Through

Why is stating a job objective in your résumé a good idea?

Education

Under the *Education* section, list the names of all schools attended from high school onward. Primary and junior high schools should not be listed. The last school you attended should appear first on the list. For example, suppose you attend a community college for two years after high school. Then your résumé would list the community college first and your high school second.

For each school, include the name, location, and dates attended. Note when you graduated (or expect to), what diploma or degree you earned (or will earn), and what program you studied. Also mention any skills acquired, such as keyboarding or carpentry. If you received good grades, you may want to mention your grade average.

Work Experience

In this section list the jobs you held and dates of employment, starting with your most recent job first. Include work-based learning experiences, part-time jobs, summer jobs, and other significant work experience. This experience is very important to employers because it shows that you can assume responsibility.

If you have never held a paying job, list any volunteer work done. Particularly mention work that directly relates to the job you seek. For example, any babysitting done voluntarily is important to list when seeking a job with a child care center. Even if you have held a job for pay, list volunteer work you have done. This shows you have an interest in your community.

For each job listed, include the title of the job, the employer's name, and the location. Also include a brief description of the work you did and any special contributions or accomplishments.

Honors and Activities

Other names for this section are *Honors and Organizations*, or just *Activities* or *Organizations*. In this section, list the school and community organizations and activities in which you participated. These experiences will help the employer get a better picture of your interests and abilities. Include any offices held and honors received. If your volunteer work is not worth mentioning as work experience, you should list it here.

Personal

Personal information, such as your interest in certain hobbies, is optional and normally not listed in a résumé. By law, employers cannot ask about personal matters. However, if you have a personal qualification that demonstrates a job-related skill or ability, you can list it here.

Reflect

Are you using your time wisely? Have you been an active participant in activities that will enhance your employability?

Resource

Your Résumé, Activity B, WB

References

Instead of including details about your references in the résumé, most simply say the information is available. They do so by including this line near the bottom of the page: *References available on request.* It is a common practice for employers to express interest in your references only when they are interested in you. Consequently, many believe that information about their references should be kept private and shared with only those who need it. Maintaining a separate list also helps prevent the information from being used dishonestly.

This means you must be prepared to provide the list of references when requested. Be sure the information you list about your references is complete and spelled correctly.

Preparing a Résumé

When you are happy with the content, the résumé is ready to be typed or entered in a computer. You should be able to include all the information on one sheet of standard white bond paper, 8½ by 11 inches. Use a standard font for text and boldface type for headings. Avoid using unusual or colored fonts that may detract from the presentation.

After completing your résumé, set it aside for a day or two. Then read it again. Did you include all the important facts about yourself? Did you organize the information well? Is it easy to read and understand? Ask your coordinator, counselor, or vocational teacher to read it. A teacher may be able to offer some constructive comments.

The information should appear neatly organized with evenly spaced margins. Be sure to review it carefully for spelling, punctuation, and grammar errors.

After the résumé is prepared, you will need to make copies. When using a computer with a good printer, you can print what you need now and make more copies later. You can also use a photocopying machine that prints sharp, clear copies. Another option is to take your résumé to a local print shop or office supplies dealer to make the master document and copies. Résumés usually look more professional when printed rather than photocopied. Check the facilities in your school first before using outside resources. Always check costs before making a decision.

Electronic Résumé

Many employers are looking for résumés to be submitted by e-mail in an electronic format that can be scanned into their databases. This requires developing an electronic version of your résumé. An electronic version is a text-only file without any of the special formatting you may have used in your original résumé, 16-6. Detailed instructions for creating electronic résumés may be found at Web sites such as www.eresumes.com. Employers may also offer instructions for submitting electronic résumés.

MARY R. POSTON

1036 Spring Street

Milwaukee, Wisconsin 53172

(414) 555-3214

mposton@provider.com

JOB OBJECTIVE

Entry-level job as a receptionist or office assistant leading to a position as an office manager.

EDUCATION

20xx-20xx

Washington High School, Milwaukee, WI

Majored in business training, graduating June 20xx. Skilled in keyboarding, accounting, Excel, and Microsoft Word. Can operative dictaphone and copy machine.

WORK EXPERIENCE

20xx-20xx

Office Assistant, Watkins Insurance Agency, Milwaukee, WI

As a cooperative education student employee, typed, filed, and operated the telephone and office machines. Handled some correspondence for the office manager.

Summer 20xx

Grill Crewperson, McDonald's Restaurant, Milwaukee, WI

Responsible for cooking and preparing the food and keeping the work area clean.

HONORS AND ACTIVITIES

Member of the Office Educational Association for two years. Secretary during senior year.

Member of the Student Council during junior year.

Member of the high school marching band for four years.

Member of 4-H for eight years.

HOBBIES

Coached youth soccer team (3 years).

16-6

This electronic résumé has been prepared for e-mail or scanning.

Resource

Preparing a Portfolio, Activity C, WB

Reflect

What samples of your work do you have that would impress a potential employer?

If you are responding to a job opening by e-mail, include both your cover letter addressed to the recipient and the electronic version of the résumé in the body of the e-mail. If you are mailing your résumé, do not fold it. If it has been folded, it may not feed properly through a scanner. Instead, mail your résumé and cover letter in a letter-size envelope.

The Job Portfolio

You may wish to prepare a portfolio to display items reflecting the education and work experience listed on your résumé. A **portfolio** is a well organized collection of materials that supports your job qualifications. It can be used during an interview to show an employer examples of your talents and capabilities.

Your portfolio should include a cover sheet, a letter of application, and a copy of your latest résumé. The cover sheet should list the contents of the portfolio in outline form. You may also want to include a list of job-related skills you have mastered. The heart of your portfolio, however, should be a collection of actual samples of your best work specifically related to the job you seek. For example, an excellent paper you wrote for an English class would show that you can effectively organize and express your ideas in writing. It could support your application for a position as an office assistant. A drawing made in drafting class or a part made in machine tool technology class show the technical skills you have mastered for related occupations. Certificates of completion and awards should also be included.

Do not limit your portfolio to items from school activities. You could include photographs and a written description of a community service project accomplished by you working with others. Cleaning a park would demonstrate your ability to help a group plan and carry out a worthwhile project. These skills are valuable in many different occupations.

You should take special care to make sure your portfolio is well organized and presented. Choose a strategy that works best for your material. For example, if you use photographs and written documents, a three-ring binder is appropriate. Photographs are an excellent way to record items you cannot take to an interview, such as a special dish made in foods class. On the other hand, a large 18×24-inch artists' envelope is best for displaying drawings from art or drafting classes. Use a method that allows you to easily add and remove materials.

The order of the materials in your portfolio is also important. You may want them organized according to their completion dates, or you may prefer groupings of similar projects or themes. Choose a strategy that shows your work to its best advantage. Temporarily remove items that should be reserved for some other job interview. For example, photos showing cooking skills are perfect for a foodservice job interview, but English papers are not.

It may take months or even years to assemble a good portfolio. Start today by working hard in each class and keeping samples of your best work. Update your portfolio on a regular basis by adding new items and replacing others as your work improves.

Developing a Home Page

Many employers today are looking for employees with strong computer skills. One way to demonstrate this skill is to develop your own home page. A *home page* is the first page that is encountered on a company or individual's Web site. Companies often use home pages to provide customers with up-to-date information about their products and services. The home page also provides links to more detailed pages on the Web site. For individuals, a home page allows the sharing of recreational interests or hobbies with others having similar interests. Another way to use a home page is to display employment information for perspective employers to view. It is an electronic version of your career portfolio.

In some cases, your home page may be part of your school's Web site. Schools that have Web sites often reserve part of their space for employment information on their students. Even if your school offers this benefit, you may want to develop your own home page tailored to your specific job skills and personality.

Your home page should include a copy of your résumé. Photos of important projects you have completed may be effective. You can even provide a direct link to the schools you attended to help prospective employers evaluate your education and training.

When developing a home page, carefully consider the information to include. Remember that anything you post becomes public and can be viewed by everyone. To help guard your privacy, do not post your home address or telephone number. To protect your safety, only post your e-mail address as a method of contact. Make sure to keep this page separate from your personal Web site.

Contacting an Employer by Telephone

Your first contact with an employer may be by telephone. You may have a job lead from a friend, relative, or newspaper want ad. In any case, you may have just a company representative's name and telephone number to contact for more information. A call will help you learn more about the job available and how to apply.

Plan ahead and be prepared when you call the company representative. Choose a quiet room for making the call. Background noise from loud music or people talking can be distracting. Make a list of the questions you want to ask. Also be prepared to briefly list your background and qualifications for the job opening. You may wish to refer to your personal fact sheet.

Enrich

Have students develop their own home page to share with employers for purposes of finding a job.

Discuss

Brainstorm the types of information not appropriate for posting on a personal home page. Explain why each is inappropriate.

Resource

Telephoning an Employer, Activity D, WB

Enrich

Role-play proper telephone techniques.

Resource

Letter of Application, Activity E, WB

Place a pencil and paper by the phone so you can take notes. Use good telephone manners when you make the call. In your best conversational voice, introduce yourself and state your purpose for calling. If there is a job opening and you are interested in applying, ask for a personal interview. Be sure to note the correct date, time, and location for the interview. You may also need to ask directions to the interview.

Letter of Application

Sometimes you may need to write a letter to an employer to apply for a job. This type of letter is called a **letter of application** or *cover letter*. The purpose of an application letter is to get an employer interested in your qualifications so she or he will ask you for an interview. A letter of application is needed in the following situations:

- answering a newspaper ad

- mailing a résumé to a prospective employer

- responding to an employer's request for an application letter

A letter of application should be written to the person in the organization who has the ability to hire you. This may be the personnel manager, department manager, or president of the company. If you do not know the name of this person, call the company and ask the receptionist for the name and title you need. Ask the receptionist to spell the name so you can write it down correctly. Some smaller companies may not have an employee with the title of *personnel director*. In this case, ask the receptionist for the name and title of the person to whom a letter of application should be written. All employers have someone in charge of employment.

When writing the letter, keep it short and to the point. You want to attract the employer's attention but not overload him or her with too many facts. Three carefully worded paragraphs should be all you need to write a convincing letter of application.

In the opening paragraph, tell why you are writing. Mention the job or type of work you seek. If you know a position is open, explain how you learned this. For example, if you learned about the job through a want ad or one of your teachers, mention this to the employer. Include a brief statement about the company to show you have done your homework.

In the middle paragraph, tell why you think you are right for the job. Briefly explain how your qualifications have prepared you for this type of work. If you are enclosing a résumé, mention it here. Encourage the employer to refer to it for further information about your qualifications.

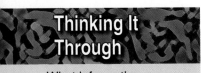

Thinking It Through

What information should be in a letter of application? What type of information should be left out?

In the Real World

Roberta Applies for a Job

Roberta stopped at Rogers Dairy on her way home from school to check possible job openings. All parking spaces for visitors were used so she parked in a space marked "Reserved for David Parks." The Security Guard asked her to move, but Roberta insisted she wouldn't be gone too long. Not until the guard threatened to have her car towed did Roberta finally leave the reserved parking space.

Roberta entered the building and said to the secretary, "You ain't got no job openings, do you?" The receptionist asked Roberta what type of position she wanted. "It don't matter 'cause I can do anything," Roberta said. The receptionist was tempted to say all jobs were filled, but knew the shipping department desperately needed help.

She reluctantly gave Roberta an application and asked her to fill it out in the lobby. Roberta promised to fill it out later and bring it back. The receptionist explained that all applicants had to fill out their applications in her presence. "But I have to meet my boyfriend at the mall at 3:00," Roberta complained. The receptionist quietly replied, "Anyone who wants a job with us must fill out the application here."

As Roberta began filling out the form, she noticed several questions she couldn't answer. She didn't know the address of her former employer or the exact dates she was employed. She could only think of one person to list as a reference. She was in such a hurry to meet her boyfriend that her writing became unreadable and full of mistakes. She scribbled over her errors, wrote corrections in the margins, and used arrows to indicate where the new information belonged. She dropped the pen and application, unsigned, on the receptionist's desk as she raced out the door.

The receptionist looked at the application, took a deep breath, and sighed. Then she dropped the application in the wastebasket when Roberta's car pulled away.

Questions to Discuss

1. Why was the receptionist tempted to tell Roberta there were no openings?
2. What mistakes did Roberta make? What should she have done or said in each case?
3. Why did the receptionist insist the application be filled out immediately in her presence?
4. Why didn't the receptionist give Roberta's application to the human resources manager?

In the last paragraph, ask the employer for an interview and thank the employer for considering your application. Make sure to mention where and when you can be reached by telephone.

Although the content of a letter of application is very important, so is its appearance. A letter of application looks best if you use word processing software and print it on standard 8½×11-inch white bond paper. Use a standard type size and style. A handwritten letter is not recommended. Remember, your business letter should follow a standard business style. Your letter should include a return address, date, inside address, salutation, body, and complimentary close. A sample letter of application is shown in 16-7. To review the proper way to prepare a business letter, turn to Chapter 5, "Communicating on the Job."

Enrich

Have a personnel director from a local business speak about effective letters of application.

1036 Spring St.
Milwaukee, WI 53172
April 25, 20xx

Mr. Robert Drake
Personnel Manager
Whitaker Publishing Company
1822 W. Meridian St.
Milwaukee, WI 53172

Dear Mr. Drake:

Through Mr. James Mitchell, career counselor at Washington High School in
Milwaukee, I learned your company plans to hire a full-time office assistant in June.
I know your company is a worldwide leader in outdoor publications and I would like to
apply for this position.

To prepare for office work, I have taken a number of business courses in high school.
As mentioned in my résumé, I am now skilled in keyboarding, accounting, Microsoft
Word, and Excel. As a cooperative education student at Washington, I am presently
gaining on-the-job experience as an office assistant with Watkins Insurance Agency.
With my education and work experience, I feel confident I can perform well as an
office assistant for your company.

May I have an interview to discuss the job and my qualifications in greater detail?
I can be reached at 414-555-3214 after 4:30 or at mposton@provider.com. I will
appreciate the opportunity to talk with you. Thank you for taking time to consider my
application.

Sincerely,

Mary Poston

Mary Poston

16-7

A good letter of application attracts attention to the sender's
qualifications.

After preparing the letter, read it carefully one more time. Make sure you have complete sentences and correctly spelled words. Word processing software can help you check spelling and grammar, but it may not catch all errors. By preparing a good first letter of application, you can use it to help prepare others.

Job Application Forms

When applying for a job, most employers ask you to fill out an application form. Employers use application forms to screen job applicants. Therefore, the information you give on a form is very important. An application that is incomplete, difficult to read, or smudged with dirt may not make it beyond the first screening. Use a black pen to increase legibility. Do not be eliminated from consideration for a job just because your application form is incorrect or sloppy, 16-8.

Now is the time to rely on the personal fact sheet you prepared earlier in the chapter. With this information, all personal facts are at your fingertips.

If the application asks for references and their phone numbers, there is no need to fumble through a telephone book. You will have the information in front of you. The personal fact sheet will help you fill out application forms accurately and completely. Always remember to carry this sheet and a pen with you when applying for jobs.

When filling out an application form, follow these tips:

- Read the entire application before you begin writing any information. Make sure you understand all the questions.

- Carefully follow the instructions for filling out the form. If you are asked to print, type, or use black ink, be sure to do so. Be careful not to write in the sections marked *for employer use only.*

- Complete every question on both sides of the form. If some questions do not apply to you, draw a dash through the space or write *does not apply.* This lets the employer know you read the question and did not overlook it.

- You may wish to omit your social security number and write *will provide if hired.* This may help protect your identity if the application is left on someone's desk or disposed of improperly.

- In the section concerning the job you desire, there may be a question about the wages or salary you expect. The best answer is *open* or *negotiable.* Consequently, you do not commit yourself to a figure too high or too low. If your salary request is too high, the employer might focus on the more affordable applicants and not even consider you. If the salary request is too low, the employer may think you have a low opinion of yourself or are not really serious about the job.

APPLICATION FOR EMPLOYMENT

Whitaker Publishing Company
1822 W. Meridian Street
Milwaukee, WI 53172

PERSONAL INFORMATION

Date _May 14, 20XX_

Social Security Number _Will provide if hired_

Name _Poston_ _Mary_ _Rachel_
      Last   First   Middle

Present Address _1036 Spring Street_ _Milwaukee,_ _WI_ _53172_
                 Street   City   State Zip

Permanent Address _1036 Spring Street_ _Milwaukee,_ _WI_ _53172_
                   Street   City   State Zip

Phone No. _(414) 555-3214_

If related to anyone in our employ, state name and department _____

Referred by _Mr. James Mitchell Career Counselor_

EMPLOYMENT DESIRED

Position _Office Assistant_

Date you can start _June 10, 20XX_

Salary desired _Open_

Are you employed now? _yes_

If so may we inquire of your present employer? _yes_

Ever applied to this company before? _no_ Where _____ When _____

EDUCATION

	Name and Location of School	Years Completed	Subjects Studied
Grammar School	Spring Grove School Brookfield, WI	8	General Education
High School	Washington High School Milwaukee, WI	4	keyboarding, accounting, and English
College			
Trade, Business or Correspondence School			

Subject of special study or research work _____

(continued on next page)

16-8

Application forms must be filled out accurately and neatly.

What foreign languages do you fluently speak? ———— Read? ———— Write? ————

U.S. Military or
Naval service ———— Rank ———— Present membership in
National Guard or Reserves ————

Activities other than religious
(civic, athletic, fraternal, etc.) *Office Education Association, Student Council,*

Washington Marching Band, 4-H Club

Exclude organizations the name or character of which indicates the race, creed, color or national origin of its members

FORMER EMPLOYERS List employers starting with last one first

Date Month and Year	Name and Address of Employer	Salary	Position	Reason for Leaving
From *9/XX* To *6/XX*	*Watkins Insurance Agency 1122 Market Street Milwaukee, WI 53177*	*$8.50/Hour*	*Office Assistant*	*Seeking full-time job after graduation*
From *9/XX* To *6/XX*	*McDonald's Restaurant 1301 Main Street Milwaukee, WI 53177*	*$8.00/Hour*	*Grill Crewperson*	*Summer job*
From To				
From To				

REFERENCES List below at least two persons not related to you whom you have known at least one year

Name	Address	Job Title	Years Acquainted
1 *Mr. James Mitchell*	*Washington High School 3300 W. Glendale Ave. Milwaukee, WI 53180*	*Career Counselor*	*3*
2 *Ms. Angelica Ortiz*	*Watkins Insurance Agency 1122 Market Street Milwaukee, WI 53177*	*Office Manager*	*1*
3			

PHYSICAL RECORD

Have you any defects in hearing, vision or speech that might affect your job performance?
no

In case of emergency notify *Mrs. Jean Poston*   *1036 Spring Street Milwaukee, WI 53172*   *(414) 555-3214*
Name   Address   Phone No.

I authorize investigation of all statements contained in this application. I understand that misrepresentation or omission of facts called for is cause for dismissal.

Date *May 14, 20XX*   Signature *Mary R. Poston*

- In the section marked *employment history*, remember to include part-time jobs such as babysitting and mowing lawns. For each job, there may be a question asking your reason for leaving the job. In the case of a summer job, your reason for leaving is simply stated as follows: *summer job only*. If you left a job for another reason, word it very carefully. Avoid writing any negative comments about yourself or a former employer.

- Be as neat as possible. Do not get the form dirty or stained. If you must change any information you wrote, neatly draw a line through the wrong words.

As soon as you finish the form, hand it to the correct person. You may also want to offer a copy of your résumé for their files. However, do not expect your résumé to substitute for a completed application form. A résumé is not necessary for getting a job, but a completed application form usually is.

Illegal Questions on Job Applications

When you apply for a job, you have certain legal rights protected by law. These federal laws state what questions employers can and cannot ask on application forms. This prevents discrimination in job hiring related to race, color, religion, national origin, sex, age, and disability.

Legally, you are not required to answer any question unrelated to your ability to do the job. The following questions are not job-focused and, therefore, are illegal: *Do you live in an apartment or house? Do you have any serious debts? Do you own a car? Do you have a disability?*

A disability can be addressed, however, if it may affect job performance. For example, if you are applying for a sales position, it may be legal to discuss if you have a hearing or speech problem that may affect your job performance. (These same laws also apply to job interviews, which are discussed in Chapter 18, "Interviewing for Jobs.").

There are other jobs that require special questions. For example, if you apply for a job delivering flowers or pizza, the job description may say *must provide transportation*. In this case, it is legal to ask if you own a car and have a good driving record. Otherwise, the employer can only ask if you have a dependable way to get to work.

Sometimes employers interpret these laws differently and may innocently ask you a discriminatory question. Knowing the types of questions employers cannot ask on applications or in job interviews can help you protect your rights, 16-9. If you suspect a discriminatory question on a form, write "willing to discuss" or "not clear." During the interview you can ask how the question and job are related. At the same time, emphasize your desire to provide accurate answers to all job-related questions.

Reflect Further

If you see a suspicious question on a job application form, what should your attitude be? Would you answer an illegal question if you felt it would help you get the job?

Illegal Questions for Job Applicants

Subject	Questions	Subject	Questions
Race or color	What is the color of your skin, hair, or eyes? What is your race?	**Personal/ family**	What is your place of birth? What is your parents' or your relatives' place of birth? Are you a naturalized citizen? Do you have any children? What child care arrangements do you have? Do you plan to have children?
Religion	What is your religion? What church do you attend? What religious holidays do you observe? Who is your religious leader?	**Sex and marital status**	Are you single, married, divorced, or widowed? Do you prefer to be addressed as Miss, MS, or Mrs.?
National origin	What nationality are you, or your spouse or parents? What is your ancestry? What language do you and your family speak at home? What is your native language?	**Age**	What is your age? What is the date of your birth?
Photographs	Do you have a current photograph to attach to your application?	**Disabilities**	Do you have any disabilities?
		Organizations	To what organizations or clubs do you belong?

16-9

It is important to know what questions should not appear on job application forms.

Discuss

Why is it illegal to ask each of these questions?

Summary

Job openings can be found through friends, relatives, networking, school placement services, and want ads. Other sources include trade and professional journals, government employment services, private agencies, and the Internet. Using as many sources as possible is best since most jobs are unadvertised.

Before applying for a job, prepare a personal fact sheet. This information is helpful when filling out a job application or preparing a job résumé. A résumé should include your education, work experience, and qualifications for employment. A well-written résumé provides all the information an employer needs to know about you. You may also want to prepare a portfolio or a home page.

When applying for a job, your first contact with an employer is usually by telephone or letter. The purpose of these contacts is to get employers interested in your qualifications so they will invite you for an interview.

Most employers will ask you to fill out a job application form when you apply in person for a job. They use these forms to screen job applicants so the forms should be filled out accurately and carefully. To prevent possible job discrimination, know your legal rights before interviewing for jobs and filling out job application forms.

Resource

Review and Study Guide for Chapter 16, reproducible master 16-3, TR

Answers to *Facts In Review*

1. Make a list of companies where you would like to work; prepare a résumé that summarizes your qualifications; contact the person with each employer who has hiring authority.
2. usually the director or manager of the personnel/ human resource department, otherwise the manager of the department you want to join or the company president
3. After learning who to contact, write or call the person to express interest in a job.
4. the types of jobs most available, the skills needed for certain jobs, the salaries paid
5. Only a small fraction of job openings are advertised.
6. The employer pays the fee.
7. *job objective, education, work experience, honors and organizations* (or *activities* or *organizations*)
8. job title, employment dates, employer's name and location, brief job description

Facts in Review

1. What three steps should be taken to successfully hunt for a job?
2. Who in a company should be contacted about a job?
3. What should a person do when contacting employers directly to find job openings?
4. What can be learned about the job market by reading want ads?
5. Why should a person *not* rely on want ads alone to find a job?
6. What does *fee paid* mean in employment agency want ads?
7. List the headings most often used in résumés.
8. For each job listed under *work experience* on a résumé, what information should be included?
9. How does an electronic résumé differ from a print version?
10. What is a portfolio? What might be included in yours?
11. List five steps to take when contacting a potential employer by telephone.
12. What is a letter of application and its purpose?
13. What points should be covered in a letter of application?
14. If a question on an application form does *not* apply to you, what should you do?
15. What is the best way to respond to questions about wages or salary expectations? Explain.

9. An electronic résumé has had all formatting removed to make it easy for an employer to enter it into a database.
10. a collection of samples of your best work (Student response for contents of portfolio.)
11. (List five:) Be prepared; choose a quiet room; have a list of questions; have paper and pencil nearby; use good telephone manners; express interest in a job; summarize your background and qualifications; request an interview; note the details of any interview scheduled.
12. A letter of application is a job request written to an employer to obtain a personal job interview.
13. purpose of the letter, type of job you seek, your abilities and qualifications for the job, a brief statement about the company, reference to a résumé enclosed, request for an interview
14. Draw a dash through the space or write *does not apply*.
15. Write *open* or *negotiable*. This prevents the applicant from committing to a figure that is too high or low.

Developing Your Academic Skills

1. **Language Arts.** Bring in newspapers and read help wanted ads. Identify the meanings for the "code" words that appear in most ads. Discuss any codes not presented in the text and give tips for interpreting their meanings correctly.

2. **Speech.** Practice contacting employers by telephone. Discuss how speaking over the telephone is different from face-to-face conversations.

3. **English.** Practice writing letters of application. Make sure you include three properly developed paragraphs in addition to checking grammar and spelling.

Information Technology Applications

1. Make a database of possible network contacts. Create a data field for information on how the network contact might be of help to you.

2. Visit the Web site for Monster's Résumé Center (resume.monster.com). List three good résumé tips you learned from the site.

3. Create a sample résumé using a résumé writing program or template commonly found in word processing software.

4. Prepare an electronic version of your résumé. E-mail a copy to yourself and a friend to see if the formatting remains the same.

Applying Your Knowledge and Skills

1. **Academic Foundations.** Visit your school or public library. Tell the librarian the career area that interests you and ask to see the related trade or professional journal(s). Note the latest developments or trends in the trade or profession, and check for job ads.

2. **Systems.** Visit the state employment office nearest you. Learn how to register with their employment service. Also learn the procedure for applying and qualifying for state and federal government jobs.

3. **Employability and Career Development.** Prepare a résumé. Ask a teacher, counselor, mentor, or supervisor to review it and offer suggestions.

4. **Employability and Career Development.** Prepare a portfolio following the suggestions in the chapter. Ask a potential employer to review it with you.

5. **Communications.** Write a sample letter of application for a job you want. Follow the guidelines in the chapter.

6. **Communications.** Collect several different application forms. Display them for classmates to see. Choose one and complete it neatly and correctly.

Developing Workplace Skills

Working with two classmates, imagine your group is assigned the task of finding the right person to hire for a job as restaurant assistant. You want a high school graduate who will check in and put away shipments of food and supplies, operate the cash register, and greet customers. What type of information should the right person's résumé contain? Using a computer and appropriate word processing software, develop the ideal résumé. Present it to the class explaining how your résumé would identify the best person for the job.

17

Taking Preemployment Tests

Key Terms

skill test

psychological test

situational test

civil service test

Armed Services Vocational Aptitude
   Battery (ASVAB)

polygraph

Chapter Objectives

After studying this chapter, you will be able to

- **explain** why employers give preemployment tests.
- **describe** the types of preemployment tests commonly given to prospective employees.
- **prepare** for preemployment tests.

Reading Advantage

After reading each section, answer this question:
If you explained the information to a friend who
is not taking this class, what would you tell him
or her?

Achieving Academic Standards

English Language Arts

- Read print and non-print texts to acquire new information and to respond to the needs and demands of society and the workplace. (IRA/NCTE, 1)
- Apply strategies to comprehend, interpret, evaluate, and appreciate texts. (IRA/NCTE, 3)
- Use a variety of technological and information processes to gather and synthesize information and to create and communicate knowledge. (IRA/NCTE, 8)

Key Concepts

- Many employers will require applicants to take preemployment tests. Most of these tests do not have right or wrong answers.

- Being prepared for preemployment tests includes being well rested, having supplies needed, and arriving at the test site early.

Discuss

What could preemployment tests reveal to an employer about a prospective employee?

Resource

Employment Test-Taking Tips, color transparency CT-17, TR

Activity

Consider a job title you would like to earn in the future. Discuss the needed training, education, skills, physical requirements, work hours, tools, and equipment.

Resource

Preemployment Perception Test, Activity A, WB

Resource

Preemployment Math Skills Testing, Activity B, WB

Thinking It Through

What preemployment tests do you think are used for jobs that interest you?

Sharika had just returned from applying for three jobs. "I was surprised I had to take so many tests," she said.

"Tests!" Dave said in alarm. "You mean you have to take tests to get a job?"

"That's right," said Sharika. "You thought teachers were the only people who gave tests? Well, employers do, too. When I was interviewed at one company, the personnel manager said practically all companies give preemployment tests to prospective employees. All government employees, such as mail carriers and civil service workers, must take one or more preemployment tests."

Why do employers give tests when hiring? Many employers give preemployment tests to screen, or examine, prospective employees. Companies want to choose the best people for the jobs available. They try to gather enough data about job applicants to make wise selections. Another reason employers give preemployment tests is to find out if an applicant is suited to a given job. Employees may give one or more of the following types of tests:

- Skill tests evaluate a person's physical or mental skills.

- Psychological tests evaluate a person's personality, character, and attitudes.

- Situational tests give the employer a better idea of how a person will perform under actual job conditions.

- Government agencies give exams to help place people fairly in government jobs.

- Polygraph tests and written honesty tests help employers judge a person's truthfulness.

- Medical exams determine a person's physical condition for the job.
  Preemployment tests can help you as well as the employer. Taking a preemployment test may reinforce your interest in your chosen career. On the other hand, test results may show that you are seeking a job for which you are not suited. You may find more training is needed to meet an employer's requirements, or your skills and interests are better matched to another career field. Preemployment tests are only a part of the job selection process, but an important part.

Skill Tests

A **skill test** is used to test the physical or mental abilities of a job applicant. An employer uses one or more of these tests to decide if an applicant has the skills to do a job.

Skill tests may be performance, written, or oral. Performance tests check your ability to operate tools and machines. Written and oral tests examine your understanding of the practices or facts needed to perform in the workplace.

In the Real World

The Missing Skill

Bob saw a want ad from a small equipment operator that repairs and rebuilds heavy diesel equipment. Since Bob had experience in auto and diesel mechanics and equipment operation, he applied for the job and was granted an interview.

At the interview, the shop supervisor explained the type of person he wanted for the job. "I need someone who can do four things: drive a truck, operate a forklift, operate a crane, and keep our equipment in good working order."

Bob quickly thought about what the supervisor said before responding. Driving a truck and operating a forklift would be no problem because he had experience doing both. He also had experience repairing and maintaining heavy equipment. However, the crane might be a problem because he never operated one. He glanced at the crane that was parked nearby, and it didn't look difficult to operate. So he said, "I can do all four, but I might need some help running the crane."

"Oh, you have never operated a crane?" the supervisor asked.

Bob made the mistake of saying, "Sure I have. It's been a while though. I'm just a little rusty."

"Well, let's find out how well you can operate it," the supervisor replied.

Bob climbed into the seat while the supervisor explained the controls. Bob was about to say he couldn't do it when the supervisor said, "Back it up about 10 feet and pick up that track to your right. Then set it down on the concrete pad to your left. Be careful, that track weighs over 1,000 pounds."

The supervisor climbed down from the crane, leaving Bob alone at the controls. Bob successfully started the engine and shifted the crane into reverse. The gears engaged and the crane moved backward. "Hey," he thought, "I'm driving a crane. I'm going to get this job after all."

Bob advanced slowly and carefully moved the crane into position. "That's far enough," the supervisor yelled to him. "Pick up the track."

Bob looked at the levers. "Here it is," he said to himself, "the lever to lower and raise the boom." He moved the lever and the boom slowly lowered. However, it wasn't directly over the track. The boom was just a few feet out of reach.

"You'll need to go forward about three feet," yelled the supervisor.

When Bob shifted into gear, the crane moved forward and kept going. "How do I stop it?" he yelled.

Bob finally stopped the crane, but not before driving the boom into the wall of the office building.

Questions to Discuss

1. Do you think Bob was hired for the job? Why?
2. Instead of lying to the supervisor, what positive things could Bob have told the supervisor about himself and his ability to do the job?
3. Do you think the supervisor would have considered Bob for the job even without experience operating a crane? Why?
4. What would you have done in Bob's situation?

17-1

Employers may have workstations set up as testing sites for job applicants.

A word processing test is a good example of a performance test, 17-1. When a person applies for a job that involves keyboarding, he or she may be asked to prepare a one-page sample or a letter. From the sample, the employer will rate the person's speed, accuracy, and computer literacy. The applicant who keys in material the fastest with the fewest errors will probably be the person who will be offered the job. A performance test may also be required for drafters, welders, X-ray technicians, machine operators, and instrument technicians.

If you apply for a job as a bank teller, clerk, or computer operator, you may be asked to take a math test. A math test is an example of a written test that checks your ability to perform needed work skills. A basic math test examines your ability to add, subtract, multiply, divide, find percentages, and work with fractions.

Clerical skill tests are examples of combined written and performance tests. These tests are often given to applicants seeking employment as office assistants. They are given to measure such abilities as performing simple math operations, copying numbers and names correctly, and placing files in alphabetical order, 17-2.

Do not be afraid to take a skill test. If you have the skills to perform the job for which you are being tested, you will not have problems. If you do poorly on a skills test, it is not the end of the world. Instead, it is an opportunity to find out how you can improve your skills. If you express a sincere interest in the job, the employer may offer to teach you the skills you need.

Whatever you do, never tell an employer you possess skills that you do not have. Eventually, the employer will discover the truth. You could then be fired for being dishonest, not being able to perform the duties of the job, or both.

Filing Speed and Accuracy Tasks

This task measures your ability to quickly and correctly file records alphabetically. Below are two lists of files identified by names—last names followed by first and middle initials. **List A** consists of files to put away. **List B** represents a drawer of files already in alphabetical order. Determine where the List A files correctly belong in the file drawer. You will do this by placing the numbers corresponding to the List A files in the appropriate spaces in List B.
For example:

LIST A (To be filed)   LIST B (Already filed)

1. Lockport, H.A.
2. Logan, K.L.

( )		( )	
Lober, D.F.		Logan, J.G.	
(1)		(2)	
Lockwood, R.E.		Long, C.F.	
( )		( )	
Lodge, H.A.		Lopez, J.M.	
( )		( )	
Loffredo, S.A.		Loren, L.P.	
( )		( )	

Mountain Bell

17-2

These directions show one example of a clerical test that measures a person's filing speed and accuracy.

Extend Your Knowledge

What Might You See on a Psychological Test?

Most psychological tests involve written multiple choice questions or short essays. A common essay instruction is: "Describe yourself in a paragraph." Oral psychological tests are given by a psychologist. The questions may be about you or your opinions on certain issues.

Psychological Tests

A **psychological test** examines a person's personality, character, and interests. These tests do not measure a person's knowledge or aptitudes. They measure factors such as cooperation, assertiveness, adaptability, loyalty, honesty, and personal likes and dislikes. Some employers give these tests to determine how well an applicant will adjust to the job and get along with coworkers, 17-3.

If you are asked to take a psychological test, do not be concerned. There are no right or wrong answers for these tests so you should not feel stressed. Simply answer the questions as well as you can. The best approach is being positive and truthful.

Situational Tests

Many employers find that traditional performance, written, and oral tests do not reveal how well a worker will actually perform on the job. Consequently, they use a **situational test** to examine the ability of job applicants in a work setting similar to the job's. These tests examine the skills, knowledge, and attitudes required by the job. For example, for a job involving frequent teamwork, applicants may be grouped with four or five other applicants. The group is then given a problem to solve. A trained observer judges how successfully each team member works with others, solves problems, and demonstrates leadership skills.

In another case, potential assembly line workers may be placed on a test assembly line. They may be judged for their dexterity and patience in performing simple routine tasks for long periods. These tests can be very helpful to both the employer and the potential employee. Often it is the applicant who decides not to take the job after getting a chance to experience the work involved.

17-3
Some employers give psychological tests to determine how well an applicant will get along with others on the job.

Activity

Obtain other examples of skill tests from guidance counselors or vocational teachers and share them in class. Take the tests, if appropriate.

Discuss

How is a driver's license exam an example of a written and performance test?

Enrich

Have a qualified individual, such as a guidance counselor, administer a personality-style inventory to the class. Discuss the results individually and relate them to career choice.

Enrich

Have students working in small teams design a situational test to help screen potential workers for a job held by at least one team member.

Thinking It Through

What is wrong with telling an employer you possess certain skills when you don't?

Reflect Further

How well do you think you would score on a psychological test? What do you think the test would reveal about you?

Government Tests

The United States Government is the nation's largest employer. It hires many people for civilian jobs as well as military jobs. In addition, a variety of jobs are filled by people working for state and local agencies. Two types of tests you may encounter if you apply for a federal or state government job or pursue a military career are discussed here.

Civil Service Test

A **civil service test** is an examination a person may be required to take in applying for a government job. The Civil Service Commission is the federal agency that administers the civil service tests and hires employees for federal government jobs. The employment service of each state administers tests and hires workers for state jobs. Both federal and state governments test job applicants to select the best qualified person for the job without regard to sex, race, religion, or political influence. The testing system attempts to give all U.S. citizens a fair chance at government jobs.

To learn about these job openings and the testing required, call your nearest state employment service. You can find the number by looking under your state's name. For example, in Illinois look under *Illinois, State of*. Then look for *jobs* or *employment*. The exact title will vary from state to state. You can also find information on your state's Web site.

Armed Services Vocational Aptitude Battery

The **Armed Services Vocational Aptitude Battery**, or **ASVAB**, is an aptitude test designed to measure strengths, weaknesses, and potential for future success. There are three versions of the test. Two versions are designed for use by military recruiters, 17-4. The third version is the student ASVAB, which is part of the ASVAB Career Exploration Program.

The student ASVAB is for juniors and seniors in high school and postsecondary students. It is given in high schools, colleges, and vocational schools. The test provides three overall scores in verbal, math, and science and technical skills. In addition, eight sub scores in areas such as auto and shop information, arithmetic reasoning, paragraph comprehension, and electronics comprehension are provided.

The ASVAB Career Exploration Program is designed to help you learn more about yourself and explore various occupations. It can help you determine if you are ready for more training in different career areas. A program will provide you with a variety of career planning tools. For example, the Find Your Interests (FYI) inventory will help you identify your work-related interests. The OCCU-Find tool will help you explore occupations in relation to the scores you received on the ASVAB and FYI. You can learn more about ASVAB at www.military.com/ASVAB and www.asvabprogram.com.

Enrich

Invite someone from a company who uses situational tests to speak about their use and effectiveness.

Discuss

What types of jobs are available through the United States government?

Enrich

Have someone from the State employment office talk to the class about the purpose and content of the civil service test.

Enrich

Arrange for the ASVAB to be administered in class.

Polygraph Tests

A **polygraph** test, also called a *lie-detector test*, is given with a polygraph machine. The machine measures and records on graph paper the changes in the subject's blood pressure, perspiration, and pulse rate when an examiner asks questions. To conduct a polygraph test, an examiner places an inflated blood-pressure cuff around the subject's arm, a rubber tube around the chest, and small electrodes on one hand. Then the examiner asks the subject questions.

A specific series of questions are asked in a specific sequence. The questions asked usually fall into two broad categories: relevant and control. A *relevant* question is very specific. For example, "Did you steal from your last employer?" A *control* question is less precise, such as, "In the last 10 years, have you ever stolen anything?" Examiners say that a person who is lying will usually react more strongly to the relevant questions.

After a polygraph test, the examiner analyzes the graph and decides whether the subject is lying or telling the truth. The machine by itself cannot do this; it only measures levels of stress. The examiner examines the stress levels and determines if the stress was caused by lying or an emotion such as anger or fear.

The Employee Polygraph Protection Act (EPPA) of 1988 prohibits most private employers from using lie detector tests for preemployment screening or during the course of employment. The EPPA does not apply to federal, state, and local governments.

The law, however, permits the use of polygraph tests by private employers in certain cases. For example, lie detector tests may be given to company employees suspected of theft, embezzlement, or other activities resulting in economic loss or injury to the employer. The test may be used on job applicants in certain firms dealing in security issues, armored cars, or alarms. The polygraph test may also be used by pharmaceutical manufacturers, distributors, and dispensers.

Polygraph tests are subject to strict standards under the law. These standards control the administration of the test and the certification of the examiner. The EPPA strictly limits the disclosure of information obtained during a test. For more information about polygraph tests, contact the Employment Standards Administration's Wage and Hour Division of the U.S. Department of Labor (www.dol.gov/esa).

17-4

If you are considering a military career, you may find the ASVAB tests helpful in your career planning.

Reflect Further

Would you feel uncomfortable taking a polygraph test? Why or why not?

Enrich

Have a polygraph examiner demonstrate the test to the class and discuss its use.

Reflect

How comfortable would you be while taking a polygraph test for employment?

Enrich

Have the students debate the pros and cons of employers administering polygraph tests.

In the Real World

Alan and Hal

Alan and Hal recently graduated from different high schools. They don't know each other, but they are alike in many ways. Both studied vocational electronics in high school and had similar work-based learning programs. Also, both applied for the following job:

Electronics

Ground floor opportunities with growing national computer firm. Must be HS grad exp'd in electronics, microcomputer assembly & repair, digital electronics, data communications. Will be trained to work for a team of experts. Contact: P.O. Box 1354, Chicago, IL 60606

After completing their application forms, Alan and Hal were scheduled for interviews on the same day—Alan in the morning and Hal in the afternoon. When Alan and Hal arrived, each was asked to take a written test. It wasn't an electronics test, but a psychological test. Here are some of the questions asked and their responses.

1. Why do you want to work in electronics?

   - Alan: I like electronics and feel it has good future opportunities.

   - Hal: I like to work in electronics, and I want to make a lot of money.

2. Would you enter a nine-month training program at a lower salary?

   - Alan: Yes, if it meant I would learn the business.

   - Hal: No. I'm prepared to go to work right now. I don't need much more training.

3. Do you prefer to work alone or with a group?

   - Alan: Either. At times I like to work alone, but I also like to work with others.

   - Hal: In a group. I like to be with people.

4. Answer yes or no to this: I always control my temper.

   - Alan: No. I try, but sometimes I get mad and raise my voice.

   - Hal: Yes. No matter how unreasonable others are, I control my temper and never get angry.

The company wanted young people with knowledge and experience in electronics who were willing to be trained according to the company's system. Who do you think was hired—Alan, Hal, or both?

Alan was offered a position, but Hal was not. The main reason for Hal not being hired was his answer to the last question about controlling his temper. Very few people, if any, never get angry. Hal's reply sounded unrealistic. His answer also gave the impression that he thinks he's always right and incapable of making mistakes. The interviewer concluded that Hal's attitude would probably lead to problems in getting along with others and accepting constructive criticism.

Questions to Discuss

1. Do you think the test questions were fair?
2. Do you agree with the interviewer's interpretation of Hal's answer? Why?
3. Whom would you hire? Why?
4. Would you feel uncomfortable taking a similar psychological test? Explain.

Written Honesty Tests

A written honesty or integrity test is another type of test designed to measure a person's honesty in the workplace. These paper-and-pencil tests are intended to help employers identify job applicants who are likely to be dishonest employees. They are often used where people handle cash or merchandise. They may also be used where individuals must work with little supervision. The results of the test may not always be accurate. The test should be used as a part of the total job screening process. It should never be used as the sole reason for hiring someone. Unlike polygraph tests, pencil and paper honesty tests can be given in most states. However, some states have laws restricting their use.

Two types of questions are commonly asked on honesty tests. There are *overt questions*, such as "Have you ever stolen anything from an employer?" A second type of question is more subtle. Some examples include "Do you think a person should be arrested for downloading songs from the Internet without paying?" or "Does everyone steal something once in a while?" These types of questions are often designed in a way that makes it difficult for a person to cheat. More than one question may be included to identify the same type of dishonest behavior. This makes it hard to know the "right answer."

You should not be afraid to take an honesty test. Just answer all questions truthfully.

Medical Examinations

Do not be surprised if you are asked to take a medical or physical examination before you are hired for a job. Some large companies even have their own clinics and doctors. One purpose of a medical exam is to identify health problems that might prevent a person from performing his or her job safely and successfully.

Another purpose is to identify applicants with health problems that may become expensive insurance liabilities for the employer. Some companies have begun to use genetic testing for this purpose, and the trend is expected to continue. Genetic testing examines inherited traits. These can reveal the likelihood of future health problems developing, such as diabetes or heart disease.

Certain jobs, such as flying passenger airplanes or playing professional sports, require top physical condition. Some hospitals, medical clinics, and restaurants require workers to have medical exams for health reasons, 17-5. It is also a common practice for workers in management or stress-related jobs to have a complete medical exam prior to employment and periodically during employment.

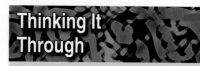

Thinking It Through

Why do you think it is legal for certain security and pharmaceutical firms to use polygraph tests?

Reflect Further

Would you rather answer an overt or a subtle honesty question? Why?

Discuss

Answer the *In the Real World* questions in writing. Then work in pairs to discuss your answers.

Reflect

What aspects of your personality would you not want a test to reveal?

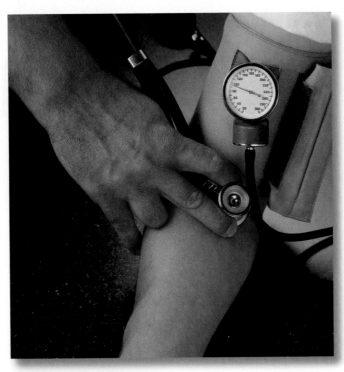

Physical Disabilities and the Screening Process

The Americans with Disabilities Act (ADA) has caused major changes in the employment of individuals with disabilities. The *Title I—Employment* section of the act prohibits discrimination against individuals with disabilities who otherwise are qualified for a given job or position.

The act requires employers to make reasonable accommodations for a person with disabilities who can perform the essential functions of the job. Employers must eliminate all attempts, intentional or otherwise, to screen out individuals with disabilities during the interview process. A more complete discussion of ADA is found in Chapter 20, "Diversity and Rights in the Workplace."

Drug Testing

Besides medical exams, many employers require drug testing as part of the job application process. Drug use in the workplace has become a major concern to employers. Workplace accidents, high absenteeism, reduced productivity, and high health costs are linked to drug use by workers. Since drug use can affect future job performance, applicants who test positively for drugs are usually not hired.

Drug abusers endanger themselves and coworkers. They have more accidents due to carelessness and poor judgment. Coworkers are endangered when drug users take risks and ignore safety rules. These problems cost employers billions of dollars every year.

To help fight the growing drug problem, many employers have started drug prevention programs for employees. The main purpose of the programs is to provide workers with a safer work environment. These programs usually include some form of drug testing. Employees may be tested periodically without prior notification of the specific time and date of the test. Company policies for employees who test positively may vary, but may include suspension or dismissal.

Drug testing is a controversial issue for both employers and employees. A difficult decision for an employer is whether to include testing in a drug prevention program. The workers most likely to be tested are those in jobs involving workplace or public safety, such as public transportation workers. Employees have concerns, too, such as the right to privacy and test accuracy.

How to Take Preemployment Tests

Unlike most tests, there are few preemployment tests for which you can study. However, there are several steps you can take to prepare yourself for any test. Follow these suggestions to help you feel calm and composed at test time:

- Try to find out in advance what type of tests you must take. If it is a skill test, such as welding, you can practice. However, do not practice so much that you tire yourself just before test time.

- Get plenty of rest the night before the test so you will feel refreshed and alert.

- If you are taking a written test, bring an extra pencil just in case you need it.

- Arrive at the test site early. Select a seat where you can see and hear the examiner well.

- While instructions are being given, be sure to ask questions about anything you do not understand. Follow directions exactly. Know how and where your answers are to be made. You may know the answer, but it will be marked wrong if you write it in the wrong place on the answer sheet.

- When taking a written test, try not to stay too long on one question. Answer the easiest questions first. Then go back and try to answer the harder questions.

- Have confidence in your ability.

Thinking It Through

What are the advantages and disadvantages of drug testing? Should employers use this type of test to screen job applicants?

Reflect Further

What additional steps might you take to prepare yourself for scoring well on a preemployment test?

Resource

Preemployment Testing, Activity C, WB

Resource

Types of Preemployment Tests, Activity D, WB

Resource

How to Take Preemployment Tests, Activity E, WB

Reflect

What kind of test taker are you? What can you do to improve your test-taking skills?

Summary

Many employers give preemployment tests as part of the job selection process. This helps them choose the best people for the jobs available. In addition, they can determine if a person will be suited to a certain job.

Several types of preemployment tests can be given to prospective employees. Skill tests may be given to test either their physical abilities or their knowledge of how to perform certain skills. Psychological tests are often used to find out more about an applicant's personality, character, and interests. Situational tests give the employer a better idea of how a person will perform under actual job conditions.

Civil service tests are often required to help place people fairly in state and federal government jobs. The military uses the Armed Services Vocational Aptitude Battery test to help place people in the military. Polygraph tests and written honesty tests help employers judge an applicant's honesty.

Medical exams are required by some employers to determine an applicant's physical condition for the job. The Americans with Disabilities Act prohibits discrimination against individuals with disabilities who can perform the essential functions of a job. Increasing concerns about drug abuse on the job have led some employers to start drug testing programs for job applicants.

Facts in Review

1. List two ways a preemployment test may be helpful to the person taking the test.
2. What is a performance test? Give an example.
3. Why do some employers give psychological tests to job applicants?
4. Who administers civil service tests?
5. Why do state and federal governments test job applicants?
6. Why may someone with no plans for a military career want to take the ASVAB?
7. What stress changes in the body do polygraph tests measure?
8. Who determines if a person taking a polygraph test is lying or telling the truth?
9. Where are honesty tests most often used?
10. What are the two main reasons for giving medical examinations to prospective employees before hiring them?
11. True or false. The main purpose of employee drug prevention programs is to provide workers with a safer work environment.

Resource

Review and Study Guide for Chapter 17, reproducible master 17-2, TR

Answers to *Facts In Review*

1. (List two:) may reinforce interest in a chosen career, may show unsuitability for a career area, may reveal a need for more training, may indicate that skills and interests better match another career field
2. a test that checks the applicant's ability to operate tools and machines (Example is student response.)
3. to determine how well an applicant will adjust to the job and get along with coworkers
4. The Civil Service Commission administers the tests for federal jobs, and the employment service within each state does so for state jobs.
5. to select the best qualified person for each job regardless of sex, race, religion, or political influence
6. to help you learn more about yourself, explore various career options, and determine if you are ready for more training in different career areas
7. changes in the subject's blood pressure, perspiration, and pulse rate
8. a certified polygraph test examiner
9. where people handle cash or merchandise or where individuals must work with little supervision
10. to identify health problems that may prevent a person from performing the job safely and successfully, to identify applicants with health problems that may become expensive insurance liabilities for the employer
11. true

Developing Your Academic Skills

1. **Science.** Research the possible future use of genetic testing to determine employees' health plans. In class, debate whether this seems to be an appropriate procedure—are there advantages or disadvantages to the employer or the employee?

2. **Social Studies.** Study examples of civil service tests. Discuss how the tests help place workers in jobs in the state and federal government. Give examples of different government jobs and discuss the qualifications necessary for each job.

Applying Your Knowledge and Skills

1. **Employability and Career Development.** Investigate the types of preemployment tests you may be asked to take when applying for jobs in your career area.

2. **Communications.** Obtain sample questions from preemployment tests and answer them in class.

3. **Problem Solving and Critical Thinking.** Assume the role of an employer. Make a list of the skills a job applicant needs to qualify for a specific job in your company. Then describe a performance, written, or oral test you could give applicants to evaluate their skill levels.

Information Technology Applications

1. Video yourself answering questions commonly asked in an oral psychological test. View the videos and critique your test.

2. Practice taking a standard keyboarding test. Rate yourself for speed and accuracy. Evaluate your results and determine areas that need more work.

Developing Workplace Skills

Working with two or three classmates, design a written honesty test for an entry-level position with one of the following employers: a child care center, a fast-food restaurant, or an auto repair shop. Talk with someone employed in the chosen career field to get a better understanding of the job. Present your written honesty test to the class. Explain why honest employees are important to the employer you selected. Also explain how your test will help identify people that may not be honest.

18

Interviewing for Jobs

Key Terms

mock interview

etiquette

follow-up letter

postmark

informational interview

Chapter Objectives

After studying this chapter, you will be able to

- **prepare** for an interview.
- **explain** how to make a good impression on the interviewer.
- **write** a follow-up letter after an interview.
- **describe** the factors to consider before accepting or rejecting a job offer.

Reading Advantage

Make a list of everything you already know about the topic of this chapter. As you read the chapter, check off the items that are covered in the chapter.

Achieving Academic Standards

English Language Arts

- Read print and non-print texts to acquire new information and to respond to the needs and demands of society and the workplace. (IRA/NCTE, 1)
- Use spoken and written language to communicate effectively. (IRA/NCTE, 4)
- Use spoken, written, and visual language to accomplish their purposes. (IRA/NCTE, 12)

Key Concepts

- A job interview is your chance to convince the employer that you are the right person for the job.

- Be sure to prepare thoroughly for your job interview by making a list of questions to ask and researching the employer.

- Before accepting a job offer, consider all the factors about the job.

The interview is usually the most important step in getting a job. Your application form, résumé, letter of application, or telephone call may have caught the employer's attention. However, it is the personal interview that will determine whether you are offered the job.

For the employer, the purpose of an interview is to evaluate the job seeker in person. The interviewer wants to find out if you have the skills to do the job and if you will work well with the other employees.

For you, the job seeker, the purpose of the interview is to convince the employer that you are the right person to hire for the job. The interview also gives you a chance to learn more about the job and the company. It may also convince you that the job is not right for you.

Preparing for an Interview

An interview is a talk between a job applicant and an employer. It can be a very important 20 or 30 minutes in your life. You should never expect to just walk into an interview without preparing yourself ahead of time. The better prepared you are for an interview, the better the impression you will make on the interviewer. To prepare for an interview, follow these tips:

- Learn about the employer and the job.

- Make a list of questions to ask.

- List the materials to take with you.

- Decide what to wear.

- Be prepared for questions.

- Practice for the interview.

- Know where to go for the interview.

Learn About the Employer and the Job

Become familiar with the employer before you go on your interview. You should know more about the company than the position for which you are applying. Find out about the company's products or services, size, reputation, and the possibilities for growth and expansion. Some companies publish annual reports that include this information.

You can generally find information about employers at your local or school library, 18-1. Descriptions of most corporations appear in business and industrial directories and library references. Ask the librarian to help you locate sources and obtain the information you need.

Ask your school-to-work coordinator and your guidance counselor if they can provide any information about the company. Talking with someone who works for the company will help you learn about the employer. Check with your chamber of commerce for information on companies in your area.

Another place to check is the company's Web site on the Internet. There you will often find information on the company's history, products, and employment needs. Companies cite their Internet addresses in TV commercials and magazine ads. You can also do an Internet search to locate their Web sites. Having some knowledge of the company will help you talk intelligently with the interviewer. It also shows the interviewer that you are interested enough in the company to do outside research.

Find out as much as you can about the job. Get information on specific duties and responsibilities, physical requirements, qualifications, hours, and opportunities for advancement. You can do this by requesting a copy of the job description. Save questions to which you cannot find answers for the interview.

Make a List of Questions to Ask

As you prepare for the interview, write down a few questions you would like to ask the interviewer about the job and the company. Asking questions, like researching the company, shows the employer that you have a serious interest in the company. The questions you ask can also help you decide if you really want to work for the company.

You may want to ask some of the following questions: "Would I receive training for this job?" "What hours would I work?" "Are there opportunities for advancement?" "May I see the work site?" "Is there anything I should read or study to get a head start on learning this job?" Do not ask questions that can be readily found on a company's Web site. It shows that you have not done your homework.

Wait until the end of the interview to ask about the job's salary range and benefits. Sometimes these topics are covered more fully in a second interview.

List the Materials to Take with You

When you go to an interview, there are a few items you will need to take with you. You will need a pen and your personal fact sheet for filling out an application. You will also need your résumé and the list of questions you plan to ask the interviewer. To keep your papers neat and clean, carry them in a file folder or large envelope.

18-1

Take the time to research an employer before you go to an interview.

Thinking It Through

What questions would you want answered during an interview?

Discuss

What should you do if you learn some negative facts about a company?

Resource

Interview Preparation, Activity B, WB

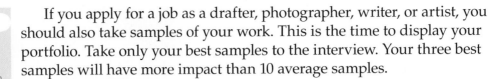

If you apply for a job as a drafter, photographer, writer, or artist, you should also take samples of your work. This is the time to display your portfolio. Take only your best samples to the interview. Your three best samples will have more impact than 10 average samples.

Decide What to Wear

Think carefully about what to wear to the interview several days in advance. Your clothes and appearance will influence the employer's impression of you. To make a good impression you should strive to look your very best, 18-2.

Let the type of job and company dictate your choice. A guideline you may want to follow when making your selection is: Dress one step above what is worn on the job. For example, if you are interviewing for a job as an auto technician, casual clothes business dress would be appropriate to wear. Avoid wearing work clothes, jeans, T-shirts, and tennis shoes. These clothes would probably appear too casual. It is always best to lean toward conservative in either professional or business attire. If you are still in doubt about what to wear, ask your instructor or counselor for advice. See 18-3.

Clothes should be clean, neat, and in good condition. Do not wear a torn shirt, a wrinkled coat, or muddy shoes. Have the shirt mended or choose something different. Get your coat pressed ahead of time, and clean and polish your shoes.

Remember, however, that neat, clean clothes will not leave a positive impression if you yourself are not neat and clean. Hair should be well styled. A beard should be neatly shaven or trimmed. Makeup and perfume should be applied sparingly.

Be Prepared for Questions

During an interview, you will be asked many questions to determine if you are the right person for the job. There are some questions that almost every job seeker can expect during an interview, 18-4. You need to become familiar with these questions and think about how to answer them. In fact, it is a good idea to write your answers on paper. Then you can read them over and decide if you phrased your thoughts clearly and positively. Sample interview questions may also be found on www.careerbuilder.com or www.monster.com. You may also want to try a Web search using the term *interview question answers*.

Early in the meeting, the interviewer is likely to say "Tell me about yourself." What do you suppose the interviewer wants to learn? He or she is exploring your educational background and

18-2

Strive to look your very best for every job interview.

Appropriate Interview Attire		
	Professional	**Casual Business**
Men	Two-piece suit—dark colors	Sport coat or blazer—not required, but avoid loud colors and patterns Pants—no jeans, avoid baggy pants
	Long-sleeved shirt coordinated with suit—white, blue or conservative stripe, no bright colors	Shirt—button-down or polo shirt—wear collar open if not wearing a tie
	Tie—coordinated with suit and shirt, conservative colors and patterns, no character ties	Tie—not required but appropriate
	Socks—calf-length coordinated with suit (usually black or brown)	Socks—conservative, mid-calf length
	Belt and shoes—leather, black or brown to match suit; no boots	Shoes—leather loafers or dress; no sandals, athletic shoes, or boots
	Jewelry—very little: conservative watch, no body piercings or chains	Jewelry—very little; no chains or body piercings
	Cologne—very little	Cologne—very little
Women	Two-piece dress or pants suit—conservative color (navy, dark gray, black, or brown); avoid short or tight skirts; no revealing slits	Skirt or pants—casual, solid conservative colors, avoid short or tight skirts, no revealing slits
	Blouse—tailored, cotton or silk, small collar, sleeves; no cleavage	Shirt or blouse—conservative, tailored, no cleavage
	Scarves—if worn, should be conservative colors that complement suit and blouse	Sweater—tailored knit or sweater set
	Shoes—pumps with low heel; color should match suit; toes should be covered	Shoes—leather or fabric loafers; dark colors to coordinate with wardrobe
	Hose—light color to match wardrobe, no patterns	Hose—light color to match wardrobe, no patterns
	Purse—small and simple	Purse—small and simple
	Jewelry—small, conservative; no body piercings except earrings	Jewelry—small, conservative; no body piercings except earrings
	Cosmetics—conservative, less is better	Cosmetics—conservative, less is better
	Perfume—very little	Perfume—very little

18-3

When in doubt, lean more toward professional than casual business dress.

Resource

Deciding What to Wear, Activity C, WB

Activity

Identify the appropriate job interview attire for five different occupations.

18-4

Be prepared to answer these questions completely before you go on your first interview.

Interview Questions	
Possible Questions	**Possible Responses**
"Won't you tell me about yourself?"	Succinctly summarize your abilities as they relate to the job qualifications or your career goals. Do not provide a general life history.
"Why do you want to work for this company?"	Tell what you know about the company. Explain how your abilities match the company's needs.
"Why do you think you will like this kind of work?"	Relate the job requirements to successful experiences you have had in the past.
"What were your best subjects in school?"	Name two or three and relate them to job qualifications.
"What were your poorest subjects in school?"	Explain what have you done to try to improve.
"What other jobs have you held?"	Focus on jobs with skills that relate to the jobs you are seeking.
"Why did you leave your last job?"	Be honest. However, avoid saying anything negative about your previous employer.
"Have you ever been fired from a job? If so, why?"	Answer honestly. If you have been fired, try to turn it into a positive by sharing what you learned from the experience. Avoid trying to blame others.
"What is your major strength?"	Select one and relate to the job qualifications.
"What is your major weakness?"	Be honest but explain what you have done to improve. Give an example.
"Have you ever had a conflict with a coworker? How did you handle it?"	Briefly describe the situation and how you handled it. Avoid placing all the blame on the other person. Explain what you learned from the experience.
"What do you expect to be paid?"	If possible, determine the salary range before the interview. Say that you are willing to discuss, or state a range you feel comfortable with.
"Are you willing to work evenings and weekends?"	Ask how much evening and weekend work would be required and then answer honestly.
"What are your future plans?"	Describe how the need to learn and grow is important to you. Confine your answer to the company with which you are interviewing.
"Why should I hire you?"	Be specific. Explain how your qualifications match the job requirements.

Activity

Write out the answers to these questions.

Resource

Interview Questions, Activity D, WB

job skills. At the same time, the interviewer is checking how well you express yourself. Provide the interviewer with responses that highlight your qualifications for the job.

Keep in mind that the subjects that interviewers cannot explore and the questions they cannot ask. A list of illegal questions for job application forms and job interviews is found in Chapter 16, "Applying for Jobs." These questions involve a job candidate's race, skin color, religion, national origin, sex, age, or disability. They are forbidden by laws that address discrimination, which is discussed in Chapter 20, "Diversity and Rights in the Workplace."

Although laws to prevent discrimination make certain questions illegal, that does not mean they will not be asked. Prepare yourself now and you will not be taken off guard if you hear an improper question. For example, you might respond by saying, "Please explain how that relates to the job" or "I would rather not answer personal questions." You could also respond to the intent of the question without answering it directly. For example, if the employer asks how old you are, you could respond by saying, "My age won't be a factor in performing the duties of this job."

If the interviewer innocently asked a borderline question, he or she will restate the question and keep the interview on a professional course. If questions or comments of a questionable nature continue, you should become suspicious of the interviewer. Remember, you are not obliged to answer illegal questions. When you suspect an interviewer of violating your legal rights, simply end the interview. Politely say that you are no longer interested in the job.

Practice for the Interview

Take some time to rehearse your interview. Ask a friend, family member, or other adult with business experience to interview you. These are known as **mock interviews**. You should also practice by interviewing yourself in front of a mirror. Practice answering questions that are likely to be asked. However, do not memorize your answers. Try to make them sound natural and positive. It is important to let your personality show through.

Most people usually feel nervous when interviewed. That is why practicing ahead of time is important. Practicing builds your self-confidence and helps you feel more relaxed during the actual interview.

Know Where to Go for the Interview

What a waste of time and energy it is to prepare for an interview and miss it by going to the wrong place. This has happened. One job seeker, for example, assumed his interview would be at the company's manufacturing plant. When he arrived at the scheduled time, he learned that all interviews were held at the company's headquarters across town. Another job seeker missed her interview because she wrote down the wrong time and did not double-check. For these reasons, it is important to keep an accurate record of each interview you schedule.

Thinking It Through

Why is it important to be prepared for interview questions? How should you react if you think an interviewer's question is illegal? Would you want to work for someone who does not carefully avoid discriminatory practices?

Thinking It Through

Why is it important to practice for an interview? What are some good ways to practice?

Resource

Interview Practice, Activity F, WB

Enrich

Invite business and industry representatives to conduct mock interviews.

Extend Your Knowledge

Interview Parking Tips

When arranging the interview, remember to ask where to park. Knowing where to park can save you valuable time. Some companies have special areas for visitor parking. If you are interviewing in a city, you may need to park in a parking garage or a parking lot. Make sure to bring extra money; parking in a city garage can be expensive.

It is a good idea to visit the company before the interview to be sure you know how to get there and where to go. The trip will help you estimate the travel time. Be sure to allow extra time on the day of the interview so you arrive early.

One easy way to keep your interviews organized is by preparing an index card for each, 18- 5. Write the date and time of the interview, the employer's name, and the exact location. Also note the name of the person to contact and the title of the job for which you are applying. Be sure to double-check all information to make sure you have recorded it correctly.

On the bottom and back of the card, leave space for comments. After each interview, make notes about what questions were asked and how well you answered them. Evaluating yourself can help you have a more successful interview next time.

18-5

Filling out a note card for every interview helps keep track of important facts about the employer and the result of each interview.

Job Interview

Date of interview __May 14, 20xx__

Time of interview __8:30__

Employer __Whitaker Publishing Company__   Contact __Robert Drake__

Location __1822 W. Meridian St.__

__Milwaukee, WI 53172__   Phone no. __(414) 555-2323__

Job title __Office assistant__

Comments __I interviewed with Mr. Robert Drake, Personnel Manager. He was__
__very interested in my business education background and keyboarding skills.__
__He plans on making a decision about the position by next Friday.__

Discuss

Is there ever a legitimate excuse for arriving late for an interview?

The Interview

Once you have prepared for an interview, you are ready to meet your interviewer face to face. However, there are a few other details you need to consider. For example, what time should you arrive at the interviewer's office? How should you greet him or her? How should you behave during the interview? How should you end the interview? Knowing the answers to these questions will help you handle yourself with confidence and make a good impression on the interviewer.

Arrive five to ten minutes early for the interview. Relax and be yourself. Tell the receptionist or person in charge who you are and who you are scheduled to see. Do not take someone with you to the interview. Taking a friend or family member may give the impression that you will not be comfortable working alone. You certainly do not want to give this impression. Be sure to turn off your cell phone.

The interview begins with a formal introduction. This may be one of the most important parts of the interview. It is the first impression your prospective employer will have of you. It is important that you make eye contact when you are introduced to someone and maintain it throughout the entire conversation.

Chances are that you will first introduce yourself to a receptionist. Smile and offer a friendly greeting such as "good morning." Clearly state your name and the purpose of your visit. You will probably be asked to take a seat to wait for your appointment. It is important that you conduct yourself professionally at this time. Sit up straight. Use this time to review your notes or look over any brochures or professional magazines in the reception area. Of course, be prepared to carry on a conversation with the receptionist if prompted.

When the interviewer arrives, the receptionist may introduce you. If so, stand and wait for him or her to complete the introduction. If not, stand and introduce yourself. In either case, be sure to include a friendly greeting and restate the interviewer's name. This will help you remember it. Ask the individual to repeat his or her name if you did not hear it clearly or are unsure of the pronunciation. It is very important to smile and act relaxed. Remove gloves if you are wearing them and shake hands firmly.

When you are offered a seat, sit in a comfortable position but do not slouch. Sit straight and look alert. Your body language often tells the employer as much about you as what you say. Avoid doing anything distracting such as smoking, chewing gum, or cracking your knuckles. It is natural to be nervous, but do your best to appear relaxed.

As the interviewer asks you questions, listen very carefully. Then respond positively and honestly about yourself and your experiences. Keep your answers brief and to the point. Do not brag about your qualifications, but do not be bashful to tell the interviewer about your accomplishments.

Throughout the interview, act interested in what the interviewer is saying. Do not look out the window, around the room, or at the floor. Look pleasantly at the interviewer and maintain eye contact. Show you are enthusiastic about the job and the company.

Reflect Further

What impression do you want the interviewer to form of you during the interview?

Reflect

Do you believe that you generally follow rules of etiquette while dining? Why might you want to brush up on your table skills before a dinner interview?

Activity

Set up a table with dinnerware, utensils, and napkins. Have students role-play a dinner interview. Have students offer constructive criticism to one another and discuss rules of dining etiquette.

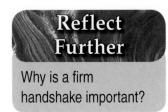

Reflect Further

Why is a firm handshake important?

When the interviewer asks if you have any questions, that is usually a signal that he or she has all the information needed about you. It is your turn to find out more about the job to help you decide if it is really for you. It is important to have your questions ready at this time. You will want to ask the questions about the job and the company that you have not been able to answer in your research on the company. For example, you might ask about the opportunity to learn and grow on the job. What are the opportunities for advancement? You might also ask about a typical workday or what the interviewer likes about working for the company. However, these types of questions should have a low priority. It is usually best to save questions about salary and benefits for a follow-up interview. After your questions are answered, the interview is just about over. At this time, thank the interviewer for seeing you and again express your interest in the job.

Seldom will you be offered a job at an interview. Most likely, the interviewer will want time to consider your qualifications and those of the other job candidates. The interviewer may promise to contact you on a certain date to let you know if you have the job. Sometimes the interviewer may ask you to call him or her at a later date. If you do not get the job, the interviewer is not likely to call you at all.

If no mention is made at the end of the interview of what happens next, it is appropriate to ask when a hiring decision will be made. You should leave an interview with a clear idea of when the newly hired person will be notified.

The Dinner Interview

It is possible that you may be asked to interview for a job over dinner. You may also be asked to attend a dinner meeting as part of your job. In these situations, it is important to follow etiquette. **Etiquette** is the code of behavior that guides social situations. Observing proper table manners is an example of etiquette. Your behavior while dining can influence whether you are offered the position or have a successful meeting.

Table etiquette begins as you approach the dining table and does not end until you have left the dining area. Wait for your host to seat you. Men should offer to pull out a woman's chair.

Begin by removing the napkin and placing it in your lap. If you are dining in a formal situation, you will notice that the dinnerware and eating utensils are placed in a specific order. The forks will be on your left and the knife and spoons on your right. If the utensils are wrapped in a napkin, you should place them in their proper place. As you begin eating, always use the utensils on the outside of your place setting first. For example, the fork farthest away from your plate will be the salad fork. The spoon on the far right will be the soupspoon. When in doubt, follow the lead of your host.

As you begin eating, it is important to note that you will be expected to engage in conversation. Of course, you should not chew or talk with your mouth full. Therefore, you will need to control the amount of food you place in your mouth at one time. Take small bites so you can chew, swallow, and still converse in a timely manner. Bread and rolls should be broken into small pieces as you eat them. Cut meat as you eat each piece. Certain foods such as olives and corn on the cob are considered finger foods. Finger foods may be picked up by hand, but other foods may not. You may place your elbows on the table between courses, but not while eating.

Try to pace your eating so you do not finish too soon or too late. Wait for your host to conclude the meal. Place used utensils back on your plate when you are finished eating.

If you have been invited to dinner for a job interview, your host will pick up the check. The purpose of other meal functions will determine who pays the check. Try to determine this prior to the meal to avoid awkward situations when the check arrives. Avoid ordering the most expensive items from the menu if others are paying. Be sure to thank your host at the conclusion of the meal.

After the Interview

After an interview, do not just sit back and hope you will get the job. At your first opportunity, immediately send a **follow-up letter**. This is a brief letter written in business form to thank the interviewer for his or her time. It should be postmarked within two days of the interview. A **postmark** is the official U.S. Postal Service stamp on delivered mail. A follow-up letter reminds the interviewer of your interest in the job. You may want to include a brief comment on how your qualifications match the job requirements. See 18-6.

If the interviewer promised to contact you by a certain date and does not, also follow up with a telephone call. Be as pleasant and positive as you were during the interview. You may want to say something like this: "Mr. Roberts, this is Terry Brooks. I interviewed two weeks ago for the auto mechanic position. You mentioned that a decision about the job would probably be made by now. I am still interested in the job and wonder if you have made your decision." You may learn the job has been filled. On the other hand, you may learn that you are still in the running and a final decision will be made in two weeks. Whatever the response, you will know where you stand.

Do not be discouraged if you do not get a job offer right away. Very few job seekers land a job after just one or two interviews. You may need to interview with a number of employers to find the best job for you. However, if you have missed out on several jobs, try to figure out why. Check the comments you have written down on your interview cards. Have you had any problems on your interviews? You may discover there is a specific reason why you are not getting job offers. To help you evaluate yourself on the job hunt, ask yourself the following questions.

- Are you qualified for the jobs for which you are applying? Perhaps you are applying for jobs that require more training and experience than you have. Be willing to start at the bottom if necessary.

- Are you applying to the wrong places? Apply where there are likely to be job openings. Consider applying for jobs in neighboring towns or moving to an area where there are more job opportunities.

Thinking It Through

Why would you want to avoid ordering the most expensive items from the menu if someone else is paying for the meal?

Resource

The Follow-Up Letter, Activity H, WB

Discuss

Is it appropriate to write a follow-up letter if you didn't get a job?

Activity

Role-play follow-up calls.

Discuss

Is it appropriate to ask an interviewer why you didn't get a job?

1036 Spring St.
Milwaukee, WI 53172
May 15, 20xx

Mr. Robert Drake
Personnel Manager
Whitaker Publishing Company
1822 W. Meridian St.
Milwaukee, WI 53172

Dear Mr. Drake:

Thank you for taking time yesterday to interview me for the office assistant position that will become available in June.

After talking with you, I am very excited about the possibility of joining your company. I am confident I have the ability to work independently, which is so important to you.

I look forward to hearing your decision and hope it will be a favorable one.

Sincerely,

Mary Poston

Mary Poston

18-6
Sending a follow-up letter after an interview is a courtesy the interviewer will appreciate.

- Are you filling out job application forms properly? If you are not filling out applications correctly and neatly, employers may think you will not be able to perform a job properly. Read the directions carefully on all applications and answer all the questions completely. Remember, you need not answer questions that violate your rights as a job applicant.

- Do you lack interest and energy? Not asking questions about the job or seeming uninterested could convince the interviewer you do not really want to be hired.

- Do you lack confidence? Appearing very nervous and ill at ease may make it difficult for the interviewer to talk with you.

- Are you being discourteous? Arriving late for the interview or not thanking the interviewer for seeing you may leave a bad impression of you.

One way to improve your job-seeking skills is to conduct an **informational interview**. Locate someone who is employed in a job area in which you are interested. Call the company and arrange for an interview with the individual. Tell the individual you are trying to learn more about an occupation and that you will not take more than 15 or 20 minutes of his or her time. Use the interview to learn more about the occupation and yourself.

Because you will not be under the pressure of applying for a job, you should be more relaxed and able to work on the interview skills discussed earlier. You may even want to ask what the interviewer seeks in a job candidate. Near the end of the interview, ask the individual to recommend how you might improve your interview skills. Be sure to express a sincere thanks at the close of the interview and send a follow-up letter, just as you would for an actual interview. This effort could even result in a future job offer.

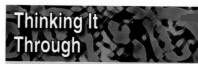

Thinking It Through

Why is it important to make notes after each interview about the questions you were asked and how well you answered them?

Accepting a Job Offer

Before accepting a job offer, consider all the factors about the job. This will help you evaluate the job and the company. An important factor to consider is whether you will be happy in this position. Excellent working conditions and good pay will not mean much if you end up hating to go to work each day. Now is also the time to ask questions about the job's responsibilities, pay, and benefits.

The salary for a job should be in line with the salaries paid for similar jobs at other companies. If the salary is a lot lower, you should probably consider a job with an employer that pays a more reasonable salary. However, a lower salary is sometimes balanced with excellent opportunities for advancement or very good fringe benefits. Check to see if your employer provides any of the following fringe benefits:

Insurance

Does the company offer group health, dental, and/or life insurance? If so, how much coverage do the policies provide? Does the employer pay all or much of the cost?

Resource

Informational Interview Practice, Activity G, WB

Resource

Fringe Benefits, Activity I, WB

Activity

Write a letter of acceptance for a mock employment offer.

In the Real World

The Perfect Interview

Sholanda was very pleased when she received an offer to interview for a job as a receptionist in the emergency room at the local hospital. It was a very good job and she knew there were many applicants. In fact, over half of her classmates in health occupations applied for the job.

Sholanda prepared herself well for the interview by finding out as much as she could about the hospital and the position. On the day of the interview she dressed appropriately and followed all the interview tips she had learned in class. The interview went extremely well, and as the interview closed Sholanda felt certain she would be offered the position.

The last step in the interview process was a tour of the emergency room. As they were about to leave, the ambulance arrived with an accident victim. The patient was covered in blood and in very serious condition with deep cuts to the face and neck. When Sholanda saw the victim she almost panicked. She felt faint and sick to her stomach. She quickly looked away and managed to hide her reaction from the personnel director and head nurse who were conducting the tour. However, she knew immediately that she would never be able to work in an emergency room.

They left the emergency room and returned to the personnel director's office. The director asked Sholanda if she had any questions and still wanted the job. Sholanda said all her questions had been answered and she knew she would be perfect for the job.

A few days later Sholanda received a telephone call from the personnel director. The job was hers if she still wanted it. Sholanda told the director she was very excited and flattered by the offer and was pleased to accept. The director told her to report to the emergency room in two weeks to begin her orientation training.

The next week was very difficult for Sholanda. She knew she didn't want the job and would take another as soon as possible. She couldn't think about anything else and began to lose sleep agonizing over her decision. She finally called the director the day before she was scheduled to start training and declined the offer. When asked why, Sholanda said she had too much schoolwork and couldn't handle both the job and school.

Questions to Discuss

1. What might be some reasons Sholanda accepted the job? What should she have done differently?
2. Do you think Sholanda should have at least tried to do the job?
3. Were her actions fair to the hospital?
4. Why do you suppose she lied to the personnel director? Do you think Sholanda's behavior affected the director's opinion of her classmates who also applied for the job?

Paid Vacation

Will you receive paid vacation time? If so, how many days? Will you receive more paid vacation days after working for a certain number of years? See 18-7.

Enrich

Contact three or four companies and obtain copies of their fringe benefits. Compare the benefits in class.

Sick Pay

Will the company pay for any days you are sick and unable to come to work? How many paid sick days are available per year?

Retirement or Profit-Sharing Plans

Does the company contribute a set amount of money to a retirement plan or a percentage of its profits to a profit-sharing plan for you? Will a portion of your income also be contributed to one of these plans? If so, how much? Must you work for a certain number of years before you are eligible to participate in plans offered by the employer?

Bonuses

Does the company give yearly or holiday bonuses? How are the amounts of bonuses determined? As discussed earlier, pay and fringe benefits are just two factors to consider about a job. Also consider the location of the job, working conditions, work hours, and opportunities for advancement before you make a final decision about a job.

If you do decide to accept a job offer, let the interviewer know. Tell him or her you are glad to accept the offer. Then find out everything you need to know to start your first day of work. Remember to ask when, where, and to whom you should report for work. Also ask whether you need to bring anything with you.

18-7

Paid vacation time is a fringe benefit of many full-time jobs.

Rejecting a Job Offer

At the end of your interview with an employer you may be offered a job. If you need more time to evaluate the job, you may want to ask the interviewer for a few days to think about it. Most employers will usually agree.

On the other hand, you may be asked to decide immediately whether to accept the offer. If you have evaluated the job and decided it is not what you really want, you will probably choose not to accept the offer. At this point, politely thank the interviewer. Explain briefly why you feel you are not the right person for the job. The interviewer will appreciate your direct, honest answer.

Many jobs are not offered at the end of the interview. You may receive a job offer later, either by telephone or by mail. In either case, let the employer know right away via phone that you will not accept the offer. Thank the employer and give a brief explanation for your decision. When rejecting a job offer made by mail, immediately send a short follow-up letter thanking the interviewer for the offer. Include a statement explaining why you are not interested in the job.

Activity

Write a letter rejecting a mock employment offer.

Summary

A personal interview with an employer is an important step in getting a job. Prepare for it carefully by learning all you can about the employer and the job. Think about the questions you may be asked during the interview. Be prepared to answer those questions before the interview.

Making a good impression on the interviewer is important. Be on time for the interview and go by yourself. During the interview, listen to the questions asked. Respond positively and honestly about yourself. Ask your questions about the company and the job after the interviewer finishes. After the interview, send a follow-up letter. Thank the interviewer and let him or her know of your interest in the job. If the interviewer does not contact you by the date promised, you may follow up with a phone call. If you do not get the job, take time to evaluate what happened during the interview and learn from your experience.

Before accepting or rejecting a job offer, carefully evaluate the job and the company. Consider several factors in making your final decision. In either case, let the interviewer know your decision right away.

Facts in Review

1. What is the purpose of the interview for the employer? for the job seeker?
2. List five ways to prepare for an interview.
3. What information about an employer should a job seeker try to learn before the interview?
4. Why is it important to have some knowledge of a company before an interview?
5. Why is it important to prepare a list of questions to ask the interviewer?
6. What items should be taken to an interview?
7. What is a good guideline to follow to help decide what to wear to an interview?
8. What information should be included in your record of each interview?
9. Why should a job seeker go alone to an interview?
10. If an interviewer does not mention when a hiring decision will be made, what can a job applicant do?
11. How can an individual evaluate his or her interviewing skills?
12. What topics should a job seeker who receives a job offer discuss thoroughly with the employer?
13. Give examples of four fringe benefits.

Resource

Review and Study Guide for Chapter 18, reproducible master 18-2, TR

Answers to *Facts In Review*

1. to evaluate a job seeker in person; to convince the employer of being the right person for the job
2. (List five:) Learn about the employer and the job. Make a list of questions to ask the employer. List the materials to take. Decide what to wear. Be prepared for questions. Practice for the interview. Know where to go for the interview.
3. the employer's products/services, size, reputation, and future plans
4. shows a serious interest in the company, helps with the interview discussion
5. helps you decide if you really want to work for the company

6. pen, personal fact sheet, résumé, list of questions to ask the interviewer, folder or large envelope for papers/portfolio
7. Dress one step above what is worn on the job.
8. interview date and time, employer's name, interview location, name of contact person, title of job, notes about questions asked and how well they were answered
9. It gives the impression that the applicant can handle matters alone.
10. Ask when a hiring decision will be made.
11. by requesting an informational interview for practice and asking the interviewer for recommendations
12. job responsibilities, pay, and fringe benefits
13. (List four:) insurance, paid vacation, sick pay, retirement or profit-sharing plans, bonuses

Developing Your Academic Skills

1. **English.** Write responses for typical interview questions. Trade papers with another student and critique each other's responses for appropriate expression of thoughts. Give suggestions for how your classmate might improve his or her responses.

2. **Speech.** Choose a partner and role-play an interview. The "employer" should prepare interview questions to ask. When the interview is finished, the "employer" should give the "applicant" feedback on his or her interview. Then switch roles.

Information Technology Applications

1. Choose a company for which you might be interested in working. Search the Internet for the company's history, products, and employment needs.

2. Participate in a mock interview using standard interview questions. Have your "interview" video recorded. Watch the video and critique your interview.

Applying Your Knowledge and Skills

1. **Problem Solving and Critical Thinking.** Assume you will be interviewed for the future job of your dreams. Prepare for the interview by doing the following:
   A. On a note card, record the important information about the interview.
   B. List three questions to ask the interviewer.
   C. List five questions that the interviewer is likely to ask you.
   D. Decide what is appropriate to wear.

2. **Communications.** Role-play the interview described in Item 1. Have a classmate interview you for the job. Be sure to give the interviewer a copy of your résumé. Discuss the interview in class.

3. **Academic Foundations.** Research proper dinner etiquette. Share your findings in an oral class presentation.

4. **Employability and Career Development.** Role-play appropriate and inappropriate ways to dress for the interview.

5. **Communications.** Write a follow-up letter for the interview described in Item 1.

6. **Employability and Career Development.** Conduct an informational interview. Share your experience with the class.

Developing Workplace Skills

Select three or four companies that interest you and research them. Search for information through your school library and the Internet. Develop a list of the strengths and weaknesses of each employer as they relate to your interests and abilities. Then rank the companies in terms of how well they suit you. Justify your rankings. Finally, write down your reply to this interviewer comment: "Tell me about yourself."

Part 5
Job Satisfaction

19

Succeeding on the Job

Key Terms

orientation

conviction

stress

job probation

performance rating

incentive

promotion

lateral move

demotion

union

collective bargaining

labor contract

Chapter Objectives

After studying this chapter, you will be able to

- **explain** how getting along with others can help you succeed on the job.
- **identify** the rules of proper workplace conduct.
- **describe** ways to recognize and handle stress.
- **evaluate** your job performance and the job itself.
- **explain** the purpose of job performance reviews.
- **describe** the options for changing your job status.
- **recognize** the signs of a stalled career and the best way to change jobs.
- **debate** the pros and cons of union membership.

Reading Advantage

Predict what you think will be covered in this chapter. Make a list of your predictions. After reading the chapter, decide if your predictions were correct.

Achieving Academic Standards

English Language Arts

- Read print and non-print texts to acquire new information and to respond to the needs and demands of society and the workplace. (IRA/NCTE, 1)
- Use spoken and written language to communicate effectively. (IRA/NCTE, 4)
- Use different writing process elements appropriately to communicate. (IRA/NCTE, 5)

Key Concepts

- Your first day on the job may include attending an orientation, meeting coworkers, and becoming familiar with your duties.

- Demonstrating proper conduct on the job includes getting along with others, following directions, taking responsibility, and controlling anger.

- Job stress can have positive and negative effects on people.

- Changes in job status can include promotions, lateral moves, demotions, or being fired.

- Unions bargain with management for better wages, working hours, working conditions, and benefits.

What does it mean to succeed on the job? To many people, being successful on the job means doing their jobs well and not getting fired. To others, job success is having more pay, more responsibilities, and a new title.

To succeed at any job, you must stick with it. Do not be surprised if it takes several weeks to adjust to your job and learn your responsibilities. You will need to work hard to learn all your duties, but you should not try to get too far ahead of yourself. You cannot expect to accomplish everything in only a few weeks.

Your First Day on the Job

Your first step toward job success begins the first day on the job. As you learn your job duties and adjust to your job, your chances for success will increase.

Starting a new job and working with new people in a new environment may make you feel a little nervous. Most people feel this way when they start a new job. Planning ahead can help you feel more prepared for that first day. Think about how you should dress for the job and have your clothes out the night before. Allow yourself plenty of time to get ready. That means getting dressed, eating, and preparing a lunch if necessary. Arrive a few minutes early at the job—definitely do not be late on your first day. Keeping a positive attitude will help you start your new job the right way.

What you do on the first day at work depends on your employer. A small business may want you to start working right away. Larger companies usually have an employee orientation for new workers. During the **orientation** you will likely learn the company's history, policies, rules, and safety procedures. You may be asked to fill out personnel forms. You may also be asked to take a drug test. After the orientation, you will report to your supervisor.

Your supervisor is responsible for your training. On your first day, he or she will show you where you work and explain your duties. You will be introduced to your coworkers. Sometimes another worker will teach you how to do the job, or you may watch an experienced worker. Depending on your job, you may attend a company training program or school. In any case, your concern at this point should be learning to do the job.

Pay close attention and show an interest in learning your job duties. Ask questions if you do not completely understand what is expected of you. Because you are new, do not try to work at full speed the first day. At this point, accuracy is much more important than speed. Try to do the job to the best of your ability, but if you make a mistake, do not worry. Inform your supervisor of your mistake and learn something from it. Making a true effort to do your best will help you succeed.

Relating to Others at Work

Learning your job duties is one of the first steps in starting a new job. To achieve success on the job, however, you also need to work well with other people. Companies function best when employees cooperate and work together as a team. Your ability to get along with your supervisor and coworkers will contribute to your success on the job.

Working with Your Supervisor

In addition to training, your supervisor is responsible for your job performance. He or she must make sure your work is completed and done well. Your supervisor will observe your work to see how well you are doing your job and getting along with others. You may be encouraged to work faster or to try a new way of doing a job. Remember, this is constructive criticism. It can help you improve your skills and work more efficiently. See 19-1.

Sometimes you may be assigned tasks you do not want to do. As a beginner, you should perform these tasks as well as you would any others. Consider them learning experiences.

Supervisors have different personalities and management styles. No matter what type of supervisor you have, make the effort to learn and to cooperate with him or her. Listen and follow through on all suggestions. Most supervisors want you to succeed on the job, but you must do your part to promote a good working relationship.

Note

The first day on the job may sometimes be a disappointment. New employees do not generally become involved in their main tasks for weeks.

19-1
When you start a new job, be prepared to listen to your supervisor, accept instructions, and ask questions.

Working with Coworkers

Resource

People's Attitudes, reproducible
master 19-1, TR

As a new employee, getting along with and being accepted by your coworkers is important. First, you will be happier and enjoy your work more in a workplace where everyone is pleasant to others. Second, you and coworkers will probably get more work done if you enjoy working together. It is important that you show an ability to work cooperatively with others. This cooperative effort could lead to future pay raises or even a better job.

Part of getting along with others depends on you. When you start your job, introduce yourself to coworkers if your supervisor has not done so. Learn their names. Try to be pleasant without overdoing it. Be friendly and most coworkers will accept you. Respect and accept them as both individuals and teammates. They have knowledge and skills to contribute to the company.

In the Real World

Dealing with Restaurant Customers

John worked as a server in a restaurant known for its fine food and excellent customer service. There were many restaurants in town, but this relatively new restaurant had quickly established many loyal customers. John was careful to place the table service correctly and present the menus properly. He did these tasks better than any of his coworkers.

John seemed to have a reserved manner with customers, however. He didn't smile much and his face often looked grim. When a customer complained about the food, the bill, or the service, John became irritable. He occasionally talked back to customers. This conduct was strictly forbidden in the restaurant's employee handbook. John also complained to his coworkers.

One night just before closing, a large group entered the restaurant. The people were seated in John's area. He took their orders and served them properly even though he wanted to go home early. When the group finished eating, it was after the closing hour. John noticed they left a smaller tip than he expected.

Just as the group was leaving John said, "That wasn't much of a tip for the service you got." His boss heard the comment and fired John on the spot.

Questions to Discuss

1. Why was John fired?
2. What rules of proper conduct did John disobey?
3. Do you think John's boss fired him too hastily? Would you have given John another chance?

Although you may not become close friends with all of them, you should respect their positive qualities. Try to be a likable person so coworkers will enjoy working with you. Remember, you are a beginner getting to know your job. Learn to accept suggestions or criticism positively as a way to improve your work. Acting like a know-it-all or being self-centered will give others a bad impression of you.

Your Conduct and Job Success

Another important factor in getting along with others and being successful on the job is worker conduct. Employers want workers who behave properly on the job. The rules of proper workplace conduct are shown in 19-2 and explained here. Employees who demonstrate proper on-the-job conduct do the following:

- *Follow directions.*—Pay close attention and show interest in learning your job duties. Make sure you perform all your responsibilities on the job. If necessary, keep careful notes about your assignments so you do not forget any directions.

- *Enjoy learning.*—Upgrade your skills whenever possible. Willingly try new tasks and believe in your ability to succeed, 19-3. Accept suggestions and constructive criticism about your work with a positive attitude.

- *Act responsibly.*—When your work is done, find other tasks to do instead of killing time. Let your supervisor know that you need more assignments added to your workload.

- *Be enthusiastic.*—Keep an upbeat attitude. Avoid letting problems at home or school interfere with your work.

- *Deal with mistakes.*—Learn from your small mistakes and avoid repeating them. Report big mistakes to your supervisor as soon as possible and discuss how to handle them. Above all, do not cover up mistakes or deny they ever happened.

- *Handle gossip.*—Avoid talking about others behind their backs and you will be trusted by everyone. Most office gossip is merely rumor or suspicion, neither of which is worth your time.

- *Control anger.*—Try to get along with everyone, and stay in full control of your emotions. When events become too heated, find a way to break the tension so everyone can take time to think. Voice legitimate complaints to the proper authorities instead of complaining to coworkers.

- *Assert yourself.*—Be "in charge" of your job assignments. Act confidently and voice your convictions. A **conviction** is a strong belief. Defend the decisions you make and the people who followed your directions and helped you.

Reflect Further

How might your work relationships with your supervisor and coworkers affect your job performance?

Rules of Good Workplace Conduct

- Follow directions.
- Enjoy learning.
- Act responsibly.
- Be enthusiastic.
- Deal with mistakes.
- Handle gossip.
- Control anger.
- Assert yourself.
- Take responsibility.

19-2
These guidelines list the employee behavior expected by employers.

Resource

Workplace Conduct and Job Success, Activity C, WB

Resource

Successful Job Conduct, reproducible master 19-2, TR

Activity

Write a one-page paper stating your views on the importance of controlling emotional reactions in the workplace.

19-3

A positive attitude is an important factor in job success.

• *Take responsibility.*—Do assignments well, meet all deadlines, and alert your supervisor if you think you may miss a deadline. Do not make excuses for poor performance or bad decisions. Accept your errors and correct them. Do not blame problems on coworkers.

The reasons employees are fired will be discussed later in this chapter. You will learn that improper conduct on the job is the main cause of most firings. If you need to improve your conduct in any of the areas discussed here, start now. It is never too late to modify behaviors that need improvement.

Handling Job Stress

No matter where you work or how well you get along with others, you are likely to face some sort of job stress. By understanding stress and what causes it, you can learn to handle it effectively.

People face some form of stress in their lives every day. **Stress** is a feeling of pressure, strain, or tension that results from change. Change can create different levels of stress. Major changes, such as the death of a friend or the loss of a job, are extremely stressful. Losing a homework assignment or being late for work is less stressful. Even positive changes like a pay raise or a vacation can be stressful.

Stress can have positive or negative effects on people. It can motivate them to get things done or face new challenges. On the other hand, stress can cause frustration, anger, and lower productivity. Too much stress can affect a person's body and the mind. It can eventually lead to health problems including headaches or high blood pressure.

Stress, no matter what the cause, can affect job performance. Workers react to stress in different ways. Those who feel great stress are likely to be less productive and have more accidents on the job. They tend to blame and criticize others. Workers who make an effort to handle stress, however, stay in control of their emotions. They may use humor to break the tension. They may try to analyze the situation to find the problem's cause. Above all, they channel their energy to getting the problem solved and the job done.

You cannot avoid stress in your life, but you can learn how to manage it. Handling stress begins by recognizing the cause and learning to deal with it. Several ways to handle stress effectively are shown in 19-4.

Evaluating Job Performance

After working at a job for several weeks, you can begin to evaluate your job performance and the job itself. To help you find out if you are succeeding on your job, ask yourself the following questions:

Handling Stress

Keep a positive attitude. Use stress in a positive way to help you set and achieve your goals.

Stay healthy. This helps you handle the causes of stress. To relieve stress, try some physical activity.

Discuss your problem. A friend, family member, or counselor may see your problem differently.

Manage your time well. List all your tasks. Do the most important first. Check off each task as you complete it.

Know your limits. Sometimes a problem may be beyond your control and cannot be changed right away. Learn to accept the situation until you can change it.

Cooperate with others. Try to give and take instead of fighting or confronting.

Find healthy ways to relieve stress. Get involved in an activity if you are lonely or sad. Try deep breaths to relieve built-up tension.

Take time to relax and have fun. Relaxing helps you slow down your pace and lessen stress. Recreation gives you a break from your everyday routine.

19-4

Learning to handle stress is the key to good mental and physical health.

Discuss

Have you used any of these techniques to handle a stressful situation?

Activity

Analyze your time-management skills by keeping a log of what you do during the next 24 hours.

Resource

Job Satisfaction, Activity E, WB

Am I making progress in this job? Have you learned how to perform all your duties and do them well? If you are having a problem learning how to do a task, ask your supervisor for assistance. If you are accomplishing your work with time to spare, let your supervisor know you are capable of taking on more responsibility. The more you can learn and accomplish, the faster you will succeed on the job.

Consider the example of Marla, who learned her job duties quickly and became a very productive worker in a few weeks. When she accomplished her assigned work, she asked the supervisor for other assignments to handle. Marla was a responsible and cooperative employee who was always willing to help others with tasks whenever asked. When the assistant supervisor was promoted to a new position, Marla was asked to take that position. She accepted and continued to work just as conscientiously at her new job. Marla's hard work paid off, and it helped her get better jobs in the future.

Does this job give me personal satisfaction? Do you enjoy the work you do? You cannot expect a job to be all fun and games, but it should not be all drudgery either. Job success depends on the way you feel about your job. To be successful, you must feel your job is useful and helpful to others. If you feel you are making important contributions on the job, you will probably feel pleased about your life and the work you accomplish, 19-5.

Am I paid adequately for the work I do? Although salary is only one aspect of job success, it is an important one. Check to see what other

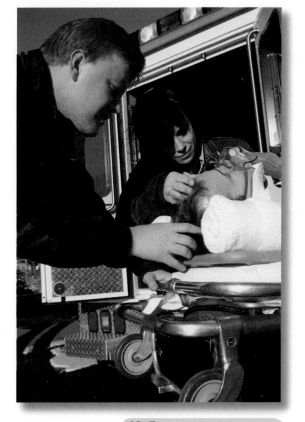

19-5

These paramedics get satisfaction from their work because their job provides important, lifesaving services to others.

In the Real World

The Stressful Boss

Chang feels constant stress on his job. He has been working as a carpenter for three months, and for the entire period his supervisor has watched him almost constantly. On a few occasions, the supervisor criticized Chang's work.

Chang likes his job, but is bothered by his supervisor's frequent checkups. Finally, in frustration he yelled to his supervisor, "This job is getting to me because you are constantly watching me. I can't stand it anymore!"

The supervisor seemed surprised. "That's my job, Chang," he replied. "It usually takes a new worker at least six months to adjust to the job. It's my responsibility to check your work, make sure it's done right, and be certain you don't have an accident."

Chang apologized for his outburst and acknowledged that the supervisor was only doing his job. As a result of their conversation, Chang's stress was greatly reduced. He was able to concentrate more on learning his job and wasn't bothered by frequent glances from the supervisor. He knew they were for his benefit.

Questions to Discuss

1. What could Chang have done to handle his stress before it became uncontrollable?
2. Could Chang have been fired for his outburst?
3. Did Chang have a legitimate reason for feeling stress?
4. Are misunderstandings a common reason for stress?

Thinking It Through

How often would you advise workers to ask themselves these questions?

Discuss

What should a person do if a job probation reveals the job is not what the worker expected?

people with similar jobs are making at other companies. Your wages should be in that range. However, do not expect to begin an entry-level job at a high salary. Normally, a worker can expect to start at the lower end of the wage scale and move up as he or she becomes more productive. If you do not get a salary review or pay increase after six months on the job, you should find out why.

Can I foresee opportunities for advancement? If you do well in your present job, will you be able to move to a higher-paying job with more responsibilities? If you find you are in a job that leads nowhere, it is doubtful that you will find much success in your work. Having a goal to work toward can motivate you to succeed at your present job, 19-6.

Keep in mind that no job is perfect. Every job has its good and bad points. When the bad points outweigh the good, however, you may find you need to change jobs.

Job Probation

Sometimes a worker is hired on a probationary basis. A **job probation** means a worker is hired for a trial period of time to see how well he or she can do the job. A probationary period can be as short as a few days or as long as a few months. During this period, a supervisor helps train the new worker and oversees his or her work. The supervisor also evaluates the worker's job skills, work habits, and ability to get along with coworkers.

Most workers complete their probationary period with very little trouble. With the help of their supervisors, they learn how to be productive at their jobs and avoid making mistakes.

If a worker does not pass probation, he or she is not hired. If this should happen to you, be sure to find out why you did not pass. You do not want to make the same mistakes again at your next job.

Students with work experience are less likely to have problems during their probationary period. This is because past work experience tends to help them adjust to new jobs more easily.

19-6
This flight attendant knows she can advance to flight attendant trainer if she does a good job.

Performance Rating

Job success depends a great deal on how your supervisor rates your performance on the job. This is called a **performance rating**. At most companies, employees are reviewed every six months or once a year and the record is kept on file. During these reviews, employees are rated on their work and social skills as well as their attitudes on the job.

Check sheets are often used by companies to rate employee performance, 19-7. Employees are rated on job factors such as accuracy of work, ability to work with others, ability to think problems through, and willingness to accept responsibility. The supervisor evaluates an employee's performance according to a rating scale.

The purpose of performance ratings is to help supervisors identify the weaknesses and strengths of their employees. After a performance rating, a supervisor may decide that an employee's skills would be better used for a different job. Therefore, the supervisor may move the employee to another position or transfer him or her to another department. For example, after a performance rating, a supervisor may decide to assign a receptionist who has shown excellent keyboarding skills to the position of secretary. A receptionist who has been especially skilled at working with the public may be transferred to the customer service department.

If the employee is having problems with certain tasks, the supervisor can work with the employee to help improve the weaker skills. The supervisor may also assign the worker to another job.

As a result of performance ratings, employees become aware of their strengths and weaknesses. Most supervisors show workers

Employee Appraisal Form

Hire Date: _____
Appraisal Date: _____
Last Appraisal Date: _____

Employee Name: _____
Job Classification: _____
Supervision: _____

( ) Exceptional

Productivity. Employee's performance (is)
( ) Meets Expectations
( ) Must Improve
in meeting company productivity standards.

Explain: _____
_____

( ) Exceptional

Quality. Employee's performance (is)
( ) Meets Expectations
( ) Must Improve
in meeting company productivity standards.

Explain: _____
_____

( ) Exceptional

Teamwork. Employee's performance (is)
( ) Meets Expectations
( ) Must Improve
in meeting company productivity standards.

Explain: _____
_____

( ) Exceptional

Dependability. Employee's performance (is)
( ) Meets Expectations
( ) Must Improve
in meeting company productivity standards.

Explain: _____
_____

( ) Exceptional

Safety. Employee's performance (is)
( ) Meets Expectations
( ) Must Improve
in meeting company productivity standards.

Explain: _____
_____

Performance Appraisal continued:

Overall Summary: _____
_____
_____
_____
_____
_____
_____
_____

Employee Comments: _____
_____
_____
_____
_____
_____
_____
_____

Signatures: _____ Personnel

_____
Appraising Supervisor _____ Employee

_____
Department Manager

19-7
Employers consider many factors when evaluating a worker's job performance.

their evaluation forms or talk to them about their past performance and future with the company, 19-8. In most cases, employees must sign their forms.

Performance reviews give employees a chance to learn how they can improve their work and become more productive employees. By improving their job performance, they will have an opportunity to get pay raises and take more desirable positions. It is important to examine your performance ratings and what they mean for your future employment.

Training Opportunities

The skills required for most jobs are changing rapidly. Your employer will consider how well you perform your present duties and how willing you are to upgrade skills and learn new ones. Employees who are unwilling to take advantage of training opportunities could lose their jobs.

Most companies value employees who are willing to further their training and education. These companies offer employees some type of incentive to do so. An **incentive** is something that inspires a person to act. Some of the ways employees may be inspired to pursue further training include the following:

- free in-house training
- a pay raise
- complete or partial payment of tuition for approved courses taken at technical schools, community colleges, and universities

Changes in Job Status

Part of being successful in the workplace is being able to handle changes in your job status in a positive way. Usually, the abilities you demonstrate on the job are the reasons for a change in your job status. The ways that a person's job status is changed include promotions, lateral moves, demotions, and firing.

Promotion

A **promotion** is a transfer to a job classification with a higher pay grade. A promotion is not something an employer gives to just any employee. It is a sign your employer appreciates your job performance. A promotion is an advancement that employees earn by being productive, cooperative, dependable, and responsible on the job, 19-9.

If you are promoted, you will probably be given a new job title, an increase in pay, and more responsibility. With increased responsibility, you may be asked to supervise the work of others. This means your role would change to that of a supervisor. Not only would you be responsible for your work, but also for the work of those under your authority.

19-8
Through performance ratings, workers learn how they can become better professionals.

Thinking It Through

What may happen if an employee receives a poor performance rating?

Activity

Interview a supervisor to identify how workers can benefit from training opportunities.

Discuss

Why is it important to weigh the positive and negative aspects of a current job before changing job status?

Discuss

If a job promotion requires a relocation, what are some reasons for turning it down?

Arizona Public Service

19-9

Employees who are productive, cooperative, dependable, and responsible are most likely to be promoted on the job.

Reflect

How will you handle being promoted? How will you handle being passed over for a promotion? Chances are both will happen to you during your career.

Thinking It Through

For what reasons do you think most promotions are made?

Not all promotions lead to supervisory positions. Some are simply a matter of reclassification. For example, Nadira was hired as a secretary at a number three classification. After working six months and receiving a good performance rating, Nadira earned a number two classification. Although her duties stayed the same, Nadira's salary increased 10 percent. When Nadira advances to the number one classification, there is no higher level for her to achieve as a company secretary. She will continue to receive small pay increases as long as she does good work, but she will not be given any new responsibilities.

The opportunity for a promotion does not come along every day. If you turn down a promotion, it may be a long time before you are offered another one.

Lateral Move

A **lateral move** is a transfer to a different department or another classification in the same pay grade. The person may receive a different title and new responsibilities, but no increase in pay. Lateral moves let workers experience different jobs or departments in a company, which makes them more valuable employees.

A lateral move may not be viewed in a positive light by some people. For example, they may consider it a demotion. To them, it signifies the boss does not consider them worthy of a promotion. However, if the company is reducing its workforce, a lateral move may be a compliment. It may mean the company wants to keep the person and is willing to find another position.

Demotion

A **demotion** is a transfer to a classification in a lower pay grade. A demotion usually indicates the company is not satisfied with the work of the employee. It usually is a final warning before an employee is fired.

A demotion is never considered a positive achievement in a person's career. When it occurs, it is important for the employee to take this last opportunity to work hard and demonstrate a desire to keep his or her job. When demoted, however, the employee usually starts looking for employment elsewhere.

Being Fired

A person who is fired no longer works for the company. This separation from the company is also called *being released* or *let go*. This change in job status is the hardest to accept. Knowing the reason for being fired sometimes helps ease the pain, but not entirely. If an employee is released because of cutbacks in the workforce, it is easier to understand.

Extend Your Knowledge

Me...A Supervisor?

The idea of becoming a supervisor may sound like a lot of work. In fact, you may be wondering if you can handle the responsibility. Chances are, if you are asked to become a supervisor, you are capable of handling the job. Many companies have training classes to help new supervisors adjust to their new responsibilities and learn how to be successful at their jobs. If you are given the opportunity to advance to a supervisory position, consider the offer carefully. Review your occupational plans and think about how this promotion can help you further your career.

Activity

Identify two or three jobs of students' parents. Ask students to list specific examples of possible lateral moves.

Discuss

What is the relationship between losing a job and negative stress? How can the stress be turned into positive energy?

Reflect

Would you hire workers fired for the reasons in the bulleted list when dependable workers with good records are available?

If an employee is let go because of poor work performance or other negative reasons, usually the employee is not really surprised. Employees who do not perform as expected are normally aware they may be fired.

Ninety percent of firings, however, are due to personal reasons such as improper conduct and difficulty working with others. Often these people have good job skills. These are the most common reasons employers give for firing employees:

- absenteeism—not showing up for work on a regular basis

- loafing—taking long breaks, leaving workstations for no good reason, or daydreaming on the job, 19-10

- personality conflicts—not getting along with the supervisor or coworkers

- violating company rules—primarily fighting, drinking, using illegal drugs, smoking in nonsmoking areas, and ignoring safety regulations

- incompetence—not demonstrating the knowledge, skills, experience, or attitude to perform the job responsibilities as requested

If you should ever find yourself out of a job unexpectedly, give yourself a couple days to recover from the shock. Then try to figure out why you were fired. Did you do or say something to contribute to the situation? Was your employer fair to you? Were there financial reasons that made the action necessary?

Be honest with yourself. If you did something you were not supposed to do, admit it. Do not lie or try to blame someone else. If you care about your future and career, you will not make the same mistake again.

Changes in job status cause employees to think about how their jobs fit their plan for the future. Usually changes in job status are positive events in employment history.

19-10
Frequent daydreaming can be a cause for dismissal from a job.

Reflect Further

Have you known or heard of people who used a negative experience, such as a firing or demotion, to change their lives in a positive way?

Discuss

Does a company owe an employee a job? Should an employer have a right to hire and fire as necessary?

Signs of a Stalled Career

- No added job responsibilities in three or four years
- Reduction of responsibilities
- No important projects or committee work
- No promotion (or a demotion)
- Frequent boredom, difficulty staying focused, and lack of enjoyment from aspects of the job that formerly were exciting
- Strained or unpleasant relationships with the boss or coworkers

19-11

These clues are signals to employees to begin looking for another job.

Reflect

What is the likely future of a person who always tries to get out of work?

Resource

Changing Jobs, Activity G, WB

Making a Job Change

Look carefully at your job status and at your performance ratings. Are you in a dead-end job? You may wonder if it is best to "stick it out" or "move on." At several points along your career, you will find yourself struggling with these questions: Should I stay with this job or find a new one? Should I leave this secure position and risk the uncertainties of another? Can I find or create my dream job right here, or must I work for someone else to achieve that goal?

In the United States, people tend to change jobs often, especially in their early years of employment. If you seem to be doing the same things over and over, then your career is not progressing and a new job may be what you need. See the clues in 19-11 to know when your career is stalled. The clues are explained here.

- *Your job responsibilities have not changed in three or four years.* If your name does not come up when a position opens, it is possible that management feels, for one or a number of reasons, you should stay in your present position.

  - *Your responsibilities are reduced.* This may be a sign your job may be eliminated. Look for another way to become involved in the company, or start networking with colleagues at other companies and prepare your résumé.

  - *You are not chosen for important projects or committees.* Management may feel you are a good, reliable worker, but does not consider you valuable for more challenging projects. Not participating in important committees and projects limits your exposure to the key people in the company.

  - *You are passed over for promotions or you have been demoted.* Either situation is a definite clue your supervisor feels you should not have a job with more responsibility. It may be time to start looking for a job outside the company.

  - *You are bored, find it hard to focus, and get little enjoyment from those things that once excited you.* If this happens every day, you may be happier with other responsibilities or another job. Everyone, however, has days that are frustrating or not very exciting.

- *Your relationships with the boss or coworkers are strained or deteriorated.* Personality clashes are part of life and something experienced by everyone. If these clashes lead to extreme unhappiness for anyone, it is important to try to resolve the differences. If they cannot be resolved, work is going to suffer and a change in job status may be next.

When you decide to change jobs, plan the change carefully. Avoid making a quick decision. Think about your career and future plans. Think about the reasons you want to leave your present job and the type of job you want next. What do you plan to accomplish by making a change? You should not just walk away. Make sure you have another job lined up before leaving the one you have.

If you decide to leave a job, you should try to leave on good terms. Quitting suddenly is not fair to your employer, and it will not leave your employer with a good impression of you. As a general rule, notify your supervisor in writing at least two weeks before you plan to leave. This will give your employer a chance to find another worker to replace you. Offer to train your replacement and finish all your work. If your job involves a great deal of responsibility and training, you should try to notify your employer even earlier.

You may be expected to give your employer an *exit interview*. This can provide the employer with information to help establish and maintain good working relationships with its employees. To prepare for your exit interview, make a list of positive comments regarding your employment. You may also want to share constructive criticisms that can be helpful to the employer in the future. It is best to be as positive as possible in an exit interview.

Do not bad-mouth anyone, even the boss. In this era of networking, your negative comments may travel back to the people you criticized. In the future, you will want the boss's approval so you can use his or her name as a reference.

Although hopping from job to job is something you should avoid, changing jobs can be a very positive move to make. All too often people stay in jobs they dislike because they do not have the courage or ambition to look for other jobs. It takes considerable courage and drive to look for a new job and make a change, but the rewards can be well worth it. Feeling satisfied with your job will make you feel happier about your life and the work you accomplish.

Unions

To work in some occupations, workers are required to join a labor union. A **union** is a group of workers who have united to voice their opinions to their employer or the employer's representatives (management). Ideally, the purpose of a union is to help workers be successful and secure on the job by bargaining with management for better wages, working hours, working conditions, and benefits.

Labor unions developed in the early days of industry because of poor working conditions, low wages, child labor, and unfair treatment of employees. By uniting together, workers found they gained strength and power to discuss these problems with management.

As a result of unions and changes in corporate attitudes, many of the problems that faced workers in the early 1900s have been solved. Workers are no longer faced with terrible working conditions. Laws have been passed to protect workers' rights and safety. Management has learned over the years that satisfied workers are more productive workers, 19-12. More productive workers make companies successful and thereby yield higher profits.

For these reasons, many workers no longer need union membership to be treated and paid fairly. They no longer want to pay expensive union dues to support their local and national union organizations, especially when they hear about misused union funds. Some people believe unions have accomplished their original purposes and are no longer needed.

On the other hand, others feel that unions still serve a useful purpose. They continue to campaign for improved working conditions and increased wages and benefits. They help retrain workers whose jobs are assumed by automation. They also influence the legislation of labor and fair trade laws.

Enrich

Role-play the many different reactions an employee may show when being fired. (Specify different conditions, such as notification of dismissal by the boss in person, via letter, or via phone.)

Discuss

Do you know anyone who learned, after changing jobs, that the new job was a mistake? Explain.

Activity

Explore the choice of adjusting to a job you dislike or taking a chance with a new job. List two benefits and two negative outcomes of each possibility.

Resource

Case Study: Linda's Negative Behavior, reproducible master 19-3, TR

Activity

Write a letter of resignation that includes a courteous opening, explanation for leaving, planned termination date, and cordial closing.

Discuss

Why do people remain in jobs that do not provide personal satisfaction? What effect may this have on customers and other employees?

Thinking It Through

For what reasons do you think most people change jobs?

The safe, clean working conditions that we take for granted primarily resulted from union efforts.

Resource

Unions, Activity H, WB

Activity

Schedule a class debate to discuss the advantages and disadvantages of union membership.

Thinking It Through

Do you think unions are needed in today's society? Why or why not?

Vocabulary

In your words, explain the differences between union shop and open shop agreements.

Discuss

Why is it important to know before you start a job whether employees are unionized?

Must You Join a Union?

The answer to this question depends on the state in which you work and the kind of job you have. Some occupations do not have union affiliations. However, others require union membership.

If a workplace has a *union shop agreement*, all its workers must join the union as a condition of employment. In such cases, if you were hired by a company, you would not be able to work beyond a certain period unless you joined the union.

If a workplace has an *open shop agreement*, its workers are free to join or not join the union. Most unions oppose this type of agreement because they represent all workers in their negotiations. Therefore, they feel every worker should be required to join the union.

To find out what type of shop agreement a company has, call the company or check with your state's labor department. If you have a choice about whether to join a union or not, do a little investigating first. To help decide if joining a union will benefit you at your job, answer key questions on the following topics:

- union's track record—What has the union accomplished? What are its plans for the future?

- size of the workplace—Are there so many workers that the help of a union is needed to negotiate terms that benefit all?

- cost of union membership—What is the initial fee to join? What monthly or weekly dues are withheld from your paycheck?

Keep in mind that if you join a union, you must abide by union rules. You must be willing to give up some independence. If you have a complaint about work, you must follow a specific procedure for getting the problem solved. It is possible that you and your manager could easily solve the problem yourselves, but you must follow union rules. If the union votes to go on strike, whether you believe it should or not, you must support the decision and live with reduced pay or without a paycheck during the strike period.

Organization of Unions

Two major types of labor unions exist in the United States—craft unions and industrial unions.

- *Craft unions* are formed by workers who have the same craft or trade. There are craft unions for carpenters, painters, plumbers, electricians, and machinists. For example, the union for carpenters is called the United Brotherhood of Carpenters and Joiners. The union for electricians is the International Brotherhood of Electrical Workers (IBEW).

- *Industrial unions* are formed by workers who belong to the same industry. Most industrial union members work in factories where cars, clothing, steel, and other products are made, 19-13. The industrial union for autoworkers is called the United Automobile Workers (UAW). The union for apparel, garment, and textile workers is the National Apparel, Garment, and Textile Workers Council.

The basic work of unions is done in the locals. A local union has its own constitution, bylaws, and set of officers. The local union also elects shop stewards who handle members' complaints about management.

National unions consist of many local unions. For example, the UAW has local unions practically everywhere cars are manufactured in the United States. Some national unions such as the UAW have more than a million members.

19-13

Most workers on large construction projects are unionized.

Collective Bargaining

Collective bargaining is the process of labor and management representatives discussing what they expect from each other in the workplace. In a way, collective bargaining is like a buyer and a seller debating the price of something to be sold. Labor may first demand much more than it expects to get. Management will offer much less than it intends to give.

Through debate, discussion, and possibly arguments, a compromise is finally reached in the form of a labor contract. A **labor contract** is an agreement that spells out the conditions for wages, benefits, job security, work hours, working conditions, and grievance procedures. A grievance procedure is a step-by-step list for handling complaints from union members.

Bargaining for a new contract can be a long process. It usually begins weeks or months before the date the existing contract expires. Representatives from management and labor each present their positions and demands. When an agreement is reached for a new work contract, union members vote to accept or reject it. If the membership rejects the contract, union representatives go back to the bargaining table and bargain for different terms.

If no agreement can be reached and the existing contract expires, there may be trouble. Sometimes union members will vote to strike until the company meets their demands or comes closer to their demands. On the other hand, management can threaten to close down the company unless an agreement is reached. Obviously, either action can be a loss to both labor and management. This is why it is important for both labor and management to be reasonable in their expectations.

Thinking It Through

What are the laws in your state concerning union membership?

Activity

Interview union employees about how successfully their complaints are handled by shop stewards.

Activity

Role-play the bargaining process for a new labor contract

Activity

Read an article about collective bargaining. Does it involve conflict resolution?

402 Part 5 Job Satisfaction

Summary

Succeeding on the job involves many steps. You begin by learning your job duties and adjusting to the job. Getting along with your supervisor and coworkers will encourage teamwork, as well as make your job more enjoyable. Proper conduct will help you deal with most situations. Stress can affect your body, mind, and job performance unless you control and manage it.

Evaluating your job performance is one way for you to judge your success on the job. A performance rating by your supervisor helps show your strengths and weaknesses. Learn to recognize if your job is stalled. If you decide to change jobs, plan the change carefully. Consider your future plans and career before you leave.

Earning a job promotion is one step to job success. A lateral move is another. Getting a demotion or losing a job can be an unpleasant experience. However, try to learn from the experience and avoid repeating mistakes.

Unions were developed to help workers be successful and secure in their jobs. Representatives of labor and management discuss work expectations through the process of collective bargaining. Decide whether joining a union benefits you. For some jobs, union membership is required.

Facts in Review

1. How can you prepare for your first day on the job?
2. Name six rules of proper employee conduct.
3. What is the main cause of stress?
4. Name an effect of positive stress.
5. What questions can help you determine if you are having success on the job?
6. What does it mean for a worker to be hired on a probationary basis?
7. What is the purpose of performance ratings for the employer and the employee?
8. List the four types of changes possible in job status.
9. List the most common reasons employers give for firing employees.
10. What are six indicators your job or career may be stalled?
11. How much notice should you give your supervisor before leaving a job?
12. Why were labor unions originally formed?
13. If you have a choice, what should you consider before joining a union?
14. Explain the difference between a union shop agreement and an open shop agreement.
15. Describe the two major types of labor unions that exist in the United States.

Developing Your Academic Skills

1. **Science.** Form groups and research stress management techniques. Give group presentations to the class demonstrating some of the techniques your group has studied. Discuss how some techniques might be performed during stressful moments on the job.
2. **Social Studies.** Research the history of unions in the United States. How are unions different today from unions of the past? Are the changes beneficial to the workers, the employers, or both? Summarize your findings in a written report.

Information Technology Applications

1. Use a spreadsheet program to create a self-evaluation sheet you could use to rate your job performance. Devise a system of rating, such as 4 for excellent, 3 for good, 2 for adequate, and 1 for poor. You may use some of the criteria listed on page 391. Use spreadsheet commands to find an average rating number for your overall performance.
2. Search the Internet for information on a recent, well-publicized strike. What conditions brought about the strike? How was the strike resolved? Did the union members accomplish their goals by striking? Summarize your findings in an oral report.

Applying Your Knowledge and Skills

1. **Problem Solving and Critical Thinking.** List five reasons why you think you are succeeding at your work-based learning experience. Also list five ways you can improve your job performance. Then, working with three classmates, share your lists and discuss ways each person in the group can improve his or her job performance.
2. **Employability and Career Development.** Invite a local employer or an employee in a supervisory position to class to discuss two topics: how to avoid the common problems of new employees and how to prepare for a supervisory position.
3. **Communications.** Talk to three people who recently changed jobs. Find out why and how each person changed his or her job and what each hopes to accomplish in the new job. Are there any similarities in the answers given by the three workers? Do you feel each person made a good decision? Be prepared to discuss your findings in class.

Developing Workplace Skills

Working with three classmates, develop a 10-minute role-play that demonstrates the rules of proper conduct in the workplace and perform the role-play for the class. The role-play should include examples of workers who do follow the rules plus those who do not. Working with the members of your group, decide how to divide the tasks. (Everyone need not be involved in every task.)

15. Craft unions are formed by workers having the same craft or trade. Industrial unions are formed by workers belonging to the same industry.

20

Diversity and Rights in the Workplace

Key Terms

ethnic group

assimilation

workplace diversity

discrimination

criminal penalties

stereotype

racism

sexual orientation

sexual harassment

quid pro quo harassment

hostile environment harassment

body language

reprisal

Chapter Objectives

After studying this chapter, you will be able to

- **relate** current population trends to their effect on workplace diversity.
- **list** the benefits of diversity to an employer.
- **describe** ways that employers and employees can promote workplace diversity.
- **provide examples** of employment discrimination forbidden by law.
- **explain** how to take action against any sexual harassment or discrimination directed at you in the workplace.

Reading Advantage

Find an article on http://news.google.com that relates to the topic covered in this chapter. Print the article and read it before reading the chapter. As you read the chapter, highlight sections of the news article that relate to the text.

Achieving Academic Standards

English Language Arts

- Read print and non-print texts to acquire new information and to respond to the needs and demands of society and the workplace. (IRA/NCTE, 1)
- Apply strategies to comprehend, interpret, evaluate, and appreciate texts. (IRA/NCTE, 3)
- Develop an understanding of and respect for diversity in language use across cultures. (IRA/NCTE, 9)

Key Concepts

- It is the responsibility of both employers and employees to promote diversity in the workplace.

- Several federal laws protect people from discrimination and sexual harassment in the workplace.

- There are steps individuals can take to discourage or end discrimination or harassment behavior.

Thinking It Through

What is your best opportunity for associating with diverse populations?

The term *diversity* refers to the many factors that make people different. Diversity involves respecting people's differences. When diversity is supported, everyone is allowed to maintain his or her individuality. People are not forced to change how they live, speak, look, or think in order to be more like those in the majority.

The United States is the most diverse country in the world because its population comes from every other nation. No other country in the world can make this claim. The diversity of the U.S. population is most evident in large cities. There you see individuals of many different backgrounds and life experiences. For people growing up in these areas, diversity is a way of life. They live, play, study, work, and develop friendships with those of different backgrounds, customs, and beliefs.

Everyone in the United States has experienced some form of diversity. If you live in an area where few differences exist among people, associating with a more diverse population may make you feel uneasy. There is a natural tendency to seek out and stay close to people who are like you. Sometimes to eliminate feelings of discomfort, people who are alike try to change those who are different. This forced change has been the cause of many clashes and conflicts between groups of people throughout history.

Diversity Trends in the United States

A country as large and diverse as the United States can point to many factors causing population differences. Many of these factors are listed in 20-1. These factors affect society in general and, therefore, affect the workplace.

Cultural Heritage

Cultural heritage is one of the biggest factors affecting U.S. diversity. Cultural heritage determines what beliefs, learned behaviors, and language pass through the generations to each individual. The cultural heritage of people in the United States has been shaped by Native Americans and immigrants who settled here. As a result, all Americans are part of some ethnic group. An **ethnic group** is a group of people who share common racial and/or cultural characteristics such as national origin, language, religion, and traditions. The major ethnic groups that exist in this country are shown in 20-2.

Presently the majority of Americans have European ancestors. Increases in the number of European Americans are not keeping pace with the rapid rise in African-American, Asian-American, and Hispanic-American populations. This trend is occurring mainly in big cities and certain agricultural areas. When different

Factors That Cause Population Differences
• Cultural heritage
• Language
• Religion
• Gender
• Age
• Disabilities/abilities
• Race
• National origin
• Sexual orientation
• Traditions

20-1

Several factors account for the wide-ranging differences in the U.S. population.

Major Racial and Ethnic Groups in the United States

Native Americans

Descended from the original North Americans

European Americans

Immigrated from European countries including Spain, England, Germany, France, and Holland

Asian Americans

Immigrated from China, Japan, Korea, the Philippine Islands, and Indonesia

African Americans

Descended from the black racial groups of Africa

Hispanic Americans

Immigrated from Mexico, Puerto Rico, Cuba, Central and South America, and other Spanish cultures

20-2

There are other U.S. racial and ethnic groups besides these five largest.

Activity

List several foods commonly associated with each of the racial and ethnic groups listed in Chart 20-2.

Note

This is not a comprehensive list of racial and ethnic groups in the United States.

Activity

As a class, see how many different languages can be used to express the following: *we are different, yet alike.*

cultures associate, there is the opportunity to share the best of what each has to offer. When people are not permitted to express their culture or are forced to change it, hostility and conflicts may result.

In the past, assimilation was considered the best way to handle diverse populations. **Assimilation** is blending people into society by helping, and sometimes forcing, them to become more like the majority. Today the focus is on allowing people to preserve and express their heritage, 20-3.

Some individuals feel very strongly about preserving their cultural heritage while others do not. Some, but not all, want to be identified as a member of their cultural group. Everyone, however, wants to be treated and respected as an individual.

Language

Diverse languages are more common in the workplace because a growing segment of workers are first-generation immigrants who know little English. When employers, employees, and customers cannot understand one another, misunderstandings often result. Using different languages in the workplace is a growing issue and one that people feel very strongly about, no matter which position they favor. Some argue that only English should be spoken for purposes of clear communication.

20-3

Preparing traditional food dishes is a positive expression of a person's heritage.

Reflect Further

Is a language other than English spoken in your community? What words do you understand? Is a language other than English spoken in your home?

Others say language is part of their cultural heritage and should be preserved. This debate is ongoing.

Religion

Religion is a private matter and, therefore, rarely discussed during work hours. Problems in the workplace usually surface when off-time is granted for observing the practices of one religion but not others. Many conflicts arise when companies have religious displays or events that express one group's beliefs but not others'. Religious diversity is rapidly increasing for two key reasons. First, new styles of religious practices are being introduced by recent immigrants. Secondly, traditional religions are splitting into factions.

Gender

Reflect Further

Are there certain jobs that you believe women (or men) should not hold?

Gender, or a person's sex, is another factor that affects the diversity of the workplace. In recent decades, millions of women took jobs outside the home, causing tremendous change in the workforce. The number of employed women increased from about 30 percent in 1970 to over 55 percent of all working-age women today.

Many women seek work to earn income needed by the household. Some female workers want the economic freedom that extra income brings. Others want the challenge of pursuing a career. In the future, women are expected to enter the labor force at about the same rate as men, 20-4.

Age

Age is fast becoming a diversity issue because the number of older workers is quickly increasing in society. The U.S. Census Bureau predicts

20-4

Compared to men, more women graduate from college but approximately the same number enter the workforce.

Enrich

Examine help wanted ads in the local paper. Do any imply or request job candidates of one or the other sex?

Discuss

Does a mandatory retirement age harm or help society?

that between 2000 and 2040, the number of Americans ages 65 and older will more than double, to 77 million. Because the U.S. population in general is aging, older workers who can relate to this fast-growing market segment will be highly valued. Their keen insight, valuable experience, and dependable work habits will be sought. See 20-5. Older workers who might have considered retiring will be lured back to at least part-time work. These workers demonstrate the value of lifelong learning and acquiring new skills, such as computer literacy.

For older workers who have not updated their skills, the outlook is quite different. In an era when updated skills are a necessity, workers with outdated skills will be the first employees let go in economic downturns. Unskilled older workers will have difficulty keeping their jobs. If these workers ever leave or lose their jobs, they may not find replacement work.

20-5
Older employees are valued for their extensive experience and in-depth knowledge of the company.

Disability

Disability covers a wide range of physical and mental impairments. These disabilities affect about eight percent of the work population at any given time. A person with a disability still has many abilities or talents to devote to producing quality work. Workers with disabilities are more visible in the workforce because of federal law and changing attitudes. Everyone is a potential candidate for some form of disability during his or her life.

The Benefits of Diversity in the Workplace

Diversity, as applied to the workforce, is a fairly new concept. **Workplace diversity** means respecting the contributions of coworkers who are unlike you. Companies have found that teaching employees to value workers' differences yields the following positive results:

- There are fewer lawsuits.—The enormous expense of money and time devoted to defending a company against charges of unequal opportunity is reduced or eliminated.

- Morale is high.—Employees feel more comfortable and at ease because the emphasis is on what they contribute, not who they are. See 20-6.

- Creativity increases.—Since all ideas are valued, people feel greater freedom to make suggestions and present alternative views.

- Productivity increases.—When people feel respected, they are committed to doing the best job possible.

- Quality workers are attracted to the organization.—Most workers seek employers who respect them and value their ideas. Employers with such a reputation usually have no trouble attracting the highest quality workers.

- The decision-making process improves.—When many different views are examined early and frequently during planning, the final plan is usually a sound one.

- Decision-making speed improves.—When frank, open discussions are common, complex issues are explored more quickly. Sensitive issues can be raised without fear of hurting coworkers' feelings. This leads to faster decisions.

- More customers are reached.—A diverse workforce understands a wider range of customers. Consequently, market opportunities are recognized quicker and products are launched faster.

- Goodwill and positive ties are formed with businesses and government groups.—Having a policy of accepting diversity can mean gaining public respect. For companies whose customers are organizations, it can also mean getting more business from the government and like-minded companies.

20-6
This landscaping crew does a quality job because members appreciate and use the special abilities of each person.

Thinking It Through

What types of companies do you think might benefit most from a diverse workforce?

Resource

Promoting Diversity,
Activity C, WB

Enrich

Invite an employer to discuss the challenges and benefits of employing people with diverse backgrounds.

Promoting Diversity in the Workplace

Managing workplace diversity is extremely important to U.S. organizations wanting to sell in a global environment. World markets are growing more diverse. Experts believe that enlightened management policies emphasizing diversity will help companies serve customers better everywhere. This will especially help U.S. companies compete more effectively in worldwide markets.

What Employers Are Doing

Diversity training in the workplace is relatively new, but rapidly increasing. Large global companies have taken the lead and report that the benefits, listed earlier, far outweigh the costs. Corporate leaders agree that diversity makes good moral and economic sense. Now that diversity has been shown to make good business sense, companies without such programs are more eager to implement diversity training.

Much of today's knowledge about what to teach and how to teach it was developed in the United States on the job through trial and error. Until recently, no courses existed on the subject, and no other country practiced it. Consequently, each company developed its own way to handle the diversity challenges. Then, companies shared information through business conferences and learned from each other. Some of the methods that are in current use are listed in 20-7. Most companies generally review and update their programs to keep them effective and relevant.

Diversity programs began as a way for companies to avoid costly legal battles and tell employees what *not* to do. Gradually managers with foresight recognized that a company's success hinged on its workforce. Workers preferred learning *what to do* instead of *what not to do*. Training programs were revised to emphasize positive behavior. The focus turned to understanding and accepting people's differences and viewing them as a positive asset.

What Employees Can Do

You, as an employee, also have a role in promoting diversity. First, consider how your behavior is affected by your cultural background. Then, recognize that your value system will probably differ from that of other coworkers. All employees have a responsibility to work in harmony toward achieving company goals.

Enrich

Invite a human resource specialist to discuss past cases from history of discriminatory company practices that involved costly legal settlements.

Reflect

Share one of your experiences teaching a person of a different culture.

Employer Strategies for Promoting Workplace Diversity

- Develop a diversity policy. Include the policy in the employee handbook and discuss it in company publications.

- Recruit employees for diversity task forces and advisory councils to guide the overall diversity policy.

- Reward behavior that reinforces diversity goals.

- Evaluate manager and employee performance based on diversity measures.

- Revise existing company policies and benefits so they support diverse needs.

- Place special emphasis on recruiting individuals from populations that are missing or underrepresented in the organization.

- Promote community volunteer work that encourages employees to work with diverse populations.

- Link diversity goals to business goals.

- Provide training programs that help employees examine assumptions and past attitudes.

- Provide training programs to help managers develop skills for removing communication barriers among workers.

- Keep employees informed about diversity efforts that have benefited the company.

20-7

Employers use one or more of these methods to encourage workers to respect their coworkers.

Vocabulary

Before reading this section, have students define *discrimination* from their perspectives.

If working in a diverse environment is unfamiliar to you, you may find this quite challenging. You will want to broaden your outlook and adjust any negative viewpoints you have. Some ways to help you make that adjustment are listed in 20-8. Ultimately, learning to work with diverse coworkers will build your character. You will become a more valuable team member and employee.

Diversity, Rights, and Discrimination

A diverse population inspires many different views on every issue. On the subject of opportunities in the workplace, however, only one view is lawful—everyone has a right to fair treatment. When that right is taken away, discrimination has occurred.

Considered on its own, discrimination is a positive trait. It actually means "distinguishing one object from a similar one." It also means "using good judgment," as in deciding what to say in a letter of application to try to get the job you want.

When the term *discrimination* is used in the workplace, it usually has a negative meaning. **Discrimination** then means treating people on a basis other than individual merit. Generally discrimination refers to the negative treatment of one or more individuals compared to that of the larger group. Discrimination may also refer to excluding some people from a special treatment offered to others.

20-8

These guidelines help workers respect and appreciate their coworkers.

Employee Actions That Encourage Workplace Diversity
• Show flexibility in adapting to your coworkers and work environment.
• Examine your assumptions about people different from you.
• Explore different cultures through cultural events, movies, plays, books, and travel.
• Show patience in understanding and communicating with others when language barriers exist.
• Politely ask for clarification if a message or gesture does not make sense to you.
• Admit your unfamiliarity with diverse customs, but express a willingness to learn.
• Show respect for everyone's ideas.
• Adjust your style of humor so jokes are not made at someone's expense.
• Look beyond everyday annoyances and see the humanity in each person.
• Recognize that you are no better than your coworkers, only different.

The Law and Discrimination

Several important laws exist to promote fairness and fight discrimination in the workplace. See 20-9. The first two laws listed here were discussed briefly in Chapter 2, "Understanding Work-Based Learning." These two laws plus the others listed here are the major laws preserving worker rights in the workplace.

Employers keep employees informed of company rules regarding the behavior expected of them while on the job.

- The *Fair Labor Standards Act (FLSA) of 1938* forbids unfair treatment of employees by employers. This law has been amended many times to raise the minimum wage. It also reduced the number of hours worked without overtime pay and extended coverage to many low-income workers. The law also addresses child labor standards.

- The *Equal Pay Act of 1963*, a FLSA amendment, forbids the practice of using different pay scales for men and women. It requires that both sexes receive equal pay for jobs in similar working conditions requiring the same level of skill, effort, and responsibility.

- The *1964 Civil Rights Act* banned employment discrimination on the basis of race, color, religion, sex, or national origin. For interfering with a person's employment rights, a 1968 amendment established criminal penalties. **Criminal penalties** usually involve one or more of the following: serving a jail sentence, doing community service, paying a fine, and periodically reporting to a court-ordered supervisor.

- The *Age Discrimination in Employment Act of 1967* banned unfair treatment of workers age 40 and older. The law was expanded by the *Older Workers Benefit Protection Act of 1990*, which permitted workers to sue employers over age-discrimination matters.

- The *Immigration Reform and Control Act of 1986* allowed the awarding of criminal penalties to employers who discriminated against U.S. citizens born outside the country. The *Immigration Act of 1990* further strengthened the law and protected these citizens by making it harder for noncitizens to obtain employment in this country.

- The *Americans with Disabilities Act (ADA) of 1990* is a wide-ranging law prohibiting discrimination of individuals with disabilities in matters involving employment, government services, and transportation. The law required public transportation services to be accessible to individuals with disabilities. It also required employers to provide such employees with reasonable accommodations in physical facilities. The law gives people with disabilities a chance to be hired for their skills rather than turned away for an unrelated disability.

- The *1991 Civil Rights Act* strengthened the ban against discrimination of races and sexes. It also gave protection to members of groups that had a history of receiving intentional job discrimination. In cases that go to court, this law allows victims to be awarded compensatory damages (money to pay for actual losses) and punitive damages (as payment to make an example of the wrongdoer).

Several government agencies deal with equal opportunity employment issues every day. The two federal offices that do most of the work are the following:

- The Office of Federal Contract Compliance Programs (OFCCP) actively seeks out cases of discrimination by monitoring contractors who hold federal contracts.

- The Equal Employment Opportunity Commission (EEOC) investigates charges of discrimination brought to it by individual workers and groups of employees. Created by the 1964 Civil Rights Act, the EEOC makes sure all laws, regulations, federal guidelines, executive orders, and collective-bargaining agreements that address discrimination are followed. Its mission is to assure equal opportunity in employment for everyone and prohibit discrimination. The EEOC's authority covers all employment practices such as interviewing, hiring, promoting, transferring, training, retiring, and firing employees. See 20-10. The EEOC's authority also covers membership opportunities in work-related groups. Important EEOC information can be accessed through the agency's Web site (www.eeoc.gov).

In addition to the work done at the federal level to maintain equal opportunity, many state and local government agencies monitor and/or investigate discriminatory practices locally.

20-10

The EEOC's authority covers local government workers such as police officers and firefighters, as well as employees of nonprofit and profit-making organizations.

Types of Discrimination in the Workplace

The EEOC has handled thousands of claims of discrimination. From these cases, guidelines have been developed to help employers identify workplace behavior that is considered unlawful. Some examples of unlawful workplace behavior are discussed here. You will read about issues involving a worker's sex, race, color, national origin, language, religion, disability, age, height, weight, or sexual orientation.

Sex Discrimination

The number of women now in the workforce almost equals that of men. At first glance, it may appear that sex discrimination, also called *gender bias*, is no longer a problem. However, complaints to the EEOC show that working women still face discrimination in the following ways:

- lower pay than men working in similar jobs and occupational areas

- restricted entry to training opportunities and higher-paying jobs

- more difficulty in gaining promotions, even with more education and experience

- less value placed on skills in which women may excel, such as human relations and interpersonal communications

- a tendency to cluster women in jobs that are extensions of their expected roles as wives and mothers, such as housekeeping, child care, nursing, and teaching

It is unlawful to label any work as *women's jobs* or *men's jobs* unless gender is a *bona fide occupational qualification (BFOQ)*. This means having a legitimate reason for specifying that a job should be held by one sex specifically. Examples of BFOQs include hiring male attendants for a men's locker room and female attendants for a women's locker room.

Much of the discrimination directed at women is due to society's concept of what types of work are appropriate for women. Throughout history, women have been the primary providers of care for the family and the home. Men sometimes, even unconsciously, believe that women in the workplace will be distracted by home matters and motherhood and less committed to their jobs. As a result, women in some situations may not be considered for important jobs that require greater dedication and responsibility. These old notions clash with today's women, who are willing to handle responsibilities on an equal level with men but expect fair treatment. See 20-11.

Several family-friendly policies now address the special problems of balancing responsibilities at home and work. These will be discussed in Chapter 28, "Managing Family, Work, and Citizenship Roles." The policies permit workers to take time off for several common family challenges. However, few men take advantage of these policies because of society's expectation that men must put their jobs first. Consequently, many men feel pressured to sacrifice time with the family in order to keep their careers on track. Labeling men who take time off to care for a sick family member as not serious about their jobs is also a form of sex discrimination.

JupiterImages

20-11

Many women enjoy traditional professions, such as teaching, but face discrimination when seeking less traditional jobs, such as school administration.

Discuss

Are any forms of sex discrimination evident in movies, TV, or other areas of life? Give examples.

Discuss

List jobs for which one or more BFOQs would make it legal to specify for *men only* or for *women only*. (This will be a challenging activity).

Thinking It Through

Give two examples of illegal sex discrimination. Can you give an example of legal sex discrimination?

Reflect Further

Have you observed any examples of racial discrimination?

Reflect

Has someone ever judged you on the basis of a misconception? How did it make you feel?

Vocabulary

What does *slur* mean? Explain why slurs are harmful.

Racial Discrimination

Discrimination based on race occurs when people belonging to a specific race are treated differently from others. Much of this is the result of stereotypes. A **stereotype** is a label given to a person based on assumptions held about all members of that person's racial or cultural group. It causes persons to be judged on the basis of assumptions instead of merit or fact. The most severe form of discrimination is racism. **Racism** is the belief that one race is superior or inferior to all others.

Racial discrimination can occur when individuals are treated unfairly because of inherited characteristics, such as skin color or other physical features unique to their race. Racial discrimination in employment can also occur when employees are treated differently from other employees because of attitudes on interracial dating or marriages, racially oriented expression of attitudes and beliefs, and/or membership in racially oriented groups. Employers are obligated to keep the workplace free of racial insults and threats.

20-12

Among people of the same race, color discrimination occurs when people are treated differently as a result of different skin tones.

Color Discrimination

Color discrimination occurs when individuals are treated differently because of skin color alone. This type of discrimination can occur among people of the same race. For example, a Mexican restaurant staffed entirely by Hispanic Americans is practicing color discrimination when it offers the best jobs to light-skinned employees. See 20-12.

National Origin Discrimination

This type of discrimination is directed at a worker because of his or her (or an ancestor's) birth outside the United States. Equal employment opportunities cannot be denied on the basis of an individual's (or an ancestor's) place of origin. Also, the physical, cultural, or language qualities of people from that place of origin cannot be a basis for unfair treatment.

Criticizing or making fun of a person's facial features and using ethnic slurs are the most common causes of complaints involving national origin discrimination. An employer has a duty to eliminate this discriminatory behavior from the workplace.

Language Discrimination

The ability to speak or read the English language may be a work requirement. Employers who make this a requirement must show that fluency in English is a business necessity for the position in question. The employer must clearly inform employees of the general circumstances requiring them to speak English only. The consequences of violating the rule must be clearly stated and understood.

Requiring employees to speak English at all times, including during work break and lunchtime, is an example of an unlawful practice. It discriminates against people whose primary language is not English. The EEOC has determined that English-only rules may be discriminatory unless required for business reasons.

Sometimes it is assumed that people who cannot speak English well lack intelligence and are not competent. This may be far from the truth, and treating them as inferior conveys a superior attitude that is discriminatory. See 20-13.

Religious Discrimination

Religious discrimination occurs when an employment role or policy requires workers to choose between a basic principle of their religion or lose an employment opportunity. The definition of *religion* is not restricted to well-known denominations. It covers all beliefs and even a lack of belief, or *atheism*. The law covers discrimination in religious observances and practices. It also extends protection to those handling church-related obligations, such as attending a business meeting called by a minister. The most common religious practices that cause complaints of discrimination in the workplace are the following:

- wearing items of dress forbidden by the company dress code, such as long hair on men or turbans

- requesting prayer breaks during work hours

- following specific dietary requirements, such as eating at times other than the designated break periods

- observing the grieving period for a dead relative by not working

- refusing to take medical examinations

Reflect Further

Have you visited any place where you were considered the "outsider"? Recall your feelings.

20-13

Many employers try to help employees improve poor language skills.

Enrich

Conduct a debate on the following: English should be declared the official language of the U.S. workplace.

Activity

Have several students role-play a group of department store managers trying to understand and resolve a worker's demand for taking Fridays off for religious observances. (Give other role-play groups similar challenges by changing one or more conditions, such as time/day requested, type of work/company, and reason for the request.)

Organizations are obliged to provide reasonable accommodations for the religious practices of employees and job applicants. Businesses must try to change rules or policies to accommodate employees' religious needs. Employers are exempt from these requirements, however, if doing so presents an undue hardship.

Discriminating Against People with Disabilities

Attitudes are changing in favor of helping people be productive members of their companies and society. According to the law, businesses must focus on *what* abilities the job requires and *whether* an applicant has them. If an applicant has a disability that is unrelated to job performance, it cannot be held against him or her. On the other hand, businesses are not required to give special preferences to people with disabilities. The law applies to businesses with more than 15 workers.

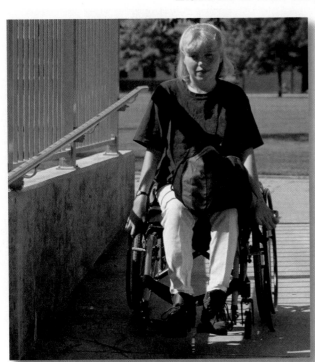

The most common cases of discrimination occur when employers turn away qualified people who have visible disabilities. Discrimination may also occur when employers do not provide reasonable assistance to employees who become disabled while employed, 20-14.

Because having a disabled person in the workplace usually involves extra time, effort, and cost, some employers try to screen out job applicants that may have invisible disabilities. This may be done by asking questions that are not lawful. Some examples of unlawful questions are: Do you have asthma (or AIDS, alcoholism, or any other disability)? What injuries have you suffered on the job? What prescription drugs are you currently taking?

When interviewing a job candidate who has a disability, care must be taken to focus on the person's abilities and the job's needs. For example, a sloppy application would normally disqualify the average job applicant. For a person with a disability, however, sloppy handwriting may simply be caused by the person's physical impairment. In this case, the appearance of the application can be considered only if excellent handwriting is a job requirement.

20-14

Ramps, handrails, and other construction details are required in new factory and office buildings to make them accessible to people with disabilities. Owners of older structures must try to make the necessary modifications.

Age Discrimination

Age is the one diversity that will eventually affect everyone. Laws forbid age-related discrimination in companies toward individuals 40 to 70 years old. In the federal government, however, the law covers everyone 40 years and older.

In the Real World

A Case of Hiring Discrimination?

The XYZ Publishing Company, which prints a major city newspaper, made plans for hiring two reporters. The position required the new employees to cover local business news and events as well as report on individual company successes and failures. Extensive interviewing of company employees and executives would be a key requirement.

Andre and Heidi applied for the positions. Both were college graduates with journalism degrees and similar work experience on college and hometown newspapers. For all practical purposes, their résumés reflected nearly identical abilities.

Both were interviewed during the same afternoon for nearly 30 minutes apiece. They were questioned intently on their people skills, communication skills, computer skills, and reporting experience. They were also questioned about their flexibility to work late or overtime as the work required. Both said their schedules were flexible.

Andre wore a dress shirt and tie, pressed trousers, and polished shoes to the interview. His hands and nails were well groomed and his hair was neatly combed. Heidi wore jeans, a wrinkled shirt, tennis shoes, a nose ring, and a row of four pierced earrings in each ear. She wore no makeup because of her religious beliefs.

A week later, both Andre and Heidi received a letter from the employment office, but only Andre was offered a job. Heidi believed she was the most qualified person for the position. She wondered if she was a victim of sex discrimination. She also wondered if she was a victim of religious discrimination. Heidi decided to write a letter to the president, charging the company with discrimination in its hiring practices.

Questions to Discuss

1. Do you believe that discrimination played a part in the hiring decision? Explain.
2. If you had to handle Heidi's complaint letter, how would you respond?
3. What advice would you give Heidi for her next interview?

Age discrimination is present when an older person is treated unfavorably in the terms and conditions of employment for no reason except age. Discrimination of older workers may also involve decisions regarding wages, benefits, hiring, firing, hours worked, and overtime work.

A common example of age discrimination is the across-the-board firing of people over age 40 in management positions to allow lower-salaried workers to fill their jobs. Another example of age discrimination is a want ad that indirectly implies what age of worker is encouraged to apply.

Height and Weight Restrictions

Limits placed on the height and weight allowed for workers may be a form of discrimination. The employer has the burden of showing the

Reflect Further

Are there any jobs that people over 50 should not hold?

Discuss

For which occupations is age seldom a barrier? Discuss reasons for each.

height and/or weight requirements are reasonable and necessary for the particular job. Some height and weight requirements have discriminated against foreign-born applicants who had lower height and weight averages than U.S. averages. See 20-15.

Discrimination Based on Sexual Orientation

A person's sexual behavior is a private matter, just as religion is. However, discrimination sometimes occurs in the workplace when an individual is thought or known to be attracted to a person of the same gender. This raises the issue of sexual orientation. **Sexual orientation** refers to the gender preferred when choosing someone for an emotional/ sexual relationship. Since most people are heterosexual, sexual orientation becomes an issue when a person chooses a same-sex partner.

People who have their sexual orientation questioned are sometimes made fun of, rejected, and even fired. Unlike other victims of unfairness in the workforce, there are no federal laws that specifically prohibit discrimination based on sexual orientation. Several states and large cities, however, include sexual orientation in their employment-protection laws. Many employers, too, stress the importance of avoiding discrimination in any form. They remind all employees to focus on job performance instead of unrelated matters.

Pregnancy and Maternity Leave Discrimination

Pregnant employees must be permitted to work as long as they are able to perform their jobs. If an employee has been absent from work as a result of a pregnancy-related condition and recovers, her employer may

20-15

Asian Americans are the most frequent victims of discriminatory height and weight restrictions.

not require her to remain on leave until the baby's birth. An employer also may not have a rule that prohibits an employee from returning to work for a predetermined length of time after childbirth.

If the employer allows temporarily disabled employees to modify tasks, perform alternative assignments, or take disability leave or leave without pay, the employer must also allow an employee who is temporarily disabled due to pregnancy to do the same.

Employers must hold open a job for a pregnancy-related absence the same length of time jobs are held open for employees on sick or disability leave.

Sexual Harassment in the Workplace

Sexual harassment is a broad term that refers to a wide variety of behaviors. **Sexual harassment** generally means unwelcome or unwanted advances, requests for favors, or other verbal or physical conduct of a sexual nature. See 20-16. Women are the most common victims, but both the victim and the aggressor can be either sex. Approximately eight percent of the cases handled by the EEOC involve female harassers.

Sexual harassment is primarily an issue of power since the victim is usually a subordinate or less influential person in the organization. Because sexual harassment is a deliberate attempt to take advantage of a person's rights, it is prohibited by law. There are two basic types of sexual harassment defined by EEOC guidelines.

20-16
Being pleasant yet professional with everyone is the best way to conduct yourself in the workplace.

- **Quid pro quo harassment** occurs when one person makes unwelcome sexual advances toward another while promising certain benefits if the person complies. The promise of a promotion or pay raise is an example. The threat of firing or demotion if the victim refuses also is a form of quid pro quo harassment.

- **Hostile environment harassment** is behavior that makes an atmosphere uncomfortable enough to interfere with a person's performance. Examples of unlawful behavior include inappropriate remarks or questions and unwanted staring or touching. It also includes posting pictures, playing music, using body language, or communicating a sexual message in any other way. **Body language** is a means of expressing a message through body movements, facial expressions, or hand gestures.

Sexual harassment undermines employment relationships. It also affects morale and interferes with workplace productivity. Victims are likely to suffer stress, depression, and inability to focus on their work. The employer suffers, too, since both the victim and the aggressor are less effective in their jobs.

Discuss

Why do you think very few cases of sexual harassment in the workplace involve females as harassers?

Discuss

Is body language a clear or unclear way to communicate?

Extend Your Knowledge

Sexual Harassment and the Law

Although it has existed throughout history, not until 1986 was sexual harassment considered unlawful. In that year the U.S. Supreme Court ruled that EEOC guidelines for preventing sexual harassment must be treated as law. The Civil Rights Act of 1991 further strengthened victim's rights by allowing victims a trial by jury and eligibility for receiving compensatory and punitive damages. Unlike other cases involving crimes, however, sexual harassment victims must prove they did not welcome or encourage the offensive behavior.

Identifying Sexual Harassment

Ask the following questions about the behavior being examined:

- Is it sexual in nature?

- Does it violate my employer's (or school) written sexual harassment policy?

- Is it offensive to me? unwelcomed?

- Does it interfere with my work (or school) performance?

- Does the harasser know that I want it stopped?

20-17

These points can help a person determine if a questionable behavior meets the definition of sexual harassment.

Discuss

Do you think a sexual harasser knows his or her conduct is illegal? How can a school or employer clarify what specific conduct is illegal?

Recognizing Sexual Harassment

Obvious acts of sexual harassment, such as threats and inappropriate physical contact, are easy to identify. However, some behavior that seems fairly innocent may still leave a person wondering. In the case of sexual harassment, there are several questions to ask to help clarify any confusion. See 20-17.

A key component of sexual harassment is *not* considering the feelings of the person receiving the aggressive behavior. If the victim does not want certain sexual behaviors to occur and says so, yet the behaviors continue, he or she is being sexually harassed. Some aggressors may try to make the matter seem less serious by saying they were simply joking. It is important for everyone to know that their behavior is not only wrong, but also illegal. The person being harassed is not at fault for the aggressor's actions.

On the other hand, if a person is comfortable with aggressive behavior or encourages it, then he or she is not considered a victim. In this case, the behavior would not be considered sexual harassment even though others would regard it as such if it happened to them.

Another factor that is considered in deciding a claim of sexual harassment is the setting. Certain behaviors that do not involve sexual contact are considered acceptable for some settings but not others. For example, gestures such as "blowing" kisses and "looks of desire" are inappropriate in the workplace. At a party or on a date, of course, these actions would not be considered sexual harassment. However, these same

Events that are extensions of the workplace require behavior appropriate for the workplace.

gestures at a restaurant dinner may be considered sexual harassment when a supervisor and his assistant are on a business trip. The reason is that the dinner is not a date, but an extension of the workplace. See 20-18.

Students in work-based learning experiences should immediately discuss any harassment they receive with their school coordinator. That person is most qualified to help determine the next steps to take. After graduation, however, you may find it helpful to discuss the problem and sort through the facts with a trusted friend who is not involved in the matter.

Thinking It Through

What is the difference between teasing and sexual harassment?

Facing Sexual Harassment or Discrimination

Most employers have programs in place to prevent sexual harassment and discrimination, but no workplace is immune to it. If you should ever believe that you are a victim of either form of unlawful behavior, prepare to take steps to stop it. Letting time go by and hoping that the aggressor will stop rarely works.

Discouraging the Behavior

If you believe that a person's actions may be illegal, you will want to discourage that person from showing any further personal attention. Follow these suggested guidelines:

- Familiarize yourself with your right to a workplace free of illegal behavior.

Discuss

What is the difference between flattering and harassing comments?

20-19

Dressing in a professional manner can send the nonverbal message to coworkers that your relationship is strictly business.

- Know your company's policy and reporting procedure.

- Be businesslike at all times. For example, always dress appropriately for the workplace and work-related events, 20-19. Avoid circumstances that leave you alone with the aggressor or that imply you want the individual's personal attention.

- Make your intentions clear and correct any misinterpretations. Let the aggressor know that you want the offensive conduct to stop.

Taking Action

When a person is the victim of discrimination or sexual harassment, there is a danger of becoming too emotional to effectively do the work that must be done. The first priority is to remain professional as you handle the following steps:

1. *Tell the aggressor to stop.* Let the person know that you consider his or her conduct illegal. Insist that the conduct stop. If it continues, write the person a letter explaining *what* you want stopped and *why.* Keep a copy and preserve it in your files. Send the letter by *certified mail, return receipt requested* to get signed proof the person received the letter.

2. *Keep detailed records.* Maintain a journal, describing each incident and its date. Start with the event that convinced you to tell the aggressor to stop. Explain the *who, what, when, where,* and *how* of each incident. Be prepared to provide names of witnesses or others who can support your claim.

3. *Report the offense.* If your company has a written policy, be sure to follow it. If not, your supervisor is generally the one to hear your complaint and receive your report unless he or she is the aggressor. In that case, go to the person's supervisor or someone of higher authority. See 20-20.

20-20
The person in charge of handling EEOC complaints at your company will treat all information you provide confidentially.

Resource
Diversity Terms, Activity E, WB

Resource
Harassment Points, Activity F, WB

Sometimes employees who resist harassment or discrimination fear reprisal from their supervisor or employer. **Reprisal** is the revenge-motivated act of retaliating, or "getting back at" someone. Workers have been demoted, transferred, and even fired for challenging harassment or discrimination. It is important to know the EEOC considers such acts of reprisal unlawful. Workers are protected from retaliation when they file discrimination complaints, oppose illegal practices, or participate in related investigations.

Thinking It Through

Are you familiar with your employer's sexual harassment policy? Does your school have one?

Summary

The U.S. population is the most varied on earth. A variety of ethnic characteristics as well as differences in age, gender, and other factors all contribute to these differences. When differences among people are not respected, conflicts can occur. When these differences are respected, everyone benefits.

In the workplace, the benefits of diversity include higher employee morale, more productivity, and better ideas. The company also reaches more customers faster. Promoting workplace diversity as a corporate policy is a relatively new goal. This goal is very important to companies trying to succeed the global market. Both employers and employees have a responsibility to promote workplace diversity.

The emphasis on workplace diversity grew as a response to avoiding discriminatory practices. Past cases of discrimination involved unfair treatment of workers based on various factors. These factors involved a worker's sex, race, color, national origin, language, religion, disability, age, height, weight, or sexual orientation. Government guidelines help employers identify workplace behavior that is unlawful.

Sexual harassment is another example of behavior that is unlawful in the workplace. People who become victims of sexual harassment must take steps to stop the action because harassers do not stop on their own.

Resource

Review and Study Guide for Chapter 20, reproducible master 20-3, TR

1. (List seven:) cultural heritage, language, religion, gender, age, disabilities/abilities, race, national origin, sexual orientation, traditions

2. (List eight:) fewer lawsuits, high morale, increased creativity, increased productivity, more quality workers, improved decision making, faster decision making, more customers reached, more positive ties with business and government groups

3. large U.S. businesses selling globally

4. (List six. See Chart 20-8.)

5. 1964 Civil Rights Act

Facts in Review

1. List seven factors that cause diversity in the U.S. population.

2. Name eight benefits of workplace diversity.

3. What organizations have taken the lead in developing policies and programs that promote workplace diversity?

4. List six guidelines that help employees promote diversity.

5. Which law established criminal penalties for interfering with a person's employment rights?

6. Which law gives people with disabilities a chance to be hired for their skills?

7. What is the primary government agency that investigates charges of discrimination brought by individuals and groups?

8. Explain the relevance of bona fide occupational qualifications to the issue of sex discrimination.

9. Explain why color discrimination is different from racial discrimination.

10. What beliefs do religious discrimination laws cover?

11. Explain why a person who is blind cannot be turned away from a job as music conductor on the basis of a vision disability.

12. Identify and describe the two types of sexual harassment.

13. List six questions that help a person decide if a behavior is sexual harassment.

14. What three steps are important in taking action against sexual harassment and discrimination?

6. Americans with Disabilities Act of 1990

7. Equal Employment Opportunity Commission

8. It is unlawful to link any work to a specific sex unless there is a legitimate reason for it, such as restricting the job of women's restroom attendant to a woman.

9. Racial discrimination involves one individual's actions toward a member of a different race. Color discrimination may involve actions toward a member of the same race.

(continued)

Developing Your Academic Skills

1. **English.** Write a paper on your family's cultural background. When did family members first come to the United States? What traditions did your family members bring with them that have been passed down to your generation?

2. **Social Studies.** Research and write reports on one of the laws listed on pages 413-414 in the text. Include conditions that existed before the law was passed. Also state a famous case in which the law was cited.

Applying Your Knowledge and Skills

1. **Ethics and Legal Responsibilities.** Role-play an example of sex discrimination.

2. **Academic Foundations.** Search newspapers or news magazines to find a news story related to discrimination in the workplace.

3. **Problem Solving and Critical Thinking.** List sociability skills teens need to become accepting of others their age from different backgrounds and ethnic groups.

4. **Communications.** Conduct a survey in your classroom and determine the number of ethnic origins represented by your classmates. Discuss the differences represented by mannerisms and dress due to these various ethnic origins.

Information Technology Applications

1. Interview an older working relative, friend, or neighbor. Ask the person what new technology skills they have had to learn in order to stay competitive as an employee and whether the person found learning these skills difficult.

2. Explore the EEOC Web site (www.eeoc.gov) including links to mediation, filing charges of employment discrimination, and current enforcement statistics.

Developing Workplace Skills

Work with three classmates to plan an employee picnic for ABC Company. Imagine the company includes employees from India and Saudi Arabia as well as some who follow Jewish dietary laws. Your team is in charge of food, activities, and scheduling the event. Decide when the event will be held; what food will be served; and what sports, games, or other activities to arrange. Your plans must be sensitive to employees' customs, traditions, and religious beliefs. Research the topics necessary for developing a plan and report it to the class. Explain the factors that prompted your decisions.

10. all beliefs plus nonbelief

11. The job primarily involves the ability to hear, not see.

12. *Quid pro quo harassment* occurs when one person makes unwelcome sexual advances toward another while promising certain benefits if the person complies. Hostile environment harassment is behavior that makes an atmosphere uncomfortable enough to interfere with a person's performance.

13. (See Chart 20-17.)

14. Tell the aggressor to stop; keep detailed records; report the offense.

21

Succeeding in Our Economic System

Key Terms

capital

free enterprise system

productive resources

needs

wants

profit

supply

demand

monopoly

proprietorship

partnership

corporation

organization chart

Chapter Objectives

After studying this chapter, you will be able to

- **describe** the economic system of the United States.
- **compare** the three forms of business ownership.
- **describe** the responsibilities involved in managing a business.

Reading Advantage

As you read the chapter, put sticky notes next to the sections where you have questions. Write your questions on the sticky notes. Discuss the questions with your classmates or teacher.

Achieving Academic Standards

English Language Arts

- Read print and non-print texts to acquire new information and to respond to the needs and demands of society and the workplace. (IRA/NCTE, 1)
- Apply strategies to comprehend, interpret, evaluate, and appreciate texts. (IRA/NCTE, 3)

Math

- Understand patterns, relations, and functions. (NCTM)
- Understand and apply basic concepts of probability. (NCTM)

Key Concepts

- The free enterprise system of the United States is based on six major factors: private ownership and control of productive resources, a free market, the profit motive, supply and demand, competition, and limited government involvement.

- Business can be organized as proprietorships, partnerships, or corporations.

- Businesses may have tall or flat management structures.

- Businesses must be well managed to succeed.

Resource

Another Economic System,
Activity A, WB

Note

Provide examples of changes
that occurred during the
industrial revolution related to
your geographic location.

Discuss

How do changes in the
economic system affect changes
in the job market?

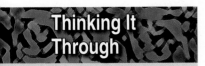

Thinking It Through

What helped the United
States develop into a
strong industrial nation?

For years, the United States has been recognized as a highly
industrialized nation that developed through a strong business economy.
This was not always the case. In the early years of our nation, agriculture
was the main industry. Land was available to farmers and ranchers who
moved freely across the country. The land was developed, and thousands
of communities sprang up. The United States did not develop into a great
producer of world goods until the 1800s.

With the industrial revolution, American industries were born.
Machines were invented to mass produce goods. The production of
goods steadily increased, which made more goods available to more
people. Manufacturers worked hard to produce more and better goods at
ever-lower prices.

Along with a good production system, the United States had great
supplies of natural resources, such as lumber, coal, iron ore, and copper.
The rivers were used to supply power and energy and provide easy
transportation of goods.

Through the United States patent system, inventions of all kinds were
encouraged. The patent system helped protect inventors. It required all
inventions to be registered with the federal government, which issued
a patent number. Once an invention was patented, it was illegal for
someone to copy the invention and assume it as his or her own. As a
result, many inventors around the world moved to the United States
for this protection. With the invention of new products and processes,
industries grew and everyone seemed to benefit.

The working people who immigrated to the United States brought
their training and skills with them. What tools they could not bring, they
made. With their skill and desire to succeed, these workers provided a
very productive labor force that industries needed to manufacture goods.

To pull the entire industrial system together required organization.
Business leaders gave the needed direction as they built their companies
and produced their goods and services for the world market. As
businesses continued to grow and expand, more emphasis was placed
on management. The owners of many companies continued to provide
capital, which are possessions and money used to increase business.
However, they eventually depended on highly trained persons to manage
their businesses and keep them profitable.

Why did the United States develop into such a strong industrial
nation? It became strong economically because it had natural resources,
a patent system, skilled labor, good management, and capital for
investments. The United States also had another very important asset—a
system of government that permitted industry to operate as a free
enterprise. It was the free enterprise system that allowed individuals and
groups the right to start businesses and earn profits from them.

The Free Enterprise System

Free enterprise is only one of many names used to describe our
economic system. It is also called a *consumer economy*, a *market economy*,

a *profit system*, and *capitalism*. Although all these words have slightly different meanings, they all represent the same basic economic system. In a **free enterprise system**, people are free to make their own economic decisions. This system is based on six major factors: private ownership and control of productive resources, a free market, the profit motive, supply and demand, competition, and limited government involvement.

Private Ownership and Control of Productive Resources

The government does not own or control business and industry. Private citizens do. Individuals and businesses decide how to use their productive resources to produce and provide goods and services. **Productive resources** are resources such as labor, land, capital, and equipment that can be used to produce and provide goods and services. See 21-1.

Consumer decisions about which goods and services to buy or use are affected by resources. Resources are limited, but needs and wants are unlimited. **Needs** are the basics a person must have to live. **Wants** are the items a person would like to have, but can live without. Having nutritious food is a need, but having your favorite fast-food meal is a want.

Individuals and families have limited resources, such as time and money. However, their needs and wants for food, clothing, and entertainment are unlimited. Because their resources are limited, they must first take care of their needs before they decide which wants to satisfy. They may choose between a play or a concert when they do not have time to do both. If money is limited, they may choose between saving money for college costs or taking a vacation. Some choices are

Resource

The Free Enterprise System, transparency master 21-1, TR

Resource

Business in a Free Enterprise System, Activity B, WB

21-1

Labor, land, equipment, and capital (money) are all productive resources.

Discuss

If you own a company and can't meet your payroll due to a lost contract, what are your options?

Discuss

Other than a profit motive, what reason(s) may drive the owner of a company? An employee?

Resource

Supply and Demand in Our Economic System, reproducible master 21-2, TR

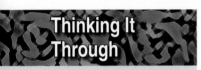

Thinking It Through

What is the one principle on which all businesses operate? Give examples of this principle in action.

more difficult than others. For instance, parents take extra part-time jobs to make extra money or use the time to devote to the family.

Free Market

In the free enterprise system, the market is not controlled by the government. People have the right to decide how and where to earn, spend, save, and invest their money. They also have the freedom to produce whatever they think they can sell, provided they follow existing rules and laws. If there is a demand for their product, they make a profit. On the other hand, if the demand is small and they make too many products, they suffer financial losses.

When losses occur, a company will search for ways to become profitable again. It may mean reorganizing the company, laying off workers, or installing newer technology. Sometimes a company cannot produce goods as cheaply as its competition. If a company cannot turn losses into profits, they may need to take more serious action. They may reduce the number of workers they employ, or in some cases close the business.

Profit Motive

The main reason for operating a business is to make a profit. **Profit** refers to the amount of money a business makes from selling goods and services beyond the cost of producing them. Businesses, motivated by their desire to earn profits, use their resources to produce goods and services. If consumers buy enough of the product and the production costs are not too high, then the business makes a profit. This reason for doing business is called the *profit motive*.

Profits motivate people to be productive. Without this opportunity to earn a profit, they would not be motivated to work or to invest their money. Productive people receive a profit in the form of income, called a *return on their investments*. Without productive people, there would be no labor or money to produce goods and services.

Supply and Demand

Our economic system is based on supply and demand. **Supply** is the amount of products and services available for sale. The amount of products and services consumers want to buy is called **demand**. Businesses decide what and how much to produce based on consumer demand. Consumers express their demand for products and services through their spending choices in the marketplace. Whatever consumers are willing to buy, there are businesses willing to supply it.

The relationship between supply and demand affects the prices of products and services. When consumer demand is high, prices tend to go up. As the supply increases and more competition enters the market, prices tend to go down.

Prices can also change as supplies increase or decrease. A product shortage can cause prices to rise. For instance, when bad weather ruins the orange crop, the supply is low and prices are high. When the supply increases, creating a surplus, orange prices go down. See 21-2.

Competition

Any individual or business has the right to enter into the same business as any other company and compete for consumer dollars. Competition encourages businesses to produce quality goods and services at low prices. If a company charges too high a price for a product or service, consumers can go to a competitor who sells a similar or better product or service and buy it for less. The company that produces the best products and services at the lowest prices will earn the most profits.

BJ's Shoe Store is an example of how consumers benefit from competition. Since no other shoe stores were in the area, customers paid BJ's prices for years. When a competitive shoe store opened about a block away, it advertised the same quality shoes at much lower prices. As a result, BJ's sales dropped. To stay competitive, BJ's owner decided to buy cheaper shoes and advertise more. To compete successfully, he knew he had to offer lower prices than his competitor.

Without competition, prices tend to be high for a couple reasons. First, businesses can charge whatever price they think consumers will pay without fear of losing business to someone selling for less. Secondly, if there is only one manufacturer and it is successful, there is little need for the company to reduce production costs. Competitors usually must work harder to get a share of the business. Consequently, they find ways to make

USDA

21-2

The price of fresh oranges is highly affected when bad weather sharply reduces the annual crop.

Resource

The Competitive Business World, Activity C, WB

Enrich

Ask the owner or representative of a company to discuss the effects of demand and competition on price.

Extend Your Knowledge

Competition Is Mightier Than the Pen

When ballpoint pens were first introduced, consumer demand was high, and the steps involved in making pens was unknown. The initial process was relatively expensive, and consumers paid several dollars to buy one. As more companies started making ballpoint pens, they offered greater variety at lower prices. Competition among businesses improves product choice and lowers prices for consumers. The desire to compete also inspires a search for breakthroughs that allow a business to offer these improvements.

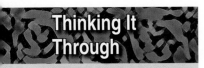

Thinking It Through

Name at least five proprietorships that exist in your community or surrounding area.

Activity

Select a small business in your community. Develop a list of ways government is involved in it. (You may interview the owner.)

Resource

Economic Systems and Employment, reproducible master 21-3, TR

Resource

Free Enterprise System, Activity D, WB

products quicker and less expensively. They also explore consumer needs and wants, then offer products and services that address them more directly.

Limited Government Involvement

To keep the free enterprise system free and fair requires some government involvement. Federal, state, and local governments establish and enforce economic laws and policies to promote economic growth and stability. They also protect consumers from unsafe and unfair business practices.

To promote fair competition among businesses, the government enforces laws that prevent monopolies. A **monopoly** is a single company that controls the entire supply of a product or service. If a monopoly was allowed to exist, it could charge consumers unfair prices for goods and services and limit their production and availability. This practice prevents competition and does not allow the economy to operate on a free enterprise basis.

How Businesses Are Organized

As a result of our free enterprise system, the United States has thousands of businesses that produce a variety of products and services. Businesses range from only one person as the owner-worker to thousands of employees in a large company. However, they all operate on the same basic principle. They must earn a profit to stay in business. This means all businesses depend on consumers to buy their goods and services, which creates a demand for more goods and services.

To understand more about the way businesses operate in our economic system, it helps to understand the three forms of business ownership—proprietorship, partnership, and corporation.

21-3

This store is a proprietorship because it is a neighborhood business that has only one owner.

Proprietorship

A **proprietorship** is a business that has only one owner. It is the simplest form of business organization because usually only one person makes the decisions and manages the business. There are no business partners or board of directors to consult. For these reasons, there are many single-owner businesses.

In a proprietorship, the owner or proprietor supplies all the money to start and operate the business. As a result, the owner receives all the profits that are made and assumes all the debts and losses.

Most proprietorships are small companies in which the owner does much of the work. Many retail and service shops such as the corner restaurant, barbershop, hair salon, dry cleaner, and auto repair shop are proprietorships, 21-3. However, a proprietorship can be a multimillion dollar business with hundreds of employees.

Partnership

A **partnership** is a form of business organization where two or more people go into business together, 21-4. Have you ever seen or heard of a company with two names in its title? *Wagner and Son* suggests a father and son in partnership. *Smith and Jones Plumbing* suggests a company formed by two friends who own and operate the business as equal partners.

21-4

The law firm of Qualls & Fry is a partnership because it is a business that has more than one owner.

In a partnership, all the partners pool their money to establish and operate the business. The partners share the work responsibilities as well as the profits and debts.

One of the advantages of a partnership over a proprietorship is that more money is available to finance the business. A partnership also brings together the skills and experiences of two or more people. This often makes it easier for a partnership to solve problems and make wise business decisions. It follows the logic that "two heads are better than one."

Partnerships may have their disadvantages as well. Problems can arise when partners do not agree on business decisions. There can also be problems when one partner feels he or she is assuming more of the work and responsibility than the other partner(s).

In addition to regular partnerships, there are limited partnerships. Limited partners, sometimes called *silent partners*, invest money or property into a business but do not work in the business. As the business makes a profit from the sale of its goods or services, limited partners receive a percentage of those profits. If the business fails, limited partners are only responsible for any debts of the business up to the amount of their investments.

Resource

Types of Business Organizations, color transparency CT-21, TR

Reflect

If you are a proprietor, what might cause you to change the company to a partnership or corporation? What might you lose as well as gain?

Corporation

A **corporation** is a business owned by many people. A corporation is formed by selling portions or shares of a business that are called *stocks*. The people who buy the stocks become part owners of the business and are called *stockholders*. See 21-5.

A stockholder is only responsible for business debts up to the amount of his or her investment. Therefore, if a stockholder invests $500 in a corporation, the most the stockholder can lose if the business fails is $500. This is called *limited liability*. Stockholders are only liable for the amounts they have invested. If the corporation makes a profit, the stockholder receives a share of those profits according to the amount he or she has invested.

Corporate ownership offers two advantages. Limited liability is one of the major advantages of forming a corporation. The other advantage of corporate ownership is that large amounts of money can be raised to expand a business and produce more goods or services.

21-5

Although this company's name implies a single owner, Sally's Beauty Supply is a corporation with shops in many states.

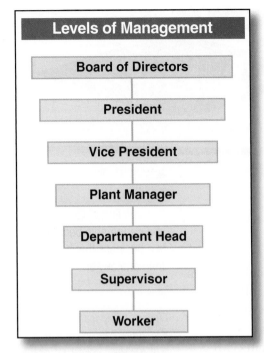

Levels of Management

- Board of Directors
- President
- Vice President
- Plant Manager
- Department Head
- Supervisor
- Worker

21-6

Many levels of management exist in some corporations. Most of the important business decisions are made by the board of directors and top level managers.

Resource

Forms of Business Ownership, Activity E, WB

Activity

Have students research what percentage of Americans are stockholders.

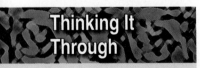

Thinking It Through

What does *limited liability* mean?

Although stockholders are part owners in a corporation, they have very little input in the decision making. A board of directors, elected by stockholders, makes most of the business decisions along with the leaders hired to run the corporation. The president and vice presidents of a corporation are the top level managers. These officials give leadership and direction to the entire corporation. They work together to see that the corporation makes a profit.

See 21-6 for an example of the levels of management that exist in some corporations. The president oversees all corporate activities and hands down decisions to the vice presidents. The vice presidents delegate responsibilities to managers (in this example, plant managers). The plant managers oversee the department heads. The department heads oversee the supervisors. The supervisors comprise the lowest level of management and oversee the workers. Each person reports to the person in the next highest position and, in turn, receives direction from that person. The larger the corporation, the more specialized the levels of management become.

How Businesses Are Structured

There are many different management structures within businesses. The type of management structure within a company may directly influence the responsibilities of your job. Two common types of management structures are *tall*, sometimes called *vertical*, versus *flat*, sometimes called *horizontal*. A chart that shows an organization's internal structure is called an **organization chart**. See 21-7.

In the tall structure, a low-level worker is quite removed from the top managers. Jobs tend to be more specialized, requiring very specific skills. Responsibilities also tend to be narrower.

In the flat structure, a worker usually has closer contact with supervisors, vice presidents, and other personnel. Employees usually have a broader range of skills. They also tend to have greater responsibility for their work. More emphasis is placed on teamwork, with each member of the team having a major role in the work being done. There may be fewer delays and mistakes with fewer layers of personnel due to improved communications.

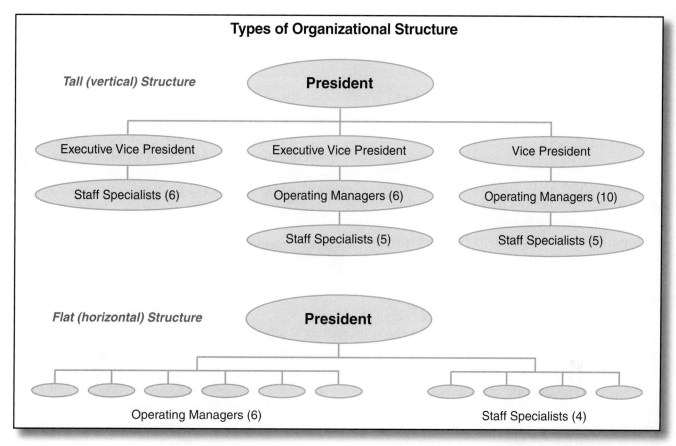

Types of Organizational Structure

Business Management

For a business to be successful, it must be well managed. Managing a business involves many responsibilities. It requires careful attention to the details of the specific business. It also requires planning, staffing, directing, marketing, and financing.

The purpose of planning is to set goals for the business to make it more successful and profitable. This involves deciding which goods to produce or services to provide and how to market them well. Planning includes researching the competition and turning out the products or services consumers prefer. Planning also includes organizing the business so it can operate efficiently and reach its goals.

Staffing involves hiring workers to help produce, market, and distribute goods and services. The larger the business, the larger this function is. In large corporations, the staffing and training of employees is usually handled by a personnel manager.

21-7

The type of organizational structure may affect the number of executives, effectiveness of communications, and job responsibilities within the company.

Thinking It Through

Explain the levels of management that exist in many corporations.

Activity

Set up a class fund-raising activity like a mock corporation. Students who are not part of management can become stockholders and earn a percentage of profit as a stock dividend.

In the Real World

Starting a Multimedia Business

Renata and Marc are close friends. Both want to start a business they can operate from a home office. They both have experience with multimedia. Coincidentally, both are considering similar business ideas.

One business idea involves creating interactive high school yearbooks. Since the majority of high school students have access to computers in their own homes, it is felt there may be high potential in this product.

The other business idea is designing Web sites for individuals and businesses. They both feel they have the background in computer language to use simple software to make Web pages come alive. They know how to use graphics, animation, and sound in Web sites and have successfully created Web sites for several local companies.

Since Renata and Marc have such similar career plans, they wonder if a partnership is a better work arrangement for them than individual proprietorships. Perhaps they should consider forming a corporation.

Questions to Discuss

1. What type of business organization would you recommend for Renata and Marc? Explain.
2. If they asked you to invest money in their business venture(s), how would you respond?
3. Which business management responsibilities will Renata and Marc probably handle well, based on their abilities? For which business management responsibilities might they need help?

Directing the production of goods is another job for management. Production managers and supervisors oversee the manufacture of goods. Managers of stores, restaurants, health clubs, and other service businesses make sure they operate efficiently and provide customer satisfaction. Production and service managers are both responsible for the quality of goods and services their businesses provide.

Marketing includes the promotion, selling, and distribution of goods and services. The purpose of marketing is to persuade customers to buy the products or services and become repeat customers.

Financing involves keeping records of accounts, paying debts, collecting payments from customers, handling the payroll, and paying taxes.

As managers plan, staff, direct, market, and finance their businesses, they must constantly make decisions. A personnel manager must decide

Resource

Business Structures,
Activity F, WB

21-8

Running a business successfully requires the input of experts on staff or outside consultants hired for specific projects.

Enrich

Many annual reports explain how profits have increased due to managerial decisions. Find some such statements and discuss in class.

who to hire. A production manager must decide how goods will be manufactured. A marketing manager must decide how products or services will be promoted. A business manager must decide how to keep accurate financial records. Because decision making is such an important part of management, workers with the most training and experience are most often promoted to management positions. The more knowledge and experience people have, the more likely they are to make wise business decisions. See 21-8.

Thinking It Through

Describe the responsibilities involved in managing a business.

Summary

The economic system in the United States is known as the free enterprise system. This means people have the freedom to make their own economic decisions and possess property. Businesses and individuals can decide how to use resources to produce products and services. The free market gives people control over their money and the ability to be both buyers and sellers in the marketplace. Competition encourages better quality products at lower prices. Profit motivates people to work and produce more goods and services. Consumer choices largely affect supply and demand in the marketplace. Government involvement helps the economy stay healthy and competitive.

Businesses are organized under three basic forms of ownership and may be structured in many different ways. Two common types of management structures are tall and flat. All types of business organizations must be well managed to be successful. Business management involves careful planning, staffing, directing, marketing, and financing.

Facts in Review

1. What are the six basic factors on which the U.S. free enterprise system is based?
2. Why is some government involvement necessary in a free enterprise system?
3. What would happen if monopolies were allowed to exist?
4. Name and describe the three forms of business ownership.
5. Name two advantages of a partnership over a proprietorship.
6. What are the disadvantages of a partnership?
7. What is a limited partnership?
8. If a business fails, for what are limited partners responsible?
9. What are the two major advantages of corporate ownership?
10. Who makes most of the business decisions in a corporation?

Resource

Review and Study Guide for Chapter 21, reproducible master 21-4, TR

Answers to *Facts In Review*

1. private ownership and control of productive resources, a free market, the profit motive, supply and demand, competition, limited government involvement
2. to establish and enforce laws and policies to promote economic growth and stability, to protect consumers from unsafe or unfair practices
3. They could charge unfair prices and limit production and availability of goods and services.
4. A proprietorship has one owner. A partnership has two or more owners. A corporation is owned by many people.
5. availability of more money, more people to offer more skills and experiences
6. disagreements between/among partners, uneven workload between/among partners
7. an investor in the business who does not work for the business
8. debts equal to the amount invested
9. limited liability, ability to raise money for the business
10. board of directors and top-level managers

Developing Your Academic Skills

1. **Math.** Prepare a presentation on current examples of products in high demand. How has demand affected the price of the products? What is likely to happen to the prices once a surplus of the product is available? Present your findings to the class.

2. **Social Studies.** Research the differences between the United States' free enterprise system and economic systems in other countries. Discuss your findings in class.

Information Technology Applications

1. Give examples of technology invented during the industrial revolution. Explain how these inventions changed America's economy.

2. Search the Internet for examples of companies that were declared monopolies in the U.S. Report to the class what actions were taken against these companies.

3. Use drawing software to draw an organization chart of the company for which you or family members work.

Applying Your Knowledge and Skills

1. **Systems.** Ask someone who has lived under an economic system different from the free enterprise system in the United States to speak to the class about life under that system. Discuss the differences between that economic system and a free enterprise system.

2. **Problem Solving and Critical Thinking.** Prepare an organization chart showing the levels of management that exist in your school system. Begin with the school board and work down to the teaching and nonteaching positions.

3. **Communications.** Invite the president of a proprietorship, a partnership, and a small corporation to your class to discuss their responsibilities as a company president. After hearing them speak, discuss the similarities and differences in their responsibilities.

Developing Workplace Skills

Work with two classmates to create a new business on paper. Imagine that your group's life savings will be invested into its development, so select one everyone believes will be successful. Then answer the following questions on paper: What product(s) and/or service(s) will your business provide? What type of business organization will it have? Approximately how many people will it employ? Will the organization chart be tall or flat? Why will consumers patronize your business instead of your competitors'? Be prepared to present your business idea to the class.

22

Entrepreneurship: A Business of Your Own

Key Terms

entrepreneur

entrepreneurship

franchise

Small Business Administration (SBA)

fraud

commission

zoning laws

license

capital expenses

fixed expenses

flexible expenses

assets

liabilities

bookkeeping

accounting

receipts

profit ratio

break-even point

Chapter Objectives

After studying this chapter, you will be able to

- **explain** the importance of small business to the U.S. economy.
- **determine** advantages and disadvantages of entrepreneurship.
- **explain** points to consider when planning a business, selecting a location, and pricing a product or service.
- **discuss** advantages and disadvantages of conducting a business from home.
- **describe** legal and financial issues associated with starting a business.

Reading Advantage

Read the summary at the end of the chapter *before* you begin reading. Reading the summary helps identify main points and important information.

Achieving Academic Standards

English Language Arts

- Read print and non-print texts to acquire new information and to respond to the needs and demands of society and the workplace. (IRA/NCTE, 1)
- Apply strategies to comprehend, interpret, evaluate, and appreciate texts. (IRA/NCTE, 3)
- Use a variety of technological and information processes to gather and synthesize information and to create and communicate knowledge. (IRA/NCTE, 8)

Math

- Understand meanings of operations and how they relate to one another. (NCTM)

Key Concepts

- Entrepreneurs and their small businesses play an important [...] the economy of the United States.

- Many people find that the advantages of being an entrepren[...] worth the risks.

- Setting up a business includes choosing the business, choos[...] the location of your business, and pricing your product or ser[...]

- Entrepreneurs often need professional help dealing with the [...] and financial issues involved with starting a business.

HOURS

Café
Monday-Saturday 8:45-5:00

Spa
Tuesday-Thursday 10:00-9:00
Friday-Saturday 8:00-6:00
Sunday 10:00-5:00

Yoga & Fitness
Classes held daily

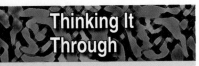
Thinking It Through

How do entrepreneurs and their small businesses play an important role in the U.S. economy?

Can you name people in your community who own their own businesses? Your list may include florists, restaurant or catering owners, and barbers who have their own shops. These people are entrepreneurs. An **entrepreneur** is a person who organizes and manages a business.

Starting a business is a serious endeavor. This chapter will give you the basics of **entrepreneurship**, which is the organization and management of a business.

The Importance of Small Business

Vocabulary

Share additional information regarding the term *entrepreneur*.

Entrepreneurs and their small businesses play an important role in the economy of the United States. Over 90 percent of all businesses in the United States are small businesses. Since the nation was founded, Americans have been free to try their hands at running their own businesses. They have been able to watch their business dreams become realities. Businesses owned by entrepreneurs help keep the economy strong by creating jobs.

The small business sector has helped the United States have a higher standard of living. When people are working, they have more money to spend. This creates more demand for the goods and services provided by small businesses. Small businesses then must hire more people to help meet the increased demand. As more people are put to work, more money is spent, and the standard of living keeps increasing.

Small businesses identify and meet consumer needs. They can provide specialized products and services that large corporations do not. They create competition for each other and for large corporations. This helps keep prices in line. It also gives consumers the freedom to choose from a range of products and services.

America's 23.7 million small businesses employ the majority of workers who are not employed by the government. Often this sector is the principal source of new jobs in the U.S. economy. See 22-1 for more facts about the impact of small businesses on the economy.

Facts About Small Businesses

Small businesses employ

- 53 percent of the private workforce
- a larger proportion of employees who are younger workers, older workers, female workers, and people seeking part-time work

Small businesses provide

- 47 percent of all sales in the country jobs and initial on-the-job training in basic skills to 67 percent of beginning workers

Small businesses account for

- 28 percent of jobs in high technology
- 51 percent of private sector output
- 55 percent of innovative products and services

22-1

Small businesses make a large impact on the U.S. economy.

Opportunities for Entrepreneurs

Resource

Importance of Small Business, Activity A, WB

Being an entrepreneur involves organizing a business, planning its direction, and taking the risks. Starting a new business, significantly enlarging it, or reorganizing a failed business are challenges few can handle. However, entrepreneurs are willing to spend the time and energy that are needed for success.

Advantages of Entrepreneurship

People go into business for themselves for many reasons. Being an entrepreneur can be very exciting and rewarding. It gives people the sense of accomplishment that comes from doing something on their own.

Entrepreneurs are their own bosses. They have the freedom to make their own decisions. They are in charge of setting their own schedules, 22-2. Entrepreneurs have the opportunity to try out new ideas that might get overlooked in a big company. If the ideas are accepted by their customers, the entrepreneurs get the credit in the form of more sales.

Profit is another factor that motivates many people to become entrepreneurs. Profit is the money left from business income after paying all expenses. Entrepreneurs get to keep the profits their companies earn. Successful entrepreneurs, therefore, can earn more money working for themselves than for someone else.

Jack Klasey

22-2
Being entrepreneurs allows these contractors the freedom to schedule their jobs whenever they want.

Disadvantages of Entrepreneurship

Being an entrepreneur is not all positive; it has drawbacks, too. Entrepreneurs must be willing to do everything connected with a new business. They must do the jobs of a bookkeeper, manager, and salesperson. They may have to do the jobs of a secretary and custodian, too. Doing all these jobs may require many extra hours of work. It is not unusual for a small business owner to work at least 60 hours per week.

Owning your own business also involves emotional strain. Small business owners worry about being able to make a profit. They must bear the burden of making decisions that can affect the success of their businesses. If they make the wrong decisions, they may not make enough money to meet their expenses. Entrepreneurs feel the pressure of knowing their businesses could fail if they make too many mistakes.

Types of Business Ventures

What kinds of businesses can entrepreneurs own? The possibilities are almost endless. As an entrepreneur, you could start any type of business you think would be successful. You could sell homemade products, such as clothing, artwork, or food. You could offer a service, such as housecleaning, child care, or car repair. See 22-3. You might even decide to build a factory and manufacture items such as tools, toys, or furniture.

Your company could involve an established business concept, or you might introduce new ideas. For instance, dry cleaners and restaurants are established concepts. These types of businesses have existed for a long time. Creating computer software is an example of a newer business idea.

Thinking It Through

Why do some people want to become entrepreneurs?

Resource

Exploring Entrepreneurship, Activity B, WB

Discuss

The hours a successful entrepreneur must work during the first years may strain home life.

Enrich

Ask a student who may be considering an entrepreneurial venture to discuss the idea in class. Students may critique the idea.

Franchises

One type of entrepreneurial opportunity you might explore is a franchise. A **franchise** is the right to market another company's product or service. Purchasing this right usually costs thousands or even tens of thousands of dollars. Fast-food restaurants, convenience stores, and dry cleaners are businesses that are often sold through franchises.

Purchasing a franchise has several advantages. It allows the entrepreneur to buy a business with a proven track record of success. Often the buyer is granted *exclusivity*. In other words, no one else could buy into the same franchise in the same area. As a franchise owner, you would also receive support from the franchiser. The company that sold you the franchise rights may help you find a good location. You may receive training and business tips the company has found successful in the past.

Buying a franchise also has some disadvantages. You need a lot of money for the initial investment. You also have to pay ongoing fees to retain the right to use the company's name. You may not be free to run the business as you wish. You may be required to follow company guidelines instead.

If you ever consider investing in a franchised business, be sure to investigate it carefully. Talk to people who own the same franchise in other areas. These owners are called *franchisees*. They have purchased a franchise from the same *franchisor*, which is the one who sells a franchise. Franchisees can provide you with insight about the franchisor and the success of their franchises. This information can help you make the right decision. If the franchisor is your only source of information, you may not get the whole picture.

You are probably familiar with several franchises, especially those that rank high in sales. See 22-4. Ranking high in sales means they have

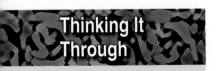

Successful Franchises

- Big Apple Bagels
- Compu-Fun
- Copy Club
- **Curves**
- **Dunkin' Donuts**
- Executive Tans Inc.
- Great Clips, Inc.
- House Doctors
- Juice Stop
- **KFC**
- Lawn Doctor
- **Liberty Tax Service**
- MaidPro
- **Mail Boxes, Etc**
- **McDonalds**
- Nursefinders
- Pets Are Inn
- **Quiznos**
- **RE/MAX International, Inc.**
- Resort Maps Franchise Inc.
- **7-Eleven**
- **Signs By Tomorrow**
- **Taco Bell**
- **TCBY Treats**
- The Athlete's Foot
- **The Coffee Beanery**
- The Little Gym
- **The UPS Store**
- We Care Hair
- **Wendy's**
- Window Works
- **Yogen Fruz Worldwide**
- **Ziebart-TidyCar**

22-4
Some of the most well-known companies are franchises.

an excellent record of meeting consumer needs. Many other franchises are successful but not as well known. The Federal Trade Commission can provide invaluable information on franchise and business opportunities (www.ftc.gov).

Buying an Existing Business

Another opportunity open to some entrepreneurs is buying a business that is already established. Business owners who want to change careers, move, or retire often put their businesses up for sale. Buying an established business can eliminate much of the work and expense of starting a business. Your location will already be decided. The business name will already be familiar in the community. You will already have loyal customers.

As with a franchise, you must investigate carefully before buying an existing business. Be sure the business has a good reputation. Make sure the equipment is in good condition. Be aware of new laws and new competition that might affect the business.

Planning Your Own Business

As a child, did you try to run a small business such as a paper route or lemonade stand? Many successful entrepreneurs started their careers with similar business ventures as youngsters. If you still have thoughts of running your own business, entrepreneurship may be for you.

Activity

Have students research the current most successful franchises.

Resource

Entrepreneur's Self-Quiz, color transparency CT-22, TR

Resource

Qualities for Success, Activity C, WB

22-5
This checklist covers the main tasks an entrepreneur must do before beginning to operate a business.

Business Planning Checklist

- ❏ Contact your local library, chamber of commerce, SBA office, and/or state Department of Commerce for information about starting a business.
- ❏ Identify the product or service your business will offer.
- ❏ Ask people already in the business for advice and insight about potential problems.
- ❏ Conduct a market survey to identify potential customers and assess their need for your business.
- ❏ Investigate the possibility of purchasing a franchise or an existing business.
- ❏ Investigate the strengths and weaknesses of your competitors.
- ❏ Choose a business location.
- ❏ Price your product or service.
- ❏ Contact a lawyer to help you set up your chosen business structure.
- ❏ Check your local government for information about local zoning laws.
- ❏ Contact your state commerce department for information about necessary licenses and permits.
- ❏ Contact an accountant to help you establish a financial record keeping system.
- ❏ Contact sources of financing to arrange for a loan, if necessary.
- ❏ Contact an insurance agent for advice about your needs for business insurance.

Making the decision to open a small business should be done only after careful study and thought. The checklist in 22-5 offers helpful guidelines for those planning to become entrepreneurs. The checklist also helps you determine if you are going to continue planning your own business. If so, it will be necessary for you to develop a business plan. A business plan is written to guide you through the life of your business. It also provides information required by most lending institutions. This is important to you if you need to borrow money to get your business started. A good reference to writing your business plan can be found at www.sba.gov/smallbusinessplanner/plan/writeabusinessplan/index.html.

What Does It Take to Succeed?

Before you plan to start your own business, you might want to know what it takes to succeed. Successful entrepreneurs seem to have certain skills or qualities that make them successful. One key quality for success is optimism. You must believe in yourself and in your business. This positive attitude will help you succeed.

You need to be a self-starter to be an entrepreneur. You must have the initiative to see what needs to be done and then do it. You cannot wait for someone else to tell you to get busy. It has to be your time, energy, and interest that make your business successful.

Activity
As a class, survey your community and suggest a potential franchise. Accomplish each item on the checklist, then review the probable success of the franchise.

Discuss
Ask students to name several famous entrepreneurs and list the qualities that helped them succeed.

Being *innovative* is another quality needed to run a business. This is an ability to come up with new ideas. The right idea for a new product, service, or sales technique can lead you to success.

Entrepreneurs need skill in making decisions. You must be able to decide about routine issues and major problems. Sometimes choices have to be made quickly. In large corporations, several people might be involved in decision making. However, if you become an entrepreneur, the ultimate responsibility for making decisions is yours.

A willingness to take risks is another success factor for entrepreneurs. Starting a business involves many risks. You might risk losing the money you have invested. You may also risk losing self-esteem and community respect if your business fails. If you believe in your ability to succeed, however, you will be willing to take those risks.

Being able to set and achieve goals is another skill for success. You will be expected to identify *when* you expect your business to become profitable. You must also set goals for the growth of your business. After setting these goals, you will need to make and carry out plans for reaching them.

Successful entrepreneurs must be good managers. Failing to use their resources wisely could cause the business to fail. They must make the best possible use of their human, material, and financial resources.

- *Human resources* include both employees and customers.

- *Material resources* include the supplies and other items needed to run the business.

- *Financial resources* is the money needed to start the business and keep it going. Financial resources also include profits.

Helpful Planning Resources

One textbook chapter cannot tell you all you need to know to become an entrepreneur. You will want to spend time doing your research before becoming too deeply involved financially in a new business. Your local library, local chamber of commerce, and state commerce department can provide you with more information. Community college classes may also help get you started.

A prime source of information for would-be entrepreneurs is the U.S. **Small Business Administration (SBA)**. This agency provides assistance to small business owners in a number of ways. Established in 1953, SBA provides financial, technical, and management assistance to help start, run, and enlarge a business. It offers a start-up kit that helps you determine if owning a business is for you. The kit also provides information on what you will need to get started. The SBA can help you develop the business plan that is required by lending institutions. While it does not make direct loans, the SBA can guide you through the process of applying. The SBA also offers workshops, seminars and courses on marketing, purchasing, and planning a small business. Many SBA resources are available online (www.sbaonline.sba.gov).

Discuss

Is there a difference between calculated and uncalculated risks?

Resource

Planning a Business, Activity D, WB

Thinking It Through

What qualities and skills do entrepreneurs need to be successful?

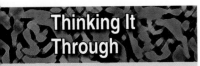
Another excellent source of information for entrepreneurs is also available online (www.workingsolo.com). This Web site contains links to important topics such as business planning, management, financial matters, government resources, sales, and marketing.

Choosing a Business

What is the best business for you? This is one of the first questions to answer if you become an entrepreneur. Answering this question takes time and study.

Your business should involve your interests and abilities. Ideally, it would relate to your work experience or a favorite hobby. See 22-6. You might choose to sell a product that you enjoy. You might choose to offer a service that uses your skills.

The needs and wants of consumers in your area should also be considered when choosing a business. You may need to conduct a survey to find out more about consumers' interests. Your product should be something that customers would be willing to buy. If you want to start a service business, that service should fill a consumer need.

Once you choose a business, you need to find out more about it. Read about it. Talk to those already in the same business. Your investigation may convince you to choose another business, but do not let that discourage you. It is better to choose another business than to open a business that will soon fail.

22-6

This man's interest in gardening led to a job as a florist.

Avoiding Fraud

People wanting to start their own businesses have been "taken" for tens of thousands of dollars by illegal and unethical marketers of franchise and business opportunities. People who rush into these businesses are prime victims of franchise and business fraud. **Fraud** is the act of deceiving or tricking.

Some examples of fraudulent businesses are advertised as follows: "Huge Profitmaker: $3,000 to $4,000 weekly income possible. Zero down and instantly qualified." Certainly something this profitable would require a substantial investment. Other fraudulent schemes claim to pay big money for assembling products at home or setting up product display racks. Yet others promote big profits for processing medical claims for health care providers.

While a business opportunity may seem ideal for you, it is important to take time to check it very carefully. A call to the consumer protection agency in your state and the local Better Business Bureau can reveal if advertisers are the subject of an existing lawsuit or state order. The Better Business Bureau will also tell you if there have been complaints filed against the company.

Choosing a Location

The importance of location depends on the kind of business you have. For instance, if you have a mail-order business, location is not very important. On the other hand, if your business is a restaurant, a good location could greatly affect your success.

Keep several factors in mind when choosing a location. Choose a site that is close to your customers and easy for your suppliers to find. Look for neighboring businesses that will help attract people to your business. Know where your competition is located. Find out if the population that would use your services is growing or shrinking in the neighborhood.

The features of any building you use should also meet your needs. Evaluate the size and number of rooms. Look at the electricity and plumbing capacity. Check out the parking facilities. See if you can find a building that is already equipped with any special fixtures you need. If a building does not meet your specific needs, think about how costly it will be to make changes.

Working from Your Home

Many entrepreneurs start their businesses in their homes, 22-7. This helps keep costs down while businesses are getting established. Entrepreneurs can move to other locations later as their businesses grow and profits increase.

Estimates from the Census Bureau's American Community Survey show that over 4.5 million people worked at home. Close to 300,000 people working from home make over $100,000 a year.

22-7
Accomplished musicians who give music lessons in their homes are entrepreneurs.

Occupations Suited for Working from Home

Some types of businesses work well as home-based operations. Caterers can use their kitchens, and garment makers can use home sewing machines. Artists, photographers, architects, and graphic designers can work out of home studios. Other professions suited for a home-based business include consultants, computer programmers and repairers, engineers, marketers, and technical writers.

Be careful of work-at-home rip-off artists. Ads like that shown in 22-8 are found every day in newspapers and magazines. While some work-at-home plans are legitimate, many are not. Be wary of schemes involving envelope-stuffing, assembly work, and craft work. Scam artists are experts at concealing the true nature and extent of the work and its cost to you.

Legitimate work-at-home program sponsors are willing to tell you—in writing and for free—what exactly is involved. Ask for a list of every

22-8
Fraudulent ads often say little but offer much. This is an example.

Discuss

What type of home-based businesses exist in the community?

Activity

Using a set of the most recent year's IRS guidelines, discuss the allowable and nonallowable deductions for a home business.

Reflect

Is your personality suited to working alone from your home?

Thinking It Through

What advantages and disadvantages might a home-based business have for an entrepreneur?

step of the job. They will answer the following questions so you can make an informed decision:

- What tasks will I be required to perform?
- Will I be paid a salary or a commission? (A **commission** is a percentage of sales paid to a salesperson.)
- Who will pay me?
- When will I get my first paycheck?
- What is the total cost of the work-at-home program, including supplies, equipment, and membership fees? What will I get for my money?

Be sure to check out the company with the consumer protection agency in your state and the Better Business Bureau in your own area. Also check those agencies in the city and state where the company's headquarters is located.

Advantages and Disadvantages of Working from Home

Working from your home has several advantages. You are not committed to pay rent or a lease for office space. You do not have to spend time getting to and from work. You avoid the problem and expense of parking. You can handle home responsibilities throughout the workday. Working out of your home also has certain tax advantages.

Working out of your home may have some disadvantages. Family concerns may disrupt your business. Neighbors may object to having a business near their homes, especially if it draws traffic. Some clients may not take your business seriously. They may feel that your worksite is very unprofessional. Also, be sure to check with your local zoning commission. **Zoning laws** regulate what types of business activities can be performed in certain areas. For instance, you may not be able to open a store in a residential area.

Loneliness from working alone is another possible hazard. Many people working from their homes solve this by using Internet sites known as *telecommunities* or *virtual communities*. A virtual community consists of friends and business acquaintances established through the Internet. These sites vary from text-only sites to those with graphics and audio options.

To curb the isolation of working from home, many people keep the online link open while they work on projects during the day. These Internet sites can help entrepreneurs keep in touch with both a professional and social network. Casual online "conversations" can give entrepreneurs the sense of associating with coworkers in an office environment. As with any job that involves a computer, there is the danger of spending too much time with unrelated matters and letting work slide. For the home-based worker, however, these sites are very valuable when used properly.

Setting Up a Home Office

Setting up a home office involves more than a desk and a chair. It involves planning carefully and making many decisions. It also involves very organized and detailed recordkeeping. See 22-9. A tax accountant or attorney can advise you on which records you need to save and for how long. It is important for tax purposes to keep copies of all business-related receipts, bank statements, charge account statements, mileage logs, and cash receipts. When making cash purchases, write the date and item purchased on the receipt. Keep your personal and business finances separate with two bank accounts. All your records should be kept in a locked file cabinet.

Under certain conditions, people who work from home can deduct a part of their utility costs and other business-related expenses from their income tax each year. However, the requirements are very specific. For example, you may not claim deductions if your office is a space used, even part time, for purposes other than running the business. Consult knowledgeable people on what is deductible and what is not.

Safety is important in a home office. Office equipment may exceed the capacity of regular home wiring. Have an electrician check your circuits and power loads. It is important to secure your windows and doors as well as have good lighting inside and outside.

Good planning can make your work area productive. Indirect lighting and supplemental lighting in key areas is helpful. Position your computer screen to avoid sun or lamp glare and use light-colored walls. Since you may spend most of your time sitting, invest in a comfortable, high-quality desk chair. Map your work area, consider space limitations, and then purchase equipment and furniture. For more tips on working successfully from home, see 22-10.

22-9

Sometimes the many hours of record keeping involved in running a business resembles a full-time job.

Pricing Your Product or Service

Are you charging enough for your products or services? Many entrepreneurs and home-based workers are not. They are not sure what a fair rate is or do not have enough confidence in the value of their goods or services. The following tips should be kept in mind when deciding what prices to charge:

- Survey other people working in the same area. Determine the highest and lowest acceptable rates. You may then set a rate within that range that will allow you to be competitive.

- If your field is not crowded with competition, you can likely charge more. If you are an expert at what you do, do not hesitate to charge appropriately.

- If you find yourself in a very busy season, or your product or service suddenly booms, you may want to consider raising your rates a bit.

Activity

Invite a lawyer or accountant to class to discuss how to set up a home-based business.

Discuss

How much should a product or service be marked up to cover overhead expenses?

22-10
Follow these guidelines for building a successful home-based business.

Guidelines for Working Smarter from Home

- **Use technology to help speed up daily tasks.** Invest in office equipment that meets your needs, such as a computer and software to organize your records, help with money/time management, and prepare tax records.
- **Keep track of your business and personal contacts.**
- **Save your energy for important matters.** Make a decision and go with it.
- **Build a reputation and make yourself known.** Market yourself by telling people who you are, what you do, and what makes your product or service better than the competition's. "Talk yourself up." Word-of-mouth marketing really works.
- **Target your customer.** Provide a sample of your product or service, free if possible.
- **Network continuously.** Join trade and industry associations in your area and attend social gatherings. Establish relationships that may lead to additional business or business information.
- **Develop a mailing list.** Send out regular mailings about your business or, better yet, about your clients' businesses. Use newsletters as another way of keeping your name in the customer's mind. Periodically review your list.
- **Be prepared to sacrifice.** You may need to lose a little sleep and do a little more work without always sending a bill. If you help a customer once or twice for no charge, you will be remembered.

You may have fewer customers but a higher profit that will create less stress and make it easier for you to maintain quality.

- How highly your customers value your product or service is another issue. If you are providing something your clients cannot do without, you can charge more for it.

There are several factors you can keep in mind to help you figure your prices. You need to charge enough to pay for the materials and labor used to produce your product or service. *Overhead expenses* are also part of your costs. These are any expenses beyond materials and labor such as rent, utilities, office supplies, postage, and advertising costs.

Legal and Financial Issues

A number of legal and financial issues will affect you if you become an entrepreneur. You will need to choose your business structure and meet any zoning and licensing requirements. You must obtain financing to start your business. You will also have to maintain accurate financial records to keep it going. If you operate a business from your home with clients coming and going, be sure to find out if your homeowner's policy protects you. You can find professional help to assist you with these matters.

Discuss

What does *talk yourself up* mean?

Activity

List five products or services considered expensive that you would rather buy than live without.

Choosing Your Business Structure

As an entrepreneur, you must decide how to set up your business. You learned in Chapter 21 about the three basic business structures—proprietorships, partnerships, and corporations. Each of these structures has advantages and disadvantages for entrepreneurs.

A proprietorship is the simplest type of business and the least costly structure to form. You would be the sole owner of a proprietorship. This gives you the freedom to run your business any way you want. However, it also makes you entirely responsible for the business and the risks associated with it.

A partnership has the advantage of giving you someone with whom to share business responsibilities, 22-11. With a partner, you may be able to borrow more money than you could by yourself. However, if you and your partner disagree, deciding who has the final say may be difficult. Getting rid of a lazy or dishonest partner may be difficult, too. If something should happen to your partner, you would be legally responsible for his or her business debts. The business could be jeopardized.

If your business is organized as a corporation, you may have an easier time raising money. You may have less risk to your personal assets. However, this form of business costs more to set up. It is subject to more taxes. Corporations also allow entrepreneurs less freedom of action.

Thinking It Through

Identify examples of a corporation, a partnership, and a proprietorship in your area.

22-11
Some entrepreneurs feel more comfortable when they have business partners with whom they can consult.

Note
Keep in mind that a proprietorship or partnership may appear attractive but owners risk assets. On the other hand, corporate taxes are high.

Zoning, Licensing, and Permits

A number of laws apply to businesses and how they must be run. Failing to follow these laws could put you out of business. Therefore, you need to find out what your legal responsibilities are before you begin operation.

If your business plan would not conform with local zoning laws, you may have to change your plan. You might also be able to apply for an exception to the law or have the law changed. Your town hall can provide you with information about zoning laws. Your local newspaper can help you keep up with changes in these laws.

You must be licensed to operate certain businesses. A **license** is a certificate showing that you have been granted permission to practice your occupation. Hairdressers and barbers, for instance, must be licensed by the state. They must pass a test to show they are qualified to perform the services of a hairdresser or barber, 22-12. Aside from a license, you may be required to obtain a permit to run your business. You will probably pay small fees for any licenses and permits you need.

Contact your state Department of Commerce before you start your business. They can tell you how to register your business. They can also help you gather information about the licenses and permits you will need.

22-12
This entrepreneur must have a license to show that he is qualified to be a barber.

Obtaining Financing

Starting a business costs money. The amount of money depends on the business. However, many entrepreneurs get into trouble because they fail to obtain enough money to keep their new businesses running.

Sources of Financing

Entrepreneurs can turn to a number of sources for the money needed to get their businesses going. Your own savings account is the best place to begin looking for money to start a business. Using your savings allows you to avoid the interest costs of borrowing from someone else. It shows others that you are willing to take a risk with your own money. It also shows that you have confidence in your ability to succeed.

Your business may require a larger investment than your savings account can cover. In this case, you can turn to other sources for financial help. Many entrepreneurs borrow money from family and friends to get their businesses started. If you decide to do this, be sure to put your loan agreements in writing. State how much you borrowed, when you plan to return it, and the rate of interest you will pay. Having this information in writing will help you avoid misunderstandings.

Sometimes money can be borrowed from a bank. However, getting a loan for a new business is usually difficult. Banks are more likely to issue loans to existing businesses that need funds to expand.

The SBA may be able to help you get a bank loan. They can review the business proposal and financial statement you plan to take to the bank. They may also be willing to guarantee the bank that the money you borrow will be repaid.

Another source of money is outside investors. Some individuals and companies are interested in investing in business ideas that have a high profit potential. You can try to persuade such investors that you have the ability to run a successful business. If you are convincing, they may be willing to take a chance on you.

Applying for a Loan

When you apply for a loan, you must be willing to provide detailed information about your business. This is true even if you are borrowing from family or friends, 22-13. Having your business plan written out in detail shows that you have thought about your business seriously. It shows that you are taking a professional approach to entrepreneurship.

Before going to the bank for a loan, prepare a business plan. This should outline the type of product or service you will offer. It should state where your business will be located and when you plan to open. It should identify your competitors and why you think you will be able to compete with them. Your business description should explain who your customers will be and your promotional plan for attracting them. It should also specify your needs for space, equipment, and employees.

Another item the loan officer will want to see is a list of your financial needs. This statement shows how much money you want to borrow and itemizes how you intend to spend it. Your statement of need should include cost estimates for all your anticipated expenses. Your expenses may be grouped into the following categories:

- **Capital expenses** are one-time costs needed to get the business started. Machines purchased for the business are a capital expense.

- **Fixed expenses** are those that must be paid regularly in set amounts. Examples are monthly rent payments, garbage pickup, and insurance.

- **Flexible expenses** are those that vary from month to month. Examples are advertising costs, repairs, utility bills, and supplies needed for the business.

22-13
In order to get a loan, a business plan must be very detailed, no matter what size the business will be.

Extend Your Knowledge

Keeping Records

If you're considering becoming an entrepreneur, you would be wise to take a class in small business accounting before starting your business. This will help you become familiar with basic terms and procedures. Even if you hire a bookkeeper, having this basic knowledge will help you evaluate his or her work.

Do not forget to include salaries, franchise fees, and legal and accounting fees when figuring your needs. Your loan request should also include a cushion to cover unexpected expenses.

You should not apply for just start-up money. You need to borrow enough to cover the cost of operation until the business becomes profitable. This usually takes at least a year.

The loan officer will want an idea of the future of your business. You should be prepared to discuss your plans for future growth. This will give the officer an idea of when you anticipate being able to repay the loan.

The loan officer needs information about your personal financial status, too. The officer can check your credit history on paying your bills. A good credit rating is essential. Some people have missed out on the opportunity of a lifetime because of an unpaid debt. You should prepare a statement showing your personal assets and liabilities. Your **assets** are items you own. They include cash, stocks, bonds, and property. Your **liabilities** are all the debts you owe, such as payments on a car or home loan.

You will also need to provide the loan officer with personal data. You must show that you have the experience and knowledge needed to run your proposed business. Your résumé would summarize this information.

All this detailed preparation may take considerable time and effort on your part. However, a complete, organized proposal will affect the loan officer's decision. If you are successful in getting a loan, your effort will have been well spent.

Financial Record Keeping

Over 50 percent of small businesses fail within the first five years of operation. The reasons for this high failure rate vary. However, lack of financial planning is often part of the problem. Keeping good financial records can help you plan wisely once your business is up and running. See 22-14.

It is not only a good business practice to keep thorough records; the law requires it. There are two basic aspects to record keeping. One is **bookkeeping**, which involves the recording of income and expenses. The other is **accounting**, which involves an analysis of the data you have recorded.

The type of record keeping system you use will depend on the type of business you own. If you have a store, you will need to keep track of the products you have in stock. If you have employees, you will need to keep track of the number of hours each works and the many related taxes and expenses. If you have a service business, you must record how much time you spend performing different tasks. A bookkeeper can help you choose a record keeping system that will work for your business. There are several excellent accounting computer programs to help with these tasks.

The way information is recorded will vary from one record keeping system to another. However, all systems will help you keep track of your receipts and expenses. Your **receipts**, also called *revenues*, include all the money you receive from your customers for cash and credit sales. You may be able to keep track of your receipts by using sales slips. When filling out a sales slip, you should record the date and the customer's name and address. You should also list what was sold, the quantity, the price per item, sales tax, and the sales total. All this information will be helpful when you review your books to make plans for the future.

Your *expenses* include all the money you paid for bills and any losses you incurred. One easy way to keep track of your business expenses is with a detailed check register. You should have a separate checking account for your business. This account should be set up before your first sale. Make a habit of paying all your business bills by check. Note the date, whom you paid, the purpose of the payment, and the amount. This will give you a record that can help you with taxes as well as decision making.

Subtracting your expenses from your receipts (income) yields your profits. To evaluate the success of your business, you need to compare your profits from one year to the next. When making this comparison, the dollar amount of your profits is not as significant as your **profit ratio**. Your profit ratio is the percentage of receipts that are profit. It is figured by dividing the total profit by the total receipts. The dollar amount of your profits may increase from one year to the next. However, if your expenses also increase, your profit ratio may drop. See 22-15.

Keeping up with your records on a regular basis is important. Depending on your business, you may do your bookkeeping daily, weekly, or monthly. The more detailed your records are, the more helpful they will be when making future business decisions.

The main goal of owning a business is to make a profit. You do not want to simply break even. The **break-even point** is when income

22-14

A computer can help entrepreneurs keep accurate financial records.

Activity

Using a computer software program, demonstrate what is involved in a basic record-keeping system for a simple business like babysitting or car washing.

Activity

Develop several reports like this to use as handouts (leaving out the profit ratio). Practice calculating the figures.

Comparing Annual Profits		
	Year 1	Year 2
Income	$100,000	$120,000
Expense	−80,000	−98,000
Profit	$ 20,000	$ 22,000
Profit ratio = $\frac{profit}{receipts}$	$\frac{$ 20,000}{$100,000}$ = 20%	$\frac{$ 22,000}{$120,000}$ = 18%

22-15

Comparing annual profit ratios can give entrepreneurs a better idea of their business success than just looking at dollar figures.

In the Real World

Joseph's Complete Editorial Services

Joseph had worked as an editor for a book publisher for four years since graduating from college. When his wife was transferred to another state, he quit his job. Rather than look for a new job in their new state, Joseph decided to start his own business.

He liked working as an editor. He already owned a computer with the necessary software. Therefore, Joseph decided to open an editing business.

First, he investigated the market. He found that many small business owners needed newsletters, flyers, and press releases. However, they often had trouble working with existing editorial services that handled only large orders. Joseph decided he could make his business more successful if he focused on handling small jobs for other entrepreneurs.

Next, he decided he would work from his home. He could use the spare bedroom as an office. This would save him the cost of renting office space. He would call on clients at their businesses. Therefore, having a home office would have little effect on his professional image.

Joseph joined a business organization and met other editors there. They gave him ideas about how much he should charge for his services and how to attract clients. They also told him where to buy office equipment at good prices.

Joseph consulted a lawyer about setting up his business as a sole proprietorship. The lawyer also helped him check local zoning laws. He wanted to be sure there were no restrictions against working from his home.

Although he didn't need to borrow money, Joseph did consult with an accountant for some other advice. Joseph's accountant helped him set up a system for billing his clients. The accountant also told Joseph how to keep his books to make it easier to file taxes.

An insurance agent helped Joseph evaluate his insurance needs. Joseph wanted to know if his homeowner's policy would cover his business.

Questions to Discuss

1. Was Joseph's choice of business wise? Explain.
2. Do you think Joseph made the right decision by choosing to work out of his home? Explain.
3. What problems might Joseph have faced if he had not consulted a lawyer, an accountant, and an insurance agent?

Note

Review calculating percentages at this time.

Thinking It Through

What types of information do entrepreneurs need to record in their financial records? Why?

equals expenses. For the business with a 20 percent profit ratio in the first year, the break-even point occurred in September of that year. See 22-16. The fact that this business was profitable in its first year makes it an exception, not the rule. As you learned earlier, most new businesses operate at a loss for more than a year.

Professional Assistance

Starting and operating a business involves a lot of details. Being sure your financial records are correct and you have met all your legal obligations can be a little unnerving. Fortunately, you can turn to a number of professionals to help you with these tasks.

A lawyer can be one of your most valuable resources when starting a business. A lawyer can help you set up your business structure. He or she can be sure you are operating within zoning laws and licensing requirements. Your lawyer can also help you with any legal problems that involve your business.

Next to your lawyer, your accountant can be your best friend when going into business. An accountant can help you choose a record keeping system that will meet your needs. He or she can help you with loan applications and handle your taxes, too. Accountants can also analyze your books and give you advice about how to increase your profits.

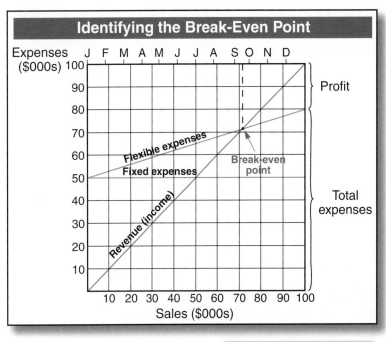

When choosing a lawyer and an accountant, look for people who have small business experience. This will assure you they have the background necessary to meet your special needs as an entrepreneur. Other business owners or your local chamber of commerce can give you references for experienced professionals.

Discuss fees before hiring a lawyer and an accountant. Legal and accounting fees are high. The money is well spent, however, if it can keep your business from failing.

An insurance agent is another professional whose advice you should seek before starting a business. Of course you will need insurance to protect you in the event of fire or theft. You will also need liability coverage in case your product or service causes an injury. You may want disability coverage to provide for you in case you become unable to work. Your agent can recommend the types of coverage that will best meet your needs. See 22-17.

22-16

A break-even point shows when the total income of a business surpasses its expenses.

Resource

Entrepreneurship Terms, Activity E, WB

Resource

Business Expenses for an Entrepreneur, reproducible master 22-1, TR

22-17

In five years, this entrepreneur's business has grown. He has found it necessary to increase his liability coverage to include additional equipment and another employee.

Discuss

What penalties might this entrepreneur be subject to in cases of carelessness?

Summary

Entrepreneurs and the businesses they run are important to the U.S. economy. Being an entrepreneur has many advantages, including the authority to make decisions and the opportunity to make money. Entrepreneurship also has some disadvantages. Owning your own business takes a lot of time and effort and usually involves risking personal assets.

The types of businesses run by entrepreneurs is extensive. Many entrepreneurs build on their own business ideas. Others invest in franchises or buy existing businesses. There are many places where an entrepreneur may seek help, particularly the Small Business Administration. Would-be entrepreneurs should be very careful in choosing a business.

Having the qualities of an entrepreneur is not enough to be successful. You need to make wise decisions about the type of business to pursue, its location, and how to price your product or service. You also need to form a good business plan that addresses the start-up period as well as plans for growth.

Having a home-based business is becoming a common practice. This, like working for someone else, has its advantages and disadvantages. It is very important to research your plans before making final decisions. Networking can be very helpful and may even steer you away from making serious mistakes.

A number of legal and financial issues must be handled before you can begin operating a business. You need to choose your business structure, adhere to zoning laws, and obtain needed licenses and permits. You also need to obtain financing to get your business going and maintain good records to keep it going.

Resource

Review and Study Guide for Chapter 22, reproducible master 22-2, TR

Answers to *Facts In Review*

1. opportunity to buy a business with a proven track record of success, exclusivity in a specific area, help in finding a good location and providing training and business advice
2. Federal Trade Commission

Facts in Review

1. What advantages does purchasing a franchise offer an entrepreneur?
2. From which federal agency can you learn about franchises and fraudulent advertising?
3. List four personal factors an entrepreneur should possess to succeed.
4. Name three sources of information about entrepreneurship.
5. What services are provided by the Small Business Administration?
6. Name two advantages and two disadvantages of working from your home.
7. What is the key factor in figuring a price for a product or service?
8. Which business structure is the most costly for an entrepreneur to establish?
9. What is the purpose of a business license?
10. Name three sources from which an entrepreneur might obtain financing to start a business.
11. Identify the three types of expenses in financing a business. Give an example of each.
12. How would an entrepreneur benefit from taking a class in small business accounting?
13. How is *profit ratio* figured?
14. Name three professionals that can assist an entrepreneur with the details of starting and operating a business.

3. (List four:) be a self-starter, be innovative, have decision-making skill, be willing to take risks, set and achieve goals, be a good manager
4. (List three:) local library, local chamber of commerce, Small Business Administration, state commerce department, community college classes, www.workingsolo.com
5. financial, technical, and management assistance to help start, run, and enlarge a business
6. (List two of each:) advantages—no rent or lease payments, no wasted commuting time, opportunity to handle home responsibilities, possible tax advantages, possible interaction with telecommunities; disadvantages—family disruptions, possible objections from neighbors, possible conflicts with zoning laws, loneliness, isolation from other workers
7. total costs

(continued)

Developing Your Academic Skills

1. **Science.** Research ergonomics. Demonstrate proper posture at the computer, as well as exercises that help prevent carpal tunnel syndrome.

2. **Social Studies.** Research a famous entrepreneur. Give an oral report on this person's contributions to the business world. Why did the entrepreneur start the business? How did the person prepare to open the business? Why did the business succeed?

Information Technology Applications

1. Search the Internet for information on one of the popular franchises listed in 22-4. Find information on company guidelines, business structure, training offered, and the investment required to open a franchise. You might also check information on the Web site for the Federal Trade Commission (www.ftc.gov).

2. Give a report on the resources available at the Small Business Administration Web site (www.sba.gov).

Applying Your Knowledge and Skills

1. **Systems.** Use library resources to research the impact of small business on the economy in the United States. Summarize your findings in a two-page report, listing three of your references.

2. **Employability and Career Development.** Make a list of all of the qualities and skills you think an entrepreneur must have to succeed. Place a check beside each quality or skill that applies to you. Then write a few paragraphs explaining why you think you would or would not be a successful entrepreneur.

3. **Leadership and Teamwork.** Work with three or four classmates to develop a business plan for a small business. Include the points outlined in the chapter.

4. **Communications.** Invite a bank loan officer to speak to your class about how an entrepreneur would qualify for a business loan.

5. **Communications.** Invite a bookkeeper or an accountant to speak to your class about financial record keeping for a small business.

Developing Workplace Skills

Work with three classmates to develop a business idea and present it to the class. Determine the following about the business: the product and/or service offered, business structure, major competitor(s), and potential customers. Also describe the location and appearance of your business. Present your plan to the class, using whatever props or visual aids would clarify your ideas. (Decide among yourselves who does which parts of this project.)

8. corporation

9. to show that permission to run the business has been granted

10. (List three:) friends, family, personal savings, bank loan, outside investors

11. capital, fixed, variable (Examples are student response.)

12. by becoming familiar with basic terms and procedures, by recognizing whether hired accountants are doing a good job

13. dividing total profit by total receipts (or income, or revenues)

14. lawyer, accountant, insurance agent

Part 6
Managing Your Income

23

Understanding Income and Taxes

Key Terms

earned income
wage
salary
piecework
tips
bonus
profit sharing
deductions
gross pay
net pay
exemption
Form W-4
FICA
Form W-2
Form 1040EZ
Supplemental Security Income (SSI)
Medicare
Medicaid
unemployment insurance

Chapter Objectives

After studying this chapter, you will be able to

- **describe** the different forms of income and fringe benefits an employee can receive for doing a job.
- **distinguish between** gross pay and net pay.
- **describe** paycheck deductions.
- **identify** the various services and facilities provided by tax dollars.
- **describe** how consumers are taxed and the types of taxes they pay.
- **simulate** filing a federal income tax return.
- **describe** the purpose of, and benefits provided by, the Social Security program, Medicaid, Medicare, workers' compensation, and unemployment insurance.

Reading Advantage

Take two-column notes as you read the chapter. Fold a piece of notebook paper in half lengthwise. On the left side of the column, write main ideas. On the right side, write subtopics and detailed information. After reading the chapter, use the notes as a study guide. Fold the paper in half so you only see the main ideas. Quiz yourself on the details and subtopics.

Achieving Academic Standards

English Language Arts

- Read print and non-print texts to acquire new information and to respond to the needs and demands of society and the workplace. (IRA/NCTE, 1)
- Apply strategies to comprehend, interpret, evaluate, and appreciate texts. (IRA/NCTE, 3)
- Use spoken, written, and visual language to accomplish purposes. (IRA/NCTE, 12)

Math

- Understand meanings of operations and how they relate to one another. (NCTM)
- Compute fluently and make reasonable estimates. (NCTM)

Key Concepts

- Earned income can include wages, salaries, commissions, piecework, tips, bonuses, and fringe benefits.

- Paycheck deductions include social security and federal income taxes, and may include state income taxes, union dues, and insurance premiums.

- The taxes you will be paying include personal income tax, social security tax, property tax, sales tax, and excise tax.

- Social security provides income when earnings are reduced or stopped because of retirement, disability, or death.

- Worker's compensation provides payments to workers when they are injured on the job.

- Unemployment insurance provides benefits to workers who have lost their jobs.

As you enter the work world, understanding what goes into your paycheck and what comes out is important. When you work, you earn an income. You need to know about the different types of income and fringe benefits you may receive.

You usually receive your income in the form of a paycheck from your employer. Most of the money you earn is yours to spend, but do you know what happens to the money taken out of your paycheck? Most of it goes toward paying taxes. Now that you are working, you are responsible for paying your fair share of taxes. You, along with all other citizens, share the benefits of taxes in the form of government protection and services.

Besides understanding your income and paycheck, you also need to learn how your tax dollars are spent. This will give you a better understanding of why you should meet your responsibilities as a taxpayer. You will also learn more about government benefits available to you.

Forms of Income

When you were hired for your job, you probably discussed how you would be paid by your employer. **Earned income** is the money you receive for doing a job. The form of income you earn may depend on the type of job you have. If you work in an office, you may be paid an hourly wage. As a cosmetologist, you would probably receive a wage plus tips. If in the future you become a manager, you may earn an annual salary instead. From these examples you can see there are many different forms of income. Understanding each form of income will help you see what goes into your paycheck. The following are the most common forms of income paid to workers:

- wages
- salary
- commission
- piecework
- tips
- bonus
- fringe benefits

Wages

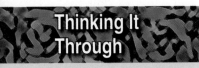

Thinking It Through

Would you prefer payment in the form of a salary or a wage? Why?

Many people earn wages as payment for doing their jobs. A **wage** is a set amount of pay for every hour of work. An hourly wage can vary depending on the type of job. Skilled or experienced workers usually earn a higher wage than unskilled or beginning workers. Unskilled or beginning workers may receive a minimum wage. *Minimum wage,* which is set by law, is the lowest amount of money an employer is allowed to pay a worker per hour for most jobs.

Workers who are paid by the hour will get a paycheck based on how many hours they work each week, 23-1. Kristy, for instance, works in a fast-food restaurant where she earns a wage of $8 per hour. When she works 20 hours per week she receives $160 before taxes. By working 40 hours per week she earns $320. If she works beyond a normal 40-hour work week, she is paid *overtime*. Overtime pay is usually one-and-one-half times the worker's regular wage. Her overtime pay, therefore, is $12 per hour for each extra hour of work. Hourly wages are most common in office, manufacturing, maintenance, retail, and service jobs.

Salary

In certain types of jobs, workers receive salaries instead of hourly wages. A **salary** is a set amount of money paid for a certain period of time. For example, an annual salary is the total amount of money for a full year of work. The salary amount is divided into equal payments. Salaried workers may be paid once a week, every two weeks, or once a month. Highly skilled or experienced workers, such as teachers, managers, and some office workers, are examples of workers who earn salaries. Salaried workers may work overtime, but they receive no extra pay. This often is the case in management or supervisory jobs, which involve more responsibilities.

Commission

Some workers in sales positions earn a *commission*, which is a percentage of the sales they make. For example, a 10 percent commission on a $100 sale is $10. The more salespeople sell, the more money they earn. The purpose of a commission is to encourage employees to sell. Good salespeople may prefer to be on commission because they can earn more money. Other salespeople prefer more stable incomes. They choose to receive a wage or salary, plus a smaller commission. Those who work on commission include some retail salespeople, real estate agents, and insurance agents.

Piecework

Some employees are paid a fixed amount of money for each piece of work they do. This is called **piecework**. For example, Ardis works in a manufacturing plant painting faces on toys. She works along with several other workers on an assembly line. Each worker is paid a set amount for each toy painted. The more toys Ardis paints, the more she earns. Pieceworkers who qualify for minimum wage must be paid no less than the minimum hourly wage.

Discuss

What are the advantages and disadvantages of both hourly and salaried work?

Discuss

What traits do commission employees need to work effectively?

Enrich

Interview two or more sales workers who earn a commission or salary plus a smaller commission. What are the advantages? What are the disadvantages?

Thinking It Through

Do you think you could earn more if you were a student working on commission? Why?

23-1

Because of their additional skills and experience, laboratory technicians usually earn more money per hour than assembly line workers do.

Thinking It Through

What form(s) of income do you receive for doing your job?

Tips

Tips are small amounts of money given by customers to service-related workers in return for service. See 23-2. Food servers, bellhops, porters, and taxi drivers are examples of workers who may get tips. Tipping is one way for a customer to reward a worker for good service. It can also encourage a worker to continue providing good service. However, giving a tip is voluntary, as is the amount of money given. Service workers may not get a tip from every customer.

Usually tips are not a service worker's only source of income. In many cases, workers receive an hourly wage plus the tips they earn. Since tips are considered part of total income, workers must keep track of them for tax purposes. If you receive tips, you may want to get Form 4070A, "Employee's Daily Reporting of Tips." It is contained in Publication 1244, *Employee's Daily Record of Tips and Report to Employer*. It is available online from the *Internal Revenue Service (IRS)* at www.irs.gov. This IRS is the federal government agency that enforces federal tax laws and collects taxes. Form 4070A will help you keep track of your income from tips.

Bonus

Some employers may offer their workers a **bonus**. This is an extra payment in addition to the workers' regular pay. Usually it is taken from the company's profits. Two types of bonuses are common: incentive and year-end bonuses.

The purpose of an *incentive bonus* is to encourage workers to increase their production. For example, a salesperson may receive a bonus if his or her sales total ranks highest in the department. Each member of a production team may receive a bonus for exceeding their scheduled production goal.

A *year-end bonus* may be given to employees, usually at the end of the calendar year. The amount of a bonus will often depend on the company's profits and the length of time a worker has been with the company. A person with 10 years of service, therefore, will receive a larger bonus than a person with one year of service. Some employers feel a year-end bonus encourages workers to stay with a company.

23-2

Restaurant servers often receive tips for the service they provide to customers.

Profit Sharing

Another form of income that some employers provide is **profit sharing**. If the employees' hard work results in greater profits for the company, the company returns some of those profits to the employees. Profit sharing is an incentive to make employees more productive. Profit sharing is often offered in the form of company stock or bonuses given periodically throughout the year. Each employee's share may be based upon seniority, productivity, employee evaluations, or other criteria.

Fringe Benefits

In addition to the types of income described, many full-time workers receive extra financial rewards called *fringe benefits*. These benefits are provided by an employer along with the worker's regular paycheck.

When Luanda's grandfather was an employee, he received only wages for the time he worked—nothing more. Today, Luanda is working at a job where she receives fringe benefits. These benefits are provided by the company in addition to a regular paycheck. Her company provides payments for time not worked, such as vacation time, holidays, and sick leave. The company also pays for employees' health and life insurance. Both the employees and the employer contribute to the company's retirement plan. Luanda does not receive cash payments for these fringe benefits, but she knows they are a significant part of her income. The company also has a child care facility available to employees that Luanda does not use.

Fringe benefits are an important factor for a worker to consider in deciding which job to take or company to join. Employers consider fringe benefits an incentive for their employees. Employees tend to be more satisfied and loyal to the company. Some employee benefits even help the employer. For example, the employer may provide tuition aid to further an employee's education. As the employee learns new skills, he or she becomes a more productive worker with more knowledge to contribute.

Understanding Your Paycheck

Upon receiving a first paycheck, many are surprised to find it smaller than expected. You may have wondered why you did not get to take home all the money you earned. From each paycheck you receive, a part of your earnings are deducted by your employer for tax payments and other expenses. Therefore, an important part of understanding your paycheck is knowing what is subtracted from your paycheck.

Your paycheck contains important information about how much pay you earned and how much was deducted from your earnings. This information is found on the *paycheck stub* attached to your paycheck. The stub states the total amount of money you made for the pay period. It also lists all deductions. **Deductions** are amounts of money subtracted from your total pay.

The paycheck stub in 23-3 gives an example of earnings and deductions. Suppose you work 27 hours for the week at a wage of $8.00 per hour. What will your pay be? You might expect to be paid $216.00 since 27 × $8.00 = $216.00. However, $216.00 is the gross pay, not the amount of your paycheck.

Gross pay is the total amount earned for a pay period before deductions are subtracted. The actual amount of pay you receive is called *take-home pay* or net pay. **Net pay** is gross pay minus deductions. How much money is deducted from your gross pay? At least two deductions are made by your employer—social security tax and federal income tax. The amount of social security tax withheld is a set percentage of your income. The amount of federal income tax withheld depends on how much you earn and the number of exemptions you are allowed. An **exemption** is a set amount of money on which you do not have to pay tax. The exemption amount is set by Congress.

The government allows you to claim certain exemptions. Each exemption you claim lowers the amount of tax deducted from your paycheck. You can claim a personal exemption for yourself, unless someone else can claim you as a dependent. Some taxpayers can take additional exemptions for a spouse, any dependents, blindness, and age.

When you begin a job, your employer will ask you to fill out **Form W-4**. This form is called the Employer's Withholding Allowance Certificate, 23-4. It gives your employer the information needed to determine how much tax to withhold from your paycheck.

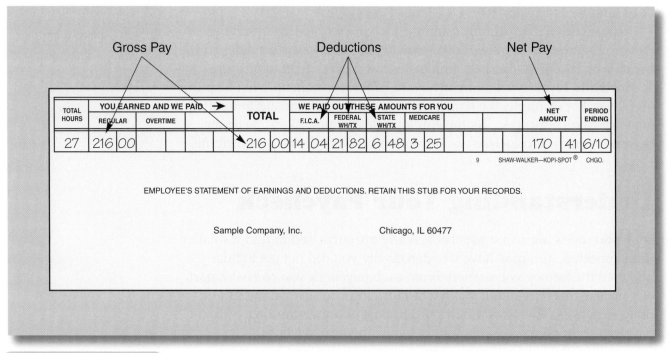

23-3

This paycheck stub shows the deductions made for state, federal, and social security taxes from a weekly gross pay of $216.00.

Form W-4 (20XX)

Purpose. Complete Form W-4 so that your employer can withhold the correct federal income tax from your pay. Consider completing a new Form W-4 each year and when your personal or financial situation changes.

Exemption from withholding. If you are exempt, complete **only** lines 1, 2, 3, 4, and 7 and sign the form to validate it. Your exemption for 2008 expires February 16, 2009. See Pub. 505, Tax Withholding and Estimated Tax.

Note. You cannot claim exemption from withholding if (a) your income exceeds $900 and includes more than $300 of unearned income (for example, interest and dividends) and (b) another person can claim you as a dependent on their tax return.

Basic instructions. If you are not exempt, complete the **Personal Allowances Worksheet** below. The worksheets on page 2 adjust your withholding allowances based on itemized deductions, certain credits, adjustments to income, or two-earner/multiple job situations. Complete all worksheets that apply. However, you may claim fewer (or zero) allowances.

Head of household. Generally, you may claim head of household filing status on your tax return only if you are unmarried and pay more than 50% of the costs of keeping up a home for yourself and your dependent(s) or other qualifying individuals. See Pub. 501, Exemptions, Standard Deduction, and Filing Information, for information.

Tax credits. You can take projected tax credits into account in figuring your allowable number of withholding allowances. Credits for child or dependent care expenses and the child tax credit may be claimed using the **Personal Allowances Worksheet** below. See Pub. 919, How Do I Adjust My Tax Withholding, for information on converting your other credits into withholding allowances.

Nonwage income. If you have a large amount of nonwage income, such as interest or dividends, consider making estimated tax payments using Form 1040-ES, Estimated Tax for Individuals. Otherwise, you may owe additional tax. If you have pension or annuity income, see Pub. 919 to find out if you should adjust your withholding on Form W-4 or W-4P.

Two earners or multiple jobs. If you have a working spouse or more than one job, figure the total number of allowances you are entitled to claim on all jobs using worksheets from only one Form W-4. Your withholding usually will be most accurate when all allowances are claimed on the Form W-4 for the highest paying job and zero allowances are claimed on the others. See Pub. 919 for details.

Nonresident alien. If you are a nonresident alien, see the Instructions for Form 8233 before completing this Form W-4.

Check your withholding. After your Form W-4 takes effect, use Pub. 919 to see how the dollar amount you are having withheld compares to your projected total tax for 2008. See Pub. 919, especially if your earnings exceed $130,000 (Single) or $180,000 (Married).

Personal Allowances Worksheet (Keep for your records.)

A	Enter "1" for **yourself** if no one else can claim you as a dependent	**A** 0
B	Enter "1" if: { • You are single and have only one job; or • You are married, have only one job, and your spouse does not work; or • Your wages from a second job or your spouse's wages (or the total of both) are $1,500 or less. } . .	**B** 0
C	Enter "1" for your **spouse**. But, you may choose to enter "-0-" if you are married and have either a working spouse or more than one job. (Entering "-0-" may help you avoid having too little tax withheld.)	**C** ___
D	Enter number of **dependents** (other than your spouse or yourself) you will claim on your tax return	**D** ___
E	Enter "1" if you will file as **head of household** on your tax return (see conditions under **Head of household** above) .	**E** ___
F	Enter "1" if you have at least $1,500 of **child or dependent care expenses** for which you plan to claim a credit . . (**Note.** Do **not** include child support payments. See Pub. 503, Child and Dependent Care Expenses, for details.)	**F** ___
G	**Child Tax Credit** (including additional child tax credit). See Pub. 972, Child Tax Credit, for more information. • If your total income will be less than $58,000 ($86,000 if married), enter "2" for each eligible child. • If your total income will be between $58,000 and $84,000 ($86,000 and $119,000 if married), enter "1" for each eligible child plus "1" **additional** if you have 4 or more eligible children.	**G** ___
H	Add lines A through G and enter total here. (**Note.** This may be different from the number of exemptions you claim on your tax return.) ▶	**H** 0

For accuracy, complete all worksheets that apply.	{	• If you plan to **itemize or claim adjustments to income** and want to reduce your withholding, see the **Deductions and Adjustments Worksheet** on page 2. • If you have **more than one job** or are **married and you and your spouse both work** and the combined earnings from all jobs exceed $40,000 ($25,000 if married), see the **Two-Earners/Multiple Jobs Worksheet** on page 2 to avoid having too little tax withheld. • If **neither** of the above situations applies, **stop here** and enter the number from line H on line 5 of Form W-4 below.

- - - - - - - - - - - - - - - - - - **Cut here and give Form W-4 to your employer. Keep the top part for your records.** - - - - - - - - - - - - - - - - - -

Form W-4

Department of the Treasury
Internal Revenue Service

Employee's Withholding Allowance Certificate

▶ **Whether you are entitled to claim a certain number of allowances or exemption from withholding is subject to review by the IRS. Your employer may be required to send a copy of this form to the IRS.**

OMB No. 1545-0074

20XX

1 Type or print your first name and middle initial. **Kristy A.**	Last name **James**	2 Your social security number 987 65 4321

Home address (number and street or rural route) **1027 Cedar Street**	3 ☑ Single ☐ Married ☐ Married, but withhold at higher Single rate. **Note.** If married, but legally separated, or spouse is a nonresident alien, check the "Single" box.
City or town, state, and ZIP code **Franklin, IL 65432**	4 If your last name differs from that shown on your social security card, check here. You must call 1-800-772-1213 for a replacement card. ▶ ☐

5	Total number of allowances you are claiming (from line **H** above **or** from the applicable worksheet on page 2)	**5** 0
6	Additional amount, if any, you want withheld from each paycheck	**6** $
7	I claim exemption from withholding for 20XX, and I certify that I meet **both** of the following conditions for exemption. • Last year I had a right to a refund of **all** federal income tax withheld because I had **no** tax liability **and** • This year I expect a refund of **all** federal income tax withheld because I expect to have **no** tax liability. If you meet both conditions, write "Exempt" here . . . . ▶	**7**

Under penalties of perjury, I declare that I have examined this certificate and to the best of my knowledge and belief, it is true, correct, and complete.

Employee's signature
(Form is not valid
unless you sign it.) ▶ *Kristy A. James*

Date ▶ *February 15, 20XX*

8 Employer's name and address (Employer: Complete lines 8 and 10 only if sending to the IRS.)	9 Office code (optional)	10 Employer identification number (EIN)

For Privacy Act and Paperwork Reduction Act Notice, see page 2.   Cat. No. 10220Q   Form **W-4** (2008)

23-4

An employee must fill out Form W-4 when he or she begins working for an employer.

On your paycheck, the amount of social security tax withheld appears under *social security* or *FICA*. **FICA** stands for the Federal Insurance Contributions Act, which began the social security tax. The amount of federal income tax deducted will appear under *federal withholding tax*.

Other deductions may also be taken from your paycheck. If your state has a state income tax, that too will be deducted. Like social security and federal income taxes, state income taxes are usually based on a percentage of your income and the number of exemptions you have. If your company has a retirement plan, a certain amount from each paycheck may be contributed to it. You may have union dues, insurance premiums, and contributions to a savings plan also subtracted from your pay. With your permission, other deductions such as charitable contributions may also be withheld.

The paycheck stub in 23-3 shows the deductions for a weekly gross pay of $216.00. After deductions were made for state, federal, and social security taxes, the net pay came to $170.41. What percentage of $216.00 was deducted for taxes? To find this answer, add the deductions together and divide the total by $216.00. The answer is 21.1 percent.

Taxes

Government plays a very important role in your life. It provides many services and benefits, such as parks, highways, public schools, and police and fire protection. It also helps people financially when they retire, become disabled, or lose their income unexpectedly. Government can provide these services and benefits because of our tax system and Social Security program.

Taxes are payments that citizens and businesses are required to pay to city, county, state, and federal governments. Very few people like or want to pay taxes. However, without taxes, governments would not be able to provide the variety of services and facilities they do. The chart in 23-5 lists many of the services provided by the different levels of government.

Types of Taxes

As you are probably aware, there are many types of taxes. The five most common taxes you will probably pay are the following:

- personal income tax
- social security tax
- property tax
- sales tax
- excise tax

The *personal income tax* is a tax on the amount of money a person earns. The *social security tax* is also a tax on a person's income. It is used to pay for the Social Security program administered by the federal government. Both of these taxes are deducted from your paychecks by your employer and sent to the federal government. Many state government and some local governments also tax personal income.

As explained before, the amount of personal income tax and social security tax withheld from your paycheck depends on how much you earn. It also depends on the number of exemptions you are allowed. Your employer uses your Form W-4 to determine how much income tax and social security tax to withhold from your pay.

Property tax is a tax on the value of personal property and real estate a person owns. This may include houses, land, cars, boats, home furnishings, and expensive jewelry. Property taxes are assessed by city, county, and/or state governments.

Sales tax is a tax on goods and services. You pay this tax at the time of purchase, 23-6. Sales taxes may be charged by the state and/or city. Food and drugs may be exempt from sales tax in some states. In other states, all merchandise is subject to a sales tax.

An *excise tax* is a tax placed on certain products or services, such as gasoline, cigarettes, liquor, and telephone service. City, state, and/or federal governments can place excise taxes on products and services.

Sometimes the five basic types of taxes may fit one or more classifications. In such a case, these taxes may have one or more of the following added titles:

- direct
- indirect
- progressive
- regressive

Direct taxes are those charged directly to the taxpayer. Personal income taxes, property taxes, and sales taxes are examples of direct taxes.

Indirect taxes are taxes that are included in the price of taxed items. They are passed on to the buyer in the form of higher prices. Indirect taxes are sometimes called hidden taxes because they are hidden within the total price of an item. Excise taxes on cigarettes and gasoline are examples of indirect taxes.

Progressive taxes take a greater share of income from the rich than the poor. For example, income tax is a progressive tax. As a person's income increases, so does the amount of tax paid. There are two reasons for this. First, with greater income, there's more pay to tax. Second, the tax rate itself increases.

Services and Facilities Funded by Tax Dollars	
Airports	Police protection
Community colleges	Public schools
Fire protection	Public transportation
Garbage collection	Public welfare
Hospitals	Road maintenance
Libraries	Scientific research
Medicaid benefits	Social security benefits
Medicare benefits	State universities
National defense	Unemployment insurance
Parks and recreation	Workers' compensation

23-5
The primary purpose of taxes is to pay for government facilities and services.

Discuss

Does each person have a responsibility to support society by paying taxes?

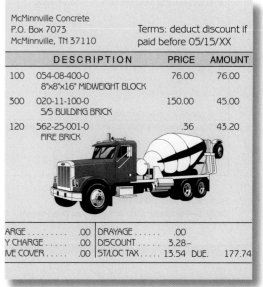

23-6
Sales tax is required on goods as well as services—even masonry products.

Regressive taxes are the opposite of progressive taxes. *Regressive taxes* take a lower percentage of income from the rich and a higher percentage of income from the poor. Sales tax is an example of a regressive tax. People with high incomes pay a smaller percentage of their incomes for sales taxes than people with low incomes.

Preparing Tax Returns

Your employer deducts taxes from every paycheck you receive. However, it is possible that too much or not enough tax is deducted at the end of a year. To declare how much income you made and how much federal tax you owe each year, you must file the required paperwork, called a *tax return*. Wage earners must file a federal tax return and, if their state taxes income, a state return. If too much tax was withheld during the year, you can receive a refund from the federal government. If too little tax was withheld, you must pay the amount owed.

In January of each year, you will receive a Wage and Tax Statement called **Form W-2**. See 23-7. This form shows the amount you were paid

22222	**a** Employee's social security number		
	OMB No. 1545-0008		
b Employer identification number (EIN)		**1** Wages, tips, other compensation	**2** Federal income tax withheld
c Employer's name, address, and ZIP code		**3** Social security wages	**4** Social security tax withheld
		5 Medicare wages and tips	**6** Medicare tax withheld
		7 Social security tips	**8** Allocated tips
d Control number		**9** Advance EIC payment	**10** Dependent care benefits
e Employee's first name and initial Last name Suff.		**11** Nonqualified plans	**12a** Code
		13 Statutory employee Retirement plan Third-party sick pay	**12b** Code
		14 Other	**12c** Code
			12d Code
f Employee's address and ZIP code			

15 State Employer's state ID number	**16** State wages, tips, etc.	**17** State income tax	**18** Local wages, tips, etc.	**19** Local income tax	**20** Locality name

Form **W-2** Wage and Tax Statement   20XX   Department of the Treasury—Internal Revenue Service

Copy 1—For State, City, or Local Tax Department

23-7

At the beginning of each year, employers send each employee Form W-2. Copies of this form must be filed with all income tax returns.

in the previous year. It also gives the amounts of income tax and social security tax (FICA) withheld during the year. You use Form W-2 to help prepare your federal income tax return.

On a tax return you must list all the income you made from wages, salaries, tips, and bonuses. You must also include any money made from savings accounts, stocks, bonds, and other financial investments.

The three common forms for filing a federal tax return are the 1040EZ, 1040A, and the 1040. *Form 1040EZ* and *Form 1040A* are called the short forms because they are the easiest and quickest to file, 23-8. Either of these two forms may be used by taxpayers whose income falls within certain limits and who do not choose to itemize deductions. There are other restrictions to using these forms. These restrictions often change from year to year as new tax laws are passed.

Form 1040 must be used by all other taxpayers. This is called the long form because it requires more information and more time to prepare. Usually the tax preparer must file additional tax forms with it. When using this form, some taxpayers consult a tax specialist to help them determine what expenses they can claim.

Deductions, adjustments to income, and *tax credits* are all expenses taxpayers can claim to lower their tax bills. However, there are a number of restrictions on these items and not everyone may claim them. Also, they may be claimed only on certain tax forms. Deductions include charitable contributions, interest on some loans, some medical and dental expenses, certain financial losses, and other expenses. Income adjustments include alimony and certain retirement deductions. Tax credits can be claimed for child care, the elderly, and the people with disabilities. See 23-9.

On a year-by-year basis, taxpayers should decide which tax form is best for their needs. The form sent to each taxpayer is usually a new version of the type they filed last time. However, if you file your taxes electronically, you may not receive a form in the mail. Since a person's financial situation may change significantly in a year, it is best to check if a different form is more beneficial. Sometimes the opportunities to reduce taxes—by declaring deductions, adjustments to income, and tax credits—are part of one form but not another.

Reducing taxes by claiming legitimate deductions, adjustments, and credits is a legal way to avoid paying unnecessary taxes. Failing to declare income or falsifying information, however, is not legal. This is considered *tax evasion*. It is a criminal offense that can involve fines and even a jail sentence.

Resource

Preparing Tax Returns, Activity E, WB

Discuss

It is important to use an accurate method to record income. Describe some methods to use.

Activity

For ease in tax preparation, create a "tickler" file to maintain records throughout the year. Label a file folder for each of the following items: income and taxable benefits, charitable contributions, medical and dental expenses, earned interest, and interest paid (for certain loans). Create other files as needed. Keep the file folders in a tabletop file or small box for easy access. File records as they are received.

Thinking It Through

How can taxpayers lower their tax bills lawfully?

Enrich

Locate the preparation instructions for Form 1040EZ and Form 1040 on the Internal Revenue Service Web site (www.irs.gov/instructions/). Compare the instructions. How are they similar and different?

Enrich

Invite a certified public accountant or other tax specialist to speak with students about taxable income, deductions, adjustments to income, and tax credits. Have students write questions for the speaker in advance of the visit.

Form 1040A

Department of the Treasury—Internal Revenue Service

U.S. Individual Income Tax Return **20XX**

IRS Use Only—Do not write or staple in this space.

OMB No. 1545-0074

Label (See page 15.)

Use the IRS label. Otherwise, please print or type.

Presidential Election Campaign ▶ Check here if you, or your spouse if filing jointly, want $3 to go to this fund (see page 15.) ▶ ☐ You ☐ Spouse

Your first name and initial | Last name

Your social security number

If a joint return, spouse's first name and initial | Last name

Spouse's social security number

Home address (number and street). If you have a P.O. box, see page 15. | Apt. no.

City, town or post office, state, and ZIP code. If you have a foreign address, see page 15.

▲ You **must** enter your SSN(s) above. ▲

Checking a box below will not change your tax or refund.

Filing status
Check only one box.

1 ☐ Single
2 ☐ Married filing jointly (even if only one had income)
3 ☐ Married filing separately. Enter spouse's SSN above and full name here. ▶
4 ☐ Head of household (with qualifying person). (See page 16.) If the qualifying person is a child but not your dependent, enter this child's name here. ▶
5 ☐ Qualifying widow(er) with dependent child (see page 17)

Exemptions

6a ☐ Yourself. If someone can claim you as a dependent, **do not** check box 6a.
  b ☐ Spouse
  c Dependents:

If more than six dependents, see page 18.

(1) First name Last name	(2) Dependent's social security number	(3) Dependent's relationship to you	(4) ✓ if qualifying child for child tax credit (see page 18)
			☐
			☐
			☐
			☐
			☐

Boxes checked on 6a and 6b

No. of children on 6c who:
• lived with you
• did not live with you due to divorce or separation (see page 19)

Dependents on 6c not entered above

  d Total number of e

Income

Attach Form(s) W-2 here. Also attach Form(s) 1099-R if tax was withheld.

If you did not get a W-2, see page 21.

Enclose, but do not attach, any payment.

7   Wages, salaries,
8a **Taxable** interest.
  b **Tax-exempt** inter
9a Ordinary dividends
  b Qualified dividend
10 Capital gain distr
11a IRA distributions.
12a Pensions and annuities.
13 Unemployment c
14a Social security benefits.
15 Add lines 7 throug

Adjusted gross income

16 Educator expense
17 IRA deduction (se
18 Student loan inte
19 Tuition and fees
20 Add lines 16 thro
21 Subtract line 20 f

For Disclosure, Privacy Act, and Paperwo

Form 1040EZ

Department of the Treasury—Internal Revenue Service

Income Tax Return for Single and Joint Filers With No Dependents **20XX**

OMB No. 1545-0074

Label (See page 8.) **Use the IRS label.** Otherwise, please print or type.

Presidential Election Campaign (page 9) ▶

Your first name and initial | Last name

Your social security number

If a joint return, spouse's first name and initial | Last name

Spouse's social security number

Home address (number and street). If you have a P.O. box, see page 9. | Apt. no.

City, town or post office, state, and ZIP code. If you have a foreign address, see page 9.

▲ You **must** enter your SSN(s) above. ▲

Checking a box below will not change your tax or refund.

Check here if you, or your spouse if a joint return, want $3 to go to this fund . . . . ▶ ☐ You ☐ Spouse

Income

Attach Form(s) W-2 here.

Enclose, but do not attach, any payment.

1 Wages, salaries, and tips. This should be shown in box 1 of your Form(s) W-2. Attach your Form(s) W-2. | 1

2 Taxable interest. If the total is over $1,500, you cannot use Form 1040EZ. | 2

3 Unemployment compensation and Alaska Permanent Fund dividends (see page 10). | 3

4 Add lines 1, 2, and 3. This is your **adjusted gross income.** | 4

5 If someone can claim you (or your spouse if a joint return) as a dependent, check the applicable box(es) below and enter the amount from the worksheet on back.
  ☐ You   ☐ Spouse
  If no one can claim you (or your spouse if a joint return), enter $8,750 if **single;** $17,500 if **married filing jointly.** See back for explanation. | 5

6 Subtract line 5 from line 4. If line 5 is larger than line 4, enter -0-. This is your **taxable income.** ▶ | 6

Payments and tax

7 Federal income tax withheld from box 2 of your Form(s) W-2. | 7
8a **Earned income credit (EIC).** | 8a
  b Nontaxable combat pay election. | 8b
9 Add lines 7 and 8a. These are your **total payments.** ▶ | 9
10 **Tax.** Use the amount on **line 6 above** to find your tax in the tax table on pages 18–26 of the booklet. Then, enter the tax from the table on this line. | 10

Refund

Have it directly deposited! See page 15 and fill in 11b, 11c, and 11d or Form 8888.

11a If line 9 is larger than line 10, subtract line 10 from line 9. This is your **refund.** If Form 8888 is attached, check here ▶ ☐ | 11a
  ▶ b Routing number | ▶ c Type: ☐ Checking ☐ Savings
  ▶ d Account number

Amount you owe

12 If line 10 is larger than line 9, subtract line 9 from line 10. This is the **amount you owe.** For details on how to pay, see page 16. ▶ | 12

Third party designee
Do you want to allow another person to discuss this return with the IRS (see page 16)? ☐ **Yes.** Complete the following. ☐ **No**
Designee's name ▶ | Phone no. ▶ ( ) | Personal identification number (PIN) ▶

Sign here
Joint return? See page 6.
Keep a copy for your records.

Under penalties of perjury, I declare that I have examined this return, and to the best of my knowledge and belief, it is true, correct, and accurately lists all amounts and sources of income I received during the tax year. Declaration of preparer (other than the taxpayer) is based on all information of which the preparer has any knowledge.

Your signature | Date | Your occupation | Daytime phone number
Spouse's signature. If a joint return, **both** must sign. | Date | Spouse's occupation

Paid preparer's use only
Preparer's signature ▶ | Date | Check if self-employed ☐ | Preparer's SSN or PTIN
Firm's name (or yours if self-employed), address, and ZIP code ▶ | EIN | Phone no. ( )

For Disclosure, Privacy Act, and Paperwork Reduction Act Notice, see page 32.   Cat. No. 11329W   Form **1040EZ** (2007)

23-8

Many taxpayers can use Form 1040EZ or Form 1040A to file their taxes.

Extend Your Knowledge

Methods for Filing Taxes

The forms needed for filing taxes can be obtained from post offices, banks, public libraries, the Internet, and the IRS. The forms provide instructions for filing. If you wish to use a personal computer to complete your taxes, you may purchase commercial software to do so or use E-filing at www.irs.gov. The federal government has made E-filing free to certain individuals. Using a computer will make your filing simpler, neater, and more accurate. E-filing will also speed any refund you deserve.

When preparing your federal income tax return, follow these helpful suggestions.

1. Get all your financial records together. You may need them to verify your deductions, adjustments, and credits. For tax purposes you may need:
   * records of income including wages, tips, and taxable benefits

   * records of interest earned and dividends received

   * canceled checks or receipts for expenses entered on tax returns as deductions

   * interest payment records for a home mortgage

   * past tax returns

23-9
Working taxpayers may be able to claim tax credits for child care expenses if they meet certain requirements.

2. Read all the instructions carefully before beginning.

3. Prepare the form in pencil first so any errors can be erased easily. Before writing the final copy in ink, check your math or have someone else check it. If you make a mistake, you can always get another form.

4. Make a copy of the completed form and keep it with other important papers.

The IRS offers a variety of sources to help you fill out your tax forms. You can telephone an IRS agent or listen to prerecorded messages on a variety of topics. You can use the IRS Web site. You can also order free copies of tax forms and helpful publications.

Thinking It Through

What financial records may be needed when preparing income tax returns?

Note

Have blank copies of
Form1040EZ and a few other
types of income tax forms
available for student practice.

Activity

Create a presentation in
presentation software showing
how to complete Form 1040EZ.

Resource

Filling Out a Tax Return Form,
reproducible master 23-2, TR

Enrich

Have students go online to
review publications related to
completing Form 1040EZ.

The final date for filing tax returns is April 15 of the following year. If that date falls on a Saturday, Sunday, or legal holiday, returns are due on the next business day. Returns must be postmarked no later than the due date. If you file late, you may have to pay penalties and interest fees. Be sure to mail the return to the IRS Center for your state or file your return electronically.

Filing Your First Tax Return

When filing a first tax return, most people can use the Form 1040EZ unless they have deductions that require a different form. **Form 1040EZ** is the simplest form to complete for filing an income tax return. You can obtain a Form 1040EZ from a local library, bank, post office, IRS office, or download a form from the IRS Web site. You should automatically receive a form in the mail each year thereafter unless you file electronically or move. If you move, the form may not be forwarded to you. Failing to receive a form in the mail is no excuse for not filing a return. As a wage earner, it is your responsibility to prepare and file a tax return on time.

Selecting Form 1040EZ

As a first-time employee, you probably meet all of Form 1040EZ's conditions. If not, you must report your income to the IRS on another type of form. You will probably be able to use a *Form 1040A* or *Form 1040*. Each form includes instructions that explain which form to use.

With the example of college student, Kristy A. James, you can see how to complete a Form 1040EZ. Kristy James worked part-time as a supermarket cashier. Income tax was withheld according to her W-4 Form. At the end of the year, Kristy received copies of Form W-2 from her employer. It showed that $1314.00 was withheld for income tax from Kristy's total earnings of $8,940.00.

Kristy can use Form 1040EZ to file her income tax return because she is single and has no dependents. In addition to her wages, Kristy's savings account earned $75.00 in interest. See 23-10.

Completing Form 1040EZ

After reading all instructions carefully, you can seek help from a knowledgeable person—such as a parent or guardian—if you have any questions about the form. Teachers and counselors are also good sources of information. The IRS also provides taxpayers with assistance regardless which form they use. Simply contact the IRS at their Web site (irs.gov). You may also call the IRS using their toll-free number (1-800-829-1040) or visit their local office.

Kristy carefully read all the instructions on Form 1040EZ. She felt confident that she could complete the form without additional help. (Refer back to Figure 23-10 frequently as you follow the steps described in this section.)

Form **1040EZ**

Department of the Treasury—Internal Revenue Service

Income Tax Return for Single and Joint Filers With No Dependents **20XX**

OMB No. 1545-0074

Label (See page 8.)
Use the IRS label. Otherwise, please print or type.

Presidential Election Campaign (page 9)

L A B E L H E R E	Your first name and initial	Last name
	Kristy A.	James

If a joint return, spouse's first name and initial | Last name

Home address (number and street). If you have a P.O. box, see page 9. | Apt. no.
1027 Cedar Street

City, town or post office, state, and ZIP code. If you have a foreign address, see page 9.
Franklin, IL 65432

Your social security number
987 : 65 : 4321

Spouse's social security number

▲ You **must** enter your SSN(s) above. ▲

Checking a box below will not change your tax or refund.

Check here if you, or your spouse if a joint return, want $3 to go to this fund . . . . . ▶ ☐ **You**   ☐ **Spouse**

Income

Attach Form(s) W-2 here.

Enclose, but do not attach, any payment.

1	Wages, salaries, and tips. This should be shown in box 1 of your Form(s) W-2. Attach your Form(s) W-2.	1	8,940 00
2	Taxable interest. If the total is over $1,500, you cannot use Form 1040EZ.	2	75 00
3	Unemployment compensation and Alaska Permanent Fund dividends (see page 10).	3	
4	Add lines 1, 2, and 3. This is your **adjusted gross income.**	4	9,015 00
5	If someone can claim you (or your spouse if a joint return) as a dependent, check the applicable box(es) below and enter the amount from the worksheet on back. ☐ You ☐ Spouse If no one can claim you (or your spouse if a joint return), enter $8,750 if **single**; $17,500 if **married filing jointly.** See back for explanation.	5	8,750 00
6	Subtract line 5 from line 4. If line 5 is larger than line 4, enter -0-. This is your **taxable income.** ▶	6	265 00

Payments and tax

7	Federal income tax withheld from box 2 of your Form(s) W-2.	7	1341 00
8a	**Earned income credit (EIC).**	8a	
b	Nontaxable combat pay election. 8b		
9	Add lines 7 and 8a. These are your **total payments.** ▶	9	1341 00
10	**Tax.** Use the amount on **line 6 above** to find your tax in the tax table on pages 18–26 of the booklet. Then, enter the tax from the table on this line.	10	25 00

Refund

Have it directly deposited! See page 15 and fill in 11b, 11c, and 11d or Form 8888.

11a	If line 9 is larger than line 10, subtract line 10 from line 9. This is your **refund.** If Form 8888 is attached, check here ▶ ☐	11a	1315 00
▶ b	Routing number	▶ c Type: ☐ Checking ☐ Savings	
▶ d	Account number		

Amount you owe

12	If line 10 is larger than line 9, subtract line 9 from line 10. This is the **amount you owe.** For details on how to pay, see page 16. ▶	12	

Third party designee

Do you want to allow another person to discuss this return with the IRS (see page 16)? ☐ **Yes.** Complete the following. ☑ **No**

Designee's name ▶ | Phone no. ▶ ( ) | Personal identification number (PIN) ▶ ☐☐☐☐☐

Sign here

Joint return? See page 6.

Keep a copy for your records.

Under penalties of perjury, I declare that I have examined this return, and to the best of my knowledge and belief, it is true, correct, and accurately lists all amounts and sources of income I received during the tax year. Declaration of preparer (other than the taxpayer) is based on all information of which the preparer has any knowledge.

Your signature	Date	Your occupation	Daytime phone number
Kristy A. James	2/15/20XX	Supermarket cashier	(815) 555-5555
Spouse's signature. If a joint return, **both** must sign.	Date	Spouse's occupation	

Paid preparer's use only

Preparer's signature ▶	Date	Check if self-employed ☐	Preparer's SSN or PTIN
Firm's name (or yours if self-employed), address, and ZIP code ▶		EIN :	
		Phone no. ( )	

For Disclosure, Privacy Act, and Paperwork Reduction Act Notice, see page 32.   Cat. No. 11329W   Form **1040EZ** (2007)

23-10

Use this form as a reference as you review the steps for filling out Form 1040EZ.

Enrich

Research the pros and cons of married couples filing a joint return or filing separately.

Activity

Demonstrate the ease of preparing tax returns electronically using a computer.

Discuss

What is adjusted gross income? How is taxable income calculated?

Enrich

Investigate the impact of receiving unemployment payments on taxable income.

Kristy printed her full name, address, and social security number in the space provided at the top of the form. This is Kristy's first year to file a tax return. Next year she will receive her 1040EZ from the IRS in the mail with a printed label containing this information. Kristy will simply transfer that label to this section of the form and correct any errors.

Kristy did not want to contribute to the Presidential Election Campaign Fund and left the *You* and *Spouse* boxes unchecked. Congress established this fund to help pay the campaign expenses of presidential candidates. If you pay income tax, you may contribute three tax dollars to this fund by checking the box.

Filing Status

Kristy did not complete either line under "Spouse" because she is single. If Kristy were married and filing a joint return, she would have filled in the line under her name with her spouse's name and inserted her spouse's social security number.

Reporting Income

Line 1. Kristy wrote in the total she received in wages, salaries, and tips on Line 1. (Tips include cash, merchandise, or services you receive directly from customers or amounts an employer pays on behalf of charge customers.) The amount shown in Box 1 of her W-2 Form is $8,939.75. Kristy wrote in $8,940.00 because taxpayers are allowed to round off figures to the nearest dollar. (If you round to whole dollars, you must round all amounts on your return. Drop amounts under 50 cents to the next lowest dollar and increase amounts from 50 to 99 cents to the next highest dollar.) If Kristy had more than one job, she would have included earnings from all of her employers.

Line 2. Kristy wrote in the rounded amount of total interest she received. In this case, she earned $75.00 from her savings account. (You should receive an interest statement from your bank and any other institution that pays you interest.)

Line 3. Kristy skipped Line 3. She would have completed this line if she had been laid off and received unemployment payments. Unemployment payments must be claimed as income.

Line 4. Kristy added Lines 1 and 2—the $8,940.00 from wages plus the $75.00 from interest on her savings. Note that Kristy wrote $9,015.00 on Line 4.

Line 5. Kristy lives in her own home and no one claims her as a dependent. Because she did not check either *You* or *Spouse* on Line 5, Kristy entered $8,750.00—the amount given for a single person. This amount is the total of the standard deduction and her exemption. (Note: If someone could claim Kristy as a dependent, she would have turned to the worksheet on the back of Form 1040EZ as directed. She then would have completed the steps of the worksheet. Kristy would have entered the number result on Line 5.)

Line 6. Kristy calculated the amount of income on which she had to pay tax by subtracting Line 5 from Line 4 ($9,015.00- $ = $8,750.00). Kristy entered the result of $265.00 on Line 6.

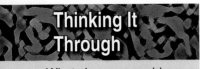

Thinking It Through

What changes would occur in Kristy's Form 1040EZ if someone else claimed her as a dependent?

Identifying Payments and Taxes

Line 7. Kristy looked at the Form W-2 she received from her employer. Box 2 of that form showed that Kristy's employer withheld $1341.00 of income tax. She wrote $1341.00 on Line 7.

Line 8. Kristy checked the instructions for the *Earned Income Credit (EIC).* Because Kristy is single, has no children as dependents, and is under age 25, she determined that she could not take this credit. (Note: The EIC is a credit available to certain people who work. This credit may result in a refund even if a person does not owe any tax. To determine eligibility for the EIC, follow the IRS instructions for lines 8a and 8b of Form 1040EZ. You may need to complete the *Earned Income Credit (EIC) Worksheet* found in the Form 1040EZ instructions to determine your earned income credit status. The IRS will also calculate this credit for you if you choose to let them.)

Line 9. Kristy added the figures on Lines 7 and 8. She wrote $1341.00 on line 9.

Line 10. Kristy is asked to look at Line 6 on her tax form. She found $265.00 on Line 6. This is Kristy's taxable income. She then looked in the back of her 1040EZ instruction booklet and found the tax table that applied to single taxpayers. The amount of tax due on $265.00 was $26.00. She wrote $26.00 on Line 10.

Determining the Refund or Amount Owed

Line 11a. Because the amount on Line 9 is larger than the amount on Line 10, Kristy subtracted the amount in Line 10 from Line 9. She entered $1315.00 on Line 11a. This is the amount of Kristy's *refund.*

Kristy can receive a refund in two ways. She can get a check from the U.S. Department of the Treasury. The check will be mailed directly to her. As an alternative, Kristy can choose to have a direct deposit made to her account. If Kristy chooses direct deposit, she must complete Lines 11b, 11c, and 11d.

Line 12. If Line 10 on Kristy's form had been greater than Line 9, she would have owed tax. She would have subtracted Line 9 from Line 10. Kristy would have entered that amount on Line 12. This would be the amount of additional tax Kristy would have to pay. She would need to attach a check for that amount to her tax form. However, since Kristy was entitled to a refund, she did not write anything on this line.

Signing the Return

Kristy marked *No* in the block titled *Third party designee* because she prepared her own return. If the IRS has questions, she is the best person to contact, not someone else. Kristy simply left the rest of the block empty.

Activity

Use the Internal Revenue Service Web site (www.irs.gov) to explore further details about *Earned Income Credit* eligibility.

Discuss

When is it best to have a tax specialist prepare a tax return? What are the pros and cons of having a tax specialist prepare a tax return?

Thinking It Through

What factors determine whether a person receives a tax refund or owes income tax?

Thinking It Through

When mailing your return, why might it be best to use a type of mail that is trackable, such as certified mail?

Kristy read the statement, "Under penalties of perjury, I declare that I have examined this return, and to the best of my knowledge and belief, it is true, correct, and accurately lists all amounts and sources of income I received during the tax year." She followed the instructions carefully. Kristy went back and rechecked her figures. To the best of her knowledge, Kristy had correctly completed her return. She signed her name and wrote the date on the form. She also wrote in her occupation and phone number.

As the last step, Kristy attached Copy B of her Form W-2 to her Form 1040EZ. She sent her return by mail to the Internal Revenue Service Center that serves her area.

As you have seen, filing a tax return using Form 1040EZ is not difficult if you carefully follow each step. A checklist appears in the instructions for Form 1040EZ to help taxpayers avoid making common mistakes when preparing their tax returns.

Social Security

You may be wondering exactly what social security is and why a portion of your paycheck is deducted for it. As you learned in Chapter 2, Social Security is the federal government's program for providing income when family earnings are reduced or stopped because of retirement, disability, or death. The purpose of social security is to provide a basic level of income that people can build on with savings, pensions, investments, or other insurance. It is not intended to replace the earnings a person formerly received. Social security taxes also help provide hospital insurance to older adults and people with disabilities through the Medicare program, which is discussed later in this chapter.

Most workers pay social security taxes and are eligible to receive benefits. Employees not covered by social security are covered by other forms of insurance. Some exceptions include federal government workers employed before 1984, railroad workers, and some state and local government employees. Another exception to paying social security tax is a teen under age 18 who works for his or her parent(s). However, that person must start paying social security taxes at age 18.

Besides employees, all employers pay social security taxes, too. The social security tax is figured as a percentage of an employee's income. Whatever an employee pays in social security taxes, the employer must pay an equal amount. The employer deducts the tax from each employee's paycheck. Then the employer sends this amount and the employer's share to the IRS under the employee's name and social security number. The amount of social security tax deducted appears on an employee's paycheck stub under the *FICA* heading.

Reflect

Draw conclusions about why the federal government includes the statement beginning with "Under penalties of perjury, and to the best of my knowledge..." preceding the signature line on a tax return form.

Enrich

Research recent newspaper and magazine articles regarding concerns about the federal government's Social Security program. What issues are of top concern? Why?

Discuss

Why should people not depend on social security income as their sole source of income after retirement?

In the Real World

Gary's First Paycheck

Gary couldn't wait to get his first paycheck. He had worked hard for two weeks and had carefully calculated how much he would be paid. He had big plans for every penny of it since Gary was usually broke on the small allowance from his parents.

First, he planned to fill his truck with gas. The gas gauge on his old pickup truck hadn't surpassed a quarter tank in the two years he owned it. Next, he would pay off the portable DVD player he had on layaway. Finally, he would celebrate on Saturday night. It had taken all his courage to ask Janet for a date, and she had accepted. Gary planned to take her to a rock concert downtown—a date that would surely impress her as he shared his new wealth.

When Gary opened his pay envelope, he was shocked! It was less than half of what he had expected. He would hardly have enough to pay for his gas and lunches for the next two weeks. The DVD player had to stay on layaway.

He'd have to borrow money from his parents again if he wanted to keep his date with Janet.

"It's not fair!" Gary shouted as he looked at his check in disbelief. He was also surprised that the pay was for one week instead of two.

He quickly focused on the check stub to try to find errors. There were deductions titled *FICA, Fed W/H, State W/H, Pension Fund,* and *Employee Stock Purchase Program.* He could only remember agreeing to the stock purchase program and wondered what all the other deductions were.

Questions to Discuss

1. Why did Gary's employer withhold one week's pay from his first paycheck?
2. What does *Fed W/H* and *State W/H* mean? Why were they automatically withheld from Gary's paycheck?
3. Why was Gary required to contribute to both FICA and a private pension fund? Why should he be required to contribute to retirement funds at all?

Social Security Benefits

The social security taxes deducted from your paycheck pay for the benefits others receive. When you retire, become disabled, or die, the taxes of others will pay for the benefits you and your family will receive. Before you can receive benefits, you must earn a certain number of *social security credits.* You earn social security credits as you work and make contributions to social security. The number of credits you receive is based on how much you earn. For example, you might earn one credit for each $1,000 in net earnings for the year. However, the amount of earnings required to earn one credit may change from year to year. It is based on the amount of money an average worker makes. You may earn a maximum of four credits for any given year.

The amount of the benefits received depends on a worker's average earnings over a period of years and the worker's age. The benefits provided by the Social Security program include the following types:

- retirement benefits
- disability benefits
- survivors' benefits
- Medicare benefits
- Medicaid benefits

Resource

Government Insurance Programs, Activity F, WB

Activity

Use the Social Security Administration Web site (www.ssa.gov) to research information on the number of social security credits needed for retirement, disability, or survivor benefits.

Retirement Benefits

Workers born before 1938 become eligible for full retirement benefits at age 65. (The age for receiving full benefits will gradually increase until it reaches age 67 for individuals born after 1959). See 23-11. Workers may retire as early as age 62, but they will receive lower retirement benefits. The amount of reduction depends on the number of months the worker gets checks before he or she reaches 65. If a worker chooses to start getting checks early, the worker may get about the same value in total benefits over the years as the worker who retires at 65. However, the amount per pay period will be smaller to take into account the longer period the worker will be getting checks. Monthly retirement benefits may also be made to a worker's children and/or spouse under certain conditions.

Disability Benefits

A worker who becomes severely disabled before age 65 can receive disability checks. Under Social Security, a worker is considered disabled if he or she has a severe physical or mental condition that prevents him or her from working and is expected to last (or has lasted) for at least 12 months, or is expected to result in death. The benefits continue for as long as a worker is disabled and cannot work. A worker with disabilities whose benefits continue for more than two years becomes eligible for Medicare benefits. Disability benefits may also be paid to a disabled worker's children and/or spouse under certain conditions.

Survivors' Benefits

If a worker dies, survivors' benefits can be paid to certain members of the worker's family. A single, lump-sum payment can also be made when a worker dies. This payment can only be made if there is an eligible surviving widow, widower, or entitled child. Monthly survivors' benefits may be paid to a deceased worker's surviving children and/or spouse under certain conditions.

23-11

Social security benefits can help people enjoy their retirement years.

Social security benefits do not start automatically. When a person becomes eligible, he or she must apply for them at the nearest Social Security office. The *Social Security Administration* calculates the benefits and issues the monthly payments.

When you are planning to retire, contact the Social Security office in your area a few months before you actually retire. This will give the office plenty of time to calculate your benefits so you can get your first payment on time. It is also a good idea to keep track of your social security earnings. The Social Security Administration mails an annual statement to workers and former workers aged 25 and older. You may also request a statement at anytime. It is also a good idea to check your social security record every three years to make sure that your earnings are being correctly reported to your record. You can get a free form at any Social Security office for this purpose, 23-12. You can also order a form at the Social Security Administration's Web site (www.ssa.gov).

Activity

Download and complete a request for social security statement with your personal information.

Reflect Further

Should the federal government provide disability and survivor's benefits? Why or why not?

Form Approved
OMB No. 0960-0446   [   ] SP

Request for *Social Security Statement*

[ ] Please check this box if you want to get your *Statement* in Spanish instead of English.

Please print or type your answers. When you have completed the form, fold it and mail it to us. If you prefer to send your request using the Internet, contact us at *www.socialsecurity.gov*.

1. Name shown on your Social Security card:

_____   _____
First Name   Middle Initial

_____
Last Name Only

2. Your Social Security number as shown on your card:

[ ][ ][ ] - [ ][ ] - [ ][ ][ ][ ]

3. Your date of birth (Mo.-Day-Yr.)

[ ][ ] - [ ][ ] - [ ][ ][ ][ ]

4. Other Social Security numbers you have used:

[ ][ ][ ] - [ ][ ] - [ ][ ][ ][ ]
[ ][ ][ ] - [ ][ ] - [ ][ ][ ][ ]

5. Your Sex: [ ] Male   [ ] Female

For items 6 and 8 show only earnings covered by Social Security. Do NOT include wages from state, local or federal government employment that are NOT covered by Social Security or that are covered ONLY by Medicare.

6. Show your actual earnings (wages and/or net self-employment income) for last year and your estimated earnings for this year.

A. Last year's actual earnings: *(Dollars Only)*

$ [ ][ ][ ] , [ ][ ][ ] . [0][0]

B. This year's estimated earnings: *(Dollars Only)*

$ [ ][ ][ ] , [ ][ ][ ] . [0][0]

7. Show the age at which you plan to stop working:

[ ][ ] *(Show only one age)*

8. Below, show the average yearly amount (not your total future lifetime earnings) that you think you will earn between now and when you plan to stop working. Include performance or scheduled pay increases or bonuses, but not cost-of-living increases.

If you expect to earn significantly more or less in the future due to promotions, job changes, part-time work, or an absence from the work force, enter the amount that most closely reflects your future average yearly earnings.

If you don't expect any significant changes, show the same amount you are earning now (the amount in 6B).

Future average yearly earnings: *(Dollars Only)*

$ [ ][ ][ ] , [ ][ ][ ] . [0][0]

9. Do you want us to send the *Statement*:
   • To you? Enter your name and mailing address.
   • To someone else (your accountant, pension plan, etc.)? Enter your name with "c/o" and the name and address of that person or organization.

_____
"C/O" or Street Address (Include Apt. No., P.O. Box, Rural Route)

_____
Street Address

_____
Street Address (If Foreign Address, enter City, Province, Postal Code)

_____
U.S. City, State, ZIP code (If Foreign Address, enter Name of Country only)

NOTICE:
I am asking for information about my own Social Security record or the record of a person I am authorized to represent. I declare under penalty of perjury that I have examined all the information on this form, and on any accompanying statements or forms, and it is true and correct to the best of my knowledge. I authorize you to use a contractor to send the *Social Security Statement* to the person and address in item 9.

▶ _____
Please sign your name (Do Not Print)

_____   _____
Date   (Area Code) Daytime Telephone No.

Form **SSA-7004-SM** (10-2006) EF (10-2006)   Printed on recycled paper

---

23-12

Use this form to request a free statement of your earnings covered by social security and your estimated future benefits.

Supplemental Security Income

Supplemental Security Income (SSI) is another program administered by the Social Security Administration. It pays benefits to individuals with disabilities who have few possessions or little income. The supplemental security income differs from other Social Security programs because it is funded through general tax revenues, not social security taxes. Unlike social security, benefits are not based on your work history and the amount of past earnings.

Medicare Benefits

Medicare is the health insurance program provided through social security. It is reserved for people 65 or older, people of any age with permanent kidney failure, and certain people with disabilities, 23-13. Until Medicare became available, health insurance coverage for older citizens and people with disabilities was very expensive and difficult to get. Medicare was created to provide these groups of people with affordable health insurance. The Medicare program provides for three types of coverage: Part A hospital insurance, Part B medical insurance, and Part D prescription drug coverage.

The hospital insurance helps pay for inpatient hospital care, inpatient care in a skilled nursing facility, home health care, and hospice care. Medicare pays for all covered services except for the hospital insurance deductible. The deductible is a set dollar amount the patient must pay before Medicare will pay a claim. After the patient pays the deductible, Medicare pays the rest. However, if the patient stays in a hospital or nursing facility beyond a specific length of time, the patient must then pay a share of the costs. There may be other limitation to Medicare hospital coverage.

Part B, the medical insurance of Medicare, helps pay for physicians' services, outpatient health care, and outpatient physical therapy. It also helps pay for some home health care and many other health services and supplies that are not covered by the Medicare hospital insurance. Enrollment in Part B is optional. Those who choose to enroll in the program pay a monthly premium. The premiums, along with government funds, help finance the program. Patients pay an annual deductible. This means they must pay a set dollar amount of their covered medical expenses each year. Then the medical insurance pays the larger percent of the approved charges for other services received during the rest of the year. The patient is responsible for the remaining amount.

23-13

Medicare helps people over age 65 meet their health care costs.

Part D coverage helps individuals defray the high costs of prescription drugs. Private companies approved by Medicare offer these insurance plans. Enrollment in this program is optional.

Individuals may choose to enroll in Medicare Advantage Plans. They replace Medicare parts A and B, and possibly Part D coverage. These plans are offered by private insurance companies approved by Medicare. You can learn more about Medicare at www.medicare.gov.

Medicaid Benefits

Medicaid is another health care program funded by the government. Medicaid pays for the health care services of those people who cannot pay for them. This may include low-income people who are aged, blind, or disabled. To receive these services, patients must apply in the state where they live. Applications are available at local public aid or welfare offices.

This medical assistance program is financed with federal, state, and local funds. However, it is managed by participating states. Each state sets an income level for acceptance into its program. People receiving public assistance or incomes below the levels set by the state are eligible. Payment levels for hospitals and for doctors who treat Medicaid patients are also set by the state. In most states, Medicaid programs cover hospital, laboratory, and clinic services. Some states pay for other services, including dental care, eye care, home health care, and family planning.

Workers' Compensation

Workers' compensation is another insurance program managed by the states. As explained in Chapter 9, workers' compensation provides payments to workers when they are injured on the job. By law, all states now have this program. However, the laws may differ slightly from state to state. The premiums are paid by the employer to the state.

When workers are injured on the job, they are entitled to certain benefits. A deceased worker's family is also eligible for certain benefits. Insurance against work-related diseases (caused by working conditions) is covered by workers' compensation, too. The major benefits provided by workers' compensation are the following:

- medical care benefits
- disability income
- rehabilitation benefits
- death benefits

Thinking It Through

What are some benefits of the Social Security program? How does a person receive them?

Thinking It Through

How is Medicaid different from Medicare?

Activity

Invite a Medicaid representative to class to discuss Medicaid programs. Have students prepare questions in advance of the speaker's presentation.

Enrich

Have students access your state's Web site to research specific requirements for worker's compensation benefits.

Reflect Further

Why are workers' compensation laws important to employees?

Medical Care Benefits

This program covers the cost of all medical expenses, usually without any time or cost limitations. It includes hospital costs, doctors' fees, and rehabilitation services, 23-14.

Disability Income

When workers are disabled and unable to return to work, they receive income benefits. They are paid a percentage (usually two-thirds) of their average weekly wage until they return to work. Permanently disabled workers receive payments for the rest of their lives.

Rehabilitation Benefits

Each state provides funding for retraining workers who must give up their jobs due to injuries. Medical and vocational rehabilitation, which includes training, counseling, and job placement, are available. Joan's case is one example.

Joan lost her left hand in a construction accident. Under workers' compensation, she received medical care and disability income. After her injury healed, she was placed in a rehabilitation program. Joan knew she did not want to go back to doing physical labor in construction. Instead, she chose to be retrained as a construction estimator. She learned how to estimate costs, prepare quality surveys, and prepare bids. After she completed the two-year program, she became a construction estimator. The rehabilitation program helped her find employment in her new career.

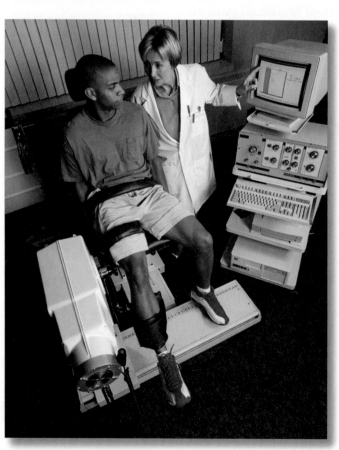

23-14

If you have been injured on the job, you may receive rehabilitation benefits through workers' compensation.

Death Benefits

The surviving spouse or children of a deceased worker receive a certain amount of income as a death benefit. The amount is usually based on the worker's average wage, but this varies from state to state.

Unemployment Insurance

Unemployment insurance provides benefits to workers who have lost their jobs. Employers are taxed by the state to help fund the program, although some states also contribute. Nothing is deducted from the employee's wages to pay for this protection. Insurance payments are managed by each state's government.

To receive benefits, unemployed workers must meet certain requirements. Each state has its rules, but some common requirements exist. Workers must have worked for a certain period of time, usually for one year, before becoming unemployed. They must have lost their job through no fault of their own. For example, if business is slow some employers may be forced to lay off workers. In this case, the workers would not be at fault. Workers must also register at their local employment office and be willing to take a job similar to the one they lost.

Unemployment benefits are temporary, not permanent. Their purpose is to provide some income security until workers find new jobs or are rehired by their employer. A maximum number of weeks for receiving benefits is set by each state. Workers receive benefits based on length of employment and amount of earnings. In most cases, this amounts to one-half their normal full-time pay. All these benefits are taxable as wages.

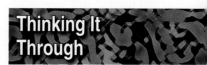

Thinking It Through

What is the purpose of unemployment insurance?

Summary

As an employee, you are paid some form of income for doing a job. Your employer may also offer fringe benefits in addition to your regular paycheck. These may include insurance, vacation time, holidays, and sick leave.

Your paycheck contains information about your earned income and deductions. Part of the money deducted from your paycheck goes toward personal income and social security taxes. Tax dollars paid to the government help provide a variety of services and facilities.

As a wage earner, you are responsible for filing an income tax return each year. The W-2 Form you receive from your employer shows the total wages and taxes withheld from your paycheck the previous year. You use it with Form 1040EZ, 1040A or 1040 to file your federal tax return.

Part of the tax deductions from your paycheck goes toward social security. Social Security is a federal program that provides benefits to eligible workers. It provides retirement, disability, and survivor benefits. Affordable health care insurance is offered to older or disabled people through Medicare. Medicaid is another social health care program managed by participating states.

Two other types of insurance programs created by the government offer benefits to workers. Workers' compensation offers medical care, disability income, and rehabilitation services to workers injured on the job. Death benefits are paid to surviving families of deceased workers. Unemployment insurance provides temporary help to those workers who have lost their jobs.

Facts in Review

1. Name four forms of income an employee may receive for doing a job.
2. Explain the difference between gross pay and net pay.
3. Name the two primary deductions made from an employee's paycheck. What other deductions may be withheld from a paycheck?
4. What is an exemption?
5. What is the primary purpose of taxes?
6. Name the five most common taxes people pay during their lives.
7. Explain the difference between direct and indirect taxes. Give an example of each.
8. Explain the difference between progressive and regressive taxes. Give an example of each.
9. What is a W-2 Form and what purpose does it serve?
10. Which two forms for filing federal income taxes are relatively simple to fill?
11. Which form for filing federal income taxes sometimes requires the help of a tax specialist?
12. What is the purpose of the Social Security program? Describe the three types of benefits it provides.
13. What is Medicare?
14. What three types of coverage are provided by Medicare?
15. List the major benefits provided by workers' compensation.

Resource

Review and Study Guide for Chapter 23, reproducible master 23-3, TR

Answers to *Facts In Review*

1. (List four:) wage, salary, commission, piecework, tips, bonus, fringe benefits
2. Gross pay is total earnings. Net pay is gross pay minus deductions.
3. federal income tax, FICA; other paycheck deductions—state/local income tax, retirement plan, union dues, insurance premiums, savings plan, charitable contributions
4. an amount of income not subject to taxes
5. to pay for government services and facilities

6. personal income, social security (FICA), property, sales, and excise taxes
7. Direct taxes are charged directly to the taxpayer. Indirect taxes are included in the price of an item. (Examples are student response.)
8. Progressive taxes take a greater share of income from the rich than from the poor, while regressive taxes do the opposite. (Examples are student response.)
9. Wage and Tax Statement; summarizes the previous year's income and deductions
10. Forms 1040EZ and 1040A

(continued)

Developing Your Academic Skills

1. **Math.** Using sample pay stubs provided by your instructor, figure out what percentages of the gross pay on each pay stub were deducted for FICA, federal withholding tax, state withholding tax, insurance, union dues, or retirement plan.
2. **Social Studies.** Investigate some government services paid for by taxes. Find out what percentage of overall tax dollars each service receives.
3. **Language Arts.** Write to the nearest state employment office to find out what requirements an unemployed worker must meet to receive unemployment benefits.

Information Technology Applications

1. Simulate filing taxes using a tax form software program. Do you think the software would be easier to use than printed forms? Explain why.
2. Investigate the Social Security Web site (www.ssa.gov) to see the most recent information posted about benefits and forms.

11. Form 1040
12. to provide a basic level of income that people can supplement with savings, pensions, investments, or other insurance; retirement, disability, and survivors' benefits
13. the federal government's health insurance program for people age 65 or older, victims of permanent kidney failure, or certain people with disabilities
14. hospital insurance, medical insurance, prescription drug coverage
15. medical care benefits, disability income, rehabilitation benefits, death benefits

Applying Your Knowledge and Skills

1. **Communications.** Contact two or three companies in your area that offer profit sharing. Find out what kinds of rewards are offered and what the employees must do to qualify for them. Report your findings to the class.
2. **Systems.** Make an appointment to visit a local government official at your village or city hall. Find out how your village or city assesses local taxes and what services they provide. If you do not live in a village or within city limits, visit the county or town hall closest to your home. Find out what services are provided that residents must pay extra to receive. Ask about police and fire department services; water and sewer service; and garbage collection.
3. **Systems.** Obtain copies of Form 1040EZ, Form 1040A, and the instructions for filing each. Underline and discuss in class any words, phrases, or instructions you do not understand on the forms. Then discuss the types of taxpayers who can use these forms and the proper way to complete them.
4. **Problem Solving and Critical Thinking.** Visit or write the Social Security office nearest you to obtain pamphlets about the Social Security program and Medicare. Using this information, explain in a one- or two-page written report who can receive social security benefits and Medicare insurance. Also, explain how a person obtains each.
5. **Communications.** Have an employee who has received rehabilitation under workers' compensation talk to your class.

Developing Workplace Skills

Organize a debate team with two or three of your classmates to examine the issue of Social Security. Debate the question: "Should citizens be required to contribute to the Social Security system?" Research and follow formal debating rules. Use the Internet and school library resources to determine current arguments on the pros and cons of Social Security.

24

Managing Spending

Key Terms

budget

emergency cash fund

consumers

goods

services

warranty

service contract

impulse buying

comparison shopping

recourse

Better Business Bureau (BBB)

Consumer Product Safety Commission (CPSC)

Food and Drug Administration (FDA)

Federal Trade Commission (FTC)

Federal Communications Commission (FCC)

consumer fraud

skimming

phishing

Chapter Objectives

After studying this chapter, you will be able to

- **prepare** a budget to help you manage your money wisely.
- **identify and use** reliable sources of consumer information.
- **explain** the methods businesses use to promote goods and services.
- **make decisions** about where and how to shop.
- **describe** your consumer rights and responsibilities.
- **explain** how your consumer rights are protected.
- **demonstrate** ways to avoid consumer fraud.

Reading Advantage

Look up this chapter in the table of contents. Use the detailed contents as an outline for taking notes as you read the chapter.

Achieving Academic Standards

English Language Arts

- Read print and non-print texts to acquire new information and to respond to the needs and demands of society and the workplace. (IRA/NCTE, 1)
- Apply strategies to comprehend, interpret, evaluate, and appreciate texts. (IRA/NCTE, 3)
- Use different writing process elements appropriately to communicate. (IRA/NCTE, 5)

Math

- Understand meanings of operations and how they relate to one another. (NCTM)
- Compute fluently and make reasonable estimates. (NCTM)

Key Concepts

- A budget helps you manage your income and expenses.

- Consumer resources are available to help you make wise shopping choices.

- As a consumer, you have certain rights and responsibilities.

- You can take steps to protect yourself from becoming a victim of consumer fraud.

Reflect

How effectively do you manage your money?

Discuss

Which is more important, the ability to make money or manage it?

Discuss

What advice would you give to Corey to help him handle his money?

Resource

Managing Your Money, Activity A, WB

Now that you are earning an income, what are you going to do with it? Are you going to spend it or save it? What expenses do you have now? What do you want to be able to buy in the future? How will you get the best value for the money you spend?

To make the most of the dollars you earn, you need to know how to manage your money. A budget is the first place to start managing your money wisely. A **budget** is a written plan to help you make the most of the money you have. Once you plan your budget, you will be more aware of how and why you spend your money.

The ability to buy wisely is just as important as planning your budget. With so many choices and temptations available in the marketplace, being a wise consumer is a challenge. Learning to spend your money wisely as you shop is a management skill you can develop with practice.

Budgeting Your Money

Consider the story of Tyrone and Cory. Both have worked for four years, earning the same income from their jobs. They each pay the same amount for rent, food, and transportation. Tyrone has a good used car, a versatile wardrobe, and a few nice pieces of furniture. He has also taken two out-of-state vacations since working. On the other hand, Cory has a beat-up car, an outdated wardrobe, and no savings. For four years, Cory has said he wants to take a vacation, but he never has enough money to do it. It seems he is constantly in debt or borrowing money.

Why is there such a difference between Tyrone's and Cory's finances? Tyrone has learned to manage his income and Cory has not. Tyrone's secret to good money management is a budget. A budget helps you do the following:

- control where your money goes
- work toward short-range and long-range goals
- keep from overspending
- reduce wasteful spending

Developing a budget involves five major steps: establishing financial goals, estimating your income and expenses, balancing your budget, keeping track of your income and expenses, and evaluating the budget. A sample monthly budget is shown in 24-1. This plan should help you organize a monthly budget of your own.

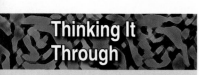
Thinking It Through

How can a budget help you manage your money?

Sample Plan for a Monthly Budget

Goals	Approximate cost	Date you want to attain the goal
Short-range _____	$ _____	_____
_____	_____	_____
Long-range _____	_____	_____
_____	_____	_____

Income	Budgeted	Actual	Difference	Expenses	Budgeted	Actual	Difference
				Fixed			
Salary	$_____	$_____	$_____	_____	$_____	$_____	$_____
Interest on savings	_____	_____	_____	_____	_____	_____	_____
Interest on investments	_____	_____	_____	_____	_____	_____	_____
Part-time work	_____	_____	_____	_____	_____	_____	_____
Other	_____	_____	_____	Flexible	_____	_____	_____
	_____	_____	_____		_____	_____	_____
	_____	_____	_____		_____	_____	_____
	_____	_____	_____		_____	_____	_____
	_____	_____	_____		_____	_____	_____
Total Income	$_____	$_____	$_____	Total Expenses	$_____	$_____	$_____

24-1

A budget should include a list of your financial goals, income, and expenses.

Establish Financial Goals

As with any plan, the first step in developing a budget is to set goals. Decide what you need and want. Start with your short-range goals; then write down your long-range goals. Short-range goals may include buying a CD player, a camera, or a new pair of shoes. Long-range goals may include saving money for a college education, a car, or a home. Another major goal should be to establish an **emergency cash fund**. This fund covers unexpected expenses, such as a new car tire. Once you have your goals listed, estimate the cost of each and the date you want to attain each goal. Then calculate how much money you would have to set aside each month to reach your goals.

Estimate Your Monthly Income and Expenses

The next step is to estimate your income. This includes your net pay and any other sources of income such as interest on savings and investments, part-time earnings, and allowances. Be conservative in estimating your income. For example, suppose you work twenty hours a week but may be able to work a few extra hours from time to time.

Discuss

What is the relationship between earning money and spending wisely?

Discuss

Why is it important to state your goals in writing? Why periodically review them?

Resource

Balance Income and Expenses, color transparency CT-24, TR

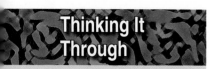

**Thinking It
Through**

Do you think most people
overestimate income or
underestimate expenses?

Estimate your income on the twenty hours, not the hours you are unsure of working. Otherwise you may end up planning to spend money you will not have if the extra hours do not come through.

The opposite is true of expenses. You will want to list all potential expenses even if you are not certain they will occur. For example, you will want to budget some money for car repair even though you do not think anything will go wrong with your automobile. That way you will more likely be able to handle all expenses that do occur.

There are certain expenses or commitments you will want to list first. A good rule of thumb is to pay yourself first. List all savings at the top of your list. Be sure to set aside money for each of the financial goals you established in step one. Setting aside money for your emergency fund is also a must. As you record other potential expenses, list them under two headings: fixed expenses and flexible expenses.

- *Fixed expenses* are the expenses that must be paid regularly. They include rent or mortgage payments, car payments, and insurance premiums. Since you have agreed to pay them by a certain due date, you must consider them first when listing expenses. You will want to keep fixed expenses to a minimum. Try not to make long range commitments for your money unless they are absolutely necessary. For example, it would be better to purchase an older, less expensive car for cash than buy a new one on credit.

- *Flexible expenses* are all the other expenses you have for which you pay varying amounts. Food, clothing, utilities, home furnishings and equipment, transportation, health care, recreation, and education are some of the flexible expenses you may have, 24-2.

24-2

Clothing accessories, such as jewelry, are flexible expenses. You can adjust these expenses to fit your income.

Balance Your Budget

To balance your budget, subtract the expenses you expect to have from the income you expect to get. If your monthly expenses exceed your income, you will need to either increase your income or decrease your expenses.

First try decreasing your expenses. Carefully examine your list of expenses. Do you really need everything on the list? You may have to make some hard choices. For example, you may have to give up that new shirt or CD you have been wanting. You still may be able to purchase a shirt but not the expensive brand name you prefer.

Your expenses should equal your income when you finalize your budget. It is very important that you account for every penny on paper before you actually start spending.

Now comes the hard part—living within your budget. Keeping accurate records of your actual income and expenses will help you accomplish this task.

Keep Track of Income and Expenses

Keep a record of all income you receive. Compare it to the income you estimated for yourself by recording it on your written budget plan. Record the difference between the estimate and the actual amount.

Keep a written list of everything you buy and the exact amount you pay for it. Record every purchase on your budget plan. Avoid spending any money that was not on your planned list of expenses. Again, compare your real expenses to the estimated total and record the difference.

Evaluate the Budget

The final step is to evaluate the budget. This step helps you to see if your budget is working for you. Consider the following questions as you evaluate your budget: Do you have enough income to cover your expenses? Is the budget flexible enough to handle unexpected expenses and emergencies? Is your money doing what you want it to do? Is your budget helping you reach important goals on schedule? See 24-3.

If you answered *no* to any of these questions, you will probably need to make some changes just as you did when planning your budget. You will need to find ways to increase your income or reduce certain expenses.

Keep in mind that your goals will change. As your goals change, your budget will need to change as well.

Managing Your Consumer Spending

You know that a well-planned budget can help you manage your money to get what you want and need. It can also help you reach your financial goals. Now that you have a budget planned, how do you get the most value from the money you have to spend? To stretch your shopping dollars, you need to manage your consumer spending and do the following:

- be an informed consumer
- understand advertising and other promotional methods
- know where to shop
- know how to shop

Thinking It Through

Why is it important to evaluate your budget?

24-3
Check your budget whenever your goals, income, or expenses change. You can expect your budget to change when you graduate, start a new job, or go to college.

Thinking It Through

What are the differences between buying goods and buying services?

Be an Informed Consumer

People who use their income to buy the items they need and want are called **consumers**. Consumers buy and use goods and services. **Goods** are any type of product consumers buy, such as food or clothing. Any type of work they pay to have done—hairstyling, repairs, or cleaning—are **services**.

Whenever you buy something—your lunch, a book, or a concert ticket—you are a consumer. You have been a consumer since your first purchase. As a consumer, you can choose from a wide variety of goods and services. Sometimes you are given so many choices that you may become confused. You may wonder how to get the most value from the money you have to spend.

To help get the most for your money, you need to become an informed consumer. With practice, you can learn to recognize the best buys among your choices and learn to shop wisely. As you learn to improve your buying habits, you can become a better consumer.

Use Available Resources

Informed consumers are smart shoppers. They make use of many resources before they make buying decisions. Resources provide up-to-date information on products, services, consumer laws, and the economy. It pays to learn as much as you can about a product or service before you buy.

Some of the resources available to you include people, places, organizations, and printed materials. For instance, if your goal is to buy a car, you have many resources available in your community to help you make your decision. An auto technician and an automotive technology teacher are examples of people resources who know about cars. The bank or library are places to go to find out about loan information or to research various models. A consumer organization could be a resource for car buying guidelines. All of these resources can provide some basic information to get you started in making your buying decision.

You can find consumer information for almost every product and service available. Talk to people who have used the product that interests you, such as salespeople and other consumers. An easy way to learn information from them is to ask questions. See 24-4.

Read and compare printed materials for information. These include advertisements, product labels and tags, use and care guides, and warranties. A **warranty** is a written promise that guarantees a product will meet certain performance and quality standards. It also tells what the manufacturer will do if the product fails to meet those promises. Although it is not found on all products, it can be used as a way to compare products. A warranty can be important for a product that may need servicing in the future. A household appliance is an example.

The type of warranty found on a product is either full or limited. A *full warranty* offers broad coverage on a product. The coverage includes free repair or replacement of the product or any defective parts within a reasonable time. If the product cannot be repaired after several attempts, it will be replaced. A

Resource

Be an Informed Consumer, reproducible master 24-1, TR

Reflect

What services do you buy? Could you do any of these yourself?

Enrich

Select an item you want to purchase and list as many resources for information about it as possible.

limited warranty offers less coverage. The customer may have to pay labor costs or handling charges to repair a product. It may cover repairs and not replacement of the product. In either case, read the warranty carefully before you buy.

You should always check the length of the warranty. Some warranties may only be good for 30 days. Others may be good for a year or two. Some companies even offer lifetime warranties on some products. In some cases a company may offer both a limited and full warranty on the same product. For example, a stereo may have a full warranty on parts and labor for ninety days and an additional five-year limited warranty on parts only.

Many stores and companies offer an *extended warranty*, which extends a warranty for an additional time period for an additional cost. An extended warranty is actually a **service contract**. The cost of a warranty is covered in the purchase price of a product. A service contract costs extra. Most consumer groups do not recommend the purchase of service contracts as a good buy. Sometimes the service contract will even cost more than the product itself.

It is important to remember that a warranty is only as good as the company that provides the warranty. A full warranty from a dishonest or disreputable company may be no better than no warranty at all. It is also important to remember to save the sales receipt and store it with a copy of the warranty. Chances are you will need to prove the date of purchase if you should ever need warranty service.

Newspapers, books, and magazines are other sources that offer information on many consumer buying issues. Newspapers provide information and advertisements about food, clothing, transportation, and home furnishings. You will find consumer-related books and magazines at your school or local library. Check the library file and reference section for buying information on consumer products and services. Relevant articles appear in many popular magazines. If you cannot find the information on your own, ask the librarian for help.

Consumer information is also published by government agencies. The purpose of these publications is to keep consumers informed about consumer issues. Many of these agencies and organizations also maintain Internet sites from which you can review consumer information and order printed copies of their publications. The U.S. Consumer Information Center (www.pueblo.gsa.gov) in Pueblo, Colorado, prints booklets with tips and guidelines for buying many consumer products. The *Consumer Action Handbook* is a particularly helpful booklet from this source.

Various nonprofit consumer organizations also test, evaluate, and rate consumer products. Perhaps the best known is Consumers Union (www.consumerreports.org), which reports its test results in a monthly magazine called *Consumer Reports*. At the end of each year, it also publishes a buying guide with summaries of product test results.

24-4
Talking to a knowledgeable salesperson and checking product tags and labels are excellent ways to gather information in the store.

Thinking It Through

Is it a good idea to purchase a service contract for a newly purchased product?

Discuss

What are the advantages and disadvantages of purchasing warranty coverage?

Reflect Further

What sources of information have you found most helpful when buying goods and services?

How do you evaluate the many sources of information available? When evaluating consumer information of any kind, use the questions listed in 24-5 as a guide.

Understand Advertising and Other Promotional Methods

Before you buy any product or service, you should be aware of the methods businesses use to promote their goods and services. They use selling methods such as advertising, sales, and incentives to attract your attention and encourage you to buy. They do this to increase sales and profits.

How can you make advertising work for you? If you understand that the main purpose of advertising is to sell goods and services, you can use the information to help buy what you need.

Advertising

Businesses use the Internet, radio, television, magazines, newspapers, direct mail, and billboards to advertise their goods and services. Using these channels, they inform you about their goods and services. Because you see and hear so many ads every day, you may not be aware of their effects on your buying behavior. Ads can influence how you spend your money. As a consumer, keep in mind the main purpose of advertising is to sell.

Advertising plays an important role in our economy. Through advertising, consumers learn more about the many goods and services available to them. Consumers can use ads to compare products and

24-5

Use these evaluation questions to sort through the consumer information you gather. Then you can use the information to make smarter buying decisions.

Enrich

Select an expensive item you want. Gather information about the item using all the resources you can find.

Resource

The Pros and Cons of Advertising, reproducible master 24-2, TR

Resource

Advertising Evaluation Checklist, transparency master 24-3, TR

Evaluating Consumer Information
Quality and Reliability of the Source
Is the source well-known and respected in the field?
Does the source have a reputation for being knowledgeable in the subject area?
Purpose of the Information
Is the information designed to be factual and informative or merely entertaining?
Is the information designed to promote one product (or service) over another?
Does the information present all the pros and cons of buying the product (or service)?
Usefulness of the Information
Is the information up-to-date, factual, and easy to understand?
Does it tell you what you want to know about the features, quality, and price of the product (or service)?

In the Real World

Cortez Buys Running Shoes

Cortez wanted to be a runner and make the school's track team. First he needed to buy running shoes so he could start training. He saved his money until he had enough to buy an expensive pair of running shoes. The shoes he chose were a popular brand advertised on television by a famous track star. Cortez thought they should be top-of-the-line running shoes. After all, a track star wouldn't wear inferior shoes!

Cortez's good friend Nathan also wanted to make the school's track team. Nathan bought a pair of running shoes too, but his shoes were less expensive than Cortez's shoes. Nathan's shoes were not endorsed by any track star, either.

Cortez and Nathan ran together every day. They had a planned route that covered several miles. After two months, Nathan's shoes were holding up well. Cortez's shoes were not. The seams were coming apart and the soles were worn.

Cortez decided to talk to the track coach about the shoes. The coach told him they were not as well made as some other brands. Cortez then realized that a track star's endorsement did not always mean a top-quality product.

Questions to Discuss

1. How was Cortez influenced in his decision to buy running shoes?
2. If a popular person uses and likes an advertised product, is the product always top quality? Explain why or why not.
3. How could Cortez have used the information he saw in the television ad to make a wiser buying decision?

prices. Businesses are also able to market their products more efficiently. Advertising helps businesses introduce new or better products to the marketplace. The economy grows as consumers buy more goods and services.

Advertising, however, can be misleading. By law, businesses are banned from using false or misleading advertising to sell their goods or services. However, many ads still make exaggerated claims about goods or services. Since ads are designed to show products in positive ways, many ads tell you only the good things about the products.

As a consumer, you must carefully evaluate all the information in ads. Select only the information most helpful to you. Beware of ads that try to persuade you to buy what you do not need, do not want, or cannot afford. This approach will help you improve your buying decisions.

Other Promotional Methods

Businesses use special sales or promotions as selling methods to attract customers and increase sales. Special sales offer products or services at reduced prices. Reduced prices benefit businesses because their sales and profits increase. Promotions draw attention to a product or service through advertising or publicity, 24-6. "Buy one, get one free" is an example.

Thinking It Through

What types of advertising messages get your attention?

Reflect

Have you ever purchased a product because of a celebrity's endorsement? If so, were you pleased with your choice?

Resource

Advertising, Activity D, WB

24-6
This store is advertising a special promotion to attract customers.

Reflect Further

How have you been influenced by advertisements or promotions to buy goods and/or services you didn't really want?

Businesses often offer *buying incentives* to consumers to help sell products. Coupons, prizes, and in-store games are examples of buying incentives. They can be found in retail stores, magazines, and newspapers.

If you are interested in buying or trying certain products or services, you may benefit from using these promotional methods. When you buy something you need on sale, you are spending your money wisely. If you do not really need it or cannot use it, it is not a good buy. Also remember that just because something is on sale does not mean that it is a good value. One store's sale price may be higher than another store's everyday price.

Decide Where to Shop

Once you have an item in mind to buy, you must decide where to shop. You will find the marketplace is made up of many different places to shop. Therefore, your choices will be affected by many factors, including what you want to buy. You may choose to shop at different stores for different items. Other factors to consider include store location, price, and product selection.

As an informed consumer, you should be aware of the many types of stores in your shopping area. Knowing this will save you time and energy when you go shopping. Besides retail shopping, you may also want to consider other types of shopping choices to meet your needs. These include direct selling, as well as catalog, mail order, television, and Internet shopping.

In deciding where to shop, location is an important factor to consider. The stores you shop at may depend on where you live, what you are buying, and what is convenient for you.

In large cities, consumers can find competitive prices and large selections in shopping malls, shopping centers, and large retail stores, 24-7. These facilities are usually conveniently located with free parking.

Discuss

What are the advantages and disadvantages of promotional methods to both the business and the consumer?

Enrich

Find examples of special sales, promotions, and buying incentives. Share them in class.

Resource

Where to Shop, Activity E, WB

24-7
Shopping malls offer the advantage of one-stop shopping for many busy consumers.

In less-populated areas, consumers may have fewer stores from which to choose. Although store locations may be convenient, merchandise selections may be limited. This may make comparison shopping more difficult.

Neighborhood stores and shops may offer more personalized service and convenient locations. However, they may have a limited selection and charge higher prices because of less competition and fewer sales.

Retail Shopping

Retail stores sell products or services directly to consumers. Consumers can choose from a variety of retail stores, including department stores, discount stores, specialty stores, and factory outlets.

Department stores offer a wide variety of merchandise to shoppers. Departments within the stores sell lines of brand name and private label (the store's own brand) products. Besides a wide selection of products, they offer customer services such as delivery and exchanges. These stores may be part of a chain of stores or independently owned.

Discount stores sell merchandise at prices lower than other retailers. Although prices on most items may be lower, fewer customer services may be offered. By selling a higher volume of goods and cutting services, they can keep most prices low.

Specialty stores sell a wide selection of one type of product or service, 24-8. Athletic shoe stores, record stores, and hair salons are just a few examples.

Factory outlets sell discontinued, slightly flawed, or overstocked items. These stores are often operated by the companies who produce the products. They have fewer employees and customer services. Although prices are lower than most retail stores, items should be carefully examined before you buy.

Reflect

What factors influence your decision regarding where to shop?

Discuss

What are some advantages of buying from department stores?

Discuss

Do discount stores always offer lower prices than department stores?

Thinking It Through

If you wanted to buy a pair of athletic shoes, which type of store would you choose?

24-8
Consumers can choose from a wide selection of candy at this type of specialty store, which is often located in a shopping mall.

Direct Selling

Buying from a door-to-door salesperson or from an in-home party is a form of direct selling. This type of shopping offers some advantages and disadvantages. The convenience of shopping from home and the chance to examine and try products are advantages. Disadvantages include a smaller selection of products, a limited return policy, or a dishonest salesperson.

Use caution when dealing with door-to-door salespeople. Most of them represent reliable companies with good products. However, it is up to you to check them out first. Ask to see their identification and selling permit or license. If you are still in doubt, call the Better Business Bureau or local chamber of commerce. Deal only with well-known sellers.

Catalog and Mail-Order Shopping

Almost every product is available through catalog and mail-order shopping. This type of shopping is very popular today. The convenience and time saved by shopping at home appeals to many consumers. However, shopping by mail does have some drawbacks.

Before making a catalog purchase, consider the pros and cons of this type of shopping, 24-9. Remember, most mail-order retailers try to provide quality items and good customer service. They depend on repeat orders to stay in business. Some mail-order retailers, however, may take advantage of customers. They may fail to deliver an item, or send a poor quality item.

Before ordering any items by mail, check out the mail-order retailer carefully. The following guidelines can help you buy wisely when shopping by mail:

- Read the ordering and warranties section of catalogs carefully before you order. Find out the company's policy for returning items in case you are not satisfied.

- Fill out the order form completely and accurately before you mail it.

- Pay by check or money order. Do not send cash. Include any shipping or handling fees and applicable taxes with your payment.

- Keep a record of your order. Write down the date, item cost, check number, company name and address, and item description.

- If your order does not arrive within 30 days, call the company. (Most companies have a toll-free number that you may call.) Ask them to check your order to see where it is.

Shopping by Mail, TV, or the Internet

Advantages

- Time savings—Busy people can avoid shopping crowds and traffic and simply shop from home.

- Money savings—Some items may be purchased for cheaper prices than at retail stores.

- Wide selection—A variety of items are offered.

- Convenience—Customers can shop at home and avoid dealing with a salesperson. They can use a credit card, phone in their order, or order by mail.

Disadvantages

- Possible extra charges—Some retailers charge extra handling fees or a cost to obtain their catalogs.

- Must rely on pictures—You can't see, feel, or try on the actual item before buying it. Colors, materials, and sizes may not be as they appear.

- Shipping delays—You have to wait for the item to be shipped, which may take days or weeks. It may not arrive in time for a special occasion, such as a birthday or holiday.

- Shipping charges—Sometimes shipping charges can greatly increase the cost of the item.

- Merchandise-return hassles—If the item you receive does not fit, is not the right color, is damaged, or is the wrong item, you are responsible for returning it. This often involves extra postage charges.

- Possible failure to deliver—The company may take your money but fail to deliver your merchandise. You are then responsible for taking action against them.

- Security—Providing personal information including credit card numbers over the Internet or by mail could result in identity theft.

24-9
An informed consumer will carefully weigh the pros and cons of shopping by mail.

- When the order arrives, check it promptly to be sure the item is what you ordered and wanted and was not damaged in shipment. If something is wrong or you are not satisfied, notify the company right away.

Television Shopping

As with catalog and mail-order shopping, almost any product may be advertised on television. Some commercials also provide an address and phone number for placing an order. There are several advantages and disadvantages to shopping by television. These advantages and disadvantages are similar to shopping by mail.

In the past, commercials were only 30 or 60 seconds long. Because of this, few facts could be conveyed. Today some TV commercials

Thinking It Through

Have you ever purchased anything by mail? What was your experience?

Discuss

Is posting your credit card number on the Internet more or less secure than using the card in a store, gasoline service station, or ATM machine?

have lengthened into a half-hour program called an *infomercial*. These are TV commercials that appear to be news or information programs. Infomercials provide more facts than standard TV commercials do, but they have the same purpose—convincing consumers to buy.

Internet Shopping

Nearly everything from automobiles to jewelry can be purchased on the Internet. You can also find repair parts for items you already own. It is a great way to do comparison shopping. You can check out the features and warranties on products by visiting the Web site of the companies that manufacture the product. See 24-10.

While many of the advantages and disadvantages of Internet shopping are similar to catalog and television shopping, there are added problems. If you purchase items on the Internet, you will need to make sure the Web site is secure and reliable. When you purchase an item over the Internet using a credit card, it may become available for others to see. If someone gets your credit card number, he or she could use it to make purchases. Most companies have security features built into their checkout sites. Look for features such as security icons that tell you the site is secure. An *s* after *http* in the Web address indicates the site is secure.

There are several things you can do if you have a problem with a product you purchase through the Internet. First, complain to the merchant who sold you the product. If that does not work and you used a credit card to make the purchase, you can contact your credit card company. Finally, you can contact the Federal Trade Commission via phone (1-877-FTC-HELP) or the Internet site (www.ftc.gov).

Develop Shopping Skills

Making wise consumer decisions means choosing carefully from many goods and services. Prices, quality, and selection can vary among businesses. With practice, you can learn how to shop wisely and develop good shopping skills. When you have certain items in mind to buy, plan your shopping before you go. To get the best price and quality, practice comparison shopping.

Plan Your Shopping

Before you leave home to go shopping, decide what you want to buy. Then make a list. With a list, you will more likely buy the

If you have a credit card, it is easy to make purchases over the Internet.

items that best meet your needs. Whether you are shopping for food or buying a car, a well-planned list will help you in many ways. It will help you avoid confusion when you shop and buy the things you really need.

Planning in advance will also help you avoid impulse buying. **Impulse buying** is making an unplanned purchase. It is buying something you see without much thought. Through impulse buying, you may pay too much for an item or buy something you really do not need or cannot use. Resisting a good deal or a sale is often difficult. However, following a list will save you time, energy, and money when you do shop.

Do Comparison Shopping

Comparison shopping is one way to compare products before you buy. Looking at several brands or models at different stores allows you to compare prices, quality, and features before buying, 24-11. This helps you save money, get better quality, and find the product that best suits your needs.

When comparison shopping, always try to get the best value for the money you spend. Does that mean price is always the most important factor to consider in your buying decision? Not always. The ability to judge quality is just as important.

Price is not always a guide to a product's quality. Although a better-quality product usually costs more, sometimes a lower-cost product offers the same or better quality. For example, some consumers buy brand-name foods for higher prices because they think the quality is better. Many grocery stores, however, offer their own brand-name foods. Smart shoppers learn that the store's own brand of food is usually very close in quality and costs less.

Shopping for value also means judging the quality of a product. Learn to inspect products when you shop so you can recognize different quality levels, 24-12. Checking the quality of an item is important if you plan to use it often or for a long time. Higher quality products usually last longer, so they are a better value. They are made to higher standards of design, material, and performance. For example, you might consider buying a higher quality winter coat if you plan to wear it for several seasons. Even though it may be more costly, it will be a better value in the long run. Quality construction features, like reinforced pockets and secured buttons, will help it wear well.

Thinking It Through

Why is a shopping list so important? Have you ever made a wrong purchase because you forgot your list?

Resource

Comparison Shopping, Activity F, WB

24-11

This couple is comparison shopping. They are checking prices and features on appliances before making a choice.

24-12

Use this chart to evaluate and then to decide which product quality level best meets your needs.

Activity

Compare several different brands (including store brands) of the same item on cost, features, and quality. Are price and brand always an indication of quality?

Discuss

Are there any disadvantages to comparison shopping?

Enrich

Have a lawyer or consumer advocate speak to the class about consumer rights and responsibilities.

Thinking It Through

What factors should you consider when comparison shopping?

Choosing Quality Products		
Quality Level	**Description**	**Buy when...**
Best	Highest price range	you can afford the best and can justify the cost
	The best and most features; top of the line	the item will be used for a long time
	Highest standards for design, performance, and materials	top quality and performance are required to meet your buying needs
Good or Better	Mid-price range	good quality sells at the best price for your budget and suits your needs; reasonable price is important
	Standard features	good quality is acceptable for the way you will use the product
	Satisfactory standards for design, performance, and materials	durability and practicality are important
Low	Lowest price range	good quality is beyond your budget and you need the item
	Few features	lower quality suits your needs and the item will not be used often
	Lowest standards for design, performance, and materials	the item will be outdated or outgrown soon or rarely used

When comparison shopping, consider what features are important to you. Make a list of the features you want at the price you want to pay. If you are buying a microwave oven for college, you will not need a large-size model with complex controls. Wash-and-wear fabric is a good choice for clothing if you do not have extra money to pay for dry cleaning.

Exercising Your Consumer Rights and Responsibilities

Part of your responsibility as a consumer is to find reliable information about the goods and services you want to buy. You then use this information to help you make an informed buying decision. You have the right to choose from a large selection of goods and services at competitive prices. You also have the right to know the products and

In the Real World

Shopping for the Right Tennis Racket

Janelle wanted to buy a tennis racket. Since she just learned how to play, she didn't want to spend too much money on it. She decided the first step was to learn as much as she could about tennis rackets before buying. She talked to a friend on the tennis team at school. Next, she checked some online stores to compare prices and features. Then she went to a local sporting goods store to look at different brands and features of tennis rackets. Janelle found a variety of rackets. She asked one of the store clerks to explain the differences in price, quality, and features. Finally, she found a good quality racket at a price within her budget that seemed to meet her needs.

Before buying the racket, Janelle decided to do some comparison shopping at a few other stores. She wrote down the most important information—brand name, model number, features, and price—for the racket she liked. She checked two other stores that carried the brand and found the racket at a much lower price. When she bought the racket, Janelle felt satisfied in finding the right quality at the best price.

Questions to Discuss

1. What steps did Janelle follow in shopping for a tennis racket?
2. What factors might have influenced her choice of a racket?
3. Did Janelle make a smart shopping decision? Explain.

services you buy are safe. When a product or service is not satisfactory, you have the right to **recourse**. That means you have the right to complain and receive some response. A more detailed list of your consumer rights and responsibilities is outlined in 24-13.

Know the Right Way to Complain

What do you do when you order a product by mail and it arrives damaged? What do you do when you buy a new product and it fails to work properly one month later? When you have a problem with a product or service, you will need to complain to the right person right away.

Before you make a complaint, make sure you have your facts straight. Your new camera is broken, but did you drop it? Your new printer does not print. Did you install it correctly?

Do not complain about a product or service when you are the one at fault. You have the right to complain only when you have a valid reason for complaining.

As soon as you discover a problem, complain promptly. Do not let weeks or months go by before you contact the seller or manufacturer. Be sure to direct your complaint to the right person and place. Routine problems, such as returning or exchanging items, can be handled by salespeople or customer service employees. For more serious problems, you may need to talk with the store manager.

Thinking It Through

Do consumers exercise their responsibilities to the same degree they exercise their rights?

Resource

The Right Way to Complain, Activity G, WB

Discuss

What are some strategies you could use to avoid buying low-quality items?

Consumer Rights and Responsibilities	
You have the right to	**You have the responsibility to**
• **information**—to be informed	• find and use information before you buy goods and services
• **selection**—to be able to choose from a variety of goods and services	• select goods and services wisely
• **performance**—to expect products to perform as they should	• follow instructions and use products as they were meant to be used
• **safety**—to get safe products and services	• use products safely; report unsafe products to sellers, manufacturers, or government agencies
• **recourse**—to be heard if you are not happy with a product or service	• tell businesses or sellers what you like or dislike about their products or services

Writing a Complaint Letter

If your problem is not settled, the next step is to write a complaint letter. Write your letter to the company's consumer affairs department. Call the company to get the name and address of the person to contact. You can try to find the telephone number of the company by calling toll-free directory assistance (800-555-1212). You may also send a formal e-mail to the customer service link on the company's Web site.

If, however, you feel the problem is so serious that top management should be told, contact a person in charge of customer relations. To find the names of officers of large business firms, use *Standard and Poor's Register of Corporations, Directors and Executives*. This book is available in most libraries.

In your complaint letter, clearly identify the product or service that is not satisfactory. Then give a brief description of the problem. If possible, give the date and place of the purchase, the product name and model number, and the purchase price. At the close of the letter, suggest some type of action. Do you expect repairs, a replacement, a refund, or an apology? Let the reader know what you would like done about the problem. A sample complaint letter appears in 24-14.

As you write, be reasonable and calm. A sarcastic or threatening letter will not help get your problem solved.

In most cases, one letter directed to the right person will get the problem solved. However, if you do not get a satisfactory response, write a second letter. In the second complaint letter, enclose a copy of the first letter. Also include the names of consumer agencies or organizations whom you intend to contact if the situation is not settled by a certain date.

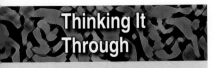

1124 E. Roberts Drive
Austin, TX 78735
July 20, 20xx

Mr. Bill Johnson
Customer Service Manager
Comfort Carpet Company
5000 S. Wood Road
Minneapolis, MN 55406

Dear Mr. Johnson:

On July 2, 20xx, I purchased a Comfort carpet from the Homerite Carpet Company in Austin, Texas. The style number is 548 and lot number is 16. I am enclosing photocopies of the sales receipt and warranty.

The carpet was installed, but it has a manufacturing defect. A bad oil stain runs the length of the carpet. When I contacted the Homerite Carpet Company, I was told they do not handle Comfort carpets anymore. They said I should write directly to you with the problem.

As the warranty shows, the carpet has a 10-year guarantee. I would like to have the carpet replaced as soon as possible. I would appreciate you contacting a carpet dealer in the Austin area to make the arrangements for replacing the carpet.

I will look forward to hearing from you regarding my carpet replacement. I appreciate your prompt attention to this problem.

Sincerely,

Ramone Barber

Ramone Barber

Your address and date

Name, title, company name, and address of contact person

Provide purchase information.

Explain the problem.

Suggest a solution to correct the problem.

24-14

A complaint letter should include a clear and complete explanation of a consumer's problem.

Extend Your Knowledge

Mailing a Complaint

When you mail a complaint letter, use *certified mail, return receipt requested*. Then you will have a record of the letter's delivery. The letter is hand-delivered and the receiver must sign for it. The sender is then sent a copy of the receiver's signed receipt. Before mailing, be sure to make a copy of your letter to keep in your records.

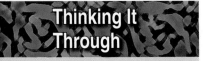

Enrich

Contact the Better Business Bureau office nearest you and find out the procedure for filing a complaint.

Thinking It Through

What should be done if a complaint about a product or service can't be settled with the local business that provided it?

Resource

Complaint Form, Activity I, WB

Activity

Have an action line reporter speak to the class on his or her experiences with consumer complaints.

Enrich

Make a collage of newspaper articles that describe lawsuits used to protect consumer rights.

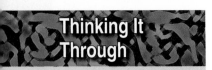

Thinking It Through

How do consumer protection agencies help protect your consumer rights?

Use Consumer Protection Services

If you fail to get satisfactory results from your complaint, you may need to contact a consumer organization or group for help. These groups can put pressure on a dishonest business or recommend a solution to the problem. Although they cannot force a business to accept their solution, they can have a strong influence. Most businesses would rather settle a complaint than risk a bad reputation with a consumer organization.

You can contact one or more of the following organizations or groups for additional help with your complaint.

- *Better Business Bureau (BBB)*—A nonprofit organization sponsored by private businesses, the **Better Business Bureau (BBB)** tries to settle consumer complaints against local business firms, 24-15. However, it has no power to prosecute. It also answers consumers' questions about the reputation of local businesses. These services are free to consumers. The national BBB may be found online at www.bbb.com.

  To file a complaint or to inquire about a company's reputation, call your local BBB. Most local BBBs also have their own Web site. It keeps files on many local businesses. The BBB can tell you how long a company has been in business and if any other consumer complaints have been filed. It will also tell you how the company resolved any previous complaints. The BBB is also a good place to start to learn about a company's reputation before doing business with them.

- *News media*—Some local newspapers and radio and TV stations have action lines to help settle complaints. This might be a good source to contact if the seller has advertised through the news media.

- *Consumer action groups*—Are you unhappy with the way an appliance company dealt with your broken stereo? Do you think a local car dealer is making unfair deals? If you have a complaint about a specific product or service, a consumer action group may be able to help. A consumer group consists of a panel of people who try to fairly judge your complaint. They listen to both sides of an issue and then give advice to settle the problem. For instance, the Direct Marketing Association (www.the-dma.org) may be able to assist with mail-order complaints. Check the Internet for the Web sites of other consumer groups.

BETTER BUSINESS BUREAU OF CHICAGO & NORTHERN ILLINOIS INC.

211 West Wacker Drive
Chicago, Illinois 60606
346-3313 – 10:00-2:30

COMPLAINT FORM

PLEASE FOLLOW ENCLOSED INSTRUCTIONS

Date of Transaction _____ Date You Complained To Company _____ To Whom _____

Sales Person _____ Identify Product/Service _____ If Advertised, When _____

Where (Enclose Ad) _____ Receipt, Contract or Policy Number _____

COMPANY_____ YOUR NAME_____

ADDRESS _____ ADDRESS _____

CITY_____ CITY_____
State   Zip Code   State   Zip Code

YOUR EMPLOYER'S FIRM NAME:_____ YOUR DAYTIME PHONE NO._____

BRIEFLY EXPLAIN YOUR COMPLAINT AND FOLLOW THE ENCLOSED INSTRUCTIONS:

_____
_____
_____
_____
_____
_____
_____
_____
_____
_____

What Adjustment Do You Consider Mutually Fair?

_____
_____

Your Signature   Date

| **BELOW THIS LINE FOR COMPANY RESPONSE** |

TO THE COMPANY: This complaint has been forwarded by one of your customers. BBB/Bureau has been furnished a copy and is prepared to assist both parties in reaching a satisfactory resolution of it. Please provide your position with regard to the facts or action taken by you to resolve the matter on the "Number 1 copy" (type or black ball point pen) and send it to the Bureau. Also advise your customer of your action. Arbitration is available through the Bureau if both parties wish this service.

Have Adjusted (Date) _____ Will Adjust By (Date) _____ Other (Explain Below)

Comments: _____
_____
_____
_____
_____
_____
_____

Company   By   Date

BBB–Follow-Up by_____

Date _____

COPY 1

24-15

You will be asked to complete a form similar to this one whenever you contact the Better Business Bureau about a company.

Use Government Protection Agencies

Government agencies serve consumers at the local, state, and federal levels. Their main function is to enforce laws, standards, and regulations to help protect consumers. They can also provide consumer-related information about products and services. In addition, they have the authority to take action against dishonest businesses.

Local and State Agencies

Local and state government agencies provide many consumer related services. One of their functions is enforcing regulations to protect your health and safety. For instance, local agencies oversee the licensing of service facilities such as hospitals or nursing homes. They also enforce food sanitation standards.

State and local agency responsibilities vary from state to state. Learning about these agencies and the services they provide in your area can be helpful to you. Then when you need assistance or information, you will know where to go.

Federal Agencies

Government agencies at the federal level help protect your consumer rights. Regulatory agencies were developed for this purpose. They have the authority to take action against dishonest businesses. Many of these agencies have offices within your own community or state to serve you.

As a consumer, you have the right to protection against unsafe products and false information about goods and services. Problems with product safety, consumer fraud, and dishonest businesses can be handled by these agencies.

They enforce safety standards for consumer goods and services. They also work to protect consumers against false or deceptive information. The four federal agencies that are most involved with protecting and helping consumers are as follows:

- The **Consumer Product Safety Commission (CPSC)** protects your right to safety. It ensures the safety of household products such as toys, appliances, tools, clothing, and furniture. The CPSC investigates consumer complaints about product safety. It can ban the sale of products found to be dangerous or require a product recall. Unsafe or hazardous products should be reported to the CPSC (www.cpsc.gov).

- The **Food and Drug Administration (FDA)** also protects your right to safety. The agency helps protect consumer safety by regulating the production, packaging, and labeling of foods, drugs, and cosmetics. See 24-16. If a product is found to be unsafe, the FDA can either ban its sale or require a safety warning on it. Medical devices and radiation-emitting products such as microwave ovens are also covered by the FDA (www.fda.gov).

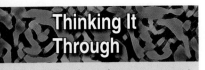

Thinking It Through

Why does the government have consumer protection agencies?

- The **Federal Trade Commission (FTC)** protects your rights to information and selection. It helps prevent unfair competition, deceptive trade practices, and false advertising. In addition, the FTC oversees laws controlling packaging, labeling, advertising, and warranties. Your right to be informed is protected by this agency. Problems with mail orders, warranties, and deceptive advertising can be referred to the FTC (www.ftc.gov).

- The **Federal Communications Commission (FCC)** protects your rights to information and selection. The agency handles complaints about the practices and charges of wired and wireless telephone systems. It also handles complaints about radio and television broadcasts and cable TV services. Problems can be referred to the Consumer Protection Division within the FCC (www.fcc.gov).

24-16
The Food and Drug Administration is responsible for making sure all cosmetics are safe for consumer use.

You can find out more about government consumer information at the FirstGov for Consumers Internet site (www.consumer.gov). This site also includes "ScamAlert," which provides current information on fraudulent and deceptive practices in the marketplace.

Your last resort for settling a complaint is to take your problem to court. Filing a lawsuit and going to court can be a lengthy and costly process. Use this method only when the problem is serious and all other alternatives have been tried.

Consumer Fraud

It is true that you may have trouble with reputable companies from time to time. However, these issues can usually be resolved to the satisfaction of both you and the company. Consumer fraud is another matter. **Consumer fraud** involves the use of trickery or deceit to gain some type of unfair or dishonest advantage over the consumer. According to government statistics, the leading reported types of fraud include identity theft, prizes and sweepstakes, and Internet services. Other common examples of consumer fraud include defective products, false advertising, fake charities, and investment scams.

Enrich

Search the large FirstGov for Consumers Web site. What types of helpful information can be found there?

Note

Share examples of class-action lawsuits filed by consumers. Discuss the legitimacy of the suits.

Discuss

Do you know anyone who has been the victim of identity theft? How did the thief obtain the victim's personal information?

Activity

Have students search for warnings of current phishing scams posted on reliable Web sites such as www.about.com. Discuss the examples in class.

Note

Phishing e-mails can be forwarded as attachments to the FTC to be investigated.

Resource

Avoiding Consumer Fraud, Activity J, WB

Thinking It Through

Have you ever received a phishing e-mail? How were you able to identify it?

Identity Theft

Modern technology has made it easier for criminals to steal your identity. *Identity theft* involves use of another's name and personal information such as social security number, address, or credit card numbers. The thief may use this information to open accounts, make purchases, and even commit fraud using your name.

Two common strategies for identity theft are skimming and phishing. **Skimming** involves stealing a credit card number. For example, a dishonest clerk could write down your credit card number during checkout. He or she could also use a pocket-size stripe reader to obtain your credit card information. This information is then used to make purchases against your card.

Phishing is tricking someone into giving out personal and financial information, such as an identification number or password. It is usually done through e-mail, but can also be done over the telephone. For example, you may receive an e-mail claiming to be from a company you trust. The sender's e-mail address may closely mimic the company's e-mail address. The e-mail may claim that there is a problem with your account or ask you to verify information. It may instruct you to click on a provided link and enter personal information on the Web site that opens. However, the Web site will actually belong to someone who can collect the information you provide and use it to steal your identity.

Phishing can also be done over the telephone. It is called *vishing*, which stands for "voice phishing." A person posing as a bank or credit card representative calls and tells you there is some type of problem with your account. You are then asked to call a toll-free number to straighten it out. If you call, any information you provide may again be used illegally.

When you shop on the Internet, you will need to be sure you are on the company's actual Internet site. There are fake sites that may look very similar to and offer items similar to those of well-known companies. At legitimate sites, security is still very important. You will be providing personal information when you purchase items over the Internet. Make sure you are checking out from a secure site.

Avoiding Consumer Fraud

There are some things you can do to avoid being a victim of fraud. Check out companies carefully before you do business with them. Do not give out your social security number and financial and account information unless you are sure there is a legitimate reason to do so. Never leave receipts casually lying around. Make sure you understand transactions and get all the details and promises in writing. Review bills and invoices for accuracy before you pay them. Shred all documents that contain identifying information when you are through with them.

If you receive an e-mail and you are unsure that it is from a legitimate company, do not open it or follow any links included. Instead, contact the company directly from their Web site or phone customer service and ask if they sent the e-mail. Legitimate retailers or financial institutions do not ask for personal information through e-mail or over the telephone. If you receive such requests, do not respond. Report the incident to your financial institution.

Follow these procedures if you think your identity has been stolen.

1. Contact the fraud departments of any one of the national consumer reporting agencies: Equifax, Experian, or TransUnion.

2. Close any accounts you think may have been tampered with or opened illegally.

3. File a report with your local police department.

4. File a complaint with the Federal Trade Commission.

See the FTC's identity theft Web site at www.ftc.gov/bcp/edu/microsites/idtheft for more information.

It is not always easy to identify consumer fraud. People who use fraudulent practices are often very convincing. By the time you realize you have been cheated, it may be too late. A good rule to follow is: "If it sounds too good to be true, it probably is." Unsolicited offers of goods or services particularly by mail, the Internet, or telephone should be suspect.

The best protection for you against consumer fraud is to be a wise consumer. Find as much information as you can about a product or service before you buy. Deal with reputable businesses. Be aware of your rights and fulfill your responsibilities as a consumer.

Note

Malware is a term used for "malicious software," or anything that can damage a computer. This includes spyware, worms, viruses, and e-mail bombs.

Reflect

Do you keep track of all your receipts? Do you file monthly bank and bill statements in a safe place?

Discuss

What other types of consumer fraud can you name? Did you ever know anyone who became a victim of these schemes?

Summary

Making the most of the money you earn begins when you learn to budget your money. A budget can be used to help manage your money wisely. It can also be used to help you work toward financial goals.

Part of managing your spending wisely is being a good consumer. Find out as much information as you can about a product or service before you buy. Understand the role of advertising in your buying choices. You also need to know where to shop in your area and the types of stores available.

Learn to shop wisely. Plan your buying before you go shopping. By making a list, you buy what you need and avoid impulse buying. Comparison shopping will help you get the most value for your money.

You have certain rights and responsibilities as a consumer in the marketplace. These include the rights to be informed, to choose, to performance, to safety, and to recourse. Each right carries a responsibility with it which you should try to meet.

Problems with goods and services should be reported to businesses so they can be corrected. Consumer and government protection agencies can be contacted to provide assistance.

Consumer fraud has become a major problem in our society. Practices such as skimming and phishing can lead to the theft of your identity. It is important that you be able to recognize fraud and know what to do about it.

Facts in Review

1. What is a budget?
2. Name the five steps involved in developing a budget.
3. Explain the difference between fixed and flexible expenses. Give two examples of each.
4. What questions can be asked to help evaluate a budget?
5. How can informed consumers get the most value from the money they have to spend?
6. List three resources to use to learn about a product or service before buying.
7. List five types of printed materials that contain consumer product information.
8. How does a limited warranty differ from a full warranty?
9. How does a warranty differ from a service contract?
10. What is the main purpose of advertising?
11. How can consumers benefit from promotional methods such as buying incentives?
12. What factors might be considered in deciding where to shop?
13. Why are the prices at a discount store usually lower than similar items at a department store?
14. List three possible disadvantages to shopping by mail or Internet.
15. List three possible advantages to shopping by television or Internet.
16. When does impulse buying result in wasted money?
17. What is the purpose of comparison shopping?
18. Identify three federal consumer protection agencies.
19. List three strategies you could use to avoid becoming a victim of consumer fraud.

Resource

Review and Study Guide for Chapter 24, reproducible master 24-4, TR

Answers to *Facts In Review*

1. a written plan to help a person make the most of his or her money
2. Establish financial goals. Estimate monthly income and expenses. Balance the budget. Keep track of income and expenses. Evaluate the budget.
3. Fixed expenses are the same amounts that are paid regularly. Flexible expenses are varying amounts due at various times. (Examples are student response.)

4. Does income cover expenses? Is the budget flexible enough to handle unexpected expenses? Is my money doing what I want it to do? Is my budget helping me meet my goals on schedule?
5. by being informed, understanding advertising and other promotional methods, deciding where to shop, and developing shopping skills
6. (List three:) people, places, organizations, printed materials

(continued)

Developing Your Academic Skills

1. **Math.** Prepare a monthly budget for yourself. Give a presentation on how you determined amounts for flexible expenses.

2. **English.** Go to the library and check out several consumer information magazines. Pick one product that interests you and find all the information on that product in the magazines. Write a paper summarizing the information you found and indicate how the information would affect your purchase decision.

Information Technology Applications

1. Identify three Web sites through which merchandise can be purchased. Describe products sold through the sites and how prices compare to those of local stores. Note any other important factors, such as ease of shopping, cost for shipping, and reliability of the sellers.

2. Search online stores for a common household appliance. Indicate if the appliance comes with a full warranty or limited warranty. Would you buy the product with that type of warranty? Why?

Applying Your Knowledge and Skills

1. **Problem Solving and Critical Thinking.** Prepare a monthly budget based on your short-range and long-range goals, income, and expenses. Keep an accurate record of your expenses for one month, then evaluate your budget.

2. **Employability and Career Development.** Using the budget you prepared above, including your long-range goals, prepare a budget you might follow when you begin working full time. Then research jobs in which you are interested. Make a list of those with salaries providing enough income to meet the needs of your projected lifestyle budget.

3. **Communications.** Select four advertisements, one from each of the following: a magazine, the Internet, a newspaper, and a television commercial. Evaluate each. How much useful information does each contain? Is any information misleading? How does each make you feel about buying the product? Share your findings with the class.

Developing Workplace Skills

Ask three or four of your classmates to help you write an original script for a television commercial for a popular product. Include examples of both honest and misleading advertising techniques. Act out and video record the commercial. Show the video to your class and have them identify the good and poor strategies you used. Then lead a discussion on the importance of ethics in advertising.

7. (List five:) advertisements, product labels and tags, use and care guides, warranties, newspapers, books, magazines, pamphlets, bulletins

8. A limited warranty covers product repairs, but paying labor costs and handling charges may be the customer's responsibility. A full warranty includes free repair or replacement of a product or any defective part within a reasonable time.

9. A warranty is a promise guaranteeing that a product will meet certain performance and safety standards for a specified period. A service contract is an extended warranty for an additional cost.

10. to sell goods and services

11. by saving money on items they would purchase anyway

12. the intended purchase and the store's location, prices, and selection

13. fewer customer services, higher sales volume

14. (List three:) extra charges, shipping delays, merchandise-return hassles, delivery failures, cannot examine merchandise

15. (List three:) time savings, money savings, wide selection, convenience

16. when spending too much, when buying something you do not need or cannot use

17. to save money, get better quality, and find the product/service that best suits your needs before buying

18. (List three:) Consumer Product Safety Commission, Food and Drug Administration, Federal Trade Commission, Federal Communications Commission

19. (List three. Student response.)

25

Using Credit

Key Terms

credit

finance charges

interest

annual percentage rate (APR)

revolving charge account

charge account

installment account

collateral

cosigner

equity

credit rating

credit bureau

grace period

debt-to-income ratio

bankruptcy

Chapter Objectives

After studying this chapter, you will be able to

- **compare** the advantages and disadvantages of using credit.
- **distinguish between** the different types of credit.
- **identify** how to establish a credit rating.
- **describe** the laws that control credit use.
- **analyze** the importance of using credit wisely.

Reading Advantage

Read through the list of key terms at the beginning of the chapter. Write what you think each term means. Then look up the term in the glossary and write the textbook definition.

Achieving Academic Standards

English Language Arts

- Read print and non-print texts to acquire new information and to respond to the needs and demands of society and the workplace. (IRA/NCTE, 1)
- Apply strategies to comprehend, interpret, evaluate, and appreciate texts. (IRA/NCTE, 3)
- Conduct research on issues and interests by gathering, evaluating, and synthesizing data from a variety of sources to communicate discoveries. (IRA/NCTE, 7)

Math

- Understand meanings of operations and how they relate to one another. (NCTM)
- Compute fluently and make reasonable estimates. (NCTM)

Key Concepts

- You can begin to establish a good credit rating without a credit card by holding a job, maintaining checking or savings accounts, and paying your rent and utilities on time.

- It is a good idea to check your credit report regularly for errors or any missing information that could affect your credit rating.

- Knowing about finance charges can help you determine the additional costs of using credit and whether or not you can afford to.

- Managing your credit wisely involves knowing when to use credit. It also involves knowing what to do if you have a financial problem.

Credit allows you to buy goods and services now and pay for them later. Many businesses make it easy to "buy now and pay later" with credit. Consumers are constantly urged to "charge it." As a consumer, you have a choice to make when using credit. Use it wisely and it can help you enjoy a more comfortable lifestyle. Use it unwisely and it can lead to serious financial problems.

Before you begin to use credit, you should have an understanding of it. You should learn what it is, how it is used, and the different types available. Once you understand credit, you can learn how to manage it wisely.

Understanding Credit

Using credit is similar to using money, but with a few important differences. When you buy with cash, you give money in exchange for goods and services. You then own your purchases. When you buy with credit instead of giving money for your purchases, you promise to pay later. In other words, you are using your future income now. Although you may make a credit purchase now, the exchange is not complete until you finish paying later.

Credit is based on trust between the *creditor* and the credit user, or borrower. A creditor may be a person or an organization. Creditors make credit available to consumers by loaning money or selling goods and services on credit. Since credit is based on trust, the creditor must believe the borrower can and will pay what is owed.

People use credit most often for personal needs. People who are good credit risks can use credit for expensive items such as cars, vacations, and furniture. They can also use credit for smaller items such as clothes, meals, and gasoline.

Before you use credit, you need to carefully consider the pros and cons of using it. By doing this, you may find credit is good to use in some situations, but not in others. Several advantages and disadvantages are discussed below and listed in 25-1.

Reflect Further

Do you think some purchases should not be made with credit?

Advantages of Using Credit

As you continue to assume more financial responsibility, you will eventually buy expensive items such as a car or a home. Unless you are very wealthy, you will not have enough money to buy an expensive item at once. It could take you years to save enough money to buy a car or a house. However, credit allows you to buy and use goods and services as you pay for them. Being able to live in a nice home or drive a car as you pay for it is one of the major advantages of credit.

Convenience is another advantage of credit. Credit eliminates the need to carry large amounts of cash. It can also be a source of cash for emergency or unexpected expenses. For example, thanks to Jim's credit

Reflect Further

What type of purchases would you consider making on credit?

Using Credit	
Advantages of Credit	**Disadvantages of Credit**
• Credit allows the use of goods, such as a car or house, as you pay for them. • Credit allows you to buy an expensive item without saving large amounts of money in advance. • Credit can offer a source of cash to provide temporary help for an unexpected expense or emergency. • Credit offers convenience. It eliminates the need to carry large amounts of cash when shopping. • Credit provides a record of purchases. Exchanges, returns, and online orders are easier with credit.	• Using credit reduces future income. By using credit now, you are spending tomorrow's income. This reduces the amount of money you will have to spend in the future. • Using credit is expensive. The more credit you use and the more time you take to repay, the greater the finance charges are. • Using credit can encourage impulse buying. Credit makes it easy to spend money you do not have and buy more than you can afford. • Misusing credit can cause serious problems, such as a bad credit rating, repossession of goods, or bankruptcy.

25-1
Before using credit, consider all the pros and cons.

Resource

Understanding Credit,
Activity A, WB

Discuss

Most creditors are in the business of making money by loaning money so they should not be viewed negatively when they collect funds.

Resource

Keeping Your Credit Card Safe,
reproducible master 25-2, TR

card, he was able to have his car fixed when the alternator had to be replaced. Without this immediate source of money, Jim could not have paid the repair bill for weeks.

Disadvantages of Using Credit

Although credit can be a very successful buying tool, it can also cause many problems if misused. Financial difficulties are one of the leading causes of marital problems and divorce. Individuals who misuse credit often develop emotional problems. They find it difficult to focus on anything except how they will deal with their mounting bills.

Credit always costs money unless a generous friend or helpful relative extends free credit to you. The more credit you use and the longer you take to repay, the higher the finance charges will be. **Finance charges** are the total amount a borrower must pay for the use of credit.

Another disadvantage of credit is the temptation. Credit makes it easy to spend money you do not have. Research shows that consumers spend more when using a credit card than when using cash. Eventually you may have more bills than you can pay. If you are unable to pay your debts, the items you bought on credit can be repossessed. You may also lose your right to obtain credit from reputable creditors. Only buy on credit as a last resort.

Thinking It Through

How can credit influence people to buy more than they can afford? What does it mean to overextend credit?

In the Real World

Eva Exceeds Her Credit

Eva decided to buy a new television on credit, even though she had monthly payments to make on two other credit accounts. At the electronics store, the salesperson went over the credit agreement with her. He showed her the sale price, tax, number of payments, finance charge, unpaid balance, and total cost including interest.

Eva was so anxious to get the television home she did not pay much attention to the figures. She did, however, notice she had a total of 36 monthly payments. Each payment was due on the fifteenth of the month.

The salesperson also showed Eva a clause in the contract. It read, "Any default by the buyer, including failure to pay when due, may, at the seller's option accelerate all of the remaining payments and seller may repossess the property." Eva was not worried about making her payments. She signed the credit agreement and went home with her new television.

Eva enjoyed her purchase and made her monthly payments on time until she lost her job. While unemployed for several months, Eva was unable to make the minimum monthly payments. She could not make payments on her other credit accounts either. All of the creditors demanded payment. A short time later, the electronics store repossessed the television.

Questions to Discuss

1. What advantages in using credit did Eva consider in buying her television?
2. What disadvantages in using credit should Eva have considered before buying the television?
3. Do you think Eva budgeted her monthly payments carefully? Explain.
4. What long-term effects might Eva's decision to buy on credit have on her ability to make future credit purchases?

Types of Credit

Various types of credit are available to consumers. Each type comes in a different form to meet different consumer needs. Some types are used to buy goods and services, while others are used to borrow money. The major types of credit available to consumers are

- credit card accounts
- charge accounts
- installment accounts
- vehicle leasing
- cash loans
- home equity loans

Credit Card Accounts

Resource

Types of Credit, reproducible master 25-3, TR

Many retail stores and businesses issue credit cards so consumers can use credit to buy their goods and services. These cards have a credit limit and can only be used at the business that issues the credit. Banks and other financial institutions also issue credit cards. These cards have a credit limit as well, but they can be used wherever they are accepted by businesses. In addition to making purchases at numerous businesses, these credit cards can also be used to obtain cash advances.

An important thing to remember is that the cost of using credit cards is often high. Many credit card companies charge an annual fee for using their card. There is usually a fine for failing to make your payments on time. Interest rates on credit cards tend to be high as well. **Interest** is the price paid for the use of money over a period of time. It is usually stated as an annual percentage rate (APR). An **annual percentage rate (APR)** is the actual rate of interest charged on a yearly basis.

Overusing credit cards is a major reason many people get into financial trouble. It is usually not a good idea to get a credit card before you are financially secure. Still, credit cards are in great demand and the competition to attract new customers is fierce. Many credit cards offer incentives to encourage you to open and use accounts. Some eliminate the annual fee. Others offer you cash rebates for using your credit card based on a percentage of your charges each month. Various credit cards offer rebates on groceries, gasoline, movie rentals, automobiles, airline tickets, and many other items.

Most credit card accounts are known as a **revolving charge account**. This type of credit account allows customers the choice of paying for purchases in full each month or spreading payments over a period of time.

Here is how a typical credit card account works. Rosita opened a revolving charge account at a retail store. In September she used her credit card to charge $56 worth of clothing purchases. In October she got a statement showing the amount she owed. Rosita had a choice of paying the full amount or making a minimum payment of $10. If she paid in full within a month, she would avoid paying finance charges. If she paid just the minimum payment, finance charges would be added to the remaining balance of $46. Rosita could continue to charge merchandise as long as she did not exceed her $500 credit limit for that card. She would also receive a monthly statement showing the amount owed. Rosita knows that finance charges on credit cards are high. She also knows that by simply making minimum payments, finance charges could eventually surpass the cost of the item purchased.

See 25-2 as an example of Rosita's concern. The chart shows a credit account that has been used to its $500 limit. After six months of paying the minimum $10 monthly payment, a total of $60 is paid. However, the $500 bill is reduced by only $15.57. The reason for this is the addition of $44.43 in finance charges during the period. If Rosita's payment was late, she would also have to pay a late fee in addition to the finance charge.

Rosita understands the high cost of finance charges and, therefore, tries to pay her credit card balance in full each month. Rosita is also very careful not to lose her credit card. She has learned about the practice of skimming. Therefore, Rosita keeps an eye on her credit card whenever she is making a purchase. She also checks her credit card statements very carefully for incorrect entries. Rosita knows that she needs to notify her creditor immediately if she finds a problem. Then, according to the law, Rosita cannot be charged more than $50 if someone else uses her card.

Note

This business is highly competitive so it is wise to shop around for a low interest rate.

Activity

Compare the interest rates and annual percentage rates of several credit card offers. Have students determine which is the best offer.

Discuss

What are the advantages and disadvantages of a revolving charge account?

Thinking It Through

What will happen if you only make the minimum payment on your credit account each month?

Effects of Minimum Payments and Finance Charges on Credit Card Balances			
Month	**Balance**	**Minimum Payment**	**Finance Charge**
January	$ 500.00	$ 10.00	$ 7.50
February	$ 497.50	$ 10.00	$ 7.46
March	$ 494.96	$ 10.00	$ 7.42
April	$ 492.38	$ 10.00	$ 7.39
May	$ 489.77	$ 10.00	$ 7.35
June	$ 487.12	$ 10.00	$ 7.31
Totals	$ 484.43	$ 60.00	$ 44.43

Charge Accounts

Some businesses allow customers to charge goods and services on a **charge account** on file at the business. This is another way businesses can extend credit to customers without using credit cards. Once a month, the business will send the customer a bill or statement. The customer is then expected to pay in full by the assigned due date. If the customer pays on time, there is no finance charge. A local clothing store or flower shop would be an example of businesses that might offer this type of credit.

Installment Accounts

An **installment account** is often used to charge expensive items such as a major appliance or piece of furniture, 25-3. The buyer pays for the merchandise according to a set schedule of payments. Finance charges are included in the payments. Buyers are usually asked to sign a contract for this type of credit purchase. A down payment in cash may also be required. If the buyer fails to make payments, the seller can repossess the merchandise.

Vehicle Leasing

There are times, especially when purchasing a car, that you may be tempted to enter into a lease agreement rather than a purchase contract. While the advertisements may sound attractive, there are both advantages and disadvantages to leasing.

Vehicle leasing is a credit transaction by which a person rents a car according to certain restrictions. The transaction usually requires a lower down payment and monthly payment. This makes a lease agreement appear attractive. With a lease, however, you do not own the vehicle. The contract may limit the driver to a certain number of miles. You may also be charged a fee for excess mileage as well as the extra wear and tear.

25-3
An expensive household purchase, like an oven, can be bought today and paid over several months with an installment credit account.

Cash Loans

It may become necessary to borrow money to buy items you need or want. This type of credit is called a *cash loan*. Commercial banks, savings banks, credit unions, loan companies, and some life insurance companies make various types of cash loans.

To get most cash loans, a borrower is required to pledge collateral. **Collateral** is something of value held by the creditor in case you are unable to repay the loan. For an auto loan, the car is collateral. For a mortgage, the house serves as collateral. If the borrower fails to pay according to the agreement, the creditor may take the property to settle the claim against the borrower.

Although a person may have nothing to pledge as collateral, getting a loan is still possible if the person has a cosigner. A **cosigner** is a responsible person who signs a loan agreement with the borrower. By signing the agreement, the cosigner promises to pay the loan if the borrower fails to pay.

Most cash loans are repaid like an installment account. The borrower makes regular monthly payments that include finance charges.

Home Equity Loans

Lenders offer a *home equity loan* to homeowners, 25-4. This type of loan provides automatic access to a sum of money separate from the amount the homeowner borrowed to purchase the house. A home equity loan is based on the homeowner's equity in the house. **Equity**

Reflect Further

In addition to a car or house, what other items could be used as collateral for a cash loan?

Discuss

What are the legal and ethical obligations of a cosigner?

Activity

Debate the advantages and disadvantages of using a home equity loan as a line of credit.

25-4

People often use a home equity loan to repair and improve their homes.

is determined by subtracting how much is owed on a house from the amount the house is worth. If your house is worth $120,000 and you still owe the bank $90,000, the amount of equity in your house is $30,000.

Once the loan is approved, it resembles a checking account. You can write yourself a check that draws money from your pre-approved loan. The advantage of this type of loan is that the interest on it is often tax deductible. Because a home equity loan is so easy to obtain, it may tempt you to make unnecessary purchases. In this case, a home equity loan may be a disadvantage.

You should think very carefully about getting a home equity loan. The collateral for a home equity loan is the house itself. Nonpayment of a loan, or sometimes a late payment, has caused some homeowners to lose their homes.

Establishing Credit

When you first try to establish credit, you may have a hard time. This is because creditors want evidence before they grant you credit that you can and will pay your debts. When you apply for credit, you will be asked to fill out a credit application form like the one in 25-5. This form helps creditors evaluate your credit rating. A **credit rating** is the creditor's evaluation of a person's willingness and ability to pay debts.

In evaluating a credit rating, creditors look for a person who is a *good credit risk*. That is, they issue credit to people who are most likely to repay the debt. Creditors consider people who have jobs with steady incomes as good credit risks. They also look for factors such as:

- making regular, on-time payments on credit purchases, loans, or fixed expenses such as rent or utilities

- owning a car, home, stocks, or bonds

- living in the same community for a period of time

Building Your Credit Rating

Resource

Applying for Credit, Activity B, WB

Note

Many of these credit-building steps may occur during this course. By the end of the course, students may establish some level of credit. (Be sure to alert parents to this activity prior to initiation.)

If you have never bought anything on credit, you can begin building a good credit rating by taking some of the following steps:

- *Get a job and stay employed.* To be a good credit risk, you must prove you can hold a job and earn a regular income.

- *Open a checking account.* A well-managed checking account shows that you can handle money responsibly.

- *Open a savings account.* Saving regularly can help you establish a good banking record that can serve as a credit reference. Your savings may also be used as collateral for a loan.

SEARS, ROEBUCK AND CO. INDIVIDUAL CREDIT ACCOUNT APPLICATION

APPLICATION TO BE COMPLETED IN NAME OF PERSON IN WHICH THE ACCOUNT IS TO BE CARRIED.

COURTESY TITLES ARE OPTIONAL   **PLEASE PRINT**

☐ MR. ☐ MRS. ☐ MISS ☐ MS. _____
                                         First Name   Initial   Last Name

Street Address _____ Apt. # ____ City _____ State _____ Zip Code _____

Phone No: _____ Phone No: _____ Soc. Sec. _____ Age ___ Number of
Home   Business   No.   Dependents _____
                                                                                                                                                              (Excluding Applicant)

Are you a United ☐ Yes If NO, explain
States citizen?   ☐ No   immigration status: _____

How Long at
Present Address _____ Own ☐   Rent-Furnished ☐   Rent-Unfurnished ☐   Board ☐   Monthly Rent or
                                                                                                                                    Mortgage Payments $ _____

Name of Landlord or Mortgage Holder _____ Street Address _____ City and State _____

Former Address (if less than 2   How
years at present address) _____ long _____

Employer _____ Street Address _____ City and State _____

How
long _____ Occupation _____ Net _____ Monthly ☐
                                                                         Income $ _____ Weekly ☐
                                                                         (Take Home Pay)

Former Employer   How
(If less than 1 year with present employer) _____ long _____

┌───┐
│ ALIMONY, CHILD SUPPORT, OR SEPARATE MAINTENANCE INCOME NEED NOT BE REVEALED IF YOU DO NOT WISH TO HAVE IT │
│ CONSIDERED AS A BASIS FOR PAYING THIS OBLIGATION.   │
└───┘

Alimony, child support, separate maintenance received under: Monthly ☐
                                ☐ Court order   ☐ Written agreement   ☐ Oral understanding   Amount $ _____ Weekly ☐

Other Income, if any: Amount $ _____ Monthly ☐ Source _____
                                                     Weekly ☐

Name and Address of Bank _____ Savings ☐ Checking ☐ _____
                                                                                                           Acc't No.

Name and Address of Bank _____ Savings ☐ Checking ☐ _____
                                                                                                           Acc't No.

Previous   ☐ Yes   Is Account ☐ Yes Date Final
Sears Account ☐ No   At What Sears Store do you usually shop? Account No. ___ Paid in Full ☐ No Payment Made _____

Relative or Personal
Reference not living
at above address _____
                       (Name)   (Street Address)   (City and State)   (Relationship)

CREDIT REFERENCES (Attach additional sheet if necessary.)   List all references (Open or closed within past two years)

Charge Accounts Loan References Bank/Store/Company Address	Date Opened	Name Account Carried in	Account Number	Balance	Monthly Payments

Authorized buyer _____
                           First Name   Initial   Last Name   Relationship to applicant

Authorized buyer _____
                           First Name   Initial   Last Name   Relationship to applicant

THE INFORMATION BELOW IS REQUIRED IF: (1) YOUR SPOUSE IS AN AUTHORIZED BUYER OR (2) YOU RESIDE IN A COMMUNITY PROPERTY
STATE (ARIZONA, CALIFORNIA, IDAHO, LOUISIANA, NEVADA, NEW MEXICO, TEXAS, WASHINGTON) OR (3) YOU ARE RELYING ON THE
INCOME OR ASSETS OF ANOTHER PERSON, INCLUDING A SPOUSE OR FORMER SPOUSE, AS A BASIS FOR PAYMENT.

Name of spouse   ☐
Name of former spouse ☐ _____
Name of other person ☐   Address   City   Age
                                        Street   and State
Employer _____ Address _____ _____

How   Soc. Sec.   Net   Monthly ☐
long _____ Occupation _____ No. _____ Income $ _____ Weekly ☐
                                                                         (Take Home Pay)

Name and Address of Bank _____ Savings ☐ Checking ☐ _____
                                                                                                           Acc't No.

Name and Address of Bank _____ Savings ☐ Checking ☐ _____
                                                                                                           Acc't No.

THE PERSON ON WHOSE INCOME OR ASSETS YOU ARE RELYING AS A BASIS FOR PAYMENT MUST SIGN BELOW, HOWEVER, YOUR
SPOUSE NEED NOT SIGN IF YOU RESIDE IN A COMMUNITY PROPERTY STATE OR IF YOUR SPOUSE IS AN AUTHORIZED BUYER.

SEARS IS AUTHORIZED TO INVESTIGATE MY CREDIT RECORD AND   X
TO VERIFY MY CREDIT, EMPLOYMENT AND INCOME REFERENCES.   _____ _____
                                                               (Signature of person on whose income or   Date
                                                                assets applicant is relying.)

25-5

A credit application form helps creditors decide if a person will be a good credit risk.

Extend Your Knowledge

Checking Your Credit Record

It is a good idea to check your credit record regularly even if you have not been denied credit. You are entitled to a free credit report each year from each of the three national consumer credit reporting agencies: Equifax, Experian, and TransUnion. You must go to www.annualcreditreport.com to obtain your free report. You may elect to receive your report online, through the mail, or by phone.

- *Buy an item on a layaway plan.* After you pay for the purchase, the store will probably be willing to grant you a charge account.

- *Apply to a gasoline company or a local store for a credit card.* When you receive a credit card, make small purchases and pay for them promptly and in full when the bills come. Keep in mind, however, that a credit card is usually not a good idea if you are just starting out with a part-time job or a low-paying, full-time job. You can establish a good credit rating without a credit card by keeping your job and paying your rent and utilities on time.

Reflect Further

How can you begin establishing credit now?

Reflect

How could a negative credit report affect your finances for several years?

Discuss

Discuss the different types of information found in the sample credit file in 25-6.

Thinking It Through

How do creditors use credit bureaus?

What Is in a Credit Record?

Once you use credit, you automatically establish a credit record at a local or national credit reporting agency. This agency, also known as a **credit bureau**, collects and keeps files of financial information on individual consumers. Businesses then use this information to decide whether to grant or deny credit to the applicant.

The information on your credit record shows only the facts collected by the credit bureau, 25-6. The credit bureau does not recommend whether you should be granted credit. Also, by law, none of the information on your record relates to your reputation, character, or lifestyle. You have the right to check your credit record. If you have problems getting credit, the creditor who denied your credit request must give you the name and address of the credit bureau they used.

By looking at your credit record, you may find errors or missing information that may affect your credit rating. You can challenge errors in your credit record by completing a written request form provided by the credit bureau. The Federal Trade Commission should be contacted if problems are not handled satisfactorily. Remember, however, there is no way to remove negative information in your credit record that is accurate. Generally, negative information stays in the report for seven years.

Please address all future correspondence to: Credit Reporting Agency
Business Address
City, State 00000

Sample Credit File

Personal Identification Information

Your Name   Social Security #:   123-45-6789
123 Current Address   Date of Birth: April 10th,1968
City, State 00000

Previous Address(es)
456 Former Rd. Atlanta, GA 30000
P.O. Box XXXX Savannah, GA 40000

Last Reported Employment: Engineer, Highway Planning

Public Record Information

Lien Filed 03/05; Fulton CTY; Case or Other ID Number-32114; Amount-$26667;
Class-State; Released 07/05; Verified 07/05

Bankruptcy Filed 12/06; Northern District Ct; Case or Other ID Number-673HC12;
Liabilities-$15787; Personal; Individual; Discharged; Assets-$780

Satisfied Judgment Filed 07/07; Fulton CTY; Case or Other ID Number-898872; Defendant-
Consumer; Amount-$8984; Plaintiff-ABC Real Estate; Satisfied 03/07; Verified 05/07

Collection Agency Account Information

Pro Coll (800) xxx-xxxx

Collection Reported 05/07; Assigned 09/06 to Pro Coll (800) XXX-XXXX Client - ABC
Hospital; Amount-$978; Unpaid; Balance $978; Date of Last Activity 09/06; Individual
Account; Account Number 787652JC

Credit Account Information

Company Name [1]	Account Number [2]	Whose Acct [3]	Date Opened [4]	Months Reviewed [5]	Date of Last Activity [6]	High Credit [7]	Terms [8]	Balance [9]	Past Due [10]	Status [11]	Date Reported [12]
Department St.	32514	J	10/96	36	9/99	$950		$0		R1	10/99
Bank	1004735	A	11/96	24	5/99	$750		$0		I1	4/99
Oil Company	541125	A	6/96	12	3/99	$500		$0		01	4/99
Auto Finance	529778	I	5/95	48	12/98	$1100	$50	$300	$200	I5	4/99

Previous Payment History: 3 Times 30 days late; 4 Times 60 days late; 2 Times 90+ days late
Previous Status: 01/08 - I2; 02/99 - I3; 03/08 - I4

Companies that Requested your Credit File

09/06/08	Equifax - Disclosure	08/27/08	Department Store
07/29/08	PRM Bankcard	07/03/08	AM Bankcard
04/10/08	AR Department Store	12/31/08	Equifax - Disclosure ACIS 123456789

25-6

Your credit record contains information about your credit history. It is used to double-check the information you provide in a credit application.

Keeping a Good Credit Rating

If you pay your bills on time and meet all terms of credit agreements, you will have a good credit rating. If you make late payments or fail to pay, you will have a poor rating. A poor credit rating will make it difficult for you to get credit in the future. It may also cause creditors to charge you higher finance charges.

Should you have trouble paying your creditors, do not ignore it. Notify each creditor promptly. Be honest about your situation. Sometimes an unexpected illness, accident, or layoff can cause financial problems. A creditor may let you delay or decrease your monthly payments for a temporary period. Working out some type of payment schedule with your creditors will help you keep your credit rating in good shape.

Credit Agreements

Before you sign any type of credit agreement, examine it carefully. A *credit agreement* is a legally binding contract between a borrower and a creditor. Reading and understanding the credit terms *before* signing an agreement is important.

Take your time and study the agreement before you sign it. Never sign an agreement that has blank spaces. Be sure that all the financial information is entered correctly. Ask questions if you are unsure of any information in the agreement. Sign the agreement only if and when you are satisfied with it.

The Cost of Credit

Anytime you use credit, it is important to find out how much it will cost you. Knowing the exact cost of credit can help you compare finance charges and find the best deal. Knowing this cost can help you decide how much credit you can afford. It can also help you decide if buying now and paying later is worth the extra price.

When you apply for credit, the following factors determine the amount of finance charges you may pay:

- amount of credit used
- interest rate
- length of the repayment period

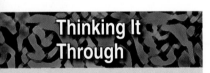

The Amount of Credit Used

The more you charge or borrow, the more interest you are likely to pay. For example, Craig buys $300 of computer software while his friend Mike buys twice as much. Both use the same type of credit account from the same creditor. Both use the same number of months to pay. Since everything is identical except the amount charged, the total finance charges on the $600 bill will usually be twice that of the $300 bill.

The Interest Rate

You will pay more in finance charges with higher interest rates. For example, Craig compared interest rates to find the best deal. One creditor charged an APR of 21 percent. At that rate, the interest on Craig's $300 purchase would total $35.16 if repaid in 12 monthly payments. Another creditor offered a 24-percent APR, totaling $40.44 in interest. Craig chose the 18-percent APR because it offered a lower finance charge of $30.00. See 25-7.

The credit agreement indicates the rate(s) that will be charged. Sometimes a creditor offers an extremely low rate as an introductory offer that increases after a specified time. Make sure you know the terms of a credit agreement before signing it. Also be aware of the grace period. The **grace period** is the number of days allowed to pay for a new purchase before interest is charged.

The Repayment Period

The more time you take to pay back the money you borrow or charge, the more you will pay in interest. For example, Craig saved money in interest by paying for his purchase in 12 monthly payments instead of 18 or 24. The finance charge for his $300 purchase totaled $27.50 for payments spread across 12 months. If he had taken twice as long to pay, he would have spent almost $60 in interest. See 25-8.

By law, creditors are required to state finance charges in credit agreements as a dollar amount and as an annual percentage rate. In Craig's case, he agreed to repay his $300 purchase in 12 monthly payments at a monthly rate of 1.5 percent. The creditor stated the dollar cost of credit as $30.00 and the annual percentage rate as 18 percent in the agreement.

Federal Credit Laws

As a credit user, you should know about your consumer rights and responsibilities under federal law. How do these laws aid credit users? They can assist and help protect consumers in choosing and using credit. They help consumers understand and compare credit costs before they use it. If you are denied credit, find a billing error, or lose your credit card, knowing what to do is important. The most important parts of these laws are explained here.

Discuss

What information will you find on a credit agreement?

Note

Stress the importance of making as large a down payment as possible.

Reflect

What would you do if you found a billing error on your statement?

Cost of Using Credit Based on Annual Percentage Rate			
Annual percentage rate (APR)	18%	21%	24%
Amount financed	$300	$300	$300
Number of monthly payments	12	12	12
Finance charge	$30.00	$35.16	$40.44
Monthly payment amount	$27.50	$27.93	$28.37
Total paid	$330.00	$335.16	$340.44

25-7

Comparing annual percentage rates helped Craig understand the differences in finance charges.

25-8
Craig reduced the cost of using credit by paying off his credit purchase in a relatively short time.

Cost of Using Credit Based on Repayment Time			
Number of monthly payments	12	18	24
Amount financed	$300	$300	$300
Annual percentage rate (APR)	18%	18%	18%
Finance charge	$30.00	$44.66	$59.46
Monthly payment amount	$27.50	$19.15	$14.98
Total paid	$330.00	$344.66	$359.46

Truth in Lending Act

The purpose of this law, passed in 1969, is to protect those who borrow money and buy on credit. Creditors are required to tell consumers what credit will cost them before they use it. This helps consumers decide if they can afford to use credit and which creditor offers the best credit terms. Under this law, a credit agreement must include the following information:

- the dollar amount financed or borrowed
- the total number, dollar amount, and due dates of the payments
- the finance charge, stated as a dollar amount and as an APR
- any charges that are separate from the finance charge
- any penalties or extra charges for late payments, missing payments, or advance payments
- a description of any security held by the creditor

The law also states that businesses cannot issue or mail unrequested credit cards to customers or potential customers. Cardholders are liable for only $50 in charges for a lost or stolen credit card if someone else uses it. However, by promptly reporting the loss or theft before anyone else uses it, cardholders are not liable for any charges.

Fair Credit Reporting Act

This law, passed in 1971, requires accuracy in credit reports. It also provides for the confidentiality of this information. If denied credit because of information provided by a credit bureau, the applicant has the right to the following:

- Know the name and address of the credit bureau issuing the report.
- Check the information on file at the credit bureau, including the source of the information and to whom it was given.
- Require the bureau to recheck any information found to be untrue by the applicant.

Resource

Federal Credit Laws, Activity D, WB

Enrich

Check several credit offers to find out what they charge for late payments, missing payments, and advance payments.

- Receive a corrected report from the bureau if any errors are found.

- Require the bureau to send the corrected report to all creditors who received wrong or incorrect information.

Equal Credit Opportunity Act

This law, passed in 1975, prohibits a creditor from denying credit for discriminatory reasons. When first passed, the law was aimed at protecting women. Many women had problems in establishing their own credit records or had been denied loans, even when they qualified.

In 1977, the law was expanded. Creditors were prohibited from discriminating against applicants on the basis of sex, marital status, race, religion, age, or for receiving public assistance. When an applicant is denied credit, it must be for financial reasons only. The creditor must also explain in writing why the credit was denied.

Fair Credit Billing Act

Passed in 1975, this law protects consumers against unfair billing practices. It describes how to settle billing disputes. Creditors are required to send their customers a written explanation of the steps to take when a billing error or question occurs. The procedure works as follows:

1. The borrower (customer) must notify the lender (creditor) in writing about an incorrect billing. This must be done within 60 days after receiving the billing.

2. The lender must answer the borrower within 30 days. Within 90 days the lender must either correct the billing or show that it is correct.
   Until the dispute is settled, the lender cannot close or collect on the account. The borrower does not have to pay the amount in question until the dispute is settled. However, the borrower must pay any amount not in question.

Electronic Funds Transfer Act

The purpose of this law, passed in 1978, is similar to the Fair Credit Billing Act. However it applies to the use of computers, automatic teller machines (ATMs), debit cards, and other electronic banking transactions. Reporting procedures are similar to the Fair Credit Billing Act. For example, you can limit your liability if you report a lost or stolen credit card promptly. Your loss is limited to $50 if you notify the institution within two business days. However, your loss could be up to $500 after two business days. If you fail to notify within 60 days, your potential loss is unlimited.

Fair Debt Collection Practices Act

This law, passed in 1978, protects consumers from abusive, unfair, or deceptive conduct by collection agencies. These agencies are hired by the creditor to collect the debts owed.

Reflect Further

What precautions can be taken to prevent a credit or debit card from being stolen?

Discuss

Spend considerable time discussing the guidelines in 25-9.

Activity

Identify two circumstances—one wise and one unwise use of credit.

Under this law, collection agencies may not reveal or publicize a debtor's debt to other people. The agencies are not allowed to make threats or use abusive language to collect debts. For example, they cannot tell the debtor that he or she has committed a crime and can be arrested for failure to pay. Also, collection agencies cannot contact debtors at inconvenient times, or make repeated and annoying phone calls to them.

Using Credit Wisely

When used carefully and sensibly, credit can help you get more of what you need when you need it. Used unwisely, credit can lead to serious financial and legal problems. Learning to use credit wisely is important, 25-9. Then you can make credit work for you, not against you. Managing your credit dollars wisely involves

- evaluating whether to use credit

- shopping for the best credit terms

- knowing what to do if you have a financial problem with credit

Should You Use Credit?

The decision to use credit is a personal choice. However, it is important to remember that many people get into serious financial and personal difficulties by misusing credit. Before using it to make a purchase, think carefully. Consider your needs, your available cash, and

25-9

Make credit work for you by following these guidelines.

Guidelines for Using Credit Wisely
• Stay within your credit limits. Use credit sparingly and only after careful thought.
• Shop around for the best credit terms before you borrow or charge.
• Deal only with reputable creditors.
• Read credit agreements before signing them. Make sure you understand all the credit terms and can fulfill your obligation.
• Keep records of all credit transactions. Include receipts, payments, contracts, and correspondence. Keep the records organized in a file, not scattered in a drawer.
• Pay off balances on revolving charge accounts each month to avoid finance charges.
• Keep a good credit rating by paying promptly.
• Contact creditors about billing errors and have them corrected quickly.
• If you have trouble making credit payments, contact your creditors right away.
• Notify creditors immediately if your credit card is lost.

the alternatives to using credit. Then evaluate your choices. You could choose not to buy the item. You could pay for the item with your savings. Finally, you could save your money and buy the item later. To help you evaluate your choices, ask yourself the following questions:

- *How important is it to buy the item now?* See 25-10.

- *Can I do without it?* If the answer is yes, you would be wise not to buy it. The extra cost of using credit can eliminate the benefit of having what you want now.

- *Should I use my savings to make the purchase?* Replacing the savings used for an unplanned purchase can be difficult and risky. This may leave you unprepared for emergencies or financial problems.

- *Should I save money and buy the item later?* This is often the wisest choice. You may find by waiting that you did not really need the item after all.

Depending on your situation, you may get more satisfaction from buying now, as Lynda did. One of Lynda's friends won a ski vacation and asked Lynda to come along. Lynda had some money for the trip in her savings account. However, to get the best airfare, she needed to buy her airline ticket right away. She decided to use her credit card to charge her airline tickets.

On the other hand, Gary got more satisfaction from his purchase by waiting. Gary wanted to buy a new computer, but did not have enough money. He decided to wait and save so he could do some comparison shopping. He also wanted to find out as much as possible about features and prices. When he finally got the computer, he enjoyed it more because it was exactly what he wanted. He was glad that he had waited instead of rushing out to buy it.

One way to help you decide if you can afford to buy on credit is to figure your **debt-to-income ratio**. First total all your monthly debts such as a car loan and credit card payments. Then divide that amount by your monthly take home pay. Ideally, the resulting debt ratio should not be more than 15 percent. Consider buying on credit only if your debt-to-income ratio will stay under 15 percent after the loan.

Shopping for Credit

If you decide to use credit, the next step is to compare credit terms from different sources. Credit charges can vary from source to source, so shopping around for the best terms is wise.

By comparing the three factors that affect credit costs, you can look for the best deal. Compare the size of the loan or the amount of credit used, the annual percentage rate, and the repayment time.

25-10

By using credit, it is easy to purchase items online.

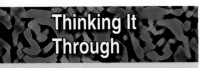

Thinking It Through

What are some disadvantages in waiting to make a purchase?

Thinking It Through

Why is it important to shop for credit? What factors should be considered when shopping for credit terms?

Also, compare the total cost of the credit, including all finance charges and other fees to make sure you are really getting the best deal. Sometimes low-priced items offer no cost savings because of high finance charges.

Dealing with Credit Problems

Using credit unwisely can lead to serious financial problems. Many people lose control of credit buying. They continue buying until they cannot afford to make payments.

Whatever the cause, as soon as you realize you are having credit problems, try to correct them. Some of the danger signals that warn credit users of credit problems are listed in 25-11.

If you have problems paying your bills, take action right away. The first step is to notify your creditors immediately. Most creditors are willing to set up a repayment schedule to reduce the size of monthly payments.

If the creditor will not work with you, the next step you may need to consider is a *debt consolidation loan*. This type of loan, financed through a financial institution, is large enough to pay off all bills. Instead of paying several creditors, you make one payment to the financial institution. However, you are still responsible for the total debt. The monthly payments may be smaller, but the repayment schedule is longer. As a result, the total finance charges may be higher.

Do comparison shopping to find the lowest fee available before entering into a contract for a debt consolidation loan. It is important to remember, however, that this type of loan will not help you unless you change your spending habits.

If you continue to charge after taking out a debt consolidation loan, you will soon find yourself in a worse situation than you were before you took out the loan.

25-11

These are some signs of a possible credit problem.

Note

Provide ample opportunity for students to compare the base and true costs of credit purchases.

Signs of Credit Problems

- Spending increasing amounts of income to pay debts.
- Using credit for purchases that could easily be paid with cash.
- Making only the minimum payments on your accounts.
- Borrowing money, taking out new loans, or using savings to pay debts.
- Getting new credit cards to pay off old ones.
- Owing so much on credit that the amount owed from month to month never goes down.
- Taking longer to pay off your account balances.
- Making payments late as a usual practice.
- Delaying payment to one creditor in order to pay another.
- Skipping some payments.
- Knowing you would have immediate financial problems if you lost your job.
- Running out of money before payday.
- Purchasing nonessential items on credit.

Credit Counseling

When financial problems get out of control, consumers can seek help from the Consumer Credit Counseling Service (CCCS). This is a nonprofit organization with offices across the country. Creditors refer consumers with serious credit problems to seek help through the CCCS. Depending on your income, the credit counseling services provided by this organization are either free or low cost. You can learn more about the Consumer Credit Counseling Service at www.moneymanagement.org or the National Foundation for Credit Counseling Services at www.nfcc.org.

Counseling services can help debtors in several ways. First, they help debtors with stable incomes work out financial programs to repay debts. Secondly, they help debtors learn to manage their money to prevent future debt. Finally, for those with more serious debts, the service tries to work out a repayment schedule with the creditor. The debtor then gives the service a set amount from each paycheck and the service pays the creditor.

Bankruptcy

Debtors with serious financial problems who are unable to pay their debts may be forced to consider filing for bankruptcy. **Bankruptcy** is a legal proceeding for the purpose of stating a person's inability to pay his or her debts. Under the U.S. Bankruptcy Act, debtors can declare bankruptcy in one of the two following ways:

- Debtors can file for *Chapter 7 bankruptcy*. They are legally declared unable to pay their debts. Their *assets* (property and possessions), except for some personal items, are sold by the court. They can lose their car, house, and furniture. The money collected from the sale is then divided among the creditors. The bankruptcy petition also becomes part of their credit record for 10 years. As a result, obtaining credit in the future becomes difficult.

- Debtors can file for *Chapter 13* protection. Under this plan, debtors with regular incomes pay back some or most of their debts over a three- to five-year period. While doing so, they are under the supervision and protection of the court. They are also protected from legal action by creditors. The court sets the payment schedule and monthly payment amounts for the debtor. A court-appointed trustee then distributes the payments to the creditors according to the plan. Filing under Chapter 13 offers debtors two advantages over straight bankruptcy. Debtors usually keep all their possessions and their credit rating suffers less.

Declaring bankruptcy is not an easy decision to make. Consider it only as a last step when all other ways of handling your debts have been tried. Filing for bankruptcy is costly, too. Lawyer fees and court costs must be paid. Remember, once you file for bankruptcy your credit rating will be affected for years. After your debts have been paid off, you can start to rebuild your credit rating.

Reflect Further

What are some personal and financial problems that may result from misusing credit?

Enrich

Invite a credit counselor to class to discuss how to avoid credit problems and bankruptcy.

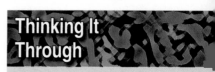

Thinking It Through

What are the advantages of filing under Chapter 13 instead of straight bankruptcy?

Summary

Credit allows you to buy now and pay later. Understanding credit can help you learn to look at the pros, the cons, and the responsibilities of using it wisely. Before charging or borrowing on credit, you should know how each type of credit works.

When you apply for credit, creditors look for evidence that you can and will pay your bills. They do this by checking the credit rating on your credit record. You can build a strong credit rating by handling money wisely and paying all bills on time. After establishing your credit record, keeping a good credit rating is important.

If you use any type of credit, find out how much it will cost you. Compare finance charges to find the best deal. The longer you take to repay, the more it costs to use credit. Several federal credit laws are designed to inform and protect credit users.

Using credit wisely can help you get more of what you need when you need it. To head off credit problems, watch for signals of credit trouble and take immediate steps to correct them. A credit counseling service may be able to assist or advise you. For severe financial debt, you may be forced to file for bankruptcy.

Facts in Review

1. Explain the difference between using cash and credit to make a purchase.
2. List four advantages and disadvantages of using credit.
3. Name four types of credit available to consumers.
4. Explain the difference between a credit card account and a charge account.
5. Why do most cash loans require some type of collateral?
6. List the steps to take to build a good credit rating.
7. What is the purpose of a credit bureau?
8. What information is usually found in a credit record?
9. Why is it important to read over credit agreements carefully?
10. What three factors determine the amount of finance charges that will be paid for using credit?
11. Describe how creditors are required to state finance charges to consumers.
12. Which credit law requires creditors to tell consumers what credit will cost them before they use it?
13. Name the credit law that prohibits creditors from denying credit to consumers for discriminatory reasons.
14. What alternatives might be considered instead of using credit to make a purchase?
15. How do credit counseling services help debtors handle credit problems?
16. Explain the difference between Chapter 7 bankruptcy and Chapter 13 protection.

Resource

Review and Study Guide for Chapter 25, reproducible master 25-4, TR

Answers to *Facts In Review*

1. When using cash for a purchase, money is exchanged. When using credit for a purchase, a promise to pay is exchanged.
2. (List four of each. See Chart 25-1 on page 525.)
3. (List four:) credit card account, charge account, installment account, vehicle leasing, cash loan, home equity loan
4. With a credit card account, customers have a credit card, use it to make purchases, then pay the entire bill when it arrives or minimum amounts for extended periods. With a charge account, a record of the purchase is kept on file and the full bill must be paid promptly when it arrives.
5. to protect the lender/creditor from the risk of nonpayment
6. Get a job; stay employed; open a checking account; open a savings account; buy a layaway item; apply to a gasoline company or a local store for a credit card.
7. to collect and maintain financial information on individuals
8. the information collected by credit bureaus

9. because they are legally binding and the borrower must fulfill the terms
10. amount of credit used, interest rate, length of repayment period
11. as a dollar amount and as an annual percentage rate
12. Truth in Lending Act
13. Equal Credit Opportunity Act
14. choosing not to make the purchase, paying for the purchase with savings, saving money to make the purchase later

(continued)

Developing Your Academic Skills

1. **Language Arts.** Using Internet or print sources, research the history of credit. Prepare a report answering the following questions: Before credit cards were used, how was credit issued? How were credit ratings tracked? What were the consequences for people who did not pay their debts?

2. **Math.** Pretend you own a credit card and keep track of any purchases you would like to make with credit for a month. Calculate any interest that would accrue if only the minimum payment was made. How much interest would be accrued in a year's time?

Information Technology Applications

1. Pick up credit card applications from three local stores and create a chart on the computer comparing the credit agreements offered. Be sure to list the amount of credit offered, annual percentage rate, finance charges, and any other fees. Write a brief summary describing which credit plan seems best based on the information listed in the chart.

2. Using the Internet, conduct a search for different types of car leases. Write a brief report of your findings.

3. Using the Internet, conduct a search for some of the online agencies offering debt consolidation loans. Do these agencies seem legitimate? Why or why not? Share your findings with the class.

15. by providing financial programs for repaying debt, by giving lessons in managing future debt, by restructuring payment schedules for people with serious debt

16. With Chapter 7 bankruptcy, a debtor's assets are sold by the court to pay the debt. With Chapter 13 bankruptcy, debtors with regular incomes pay back some or most of their debts over a three- to five-year period.

Applying Your Knowledge and Skills

1. **Problem Solving and Critical Thinking.** Suppose you want to buy a $300 digital camera on credit. Find out what the credit terms would be if you bought the camera at an electronics store, department store, or with a bank credit card. For each of the three ways, check the credit contract, finance charges, annual percentage rate, monthly charges, and the length of the repayment period. Where would you get the best deal?

2. **Employability and Career Development.** Contact a local credit counseling service. Interview a representative about the types of service available. Write a brief report of your findings.

3. **Communications.** Collect several credit plans from local businesses and banks. Compare and discuss the credit terms in each plan. Which business or bank has the best deal?

4. **Leadership and Teamwork.** Contact a private credit bureau. Find out what information they include in a credit record. Ask them for recommendations on how to maintain a good credit record.

Developing Workplace Skills

Name two purchases you would like to make in the next ten years that represent considerable expenses. Buying a new car and paying for post-secondary education are examples. Find out the current cost of each and add ten percent to estimate their future costs. (Use these estimates for your calculations.) Identify when each purchase would be made and how you would pay. If you plan to earn money by working at a job, include a realistic estimate of your future annual earnings. If borrowing or saving money is part of your plan, use the current interest rates for your calculations. Summarize your plan in a brief report.

26

Banking, Saving, and Investing

Key Terms

online banking

electronic funds transfer (EFT)

debit card

smart card

cash card

endorse

canceled check

traveler's check

cashier's check

certified check

money order

simple interest

compound interest

certificate of deposit (CD)

inflation

Consumer Price Index (CPI)

securities

stock

preferred stock

common stock

bond

mutual fund

money market fund

401(k) plan

individual retirement account (IRA)

Keogh plan

Chapter Objectives

After studying this chapter, you will be able to

- **select** the financial institutions and banking services that will best meet your financial needs.
- **endorse**, deposit, write, and cash checks correctly.
- **balance** a checkbook.
- **describe** the special types of checks that can be used in place of personal checks and cash.
- **evaluate** the basic types of savings plans.
- **compare** different types of investments.

Reading Advantage

Using all of the chapter vocabulary words, create a crossword puzzle on www.puzzle-maker.com/CW . Print out the puzzle and complete it before reading the chapter.

Achieving Academic Standards

English Language Arts

- Read print and non-print texts to acquire new information and to respond to the needs and demands of society and the workplace. (IRA/NCTE, 1)
- Apply strategies to comprehend, interpret, evaluate, and appreciate texts. (IRA/NCTE, 3)
- Use a variety of technological and information processes to gather and synthesize information and to create and communicate knowledge. (IRA/NCTE, 8)

Math

- Understand meanings of operations and how they relate to one another. (NCTM)
- Compute fluently and make reasonable estimates. (NCTM)
- Apply and adapt a variety of appropriate strategies to solve problems.

Key Concepts

- Commercial banks, savings banks, and credit unions provide financial services to consumers.

- Online banking provides more electronic services for the consumer than any other form of banking.

- Having a savings and checking account is a good method of establishing a credit rating and saving money.

- Investments involve some degree of risk so you need to be sure to investigate before you invest.

Having a job means earning money. That first paycheck makes you think about what to do with your money. One option is to spend it, but spending is only part of managing your money. Managing your money also involves finding a place to put it when you receive it. You will want to keep it in a safe place because you worked so hard to earn it. You may also want to save some for future needs. In that case, you should decide where to put money to earn the most interest and still remain safe. You may want to invest some money to meet long-term financial goals.

After reading this chapter, these money management decisions will be easier for you to make. You will learn about the various types of financial institutions and be able to evaluate the services they provide. You will also learn which saving and investment options you might want to consider using.

Types of Financial Institutions

There are three types of financial institutions that provide a variety of financial services. They are commercial banks, savings banks, and credit unions.

Commercial banks are often called full-service banks because of their many services. At a commercial bank you can open a checking or savings account and buy special types of checks. You can also buy U.S. Savings Bonds, take out a loan, and rent safe-deposit boxes. In most commercial banks, the money you deposit is safe because the *Federal Deposit Insurance Corporation (FDIC)* insures it. The FDIC is the governing agency that insures commercial banks for deposits up to $100,000. For example, if you have $75,000 in a savings account and $30,000 in a checking account at the same bank, $5,000 of it would not be insured. You can find out more information about the FDIC at www.fdic.gov/. The site provides information on topics such as identity theft and consumer protection as well.

Savings banks provide many of the same services offered by commercial banks. In the past, they focused more on savings plans for investors and mortgage loans for home buyers. They still provide these services, but changes in the law now allow them to offer many of the same services as commercial banks. For example, savings banks can offer checking accounts to their customers. The FDIC also insures each savings banks depositor's funds up to $100,000.

A *credit union* differs from a commercial bank and a savings bank in that its services are for members only. Members of credit unions are people who share a common bond, such as members of a union, a company, or a professional organization. Since credit unions are nonprofit organizations run by their members, operation costs are usually low. Therefore, credit unions typically charge lower interest rates on loans and offer higher interest rates on savings. Credit unions can also offer checking accounts to their members. The *National Credit Union Administration (NCUA)* is the governing body that insures credit union depositor's funds up to $100,000. You can learn more about the NCUA by visiting their Web site at www.ncua.gov/.

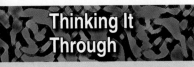

Choosing a Financial Institution

All three types of financial institutions compete with each other to provide financial services and convenience for customers. Therefore, you will need to compare several factors to decide where to put your money. Look not only at the services offered, but also consider convenience and costs as well.

In selecting a place to do your banking, you will want to find one that is conveniently located. The financial institution or a branch office should be close to your home or workplace. Consider the hours the financial institution is open when making your decision. Is it open when you need to do your banking? Some have early morning, evening, and Saturday hours. See 26-1. For further convenience, investigate whether the financial institution has any online banking options available.

You will also want to be certain that your money will be safe. In evaluating the safety of a financial institution, look for either the FDIC or NCUA to protect your account.

Sometimes there may be a charge for some services but not others depending on the type of account you have. This is another factor to consider when deciding where to deposit your money. Compare the fees charged for the services you are considering.

Financial institutions are able to offer many more services today than ever before. Understanding these services will help you decide which ones will best meet your financial needs.

Reflect

What banking services are important to you?

Resource

Compare Financial Institutions, Activity A, WB

Enrich

Have someone from a financial institution speak about online banking.

Electronic Banking

Many of the more convenient services offered by financial institutions are a result of advances in computer technology. The most popular of these services are online banking, electronic funds transfer, banking by phone, automated teller machines, and debit cards.

Online Banking

Online banking offers you the convenience of using your computer to manage your finances through an Internet connection. You can access most services directly. Your financial institution will provide you with security information such as your own identification number and password. This prevents others from easily accessing your accounts.

Online banking provides more electronic services for the user than any other form of banking. It is like having your own 24-hour bank. Transactions can take place at any time of the day or night. You can perform most of the tasks you would normally perform at the bank. You

26-1

Financial institutions that provide drive-up convenience often have extended hours for depositing and withdrawing money.

Discuss

What are some advantages and disadvantages of having your payroll check deposited directly into the bank?

can see your account statement to review your current balance and the checks that have been cashed. If you have a credit card through the bank, you can check the charges you made with it. You can also check to see if you are near your credit limit. Many bills can be paid directly through the automatic transfer of funds. Some banks will even let you write and send electronic checks. Electronic checks allow you to pay your bills right away. See 26-2.

Many financial institutions prefer online banking because it is less expensive than hiring a teller. As a result, most online banking services are offered free or for a low monthly fee. In fact, there are some financial institutions that operate entirely online.

One concern you may have about online banking is the security of your personal information. Financial institutions use firewalls and many other protective means to keep your information safe. However, you should be aware of phishing. This occurs when someone sends you an e-mail that appears to come from your financial institution. When you click on the link in the e-mail, it sends you to a false Web site that looks just like your bank's Web site. From this Web site, criminals can use any information you provide to access your accounts or even commit identity theft.

Electronic Funds Transfer

The **electronic funds transfer (EFT)** is the automatic transfer of funds to and from your accounts electronically. For example, you may want to use an EFT such as *direct deposit*. This is when you have your paychecks deposited directly into your checking and/or savings accounts each payday. With this service, you know your paycheck will automatically be deposited in your account on payday. You can also save money by designating a portion of your check to be deposited in a separate account each payday.

Your money goes straight into your account before you have a chance to spend it. Direct deposit requires your authorization and is possible only if your bank and employer are participants.

Another convenient service allows you to pre-authorize your bank to electronically pay certain bills for you each month. This type of arrangement is often used for monthly mortgage or loan payments that stay the same. A variety of other payments such as electric, gas, telephone, and credit card accounts can also be handled automatically with pre-authorization. Such electronic transfers can save you time, postage, and help you avoid late payments.

26-2

Online banking allows you to see your bank records instantly while offering the convenience of banking from home.

Banking by Phone

The telephone is another way to pay bills and transfer funds. Bank-by-phone accounts allow customers to handle certain transactions through a push-button phone. Some financial institutions are now developing services that will even allow customers to use their cellular phone. Each customer has a specific numbered code that he or she enters using the telephone. The customer can automatically pay bills to participating merchants, transfer funds between accounts, or check on the balance in an account. The financial institution's computer automatically handles all of the transactions. It is very important that you record these transfers as they occur so you have an up-to-date record and do not overdraw your account.

Automated Teller Machines

Automated teller machines (ATMs) are remote computer terminals that customers use to make financial transactions. These terminals can be used 24 hours a day, seven days a week. Banks try to locate ATMs for their customers' convenience. They may be found in shopping centers, office buildings, airports, and many other places, 26-3.

Automated teller machines can handle many of your financial transactions. You can withdraw money from your checking and/or savings accounts or transfer funds between these accounts. You can make deposits as well as loan payments. You can easily obtain information about your account from an ATM.

Before you can use an ATM, you must apply for a specially coded ATM card from your financial institution. To use an automated teller machine, you first insert your ATM card into the machine. The machine will then provide directions on how to proceed. You will be asked to enter your personal identification number (PIN). The ATM reads the card information and your PIN. Upon verification of your account and number, you will be asked to indicate the service you want. If, for example, you want to make a withdrawal, you first indicate which account you wish to use (if you have more than one). You then enter the amount of cash you want to withdraw. The machine will dispense your money through a small opening. Be sure to take your ATM card and the receipt documenting your transaction before you leave.

What makes an ATM convenient—its remote location and 24-hour accessibility—also introduces the possibility of danger. Most ATMs have security cameras and a well-lighted location to discourage would-be thieves. Nonetheless, taking extra precaution when using an

26-3
An ATM offers quick, easy, 24-hour access to your money.

Resource

Precautions for ATM Card Users, color transparency CT-26, TR

Note

Emphasize the importance of recording your withdrawals.

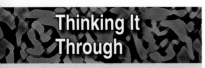

ATM alone or at off-hours is always good advice. You also need to be aware of skimming. Thieves will often attach a pocket-size stripe reader along with a pinhole camera to an ATM. As a result, your ATM card number and PIN are recorded. Thieves can then use this to obtain more financial information from your bank. Be sure you check your bank statements very carefully for incorrect entries. Notify your financial institution immediately if you find a problem. See 26-4 for a list of guidelines to follow when using an ATM.

Debit Cards

A **debit card** allows you to withdraw funds from your checking account without writing a check. It can also be used at ATMs to withdraw money. A debit card resembles a credit card. It will bear the name of a credit card company such as VISA or MasterCard. It is used like a credit card, but purchases are deducted directly from your checking account. In fact, the cashier may not know if your card is a debit card or a credit card. You approve your purchases using either a personal identification number or your signature. Cards that require a PIN are more secure than those that do not.

There are several advantages to using a debit card. It helps you avoid carrying large amounts of cash. You will not need to provide the store with personal information, such as your telephone number and address—information usually requested when paying by check. If you use it in place of your credit card, it will prevent you from running up large balances and possible interest charges. You will also have a detailed receipt for each item you purchase. This will help you keep track of your spending and provide documentation if you need to return an item or

26-4

Following these tips will make it less likely for someone to steal your PIN or your money.

Guidelines for Using an ATM
• Avoid an ATM located in a secluded place.
• When using an ATM at night, make sure the machine and the area surrounding it are well lighted.
• Beware of who is near the machine. If you observe someone suspicious, use a machine at another location.
• Have your ATM card ready as you approach the machine. This will make your transaction faster because you will not waste time searching for your card.
• Memorize your PIN number. Do not write it down and carry it with you. If your card is ever lost or stolen with your PIN number, anyone who finds it will have access to your account.
• Do not let anyone have a clear view of your PIN number as you enter it.
• Put away cash from the ATM immediately. Count it later after you leave the location.
• Check your bank statements very carefully for incorrect entries. Notify your financial institution immediately if you find a problem.

use a warranty. Debit cards are easier to use than checks when you are away from home. Some merchants will not accept out-of-town checks.

There are also some disadvantages to using a debit card. The amount of your purchase is sent to the bank electronically and deducted immediately from your checking balance. If you do not keep an accurate, up-to-date record of your purchases, you may overdraw your account without realizing it. This will result in your bank charging you a penalty fee. You will also want to keep your receipts to avoid someone else using the information to obtain access to your account. Debit cards are not ideal for purchasing mail-order items since payment is made long before your purchase arrives. Debit cards, like credit cards, are so convenient to use that you may be tempted to purchase items you do not really need. If you lose your debit card and someone else uses it, they will be stealing money directly from your checking account. This could make you bounce checks and it could take the bank 10 or more days to straighten out your account. In addition, you may still be held responsible for part or all of the other person's purchases. It is extremely important to notify your bank immediately that your card has been lost or stolen.

A **smart card** is an advanced type of debit card and much more. The magnetic strip found on a debit card is replaced by a microchip. This chip can hold a great deal of information. For example, your entire medical history could be stored on a smart card. Doctors could then use this information to provide fast and effective treatment in case of an emergency. Smart cards could also be used as debit cards to purchase items from a variety of sources including stores, vending machines, and the Internet, 26-5. The government might use a single smart card in place of your driver's license, passport, and social security information.

A **cash card** is a prepaid type of debit card. You purchase a cash card for a specific amount and then use it to make purchases up to that amount. It is also called a *stored-value card* because it is worth a specific

Reflect Further

How does a debit card differ from a credit card? When might you want to use a debit card?

Reflect Further

What problems could arise from carrying cards that contain a lot of personal information?

26-5

You can use a smart card just like a debit card to make purchases in stores or online.

Discuss

Brainstorm the potential benefits and dangers of having smart-card information recorded and stored by various agencies.

Extend Your Knowledge

Cash Cards

Cash cards have a variety of uses. Many stores now issue cash cards instead of gift certificates. Long-distance telephone cash cards are especially popular. A cash card can be helpful in budgeting your money. For example, you could purchase a long-distance telephone card to limit yourself to the amount of the card for a certain period. This could help you control the amount of money you spend on long-distance telephone charges.

cash value. For example, by purchasing a gasoline card for $50.00, you can use the card to fill your car at any station owned by that company. When all is spent, the card becomes worthless and can be discarded.

Some cash cards are *reloadable*. This means they can be reused when cash value is returned to them. When you use the cash value of the card, you may have it reloaded by paying the card issuer more money. Cash value can be returned to the card as often as you desire for whatever amount you wish.

Checking Accounts

Most people do not like to have a large amount of cash with them or in their homes. Cash is too easy to spend, lose, have stolen, or even destroyed by fire. To avoid these risks, many people put their money in a checking account. Although you may pay a small fee to have a checking account, this service has many advantages. A checking account provides the following:

- safe place to keep cash
- easy way to withdraw cash
- convenient way to make purchases and pay for them by mail
- detailed record of spending and receipts of payment
- method of establishing a credit rating

Types of Accounts

Financial institutions offer many types of checking accounts. Three types are: the basic account, express checking, and an interest-bearing account. The type of checking account you choose will depend on the amount you can afford to leave in your account. It will also depend on the number of checks you plan to write each month and on how you plan to do your banking.

A *basic checking account* allows you to deposit money and write checks. This type of account is ideal if you plan to write few checks and keep a low monthly balance. The specific details of the account vary greatly among different financial institutions. Some banks charge a basic monthly fee while others may charge for each check you write over a certain minimum. Some banks may eliminate the fee altogether if you use direct deposit or maintain a minimum balance in your account. However, you should not maintain a high balance in this type of account because they do not pay interest. Some banks even offer free checking with few or no restrictions on your monthly balance, types of deposits, or the number of checks you write.

Express checking is for people who use online banking, banking by phone, or ATMs to do all their banking. This type of account usually offers very low or no fees since you seldom work with bank employees. However, you may be charged a fee to speak with a bank employee.

The *interest-bearing checking account* allows you to earn interest and write checks on the same account. It is a savings and checking account all in one. However, this type of account usually pays a lower rate of interest than a savings account. There is usually a minimum balance requirement. In credit unions, this account is called a *share draft*. In commercial banks and savings banks, it is called a *negotiable order of withdrawal (NOW) account*. A *super-NOW account* is also available. This account is similar to the NOW account but you will receive a higher rate of interest. The minimum balance requirement is also higher with a super-NOW account.

Since checking accounts may vary from one financial institution to another, compare plans carefully. Make sure you find out the service charges, check fees, and/or minimum balance requirements for each account. Then choose the account that best meets your needs.

Opening a Checking Account

Opening a checking account is very easy once you decide what type of account to open and where to open it. All you need to do is talk to the person in charge of opening new accounts, fill out a signature card, and make a deposit. On the signature card, you will be asked to sign your name as you will sign it on all the checks you write. You should sign the card with the signature you intend to use for all financial transactions. This becomes the only signature the financial institution will honor on checks and withdrawal slips that have your name and account number. Always remember to keep your signature consistent for all transactions.

After you open your account, you will receive a checkbook with personalized checks and a register. Each check will include your name, address, and account number. The register is used for recording checks written as well as all deposits and withdrawals. To help you handle your checks and account successfully, follow the tips in 26-6.

If you want another person to be able to write checks on your account, that person must sign the signature card also. When two or more people share an account, it is called a *joint account*. If you choose to have a joint account, make sure you and your partner(s) decide how records of transactions will be recorded.

Thinking It Through

Why should you compare checking accounts at different financial institutions before opening one?

Activity

Obtain and compare checking account application forms from several banks.

Enrich

Write a short paper comparing the advantages and disadvantages of joint checking accounts.

Thinking It Through

What is the procedure for opening a checking account?

26-6

These guidelines can help you manage your checking account successfully.

Tips for Successful Checking
1. Treat your checks as you would treat cash. Keep them as safe and secure as possible.
2. Do not make changes on the face of a check that is issued to you. Do not take a check that looks altered. The bank may refuse to honor such checks.
3. Avoid carrying checks made out to "Cash." If they are lost or stolen, you have no control over who can cash them.
4. For the same reason, never sign your personal check until you have filled in the amount and the payee.
5. Check all deposit slips to make sure they are legible and correct. If you are taking cash back from the deposit, count your money carefully to make sure it is the correct amount. Do so before leaving the bank.
6. Always inspect new check orders for accuracy. Check the spelling of your name and address. Also make sure your account number is properly encoded. Any errors should be reported.
7. If you do not understand a checking procedure, ask an officer at your bank to explain it.

Making Deposits

To put money into your checking account, you will need to fill out a deposit slip so there will be a record of the transaction. See 26-7. A deposit slip states what is being deposited—currency, coins, or checks—and the amount of each. When filling out a deposit slip, follow these steps:

1. Write in the date.

2. Enter the amount of money being deposited. Write the amount of cash being deposited beside the word *Currency*. Write the amount of coins being deposited beside the word *Coin*. Write the amount(s) from the check(s) being deposited beside the word *Checks*, listing each check singly. (There is more room on the back of the deposit slip to list additional checks.) Then add these and record this amount next to *Total*.

3. Enter the amount of cash you want to receive, if any, after the words *Less cash received*.

4. Subtract the amount written next to *Less cash received* from the *Total* amount directly above it.

5. Record the actual amount of the deposit next to *Total deposit*.

6. Sign your name on the line below the date if you are receiving cash back.

Every time you make a deposit, you will be given a receipt. At that time you should enter the amount of the deposit in your checkbook register and save the receipt for future reference.

Enrich

Design an illustrated poster to reinforce the tips for successful checking in 26-5.

Activity

Practice filling out deposit slips.

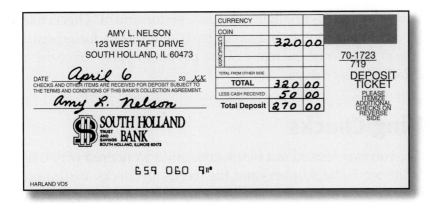

26-7

A deposit slip is a record of the money you deposit into your account.

Discuss

Why do banks restrict where a check may be endorsed?

Discuss

Under what conditions will a bank deposit a check that has not been endorsed?

Activity

Practice writing restrictive endorsements.

You should know that you may not have immediate access to deposited funds. Your bank may delay crediting your account from as little as twenty-four hours to as long as a week. This is to ensure the check clears the bank.

Endorsing Checks

To deposit a check, cash a check, or use a check to pay someone else, you must **endorse** it first. This means you must sign your name on the back of the check along the left end. Your signature must be written in the area indicated. It must also match the name entered on the front of the check. Checks may be endorsed by using a blank endorsement or a restrictive endorsement. See examples in 26-8.

A *blank endorsement* only requires your signature (the payee's signature). A check with this type of endorsement can be cashed by anyone who possesses it. If such a check were ever lost or stolen, it could be cashed easily. Therefore, you should make a blank endorsement only at the time and place the check is being cashed or deposited.

A *restrictive endorsement* states what is to be done with the check. *For deposit only* is a common restrictive endorsement. You write *For deposit only* and then sign your name underneath. This means the check can only be credited to your account. Someone else cannot cash it.

26-8

You must endorse a check before you can cash or deposit it. A blank or restrictive endorsement may be used.

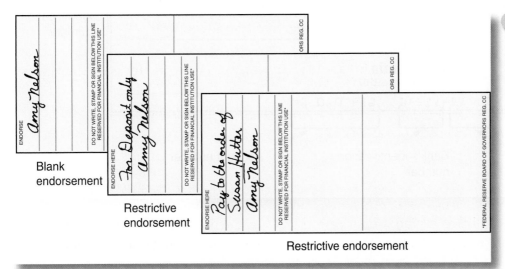

Blank endorsement

Restrictive endorsement

Restrictive endorsement

Resource

Writing Check Amounts Correctly, reproducible master 26-1, TR

Pay to the order of is another restrictive endorsement. This is used to transfer a check to another person or party. For this endorsement, you write *Pay to the order of*, the name of the person or party to receive the check, and your signature.

Writing Checks

Have you ever looked at a blank check and wondered why it has so many numbers? The numbers and the words on checks are important information. This information helps financial institutions process checks. See 26-9.

In order for a check to be processed, it must be written correctly. See 26-10. When writing a check, you need to enter the following items in the correct spaces:

- *date*, including the month, day, and year

- *name of the payee*—This is the person, business, or organization receiving the check.

- *amount of the check in numbers*—Write the numbers as close to the dollar sign as possible to prevent anyone from adding or changing the amount.

- *amount of the check in words*—Begin at the far left. Write *and* after the amount of dollars. Then write the amount of cents as a fraction of 100 (for example, *45/100*, *00/100*, or *no/100*). Draw a line through the remaining space.

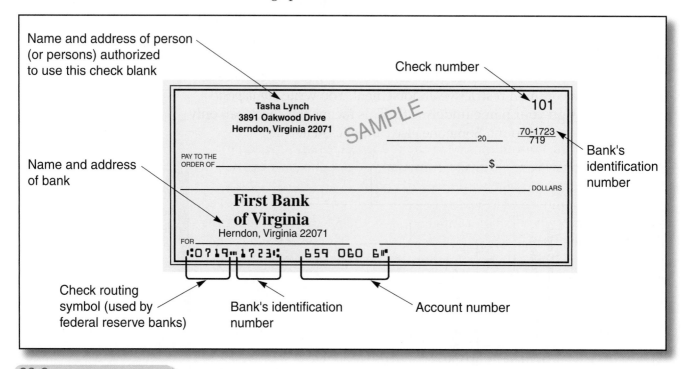

26-9

The information on checks helps financial institutions process them correctly.

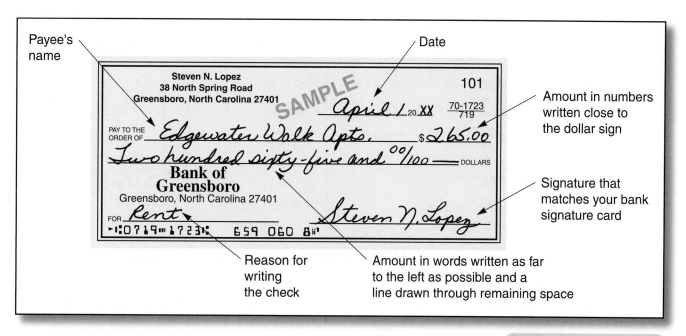

Payee's name — Date — Amount in numbers written close to the dollar sign — Signature that matches your bank signature card — Reason for writing the check — Amount in words written as far to the left as possible and a line drawn through remaining space

- *purpose of the check*, stated in a few words
- *your signature*—Sign your name the same way each time, using the signature you used on the bank signature card.

Recording Changes to Your Account

You will need to update your checkbook register each time funds enter or leave your account. Be sure to record all deposits and add them to your account balance. For recording checks, include the check number, date, payee, purpose of the check, and check amount. For recording debit card transactions, include the date, name of the merchant or ATM location, purpose, and amount. Then subtract the amount of each transaction from your existing balance.

See an example of a well-kept check register in 26-11. Notice the debit card transaction is recorded promptly on April 6. You will also notice items at the bottom that were entered late. There is a reason for the late entries. Two are electronic funds transfers authorized by the owner of this account. The telephone bill changes each month, so the correct amount must be recorded when the exact amount is known. This usually happens when the monthly bank statement arrives. At that time, electronic funds transfers for other items are also recorded, such as the regular $15 paper bill. The bank statement also showed a $3.60 service charge by the bank, so this was deducted, too.

It is important to keep an up-to-date record of changes to your account. If you authorize funds to be paid electronically, you must leave enough in your account to cover them. Knowing how much you have in your account helps to prevent you from exceeding your account balance. If you exceed your balance, your account is overdrawn. The bank charges a fee each time you overdraw your account. You will also be charged a fee by an individual who cashes an overdrawn check. It is common to pay $10 or $15 to an individual and $20 to the bank for a single overdraft.

26-10
This check has been written correctly.

Thinking It Through

What important information appears on a blank personal check? How does a financial institution use this information? What is the correct way to write a check?

Discuss

Why is it important to record the purpose of each check? How might you use this information later?

Note

It is especially important to record debit card withdrawals.

RECORD ALL CHARGES OR CREDITS THAT AFFECT YOUR ACCOUNT

NUMBER	DATE	DESCRIPTION OF TRANSACTION	PAYMENT/DEBIT (−)	√ T	FEE (IF ANY) (−)	DEPOSIT/CREDIT (+)	BALANCE
							336 27
101	4/1	Edgewater Walk Apts. Rent	265 00				265 00
							71 27
102	4/3	Family Food Stores groceries	18 35				18 35
							52 92
103	4/4	K-Mart weights	13 49				13 49
							39 43
	4/6	Deposit				270 00	270 00
							309 43
	4/6	Debit card Bob's Restaurant	9 73				9 73
							299 70
104	4/9	Commonwealth Edison electricity bill	15 60				15 60
							284 10
105	4/15	Family Food Stores groceries	20 02				20 02
							264 08
	4/20	Deposit				270 00	270 00
							534 08
106	4/23	Martin's Shoe Store black shoes	23 58				23 58
							510 50
107	5/1	Edgewater Walk Apts. Rent	265 00				265 00
							245 50
108	5/2	Family Food Stores groceries	16 98				16 98
							228 52
	4/15	Bell South telephone bill	39 83				39 83
							188 69
	4/20	Courier paper bill	15 00				15 00
							173 69
		April service charge	3 60				3 60
							170 09

REMEMBER TO RECORD AUTOMATIC PAYMENTS / DEPOSITS ON DATE AUTHORIZED.

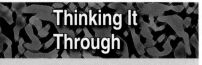

26-11

Whenever money enters or leaves your account, always record the transaction in your checkbook register.

Resource

Checks, Activity B, WB

Thinking It Through

Why is it important to keep your checkbook register up to date?

If you overdraw your account several times, your financial institution may report your poor banking record to the local credit reporting agency. This may cause you to have a low credit rating. Then it will be harder for you to get credit cards or borrow money. Excessive overdrafts could result in loss of your checking account or in criminal charges being placed against you.

Cashing Checks

With a checking account, you should have no problem cashing checks at your bank. However, if you write a check to obtain cash, be prepared to show some identification (ID). This is for the protection of the check writer as well as the person accepting the check. Wherever you cash a check, whether at a bank or another place of business, plan on showing identification.

Many places ask for two forms of identification, with one having your picture or a physical description. The common forms of ID include a driver's license, a credit card, or an employee identification badge.

In the Real World

Cashing Terrell's Paycheck

After work on his first payday, Terrell Smith stopped at the nearest bank to cash his paycheck. He endorsed his check while waiting in line for a teller. That was the first of several mistakes he made.

Arriving at the teller's window, Terrell said, "I would like to cash my paycheck."

"Do you have an account with us?" the teller asked.

"No, I don't. This is my first paycheck."

The teller smiled. "Well, your check has been issued through the Century Bank and this is the National Bank. I will have to charge you a $4 fee to cash this check. If you had an account with us, there would be no charge. Would you like to open an account with us?"

Terrell was getting impatient and grumbled, "No. Maybe I'll just go to the Century Bank."

"The nearest branch is three miles west of here. Let me talk to my supervisor," the teller replied.

When the teller returned, she said, "Since this is your first time, we will charge you only $1 to cash the check, but you should open a checking account."

"Maybe next time," replied Terrell. "Just cash the check."

"Okay, but you endorsed the check on the right end instead of the left end. Also, you wrote T.T. Smith, but the check is made out to Terrell T. Smith. Please endorse it on the left end as shown on the front of the check," the teller instructed.

After correctly endorsing the check, the teller asked to see Terrell's driver's license and second form of ID containing a photo. The teller explained that if he had a checking account, he would be given a bank guarantee card. This card would make it easier for him to cash checks in the future.

Questions to Discuss

1. Do you think Terrell should have opened an account? Explain.
2. Should Terrell have signed the check while waiting in line? Explain.
3. Is Terrell likely to have the same trouble when he tries to cash his next check?

When you endorse a check for cash, wait to do so in the presence of the bank teller. Signatures are usually compared when cashing checks, so one ID should have your signature.

A two-party check may be more difficult to cash. A two-party check is one that was made out to someone else who then endorsed it to you. When you try to cash or deposit a two-party check, you may be asked to verify the other signature as well as your own. Payment may be withheld until the check has cleared the original account. The easiest way to cash a two-party check is to have it deposited directly in your checking or savings account.

Balancing a Checkbook

After you open a checking account, you will start receiving bank statements monthly, bimonthly, or quarterly, 26-12. Each time you receive a bank statement, you will need to make sure your record of deposits and withdrawals (checks, debits, and cash) agrees with the bank's record. This is called balancing your checkbook.

Reflect

What forms of identification do you carry? Would they be sufficient for cashing checks?

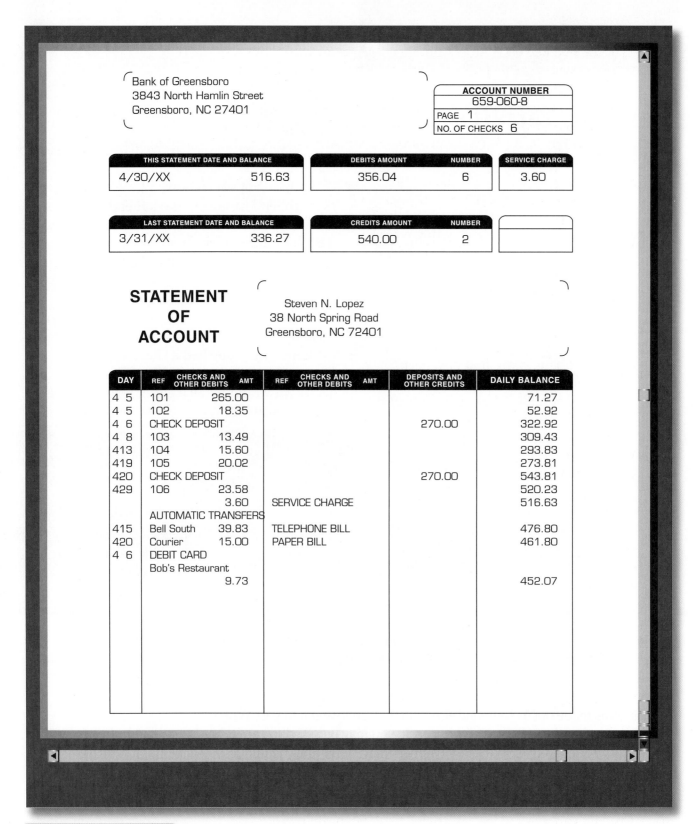

DAY	REF	CHECKS AND OTHER DEBITS	AMT	REF	CHECKS AND OTHER DEBITS	AMT	DEPOSITS AND OTHER CREDITS	DAILY BALANCE
4 5	101		265.00					71.27
4 5	102		18.35					52.92
4 6		CHECK DEPOSIT					270.00	322.92
4 8	103		13.49					309.43
413	104		15.60					293.83
419	105		20.02					273.81
420		CHECK DEPOSIT					270.00	543.81
429	106		23.58					520.23
			3.60		SERVICE CHARGE			516.63
		AUTOMATIC TRANSFERS						
415		Bell South	39.83		TELEPHONE BILL			476.80
420		Courier	15.00		PAPER BILL			461.80
4 6		DEBIT CARD						
		Bob's Restaurant						
			9.73					452.07

Statement header:

Bank of Greensboro
3843 North Hamlin Street
Greensboro, NC 27401

ACCOUNT NUMBER
659-060-8
PAGE 1
NO. OF CHECKS 6

THIS STATEMENT DATE AND BALANCE		DEBITS AMOUNT	NUMBER	SERVICE CHARGE
4/30/XX	516.63	356.04	6	3.60

LAST STATEMENT DATE AND BALANCE		CREDITS AMOUNT	NUMBER	
3/31/XX	336.27	540.00	2	

STATEMENT OF ACCOUNT

Steven N. Lopez
38 North Spring Road
Greensboro, NC 72401

26-12

A bank statement is a summary of your checking account for a specific length of time—usually a month.

The first step in balancing your checkbook is to mark off, in your checkbook register, each transaction listed on your statement. Check to make sure you have recorded the amounts correctly. Be sure to record in your register any transactions appearing on the bank statement that you forgot to record in your register (after verifying they are yours). If any service charge is listed on the bank statement, be sure to enter it in your register and subtract it. If you have an account that earned interest, be sure to add it to the balance in your register.

The next step is to account for the transactions that do not appear on the statement. The back of most bank statements has a worksheet provided for this purpose, 26-13. On the worksheet, follow these steps:

1. On the top line, write the ending balance shown on the bank statement.

2. Record any deposits that are not listed on the statement.

3. Add the amounts from steps 1 and 2 and record it on the line labeled *Total*.

4. List (by number and amount) any checks you have written that are not included on the statement. Also list electronic transfers and debit card transactions that are not included. Add these amounts and enter the total on the line labeled *Checks outstanding*.

5. Subtract the amount in step 4 from the amount in step 3.

The balance on your worksheet should be the same as the balance in your checkbook. If these figures do not agree, go through the steps again and recheck your arithmetic. Also check the addition and subtraction in your checkbook register. You may have made a mistake. If your figures still do not agree after checking for errors, take your statement, canceled checks, and checkbook to your bank for assistance.

A check listed on your bank statement is called a **canceled check**. The canceled checks shown on your statement have been processed by your bank. Some banks return canceled checks or photostat copies to their customers with the bank statements. Other banks issue *carbon checkbooks* that create a carbon copy of each check as it is written. Because customers keep their carbon copies, they do not receive canceled checks with their bank statements. If you should ever need a copy of a canceled check for proof of payment, you will need to contact the bank.

Computerized Personal Financial Management

There are several easy-to-use software programs available that will help you manage your finances. These programs make it easy to keep track of savings and checking accounts, investments, credit cards, and loans. You can use them to write checks if you have a printer and specially designed checks. They can help you plan your finances and organize your income and expenses in a format that will make filing income taxes easier. If you are using online banking, you can even download account information from your bank or credit card company. Once information is downloaded, it can simplify data entry for purposes such as budgeting and bill paying.

Resource

Using a Checking Account,
Activity C, WB

Vocabulary

Collect brochures from a variety of financial institutions and locate as many of this chapter's "Key Terms" as possible.

Thinking It Through

What are the steps in balancing a checkbook? What should you do if your checkbook does not balance?

MONTH _April_ 20 _XX_

THIS FORM IS PROVIDED TO HELP YOU BALANCE YOUR ACCOUNT STATEMENT

CHECKS OUTSTANDING
NOT CHARGED TO YOUR ACCOUNT

NO.	$	
107	265	00
108	16	98
TOTAL	$281	98

ENDING BALANCE SHOWN
ON THIS STATEMENT $ _452.07_

ADD +

DEPOSITS NOT CREDITED
IN THIS STATEMENT

(IF ANY) $ _____

_____

TOTAL $ _452.07_

SUBTRACT –

► CHECKS OUTSTANDING $ _281.98_

BALANCE $ _170.09_◄

CURRENT CHECK
BOOK BALANCE $ _170.09_

ADD +

INTEREST PAID
(IF ANY) AS SHOWN
ON THIS STATEMENT $ _____0_____

SUBTRACT –

SERVICE CHARGES AND
OTHER CHARGES (IF ANY)
AS SHOWN ON THIS
STATEMENT BUT NOT
RECORDED IN YOUR
CHECKBOOK. $ _____0_____

NEW CHECK BOOK
BALANCE
  should agree with $ _170.09_◄

NOTE Be certain to add to your register any
interest paid and subtract from your register any
miscellaneous charges (service charge, check
printing charge, NSF charge, etc.) applied in the
current statement period

26-13

A worksheet and directions
for balancing a checkbook
can be found on the back of
most bank statements.

Special Types of Checks

Paying by personal check instead of cash is a safe and convenient way to make a payment. Other types of checks are used for the same reason. These include traveler's checks, cashier's checks, certified checks, and money orders. They are available at most banks, savings banks, and credit unions for a small fee.

If you plan to travel, a **traveler's check** is a convenient type of check to use. Personal checks may be accepted only in your community or state, but traveler's checks are cashed in most places around the world. Traveler's checks can also be replaced if lost or stolen.

If you are paying a large sum of money, a **cashier's check** may be a more acceptable form of payment than a personal check. The person receiving the check may feel more secure being paid with a cashier's check because it is drawn on a bank's own funds and signed by a bank officer. The receiver is then assured of sufficient funds in the payer's account to cover the check.

Another way to make a payment to someone who does not want to accept a personal check is by certified check. A **certified check** is a personal check with a bank's guarantee that the check will be paid. When a bank certifies a check, the amount of the check is immediately subtracted from the payer's account. The receiver of the check, therefore, is assured of getting paid the amount of the check.

Instead of using a personal check, you can use a money order to make a payment safely by mail. A **money order** is an order for a specific amount of money payable to a specific payee. Money orders can be bought at a number of places besides financial institutions, such as post offices and drug stores.

Safe-Deposit Boxes

In addition to the services already discussed, banks and some other financial institutions rent *safe-deposit boxes* in their vaults. Safe-deposit boxes are small metal containers that people rent to protect their valuables from fire and theft. Jewelry, wills, deeds, birth certificates, stocks and bonds, insurance policies, and other important items are often kept in safe-deposit boxes.

If you rent a box, you will be given a key for it. Each time you use the box, you will sign your name and present personal identification and your key to the attendant. It takes two keys to open a safe-deposit box. Therefore, no one else can open your box unless you give him or her your key.

Enrich

Make a bulletin board display showing the different types of special checks and describing the purpose of each.

Resource

Safe-Deposit Boxes, Activity D, WB

Thinking It Through

How does a cashier's check differ from a certified check?

Discuss

How do financial institutions use your money?

Activity

Calculate interest over a period of time on the same base amount compounded daily, monthly, quarterly, and yearly.

Savings Accounts at Financial Institutions

Instead of keeping all your money in a checking account, you may want to put part of it into some form of savings. Saving money in a financial institution has two major advantages. It provides a safe place to keep your money and it pays interest. A savings program can also help you establish a good credit rating and save money for a specific purpose. Financial institutions offer a variety of savings programs. These include regular savings accounts, money market deposit accounts, and certificates of deposit. In order to choose the best savings plan for your needs, you should first understand how interest is determined.

Understanding Interest

The money a financial institution pays you for the use of your money is called *interest*. The amount of interest you earn depends on a number of factors. First, look at the rate of interest. The higher the rate of interest, the more money you will earn. The amount of interest paid is usually expressed as an annual interest rate based on a one-year period.

A second factor to consider is how the bank calculates the interest. There are two general methods used. One method is called **simple interest**. Interest is paid only on the money initially deposited. For instance, a $1,000 deposit would earn $100 in one year if the simple annual interest rate was 10 percent. A second method, called **compound interest**, is more often used to calculate interest. Using this method, interest is paid on your initial deposit as well as on any interest you have already earned. In other words, you earn interest on the interest. Therefore, compound interest pays more than simple interest.

Be sure to look at how often interest is compounded. The more often interest is compounded, the more money you will earn. Interest can be compounded daily, monthly, quarterly, or yearly. A $1,000 deposit would earn $105.20 in one year if the annual interest rate was 10 percent compounded daily. The true annual interest rate in this case is 10.52 percent. If the interest rate of 10 percent on $1,000 was compounded quarterly, however, it would earn $103.81 in one year. The true annual interest rate would be 10.38 percent.

Time is also a factor in determining how much interest you will earn. The longer you invest your money, the more impact it will have on your earnings. For example, if you invest $50.00 a month for 10 years at eight percent interest you would have $9,258.28 at the end of the 10 years. If you invest $25.00 a month for 20 years, you will have $14,848.68 at the end of the 20 years. In each case you would have invested $6,000.00. However, by investing your money over twenty years instead of ten, you will have earned $5,590.40 more in interest. Therefore, it is important to begin saving on a regular basis early in your life.

If you expect to deposit and withdraw money from your account at various times during the year, you may not receive interest for the entire period. There are several methods used by financial institutions to determine what constitutes an interest period. Find out the policies concerning deposits and withdrawals when choosing a savings plan.

Once you recognize the type of savings plan you prefer, compare that plan at various financial institutions. Find out what the interest rates are and how interest is paid. Look for a financial institution and a savings plan that will pay the highest rate of interest with the fewest number of restrictions.

Regular Savings Accounts

A *regular savings account* can be started with only a few dollars. It allows you to make deposits and withdrawals in varying amounts at any time. Funds can be withdrawn at any time and will not involve a penalty fee. Although a regular savings account is a convenient form of savings, it pays the lowest rate of interest.

Money Market Deposit Accounts

A *money market deposit account* is another type of savings account offered by financial institutions. These accounts pay a slightly higher interest rate than regular savings accounts, but require a minimum deposit, often $1,000 or more. You must also maintain a minimum balance before the account earns interest. You can make withdrawals from a money market account by writing checks, but the number and the amount of the checks may be restricted. These accounts are federally insured, so your money is safe.

Certificates of Deposit

If you have money to deposit for a set period of time, you might want to buy a **certificate of deposit (CD)**. A CD pays a higher rate of interest because it requires you to commit your money for a specific period. The time period may range from 30 days to ten years. A minimum deposit is usually required and there is a set annual rate of interest. The longer you agree to hold a CD, the higher the rate of interest you earn. If you cash in the certificate before the time period is over, you lose a significant amount of interest. Interest rates are also higher when deposits are larger.

The more money you can save, the more important it is for you to choose the right savings plan, 26-14. For example, if you are just starting to put aside money for savings, a regular savings account would probably be the best one for you. Suppose you already have $1,000 or more saved, however, and do not intend to use the money for at least two years. It may then be better for you to buy a two-year certificate of deposit and earn a higher rate of interest. If you left your money in a regular savings account, you would probably earn less interest.

Thinking It Through

Why is it important to know how your bank calculates interest?

Discuss

Why is the interest rate higher when you agree to hold a CD longer?

Reflect Further

What factors should be considered in choosing a savings plan? How might rising or falling interest rates affect your savings decision?

26-14

Determining the right savings plan can help you earn more money.

The fixed rate of interest on a CD can be a disadvantage, however, if rates rise. If you commit your money to a CD for a long period while rates go up, you may earn less than if you had deposited your money in a regular savings account. Once you have $2,000 or more saved, you would want to consider other ways of using your money to earn interest, such as some form of investment.

Investing Your Money

As you continue to work and earn money, you will have more money to spend. What will you do with the money you have left after paying all your necessary expenses? What about the financial goals you established when you developed a budget? Will you be able to achieve these goals simply by depositing a little money each month into a savings account? There is another way to work toward important goals. You can invest some of your money.

Investments can be a good way to protect against **inflation**. Inflation is a general increase in prices. This general price hike decreases what you are able to buy with the same amount of money. For example, it may cost you more to go to your favorite movie theatre today than it did two years ago.

One frequently used measure of inflation is the **Consumer Price Index (CPI)**. CPI is a measure of the average change in prices for consumer goods and services over time. For example, the CPI in 1983 was 99.6, but it more than doubled by 2007 to 207.3. This means the average 2007 basket of groceries cost over twice as much as the 1983 basket. One way CPI is used is to provide a basis for calculating annual cost-of-living increases for many current and retired workers. This adjustment to income gives consumers the same buying power from year to year, even though prices have risen. You can learn more about the CPI by visiting the U. S. Department of Labor Web site at www.bls.gov/cpi/.

Although most investments involve some degree of risk, there are many safe, low-risk investments that can yield higher returns than regular savings accounts. Learning a few basic investment facts may help you reach your financial goals faster. The three basic types of investments discussed here are securities, retirement accounts, and real estate.

In the Real World

Kim's Account Interest

Quietly putting money aside for a year, Kim had built her checking account to $1,000. Since she did not write that many checks, Kim felt that $1,000 was too much for a checking account. Also, she wanted her money to earn interest.

Kim decided to open a regular savings account with $500 transferred from her checking account. She would earn 5.5 percent interest compounded quarterly. Her plan was to leave the $500 in the account so she would earn $28.05 in interest by the end of the year.

During the year, Kim had to withdraw $200 for unexpected car expenses and $100 for holiday gifts. In each case, she replaced the money as quickly as she could to bring the balance back up to $500.

At the end of the year, Kim was surprised to find that she had earned only $23.84. She asked a cashier at the bank why she had not received more interest. She was told that, although interest was compounded quarterly, it was based on the lowest balance in the account during the quarter. In other words, the interest was computed on less than $500 during two quarters of the year. Kim decided to shop for a better savings plan.

Questions to Discuss

1. What questions should Kim have asked when she opened her savings account?
2. Would she have been better off borrowing the money she needed for her car expenses and holiday gifts? Explain.
3. What other types of savings plans might Kim consider?

Securities

Stocks, bonds, mutual funds, and money market funds are all securities. **Securities** represent either ownership or indebtedness. Corporations and governments issue securities to get money to operate and expand. Many securities are sold and traded on security exchanges and markets. Securities can also be bought and sold at some banks and savings banks through their investment divisions. Investments in securities are generally not insured and can be risky.

Stocks

A **stock** is a share in the ownership of a corporation. When you buy stock in a corporation, you become part owner of that company. If the company is profitable, you and other stockholders share in the profits after debts and operating expenses are paid. You also stand to make or lose money when you sell stocks. If you sell a stock for more than you paid for it, you will make a profit on your investment. If you sell a stock for less than you paid for it, you will take a loss. See 26-15.

Most corporations issue two types of stocks, preferred stock and common stock. **Preferred stock** is a more conservative investment that involves less risk than common stock. Preferred stockholders are paid set dividends (profits) at stated rates, regardless of the profit the company

Vocabulary

How are stocks and bonds different? alike?

Enrich

Chart the Dow-Jones industrial average for one month. Chart current events for that same period. Discuss the effects of current events on the stock market.

26-15

Stocks can be checked online or by looking in the business section of most daily newspapers.

Reflect Further

Would you invest money in preferred stock or common stock? Why?

Discuss

How does the federal government use the money you invest in government bonds?

earns. Preferred stockholders also have a better chance of getting some of their money back if a company fails. However, since the dividend rate is set, preferred stockholders could get paid a smaller dividend than common stockholders when the company shows a profit. The value of preferred stock also increases and decreases more slowly than common stock.

Common stock involves more risk because the value of the stock and the amount and frequency of dividends depend on company earnings and economic conditions. When company earnings are good and the economy is expanding, a company's common stock tends to increase in value. This will provide the investor with a profit if he or she chooses to sell the stock. When the economic outlook is poor, common stock tends to decline in value.

Because of the higher degree of risk involved, common stocks offer greater opportunity for large gains and losses.

Bonds

A **bond** is a certificate of debt or obligation issued by a corporation or a government. It is like an IOU. The issuing government or corporation promises to repay the bondholder the face value of the bond after a certain number of years. The bond issuer also promises to pay a fixed rate of interest on the face value of the bond during the loan period.

Bonds are among the safest investments you can make. However, the safety of the bond depends on the credit rating of the bond issuer. Rating agencies, such as Standard and Poor's and Moody, rate bonds. Bonds with high ratings carry little risk. Bonds with low ratings tend to be risky, but they can also provide greater returns.

Drawbacks to investing in bonds are a minimum (usually $1,000) investment and a required length of time when your money is tied up. For these reasons, investors who have limited funds and who cannot afford to make a long-term investment may choose another form of investment such as a bond fund.

The most common types of bonds are corporate, municipal, and U.S. Government bonds. *Corporate bonds* are issued by corporations. *Municipal bonds* are issued by state, county, and city governments. *U.S. Government bonds* are issued by the federal government. Interest rates and yields on all three types of bonds depend on market interest rates and the financial soundness of the issuing corporation or government.

U.S. Government bonds are the safest bonds you can buy. *Treasury Bills*, *Treasury Notes*, and *Treasury Bonds* are all types of U.S. Government bonds. They vary with the minimum investment required and the length of maturity dates.

U.S. *Savings Bonds* are also government bonds. However, they are more a source of savings rather than an investment. They are issued for as little as $50 at a variable interest rate for a set length of time.

Mutual Funds

A **mutual fund** is offered by a company that collects money from a number of investors and invests that money in securities. If you buy shares in a mutual fund, you automatically become part investor in all the securities included in the fund. A mutual fund pays dividends on shares just as any stock does.

Different mutual funds invest in different securities. A company may offer balanced funds, growth funds, and/or specialized funds. *Balanced funds* are investments in a variety of securities, such as preferred stock, common stock, and bonds. They provide a safer investment with dividend income. *Growth funds* are investments in common stocks with growth potential. Emphasis is placed on growth of the principal instead of dividend income. See 26-16. *Specialized funds* are investments focused on either of the following:

- one specific industry, such as only health care companies or only apparel retailers

- one type of security, such as all government bonds or all common stocks

Investing in a mutual fund has many advantages. It allows you to invest in a variety of securities instead of just one or two you might only be able to afford. Having several types of securities instead of just one reduces the amount of risk involved. Mutual funds can be bought and sold at any time. They are managed by experienced investors who work to earn the highest rate of return for their shareholders.

Money Market Funds

A **money market fund** is a type of mutual fund that deals only in high interest, short-term investments. These investments include government securities and certificates of deposit. Money market funds are managed and sold by mutual funds, investment firms, and some insurance companies. The rate of interest earned on these funds varies with money market rates.

Reflect Further

What is the difference between the three major types of bonds? In which type of bond would you prefer to invest your money?

Resource

Investment Terms, reproducible master 26-2, TR

26-16

Millions of consumers invest money in hundreds of mutual funds. They can develop their own plans or get investment advice from financial planners.

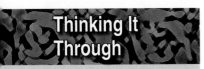
Money market funds offer many advantages for the investor. They can provide a higher rate of return than savings accounts. They can be cashed in at any time since they have no term. Some offer check-writing privileges.

Money market funds have some disadvantages, too. The rate of return on money market funds is not a set rate; it can change daily. If money market rates drop, so does the rate of return on the fund. Also, a minimum of $1,000 or more is usually required to invest in a money market fund. Unlike money market deposit accounts discussed earlier, these funds are not FDIC insured.

Retirement Accounts

Though retirement may seem like a long time away, it is best to start saving for it early in your career. See 26-17. One good way is to take advantage of a 401(k) plan during the years you work. A **401(k) plan** is a retirement savings plan offered through an employer. Workers participate in these plans by agreeing to save a certain dollar amount from each paycheck. This is automatically deducted and put into a special account. An employee can usually split their savings into two or more types of investments. Some companies also match employee contributions, which helps savings grow more quickly.

Another common type of retirement savings plan is called an **individual retirement account (IRA)**. The amount you can save annually depends on your age, income level, and your ability to participate in a company-sponsored pension plan. Two basic types of IRAs are available.

- With a *traditional IRA*, you pay taxes on your earnings and withdrawals after retirement.

- With a *Roth IRA*, the amount you contribute is taxed but, if all requirements are followed, withdrawals and earnings are not.

26-17

One of the best ways to assure a comfortable lifestyle after retirement is to begin saving for it early in life.

Generally, you pay a stiff penalty if money is withdrawn from an IRA before you reach age 59½. Usually the penalty does not apply to first-time home buyers, qualified higher education expenses, and some long-term disabilities and medical expenses.

An IRA can be set up at most financial institutions. You can choose almost any type of investment for your IRA account. You simply fill out a form designating the type of IRA you want. The financial institution becomes the trustee or custodian of the account. In many cases, some or all of your annual contribution is tax deductible.

Another type of retirement plan is a **Keogh plan**. This is a tax-deferred retirement plan for self-employed people or employees of unincorporated companies that do not have their own pension plans. It is similar to an IRA. Those eligible can invest as much as 25 percent of their annual incomes, up to $30,000 per year. Your financial institution can set up a Keogh account. There are provisions and restrictions that must be followed, just as with an IRA. For small business owners and self-employed individuals who qualify for a simpler retirement plan, a *SEP IRA* is available.

By investing in an IRA or Keogh account for each year you work, you can build a sizable fund for your retirement. You can find out more about saving for retirement by checking the Web site of the American Savings Education Council (www.choosetosave.org/asec/).

Real Estate

An investment in real estate is an investment in land or buildings. Real estate is used as a hedge against inflation. When inflation occurs, real estate values also tend to rise. Real estate should be considered a long-term investment. Since most real estate is expensive compared to other investments, a large amount of money may be needed to make the investment. Investing in real estate can yield big returns, but considerable risk may be involved.

Owning your own home or apartment is one type of real estate investment. It is generally considered one of the best real estate investments you can make. Throughout history, most homeowners have been able to sell their property for a profit. While living in your home, the interest you pay on your mortgage and your property taxes can be deducted from your taxable income. The difficulty is in saving enough money for the down payment on a home. You also have to keep up your monthly payments, which include taxes and insurance. These payments are usually higher than rent payments, but eventually you will own the property. See 26-18.

There are other ways to invest in real estate in addition to buying your own home. Some investors buy income-producing properties, such as apartments and office buildings. Income is provided in the form of rent receipts. A well-chosen income property will also appreciate in value over time. Other investors buy undeveloped land that, they believe, will increase in value. Both of these forms of real estate investing can be very risky. They should be undertaken only by people who know what they are doing and can afford the risk.

Thinking It Through

What are the pros and cons of investing in retirement plans?

Activity

Calculate the amount earned at age 65 by setting aside $100 a month for 10 years at 10 percent interest beginning at age 18. Do the same starting at age 28 and compare the results. Note: In each case, let the interest accumulate until age 65.

Enrich

Invite a real estate broker to speak to the class about investing in real estate.

Resource

Banking and Investment Terms, Activity F, WB

26-18
Buying a home often requires a 10-percent down payment and monthly mortgage payments for 30 years.

Reflect Further

To make wise investments, what should a person do?

If you want to invest in real estate, but do not have a large amount of money to invest, you might consider a limited partnership. Professional managers invest in various types of real estate properties. You risk only the amount of your investment. You can usually invest as little as $1,000 in a real estate limited partnership.

Real estate investments can be very complex. There are many factors to consider when buying property. Before investing your money, you may want to take a class on real estate investing. Also, read as much as you can on the subject.

Making Investments

The advice to follow before making an investment is *investigate before you invest*. Here are several tips to help you get the most from the money you invest.

- Set an investment goal. Begin with a small investment and build from there.

- Do not invest money you cannot afford to lose. Very few investments are completely safe from loss.

- Thoroughly examine your investment plans first. Research the current outlook for the economy, and look for an investment that is expected to increase in value.

- Find reliable professionals to help you make investments. Check their credentials and record of achievements. Do not deal with anyone whose experience and knowledge are questionable.

Note

Share strategies for selecting a reliable investment broker.

In the Real World

Kirby's Investment

It was the beginning of Kirby's senior year in high school. He had just inherited $2,500 from his grandmother. He had to decide what to do with the money. He thought about spending it on a trip or a better car. Kirby's father suggested he save the money for his education, but Kirby was not sure what he wanted to do after graduation. One of his friends suggested that he invest the money in stocks where he could "make a lot of money." His friend told Kirby that his uncle had bought some stock and doubled his money in a year. That sounded good, but Kirby had some doubts about investing in stocks.

While waiting for the train one day, Kirby overheard two businessmen talking about the stock market. One of them said to the other, "Let me give you a tip on a good stock. Buy some Everett Gas and Electric. Believe me, this utility stock pays good dividends and is about to go up. If you have any spare cash, buy Everett."

Kirby became excited and thought he was really getting in on a good tip. He checked the stock quotation table in the financial section of the newspaper. He found Everett Gas and Electric. It had closed at 12½ dollars per share the previous day. He decided to talk to his father and mother about buying some shares.

They both exclaimed, "No! Stay away from the stock market." His dad went on to explain that buying stock can be risky if you do not take the time to research and follow the stocks you are interested in buying. You also have to pay a fee to have the purchase made for you. His mother suggested that Kirby investigate the various savings and investment plans offered where he held his checking account.

Kirby followed his mother's suggestion and visited his local bank where an account representative described several options. Kirby decided to purchase a two-year certificate of deposit for $2,000. He put the remaining $500 in the company credit union where he worked. This account allowed him to write checks and still receive monthly interest on the balance.

Kirby continued to check the stock listings for Everett Gas and Electric. The price of a share went up, as the man had predicted. When the stock reached 18, Kirby told his parents that the stock would have been a better investment. His dad said he should wait and see.

The next week Everett stock began to fall. Kirby read in the paper that the company was having management problems after one of the power plants had shut down. Four weeks later the stock had dropped to 9½. Kirby was glad he had followed his parents' advice.

Questions to Discuss

1. Do you think Kirby made the best investment decision? Explain.
2. If Kirby decides to go to college right after graduation, will his investment decision help or hinder that plan?
3. Suggest steps to follow before buying shares of stock in a company.

Summary

There are three types of financial institutions: commercial banks, savings banks, and credit unions. All three offer many of the same types of financial services so compare conveniences and fees before choosing one. Credit unions are available only to members of specific groups.

Electronic banking allows customers immediate access to their money and bank records. With online banking, money can be transferred between accounts at any time. Bills can also be paid through online banking. With the use of an ATM card, money can be withdrawn, deposited, or transferred between accounts at any time.

A checking account keeps money safe while offering a convenient way to buy goods and services and pay bills. There are different types of checking accounts and some can be accessed with a debit card. Traveler's checks, cashier's checks, certified checks, and money orders are checks that serve special purposes. An individual does not need a checking account to buy these.

A financial institution keeps your savings safe and pays interest on it. Savings accounts that require larger balances and fewer withdrawals usually earn more interest. You may also designate some of your savings into retirement accounts, securities, or real estate. Because investing often involves risk, you need to learn as much as you can about any investment plan before putting money into it.

Facts in Review

1. List three factors to consider when choosing a financial institution.
2. List two advantages of online banking.
3. What is an electronic funds transfer? Give an example.
4. List five guidelines for using an ATM safely.
5. How does a debit card differ from a credit card?
6. Name three types of checking accounts.
7. What must be done to a check in order to deposit or cash it?
8. List two examples of a restrictive endorsement.
9. What happens if you overdraw your checking account?
10. What is a bank statement?
11. What type of check is drawn on a bank's own funds rather than the payer's?
12. What is the difference between simple interest and compound interest?
13. What type of savings account also includes some features of a checking account?
14. Define inflation.
15. List four types of investments.
16. What is the difference between a bond and a stock?
17. When should an individual start saving for retirement?

Resource

Review and Study Guide for Chapter 26, reproducible master 26-3, TR

Answers to *Facts In Review*

1. (List three:) convenient location, convenient hours, online banking options, financial safety of the institution, service fees
2. 24-hour access to your money, convenience of banking from your own computer
3. An electronic funds transfer (EFT) is the automatic transfer of funds to and from your accounts electronically. (Student response.)
4. (List five. See Chart 26-4 on page 550.)
5. A debit card allows you to spend money directly from your checking account.
6. basic, express checking, and interest-bearing accounts

7. It must be endorsed, which is signing your name on the back along the left end.
8. for deposit only, pay to the order of
9. Your bank and the party that cashed the check both charge fees. After several overdraws, your poor banking practices may be reported to the local credit reporting agency.
10. the record of checks, deposits, and service charges to your account
11. cashier's check
12. Simple interest pays money only on the deposit. Compound interest pays money on both the deposit and interest earned.
13. money market deposit account
14. a general increase in prices

(continued)

Developing Your Academic Skills

1. **Language Arts.** Choose a company and pretend to buy stock in it. Keep track of your stock for a month. At the end of the month, write a report and give a presentation on the status of your companies stock, how it fluctuated during the month, and whether or not the stock would have been a good investment.

2. **Math.** Calculate the amount of return you would earn after one year if you invested $1,000 in each of the following three ways: regular savings account, certificate of deposit, and money market deposit account. Compare the results with other students. Which investment yields the highest rate of return?

Information Technology Applications

1. Using the Internet, research how ATMs work and what security measures help prevent fraud. Also research possible future uses of ATMs. How soon will this technology be available? Write a brief report of your findings.

2. Using the Internet, research what online services several local banks offer. Find out what kinds of services are available at what costs. Prepare a chart of your findings.

3. Research and use a personal financial management computer program. Is this a good way to keep track of your finances? Explain why or why not.

15. (List four:) stocks, bonds, mutual funds, money market funds, retirement accounts, real estate

16. A bond is a certificate of debt or obligation issued by a corporation or government. A stock is a share in a corporation's ownership.

17. early in his or her career

Applying Your Knowledge and Skills

1. **Communications.** Visit at least three financial institutions in your area. Make a list of the services offered by each. Share your list with the class.

2. **Technical Skills.** Set up a model ATM and demonstrate the procedure for depositing and withdrawing money.

3. **Academic Foundations.** Demonstrate the correct way to endorse, deposit, and write checks.

4. **Problem Solving and Critical Thinking.** Find out the interest rates being offered on money market deposit accounts at three financial institutions in your area. Determine which financial institution offers the best interest rate.

5. **Systems.** What is the minimum deposit required for a CD at the three financial institutions you visited? Compare the minimum required with information you obtain from a financial institution in another state.

6. **Problem Solving and Critical Thinking.** Assume you have $1,000 to put in a savings plan for three years. Investigate savings plans offered at three or more financial institutions in your area. Then determine which savings plan you would choose and why. Present your findings to the class.

Developing Workplace Skills

Working with four classmates, form an investment team. Assume you have $50,000 to invest. Using current security prices listed online or in your daily newspaper, decide as a team how to invest the money. Research your investments and be able to document why you made your selections. You may hold some cash back or deposit it in a regular savings account for future use. Review your investments each week and decide as a team whether or not to sell and/or purchase additional securities. Sell your investments at the end of twelve weeks and determine if you made a profit or loss. Be sure to figure the cost of buying and selling the securities for any transactions made. Summarize the team's results in a brief presentation to the class.

27

Insurance

Key Terms

premium

deductible

claim

basic medical insurance

major medical insurance

Health Savings Account (HSA)

disability insurance

coinsurance

fee-for-service (FFS) plan

health maintenance organization (HMO)

preferred provider organization (PPO)

point-of-service (POS) plan

beneficiary

whole life insurance

cash value

term insurance

universal life insurance

Chapter Objectives

After studying this chapter, you will be able to

- **describe** the different types of auto insurance coverage you need to be aware of when buying a car.
- **distinguish between** the types of health insurance coverage.
- **summarize** the two basic types of home insurance coverage.
- **analyze** the different types of life insurance and the purposes of each.

Reading Advantage

Find a magazine article on www.magportal.com **that relates to this chapter. Read the article and write four questions that you have about the article. Next, read the textbook chapter. Based on what you read in the chapter, see if you can answer any of the questions you had about the magazine article.**

Achieving Academic Standards

English Language Arts

- Read print and non-print texts to acquire new information and to respond to the needs and demands of society and the workplace. (IRA/NCTE, 1)
- Apply strategies to comprehend, interpret, evaluate, and appreciate texts. (IRA/NCTE, 3)
- Use a variety of technological and information processes to gather and synthesize information and to create and communicate knowledge. (IRA/NCTE, 8)
- Use spoken, written, and visual language to accomplish their purposes. (IRA/NCTE, 12)

Math

- Compute fluently and make reasonable estimates. (NCTM)

Key Concepts

- Most states require you to have bodily injury liability and property damage liability auto insurance coverage if you own a vehicle.

- The three types of health coverage you need to be aware of include basic medical, major medical, and disability.

- When purchasing home insurance, make sure you take an inventory of your possessions. Be sure to keep the inventory in a safe place outside of the home.

- Buying life insurance is important if you have dependents to provide for in the event of your death.

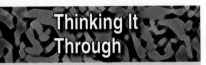

Thinking It Through

When is it important for a person to have insurance?

How does insurance work?

You may wonder, "Why do I need insurance? Is it really worth the money I pay for it?" Insurance is a plan for financial compensation that protects people from specific unexpected future losses. People need insurance to help recover financially from accidents, serious illnesses, theft, fire, and other misfortunes that may affect them.

Insurance works like this. When you buy an insurance policy, you are entering into a contract with an insurance company. You then become a policyholder. As a policyholder, you agree to pay a premium. A **premium** is a set amount of money that you pay to the insurance company on a regular basis. In return, the insurance company provides financial protection for you in the event of a misfortune covered by your policy. The premiums you and other policyholders pay are invested by the company to earn money. Part of these earnings is used to cover the expenses of operating the company.

Some people tend to think insurance is something that only people with a lot of money or possessions should have. However, it is not. Whenever a person has something of financial value that would be costly or difficult to replace, that person needs insurance to protect it. The amount of protection a person needs depends on his or her potential for financial loss. For example, a person with a new car would need more insurance coverage than a person with an older, used car. This is because the person with the new car has a higher potential for financial loss. More money would be needed to replace the new car than the older one.

The four types of insurance you are likely to need during your lifetime are automobile, health, home, and life insurance. You will learn more about each of these types of insurance on the following pages.

Automobile Insurance

Anyone who drives or owns a car takes certain financial and personal risks. If you are involved in a car accident, you may have to pay thousands of dollars in bodily injury and property damages. Very few people are able to afford such large expenses unexpectedly. Therefore, the possibility of a car accident makes auto insurance essential for all drivers, 27-1.

Auto Insurance Coverage

For an individual or a family, an auto insurance policy may include the following six types of coverage:

- bodily injury liability
- property damage liability
- medical payments
- uninsured/underinsured motorists
- comprehensive
- collision

Bodily injury liability coverage protects you if you are legally at fault for an accident in which others are injured or killed. It may pay for the legal fees and the damages assessed against you, up to the limits of the policy. Liability insurance covers the car owner and anyone else who drives the car with the owner's permission. The amount of coverage is usually stated in two amounts. For example, suppose under liability coverage you see *$100,000-$300,000*. This means the insurance company could pay up to $100,000 for any one injured person and $300,000 for any one accident.

Property damage liability coverage pays for damages your car causes to the property of others if you are responsible for the accident. Usually the property is another car. The coverage also pays for damages to other properties such as lampposts, telephone poles, or buildings. It does not, however, cover damage to your car. Like bodily injury liability, it may also pay for legal fees. Limits stated in the policy apply to both bodily injury and property damage.

Both bodily injury and property damage liability coverage may be indicated on insurance policies in the following format: *100/300/50*. In this example, the first number ($100,000) refers to the maximum liability that can be paid for any one injured person. The second number ($300,000) is the maximum payable for any one accident. The third number ($50,000) is the maximum payable for property damage.

Medical payments coverage pays for the medical expenses resulting from an accident, regardless of who was at fault. It covers you, your family, and any guests in your car if it is involved in an accident. It also covers you and your family if you are injured while riding in another car or walking. Your automobile and health insurance providers coordinate payments.

Uninsured/underinsured motorist coverage pays for bodily injuries for which an uninsured or underinsured motorist or hit-and-run driver is responsible. You and your family are covered as drivers, passengers, and pedestrians. Guests in your car are also covered. Underinsured motorist coverage pays for your bodily injury and/or property damage if the other at-fault motorist's policy limits are exhausted.

Comprehensive coverage pays for damage to your car caused by something other than a collision. It will pay for damage caused by such things as fire, theft, vandalism, hail, water, and collision with animals or falling objects.

Collision coverage pays for the damage to your car caused by a collision with another vehicle or object even if you are at fault.

If your car is older, you may not want to obtain collision insurance. The car may not be worth the cost of the premiums and deductible.

27-1

If you are a car owner, you need insurance to cover your financial responsibility in case you are involved in an accident.

Reflect

Do you know someone who has endured financial hardship because of not having insurance?

Discuss

How does a person determine the maximum amount of coverage to purchase?

Reflect Further

What kinds of auto insurance coverage do you or your family have?

In the Real World

Myles's Big Mistake

Myles was proud of the improvements he made to his 1998 car. He had spent a great deal of money and time improving the body and the engine, both of which were abused by the previous owner. Unfortunately, this took most of his extra money. For car insurance, he could only afford a policy that provided the minimum liability required by state law.

While driving one night, Myles saw the lights of an oncoming car cross the centerline. The car was coming directly at him. He swerved to the right to avoid a collision, and his right fender struck a tree. The car continued its forward motion until it hit another tree.

Myles was taken to a hospital emergency room where he was treated for a broken arm, cuts, and bruises. His parent's family health insurance paid his medical bills.

Myles later went to his insurance agent to see about his damaged car. He was told that his car was not covered and the insurance company owed him nothing.

"You don't have collision insurance," his agent explained. "If you remember, I tried to convince you to include collision coverage with a deductible of $300, but you said you couldn't afford it. Your policy does not cover the towing charges either."

Myles was angry with himself. He wondered how he could have been so stupid. He did not have enough money to repair his car, and it could not be driven in its current condition. It had a badly damaged grill, radiator, lights, fenders, and front end. Now he had no way to get to work, except to rely on his parents and friends until he could afford another car.

Questions to Discuss

1. What auto insurance coverage should Myles have purchased?
2. What is the advantage of a deductible?
3. What factors should be considered when determining how high a deductible to get in the insurance policy?

Buying Auto Insurance

When buying auto insurance, compare premiums carefully. Premiums can vary greatly because they are usually based on a number of factors. Some of these factors include your age, driving record, the year and model of your car, where you live, the distances you drive, and the amount of your deductible. See 27-2. Being a financially responsible person with an above average credit rating can also lower your insurance premiums.

Other factors also affect your premium rate. The older you are and the older the year and model of your car (unless it is a classic model), the lower your premiums are likely to be. Some insurance companies also give premium discounts for one or more of the following conditions:

- a good driving record (no accidents or traffic tickets)
- completion of a driver education or safety course
- installation of an antitheft or safety device
- good grades as a student
- insurance coverage on multiple vehicles
- below-average mileage per year

Enrich

Invite an insurance agent to recommend coverage amounts for a new driver.

27-2
Auto insurance rates are very high for teen drivers because of the high percentage of accidents they cause.

Discuss

Where will the money come from to pay for costs if a person is not insured?

Be sure to find out what discounts you may be eligible to receive. As you check several insurance companies for the lowest premium, do not forget the importance of having adequate coverage. Also be sure you do not give up important coverage just to save a few dollars on premiums. Inadequate coverage will do you little good if you are involved in a serious auto accident.

Auto coverage usually requires the payment of a deductible. The **deductible** is an amount the policyholder must pay before the insurance company will begin to cover the expense. For instance, if a policy has a $100 deductible, the policyholder must pay the first $100 of expenses. Usually, the higher the deductible you have in your policy, the lower your premiums will be.

No-Fault Auto Insurance

No-fault auto insurance eliminates the legal process of proving who caused an accident. This type of insurance is thought to lower insurance rates because it reduces costly court trials to determine who is at fault. When an accident occurs, each policyholder makes a claim to his or her own insurance company. A **claim** is a formal request to an insurance company requesting compensation for a loss covered under a policy. With no-fault auto insurance, the insurance company pays its own policyholder for medical and other expenses caused by the accident. Each company pays its policyholder regardless of who is at fault. No-fault insurance is required in some form in many states. However, state laws vary in the amount awarded for medical costs, funeral and burial expenses, loss of income, and other benefits.

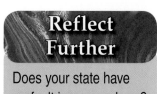

Reflect Further

Does your state have no-fault insurance laws? How do the limits vary from other states?

Financial Responsibility Laws

Most states now have *financial responsibility laws* related to auto liability insurance coverage. These laws are designed to make sure that motorists can pay for any damages or injuries they may cause while driving their cars. The two types of liability insurance—bodily injury liability and property damage liability—are required.

The amount of liability coverage required varies for each state, as does the method of enforcing the laws. For instance, some states require car owners to show proof of liability insurance in order to register their motor vehicles. In other states, proof of liability coverage must be in the vehicle at all times. If a driver is involved in an accident, he or she must be able to show proof of liability insurance. Failure to do so can result in the suspension of the driver's license or car registration. If you are involved in an accident, follow the procedures listed in 27-3.

Health Insurance

With health care costs so high, major surgery or a long hospital stay could cause financial ruin for most people. That is why everyone needs to be covered by some form of health plan. The three types of health coverage to consider are the following:

- basic medical
- major medical
- disability

What to Do After a Car Accident

1. STOP immediately. Do not leave the scene of the accident.
2. Notify the police immediately. Do not move the vehicle(s) until the police have arrived.
3. Do not admit fault. You may be entirely blameless, but witnesses will help prove it.
4. Avoid discussing the accident with anyone except the police or an identified representative of your insurance company.
5. Exchange information with the other driver. Write down the following information:
   - the other driver's name, address, telephone number, car license number, driver's license number, and insurance carrier
   - names and addresses of all witnesses
   - names and addresses of any injured persons
   - names and addresses of any passengers
6. Notify your insurance agent or insurance company as soon as possible.
7. Promptly notify the state's motor vehicle department or similar authority, as required by law.

Basic medical insurance covers the costs of hospitalization. This includes room, board, and nursing services. It also pays for other services such as laboratory tests, X-rays, and medicine. Depending on the policy, it may pay some of the costs of doctor visits and surgical procedures.

Major medical insurance protects individuals and families from huge medical bills. Major medical coverage begins paying where basic coverage stops. It pays the largest share of expenses resulting from a major illness or serious injury. Major medical insurance may also pay for additional services such as doctor visits, prescription medications, and preventative care.

Resource

Health Insurance, Activity C, WB

Individuals with major medical insurance may qualify for a **Health Savings Account (HSA)**. The federal government created Health Savings Accounts in 2003. They allow you to set money aside on a tax-free basis to pay for future qualifying medical expenses. If the money is not used, it rolls over from year to year. When you reach retirement age you can use the money for retirement or continue to save it for medical expenses.

Disability insurance provides regular income payments when a person is unable to work for an extended period of time because of an injury or illness. See 27-4. It is designed to pay you a percentage of your salary on a tax-free basis. *Short-term disability* is available when you are sick or injured for a few months. *Long-term disability* is available when you are sick or injured and permanently unable to work.

When buying health insurance, check policies for exclusions and limitations on coverage. Some companies may exclude certain preexisting illnesses and treatments from their policies. Also check the renewal conditions and cancellation clauses. Make sure you will be able to continue the policy even if you file certain claims.

Another factor to consider with health insurance is the amount of the deductible. This is the amount you must pay before the insurance company will pay a claim. Also look for coinsurance provisions. **Coinsurance** requires you to pay a percentage of the medical costs. For instance, you may have to pay 20 percent of your medical expenses and the insurance company would pay 80 percent. A larger coinsurance provision will reduce the cost of your premiums.

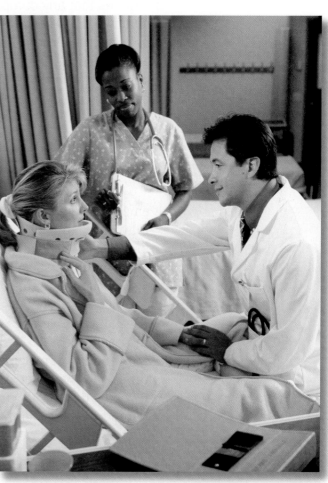

27-4
Disability insurance provides income while a person is out of work due to an injury or illness.

Thinking It Through

If you had a $40,000 hospital bill and had to pay 20 percent, how much would you owe?

Extend Your Knowledge

COBRA Insurance Coverage

If you leave a job that provided group health insurance, you may be able to continue your health insurance coverage for a short while. The Consolidated Omnibus Budget Reconciliation Act of 1986 (COBRA) requires that any company with 20 or more employees will allow you to retain your insurance coverage for at least 18 months. However, you will be required to pay both your share of the insurance premiums as well as your employer's share. You will also have to pay an additional two percent to cover administrative costs. This arrangement allows you to continue your health insurance coverage while you are between jobs.

Discuss

How much does it cost to have a baby at a local hospital with and without group insurance?

Enrich

Prepare a written report on the COBRA Act of 1985.

Group Health Insurance

Many people are able to get group health insurance coverage through employers, unions, or professional associations. If group health insurance is available to you, consider it carefully. Generally, group health insurance provides more coverage at a much lower cost than individual coverage. Some employers pay part or all of the costs of group health coverage.

If you have a group health insurance policy from an employer, union, or association, check to see how much coverage you have. You may have all the coverage you need. If not, you may need to purchase more insurance. See 27-5.

Groups can provide health insurance for their members in several different ways. They can pay premiums to insurance companies that in turn pay health care providers for their services. Some groups choose to reimburse their members directly for their medical expenses. The most

27-5

Major medical expenses, such as surgery, can cost a large sum—the equivalent of one or more years of a person's annual salary. With group health insurance, you pay for only part of these costs.

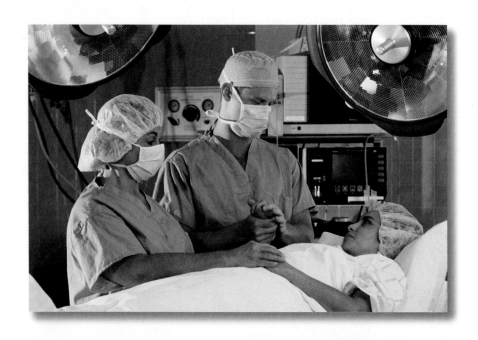

common group health insurance options are fee-for-service plans, health maintenance organizations, preferred provider organizations, and point-of-service plans.

Fee-For-Service Plan

A **fee-for-service (FFS) plan** is the traditional type of health care policy. It allows you to use any doctor or hospital you wish. There is usually a yearly deductible amount that you must pay before coinsurance begins. Once you have met your deductible, the insurance company will then pay a percentage of the charges. Based on your coinsurance percentage, you are then responsible for paying the remaining amount. A disadvantage of this type of plan is that you will probably pay more than you would in an HMO, PPO, or POS plan.

Health Maintenance Organizations

A **health maintenance organization (HMO)** is an organization of medical personnel and facilities that provides health care services to its members. HMOs differ from traditional health insurance plans because they provide health services rather than pay medical bills. As a member of an HMO, you or your group pay a lump sum or a monthly fee. The fee usually covers the costs of many hospital and medical services.

If you need to receive medical services, you must first go to the doctor you have selected from the HMO plan. He or she will be your *primary care physician*. This physician coordinates all your medical treatments eligible under the insurance plan. Only the medical treatments coordinated through your primary care physician will be covered by your insurance. An exception to this may be an emergency. Even in this case, however, certain steps must be taken to have the cost of the emergency treatment covered by HMO insurance.

Depending on the policy, the cost per doctor visit ranges from no charge to a minimal fee. In many cases, treatment is handled at the HMO facility. Sometimes the HMO facility is located within a hospital and, therefore, has access to a full range of medical experts and specialized equipment. Some HMOs, however, contract with doctors in private practice to provide medical services outside the HMO facility. If it is necessary to see a specialist or enter the hospital, the patient pays only a small fee. Though HMOs provide medical care at reduced costs, you can use only those physicians who are in the HMO.

Preferred Provider Organizations

A **preferred provider organization (PPO)** is an organization that has made arrangements with doctors and hospitals who have agreed to accept lower fees for their services in providing health care for group members. Fees for medical services are usually discounted 10 to 20 percent. If you use a doctor or hospital from the approved PPO list, you pay a minimal fee. You may choose other doctors or hospitals, but the fees will be higher.

Enrich

Invite a resource manager from a local company to speak about each of the group insurance plans.

Discuss

If you know someone who belongs to an HMO, how satisfied are they with their group medical insurance? Note: This is a major complaint about HMOs.

Point-of-Service Plans

Reflect Further

What factors might you consider in choosing a health care plan?

A **point-of-service (POS) plan** allows members to choose either an HMO or PPO each time they seek medical services. With this plan you are encouraged to select a primary care physician from the preferred list but you are not required to do so. However, the cost of services will be higher if you do not choose a primary physician from the preferred list. POS plans are becoming more popular because they provide more options than an HMO when choosing medical care.

Resource

Home Insurance Possessions Inventory, Activity D, WB

Discuss

Why should a renter carry insurance?

Note

The larger the deductible, the more cash you will need to have available for replacing your personal possessions.

Home Insurance

There is another type of insurance policy to consider—home insurance. Depending on whether you own or rent property, the following types of home insurance are available:

- homeowner's insurance
- renter's insurance

Homeowner's insurance provides two basic types of coverage—property and liability. Property coverage insures you against disasters such as fire, storms, burglary, theft, vandalism, and explosions. A standard homeowner's policy does not cover floods or earthquakes. Some policies do not cover hurricanes either. Property coverage also insures the damage or loss of the dwelling and your personal property and possessions, such as clothes and furnishings. It also pays for your living expenses if you must move out of your home while it is being repaired or rebuilt. Additional insurance, or *supplemental insurance*, can be bought to cover damages from disasters that are excluded from the homeowner's policy.

Liability coverage protects you against financial loss if others are injured on your property, 27-6. It also provides coverage if you, a family member, or a pet accidentally damages the property of others. Liability coverage pays your defense court costs if you are sued for damages to someone's property. It also pays any damages, up to the limits of your policy, if you are held legally liable for injuries or property damage.

Renter's insurance provides coverage if you are living in a rental unit. It offers protection similar to homeowner's insurance. However, renter's insurance only covers your personal possessions. Coverage of the unit is not included in renter's insurance because it is covered under the owner's insurance.

Whether you own or rent, your insurance policy will only pay up to a certain amount to replace your possessions. Be sure you review your policy to know what is covered. You can also buy supplemental insurance for additional coverage of your more expensive possessions such as jewelry and electronics. Therefore, it is a good idea to complete an inventory of all your personal possessions. Be sure to record the item name, how much it cost, when you purchased it, and where the item was purchased. Include the model or serial number and brand name whenever possible. You may also want to make a video or take pictures of your possessions. Do not keep this inventory in the dwelling. Store it in a safe place such as a safe deposit box. When you need to buy home insurance, follow the guidelines in 27-7.

Thinking It Through

Why is it important to store an inventory of your possessions in a place other than your home?

Liability Insurance

Lawsuits against individuals for negligent conduct at home or work and in automobile accidents are becoming more and more frequent. Courts have awarded large settlements in many cases. Your typical homeowner's or auto insurance may not provide sufficient coverage.

Umbrella liability insurance policies are specifically designed to protect you against claims that your inappropriate actions resulted in injury or property damage. They provide coverage above and beyond the amounts in your other insurance policies. If you think your existing insurance policies do not provide enough liability coverage, you may want to consider purchasing a liability insurance policy.

Life Insurance

Life insurance protects against the loss of income due to death. The main purpose of life insurance is to provide income for anyone who depends on it, such as a spouse, children, or elderly parents. If you do not have any dependents, you may not need life insurance.

When a life insurance policyholder dies, the insurance company pays the face value of the policy to the beneficiary. The **beneficiary** is the person named by the policyholder to receive the death benefit.

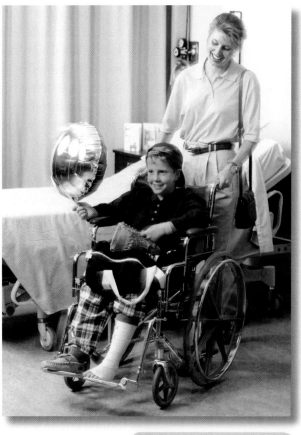

27-6
When a child is injured while playing on your property, the liability coverage of your homeowner's policy covers the medical costs.

27-7
Before buying home insurance, consider these important points.

Guidelines for Buying Home Insurance

- Make a complete inventory of household possessions.

- Photograph or video your possessions and store the photos or video off premises.

- Estimate the value of household and personal possessions. This will help you determine how much coverage to buy and, if necessary, make future claims.

- Find out the current replacement value of your home and insure it at 100 percent of that value. (Many insurance companies apply an annual inflation rate to a policy's premium to assure that the replacement value keeps pace with increasing costs.)

- Consider securing a special endorsement if household belongings and personal possessions exceed 50 percent of the value of your home.

- Consider a larger deductible to reduce premiums. A deductible can help you get maximum coverage at lowest rates for major losses if you are able to pay minor losses.

Resource

Comparing Types of Life Insurance, reproducible master 27-1, TR

The amount of life insurance a policyholder should buy requires careful consideration. For instance, the amount of income that would be lost if the policyholder died prematurely should be considered. Social security benefits, savings, investments, and other sources of income should be determined. The financial needs of the survivors must then be taken into consideration. The policyholder must determine how much money would be needed by his or her survivors to maintain their standard of living.

These factors and others need to be analyzed to determine the amount of protection needed. See 27-8. Once an amount is determined, a person can then decide which of the following basic types of life insurance to buy: whole life, term, or universal life insurance. Each type of life insurance is available in different forms and combinations with different benefits.

Reflect Further

Does anyone in your family have a life insurance policy? Who is the beneficiary?

Whole Life Insurance

Whole life insurance covers the policyholder for a lifetime. It can also be a form of savings. As the policyholder pays premiums, the policy builds a cash value. **Cash value** is the amount the policy is worth in cash upon surrender of the policy. The policyholder can borrow against this cash value or collect the cash value if the policy is canceled. Therefore, a whole life policy pays benefits when the policyholder dies or when the policyholder turns it in for its cash value.

When choosing whole life policies, policyholders have two basic options. They may choose a straight life policy or a limited payment policy. With a *straight life policy*, the policyholder pays premiums throughout his or her life. With a *limited payment policy*, the policyholder pays higher premiums, but for a limited number of years. By paying higher premiums, the policyholder can buy whole life protection in a certain number of years and still receive coverage for life.

Resource

Insurance Terms to Know, Activity E, WB

Enrich

Videotape various televised insurance ads. Solicit the information at no cost and share it in class. Compare the costs of the insurance purchased from a local insurance agent.

27-8

The finances needed to pay the bills and support the family are the major factors to consider when determining how much insurance to buy to cover the possible loss of a household head.

In the Real World

Juanita's Thank-You Gift

Juanita, who just turned 22, has a good job. The years she spent in college are beginning to pay off. She lives in an apartment with a friend. They share rent and expenses, and Juanita is beginning to save part of her income. She has no dependents.

Juanita's mother (age 47) and father (age 48) are both employed. While Juanita was in college, much of what they earned went to pay for her education. Juanita feels she owes her parents for the sacrifices they made to put her through school.

Wanting to do something for them, she went to an insurance agent and bought a term life insurance policy on her life. For a few dollars each month, her life is insured for $30,000 and her parents are the beneficiaries. Though her parents appreciated her thoughtfulness, they told her that her money could be used in better ways.

Questions to Discuss

1. Is term insurance the best type of life insurance for Juanita? Explain.
2. Is it likely that Juanita's parents will outlive her?
3. Do you believe Juanita made a smart purchase for her parents? Explain.
4. What might Juanita have done for her parents instead of insuring her life?

Endowment insurance is a form of whole life insurance in which payments are limited to a set period of time—usually 10, 20, or 30 years. At the end of that time period, the cash value of the policy is paid to the policyholder. If the policyholder should die before the end of the endowment period, the death benefit is paid to the beneficiary. Premiums are higher on endowment policies because the cash value builds up faster.

Term Insurance

Term insurance covers the policyholder for a set period of five, 10, or 20 years, or whatever term is specified in the policy. This type of life insurance is simply for protection; it builds no cash value. It pays benefits only if the policyholder dies during the term of the policy. That is why premiums for term insurance are lower than those for whole life insurance. Many people consider term insurance to be a better investment than whole life insurance because of this lower cost. They would recommend investing the difference in premiums in a good mutual fund. This could result in a greater return on your money.

When choosing term insurance, policyholders should check to see if a term policy is renewable and convertible. A *renewable* privilege allows the policyholder to renew the policy at standard rates, regardless of any changes in health. Without this privilege, the policyholder would not be able to renew the policy at regular rates if his or her health had declined. A term policy with a *convertible* option lets the policyholder switch from term insurance to whole life insurance at standard rates, regardless of the state of his or her health.

Thinking It Through

What two options does a policyholder have when choosing a whole life policy?

Resource

Life Insurance, Activity F, WB

Thinking It Through

Why should a policyholder check to see if a term insurance policy is renewable and convertible?

Universal Life Insurance

In recent years, a third type of life insurance has gained in popularity. **Universal life insurance** combines death benefits, similar to term insurance, with a savings and investment account that earns current market rates. This form of insurance also allows more flexibility in the amount and frequency of the premium payments as well as the level of protection. Interest earnings keep pace with market rates and are taxed only when you cash in the policy. Interest rates can be no lower than a guaranteed minimum rate specified in the policy.

Employer-Sponsored Insurance Programs

When evaluating job offers, consider the insurance programs the companies offer as a part of their fringe benefits. The types of insurance offered and the amounts of coverage will be important to you. An added benefit to you is that federal law exempts taxes on employer-paid health and disability insurance and up to $50,000 of life insurance.

The insurance program offered should be reviewed carefully before deciding on any full-time position. Employers' insurance packages can vary a great deal. A group auto insurance plan is offered by some employers but not others. The same is true for life insurance. Some employers will provide only one health insurance plan, while others will offer a choice of two or more.

For all insurance coverage, you will want to find out what the premiums are and who pays them. For instance, one employer may provide an insurance plan at no cost to you, while another may require you to pay a large share of the premiums. Some employers provide benefits only to the employee while others provide benefits to dependents as well. If some portion of the insurance coverage is your expense, the premiums are deducted from your paycheck. Your employer then sends the premium payments to the insurance company.

In some cases, your employer's insurance package may not meet all your needs. If this is the case, see your own insurance agent for more coverage, but do not buy more insurance than you need. Your employer's insurance package may be enough for you.

Reflect Further

What questions would you ask a potential employer about the company's insurance program?

Choosing an Insurance Company, Agent, and Policy

The company and agent from whom you choose to buy insurance are just as important to consider as the policy you select. Choosing the right company and agent can make a big difference in the coverage you receive and the premiums you pay.

Before choosing an insurance company, do a little research. Make sure a company has a reputation for settling claims fairly and promptly before you buy any insurance from it. Also, take a close look at the policies at various companies. Buy from a company that offers policies with the benefits and options that are most important to you.

Select an agent or broker just as you would select a doctor or lawyer. Find someone with good training and experience in insurance and financial planning. A good agent is one who will advise you honestly about the type and amount of coverage you need. A responsible agent will also help you evaluate your coverage periodically and will process policy revisions and claims promptly.

After you have chosen a company and agent, then concentrate on choosing a policy for your insurance needs. Before you agree to a policy, look it over carefully. Be sure to ask questions about any terms, provisions, options, or sections you do not understand. Also, make sure the policy provides the coverage you and your agent discussed specifically for you.

Note

Videotaping possessions is an excellent idea that is often discussed but seldom done. A copy of the videotape should be stored safely in another location in case of fire.

Reflect Further

How would you select an insurance company, agent, and policy?

Filing an Insurance Claim

It is best to understand your insurance policies before you have a claim. Look through your insurance policies to see what is and is not covered. Suppose you are involved in a car accident or your car is stolen. Maybe your home is burglarized or a storm damages it. You can put your insurance to work for you by filing an insurance claim. Simply follow the steps in 27-9.

Filing an Insurance Claim
• Report any accident, burglary, or theft to the police.
• Phone your insurance agent or insurance company immediately. Ask your agent what you should do and what forms or documents are needed to support your claim.
• Your insurance agent or company may ask you to provide a written explanation of what happened.
• Cooperate with your insurance company by supplying any information your insurer needs as it investigates, settles, or defends any claim. Turn over any legal papers you receive in connection with your loss.
• Keep records of your expenses. Save receipts for what you spend and submit them to your insurance company for reimbursement.
• Keep copies of your paperwork in your own files. You may need to refer to them later.
• Check your policy to find out what settlement steps are outlined. If you are dissatisfied with a settlement offer, discuss it with your agent or adjuster.

27-9

Follow these important steps when filing an insurance claim.

Summary

People need insurance to protect themselves from unexpected financial losses. To be insured, a policyholder must pay a set premium on a regular basis. In return, the insurance company provides financial reimbursement in the event of a specified misfortune.

Automobile insurance usually includes several types of coverage. A number of factors, such as the age of the driver, the distance typically driven, and the type of car, all influence the cost of auto insurance.

Because of the high cost of health care, you should consider getting health insurance. Your employer may provide one or more types of health insurance as a part of the group insurance plan.

If you own or rent property, you should consider homeowner's or renter's insurance. It should include property protection and liability protection.

Life insurance provides for the financial needs of dependents if the policyholder dies. Not everyone needs life insurance. If a person does need life insurance, the amount of coverage and the type of insurance to buy are the biggest buying decisions.

Resource

Review and Study Guide for Chapter 27, reproducible master 27-3, TR

Answers to *Facts In Review*

1. when a person has something of value that would be costly or difficult to replace
2. automobile, health, home, life
3. property damage liability
4. The *deductible* is the amount a policyholder must pay before the insurance company will begin to cover an expense.
5. (List five:) age of driver, year and model of car, completion of a driver education course, good grades, insurance coverage on more than one car, mileage driven, owner's driving record, installation of antitheft device, amount of deductible
6. a type of insurance that eliminates the legal process of proving who caused an accident
7. Basic medical insurance covers the costs of hospitalization. Major medical insurance picks up where basic coverage ends. Disability insurance provides regular income payments to a person unable to work for an extended period of time because of injury or illness.
8. provides more coverage at much lower cost to the individual

Facts in Review

1. When does a person need insurance protection?
2. Name the four types of insurance you are likely to need during your lifetime.
3. Which auto insurance coverage pays for damages your car causes to the property of others if you are responsible for the accident?
4. Define the word *deductible* as it pertains to insurance.
5. List five factors that influence the amount of auto insurance premiums.
6. What is no-fault auto insurance?
7. Describe the three types of health insurance coverage.
8. What is an advantage of having group health insurance?
9. Name and describe the four group health insurance plans.
10. Describe the property protection provided by a homeowner's insurance policy.
11. Describe the liability protection provided by a homeowner's insurance policy.
12. What is the main difference between homeowner's insurance and renter's insurance?
13. Why might a separate liability insurance policy be needed?
14. What is the main reason for having life insurance?
15. Describe the three basic types of life insurance.

9. A fee-for-service (FFS) plan allows you to use any doctor or hospital. A health maintenance organization (HMO) provides health services rather than pay medical bills. A preferred provider organization (PPO) makes arrangements with doctors and hospitals that agree to accept lower fees for health care. A point-of-service (POS) plan allows members to choose either an HMO or PPO each time they seek medical services.
10. protection against damage or loss of the dwelling and/or personal property due to fire, storms, burglary, theft, vandalism, and explosion; payment of living expenses while the homeowner lives somewhere else due to property damage

(continued)

Developing Your Academic Skills

1. **Math.** Pick one type of insurance and research the options offered by different companies. Calculate the differences in price and benefits. Decide which company offers an overall advantage. Create a presentation based on your findings.

2. **Social Studies.** Using Internet or print sources, research famous disasters such as the Chicago fire of 1871, the Johnstown flood of 1889, and the San Francisco earthquake of 1906. Find estimates in dollar amounts of how much property damage was caused by these events. How do the insurance claims for these disasters compare today to those caused by more recent events, such as Hurricane Katrina? Write a brief report of your findings.

Applying Your Knowledge and Skills

1. **Communications.** At three different insurance companies, compare insurance costs for a new car and a used car (five years old) of the same model based on the same coverage. Report to the class how insurance rates for a new and used car differed at each company.

2. **Problem Solving and Critical Thinking.** Obtain copies of life insurance policies from three or four different insurance companies. Compare coverages, benefits, options, premiums, and claim procedures.

Information Technology Applications

1. Using the Internet, conduct a search for the three types of life insurance discussed in this chapter. Create a chart on the computer listing the differences in cost, advantages, and disadvantages of each type of life insurance. Share your chart with the class.

2. Create an inventory form on the computer for your personal possessions. Be sure to include the item name, how much it cost, when you purchased it, and where the item was purchased. Include the model or serial number and brand name. Use the form to complete an up-to-date inventory of your possessions. Be sure to use a camera or video camera to take pictures of your possessions.

Developing Workplace Skills

Working with three classmates, determine which is a better buy—whole life insurance or term insurance. Decide with your teammates how to divide the following tasks. Visit an insurance agent and determine the premium costs of a whole life insurance policy and a twenty-year term life policy for the same amount of coverage. Compare the interest you might earn after twenty years if you invested the difference in premium costs in a straight savings account, a certificate of deposit, or a mutual fund. Visit a bank or other type of lending institution and determine current interest rates for each type of investment. At the end of the twenty-year period, which of the four investment strategies (whole life, term plus savings, term plus certificate of deposit, term plus mutual fund) will have the greatest value? Summarize your findings in a brief oral report to the class. Be sure to cover the advantages and disadvantages of each type of investment.

11. protection against financial loss if others are injured on or by your property, you or your property damages another's property; you are sued for injuries to others or damage to their property, you are held legally liable for injuries or property damage

12. property protection does not cover the dwelling itself

13. If existing insurance policies do not provide enough liability coverage then a separate policy may be needed.

14. to protect against the loss of income due to death

15. Whole life insurance provides death benefits for a lifetime and is a form of savings. Term insurance provides death benefits for a set period specified in the policy. Universal life insurance provides death benefits for a set period as well as a savings and investment account.

28

Managing Family, Work, and Citizenship Roles

Key Terms

role
ownership
burnout
procrastination
support system
Family and Medical Leave Act (FMLA)
flextime
job sharing
telecommuting
public laws
civil laws
felony
misdemeanor
tort
jury
plaintiff
defendant

Chapter Objectives

After studying this chapter, you will be able to

- **explain** your responsibilities in the role of family member.
- **describe** several strategies for balancing family and work roles.
- **list** factors that contribute to a family-friendly workplace.
- **explain** the responsibilities of citizenship.
- **describe** the two major categories of law.
- **explain** how to select and deal with a lawyer.

Reading Advantage

Write all of the chapter terms on a sheet of paper. Highlight the words that you *do not* know. Before you begin reading, look up the highlighted words in the glossary and write the definitions.

Achieving Academic Standards

English Language Arts

- Read print and non-print texts to acquire new information and to respond to the needs and demands of society and the workplace. (IRA/NCTE, 1)
- Apply strategies to comprehend, interpret, evaluate, and appreciate texts. (IRA/NCTE, 3)
- Use spoken and written language to communicate effectively. (IRA/NCTE, 4)

Key Concepts

- Throughout your life you will have many different roles and responsibilities as a family member.

- Learning how to manage your time effectively can help you balance your family and work roles.

- Work arrangements such as flextime, job sharing, and telecommuting assist employees in handling their work and family roles.

- Learning about your rights, responsibilities, and privileges helps you assume your role as a citizen.

A **role** is a pattern of expected behavior. When you first entered school, you began the process of balancing two different roles—student and family member. Once you enter the workforce, you add the new role of employee. This role shares your time and energy with the other two roles. As you move through adulthood, you will continue to add a variety of new roles and responsibilities related to family, work, and citizenship. How well you balance your priorities, time, and energy will have a great impact on how successful you will be in each of these important roles.

Family Roles

In the not too distant future you may begin to think about starting a family. Your role as family member will often be more complex and difficult than your work role. It may also be more rewarding. It is definitely more important. How well you perform as a family member is determined primarily by your commitment to your family and the importance you place on that commitment.

Throughout your lifetime you will play a number of different roles as a member of different families. You began in the self-centered role of a small child. As you grew, you took on more responsibilities for your own care and the care of others. When you become independent, you may take on additional roles, such as wife, mother, husband, or father. You may also take on responsibilities in extended families, such as that of son-in-law or daughter-in-law.

Each of these family roles involves building effective relationships with other family members. See 28-1. Having a role as a family member also means sharing the responsibility for maintaining the home and using leisure time effectively.

28-1

Your role as a teenage member of the family is to maintain a good relationship with your parents and siblings as well as members of your extended family.

Building Relationships

Successful families are built on successful relationships. These relationships involve love, trust, and mutual respect. They begin with honesty and commitment.

Honesty has two sides. It involves being honest with yourself and with those around you. Being honest with yourself can be very difficult. Sometimes it is too easy to make excuses for your behavior. You may tell other family members you did not do your share of housework because you were too tired after working all day. However, you know the real reason was that you could not motivate yourself to do it. There were other things you wanted to do more. Making excuses for yourself can become a habit and lead to a continual pattern of failure.

A commitment is a promise you make to yourself or to others. Commitment means taking care of your duties and responsibilities. A commitment can be as small as agreeing to take out the garbage or as important as taking marriage vows. Keeping your commitments, both large and small, is very important. If people know you honor your commitments, they are more likely to believe and trust you. It is very important for you to follow through with your commitments if you are to build strong relationships with your family, friends, and coworkers.

Reflect Further

Has someone ever broken a promise to you? How did you feel? Is it ever okay to break a commitment? Why or why not?

Maintaining the Home

Everyone benefits from a well-kept home. That is the primary reason everyone should contribute to its maintenance to the best of their ability.

Maintaining a home involves a variety of responsibilities. There are the physical tasks of preparing meals, keeping the home clean, and making routine repairs. There are also the financial responsibilities of developing and maintaining a household budget. If you are sharing your house or apartment with someone else, these should become shared responsibilities.

It is very important to reach an agreement on who will handle each responsibility. It is also important to establish a spirit of cooperation. There will be times when you will need to help finish tasks assigned to another family member.

This spirit of cooperation becomes even more important in families where all adult members work outside the home. The tradition of one person doing the cooking and housework and another being responsible for yard work or other chores may no longer apply, 28-2. Because work schedules vary, it may be best for each person to share in cleaning, cooking, and home maintenance as his or her schedule allows.

It also becomes very important for younger members to help out. Children must take on responsibilities that were considered adult responsibilities at one time. Careful consideration must be given to the age and maturity of the child when this is done.

In many cases there is not enough time to handle all the work and home responsibilities. As a result, more and more households now employ domestic help. In the future you may need to decide whether to work more hours to afford household help or work fewer hours and do your own housework.

Discuss

How is being honest with yourself different from being honest with others? Explain.

Reflect

Are the household responsibilities divided in your home? Are they shared equally?

Discuss

Should household tasks be distributed on a gender basis, such as housework for females and yardwork for males?

28-2
Saving time is a high priority with today's families. For example, whoever has time to grocery shop on the way home from work is the person assigned the task.

Reflect Further

Are you doing your fair share of household responsibilities? Develop a system for assigning household chores that you believe is fair.

Reflect

Would handling tasks with a team approach work in your home? Explain.

A good team effectively uses the time and talents of each member to pursue a common goal. As in the workplace, a team approach may be the best way to decide how to distribute household responsibilities. Household members could meet on a weekly basis to review the necessary tasks and a plan for completing them. Both household and outside responsibilities would need to be considered. Then assignments for each person could be determined based on information provided to the group. Individuals who share in this type of decision-making process are more likely to take ownership of their responsibilities. **Ownership** is when an individual understands the importance of a task and makes sure it is done well.

Using Leisure Time Effectively

How effectively you use your leisure time impacts the quality of your life and directly affects your family. As a teen, you enjoy some leisure time apart from your family. As an adult, however, your leisure time will probably revolve around your family.

An important part of maintaining a balanced lifestyle is how well you use your leisure time. An overemphasis on work can lead to burnout at home and on the job. **Burnout** is a loss of physical and emotional strength and motivation. Some job behaviors that may result from burnout include tardiness, absenteeism, low productivity, irritability, and fatigue.

Burnout can also strain family relationships. To prevent it, individuals must allow time in their schedule for a balance of restful and active leisure pursuits with the family, 28-3. Balancing your leisure time well keeps you refreshed. It helps you maintain good family relationships. It also helps you be more productive on the job.

Balancing Family and Work Roles

A meaningful and happy family life does not just happen. It takes the effort and sacrifice of all family members. There are times when your commitment to your family may affect the quality of your work or that of your partner's. A sick child may need attention on the same day an important project is due at work. Do you help the child or finish the project at work? Which is more important to you? How can you effectively handle both?

If you are not careful, work can overwhelm you. Important deadlines or the need to work overtime may be more pressing than family matters. In other cases, the problems at work may be brought home and affect your family relationships. Sometimes it is possible to become trapped in a job you hate and bring your negative attitudes home with you. There will also be times when a problem at home may affect your ability to concentrate at work.

Meeting both the demands of family and work can be very challenging, especially when both heads of the household work outside the home. Single parents trying to manage everything feel intense stress, too. By managing time well and using available resources, balancing family and work roles will be easier.

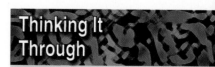

Reflect Further

What are some leisure activities in which all members of your family benefited?

Managing Your Time

A key strategy for balancing family and work roles is managing your time. Time management is the ability to plan and use time well. It involves organizing your daily schedule so everything important gets done.

No one system works for everyone. As you schedule your time, you will find that some strategies work and others do not. The following strategies have proven effective for many people in developing and implementing time management plans. They include setting goals, making to-do lists, and staying focused.

Thinking It Through

Why is time management important?

Set Goals

An important key to managing time is deciding what is important to you. There are only 24 hours in the day so you cannot possibly do everything. First, ask yourself some important questions. Where do you see yourself five, ten, or twenty years from now? What do you plan to do with your life? What is the relative importance of work, family, and friends in your life? Answers to these questions will help you establish your goals.

As you learned in Chapter 12, goals help you look at the big picture. They focus on where you want to be, not on how to get there. For example, you might establish an occupational goal of owning and operating a small engine repair shop by the time you are 30. You can then focus your time and effort on what is really important for accomplishing that goal. The tasks you consider important become your priorities.

Make To-Do Lists

To get yourself organized for each day, you begin by seeing what needs to be done to meet coming deadlines. What must absolutely be done today? What should you do today to be prepared for tomorrow? What project needs to be started today to meet a deadline later? An appointment calendar will help you do this. An *appointment calendar* provides space for hour-by-hour listings of things you need to do each day. It is available in print or electronic format. You can keep track of all your important appointments with the use of an appointment calendar. For example, you can list when class assignments are due and the dates and times of school or work meetings. You can also list any social and medical appointments you may have.

The calendar becomes the starting point for your to-do list. Use it to develop a list of all the things you need to accomplish. Then add any other important items that may have been omitted from your calendar. You may want to develop separate lists for school, home, and work. Once you have your list(s) developed, then identify the most important items. You can do this by numbering them in order of priority.

Some individuals use a system of assigning a separate number to each task. They label the most important task *number one* and the others accordingly. It is a good idea to work on tasks in their numbered order and finish each before going to the next. Check off each item as you complete it. This gives you a feeling of accomplishment and encourages you to do more. At the end of the day it is very rewarding to see all the items you have been able to check off. This system is ideal when working with a short list (about a dozen items) or when each item must be accomplished in a specific order. See 28-4.

Some individuals have dozens of daily tasks, so they use a simpler, four-number system. They number the must-do tasks *one*; the next-do tasks *two*; the should-do tasks *three*; and the remaining tasks for later deadlines *four*. This simplifies the process of prioritizing tasks and allows more flexibility in deciding what to do next. Number-three and number-four tasks can wait till tomorrow, but eventually they become number-one and number-two tasks. This type of system is especially helpful when you have many tasks to do of similar priority that can be done in any order.

Determine your most productive time of day and schedule your work accordingly. For example, try to do the difficult, unpleasant, or urgent work at your most productive time of day. Some people enjoy getting up early and doing challenging work in the morning. Others prefer to work in the afternoon or late into the evening. You will accomplish more if you schedule tasks during your most productive hours whenever possible.

Stay Focused

Having a set of goals and a to-do list is very important, but distractions can destroy your best intentions. Do you telephone a friend to chat when you should be doing your laundry instead? If you are completely honest, you will know when you are not applying yourself. To help stay focused, use the following tips:

A to-do list itemizes what must be done and prevents you from forgetting important tasks.

- *Identify your time-wasters and try to avoid them*. If having the TV on distracts your attention and takes you away from your work, turn it off.

- *Avoid postponing unpleasant work*. This is known as **procrastination**. When you have an unpleasant or difficult task, handle it as soon as possible. In that way, the unpleasant feelings you have about the task are brief and quickly replaced by satisfaction in getting the job done.

- *Set realistic deadlines*. Do you only feel motivated to complete an assignment the night before it is due? When you review your to-do lists and set priorities, you will have a better picture of *what* needs to be done *when* in order to meet deadlines.

- *Stay motivated by keeping your goals in mind*. For example, it is under-standable that you do not always feel like studying. However, if you recognize the importance of each class and each grade to your overall career goal, you will have more desire to study. Keeping "the big picture" in mind will increase your motivation level.

- *Just say no*. You have many important demands on your time. But do not try to do everything. Learn to say no to requests you do not have time for.

- *Be flexible*. As you try to stay focused and manage your time well, you will notice that some days are more productive than others. You should not feel guilty if you have tried your best. Learn from your successes and failures, and make adjustments to your plan accordingly.

Reflect Further

Which type of to-do list works best for you?

Reflect Further

What are your most and least productive times in an average day?

Reflect Further

Do you know a person with special needs? If so, how do family members adjust to assist this person?

Using Community Resources

There may be occasions when, in spite of your best efforts, you will not be able to handle all your responsibilities. Often this is the case in families with members who need special care. Small children need special care, as do some older children with special needs. Adult family members with limited physical or mental ability may also need special care and attention.

A number of community-based services and programs can be used to respond to the needs of the modern family. Help can be arranged through the efforts of concerned individuals. See 28-5. In addition, there are many low-cost community programs to use as well as private services that provide help.

A Support System

Practically every community has neighbors who are willing to help you in exchange for your helping them on occasion. Perhaps relatives live nearby and can assist, too. This group of caring, concerned friends and relatives is called a **support system**. A support system can be formed through the efforts of friends and neighbors, community service programs, and even local businesses.

A support system can be as simple as being a good neighbor. For example, you ask your neighbors to check your ailing parent during the day when you are at work. In return, you watch their son for an hour each day until his older sister comes home from school. Several supportive families working together can form a network of care that makes family challenges easier to handle.

28-5

A reading group for children at the library is one way families can use their community resources.

Reflect

What are some strategies to motivate yourself?

Resource

Support Systems, Activity C, WB

Community Programs

Many times there are community programs and events designed around the special interests and needs of children, teens, and older adults. For children and teens, there are after-school and weekend programs devoted to crafts, sports, and games. For older, retired adults, there are daytime workshops, lectures, tours, exercise programs, and other events.

These programs may be available through local park districts and recreation departments. Tax-supported community service agencies and private nonprofit groups also provide similar programs. By knowing what your community offers, you can take advantage of free or low-cost ways to benefit your family. When family members are occupied, you can devote attention to other matters. To learn all the programs and events available in your community, read the local newspaper and contact your local government office.

Extended Programs in School

The length of the normal workday plus commuting time is much longer than an average school day. As a result, some parents leave children home alone for a period before and/or after school. Since this is not a safe situation for young children, schools and communities are addressing the problem. One answer is extended programs offered by schools.

Some public and private schools are open for several hours before and after school to provide a safe place for children who have no adult at home. During this time, children can do homework or participate in recreational activities, 28-6. Children can also choose to attend special programs such as foreign language instruction. Extended school programs are usually available full-time on weekdays during summers and holidays.

Care Centers and Professional Help

For families that need more or specialized assistance, there are private centers to help. Child care centers provide all-day care for preschool children. For school-age children, the centers provide supervision before and/or after school. There are elder-care centers, too. These generally provide hourly, daytime, and 24-hour care.

Before using a private care center, learn about its reputation in the community. What services does it provide? What are the costs? What will the center expect of you when a family member is enrolled? Compare what different centers offer in terms of programs, price, and convenience to you.

Reflect Further

In which community programs can (or do) you participate now?

Discuss

Why is today's need so great for community-based support?

Enrich

Have the class research and list free or low-cost programs in the community.

28-6

Playing with friends, working on a hobby, or finishing homework are some of the choices open to children in extended school programs.

Extend Your Knowledge

Family Counseling Services

Most communities offer a variety of family counseling services to deal with the stress of modern family life. These may be offered at no or low cost by nonprofit organizations and churches. They are also offered through private counselors. Counseling services help families deal with drug and alcohol abuse, marital problems, child or spousal abuse, stress management, and other family problems. Some employers offer counseling as part of their employee benefits.

Reflect Further

What types of programs and services are available in your community for small children and older adults?

If you need a more specialized type of care arrangement, businesses and self-employed individuals can provide professional care in your home. Private care can be arranged for children as well as adults. This care can be scheduled for certain hours on certain days or for 24-hour periods. As with other types of care, you will want to check the service thoroughly before using it. You will also want to see if a similar service is offered at a more affordable cost through a government agency or nonprofit group.

The Family-Friendly Workplace

An employee who is worried about a family member cannot do a good job at work. Family emergencies may cause an employee to arrive late or miss full days of work, 28-7. If the family problem persists, workers are sometimes forced to resign and find jobs that allow more flexible schedules.

Some employers believe that the demands of work should always come ahead of family demands. However, some employers know that finding ways to help employees balance their many roles and stay employed makes good business sense. It is very costly to hire and train new employees to fill the jobs left vacant by experienced workers who leave. In the long run, programs that provide options for handling family matters are a relatively small business expense.

The cost-effectiveness of family-friendly programs has been well documented. Companies that offer the programs tend to attract the most talented and productive workers, too. Because of this record of success, many employers are voluntarily implementing family-friendly programs and policies. To make sure most workers are offered some flexibility in handling family responsibilities, a law provides workers with some guarantees.

Activity

Have the class develop a chart comparing services, costs, requirements, and quality of community, school, and private care programs.

Reflect

Would you be willing to volunteer as a tutor or activities assistant in an extended school program?

Enrich

Invite a human resource manager to speak about family-friendly programs offered by employers.

The Family and Medical Leave Act

The **Family and Medical Leave Act (FMLA)** was passed in 1993. The FMLA was designed to help families handle special family matters by permitting employees to take time off without pay. The law is intended to help preserve the stability and economic security of the family. It generally applies to employers with 50 or more employees.

Families with young children are not the only beneficiaries of this law. More and more, employees are using an FMLA leave to provide care to an aging parent or sick spouse. Under this law employees are entitled to take up to 12 weeks off during any 12 months for the reasons shown in 28-8. In 2008, the FMLA was amended to add care for a seriously injured or ill family member of the Armed Forces. FMLA leave for this reason allows employees to take up to 26 weeks off without pay in a 12-month period instead of the 12 weeks. When employees return from an FMLA leave, they are entitled to their same jobs or an equivalent one with the same level of pay, benefits, and responsibilities.

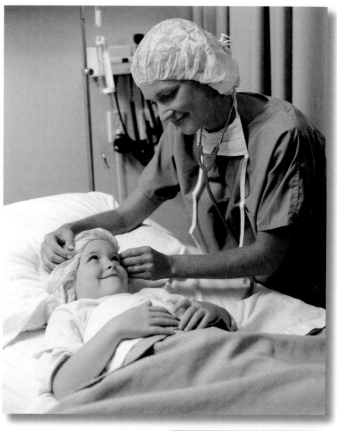

28-7

Doctor's visits and bedside care for a sick child often cause a parent to miss several days of work each year.

Family-Friendly Benefits and Policies

Family-friendly programs evolved as companies listened to workers' concerns and tried different approaches to address them. This has resulted in work arrangements such as flextime, job sharing, and telecommuting. Special programs and services are also being developed to help with child care and other home responsibilities.

Work Arrangements

Factory work and assembly line jobs require all workers to stay at their workstations during the posted work hours. Many of today's jobs dealing with information or ideas no longer need to have workers stay in one place or maintain identical work schedules. Because the nature of work itself is changing, so is the way people work. Here are several types of work arrangements that you may experience in the workplace.

Flextime is a program that allows workers great flexibility in setting their own hours. An individual may work four or five hours early in the day, then several hours late at night. In many cases, workers have certain days or "core" hours when they must be at the work site. Beyond these, they may have complete freedom in choosing when and where they

Thinking It Through

Can you take time off to care for a sick sibling or grandparent under the Family and Medical Leave Act?

Provisions of the Family and Medical Leave Act

If your employer has 50 or more employees, you are entitled to take up to 12 weeks off without pay during any 12 months for the following reasons:

- Having and caring for a baby

- Adopting a child or adding a foster child to the family

- Caring for a sick child, spouse, or parent

- Being unable to work because of serious illness

You are entitled to take up to 26 weeks off without pay during any 12 months for the following reason:

- Caring for a seriously injured or ill family member of the Armed Forces

28-8

Workers can take an unpaid leave from their jobs for these family-related reasons.

accomplish the rest of their work. This type of scheduling allows employees to balance family and work roles more effectively. Workers can be with their children for that important concert, parent conference, or sports event and still attend important meetings at work.

Job sharing is when a single job is split between two or more employees, 28-9. For example, one person may work four hours in the morning while the other works at the same job for the same time period in the afternoon. Normally, both employees receive reduced company benefits. This type of program enables individuals to earn an income and stay up-to-date in their field while devoting considerable time to personal or family matters.

Telecommuting is the process of working at home or from some other site through an electronic link-up to a central office. This usually involves a computer, fax, and telephone. You send your work to the central job site electronically rather than carry it there by car or train. Telecommuting also allows you to work at times when the company is not open, such as evening and weekend hours. Telecommuters report to the central office as occasions require. Traveling salespeople are good examples of modern telecommuters.

28-9

Workers who share jobs must keep each other informed about facts both need to know to do the job well.

Employer-Sponsored Services

There are a wide variety of services offered by employers to help workers balance their work and family roles. Many of these services help workers care for small children. Others help workers with other concerns, such as finding ways to spend more time with their families.

The problems of offering quality child care affect both the employer and employee. The quality and quantity of work may suffer if a worker is concerned about the well-being of a child or must take time off for a doctor visit. As a result, employers now offer a variety of options for the care of their employees' children.

Some employers operate child care centers at or near the company. Sometimes several employers work together to provide child care at a jointly operated center. These centers provide care for preschoolers and may also serve school-age children before and after school and during vacations. The centers provide cribs, toys, play stations, food, medical services, and professionally trained child care workers. Employees are encouraged to visit their children during work breaks and mealtimes. These centers may also provide emergency care when an employee's regular child care arrangements fall through.

Some employers provide financial support for child care through a *voucher system*. With such a system, the employee is reimbursed by the employer for all or a portion of the child care costs. This gives employees control over the type and quality of child care they use. It also avoids the expense of building or operating a special care facility.

A *Federal Flexible Spending Account (FSA)* is another program designed to provide child care assistance. Employees who participate in this program have a regular deduction taken from their paycheck. This amount is then placed in a special fund to pay for child care. As you pay your child care expenses you can request reimbursements from these funds. An advantage of this system is that neither the employee nor the employer are taxed on the money set aside and spent for child care. (A separate FSA can be set up to cover medical expenses not covered by your health insurance.)

A shortage of openings in child care centers has resulted from the increased demand for quality care. As a result, some employers guarantee slots at private centers. This ensures that employees will have a place to send their children, 28-10. The employee still pays for the child care but the employer picks up the cost of guaranteeing any unfilled spaces.

Although not a direct child care service, many companies offer seminars and workshops on skills related to parenting. These programs help employees learn to balance family and work responsibilities. Program topics include selecting a quality care facility and managing child care finances.

Besides care-focused programs, some companies offer time-saving services that allow employees more time with their families. A dry cleaning pickup and delivery service returns dry-cleaned garments directly to the work site. A food delivery service allows grocery orders to be placed one day and picked up the next. Usually this service excludes refrigerated and

Reflect Further

Do you know anyone whose job involves flextime, job sharing, or telecommuting?

Enrich

Survey at least five area employers to determine what types of child care services are offered, if any. Prepare a brief report.

Activity

Tour a company that offers child care services on site. Write a brief report of your visit findings.

Discuss

Brainstorm ideas for time-saving services that could benefit both employers and employees.

Activity

Use the Internet to learn more about Federal Flexible Spending Accounts. List the advantages of participating in an FSA program.

28-10

Some businesses help parents find openings in quality child care centers.

Discuss

Do you think medical advances will lessen or increase the need for elder care in the future?

Enrich

Invite an entrepreneur who works from his or her home to discuss the pros and cons of at-home work settings.

frozen items unless the company has the necessary storage appliances. As an ultimate convenience, sometimes take-home meals can be picked up at the job site after work and carried home for dinner.

For employees with serious problems, a variety of employee counseling programs are available. These programs address issues such as emotional health, substance abuse, marital conflict, and financial problems. The goal is to help employees get their lives in order so they can more easily handle routine work and family challenges.

The growing dilemma of finding elder care is a relatively new issue for today's workers and one that employers have generally not started to address. A 12-week FMLA leave, flextime, job sharing, and telecommuting are the general options open to workers dealing with a sick or aging parent. Some predict that future family-friendly programs for employees' parents will offer almost as much variety as today's selection of child care programs.

Working from Home

As you learned in Chapter 22, most *entrepreneurs* begin their businesses by working from home. As the boss of their home-based business, they enjoy total control over how to balance work and family responsibilities. Since entrepreneurs work for themselves, they can divide their time between family and work according to whatever best suits them.

Some people became entrepreneurs for the various business and personal reasons discussed in Chapter 22. Others, however, did so to spend more time with their families while earning a living. This is especially true of female entrepreneurs who operate home-based businesses. Their numbers have grown dramatically in recent years because of difficulty in finding flexible work arrangements. See 28-11.

Thinking It Through

What personal attributes would a worker need to work effectively from home?

Citizenship Responsibilities

You play an important role in contributing to society. When you get a job and become a wage earner, you become a productive member of the economy. There are additional responsibilities to being a good citizen, however. Learning about your rights, responsibilities, and privileges will help you assume your role as a citizen.

Community Involvement

One way to measure the success of a democracy is in terms of the involvement of its citizens. Keeping communities clean and citizens safe involves many jobs. Some jobs are handled through government and paid by taxes. However, there is always more work to do than people to do it, so the need for extra help is ongoing. Some groups that use volunteer help are the following:

- park and recreation departments—to help supervise children's activities, help with cleanup projects that beautify the neighborhood, or serve as a craft instructor

- local hospitals—to help run errands, read to patients, and deliver their food

- community service agencies—to help with office work or babysit the children of adult volunteers

- local churches and food pantries—to assist with collecting, storing, and distributing food to needy families

Community involvement can also be measured in less formal ways. You do not need to find a group to demonstrate community involvement. Look around your immediate neighborhood and see what needs to be done.

Does an older neighbor's lawn need mowing? Does a person without transportation need an errand run? Does a youngster on your street need tutoring in math? Did someone carelessly toss candy wrappers that you could pick up in the street?

Besides helping your immediate neighborhood, there are many charity fund-raisers and community programs that would benefit from your involvement. The extent of your volunteer work depends on how much time you can devote. See 28-12. During some periods in your life, you will have less time than others. It is important to remember, however, that success can be measured in many ways. Often what you give in your volunteer work is more personally rewarding than what you receive.

Reflect Further

How have you been involved in your community? If you have voluntarily helped others, how did it make you feel?

Activity

Review your state's voter registration laws.

Discuss

What are the benefits and drawbacks of political party affiliation?

Voting

In some countries, citizens have no control over who governs them. In the United States, however, citizens can choose who their leaders will be. They do this by voting for political candidates. Elected candidates are responsible for passing laws that are used to govern the people. By helping to elect certain candidates, voters help determine what types of laws will be passed. Voters are also given the opportunity to vote directly for or against laws from time to time.

In order to vote in the United States, you must *register*. This simply means adding your name to the list of people who are allowed to vote. You must be a citizen and at least 18 years old to register. You can register at the offices of the county commissioner, election supervisor, municipal clerk, or, in some states, the department of motor vehicles.

As a registered voter, you need to be aware of current issues and how political candidates view these issues. This will allow you to make informed decisions when you vote. You can cast your ballot for candidates who view issues as you do. You can vote for laws and candidates that will most benefit you and your community. One of the best ways to stay informed is to follow newspaper, television, and radio reports.

As a voter, you have the opportunity to elect leaders on three levels—local, state, and national. Mayors often head local governments. Trustees or city council members may also be elected to represent people locally. Governors are elected to lead states. State senators and representatives are also elected to serve

28-12

A volunteer activity, such as coaching a little league team, is important to mention in your résumé.

on state legislatures. The President of the United States heads the federal government. Representatives and senators are elected from each state to serve as members of the U.S. Congress.

Obeying the Law

The government officials the voters elect pass laws on the local, state, and national level. Laws are written and enforced to help people live in harmony with each other. They are established to protect the safety and rights of individuals as well as society as a whole. As a citizen, you need to become aware of the many laws that may affect you.

Within the U.S. legal system, there are two major categories of law—public and civil. **Public laws** govern the association between citizens and the government. **Civil laws** outline citizens' rights in relation to one another.

Public laws include the following:

- *International laws* outline policies for dealing with foreign governments.

- *Administrative laws* relate to the duties and powers of presidents and governors.

- *Criminal laws* protect society from offenses considered wrong and unjust.

- *Constitutional laws* establish the basic rights and freedoms of all citizens.

The U.S. Constitution and the constitution of each of the 50 states form the foundations upon which all laws are based. These constitutions describe how governments are to be organized. Any new law enacted by local, state, or federal governments must not go against the state or federal constitutions. If a law does not agree with these constitutions, it can be challenged in court. If declared unconstitutional, it cannot be enforced.

Criminal Law

A crime committed under criminal law is an offense against the public or the state. Crimes are generally classified according to their degree of seriousness. A **felony** is considered the most serious type of crime. It is punishable by imprisonment or even death. Murder, rape, kidnapping, armed robbery, arson, narcotics sales, and other such offenses are felonies. A **misdemeanor**, such as disorderly conduct or speeding, is a less serious crime, 28-13. Penalties for a misdemeanor are a fine or imprisonment for 18 months or less.

Being convicted of a crime is very serious. In addition to being fined or ordered to serve a prison sentence, a crime conviction creates a criminal record. A criminal record can handicap a person's future. For instance, a convicted felon might have a difficult time getting a job.

Thinking It Through

Why should you exercise your right to vote?

Enrich

Write a paper describing the political structure at the local, state, or national level.

Enrich

Visit the state legislature when it is in session.

Discuss

What is the difference between a felony and a misdemeanor in terms of the defendant and the victim?

Thinking It Through

What is the purpose of laws? What is the likely result of a society without laws?

Thinking It Through

How can a criminal record affect a person's future?

28-13
Burglary can be prosecuted as a felony or a misdemeanor.

Civil Law

The laws that cover property transactions and agreements between people or groups are civil laws. The issues covered by civil law include contracts, real estate sales, divorces, child custody cases, personal injury suits, and claims of wrongful acts.

Contracts

Many civil law cases deal with contracts. A *contract* is a legally binding agreement between two or more people. Suppose a company fails to deliver supplies to a shop by the date specified in a contract. The resulting lack of supplies could cause the shop to lose business. According to civil law, the shop owner could sue the company for damages. This would help the shop owner recover the losses.

In order for a contract to be valid, it must meet certain criteria. If all of the criteria were not met, the contract would not be upheld in court.

One criterion needed to make a contract binding is mutual agreement. Both *parties*, persons entering into the contract, must willingly and completely agree to the terms of the contract. One party cannot force the other to sign the contract. See 28-14.

Secondly, both parties must be *competent*. In other words, they must be able to understand the terms of the contract. They must also be able to evaluate the consequences of accepting those terms. State laws define who is legally considered competent.

If you are under age 18, you are considered a *minor* in most states. In many states, minors cannot be legally bound by written contracts. In order to make a contract valid, you may have a parent or another adult

28-14
Both parties who enter into a contract, such as health insurance coverage, must fully accept the terms of the agreement.

countersign the contract with you. The adult would then be held responsible if you failed to abide by the contract. If minors lie about their age, they lose the right to back out of contracts.

Another requirement of contracts is that both parties must give *consideration*. This means that each party must give up something in order to receive what the other party is offering. Consideration is often money, property, or a service. For instance, one party may pay the other party money to buy a television. One party may perform lawn care services in exchange for free piano lessons.

The final condition contracts must meet is that they must relate to legal activities. If a contract were made in regard to an illegal act, like theft, the contract would not be valid.

Contracts can often be spoken agreements. However, some contracts must be written to be valid. If the terms will not be enacted for over a year, the contract must be in writing. If the terms of the contract can be transferred, as to a cosigner, the contract must be written. Contracts for installment payments, real estate, or items over $500 must be written, too.

Just about everyone will sign a contract at one time or another. Teachers and professional athletes sign job contracts specifying their salaries and benefits. Authors sign contracts with publishing companies when they write books. Consumers sign contracts when they buy insurance or hire home builders.

Before you sign a written contract, read it carefully. Be sure you understand and agree to all the terms. Be sure all the required elements are contained in the contract. If you are uncertain about anything stated in the contract, ask for an explanation. After you have signed the contract, keep a copy for your records. An example of a contract is shown in 28-15.

Torts

Another area of civil law deals with torts. A **tort** is a wrongful act committed against another person, independent of a contract. It involves injuries to another person's body, property, business, emotional well-being,

Discuss

What are the advantages and disadvantages of both a written and an oral contract? Under what circumstance would you prefer an oral contract?

Activity

Collect examples of torts from newspaper articles.

Resource

Legal Terms, Activity D, WB

Thinking It Through

What four criteria are required to make a contract legally binding?

28-15

A legally binding contract must clearly outline the terms to which both parties are freely agreeing.

I, Sarah Goldsmith, of 1627 West Park Avenue, Bensonville, Maryland, agree to provide pet care service for Cary Reagan, of 705 South Dayton Road, Bensonville, Maryland. Services will include, but are not limited to, feeding, brushing, and walking Brisket, a three-year-old, 11-pound, West Highland white terrier. Services will be provided for 30 minutes between 8:00 and 9:00 each morning and between 5:00 and 6:00 each evening, beginning July 20, 20XX and ending July 28, 20XX. Consideration for these services will be $15.00 per day, or a total of $135.00.

Date: 6/30/XX
Signed: *Sarah Goldsmith*
           Cary Reagan

or reputation. Injuring someone in an auto accident is a tort. Slander (attacking someone's reputation) and assault (attempting to physically harm another person) are torts, too.

Torts may be classed as intentional or unintentional. For example, if someone purposely hits your car and damages it, then that is an intentional tort. If someone accidentally hits your car, that is an unintentional tort.

Committing a wrongful act can be a tort and a crime at the same time. For instance, if Marvin stole $100 from Carl, Marvin would be committing a tort against Carl. Marvin would also be breaking a criminal law. Therefore, Carl could bring a civil suit against Marvin to recover his $100. The state could bring a criminal suit against Marvin because he broke a public law.

Consulting a Lawyer

When you have problems or questions relating to public or civil laws, you may wish to consult a lawyer. A good lawyer can help you make wise decisions about a variety of legal and financial issues. See 28-16. People tend to seek out lawyers as a last resort. At this point, however, a lawyer may have a difficult time protecting a person from legal problems. The best time to consult a lawyer is before a serious problem arises. Such a consultation can help you avoid costly legal mistakes. The following situations may require the help of a lawyer:

- buying or selling real estate
- writing or entering into a contract
- getting divorced
- not being able to pay your bills
- writing a will

28-16

A qualified lawyer can help people make wise decisions about major financial investments, such as real estate.

- being charged with a criminal action

- facing a civil suit

- having trouble obtaining satisfaction in regard to a consumer complaint

Choosing the best lawyer for your situation should be done carefully. Do not be in a hurry. Keep in mind that the field of law is specialized. Some lawyers specialize in divorce cases, others in business law, and others in criminal law. The more specialized the case, the more important it is to choose a lawyer who has handled such cases before.

How do you find a good lawyer? One way is to ask a trusted family member, teacher, or friend to suggest a lawyer. Another way is to call Lawyers Referral and Information Service (LRIS), sponsored by local bar associations. The number for LRIS can usually be found in the Yellow Pages under *Attorneys* or *Lawyers*. You may also find a link through the American Bar Association Web site at www.abanet.org. This service can refer you to competent, reliable lawyers for the assistance you need.

Under the LRIS plan, a lawyer will consult with you for a short period of time, usually less than an hour. You will be charged an attorney's regular consulting fee for this meeting. During the meeting, be sure to discuss if any additional services will be needed and how much they will cost. If that lawyer cannot handle your problem, he or she will refer you to another attorney who can.

For people who cannot afford to hire a lawyer, there are places to get help. Many cities and communities have *legal aid* offices. Lawyers at these offices will handle problems involving civil laws for free or a low fee. Legal aid clinics are also available at many law schools. These clinics help law students gain practical experience while helping those who cannot afford a lawyer. Legal aid offices and clinics give advice in three main areas:

- small claims for wages

- disputes between the client and a lender, installment seller, or landlord

- domestic matters (divorce, child custody, contesting a will, and other family disagreements)

In the United States, everyone is entitled to a defense even if they cannot pay for it. Consequently, in criminal cases, the state will appoint a public *defender* if the accused cannot afford a lawyer.

Once you have chosen a qualified lawyer, take an active role in your case. Take your lawyer's advice, but do not hesitate to ask questions about how he or she plans to handle your case. See 28-17. It is a good idea to request copies of all letters and documents prepared on your behalf. This will help you know exactly how your case is progressing. Preparing legal cases takes time so do not badger your lawyer.

An important fact to remember when dealing with your lawyer is to be honest. Tell him or her all the facts related to your case. An attorney cannot give you well-reasoned advice if you withhold information or fail to tell the truth. Also, keep your lawyer informed of any new developments that might affect your case.

Resource

Consulting a Lawyer, Activity E, WB

Enrich

View a portion of a popular movie about the legal profession. Use it to start a discussion of the role and image of the legal profession.

Thinking It Through

Why should a person avoid hiring a real estate attorney for preparing a defense against criminal charges?

The Court System

28-17

Asking questions can help a client feel more comfortable about the way a lawyer is handling the case.

Thinking It Through

What factors determine the court in which a case is heard?

28-18

Different types of state and federal courts exist to handle different types of cases.

If you have a problem with a law, you may have to settle it through the court system. Courts try and punish people who have committed criminal offenses. They also interpret laws and settle legal problems between people involved in civil disputes.

The United States has two court systems—one at the state level and one at the national level. The court system in each state and the federal court system all follow a similar organization. Most criminal and civil cases involving people within a state are resolved in state courts. Cases involving federal laws or people from more than one state are heard in federal courts. Federal courts may also review cases previously tried at the state level.

There are many different types of state and federal courts. The type in which a given case is presented depends on a number of factors. The type of criminal offense or the value of a civil claim are also factors. See 28-18 for a brief description of the various types of courts.

The type of court also depends on whether an original ruling or a review of a previous ruling is being sought. Court cases are first heard in *trial courts*. A **jury** is a panel of citizens selected to help decide a case in a trial court. The decision of the judge or jury in a trial court may be *appealed*. The case then goes before a panel of justices in a higher court. The justices review the case and may uphold or overturn the decision of the trial court.

Resource

The Court System, transparency master 28-2, TR

Resource

Examining the Court System, Activity F, WB

State Courts

Trial Courts (limited jurisdiction)—have original jurisdiction in local misdemeanor and minor civil cases.

Trial Courts (general jurisdiction)—handle more serious criminal and civil cases for a larger geographic area. These courts are also known as circuit, county, district, common pleas, and superior courts.

Appellate Courts—review cases previously tried in a lower court.

Supreme Court—handles cases involving state constitutional law and reviews cases previously appealed in appellate courts. Cases may be further appealed to the U.S. Supreme Court.

Federal Courts

District Courts—have original jurisdiction in cases involving federal laws and/or citizens of different states.

Circuit Courts of Appeals—handles appeals of cases originally tried in district courts.

Supreme Court—has original jurisdiction in cases involving a state; reviews cases from state and federal courts involving constitutional law.

In the Real World

Del's Day in Court

When Del graduated from high school, he interviewed for a job as a lifeguard at a summer camp. The camp director, Mr. Stintsen, liked Del and hired him.

During the interview, Del told Mr. Stintsen he would be leaving to go to college in mid-August. However, when the time came for Del to leave, Mr. Stintsen became angry. He did not want Del to leave before the camp closed for the year. Mr. Stintsen decided to show his displeasure by failing to send Del his final paycheck.

Del called Mr. Stintsen several times and sent him a letter asking for the money. However, Mr. Stintsen refused to pay.

Del didn't have a lot of time and money to spend, but he wanted to get what he was owed. His mother suggested that Del take his case to small claims court since the unpaid wages totaled less that $500. She said the court fees would be only a few dollars and Del wouldn't need a lawyer. She also said that it would probably take only a few weeks until the case would be heard.

Del took his mother's advice. He summoned Mr. Stintsen, and when his court date arrived, they both appeared before a judge. Del explained the situation and showed the judge a copy of the letter he had sent Mr. Stintsen. Mr. Stintsen also gave his side of the story, but the judge found in Del's favor. He ordered Mr. Stintsen to pay Del the wages he was due.

Questions to Discuss

1. Do you think Del made the right decision to take his case to small claims court? Explain.
2. What do you think would have happened if Del had not taken his case to court?
3. What other steps might Del have taken to get his money?

Small Claims Court

One type of court that is more accessible to more people is small claims court. Small claims courts hear cases involving small amounts of money. The maximum amount for a suit varies from state to state. Usually the maximum is between $500 and $1000. You can sue only for the actual dollar loss.

Small claims courts are less formal than other trial courts. They are also less costly for people filing suits. Filing fees are low and lawyers are not required. In fact, lawyers are discouraged or forbidden from being in some small claims courts.

The person who files a lawsuit, taking his or her case to court, is called the **plaintiff**. The person accused of wrongdoing is the **defendant**. There is no jury in small claims courts. Cases are decided based on the facts plaintiffs and defendants present to the judge.

Enrich

Set up a small claims court in class. Use it to discuss job-related complaints students have.

Summary

You will play many roles during your lifetime. There will be conflicting demands on your time as you try to handle all your responsibilities. Your role as a family member can be one of your most rewarding and demanding. Support groups, community programs, and other professionals can be good sources of help.

Being a good citizen is both a privilege and a responsibility. Community involvement is one measure of a good citizen. Voting regularly is another. Voting gives citizens a right to choose who their leaders will be.

Elected officials at all levels of government pass laws. Public laws deal with the relationship between people and the government. Criminal laws are a type of public law.

Civil laws define citizens' rights in relation to other citizens. Many civil laws relate to contracts, which are agreements that meet certain conditions to be legally binding. Civil laws also deal with torts, or wrongful acts.

People who need advice concerning legal questions often seek the help of a lawyer. For people who cannot afford one, free legal services are available.

Resource

Review and Study Guide for Chapter 28, reproducible master 28-3, TR

Answers to *Facts In Review*

1. building relationships, maintaining the home, using leisure time effectively
2. because it builds strong relationships and people are more likely to believe and trust you
3. because it effectively uses the time and talents of each member to pursue a common goal
4. It helps in deciding what is important.
5. (List three:) Identify time-wasters and avoid them; avoid postponing unpleasant work; set realistic deadlines; stay motivated by keeping your goals in mind; be flexible.
6. (List four:) a support system, community programs, extended programs in school, care centers, professional help, family counseling services
7. having and caring for a baby; adopting a child or adding a foster child to the family; caring for a sick child, spouse, or parent; being unable to work because of serious illness
8. (List three:) flextime, job sharing, telecommuting, a home-based business

Facts in Review

1. What are the three basic responsibilities associated with the role of family member?
2. Why is it important to stand by your commitments?
3. Why is a team approach a good way to decide how to distribute household chores?
4. Why is setting goals an important aspect of time management?
5. What are three ways to stay focused?
6. List four community resources that help individuals balance their family and work roles.
7. List the five reasons that someone may take unpaid leave under the Family and Medical Leave Act.
8. What are three examples of work arrangements that give workers more control over their time?
9. What requirements must be met in order to register to vote in the United States?
10. What are four types of public laws?
11. What is the difference between a felony and a misdemeanor?
12. What are the two ways torts may be classified?
13. What sources of help are available for people who cannot afford to hire lawyers for civil cases? What sources are available for criminal cases?
14. Describe what may happen if a citizen is not satisfied with the decision made in a trial court.
15. How is small claims court different from other trial courts?

9. must be a citizen and at least 18 years old
10. international, administrative, constitutional, and criminal laws
11. A misdemeanor is a less serious crime, punishable by a fine or imprisonment for less than a year. A felony is a serious crime, punishable by imprisonment or even death.
12. intentional or unintentional
13. legal aid offices or clinics; public defenders appointed by the state
14. The case may be appealed, after which the first court decision is either upheld or overturned.
15. less formal, lower filing fees, no lawyers

Developing Your Academic Skills

1. **Social Studies.** Write an example of a case that might be taken to small claims court. Set up a mock court in class to decide the case. Make sure you have a defendant, plaintiff, and judge.

2. **Language Arts/Speech.** Interview someone who participates in a special work program such as job sharing, flextime, or telecommuting. Ask the person to give some advantages and disadvantages of the program. Summarize the interview and give an oral report of your findings.

Information Technology Applications

1. Debate the practicality of using computers for leisure-time activities. How can computers be used for leisure? What are some reasons you might not want to use computers in leisure time? How do computers affect the family's leisure time?

2. Electronically create a combined daily schedule/to-do list for yourself broken down by hours. Enter your goals for the day in the schedule. A column should also be added in which you can check off each task after it is finished. How can this schedule help you manage your time more wisely? Write a brief report of your findings.

3. Using the Internet, research a company to find out what family-friendly policies and benefits the company offers.

4. Develop a survey on a word processing program. Survey the school to see how many students have parents that participate in job sharing, flextime, or telecommuting. Electronically make a chart showing the percentages.

Applying Your Knowledge and Skills

1. **Systems.** Interview several people who appear to be well organized and use their time effectively. Make a list of the strategies they use that may work for you. Develop a plan to use these strategies over the next few weeks. At the end of that time determine which strategies worked for you and which did not and why.

2. **Communications.** Interview a police officer about the types of crimes that are felonies and misdemeanors. Ask the officer to discuss possible punishments that might result from the various crimes described.

3. **Problem Solving and Critical Thinking.** Using Internet or print sources, develop a list of lawyers and their areas of specialization. Discuss in class how you would choose one of those lawyers if you had a specific legal problem.

4. **Employability and Career Development.** Research local child care facilities. Arrange to observe for a short period of time at a few centers. Write reports on the advantages and disadvantages of various types of child care, citing examples from your observations.

Developing Workplace Skills

Work with three or four classmates to develop a community volunteer project for your class. Identify three or four community organizations that need volunteer help. Interview at least one representative of each organization. Determine what services they provide and what type of volunteer work is available. Are special skills required? Is there an age requirement? Etc. Prepare a plan to involve yourself in at least one worthwhile project during the summer months. Present your plan to the class. Implement and monitor the project.

Glossary

A

ability. A task or skill a person has already developed that is learned through training and practice. (12)

accounting. An analysis of the record keeping data of a business. (22)

advanced-level job. Work that requires special skills, knowledge, and experience. (15)

annual percentage rate (APR). The actual rate of interest charged on a yearly basis. (25)

apprenticeship. A type of education by which a student or worker learns the knowledge and skills of a specialized trade or craft under the direction of a skilled worker while working on the job. (9)

aptitude. A person's natural physical and mental talent for learning. (12)

area measurement. The process of finding how much space is within the border of a geometric shape, such as square, rectangle, parallelogram, triangle, or circle. (6)

Armed Services Vocational Aptitude Battery (ASVAB). An aptitude test designed to measure strengths, weaknesses, and potential for future success. (17)

assets. Items an individual owns, including cash, stocks, bonds, and property. (22)

assimilation. The blending of people into society by helping or forcing them to become more like the majority. (20)

associate degree. A two-year college degree. (13)

attitude. A person's outlook on life that reflects how he or she feels and thinks about other people and situations. (3)

B

bachelor's degree. A four-year college degree. (13)

bankruptcy. A legal proceeding for the purpose of stating a person's inability to pay his or her debts. (25)

bar graph. A chart that shows comparisons between categories. (6)

basic medical insurance. Health insurance coverage that pays for the costs of hospitalization, which usually includes room, board, nursing services, laboratory tests, X-rays, and medicine. (27)

beneficiary. The person named by a life insurance policyholder to receive the death benefit. (27)

Better Business Bureau (BBB). A nonprofit organization sponsored by private businesses to help settle consumer complaints against local business firms. (24)

blind ad. An ad that does not include the name of a company or contact person but may require a response to a post office box or fax number. (16)

block form. A style of business letter in which all parts begin at the left margin and are not indented. (5)

body language. A means of expressing a message through body movements, facial expressions, or hand gestures. (20)

bond. A certificate of debt or obligation issued by a corporation or a government. (26)

bonus. An extra payment given by an employer to an employee in addition to the workers' regular pay. (23)

bookkeeping. The recording of income and expenses. (22)

brainstorming. Group technique used to develop many ideas in a short time. (4)

break-even point. The time at which the income for a business equals its expenses. (22)

budget. A written plan to help a person make the most of the money earned. (24)

burnout. A loss of physical and emotional strength and motivation. (28)

bylaws. The rules and regulations that govern an organization. (11)

C

canceled check. A check that has been processed/paid by the bank. (26)

capital. Possessions and money used to increase business. (21)

capital expenses. One-time costs needed to get a business started. (22)

career. A progression of related jobs that result in employment and personal growth. (1)

career and technical student organizations (CTSOs). Student organizations with leadership and teamwork skills as major objectives. (10)

career clusters. The 16 groups of occupational and career specialties that are similar to each other by common interests. (1)

career ladder. A sequence of related jobs—from entry-level to advanced—available at different education levels. (15)

career plan. A list of steps to take to reach a career goal. (15)

Career Voyages. A Web site sponsored by the U.S. Department of Labor and Education that contains valuable information for students, parents, job seekers, and career advisors. (14)

CareerOneStop. A Web site sponsored by the U.S. Department of Labor and Education that helps students, job seekers, and career professionals explore the outlook and trends for all types of careers. (14)

cash card. A prepaid type of debit card. (26)

cash value. The amount a life insurance policy is worth in cash if the policy is surrendered. (27)

cashier's check. A check drawn on a bank's own funds and signed by a bank officer. (26)

cellular phone. A type of wireless telephone. (5)

Centers for Disease Control and Prevention (CDC). Part of the United States Department of Health and Human Services that works with worldwide, state, and local health agencies to protect the public from health threats. (9)

central processing unit (CPU). The part of a computer system, also called the *processor*, that controls what is done with data received. (7)

certificate of deposit (CD). Money deposited for a set period of time that earns a set rate of interest. (26)

certified check. A personal check with a bank's guarantee that the check will be paid. (26)

channel(s). How a message is delivered during the communication process. (5)

charge account. A type of credit account that allows a customer to buy merchandise, then pay in part or in full by the billing date. (25)

circle graph. A chart that shows the relationship of parts to the whole. (6)

citation. A summons to appear in court. (9)

civil laws. Laws that outline citizens' rights in relation to one another. (28)

civil service test. A preemployment test that is required when applying for most government jobs. (17)

claim. A formal request to an insurance company requesting compensation for a loss covered under a policy. (27)

coinsurance. An insurance provision that requires the insured to pay a percentage of the medical costs. (27)

collateral. Something of value held by a creditor in case a person is unable to repay a loan, such as a car or house. (25)

collective bargaining. The process that labor and management representatives use to discuss what they expect from each other in the workplace. (19)

commission. A percentage of sales paid to the salesperson. (22)

common fraction. One or more parts of a whole number. (6)

common stock. Stock that pays dividends based on company earnings and economic conditions. (26)

communication. The process of conveying a message, thought, or idea so it is accurately received and understood. (5)

commuting. Regularly traveling back and forth to work. (5)

comparison shopping. Looking at different brands and models of a product in several stores to compare price, quality, and features before buying. (24)

compound interest. Interest paid on an initial deposit as well as on interest already earned. (26)

comprehension. The ability to understand materials, such as memos, reports, books, directions, and other documents associated with a job. (5)

compromise. When opposing sides give up something of value to help solve a problem. (4)

computer literate. Knowing how to operate a computer and basic software programs. (7)

confidential. Private. (3)

conflict. A hostile situation resulting from opposing views. (4)

consensus. Full acceptance and support for a decision by all members of a group. (4)

constraint. Factors that may restrict or hinder a person's ability to solve a problem. (4)

constructive criticism. Pointing out and analyzing a weakness to cause improvement without embarrassment. (3)

consumer fraud. The use of trickery or deceit to gain some type of unfair or dishonest advantage over the consumer. (24)

Consumer Price Index (CPI). A measure of the average change in prices for consumer goods and services over time. (26)

Consumer Product Safety Commission (CPSC). A government agency that sets and enforces safety standards for consumer products and investigates product safety complaints. (24)

consumers. People who use their income to buy the items they need and want. (24)

conviction. A strong belief. (19)

cooperative education. A school program offering a paid job experience in which students alternate time between the classroom and a work site; also called *co-op program.* (1)

copyright. The legal ownership of original items, such as writings, art, and music. (7)

corporation. A business owned by many people called stockholders. (21)

cosigner. A responsible person who signs a loan agreement with a borrower and shares the obligation of repayment. (25)

credit. The present use of future income that allows consumers to buy goods and services purchased now and pay later. (25)

credit bureau. An agency that collects and keeps files of financial information on individuals. (25)

credit rating. A creditor's evaluation of a person's willingness and ability to pay debts. (25)

criminal penalties. A court order to serve a jail sentence, perform community service, pay a fine, and/or report to a court-ordered supervisor for a specified period. (20)

criteria. Standards used to find the best solution to a problem. (4)

cross-functional team. A team of workers from different areas within a company who are assigned to work on a specific project, contributing different types of expertise. (4)

D

debit card. A card that allows the immediate withdrawal of funds from a checking account without writing a check. (26)

debt-to-income ratio. The result of dividing total monthly debt by monthly take-home pay, which should not exceed 15 percent. (25)

decimal fraction. A fraction with a denominator (or multiple) of 10, such as 100, 1,000, and 10,000. (6)

decision-making process. A proven way to make important decisions carefully and logically. (15)

decoder. The communication receiver's mind, which forms a mental image of the message received. (5)

deductible. The amount a policyholder must pay before the insurance company will begin to cover the expense. (27)

deductions. Amounts of money subtracted from total pay; can be claimed on Form 1040 to lower a person's tax bill. (23)

defendant. The person accused of wrongdoing in a court suit. (28)

degree Celsius. The metric measure for temperature. (6)

delegate. To assign responsibility or authority to another person. (10)

demand. The amount of products and services consumers want to buy. (21)

demotion. A transfer to a classification in a lower pay grade. (19)

dermatologist. A doctor who specializes in treating skin. (8)

Dietary Guidelines for Americans. A set of guidelines developed by the U.S. Department of Agriculture designed to promote good health and nutrition. (8)

Dietary Reference Intakes (DRIs). Guidelines established by the U.S. government to help people know how much of each nutrient they need daily. (8)

disability. A permanent job-related injury. (9)

disability insurance. Coverage that provides regular income payments when a person is unable to work because of injury or illness for an extended period of time. (27)

discrimination. Treating people on a basis other than individual merit. (20)

dual-career family. A family in which both spouses have careers outside the home. (14)

dynamics. The underlying causes of change or growth. (10)

E

earned authority. Power granted to a person by the other members of the group. (10)

earned income. The money a person receives for doing a job. (23)

E-learning. Electronic learning, or teaching through the use of computers or related technology. (7)

electronic funds transfer (EFT). The automatic transfer of funds to and from a person's bank accounts electronically. (26)

e-mail. A message, also called electronic mail, delivered to a computer from another. (7)

e-marketing. The use of computer technology to market goods and services. (13)

emergency cash fund. Money saved to cover unexpected expenses. (24)

encoder. The communication sender's mind, which forms a mental image of the message. (5)

endorse. Signing one's name on the back of the check along the left end within the area indicated. (26)

entrepreneur. A person who organizes and manages a business. (22)

entrepreneurship. The organization and management of a business. (22)

entry-level job. Work for beginners who lack experience or specialized training. (15)

environmental hazards. Possible dangers or unsafe conditions that exist in the workplace. (9)

Environmental Protection Agency (EPA). A government agency that works to eliminate environmental hazards, such as air and water pollution. (9)

Equal Employment Opportunity Commission (EEOC). A U.S. agency that oversees and enforces equal employment opportunities nationwide. (2)

Equal Pay Act. A law that requires employers to pay employees of both sexes equally for equal work. (2)

equity. The amount remaining once the amount of debt a person owes on a house is subtracted from the amount the house is worth. (25)

ergonomics. The science of examining motions and how to perform them properly. (9)

ethics. A guiding set of moral values. (3)

ethnic group. A group of people who share common racial and/or cultural characteristics, such as national origin, language, religion, and traditions. (20)

etiquette. The code of behavior that guides social situations. (18)

exemption. A set amount of income on which a person does not have to pay tax. (23)

F

Fair Labor Standards Act (FLSA). A law designed to protect workers from unfair treatment by their employers. (2)

Family and Medical Leave Act (FMLA). A law designed to help families handle special family matters by permitting employees to take time off without pay. (28)

Federal Communications Commission (FCC). A government agency that helps protect your rights to information and selection. It handles complaints about charges and practices regarding wired and wireless telephone services, TV, and cable services. (24)

Federal Trade Commission (FTC). A government agency that helps prevent unfair competition, deceptive trade practices, and false advertising in the marketplace. It also enforces laws related to packaging, labeling, advertising, and warranties. (24)

feedback. A clue that reveals what message was received by the receiver. (5)

fee-for-service (FFS) plan. The traditional type of health care policy. (27)

felony. The most serious type of crime punishable by imprisonment or even by death. (28)

FICA. The amount of social security tax withheld from a paycheck; also the Federal Insurance Contributions Act. (23)

finance charges. The total amount of money a borrower must pay for the use of credit. (25)

first aid. Giving an ill or injured person immediate, temporary treatment before proper medical help arrives. (9)

fixed expenses. Expenses that must be paid regularly in set amounts, such as monthly rent, garbage pickup, and insurance. (22)

flammable. Liquids that ignite easily and burn rapidly, such as gasoline. (9)

flexible expenses. The expenses that vary in amount from month to month, such as advertising costs, repairs, utility bills, and supplies needed for the business. (22)

flextime. A program that allows workers greater flexibility in setting their own hours. (28)

follow-up letter. A brief letter written in business form to thank the interviewer for the interview. (18)

Food and Drug Administration (FDA). A government agency that protects consumer safety. It regulates the production, packaging, and labeling of foods, drugs, and cosmetics. (24)

Form 1040EZ. The simplest form to complete for filing an income tax return. (23)

Form W-2. A Wage and Tax Statement that shows the amount an employee was paid in the previous year. It also shows the income tax and social security tax (FICA) withheld during the year. (23)

Form W-4. The Employer's Withholding Allowance Certificate that shows the employer how much tax to withhold from an employee's paychecks. (23)

401(k) plan. Retirement savings plan offered through an employer. (26)

franchise. The right to market another company's product or service. (22)

fraud. The act of deceiving or tricking. (22)

free enterprise system. An economic system in which people are free to make their own economic decisions. (21)

fringe benefits. Financial extras in addition to the regular paycheck, such as medical and life insurance coverage, paid vacations, bonuses, and retirement plans. (14)

functional team. A team of workers with similar skills and expertise, usually from the same department. (4)

G

Gantt chart. A graph that shows the steps of a task divided across a timetable. (4)

General Aptitude Test Battery (GATB). A series of tests that measure nine aptitudes. (12)

globalization. Strengthening interrelations among nations of the world with particular effects on the global economy. (7)

goal. Whatever a person wants to attain. (4)

goods. Any type of product that a consumer buys, such as food or clothing. (24)

grace period. The number of days allowed to pay for a new credit purchase before interest is charged. (25)

gram. The metric measure for weight. (6)

grooming. Taking care of one's self and looking one's best through cleanliness and neatness. (8)

gross pay. The total amount of money earned for a pay period before deductions are subtracted. (23)

group dynamics. The interacting forces within a human group. (10)

H

habit. Doing something in the same way every time. (12)

hardware. The physical equipment in computer systems. (7)

health maintenance organization (HMO). A health plan that provides a variety of health care services to members for a lump sum or set, monthly fee. (27)

Health Savings Account (HSA). Accounts that allow people to set money aside on a tax-free basis to pay for future qualifying medical expenses. (27)

hearing. Recognizing sound. (5)

hostile environment harassment. Behavior that makes an atmosphere uncomfortable enough to interfere with a person's performance. (20)

human resources. Resources a person has within himself or herself, such as skills, knowledge, and experience. (12)

hygiene. Keeping one's body clean. (8)

I

impulse buying. Making an unplanned purchase; buying something without thinking about it first. (24)

incentive. Something that inspires a person to act. (19)

individual responsibility. Willingness to answer for one's conduct and decisions. (3)

individual retirement account (IRA). A type of retirement savings plan for employed people; can be tax-deferred (traditional IRA) or pre-taxed (Roth IRA). (26)

inflation. A general increase in prices. (26)

informal communications. Unscheduled communication with coworkers occurring by chance inside or outside the workplace. (5)

informational interview. A planned meeting in which a job applicant learns more about an occupation from a person employed in that job area. (18)

initiative. Making oneself do what is necessary. (3)

installment account. A credit account that allows the buyer to pay for expensive items according to a set schedule of payments. (25)

integrity. The quality of firmly following one's moral values. (3)

interest. The price paid to a financial institution for the use of money over a period of time. (25)

interests. The activities, events, and ideas a person likes. (12)

Internet. Thousands of computer networks around the world joined together. (7)

internship. A school program providing paid or unpaid work experience to help students learn about a job or industry. (1)

interpersonal skills. A display of friendliness and sensitivity to the needs of others through communication and listening. (4)

interview. A planned meeting between a job applicant and an employer. (2)

J

job. A task performed by a worker, usually to earn money. (1)

job evaluation. A supervisor's written review of an employee's work performance. (3)

job probation. A trial period to test how well a new worker can do the job. (19)

job shadowing. Following a worker on the job and observing what the job involves. (1)

job sharing. A job split between two or more employees. (28)

jury. A panel of citizens selected to decide the outcome of a case in a trial court. (28)

K

Keogh plan. A tax-deferred retirement plan for self-employed people or employees of unincorporated companies that do not have their own pension plans. (26)

L

labor contract. An agreement that spells out the conditions for wages, benefits, job security, work hours, working conditions, and grievance procedures. (19)

lateral move. A transfer to another department or classification in the same pay grade. (19)

leadership. The capacity to direct a group. (10)

letter of application. A letter written to an employer to apply for a job. (16)

liabilities. Debts such as payments on a car or home. (22)

license. A certificate showing permission a person has been granted by the governing authority to practice a certain occupation. (22)

lifelong learning. The process of ongoing learning over a worker's entire career. (7)

lifestyle goals. A list of what a person really wants out of life. (12)

line graph. A chart showing the relationship of two or more variables. It can also show trends across periods of time. (6)

listening. Understanding what is heard. (5)

liter. The metric measure for volume. (6)

logistics. The handling of operational details. (13)

long-term goal. A goal that may take several months or years to achieve. (12)

M

main motion. A suggestion for the group to consider that includes one item of business. (11)

major decisions. Tough choices requiring careful thought because they affect a person's career and personal life. (15)

major medical insurance. Health insurance coverage that begins paying where basic coverage stops. It pays the largest share of expenses resulting from a major illness or serious injury, protecting individuals and families from huge medical bills. (27)

margin. The blank space around the printed or written material. (5)

material data safety sheet (MSDS). A sheet of information on the hazards involved with a specific material and the procedures for its safe use. (9)

mean. The mathematical average of data. (6)

median. The number exactly in the middle when a group of numbers is listed in ascending or descending order. (6)

Medicaid. The federal government's program that pays for health care services for people who can't afford to pay them. (23)

Medicare. The health insurance program for people 65 or older, people of any age with permanent kidney failure, and others with certain disabilities. (23)

memo. An informal written message, also called memorandum, sent from one person or department to another employee or department within the company. (5)

message. Something that is understood by the senses—usually something spoken, written, or printed. (5)

meter. The metric measure for distance. (6)

metric system. A decimal system of weights and measures used by most countries. (6)

minimum wage. The lowest hourly rate of pay that most employees must receive. (2)

misdemeanor. A less serious crime, punishable by a fine or imprisonment for less than a year. (28)

mock interview. A practice interview conducted by an applicant's friend, family member, or other adult with business experience. (18)

mode. The number that occurs most frequently in a group of numbers. (6)

modified block form. A style of business letter in which all parts begin at the left margin except the return address (if keyed in), date, complimentary close, name, and signature. Paragraphs in the letter are indented. (5)

money market fund. A type of mutual fund that deals only in high-interest, short-term investments, such as government securities and certificates of deposit. (26)

money order. An order for a specific amount of money payable to a specific payee. (26)

monopoly. A single company that controls the entire supply of a product or service. (21)

multifunctional team. A team of cross-trained workers who can perform the duties of all other members on the team. (4)

multimedia. The use of two or more communication methods, such as audio, video, images, and text. (7)

multitasking. Doing more than one job at a time. (5)

mutual fund. A company that collects money from many investors and invests it in securities. (26)

MyPyramid. A personalized eating plan that gives amounts of food to consume in five basic food groups. (8)

myth. An unfounded belief or notion. (13)

N

National Institute for Occupational Safety and Health (NIOSH). An arm of the Centers for Disease Control and Prevention that is responsible for conducting research and making recommendations for the prevention of work-related injury and illness. (9)

National Safety Council. The leading advocate for safety and health in the U.S whose mission is to educate and influence people to prevent accidental injury. (9)

needs. The basics a person must have to live. (21)

net pay. The gross pay minus taxes and deductions. (23)

networking. Talking with people and establishing relationships that can lead to more information or business. (16)

noise. Anything that interrupts a message during the communication process. (5)

nonhuman resources. Time and material things a person has or can use to achieve goals, such as money, tools, clothes, and community resources. (12)

nonverbal communication. Any message that does not use written or spoken words. (5)

norm. A pattern that is typical in the development of a social group. (4)

nutrients. The chemical substances in food that nourish the body. They build and repair body cells and help the body function properly. (8)

O

Occupational Safety and Health Administration (OSHA). A U.S. government agency that sets and enforces job safety and health standards for workers. (2, 9)

occupation. Work that requires the use of related skills and experiences. (1)

occupational training. Training that prepares a person for a job in a specific field. (14)

occupational trends. Research predictions regarding the jobs that will most likely be needed in the future. (13)

One-stop Career Centers. Centers that coordinate government employment offices at local, state, and national levels to provide a wide range of employment, education, and training services. (14)

online banking. The use of a computer to manage finances through an Internet connection. (26)

organization chart. A chart that shows an organization's internal structure. (21)

orientation. A meeting at which a new employee learns the company's history, policies, rules, and safety procedures. (19)

ownership. When a person understands the importance of a task and makes sure it is done well. (28)

P

Pareto Principle. A principle stating that as a general rule, 20% of causes produce 80% of the effects, or 20% of the effort produces 80% of the results. (4)

parliamentary procedure. An orderly way of conducting a meeting and discussing group business. (11)

partnership. A form of business organization involving two or more people who go into business together. (21)

percent. Per one hundred. (6)

performance rating. A supervisor's periodic rating of a worker's job performance. (19)

peripherals. Output and input devices that can be plugged into your CPU, such as monitors and printers (output), and keyboards, mice, scanners, digital cameras, and webcams (input). (7)

personal fact sheet. A brief written summary of key facts—including education, work experience, and skills—that helps a person write letters of application, prepare a job résumé, and fill job application forms. (16)

personality. How a person thinks or feels. (12)

personnel/human resource department. The part of a company that handles hiring, pre-employment testing, and other responsibilities related to employment. (16)

phishing. Tricking someone into giving out personal and financial information, such as an identification number or password; usually done by e-mail or over the telephone. (24)

pictograph. A graph that presents information with the use of eye-catching images. (6)

piecework. A form of income in which an employee is paid a fixed amount of money for each piece of work done. (23)

plaintiff. The person who files a civil suit. (28)

point-of-service (POS) plan. A health care plan that allows members to choose either an HMO or PPO each time they seek medical services. (27)

polygraph. A test, also called a *lie-detector* test, given with a polygraph machine that measures and records on graph paper the changes in a subject's blood pressure, perspiration, and pulse rate when an examiner asks questions. (17)

portfolio. A collection of work samples that support job qualifications. (16)

position authority. Specific powers given to a person as defined by the source of the title, which usually is the company management. (10)

postmark. The official U.S. Postal Service mark on delivered mail. (18)

preferred provider organization (PPO). An organization that has made arrangements with doctors and hospitals who have agreed to accept lower fees for their services in providing health care for group members. (27)

preferred stock. Stock that pays set dividends (profits) at set rates regardless of the amount of profits the company earns. (26)

premium. A set amount of money paid on a regular basis to an insurance company for coverage. (27)

priority. The first ranking in a "to do" list when items are listed by importance from first to last. (2)

problem. The difference between reality and expectation. (4)

problem solving. The process of making an expectation a reality. (4)

procrastination. Postponing unpleasant work. (28)

productive resources. Resources such as labor, land, capital, and equipment that can be used to produce and provide goods and services. (21)

profit. The amount of money a business makes from selling goods and services beyond the cost of producing them. (21)

profit ratio. The percentage of receipts that are profit, figured by dividing total profit by total receipts. (22)

profit sharing. A form of income, usually company stock or bonuses, used to reward employees' hard work and as an incentive to make them more productive. (23)

program coordinator. A special teacher or counselor at school who assists a student in a school-to-work program; also called *school-to-work coordinator.* (1)

promotion. A transfer to a job classification with a higher pay grade. (19)

proprietorship. A business that has only one owner. (21)

psychological test. A preemployment test given to find out more about a job applicant's personality, character, and interests. (17)

public laws. Laws that govern the association between citizens and the government. (28)

Q

quality. A commitment by everyone in an organization to exceed customer expectations. (4)

quality assurance. A commitment by everyone in an organization to exceed customer expectations; also strategies that ensure products and services are of the highest quality. (4)

quality control. A commitment by everyone in an organization to exceed customer expectations; also strategies that ensure products and services are of the highest quality. (4)

quid pro quo harassment. Making unwelcome sexual advances toward another person while promising certain benefits if the person complies. (20)

quorum. A majority of members, or the number of members stated in the rules of the group, that must be present in order to proceed with the business part of a meeting. (11)

R

racism. The belief that one race is superior or inferior to all others. (20)

receipts. All the money a business receives from customers for cash and credit sales; also called *revenues*. (22)

receiver. The person who gets the message during the communication process. (5)

recourse. The consumer's right to complain and receive a response for any product or service that does not meet his or her expectations. (24)

reference. A person who knows a job applicant well and who would be able to discuss the applicant's personal and job qualifications with employers. (16)

registered apprenticeship. An advanced training program for a highly skilled occupation that operates under standards approved by the Office of Apprenticeship, a division of the U.S. Department of Labor. (14)

reprisal. The revenge-motivated act of retaliating or "getting back" at someone. (20)

resources. All the things a person has or can use to help reach his or her goals. (12)

résumé. A brief history of a person's education, work experience, and other qualifications for employment. (16)

revolving charge account. A type of credit account that allows customers a choice of paying for purchases in full each month or spreading payments over a period of time. (25)

role. A pattern of expected behavior. (28)

routine decisions. Choices that most people make automatically about everyday matters, such as what to eat and wear. (15)

S

safety-conscious. Knowing job hazards and taking appropriate steps to avoid accidents. (9)

salary. A set amount of money paid for a certain period of time. (23)

school-to-work coordinator. A special teacher or counselor at school who assists a student in a school-to-work program; *also called program coordinator.* (1)

school-to-work programs. Another term for work-based learning programs. (1)

secondary motion. A motion that can be made while a main motion is being considered to amend the main motion or postpone action on the motion. (11)

securities. Investments that represent either ownership or indebtedness, such as stocks, bonds, mutual funds, and money market funds. (26)

self-assessment. The process of taking stock of one's interests, aptitudes, and abilities. (12)

self-concept. The mental image a person has of himself or herself. (12)

self-directed team. A work team that has been given full responsibility for carrying out its assignment. (4)

self-esteem. Having confidence and satisfaction in oneself. (3)

self-management. Initiative. (3)

sender. A person who starts the communication process and has a mental image of what he or she wants to communicate. (5)

service contract. An extended warranty to cover an extra time period for additional cost. (24)

services. Any type of work that a consumer pays to have done, such as a repair, dry cleaning, or hairstyling. (24)

sexual harassment. Unwelcome or unwanted advances, requests for favors, or other verbal or physical conduct of a sexual nature. (20)

sexual orientation. The gender preferred when choosing someone for an emotional/sexual relationship. (20)

short-term goal. A goal that a person wants to reach tomorrow, next week, or within a few months. (12)

simple interest. Interest is paid only on the money initially deposited in the account. (26)

situational test. A preemployment test that examines the ability of job applicants in a work setting similar to the job. (17)

skill test. A preemployment exam used to test the physical or mental abilities of a job applicant. (17)

skimming. Stealing a credit card number. (24)

Small Business Administration (SBA). An agency that provides a prime source of information for would-be entrepreneurs. (22)

smart card. An advanced form of debit card with an embedded computer chip to track certain purchasing information. (26)

sociability. Interacting easily with people. (3)

social security. The federal government's program for providing income when earnings are reduced or stopped because of retirement, disability, or death. (2)

social security tax. A tax, identified as FICA, on personal income that is used to pay for the social security program. (23)

software. The program instructions that tell a computer what to do. (7)

special committees. Committees established for a special purpose or for a short period. (11)

standard of living. The goods and services a person considers essential for living. (12)

standards. Accepted levels of achievement. (12)

standing committees. The permanent committees of a group, such as membership and program committees. (11)

stereotype. A label given to a person based on assumptions held about all members of that person's racial or cultural group. (20)

stock. A share in the ownership of a corporation. (26)

stress. A feeling of pressure, strain, or tension that results from change. (19)

summarizing. Writing down the main ideas of an assignment; expressing key thoughts. (2)

supervisor. The person at the training station assigned to help the student learn the job. (1)

Supplemental Security Income (SSI). A Social Security Administration program that pays benefits to individuals with disabilities who have few possessions or little income. (23)

supply. The amount of products and services available for sale in the economy. (21)

support system. A group of caring, concerned friends and relatives. (28)

T

table. A type of chart that arranges data in rows and columns. (6)

team. A small group of people working together for a common purpose. (4)

telecommuting. Working at home or from another site through an electronic link to a central office. (28)

teleconferencing. Using a speakerphone to conduct a meeting with participants in different locations. (5)

term insurance. Insurance that covers the policyholder for a set period of time specified in the policy, such as 10 years. (27)

The Occupational Information Network (O*NET™). An Internet system that provides the latest information needed for effective training, education, counseling, and employment of workers. (14)

tips. Small amounts of money given by customers to service-related workers in return for good service. (23)

tort. A wrongful act committed against another person, independent of a contract. (28)

tourniquet. A long, thin strip of cloth or other material twisted tightly around the body to restrict blood flow. (9)

training agreement. An agreement that outlines the purposes of a work-based learning program and defines the responsibilities of everyone involved. (2)

training plan. A list of skills, attitudes, and habits that a student plans to learn during his or her work-based learning experience. (2)

training sponsor. An employee who works with the student at the training station; also called *work-based mentor*. (1)

training station. Job site where a student works to learn job skills. (1)

training station report. A periodic record of the duties performed and skills/attitudes learned at work by a student in a work-based learning program. (2)

transfer. The acceptance of credit by one school of courses taught at another school. (14)

transferable skills. Job skills that can be easily transferred from one job to another. (1)

traveler's check. A convenient type of check used by travelers that can be replaced if lost or stolen. (26)

troubleshooting. The basic steps a person can take to solve a computer problem. (7)

U

unemployment insurance. Insurance that provides benefits to workers who have lost their jobs. (23)

union. A group of workers who have united to voice their opinions to their employer or the employer's representatives (management). (19)

universal life insurance. A type of life insurance that combines death benefits with a savings and investment account that earns current market rates. (27)

universal precautions. Steps taken to prevent the spread of infection. (9)

USB flash drive. A tiny unit used to store data for extended periods of time, also known as a *thumb drive, keychain drive,* or *jump drive.* (7)

V

values. The principles and beliefs a person considers important. (12)

videoconferencing. Two or more people communicating through a video and voice link-up. (5)

vision. Knowing what is most important to a group and how to achieve it. (10)

voice mail. A telephone feature that allows callers to leave a recorded message. (5)

W

wage. A set amount of pay for every hour of work. (23)

walkie-talkie. A communication tool similar to a cellular phone but is limited to calling short-distances. (5)

wants. The items a person would like to have, but can live without. (21)

warranty. A written promise made by a manufacturer guaranteeing a product's performance and quality standards and indicating what will be done if the product does not meet the standards. (24)

whole life insurance. Insurance that covers the policyholder for a lifetime. (27)

work ethic. How a person feels about his or her job and the effort he or she puts into it. (3)

work permit. A written document that makes it legal for an underage student to work for an employer. (2)

work-based learning programs. School programs designed to prepare students for the workplace. (1)

work-based mentor. An employee who works with the student at the training station; also called *training sponsor.* (1)

workers' compensation. A type of insurance, paid by employers, to protect employees against loss of income from work-related accidents. (9)

workplace diversity. Respecting the contributions of coworkers who are unlike you. (20)

workplace violence. Violent acts or threatening behavior that occur in the workplace or at a company function. (9)

World Wide Web. A part of the Internet that carries messages with picture, color, motion, and/or sound. (7)

Z

zoning laws. Laws that regulate what types of business activities can be performed in certain areas. (22)

Index